THE FOUNDATIONS OF EUROPEAN COMMUNITY LAW

*An Introduction to the Constitutional
and Administrative Law
of the European Community*

BY

T. C. HARTLEY

B.A., LL.B. (Cape Town); LL.M. (London)
Professor of Law
London School of Economics and Political Science

Second Edition

CLARENDON PRESS · OXFORD

Oxford University Press, Walton Street, Oxford OX2 6DP

Oxford New York Toronto
Delhi Bombay Calcutta Madras Karachi
Petaling Jaya Singapore Hong Kong Tokyo
Nairobi Dar es Salaam Cape Town
Melbourne Auckland
and associated companies in
Berlin Ibadan

Oxford is a trade mark of Oxford University Press

Published in the United States
by Oxford University Press, New York

First edition 1981
Second edition 1988
Reprinted with corrections 1989, 1990, 1991

British Library Cataloguing in Publication Data
Hartley, T. C.
The foundations of European
community law: an introduction to
the constitutional and administrative
law of the European Community.—2nd ed.
(Clarendon law series)
1. Law—European Economic Community countries   2. European communities
I. Title   341'.094
ISBN 0-19-876208-9
ISBN 0-19-876207-0 (pbk)

Library of Congress Cataloging in Publication Data
Hartley, Trevor C.
The foundations of European community law.
(Clarendon law series)
Includes bibliographies and index.
I. Law—European Economic Community countries.
I. Title   II. Series.
KJE947.H37   1988   341.24'2   87-31403
ISBN 0-19-876208-9
ISBN 0-19-876207-0 (pbk.)

Printed in Great Britain
by Biddles Ltd.
Guildford and King's Lynn

CLARENDON LAW SERIES

Edited by

TONY HONORÉ AND JOSEPH RAZ

CLARENDON LAW SERIES

The Concept of Law
by H. L. A. HART

Introduction to Roman Law
By BARRY NICHOLAS

Legal Reasoning and Legal Theory
By NEIL MACCORMICK

Natural Law and Natural Rights
By JOHN G. FINNIS

The Law of Property (2nd edition)
By F. H. LAWSON and BERNARD RUDDEN

An Introduction to the Law of Torts (2nd edition)
By JOHN G. FLEMING

An Introduction to Administrative Law
By PETER CANE

Conflicts of Law and Morality
By KENT GREENAWALT

Bentham and the Common Law Tradition
By GERALD J. POSTEMA

An Introduction to the Law of Contract (4th edition)
By P. S. ATIYAH

The Principles of Criminal Evidence
By A. A. S. ZUCKERMAN

An Introduction to the Law of Trusts
By SIMON GARDNER

Public Democracy in the United Kingdom and the United States of America
By P. P. CRAIG

Philosophy and the Development of Modern Contract Doctrine
By JAMES GORDLEY

CONTENTS

PART I. COMMUNITY INSTITUTIONS

v

Chapter 2. The European Court   49

PART II. THE COMMUNITY LEGAL SYSTEM

PART III. COMMUNITY LAW AND THE MEMBER STATES

Chapter 7. Direct Effect and the Supremacy of Community Law   183

FOREWORD

In preparing the second edition of this book, I have had a number of considerations in mind. First, of course, I have tried to bring it up to date. This has involved the inclusion of much new material; in particular, Chapter 12 (Locus Standi) has been largely rewritten. Secondly, I have tried to make the text more concise by omitting some of the speculative passages and eliminating much of the detail in case discussions. Thirdly, I have tried to improve the balance of the book by shortening the treatment of non-contractual liability (the former Part V is now contained in Part IV) and expanding the chapter on the political institutions. Finally, I have added an alphabetical, as well as a numerical, table of European Court cases. I hope that these changes will enable the book to fulfil better its main purpose, that of a student textbook.

I am grateful to Professor Francis Jacobs for commenting on Chapter 12, to Professor Vlad Constantinesco for commenting on the part of Chapter 8 dealing with France and to the staff of the European Court for supplying me with much useful information. I also wish to thank my research assistant at the London School of Economics, Mr Joseph Horn, and my assistant at the College of Europe, Mr Jorge Marti Moreno. My greatest debt, however, is to my wife, Sandra, who read all the new material in manuscript and proof-read the entire book.

I have tried to state the law as it existed on 1 January 1988 and have endeavoured to cover decisions of the European Court up to that date.

T.C.H.
15 January 1988

BIBLIOGRAPHY

Only general works are listed here; specialized materials are found in the 'Further Reading' after each chapter.

G. Bebr, *Development of Judicial Control of the European Communities* (1981).

L. Neville Brown and Francis G. Jacobs, *The Court of Justice of the European Communities* (2nd. ed., 1983).

Lawrence Collins, *European Community Law in the United Kingdom* (3rd ed., 1984).

René Joliet, *Le droit institutionnel des Communautés européennes: Le contentieux* (1981).

René Joliet, *Le droit institutionnel des Communautés européennes: Les institutions; Les sources; Les rapports entre ordres juridiques* (1983).

P. J. G. Kapteyn and P. VerLoren van Themaat, *Introduction to the Law of the European Communities* (1973).

D. Lasok and J. W. Bridge, *An Introduction to the Law and Institutions of the European Communities* (4th ed., 1987).

R. H. Lauwaars, *Lawfulness and Legal Force of Community Decisions* (1973).

Henry G. Schermers (assisted by Denis Waelbroeck), *Judicial Protection in the European Communities* (4th ed., 1987).

Hans Smit and Peter Herzog, *The Law of the European Economic Community* (1976: loose leaf)

A. G. Toth, *Legal Protection of Individuals in the European Communities* (1978).

G. Vandersanden and A. Barav, *Contentieux Communautaire* (1977).

These books are cited by name of author alone.

ABBREVIATIONS

AG: Advocate General

AJDA: L'Actualité Juridique: Droit Administratif

Am. Jo. Comp. L.: American Journal of Comparative Law

BYIL: British Yearbook of International Law

CDE: Cahiers de Droit Européen

CLP: Current Legal Problems

CMLR: Common Market Law Reports

C.M.L.Rev.: Common Market Law Review

COREPER: Committee of Permanent Representatives

EC: European Community/Communities

E.C. Bull.: Bulletin of the European Communities

ECJ: European Court of Justice

ECOSOC: Economic and Social Committee

ECR: European Court Reports (official reports of the judgments of the European Court, English version)

ECSC: European Coal and Steel Community

EEC: European Economic Community

E.L.Rev.: European Law Review

EP: European Parliament

EPC: European Political Co-operation

Euratom: European Atomic Energy Community

FIDE: International Federation for European Law

ICJ: International Court of Justice

ICLQ: International and Comparative Law Quarterly

JO: Journal officiel (French version of OJ)

LIEI: Legal Issues of European Integration

LQR: Law Quarterly Review

MCA: Monetary Compensatory Amount

MLR: Modern Law Review

MT: Merger Treaty

OJ: Official Journal (of the European Communities)

Rec.: Recueil de la jurisprudence de · la Cour de Justice des Communautés européennes (French version of ECR)

RMC: Revue de Marché Commun

RTDE: Revue Trimestrielle de Droit Européen

SEA: Single European Act

SEW: Sociaal-economische Wetgeving

YEL: Yearbook of European Law

LIST OF TABLES

TABLE OF COMMUNITY
TREATIES

(Only those provisions discussed in some detail are included.)

TABLE OF UNITED KINGDOM STATUTES

TABLE OF CASES

xxiii

EUROPEAN COURT (Alphabetical Order)

Part I
Community Institutions

INTRODUCTION

Although people often think of 'the Community' as a single entity, there are in law three Communities: the European Coal and Steel Community (ECSC), the European Economic Community (EEC) and the European Atomic Energy Community (Euratom). The ECSC and Euratom are limited to particular sectors of the economy but the EEC is general in scope. Thus the EEC covers, in principle, all sectors of the economy not covered by the other Communities.

The ECSC is the oldest. The ECSC Treaty was signed on 18 April 1951 and entered into force on 25 July 1952. The signatories were the six original Member States: Germany, Belgium, France, Italy, Luxembourg and the Netherlands. The United Kingdom was invited to take part but declined to do so. The signing took place in Paris – for this reason it is sometimes called the 'Treaty of Paris' – and the French version is the sole authentic text. Four principal institutions were created: the Council (representing the Member States), the High Authority (intended as a supranational executive), the Assembly and the Court. They were originally located in Luxembourg (except for the Assembly, which normally met in Strasbourg).

The EEC and Euratom[1] Treaties were signed in Rome on 25 March 1957 and entered into force on 1 January 1958. The United Kingdom was again invited to participate but dropped out of the preliminary discussions. The signatories were therefore the same six States, but this time the texts in each of their official languages – German, French, Italian and Dutch – were equally authentic. Separate Commissions (equivalent to the High Authority in the ECSC) and Councils were created for each of the new Communities but all three shared the same Assembly and Court.[2] The new Councils and Commissions met in Brussels.

[1] The reason why a separate Treaty was signed governing the non-military use of atomic energy was the fear that the EEC Treaty might be rejected by the French Parliament. It was hoped that, in such an eventuality, at least the Euratom Treaty could be saved: see Kapteyn and VerLoren van Themaat, p. 15.

[2] The establishment of a single Assembly and Court for the three Communities was effected by a separate Treaty, the Convention on Certain Institutions Common to the European Communities, which entered into force on the same date as the EEC and Euratom Treaties.

3

The three Treaties contain many common features but there are also important differences. One difference is that the ECSC Treaty is more specific as regards the policy to be pursued; the EEC Treaty, on the other hand, is concerned mainly with creating a framework, and leaves the creation of policy to the Community institutions. The consequence of this is that the institutions are required to play a more creative role in the EEC. This difference is in turn responsible for another difference between the ECSC and EEC Treaties: under the former, the High Authority (Commission) has much more independent power (and the Council, correspondingly less) than is the case under the EEC Treaty. In the EEC, therefore, the balance of power is more in favour of the Council. This is understandable in view of the fact that the High Authority is to a greater extent concerned with carrying out policies laid down in the Treaty, and has less opportunity for policy creation, than the EEC Commission.

On the purely legal level the EEC and Euratom Treaties are very similar – many provisions concerning legal remedies are identical – while significant differences are to be found in the ECSC Treaty. This can be explained by virtue of the fact that the EEC and Euratom Treaties were drafted at the same time and the drafters were obviously influenced by the experience gained from the operation of the ECSC Treaty.

It was, of course, illogical and inconvenient for the two most important Community organs to be triplicated; so a Merger Treaty (officially known as the Treaty Establishing a Single Council and a Single Commission of the European Communities) was signed in Brussels on 8 April 1965 and entered into force on 1 July 1967. This Treaty did not merge the Communities themselves but merged the High Authority and the two Commissions to form a single Commission and merged the three Councils to form a single Council. The official title of the former is the 'Commission of the European Communities' and of the latter, the 'Council of the European Communities.' The new Council and Commission are located in Brussels. In order to compensate Luxembourg for this loss it was agreed that some Council meetings would be held there. In addition, certain other Community activities are run from Luxembourg and the European Court still sits there. The end result is highly inconvenient and inefficient and shows that, even in the simplest matters, the common interest often has to give way to national interests.

The next step was the widening of Community membership. Britain's original attitude of disdain changed in the early Sixties and in 1961 the Conservative Government of Mr Harold Macmillan took the decision to seek entry. Initially Britain's application was blocked by General De Gaulle; but Britain persevered and on 22 January 1972 the Final Act was signed which embodied the instruments of accession of the United Kingdom, Ireland, Denmark and Norway.[3] Norway dropped out when a referendum showed that a majority of the Norwegian electorate opposed entry; but the other three new Member States joined the Community on 1 January 1973. English, Danish and Irish became official Community languages and the translations into these languages of the EEC and Euratom Treaties were declared to be authentic texts.

Greece was the next country to join. On 28 May 1979 the Treaty of Accession and other relevant instruments were signed in Athens, and Greece became the tenth Member State on 1 January 1981. Spain and Portugal followed. The relevant instruments were signed on 12 June 1985 and membership came into effect on 1 January 1986. The Community now has twelve Member States, a number which is not likely to be increased in the near future; the official languages include Greek, Portuguese and Spanish.

In 1985 Greenland left the Community following a referendum held in 1982 in which there was a narrow majority in favour of withdrawal. Greenland was not a Member State but, being associated with Denmark (though with internal self-government), was part of the Community.[4]

The structure of the Community has already undergone considerable change in the course of its development. In addition to the treaties previously mentioned, amendments have been made by the first and second Budgetary Treaties, 1970 and 1975, and by the Single European Act of 1986, which came into force on 1 July 1987. Other changes have resulted from the establishment of political (constitutional) conventions and practices which have developed without any formal legal foundation. However, in law there are still three Communities, though there is only one set of institutions. The

---

[3] The new Member States actually joined the EEC and Euratom through ratification of the Treaty of Accession and the ECSC by depositing an instrument of accession on the basis of the Decision of Accession. The latter was a decision of the Council of the European Communities under Art. 98 ECSC. The terms of admission are laid down in the Act of Accession which is an integral part of both the Treaty of Accession and the Decision of Accession. This complicated procedure was made necessary by the differences in the Treaties: compare Art. 98 ECSC with Arts 237 EEC and 205 Euratom.

[4] It is now associated with the Community. For further details, see Weiss, 'Greenland's Withdrawal from the European Communities' (1985) 10 E.L. Rev. 173.

powers of the institutions vary, depending on the Treaty under which they are acting. One cannot tell when the step of merging the Communities themselves will be taken but it is clear that there already exists a single institutional and political entity for which the phrase 'the European Community' is an apt description. The best analogy is perhaps that of three commercial companies with the same shareholders and the same board of directors: in law there are three legal persons, in reality there is only one.

It is not easy to compare the Community with other political entities: it contains some of the features of an ordinary international organization and, less prominently but nevertheless quite distinctly, some features of a federation.[5] This dualism reflects the fact that the Community was intended, by at least some of its founders, to be a first step towards a European federation, a United States of Europe, and it is probably somewhat unstable in its present form: either it will go forward to become a federation or it will regress and eventually break up.

The hybrid nature of the Community must constantly be borne in mind when considering its structure. The three political organs – the Council, the Commission and the Parliament – each contain both international and 'proto-federal' elements, though the former are more noticeable in the case of the Council and the latter in the case of the Commission.

The most important characteristic of a typical international organization is that it is basically only a form of institutionalized inter-governmental co-operation. It is based on the principle that no member state may be bound without its consent. If the decisions of the organization are taken by majority vote, they are no more than mere declarations; if, on the other hand, they are to have any real 'bite', they must be approved by each member state.

In the Community, the organs have at least some measure of autonomy and in at least some cases unanimity is not required. Nor can it be doubted that the Community has real teeth: Community law is binding on the Member States and is frequently binding on individuals and applicable by national courts; moreover, in certain

[5] Interestingly, the federal elements are strongest with regard to the judicial and legal system of the Community; they are weakest in the political area, including such vital matters as legislative and executive powers, taxation, defence and monetary questions: see Hartley, 'Federalism, Courts and Legal Systems: The Emerging Constitution of the European Community', (1986) 34 Am. Jo. Comp. L. 229. For a full and detailed study of this question, see M. Cappelletti, M. Seccombe, and J. Weiler (eds), *Integration Through Law* (3 vols) (1986).

cases the Commission has power to levy fines on companies and individuals for breach of Community law. The decisions of the Community derive their binding force from the fact that they are taken by organs endowed with the appropriate power by the Treaties – the constitution of the Community – and not because they have been agreed to by the Member States.[6] To describe this new type of political organism, the word 'supranational' has been used.[7]

[6] In certain special cases, however, the Treaties provide for decisions to be taken by the Member States as such. One example is the appointment of members of the Commission under Art. 11 of the Merger Treaty. See further Chapter 3, pp. 96–7.

[7] For an analysis of this concept, see Weiler, 'The Community System: the Dual Character of Supranationalism' (1981) 1 YEL 267.

1

THE POLITICAL INSTITUTIONS

According to the Treaties,[1] the Community has four institutions – the Commission, the Council, the European Parliament and the Court of Justice.[2] The first three are political institutions; they will be dealt with in this chapter. The Court of Justice will be considered in Chapter 2.

THE COMMISSION[3]

The Commission is the body in which the supranational aspects of the Community are most apparent. It was originally intended that it would give expression to the Community interest and provide the motive force for further integration. Its most important activities today are formulating proposals for new Community policies, mediating between the Member States to secure the adoption of these proposals, co-ordinating national policies and overseeing the execution of existing Community policies.

Composition

The Commission consists of 17 persons[4] who are appointed by the governments of the Member States. They must all be nationals of one of the Member States and no more than two may be nationals of the same state.[5] In practice the five largest countries – Germany, France, Italy, Spain and the United Kingdom – have two each and the others one each. Each appointment must, however, be agreed to by all the

[1] See Arts 7 ECSC, 4 EEC, 3 Euratom, 1 and 9 Merger Treaty and 1, 2(1), 3 and 4(1) of the Convention on Certain Institutions Common to the European Communities.
[2] The institutions are now designated in this way: see Arts 3(1) *et seq.* SEA. Other important organs, which do not have the status of institutions, are the Economic and Social Committee, the Court of Auditors and the European Investment Bank.
[3] The basic legal framework is laid down in Arts 9–19 of the Merger Treaty.
[4] The number of Commissioners may be altered by the Council, acting unanimously: Merger Treaty, Art. 10(1).
[5] Merger Treaty, Art. 10(1).

Member States[6] and a government does not have *carte blanche* to nominate anyone they like as 'their' Commissioner. Normally governments have to consider internal political claims as well as acceptability to other Community countries. Thus, in the case of the United Kingdom, one Commissioner has so far always been appointed from the Conservative Party and one from the Labour Party.

Commission members are appointed for renewable four-year terms. These terms expire together so that the whole Commission is reappointed at the same time. Commissioners cannot be dismissed during their term of office by the national governments, but the whole Commission can be removed *en bloc* by a vote of no confidence in the European Parliament.[7] Commissioners cannot be dismissed individually in this way; but the European Court can compel a Commissioner to retire on grounds of serious misconduct or because he no longer fulfils the conditions required for the performance of his duties.[8]

It is important to stress that Commission members are in no sense representatives of their countries. They are required to be above national loyalties. To ensure this, it is provided by Article 10(2) of the Merger Treaty:

The members of the Commission shall, in the general interest of the Communities, be completely independent in the performance of their duties. In the performance of these duties, they shall neither seek nor take instructions from any Government or from any other body. They shall refrain from any action incompatible with their duties. Each Member State undertakes to respect this principle and not to seek to influence the members of the Commission in the performance of their tasks.

Any breach of these principles could lead to the compulsory retirement of the Commissioner concerned.[9]

[6] The Merger Treaty, Art. 11, states that appointment is 'by common accord of the Governments of the Member States'.

[7] Arts 24 ECSC, 144 EEC and 114 Euratom.

[8] Merger Treaty, Art. 13. The procedure is set in motion by an application by the Council or Commission. This means that there are five different ways in which a Commissioner may cease to hold office: – 1. death; 2. expiry of his term of office; 3. individual (voluntary) resignation; 4. collective (compulsory) resignation (following a motion of no confidence in the European Parliament); and 5. compulsory retirement by the Court. Except in the first and last of these cases, he remains in office until his successor has been appointed.

[9] Art. 10(2) of the Merger Treaty also provides that a Commissioner must not engage in any other occupation, whether gainful or not, during his term of office (though in practice certain academic activities are allowed). After he has ceased to hold office, he must behave with integrity and discretion as regards the acceptance of appointments and benefits. Disregard of these obligations could lead to compulsory retirement (if he is still in office) or loss of pension.

Though direct personal pressure is illegal,[10] this does not prevent political pressure from being exerted on the Commission as a whole. The balance of power in the Community is such that, though the Commission is an independent force in its own right, it cannot fulfil its functions without the co-operation of national governments. Consequently, it is very much concerned with national interests and one of its most important tasks is the reconciliation of national policies with Community objectives. Therefore, even in those cases where the Commission is legally empowered to take action independently of the Council, it will still pay careful attention to national susceptibilities in order to avoid antagonising any Member State (which can always retaliate in other fields if its displeasure has been incurred).

The President of the Commission is appointed from among the Commissioners by common accord of the Member States.[11] He holds office for a renewable term of two years.[12] It is customary for portfolios to be allocated to Commissioners so that each is responsible for one or more subjects. This is done by agreement among the Commissioners themselves, with the President playing a pivotal role. There is often fierce lobbying by the Member States to ensure that their Commissioners get the key jobs.[13]

The Commission is divided into twenty departments known as Directorates General, ranging from External Relations (DG 1) to Financial Control (DG 20). Not all of these are of equal importance or prestige; hence the scramble for portfolios. Each Directorate General is headed by a Director General, who is responsible to the relevant Commissioner. Directorates General are sub-divided into Directorates (headed by a Director) and these in turn are made up of Divisions (each under a Head of Division). There are also a number of specialized services. One of these is the Legal Service, which gives legal advice to all Directorates General and represents the Commission in legal proceedings. The total staff of the Commission is over 10,000. Appointments to the higher posts (Head of Division and

---

[10] It may nevertheless still occur.

[11] Art. 4 of the Merger Treaty. There are also six Vice-Presidents, appointed in the same way.

[12] It was apparently at French insistence that it was limited to half the term of office of the Commission as a whole, but in practice appointments are usually renewed for one further term, making a total of four years in all. By convention, the office of President rotates among the Member States.

[13] In 1981 Mrs Thatcher actually telephoned the President of the Commission to press her case.

above) are subject to intense national rivalry. The decision is taken by the Commissioners themselves and depends in part on ensuring that each country maintains its share of posts. This means that the best man (or woman) will not always get the job, a fact which is damaging to morale.

Each Commissioner is assisted by his *Cabinet*, a group of officials personally appointed by him and directly responsible to him, who are not necessarily on the permanent staff of the Commission. The head of the *Cabinet* (*Chef de Cabinet*) plays an important role as his Commissioner's right-hand man. The *Chefs de Cabinet* of all the Commissioners meet regularly to co-ordinate activities and prepare the ground for Commission meetings. If the *Chefs de Cabinet* reach unanimous agreement on a question, their decision is normally adopted by the Commission without debate.[14]

Officials of the Commission (and the other Community institutions) enjoy various privileges and immunities under Community law,[15] the most important of which are immunity from legal proceedings in national courts in respect of acts performed by them in their official capacity[16] and immunity from national income tax on their Community salary.[17] They are, however, subject to a special Community income tax, though the rate of taxation is low. All the privileges and immunities enjoyed by Community officials are granted to them solely in the interests of the Community and the institution concerned is obliged to waive the immunity whenever such waiver is not contrary to the interests of the Community.[18]

Decision-Making

The Commission meets in private (its deliberations are confidential) and takes decisions by a simple majority vote. Frequently, however, use is made of the so-called 'written procedure' under which draft decisions are circulated among the Commissioners and, if no objec-

[14] Compare the role played by COREPER with regard to the Council: see p. 15, below.
[15] See the Protocol on the Privileges and Immunities of the European Communities (a protocol to the Merger Treaty), Arts 12–16. These privileges and immunities also apply to members of the Commission.
[16] As to the meaning of this, see *Sayag* v. *Leduc* (No. 1), Case 5/68, [1968] ECR 395.
[17] Member States are also prohibited from taking an official's salary into account for the purpose of determining the tax payable by the official's spouse: *Humblet* v. *Belgium*, Case 6/60, [1960] ECR 559.
[18] Protocol on the Privileges and Immunities of the European Communities, Art. 18.

tions are made within a given period, the proposal is regarded as adopted.

Special procedures are followed where powers are delegated by the Council to the Commission. It is common practice for the Council to lay down the general principles governing a matter and to delegate the power to deal with detailed questions. In order to retain some measure of control, however, the Council may provide for the establishment of a committee to which the Commission must submit drafts of measures it intends to adopt under the delegated power. These committees are composed of representatives of the national governments under the chairmanship of a member of the staff of the Commission. They employ the same system of weighted voting as the Council itself (see below[19]) and a decision can be adopted only if a 'qualified majority' of votes is obtained. The chairman has no vote.

The powers of the committee vary from case to case according to the provisions of the Council measure, but they usually follow one of three basic patterns. Under the first system, known as the consultative committee procedure, the committee's functions are purely advisory: even an unfavourable opinion does not affect the Commission's powers. Under the second system, known as the management committee procedure, the Commission may adopt the draft whatever the opinion of the committee, but if the Commission does not follow the opinion, it must immediately communicate the measure to the Council. The Council may then adopt a different measure, which replaces the Commission measure, provided it acts within a specified period. If it does not act within that period, the Commission's measure is definitive. It is also definitive if the Commission follows the committee's opinion or if the committee was unable to give an opinion within the relevant time limit.[20]

The third system, which is the least favourable to the Commission, is known as the regulatory committee system. Under it, the Commission may proceed immediately to adopt the measure only if it follows the committee's opinion. If it does not, or if no opinion is given, the matter is referred to the Council, which may adopt either the Commission draft, or its own measure, within the prescribed period. If it does neither, the Commission may adopt its draft.

Article 145 EEC, as amended by Article 10 SEA, provides for the adoption of a frame-work measure to lay down the general principles

---

[19] See pp. 16–17.
[20] This may be because sufficient votes to attain a qualified majority cannot be mustered in favour of any opinion.

applicable to these systems. The Council adopted such a decision in 1987.[21] It broadly confirms the procedures described above but provides a variant[22] to the regulatory committee system under which, if the Commission does not follow the committee's opinion or if no opinion is given, the Council can veto the Commission draft without adopting any measure of its own. Such a veto needs only a simple majority of votes. The Commission expressed reservations regarding this procedure;[23] the Parliament objected so strongly to the whole measure that it commenced proceedings before the Court to annul it,[24] but these were dismissed on procedural grounds.[25]

Effectiveness

One can sum up the overall position of the Commission by saying that it can achieve a great deal so long as it retains the confidence of the Member States. Its greatest asset is its impartiality. Member States are prepared to accept its role because they believe that it stands above national rivalries. Its greatest weakness is that it lacks an independent political base. It is not in a position to appeal to public opinion over the heads of the national governments as it could if it were appointed by, and fully responsible to, a directly elected European Parliament. In such a case it could claim a political mandate from the European electorate and might be able to force national governments to give way. For this very reason, of course, the Member States are unlikely to agree to such a change in the foreseeable future.

THE COUNCIL

The Council of the European Communities (to give it its official title) is the body where the interests of the Member States find direct expression. It takes the final decision on most EEC legislation,

---

[21] Decision 87/373, OJ 1987, L 197/33. This decision differed considerably from the Commission proposal: see OJ 1986, C 70/6.

[22] Procedure III, Variant (b), Art. 2.

[23] See the declarations in the Council minutes for the proceedings at which the decision was adopted, published by the news agency "Europe", 28 October 1987 (Documents – No. 1477). The Commission also objected to the provisions on safeguard measures in Art. 3 of the decision.

[24] *European Parliament* v. *Council*, Case 302/87, 27 September 1988 (not yet reported); see, further, p. 338, below.

[25] For a discussion of earlier cases on the management committee procedure, see pp. 111–13, below.

concludes agreements with foreign countries and, together with the
Parliament, decides on the Community budget. It consists of the
delegates of the Member States, each state being represented by a
government minister.[26] When general matters are discussed,
Member States will normally be represented by their foreign ministers; but other ministers will be sent for specialist discussions: for
example, ministers of agriculture for meetings dealing with agriculture and ministers of finance for financial meetings. Meetings of
foreign ministers are often called the 'general Council' and meetings
of other ministers are referred to, collectively, as 'sectoral', 'specialized' or 'technical' Councils and, individually, as the 'agricultural
Council', 'the financial Council', etc. All Council meetings are held in
private and no record of the proceedings is published.[27] The Council
will not reveal the position taken by a particular minister, though the
latter may sometimes do so himself. Ministers attending Council
meetings are usually accompanied by officials. A representative of
the Commission also takes part in the proceedings.[28]

The Presidency of the Council rotates among the Member States at
six-monthly intervals.[29] While it holds the Presidency, a Member
State will provide the President (chairman) for all meetings of the
Council and other Community bodies on which the Member States
are represented.[30] The functions of the President are to call meetings,
to preside at them, to call for a vote and to sign acts adopted at the
meeting.[31] The Presidency also involves a general responsibility to
ensure the smooth running of the Council. The Member State
holding the Presidency has the role of mediator between the Member
States in the search for agreement; it also acts as representative of the
Community *vis-à-vis* the outside world. Both these latter functions
parallel those of the Commission. With the shift of power from the

[26] Art. 2 of the Merger Treaty.
[27] Arts 3(1) and 18 of the Council Rules of Procedure, 79/868, OJ 1979, L268/1.
[28] Ibid. Art. 3(2). The Commission has a right to be invited unless the Council decides
otherwise.
[29] Art. 2 (second para.) of the Merger Treaty.
[30] These bodies include the European Council, COREPER, committees and working
groups of COREPER (see Art. 16(4) of the Council Rules of Procedure (*supra*)) and
meetings of the Representatives of the Governments of the Member States. The Member
State holding the Presidency of the Council also holds the Presidency of European Political
Co-operation: Art. 30(10) (a) SEA.
[31] Meetings of the Council are called by the President on his own initiative or at the
request of one of the other members or of the Commission: Rules of Procedure (*supra*), Art.
1(1). The agenda is drawn up by the President; it contains the items requested by members
or the Commission: ibid., Art. 2. For other functions of the President, see ibid., Arts 7, 9, 15
and 19.

Commission to the Council, the Presidency has become increasingly important, and the Member States vie with each other to achieve maximum progress during their term of office.

The Council has its own General Secretariat staffed by permanent officials. It is similar to, but much smaller than, the Commission staff. It is divided into Directorates General and headed by a Secretary General. It has its own Legal Service.

COREPER

The ministers are able to be present in Brussels only for short periods. In order to provide continuity, a Committee of Permanent Representatives, usually known by its French acronym 'COREPER', was set up.[32] It consists of the Permanent Representatives (ambassadors) of the Member States to the Community and represents the Member States at a lower level than the ministers. COREPER itself meets on two levels, deputy Permanent Representatives (COREPER I) for more technical questions and the Permanent Representatives themselves (COREPER II) for the more important political questions. At a lower level still, there are many COREPER committees and working groups, staffed by national officials based in Brussels or in their home countries.

COREPER plays an important role in the Council mechanism. Matters to be decided by the Council come to it first. If unanimous agreement is reached in COREPER, the item will be listed under Part A of the Council agenda; it will then be adopted without discussion.[33] (There are normally more items in Part A than in Part B, though the latter are the important ones.) Negotiations with the Commission take place in COREPER: if a Commission proposal is unacceptable, attempts will be made to induce the Commission to amend it in order to secure agreement. The result of this is that in fact, though not in law, COREPER is an integral part of the Council decision-making process and could be regarded as an extension of the Council itself.

[32] Originally set up on an informal basis, it was given official recognition by Art. 4 of the Merger Treaty.

[33] Rules of Procedure (*supra*), Art. 2(6).

Voting

Since the most important decisions are taken by the Council, the question of voting is crucial. At first sight, the Treaties[34] give the impression that the supranational element is strong. Thus Article 148(1) EEC states:

Save as otherwise provided in this Treaty, the Council shall act by a majority of its members.[35]

In fact, however, the specific provisions dealing with almost every matter of importance *do* provide otherwise: only matters of minor significance are decided by this system.[36] There are some matters (for example, the admission of new members[37]) which must be decided unanimously.[38] Most matters, however, are decided by a 'qualified majority', as defined in Article 148(2) EEC. Under this procedure the votes of the Member States are weighted as follows:

Germany, France, Italy, United Kingdom:	10 votes each
Spain:	8 votes
Belgium, Greece, Netherlands, Portugal:	5 votes each
Denmark, Ireland:	3 votes each
Luxembourg:	2 votes

The total number of votes is 76; a qualified majority is 54. Where the decision is not taken on a proposal from the Commission there is an additional requirement that at least eight Member States must vote in favour.

Two points should be noted about this system. First, it gets away

[34] The discussion in the text concerns only the EEC Treaty. The position is the same under the Euratom Treaty (see Art. 118) but is different under the ECSC Treaty (see Art. 28). It should be remembered that the Council has much less extensive powers under the ECSC Treaty than under the other two.

[35] Note that this is a majority of members (absolute majority), not a majority of votes: abstentions count as votes against the proposal. It should also be mentioned that, while most of the other versions of Art. 148 (including the French and German texts) are the same as the English version, the Dutch and Danish versions talk of a majority of 'votes'.

[36] For examples, see Arts 128, 153, 213 and 236 EEC; and Art. 5 of the Merger Treaty. Art. 49 EEC originally did not require a special majority but this was changed by Art. 6(3) SEA.

[37] Art. 237 EEC. Other examples under the EEC Treaty are Arts 51, 76, 93(2), 99, 100 (but see 100A and 100B), 103(2), 121, 165 (last para.), 235 and 238. See also Art. 10(1) (second sub-para.) of the Merger Treaty.

[38] However, an abstention by one or more members of the Council does not prevent such a decision from being adopted, provided that the members in question were 'present in person or represented' at the meeting: Art. 148 (3) EEC. Such decisions can be blocked if one member boycotts the meetings, as France did during the crisis of 1965-66.

from the principle of equality for all states irrespective of size and importance (though it does so only to a limited extent: the smaller states still have greater voting power than they would be entitled to according to the criterion of population; moreover, a two-thirds majority of states is required if there is no Commission proposal). Secondly, the magic figure of 54 votes, which is a little more than a two-thirds majority, means that the five biggest countries (France, Germany, Italy, Spain and the United Kingdom) cannot outvote the small states.[39]

In every constitution, however, the provisions of strict law are supplemented, and sometimes modified, by convention. Constitutional conventions are rules of political practice based on the realities of political life. They reflect political power and do not normally endure for long, once the assumptions on which they are based have disappeared. Conventions operate in the Community as they do in national constitutions.

International bodies usually work on a system of give and take. States try to achieve what they want by influencing other Member States either by offering something in return – 'We will vote for you on issue X if you support us on issue Y' – or by threatening to cause trouble. In the latter category three tactics (in order of stringency) are: threatening to block progress on other, unrelated issues; threatening to boycott future meetings; and threatening to withdraw. Negative tactics of this kind can, if the threats are credible, be very effective, but there is a price to be paid. Bad feeling is created and other states will be less co-operative. Moreover, boycott or withdrawal will hurt the state concerned more than the others. For these reasons manoeuvres of this kind will be used only if a country feels that its vital interests are at stake (though a relatively powerful country will feel able to take tougher measures than a weaker one).

In view of this it would be surprising if a 'constitutional convention' had not sprung up in the Community to the effect that majority voting should not be used to push through a measure regarded by one Member State as harming its vital interests. Such a convention indeed exists but its exact scope is unsettled. To understand it, one must look at its history. The EEC Treaty envisaged the establishment of the common market in three stages. In many instances, it provided that the Council would take decisions unanimously during the first two stages and by a qualified majority thereafter. The third

---

[39] However, as a fixed number of votes must be obtained, abstentions have the same effect as negative votes: it is not sufficient to attain two-thirds of the votes cast.

stage began on 1 January 1966 and should have marked the transition to qualified majority voting. However, General de Gaulle was
not prepared to accept this. From the middle of 1965 France boy-
cotted the Community institutions (the so-called 'empty chair' policy) in protest against various developments, including the imminent
onset of qualified majority voting.[40] This precipitated a crisis in the
Community which was settled only when France agreed to a meeting
with the other five Member States. It was held in Luxembourg in
January 1966 and resulted in a press release containing the famous
'Luxembourg Accords'.

The main provisions of the Luxembourg Accords dealing with
majority voting are as follows:

I. Where, in the case of decisions which may be taken by majority vote on a
proposal of the Commission, very important interests of one or more partners are
at stake, the Members of the Council will endeavour, within a reasonable time, to
reach solutions which can be adopted by all the Members of the Council while
respecting their mutual interests and those of the Community, in accordance
with Article 2 of the Treaty.

II. With regard to the preceding paragraph, the French delegation considers
that where very important interests are at stake the discussion must be continued
until unanimous agreement is reached.

III. The six delegations note that there is a divergence of views on what should
be done in the event of a failure to reach complete agreement.

There is also a fourth paragraph under which the Six agreed that five
specified matters, all concerned with agriculture, should be decided
by common consent.

It should be noted that this is in part an agreement between the
Member States (of which the legal effect is uncertain) and in part an
agreement to disagree; nevertheless, for a long time afterwards the
French view prevailed in practice and when the United Kingdom
joined the Community it was confidently asserted by the British
Government that each Member State enjoyed a veto.[41] Even at this
time, however, qualified majority voting was practised in one special
case, the Community budget.

The next development occurred in 1982 when the Council adopted
an agricultural price increase despite an attempted British veto. In
what appears to have been a pre-planned move, the Belgian

---

[40] Initially the French were more concerned with agricultural markets, Community
financing and the budgetary powers of the European Parliament but they subsequently
broadened their demands to include the suppression of qualified majority voting.

[41] See *The UK and the European Communities*, Cmnd. 4715 (1971), para. 29 and *Membership
of the European Community – Report on Renegotiation*, Cmnd. 6003 (1975), para. 124.

President of the Council called for a vote, ignoring the British representative's claim that very important interests of the United Kingdom were at stake. The United Kingdom, Denmark and Greece refused to vote;[42] the others voted in favour, thus ensuring the qualified majority required by the relevant Treaty provision. The United Kingdom was outraged, but a month later, after a meeting of the general Council called specially to discuss the matter, Mr Francis Pym, the British Foreign Secretary at the time, expressed the view that the veto remained intact.

How is one to explain this? It is not known what was said in that meeting, but one explanation is that the events of the previous month did not constitute a violation of the convention, because the United Kingdom's attempt to use the veto was improper. Britain admitted that the price increases were not unacceptable in themselves: they were being blocked in order to force the other Member States to make concessions on Britain's budgetary contribution. Therefore, if one takes the view that the right to veto a measure exists only when *that* measure is contrary to the vital interests of the state concerned, the other Member States were fully entitled to press the matter to a vote.[43]

However this may be, it is obvious that the principle of unanimity had been weakened.[44] Moreover, in the years that followed, it became increasingly clear that greater use of majority voting would be essential if reasonable progress was to be made towards the attainment of the objectives of the Community. How this might be brought about was considered in the discussions leading up to the Single European Act and, though the latter does not directly refer to it,[45] there seems to have been an understanding that more votes

---

[42] Denmark and Greece both supported the measure but regarded the principle of the veto as sacrosanct.

[43] See the statement in the House of Commons by the present Foreign Secretary, Sir Geoffrey Howe, on 23 April 1986, H C Deb., Vol. 96, cols 320–321.

[44] See Nicoll, 'The Luxembourg Compromise' (1984) 23 JCMS 35, 40–41, where it is said that further votes took place in 1984.

[45] Certain provisions, for example Art. 16 SEA, amend or supplement the EEC Treaty by requiring a qualified majority in place of unanimity, but this does not in itself affect the issue, since, without a change of attitude on the part of Member States, the new provisions would be no more used than the original ones. However, in the special case of Art. 100A EEC (inserted by Art. 18 SEA), it could be argued that the veto has been implicitly discarded in view of the fact that para. 4 allows Members States, under certain conditions, to opt out of harmonization measures adopted by the Council acting by a qualified majority: the existence of this right would make it impossible for a Member State to argue that its vital interests are affected.

would take place.[46] This does seem to be happening;[47] however, it does not follow that the veto no longer exists, only that its use has been curtailed: since it is a mere matter of convention, its scope will always depend on the consensus among the Member States at any given time.

The European Council[48]

In 1974 it was agreed that the Heads of State or of Government[49] of the Member States, together with their foreign ministers, would hold summit conferences at regular intervals. In time these meetings became formalized and were known as the 'European Council' (not to be confused with the Council of the European Communities). In 1986 they attained official status in Community Law by virtue of Article 2 SEA, which confirms the right of the President of the Commission and one other Commissioner to attend. The meetings, which take place at least twice a year, are chaired by the representative of the Member State holding the Presidency of the Council of the European Communities and the discussions cover both Community matters and matters relating to European Political Co-operation (explained below). When it discusses Community matters it acts as the Council of the European Communities: there is nothing in Community Law preventing Member States from being represented at Council meetings by their Heads of State or of Government.[50] In practice, however, it seems that, even when it is dealing with Community matters, the European Council takes only general political decisions; these are then translated into legal form at meetings of the Council of the European Communities held at ministerial level.

[46] However, in his statement in the House of Commons on 23 April 1986, the British Foreign Secretary said that the Luxembourg Accords were 'in no way affected one way or the other by the Single European Act.' See H C Deb., Vol. 96, cols 320–321.

[47] It is interesting to note that on 20 July 1987 the Council amended its Rules of Procedure so that a vote can now be taken not only on the initiative of the President, but also on the initiative of any member of the Council (or on the initiative of the Commission), provided that a (simple) majority of the members of the Council is in favour. This means there are two votes: a procedural vote (on whether the substantive question should be put to the vote) and, if the procedural motion is supported by a majority of Member States, a substantive vote. See OJ 1987, L 291/27. Previously a vote on a substantive question would be taken only if the President so decided.

[48] See, generally, the Solemn Declaration on European Union 1983, Point 2.1, E.C. Bull., 6–1983, p. 25.

[49] This means the British Prime Minister, the German Chancellor, the French President, etc.

[50] Solemn Declaration on European Union 1983, Point 2.1.3, E.C. Bull., 6–1983, p. 25.

EUROPEAN POLITICAL CO-OPERATION

As far back as the early Fifties, attempts were made to promote European integration in the fields of defence and foreign policy, but these collapsed in 1954 when the French National Assembly rejected the European Defence Treaty. It was another fifteen years before a new effort was made.[51] This deliberately avoided any element of supranationalism and concentrated instead on establishing an inter-governmental framework for political co-operation, mainly in the field of foreign policy. The Member States agreed to regular consultations and exchanges of information in the hope that this would lead to common positions and joint action in international affairs.

A striking feature of the system in its initial stage was that it operated almost entirely outside the institutional structure of the Community. There was a rigid division between the European Community (EC) and European Political Co-operation (EPC): the Commission was largely excluded from EPC meetings, which took place in the capital of the Member State holding the Presidency, rather than in Brussels. The argument was that the subject-matter of EPC was outside the scope of the Treaties; therefore, it was outside the jurisdiction of the Community institutions. It soon became apparent, however, that this distinction could not be fully maintained. For example, if it were wished to adopt economic sanctions against a third country, would this be a matter for EPC (because it concerns foreign policy) or a matter for the Community (because it concerns commercial policy, a subject covered by Articles 110–116 of the EEC Treaty)? In fact, when the Falklands War broke out, sanctions against Argentina were adopted by the Community after 'discussions in the context of European political co-operation', but 'in accordance with the relevant provisions of the Community Treaties'.[52] Thus both systems came together to produce the desired result.

Recently there has been a slight blurring of the distinction between EC and EPC activities and the Single European Act now provides that the Commission has the right to be 'fully associated' with EPC;[53] it also requires the national governments to ensure that the

---

[51] The origin of European Political Co-operation is usually traced to the Hague Summit of December 1969 and the Luxembourg Report of October 1970.

[52] See the preamble to Council Regulation (EEC) 877/82, O J 1982, L 102/1.

[53] Art. 30(3)(b).

European Parliament is 'closely associated' with it.[54] Moreover, it is expressly stated in Article 30(5) SEA that the external policies of the Community and EPC must be consistent: the Presidency and the Commission have special responsibility for ensuring this.[55]

Until 1986 there was no legal framework for EPC. This has now been provided by Part III of the Single European Act,[56] which imposes a number of general obligations on the 'High Contracting Parties', as the Member States are called in Part III – no doubt in order to maintain the distinction between the EC and EPC. The most important of these obligations are:[57]

1. To endeavour jointly to formulate and implement a European foreign policy;
2. To keep each other regularly informed and to consult each other before adopting a final position on foreign policy matters;
3. To take full account of each other's positions and of the desirability of common European positions;
4. To avoid actions which would impair the effectiveness of the Member States as a cohesive force in international relations or in international organizations.

Part III also gives legal standing to the EPC machinery. This is now highly developed and to some extent parallels the Council decision-making machinery. Table 1 (below, p. 25) is an attempt to illustrate this in the form of a chart. The European Council stands at the top of both systems and unites them at the highest level. The next level is that of the Foreign Ministers' meetings, which take place at least four times a year. A representative of the Commission always attends. In effect, these are meetings of the general Council under a different name; Article 30(3)(a) SEA also permits the general Council itself to discuss EPC matters, thus further enhancing the unity of the two systems. The next level is the Political Committee, which consists of

[54] Art. 30(4). The Member State holding the Presidency has the duty of keeping the Parliament regularly informed of foreign policy issues being examined within the framework of EPC and of ensuring that the latter's views are duly taken into consideration.

[55] See also Art. 30(9) SEA, which requires co-operation between the representatives of the Member States and the Commission in non-member States and in international organizations.

[56] However, Art. 31 SEA expressly states that the powers of the European Court do not apply to Part III SEA. This means that the Court can provide no remedy for a breach of Part III.

[57] See Art. 30(1) and (2) SEA. Art. 30(6) SEA also recognizes the desirability of closer co-operation over security, an acknowledgment that this field is not excluded from EPC.

the Political Directors from the twelve Foreign Ministries.[58] This body has the task of preparing the ground for Foreign Ministers' meetings and is to some extent analogous to C O R E P E R. Beneath it is the European Correspondents' Group.[59] They are the officials in each Foreign Ministry charged with handling E P C matters. The Political Committee can set up working groups.[60] Finally, Article 30(10)(g) provides for an E P C Secretariat, based in Brussels and acting under the authority of the Presidency.[61]

THE EUROPEAN PARLIAMENT

Composition

The European Parliament[62] is intended to represent the peoples of the Community. This is made clear by Article 137 EEC[63] which states that it consists of 'representatives of the peoples of the States brought together in the Community'. In spite of this, however, the members of the European Parliament were for a long time selected by the national legislatures and it was only in 1976 that agreement was reached on direct elections.[64] The Treaties provided that the Parliament would draw up proposals for direct elections and that the Council, acting unanimously, would 'lay down the appropriate provisions', which it would recommend to Member States for adoption in accordance with their respective constitutional requirements.[65] The Parliament first drew up proposals as long ago as 1960, but it took the intervening 16 years for the Council to reach a decision. Thereafter, the provisions had to be adopted at national

---

[58] Art. 30(10)(c). It will meet within forty-eight hours at the request of at least three Member States: Art. 30(10)(d).

[59] Art. 30(10)(e).

[60] Art. 30(10)(f).

[61] For a discussion of the effectiveness of this machinery, see William Wallace, 'Political Cooperation: Integration Through Intergovernmentalism' in H. Wallace, W. Wallace and C. Webb, *Policy-Making in the European Community* (2nd ed., 1983).

[62] Referred to in the original Treaties as the 'Assembly', the European Parliament adopted its present name in 1962 (E P Resolution of 30 March 1962, J O 1962, p. 1045). This has been recognised by the Member States in the Single European Act: see Art. 3 (1) and subsequent provisions.

[63] See also Art. 20 ECSC and Art. 107 Euratom.

[64] Council Decision 76/787, and annexed Act concerning the election of the representatives of the Assembly by direct universal suffrage, OJ 1976, L 278/1. See further Forman, (1977) 2 E.L. Rev. 35.

[65] Arts 138(3) EEC, 21(3) ECSC and 108(3) Euratom.

level and this involved further difficulties and delays, not least in the
United Kingdom; so the first elections were not held until 1979.
Thereafter they have been, and will be, held on fixed dates every five
years.[66]

The instrument providing for elections took an unusual form since
all its substantive provisions are in an Act annexed to the Council
Decision. The legal nature of this Act is controversial. Does it take
effect as an international agreement between the Member States
based on a draft recommended by the Council? Or does it take effect
as a decision of the Council to which the Member States have agreed?
Perhaps the best view is that Articles 138(3) EEC, 21(3) ECSC and
108(3) Euratom lay down a special procedure for amending these
Treaties which derogates from that in Articles 236 EEC, 96 ECSC
and 204 Euratom.[67] If this view is correct, it takes effect as an act of
the Member States but forms part of the three Treaties. The importance of this question is that the jurisdiction of the European Court to
annul,[68] interpret[69] or enforce[70] the Act depends on the Act's legal
status.[71]

Seats in the European Parliament are at present allocated among
the Member States as follows:

Germany, France, Italy and the United Kingdom . . . . 81 (each)
Spain 60
Netherlands 25
Belgium, Greece and Portugal . . . . 24 (each)
Denmark 16
Ireland 15
Luxembourg 6
                                                    TOTAL   518

It will be noticed that these allocations are not proportional to
population: the population of the United Kingdom is more than 150
times that of Luxembourg; yet it has less than 14 times the number of
seats. To put it another way: a Luxembourger's vote is worth the

---

[66] See Art. 3 of the Act providing for direct elections (above).
[67] See Joliet, *Institutions*, pp. 75–77, where the problem is fully discussed.
[68] See Arts 173 EEC, and 146 Euratom (direct actions); and 177 EEC, 41 ECSC and
150 Euratom (preliminary rulings on validity).
[69] See Arts 177 EEC and 150 Euratom.
[70] See Arts 169–171 EEC, 88 ECSC and 141–143 Euratom.
[71] If the third view is correct, the European Court cannot annul the Act, even if it
infringes the Treaties, but it can interpret or enforce it where the Treaties so provide.

Table 1
The Structure of Co-operation among the Twelve

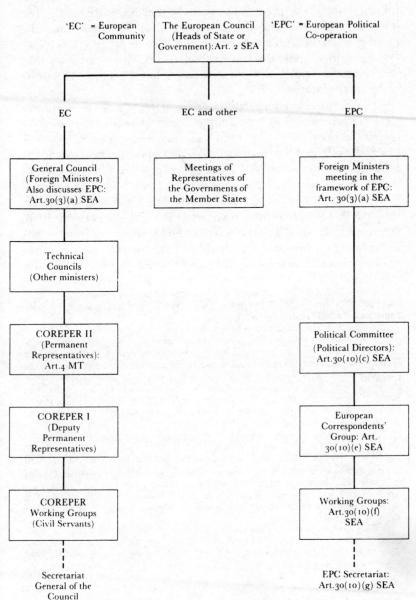

'EC' = European Community

The European Council (Heads of State or Government): Art. 2 SEA

'EPC' = European Political Co-operation

EC | EC and other | EPC

General Council (Foreign Ministers) Also discusses EPC: Art. 30(3)(a) SEA

Meetings of Representatives of the Governments of the Member States

Foreign Ministers meeting in the framework of EPC: Art. 30(3)(a) SEA

Technical Councils (Other ministers)

COREPER II (Permanent Representatives): Art. 4 MT

Political Committee (Political Directors): Art. 30(10)(c) SEA

COREPER I (Deputy Permanent Representatives)

European Correspondents' Group: Art. 30(10)(e) SEA

COREPER Working Groups (Civil Servants)

Working Groups: Art. 30(10)(f) SEA

Secretariat General of the Council

EPC Secretariat: Art. 30(10)(g) SEA

same as that of 14 United Kingdom voters.[72] This is not exactly
consistent with the principle of 'One person – one vote – one value';
though it should be pointed out that the previous system was even
less fair: under that the United Kingdom had only six times the
number of seats granted to Luxembourg.[73] Some progress has therefore been made; but the existence of such disparities shows that
democratic principles must still give way before the national interests
of the smaller states.[74]

The Act providing for direct elections states that, until a uniform
electoral procedure has been adopted, each Member State is free to
choose its own electoral system.[75] So far no agreement has been
reached on a uniform system, largely, it appears, because of the
reluctance of the United Kingdom to accept proportional representation; so the matter depends on national law[76] and the electoral
system differs from country to country. The United Kingdom has
decided to use its normal 'first past the post' system (except in
Northern Ireland).[77] The result is that the Liberal/SDP Alliance has
so far failed to win a single seat, although in the 1984 elections they
obtained over 19 percent of the vote in Great Britain.[78] With one

[72] The United Kingdom has an electorate of approximately 41 million, which gives
about 506,000 voters per MEP; Luxembourg has an electorate of roughly 214,000, making
approximately 36,000 voters per MEP.

[73] See Art. 138(2) EEC and the corresponding provisions in the other Treaties.

[74] It is sometimes said that this unequal allocation of seats is necessary in order to
ensure that all parties in the smaller countries can gain representation. Such an argument
cannot, however, justify a departure from the basic principle of equality of voting rights,
nor can it explain why Northern Ireland, with its distinctive and diverse political scene,
should have only half as many seats as Luxembourg, even though it has more than four
times as many voters. The fact that Northern Ireland is not an independent state is
irrelevant, since the European Parliament is not intended to provide a forum to represent
the Member States, a function fulfilled by the Council.

[75] Art. 7(2). This is subject to the other provisions of the Act; as to these, see Joliet,
Institutions, pp. 77–82. It could be argued that Art. 7(2) is invalid, since the Treaty
provisions (Arts 138(3) EEC, 21(3) ECSC and 108(3) Euratom) require the procedure
to be uniform in all Member States. The counter argument is that this requirement applies
only to the Parliament's proposals, not to the final measure, which can give effect to the
Treaty requirements in stages (see Joliet, *op. cit.*, p. 77); in any event it is doubtful whether
the European Court would have jurisdiction to annual the Act: see the discussion above on
the legal nature of the Act.

[76] For this reason a grant by the European Parliament to the political parties to cover
election expenses was held invalid by the European Court: *Les Verts – Parti Ecologiste* v.
European Parliament, Case 294/83, [1987] 2 CMLR 343. (The Ecologist Party (the Greens)
had challenged the grant on the ground that it was distributed in a way that was unfair to
the newer parties).

[77] European Assembly Elections Act 1978, Sched. 1. Minor amendments were made to
this Act by the European Assembly Elections Act 1981.

[78] On a proportional basis, they would be entitled to 15 seats.

minor exception,[79] the same persons are entitled to vote as in elections for the United Kingdom Parliament – British citizens, Commonwealth citizens and Irish citizens (provided they are resident in the country at the appropriate time).[80] This means that Nigerians and Canadians, for example, are entitled to vote in the United Kingdom in elections for the European Parliament, but Belgians and Italians are not.

Members of the European Parliament are permitted also to be members of their national parliaments[81] but Article 6(1) of the Act specifies a number of offices with which the office of MEP is incompatible. The most important are: member of the Government of a Member State; member of the Commission; Judge, Advocate General or Registrar of the European Court; or active official of a Community institution. Article 6(2) permits Member States to lay down additional incompatibilities at national level and in the United Kingdom most of the disqualifications for membership of the House of Commons apply also to membership of the European Parliament.[82]

Seat of the Parliament

Determining where the Parliament is to sit has caused considerable difficulties. Under the Treaties, the Member States have the power to decide where the institutions of the Community are to be located.[83] They have never been able to agree on the permanent seats of any of the institutions but have assigned them temporary seats. In the case of the Parliament, plenary sessions are held in Strasbourg[84] and committee meetings in Brussels; the secretariat, however, is located in Luxembourg. This is an absurd situation but the Member States have failed to respond to the Parliament's pleas to fix a single location for all its activities. Attempts by the Parliament itself to rationalize

---

[79] Peers are also entitled to vote.

[80] See para. 2(1) of Sched. 1 to the European Assembly Elections Act 1978; for further discussion, see Hartley, (1979) 4 E.L. Rev. 50.

[81] Art. 5 of the Act.

[82] European Assembly Elections Act 1978, Sched. 1, para. 5.

[83] Arts 216 EEC, 77 ECSC and 189 Euratom.

[84] The Luxembourg Government gave the Parliament a luxurious building in Luxembourg in an attempt to lure them there. This worked for a time, during which the Parliament divided its plenary sessions between Luxembourg and Strasbourg, but it later decided to hold them all in Strasbourg. Luxembourg sued the Parliament but was unsuccessful: *Luxembourg* v. *European Parliament*, Case 230/81, [1983] ECR 255.

the situation by moving its staff to its places of work have been declared illegal by the European Court at the suit of Luxembourg.[85]

Pay of MEPs

MEPs are paid the same salaries as their national counterparts, which means, for example, that United Kingdom MEPs are paid considerably less than their German colleagues. These salaries are subject to income tax in the MEP's home country. They also receive substantial allowances (often greater than their salaries), which are not subject to national tax.[86]

Privileges and Immunities

MEPs are entitled to various privileges and immunities[87] of which the most important are, first, freedom of movement to and from the meeting place of the Parliament; secondly, immunity from legal proceedings in respect of opinions expressed, or votes cast, in the performance of their duties; and thirdly, in their own Member State, the same immunities as are enjoyed by members of their national parliament and, in other Member States, freedom from detention and immunity from legal proceedings. Immunities in the third category apply only during parliamentary sessions but, as these last virtually all the year,[88] this limitation is of little importance. Immunities in this category may be waived by the Parliament itself.

Political Parties

Members of the European Parliament sit according to their party, not their country. The Rules of Procedure provide for the official recognition of parties (usually called 'political groups') and there are

[85] *Luxembourg* v. *European Parliament*, Case 108/83, [1984] ECR 1945. The Court held in this and the previous case that staff may be moved to Strasbourg and Brussels only to the minimum extent necessary to ensure the efficient working of the Parliament.
[86] *Lord Bruce* v. *Aspden*, Case 208/80, [1981] ECR 2205.
[87] See the Protocol on the Privileges and Immunities of the European Communities (a protocol to the Merger Treaty), Arts 8–10.
[88] The length of the sessions is a matter for the Parliament itself to decide. Although it does not actually sit throughout the year, it holds various ancillary activities, such as committee meetings, during most of the year and for the purpose of Parliamentary immunity is regarded as in session until the formal closing of the session, which takes place immediately before the opening of the new session. See *Wybot* v. *Faure*, Case 149/85, [1987] 1 CMLR 819.

various advantages, both procedural and administrative, in being so recognised. To gain recognition, a party must have a certain minimum number of MEPs.[89] Most of the parties are coalitions of national parties though in some cases one national party is dominant. As might be expected, the cohesiveness of these parties varies and on some issues national allegiances are more important than party loyalty. The Socialists are the largest party; they include Labour MEPs from Britain and social democrats from the other Member States. The next largest is the European People's Party, which contains Christian Democrats from Germany, Italy and various other countries. The European Democrats consist of the British Conservatives together with four Danish conservatives. The full party representation is as follows:

Party Representation in the European Parliament
(*August 1987*)

Socialists	164
European People's Party	115
European Democrats	66
Communists and Allies	48
Liberal and Democratic Reformists	43
European Alliance for Renewal and Democracy	31
Rainbow Group	20
European Right	17
Independents	14
TOTAL	518

Committees

A characteristic feature of the European Parliament is the role of committees. There are a number of standing committees, such as the Legal Affairs Committee, the Committee on Agriculture and the Committee on Budgets, and much of the work of the Parliament is done in these committees. When matters come before the Parliament for discussion, they are usually considered first in the appropriate committee and the subsequent debate on the floor of the House is based on the Committee's report.

To a large extent the functions of the Parliament are advisory and relate to the communication of ideas, the gathering of information

---

[89] If the members all come from the same Member State the minimum number is 23; if they come from two Member States, it is 18; if they come from three or more Member States, it is 12: see Rule 26(5) of the Rules of Procedure (4th ed., June 1987).

and, to some extent, the formation and expression of public opinion on Community matters. It holds debates and passes resolutions on a variety of topics but, though these generate publicity, they have in general no legal effect.

Parliamentary Questions

Parliamentary questions have become an important part of the Parliament's proceedings. Article 140 EEC[90] provides that 'the Commission shall reply orally or in writing to questions put to it by the Assembly or by its members'. In fact questions are put to, and answered by, the Council and the Foreign Ministers of the Member States meeting in the context of European Political Co-operation, as well as the Commission.[91] The answers are published in the Official Journal and they are an important means of gaining information on Community affairs. It is sometimes noticeable, however, that the replies given are uninformative to a degree which would hardly be acceptable in the House of Commons.

Legislation

In many (though not all) cases, the EEC and Euratom Treaties give the European Parliament a right to be consulted on proposed legislation.[92] The normal procedure is for the Commission to send a proposal to the Council, which in turn forwards it to the Parliament for its opinion. The proposal is first considered by one of the Parliament's committees, which produces a report and a draft resolution. These go to the full Parliament, which will give its opinion (either positive or negative) and may suggest amendments to the proposal.[93] The Commission may modify its proposal on the basis of the Parliament's opinion but there is no obligation on either it or the Council to follow the opinion or even to give reasons for rejecting it.

[90] See also Arts 23 ECSC and 110 Euratom.

[91] See the letter of 6 March 1973 from the President of the Council to the President of the Parliament, E.C. Bull. 1973, No. 3, p. 78 (para. 2402); see also Rule 58 of the Rules of Procedure (4th ed., June 1987).

[92] In other cases the Parliament is consulted by virtue of an inter-institutional agreement between the Parliament and the Council: see E P Resolution 65 of 27 November 1959, JO 1959 p. 1267. It is doubtful, however, whether failure to consult in these circumstances would have the same consequences (discussed below) as in the cases where consultation is required by the Treaties. For consultation on international agreements, see pp. 154–5, below; for association agreements, see p. 34, below.

[93] For further details, see Rules 36 *et seq.* of the Rules of Procedure (4th ed., June 1987).

In practice the Council is more concerned with accommodating the interests of the Member States than giving effect to the views of the Parliament.

Under this procedure the Parliament has no power to affect the content of legislation but its right to be consulted must be respected. If it is not, the European Court will declare the measure invalid. This happened in *Roquette* v. *Council*,[94] where the Council sent a proposal for legislation to the Parliament in March 1979. As the measure was to enter into force on 1 July of that year, the Council asked that the opinion be given during the April session. This proved impossible because the draft resolution proposed by the Parliamentary Committee on Agriculture, to which the proposal had been sent, was rejected by the Parliament in plenary session. This meant that the matter had to go back to the Committee for reconsideration and the resulting delay made it impossible to complete the procedure during the April session. The Parliament was willing to convene an extraordinary session should the Council or Commission so desire but the Council made no such request. Instead it adopted the measure on 25 June 1979, referring in the preamble to the fact that the Parliament had been 'consulted', rather than (as is normal) referring to its opinion.

Is it sufficient that the Parliament has been *asked* for its opinion or must it actually *give* its opinion? If the latter were the case, the Parliament could delay legislation indefinitely by the simple expedient of not giving an opinion. If such stone-walling were possible, the Parliament would in effect have a power of veto over legislation.

In its judgment the Court said that observance of the requirement of consultation 'implies that the Parliament has expressed its opinion. It is impossible to take the view that the requirement is satisfied by the Council's simply asking for the opinion.'[95] The Council had argued that the Parliament, by its own conduct, had made observance of the requirement impossible. The Court, however, pointed out that the Council had not exhausted all the possibilities of obtaining an opinion; in particular it had not asked for an extraordinary session. The Council had not, therefore, proved its allegations; and the Court declared the measure void. It was, however, careful to leave open the questions of principle raised by the Council and it is likely that if the Parliament were deliberately

---

[94] Case 138/79, [1980] ECR 3333. See also *Maizena* v. *Council*, Case 139/79, [1980] ECR 3393.

[95] Paragraph 34 of the judgment.

obstructive, the Council could go ahead without waiting for the opinion.

What is the position where, after the Parliament has given its opinion, the proposal is amended? If it was necessary to ask the Parliament for a new opinion on the amended proposal, the procedure would become very cumbersome, since amendments are frequently necessary in order to secure the assent of the Member States in the Council. In view of this, the Court has held that if the provisions of the final text of the measure are 'substantially identical' to those in the version submitted to the Parliament, there is no need for a second consultation.[96]

The Co-operation Procedure

The limited powers of the European Parliament in the legislative process were increased in 1986 by Articles 6 and 7 of the Single European Act, which provide for a 'co-operation procedure' applicable in some (but by no means all)[97] of the instances in which the EEC Treaty[98] requires the Parliament to be consulted. This procedure, which is laid down in Article 149(2) EEC (as amended by Article 7 SEA), is depicted diagrammatically in Table 2 (below, p. 35). When it applies, the legislative procedure, including the consultation of the Parliament, proceeds in the usual way until the point is reached at which the Council would normally be ready to adopt the act. Instead of doing so, however, it merely adopts a 'common position', acting by a qualified majority. This common position could be regarded as a first reading of the measure. Under Article 149(1), which applies in all cases in which the Council acts on a proposal from the Commission, a Commission proposal can be amended only if the Council is unanimous; consequently, the common position will correspond to the Commission proposal (including any amendments adopted by the Commission) unless the Council is unanimous.

The common position is then sent to the Parliament together with a statement of the reasons which led the Council to adopt it and a statement of the Commission's position. This will be the second occasion on which the Parliament considers the matter, the first being under the normal consultation procedure. The Parliament now

[96] *Chemiefarma* v. *Commission*, Case 41/69, [1970] ECR 661 (paragraphs 68 and 69).
[97] See Art. 6 SEA for a list of the cases in which the procedure applies.
[98] The procedure applies only under the EEC Treaty.

has three months[99] in which to act; it can approve or reject the common position, or propose amendments to it.[100] If the Parliament approves the common position, or fails to take any action by the deadline, the Council will adopt the act in accordance with the common position. If, on the other hand, the Parliament rejects the common position, the Council can adopt the act only by unanimity.[101]

Where the Parliament proposes amendments, the position is more complicated. The next step is for the Commission to re-examine its proposal in the light of the Parliament's proposed amendments.[102] It may adopt some or all of the Parliament's amendments but is not obliged to do so. It then forwards the proposal to the Council. If it does not adopt the Parliament's amendments, it must also send them to the Council, together with a statement of its reasons for rejecting them.

At this stage, the Council can either accept the proposal as amended by the Commission, for which a qualified majority is sufficient, or it can amend it, either by adopting amendments proposed by the Parliament but rejected by the Commission, or by adopting amendments of its own. In both these latter cases it can act only by unanimity.[103]

The co-operation procedure was adopted because of widespread dissatisfaction with the lack of democracy in the Community. The European Parliament was not happy with the procedure: it felt that its powers should be greater. If analysed, the co-operation procedure appears in fact to grant the Parliament very little. If the Parliament rejects the common position, the Council can adopt the act only by unanimity. Under the Luxembourg Accords, a Member State could, in practice, block a measure by claiming that its vital interests were at stake. Now, one assumes, this will happen less often; instead, where the co-operation procedure applies, the measure can be blocked by an alliance between one Member State and the Parliament. Being based on the Treaties, this new veto cannot be overridden by the

[99] This period may be extended by a maximum of one month by common accord between the Council and the Parliament.
[100] In the latter two cases, it acts by an absolute majority (majority of members, not votes).
[101] The Council must act within three months (a period which may be extended by not more than one further month by common accord between the Council and the Parliament); otherwise the proposal is deemed not to have been adopted.
[102] It must do this within one month.
[103] It must act within three months (four months, if the Parliament agrees); otherwise the proposal is lost.

other Member States. The result is a real, though small, increase in the powers of the Parliament.

With regard to amendments, on the other hand, the Parliament's powers have not been significantly increased. If the amendment is adopted by the Commission, the Council can reject it only on a unanimous vote. This, however, has always been the case, since the Council has never been able to amend a Commission proposal except by unanimity, and the Commission has always had the power to amend its proposal so as to give effect to amendments proposed by the Parliament.[104] All the new procedure does is to impose a legal obligation on the Commission to consider the Parliament's proposals (in the past it did this as a matter of practice, rather than legal obligation) and to give reasons if it rejects them. This can hardly be regarded as very significant.

Admission of New Member States and Association Agreements

The Single European Act significantly increased the Parliament's powers with regard to the admission of new Member States to the Community[105] and the conclusion of association agreements with non-member countries.[106] In both cases the Parliament must give its assent, acting by a majority of its members (absolute majority, not a majority of votes). In these special situations, therefore, the Parliament has a veto.

Censure of the Commission

In what at first sight appears to be its most important power, the Parliament can obtain the resignation of the Commission by passing a vote of censure. This is laid down by Articles 144 EEC, 24 ECSC and 114 Euratom which provide that the Commission must resign *en bloc* if such a motion is passed by a two-thirds majority of votes cast representing a majority of all members.[107] Since, however, the Parliament has no say in the appointment of a new Commission, and since it is provided that the old Commission will continue to deal with 'current business' until it is replaced, this power is of only limited

---

[104] See Article 149 EEC, second paragraph, in its original form.
[105] See below, pp. 91–2.
[106] See below, p. 154.
[107] The motion may be moved only by a political party or by one-tenth of all MEPs; a vote cannot be taken until at least three days after the motion has been tabled: see Rule 30 of the Rules of Procedure (4th ed., June 1987).

Table 2
The Co-operation Procedure

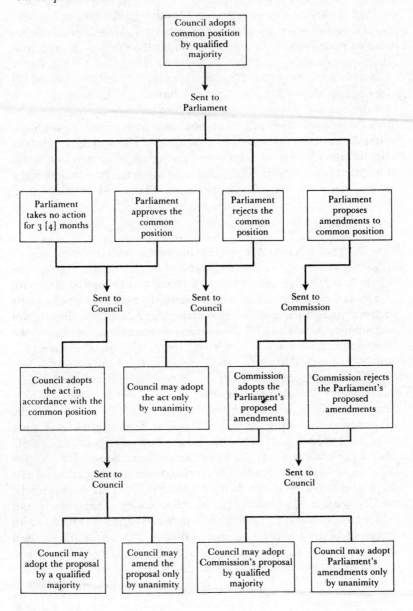

value. It has in fact never been used (partly because the Commission and the Parliament, being the most pro-European of the political institutions, are usually on the same side) though in 1972 a motion of censure was tabled, but withdrawn; the cause was the Commission's delay in making proposals to increase the Parliament's budgetary powers.

Conclusions

One of the most serious defects in the constitution of the Community is that the Parliament has only limited powers. This will be clear from what has already been said. However, the picture is not quite as bleak as might appear, since the most important powers, those concerning the budget, have yet to be considered. These will be discussed below.[108]

THE ECONOMIC AND SOCIAL COMMITTEE

Article 4(2) EEC provides that the Council and Commission are to be assisted by an Economic and Social Committee. This is an advisory body intended to represent various sectional interests. According to Article 193 EEC it consists of representatives of, among others, producers, farmers, carriers, workers, dealers, craftsmen, professional occupations and the general public. In practice it consists of three groups: employers, workers (largely represented by trade unionists) and others (the last group includes spokesmen for farmers, consumers and the professions). Its 189 members are appointed by the Council for renewable four-year terms on the basis of national allocations: the largest (for the United Kingdom and the other large countries) is 24; the smallest (Luxembourg) is 6. Each Member State draws up a list containing double its allotted number of members and the Council chooses from that list after consulting the Commission. The members, though intended to represent particular groups, are appointed 'in their personal capacity and may not be bound by any mandatory instructions'.[109] In certain cases the Committee has a right to be consulted on proposals for Community measures; it gives its opinion by an absolute majority (majority of members, not of votes). The Economic and Social Committee func-

---

[108] See pp. 39–45.
[109] Arts 194 EEC and 166 Euratom.

tions only with regard to the EEC and Euratom; there is an
equivalent body for the ECSC called the Consultative Committee of
the ECSC.[110]

THE DECISION-MAKING PROCESS

The powers of the Community to take legislative or executive action
are granted by various provisions in the Treaties,[111] and the procedure which must be followed in their exercise depends on the
particular provision in question. Although some legislative powers
are exercised by the Commission alone,[112] in most cases the Commission makes a proposal and, after the Parliament (and sometimes the Economic and Social Committee) have been consulted, the
Council takes the final decision. Under this procedure the Council is
in the strongest position; but no decision can be taken unless the
Commission initiates the process and, since the Commission can
amend the proposal at any time until a final decision has been taken
but the Council cannot do so unless it is unanimous,[113] the Commission is not without tactical advantages. In theory, complete deadlock
could be reached if the Commission (supported by at least one
Member State) insisted on a particular provision and the majority of
Member States wanted something different. In practice, however,
the Commission will usually amend its proposals in order to secure
the agreement of the Council.

Table 3 (below, p. 39) represents the normal decision-making process in diagrammatic form.[114] The first stage is the formulation of

[110] See Arts 18 and 19 ECSC.
[111] See Chapter 4.
[112] The EEC and Euratom Treaties grant the Commission legislative powers in only a
few cases, though, where granted, these powers enable the Commission to enact legislation
in the true sense: *France, Italy and United Kingdom* v. *Commission*, Cases 188–190/80, [1982]
ECR 2545 (paras 4–7 of the judgment). Moreover, the European Court has recently held
that whenever the EEC Treaty confers a specific task on the Commission, it impliedly
confers on the Commission the powers (including legislative powers) which are indispensable in order to carry out that task: *Germany* v. *Commission*, Cases 281, 283–5, 287/85,
[1988] 1 CMLR 11 (para. 28 of the judgment). In a much wider range of cases, the
Commission enjoys powers delegated to it by the Council. These powers, which apply only
where the basic principles have been laid down in Council legislation, are discussed below
at pp. 111–13. See, further, Hartley, "The Commission as Legislator under the EEC
Treaty" to be published in the E. L. Rev. for April 1988. The position is different under
the ECSC Treaty: there, the Commission is the main legislative authority.
[113] Arts 149 EEC and 119 Euratom.
[114] Where the co-operation procedure applies, it comes into operation after Point 15 on
the chart. In such cases, Table 2 (p. 35, above) may be regarded as beginning where Table
3 ends.

the Commission proposal. A working group is established, made up
of persons nominated by the national governments, who are usually
civil servants but are sometimes academics or other independent
experts. The powers of the group are only advisory: at this stage the
final decision rests with the Commission; but the views of the national
experts are listened to very carefully, since the consent of the national
governments will have to be obtained at a later stage. After the
working group has held a number of meetings and careful consideration has been given to the opinions of the national governments and
appropriate non-governmental interest groups (for example, the
relevant trade associations), the Commission will draft its proposal.

The proposal is sent to the Council, which in turn sends it to the
Parliament, and possibly also the Economic and Social Committee,
for their opinions. After these opinions have been received, the
proposal (which may have been amended by the Commission in the
light of these consultations) is sent to the Committee of Permanent
Representatives (COREPER). A working group of national officials is now set up within COREPER to prepare a report for the
Council. Commission representatives attend the meetings of these
groups. Amendments are usually put forward by the national representatives and these may, or may not, be accepted by the
Commission.

Finally the proposal, together with the report of the COREPER
working group, goes to the Council. The Commission is also represented at the Council meetings in which it is considered. If full
agreement was reached in COREPER, the proposal will be adopted
by the Council without debate, unless a last minute objection is
made. If no agreement was reached in COREPER, the matter will
be thrashed out in the Council. Sometimes this takes a long time and
in very important matters the Council may resort to one of its
'marathon' sessions. In the end, agreement may be reached on the
basis of a package deal in which several decisions are combined so
that concessions made by a state on one issue are balanced by gains
on another. In such a situation the Commission plays a crucial role in
suggesting possible compromises. If no agreement can be reached in
the appropriate technical Council, the matter may go up to the
general Council or even to the European Council. This will almost
always be necessary where a package deal contains elements from
different policy areas.[115]

[115] If the measure is one to which the co-operation procedure applies, the Council will
adopt a common position (rather than a formal decision) at this point and the co-operation
procedure will begin: see above, pp. 32–5.

Table 3
The EEC Decision-Making Process (Basic Procedure)

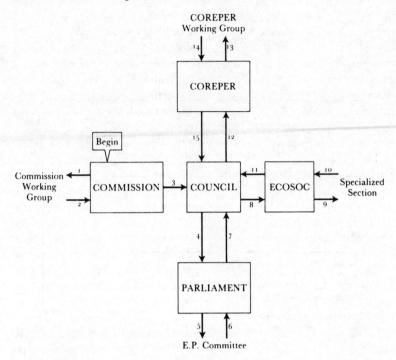

THE COMMUNITY BUDGET[116]

The revenue of the Community, which originally depended mainly on contributions from the Member States, is now mainly derived from the Community's 'own resources'. These are largely made up of agricultural levies imposed by the Community, customs duties on imports into the Community from outside (Common External Tariff) and VAT levied throughout the Community (up to a maximum at present of 1.4 per cent). The procedure for the budget is rather complex and has been varied on several occasions, notably by the first Budgetary Treaty of 1970 (which came into force on 1 January 1971) and the second Budgetary Treaty of 1975 (which came into force on 1 June 1977). These Treaties both amended the original

[116] The main provisions on finance are Arts 199–209 EEC, 78–78h ECSC and 171–183 Euratom.

Table 4
The Budgetary Procedure

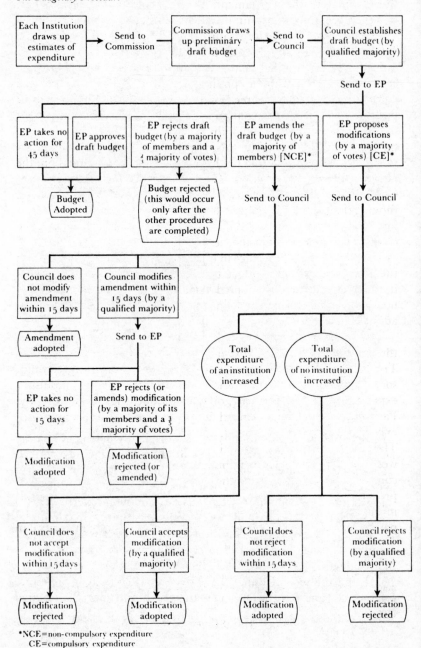

*NCE=non-compulsory expenditure
 CE=compulsory expenditure

Community Treaties; their effect was to transfer certain powers from the Council to the Parliament.[117] One important principle has, however, remained constant: the Community budget must balance.

The budgetary procedure is illustrated diagrammatically in Table 4 (opposite). The first step is for each institution to draw up its estimates of expenditure. These are sent to the Commission, which consolidates them into a 'preliminary draft budget' (there is a common budget for the three Communities). This preliminary draft budget, which must also contain an estimate of revenue, is then sent to the Council. The next step is the establishment of the 'draft budget' by the Council. In doing this, the Council acts by a qualified majority.[118] It is not bound by the proposals of the Commission: the normal rules which prevent the Council from making amendments to Commission proposals except by unanimity do not apply here, though the Council is obliged to consult the Commission when it intends to depart from the Commission's proposals. In all cases the Council will also consider the views of the Parliament.

The third stage takes place in the Parliament. The Parliament has the power to accept the budget, to amend it or to reject it. If it accepts it, the budget is thereby adopted; in addition, if the Parliament takes no action at all during the following 45 days, it is deemed to have adopted it.

The Parliament's right to make changes in the budget depends on the distinction between expenditure necessarily resulting from Treaty provisions or Community legislation (known as compulsory expenditure) and other expenditure (non-compulsory expenditure).[119] In the case of non-compulsory expenditure the Parliament may make amendments; in the case of compulsory expenditure, on the other hand, it may only propose 'modifications'. The significance of this distinction is that the Parliament has the last word in the case of amendments to provisions regarding non-compulsory expenditure; but the Council has the last word as regards proposed modifications to compulsory expenditure. Since amendments carry more weight, it is not surprising that they have to be passed by a majority of *members* of Parliament (absolute majority); in

[117] See, in particular, Arts 203 EEC, 78 ECSC and 177 Euratom.
[118] Defined above, p. 16. As previously mentioned, this is one occasion on which majority voting has always actually been practised in the Council. Were this not the case, it would probably be impossible to meet the strict deadlines which apply in the budgetary procedure.
[119] See Arts. 203(4) EEC, 78(4) ECSC and 177(4) Euratom.

the case of proposed modifications, on the other hand, only a majority of *votes cast* is required.

If amendments are made, or modifications proposed, the draft budget is sent back to the Council. The procedure in the Council depends on whether an amendment or modification is involved and, in the case of a modification, on whether or not the effect of the proposed modification is to increase the total expenditure of the institution in question. (This, in turn, depends on whether increases in particular items of expenditure are balanced by cuts in other items for the same institution.)

The procedure is as follows:

1. *Amendments:* amendments passed by the Parliament may be modified by the Council provided there is a qualified majority in favour.[120] If no such motion is passed within 15 days, the amendment is deemed to have been accepted.
2. *Modifications which do not increase total expenditure of an institution:* these modifications may be rejected by the Council if a motion to this effect is passed by a qualified majority; if no such motion is passed, the modifications are deemed to have been accepted.
3. *Modifications increasing total expenditure of an institution:* in this case the modification is deemed to have been rejected unless it is accepted. A motion accepting it must be passed by a qualified majority.

If, within 15 days, the Council has not modified any of the Parliament's amendments, and has accepted its modifications, the budget is deemed to have been finally adopted. If this is not the case, it goes back again to the Parliament.

When the budget comes back to it, the Parliament no longer has power to change provisions dealing with compulsory expenditure: if its modifications to these provisions have not been accepted by the Council, there is nothing it can do unless it decides to reject the budget as a whole. In the case of the non-compulsory expenditure, on the other hand, the Parliament has the right to reject the Council's modifications to its amendments and such a rejection is definitive. A motion to this effect must, however, be passed by a majority of the *members* of the Parliament; in addition, three-fifths of the *votes* must be

---

[120] It should be noted that, since such a decision is not taken on the basis of a Commission proposal, there must be at least eight Member States in favour: see Arts 148(2) EEC, 28 (fourth para.) ECSC and 118(2) Euratom.

in favour. If, however, no such action is taken within 15 days, the budget is deemed to have been adopted.

Under the second Budgetary Treaty the Parliament now has the right to reject the budget *in toto* if there are 'important reasons' for doing so.[121] Such a motion must be passed by a majority of all the members of the Parliament and also by two-thirds of the votes cast. This happened for the first time in December 1979. When this occurs, a new budget must be drawn up by the Council and put before the Parliament. If no budget has been passed at the beginning of a financial year, a sum equal to one-twelfth of the previous year's budget may be spent each month, provided that the Commission may not be granted more than one-twelfth of the appropriation in the draft budget under consideration. The monthly sums available may be increased by the Council, provided the consent of the Parliament is obtained with regard to non-compulsory expenditure.

It will be seen from this that the Parliament has substantial powers with regard to non-compulsory expenditure. These are, however, restricted by a rule that the annual growth of expenditure of this kind is subject to a limit (known as a 'maximum rate'), based on the increase in GNP, national budgets and inflation within the Community.[122] This limit may, however, be increased by agreement between the Council (acting by a qualified majority) and the Parliament (acting by a majority of members and a three-fifths majority of votes cast).[123]

The greatest weakness of the system from the point of view of the Parliament is that the latter has only limited powers over compulsory expenditure, which in practice constitutes the major part of the budget.[124] This deficiency has been somewhat alleviated, however, by two Joint Declarations of the Parliament, the Council and the

---

[121] Arts 203(8) EEC, 78(8) ECSC and 177(8) Euratom.

[122] It is fixed by the Commission and usually works out somewhere between 5 and 15 per cent. When the Parliament refused to abide by this limit in 1985, the European Court declared the budget invalid: *Council* v. *European Parliament*, Case 34/86, [1986] 3 CMLR 94.

[123] There is also a rule that, if the draft budget established by the Council provides for increases in non-compulsory expenditure which are greater than half the maximum rate laid down by the Commission, the Parliament is nevertheless entitled to make further increases amounting to not more than half the maximum rate, even though the end result will be that the total increases will then be over the maximum. The idea of this rule is to prevent the Council from pre-empting the Parliament's right to make increases by taking up the whole of the permitted amount. The amount by which the Parliament is entitled to increase the non-compulsory expenditure is known as its 'margin of manoeuvre'.

[124] In 1983, for example, only 28 per cent was classified as non-compulsory.

Commission, the first of 4 March 1975[125] and the second of 30 June 1982.[126]

The first Joint Declaration establishes a conciliation procedure intended to reconcile the views of the Parliament and the Council regarding Community legislation with 'appreciable financial implications' the adoption of which is not required by pre-existing legislation. This is intended to give the Parliament a say in the enactment of legislation giving rise to compulsory expenditure. The procedure is initiated, at the request of either the Parliament or the Council, when the Council does not intend to follow the Parliament's opinion on the legislation. A Conciliation Committee is convened, consisting of the Council and representatives of the Parliament, with the participation of the Commission. Its object is to seek agreement on the legislation between the Parliament and the Council. The procedure does not normally continue for more than three months and, where necessary, the Council may set a deadline. The Joint Declaration concludes by saying, 'When the positions of the two institutions are sufficiently close, the European Parliament may give a new Opinion, after which the Council shall take definitive action.' In such a case, the Council will presumably be able to follow the Parliament's opinion. The Joint Declaration is, however, silent as to what will occur where this is not possible. The Council apparently takes the view that it can then go ahead and adopt the measure without following the Parliament's opinion, but the Parliament is reluctant to accept this.[127]

The Second Joint Declaration clarifies the definition of compulsory expenditure by restricting it to expenditure which is necessary to meet the Community's legal obligations towards third parties (who may be individuals, Member States or non-member States).[128] It also classifies all the items in the 1982 budget and lays down a procedure for resolving future disputes.[129]

---

[125] OJ 1975, C 89/1.

[126] OJ 1982, C 194/1.

[127] See Joliet, *Institutions*, p. 107, where it is said that the Parliament takes the view that, in such a case, the Council can adopt the measure only by unanimity.

[128] See para. 1, which defines it as 'such expenditure as the budgetary authority [this means the Council and the Parliament acting together according to the budgetary procedure] is obliged to enter in the budget to enable the Community to meet its obligations, both internally and externally, under the Treaties and acts adopted in accordance therewith.'

[129] The Commission classifies each item in the preliminary draft budget. If either the Council or the Parliament cannot accept the classification of any item, the matter is referred to a meeting of the Presidents of the Parliament, the Council and the Commission (under the chairmanship of the Commission), where an attempt is made to reach agreement.

To ensure sound financial management in the Community, a Court of Auditors has been established.[130] It consists of twelve members of suitable qualifications who are appointed by the Council, acting by unanimity. Their status is comparable to that of the judges on the European Court. They have the task of examining the revenue and expenditure accounts of the Community in order to establish that revenue has been received, and expenditure incurred, in a regular and lawful manner. The budget is implemented by the Commission.[131] At the end of the financial year, the Parliament, acting on a recommendation from the Council (which itself acts by a qualified majority), gives a discharge to the Commission after considering the accounts and financial statement submitted by the Commission and the annual report of the Court of Auditors.[132]

CONCLUSIONS

Two facts will by now have become apparent: first, the supranational element in the Community, though real, is limited; secondly, the democratic element, though also real, is even more restricted. It seems probable that a link exists between these two facts: the supranational element is unlikely to grow significantly stronger – in particular, there is no prospect of a European federation – unless the democratic element is greatly strengthened. Significantly increased powers are not going to be given to a bureaucracy, however well-intentioned it may be: this would not be acceptable to public opinion. It is only by increasing the powers of the European Parliament that further integration can be brought about.

The most important powers that would have to be given to the European Parliament are:

1. Full legislative power within the areas of Community competence (possibly subject to the consent of a 'senate' representing the Member States);
2. Full budgetary power;
3. Power to control the executive.

It hardly needs saying that these developments are unlikely to take place in the near future. If they do come about, the Commission would be transformed into a government – responsible to the Parlia-

---

[130] See Arts 206–206a EEC, 78e–78f ECSC and 180–180a Euratom.
[131] Arts 205 EEC, 78c ECSC and 179 Euratom.
[132] Arts 206b EEC, 78g ECSC and 180b Euratom.

ment – and the Council would become a 'senate' representing national interests.

Though this may have been intended by the founders of the Community, the intervening years have shown little sign of its being realized. It is true that the European Parliament, being directly elected for the first time in 1979, has significantly increased its powers, mainly in the field of the budget[133] but also in other fields.[134] Overall, however, the most striking change has been a shift of power from the Commission to the Council. The power of the Commission relative to the other institutions was at its height in the days when only the ECSC existed, since under that Treaty it was intended to be the dominant authority. (It is interesting that the original draft of the ECSC Treaty contained no mention of the Council: it was included only to allay the fears of the smaller countries that the Commission would be dominated by the big countries.) The EEC and Euratom Treaties show a diminution of the Commission's role and an enhanced position for the Council. Perhaps this was only to be expected in view of the fact that, unlike the ECSC Treaty, the EEC Treaty sets out only the basic, initial policies to be pursued; beyond this, everything is left to the discretion of the institutions. In such circumstances, it is hardly surprising that the Member States insisted that the Council should have the dominant position.

A further shift in power, probably not intended by the authors of the EEC Treaty, has taken place over the last twenty years. The refusal to apply majority voting has meant that the adoption of legislation depends on negotiations carried on in COREPER and the Council, a development which has lessened the importance of the Commission's power to make proposals; the increased prestige and effectiveness of the Presidency has diluted the role of the Commission as mediator, and the establishment of the European Council (itself in part a response to the paralysis of the Council under the unanimity system) has involved a move back to traditional intergovernmental procedures, as has the emergence of European Political Cooperation: these and many other factors have combined to alter the political balance between the two main Community institutions.

This shift in power is usually regarded as indicating a decline in supranationalism. Up to a point, this is true. The same period has, however, seen the rise of another kind of supranationalism: in a series of key judgments, the European Court has enhanced the status of

[133] Budgetary Treaties of 1970 and 1975.
[134] See Arts 6, 8 and 9 SEA.

Community law to the point where, as far as its legal system is concerned, the Community now possesses most of the characteristics of a federation.[135] The most noticeable feature of this process has been the development, beginning in 1963 with the *Van Gend en Loos* case,[136] of the doctrine of direct effect (the principle that Community law must be applied by national courts as the law of land) and the establishment of the supremacy of Community law over national law.[137] Another feature has been the widening of Community jurisdiction, especially in the international sphere.[138] This apparent paradox may perhaps be explained by pointing to a possible link between these two developments: the growth of juridical supranationalism has made it all the more important for the Member States to control the policies of the Community, while the decline of political supranationalism has made the European Court's activism less objectionable.[139]

In the mid-1980s the first signs appeared of a possible revival of political supranationalism as it became evident that, in the Community of the Twelve, some sacrifice of national prerogatives was necessary if further progress was to take place. How far this will go, however, remains to be seen.

FURTHER READING

Joliet, *Institutions*, pp. 1–109.
Kapteyn and VerLoren van Themaat, Chapters 1, 2, 4, and 5.
Lasok and Bridge, Chapters 1 and 5–8.
H. Wallace, *Budgetary Politics: The Finances of the European Communities* (1980).
Ehlermann, 'Applying the New Budgetary Procedure for the First Time', (1975) 12 C.M.L. Rev. 325.
Hartley, 'Federalism, Courts and Legal Systems: The Emerging Constitution of the European Community', (1986) 34 Am. Jo. Comp. L. 229.
Henig, 'The European Community's Bicephalous Political Auth-

[135] See Hartley, 'Federalism, Courts and Legal Systems: The Emerging Constitution of the European Community', (1986) 34 Am. Jo. Comp. L. 229.
[136] Case 26/62, [1963] ECR 1.
[137] See Chapter 7.
[138] See Chapter 6.
[139] For a full discussion, see Weiler, 'The Community System: The Dual Character of Supranationalism', (1981) 1 YEL 267.

ority: Council of Ministers-Commission Relations' in J. Lodge (ed.) *Institutions and Policies of the European Community* (1983).

Kranz, 'Le vote dans la pratique du Conseil des ministres des Communautés européennes', (1982) RTDE 403.

Lauwaars, 'The European Council', (1977) 14 C.M.L. Rev. 25.

Nicoll, 'The Luxembourg Compromise', (1984) 23 JCMS 35.

Nuttall, 'European Political Co-operation and the Single European Act', (1985) 5 YEL 203.

Weiler, 'The Community System: The Dual Character of Supra-nationalism', (1981) 1 YEL 267.

Weiler, 'The Evolution of Mechanisms and Institutions for a European Foreign Policy: Reflections on the Interaction of Law and Politics', European University Institute, Working Paper No. 85/202.

Wooldridge and Sassella, 'Some Recent Legal Provisions Increasing the Budgetary Powers of the European Parliament and Establishing a European Court of Auditors', 1976/2 L I E I 13.

2

THE EUROPEAN COURT

The supranational element in the Community constitution would be ineffective without a court. The most important functions of the Court of Justice of the European Communities – to give it its full official name – are to ensure that the law is enforced, irrespective of political considerations (especially against Member States); to act as referee between the Member States and the Community as well as between the Community institutions *inter se*; and to protect the rights of the individual from infringement by the Brussels bureaucracies. These functions are especially important in view of the fact that the democratic element is still weak in the Community.

The powers of the Court and the law which it administers are considered in detail in the following chapters of this book. Here the stage will be set by discussing the Court as an institution.

STRUCTURE

Judges

There are thirteen judges on the Court, appointed by the common accord of the Member States.[1] It is stated in the Treaties[2] that judges must be 'persons whose independence is beyond doubt and who possess the qualifications required for appointment to the highest judicial offices in their respective countries or who are jurisconsults of recognised competence'. The latter provision permits academic lawyers to be appointed, even if they are not eligible for appointment to the judiciary in their own countries. Though this is not specified in the Treaties, there is one judge from each Member State and one additional judge to make up an odd number.[3] This political conven-

---

[1] Most Treaty provisions concerning the judges are to be found in Arts 165 and 167 EEC, 32 and 32(*b*) ECSC and 137 and 139 Euratom. The provisions in each of the three Treaties are identical.
[2] Arts 167(1) EEC, 32(*b*)(1) ECSC and 139(1) Euratom.
[3] The Treaties lay down no requirement as to the nationality of judges; in theory they could even be nationals of a non-member State.

tion is the consequence of the method of appointment: since each government must agree to every appointment, a country whose nominee was rejected could block all other candidates.[4]

Judges are appointed for staggered terms of six years, so that every three years either six or seven of the posts fall vacant. They are eligible for re-appointment and this frequently occurs; there is no retirement age. The Member States cannot remove a judge during his term of office, but he may be dismissed if, in the unanimous opinion of the other judges and advocates general, 'he no longer fulfils the requisite conditions or meets the obligations arising from his office'.[5] So far this procedure has never been put into operation.

The President of the Court is elected by his brother judges for a renewable term of three years. The election is by secret ballot.[6] The President's function is to direct the judicial and administrative business of the Court and to preside at sessions of the full Court. The Court is divided into Chambers and the President of each Chamber is elected annually by a similar method.[7]

On taking office, a judge swears to perform his duties impartially and conscientiously and to preserve the secrecy of the Court's deliberations. During office, he is not permitted to hold any political or administrative (governmental) office; nor may he engage in any occupation, whether gainful or not, unless exemption is granted by the Council.[8] Several judges have in fact been permitted to undertake academic functions. Even after they have ceased to hold office, judges must behave with integrity and discretion as regards the acceptance of appointments or benefits.[9]

At the present time, the quorum for a full Court (plenary session) is seven. As the Court reaches decisions by a majority, and the President has no casting vote, there must always be an uneven number of judges deciding a case. If one judge has to withdraw – for example, through illness – the most junior remaining judge will abstain from taking part in the deliberations.[10]

---

[4] There seems to be an understanding that the additional judge will be from one of the large countries.

[5] See Art. 6 of the Statute of the Court of Justice of the EEC and of the Statute of the Court of Justice of Euratom; under Art. 7 of the ECSC Statute there is a slightly different provision: the only ground is failure to fulfil the 'requisite conditions' and the concurrence of the advocates general is unnecessary.

[6] Art. 7(3) of the Rules of Procedure of the Court.

[7] Art. 10(1) of the Rules of Procedure.

[8] Art. 4 of the Statute for each Community.

[9] Ibid.

[10] Rules of Procedure, Art. 26(1).

A Chamber consists of either three or five judges.[11] The Court may assign to a Chamber any reference for a preliminary ruling or any action instituted by a private person 'in so far as the difficulty or the importance of the case or particular circumstances are not such as to require that the Court decide it in plenary session'.[12] Actions brought by a Member State or Community institution are always heard by the full Court; any other action will be heard by it if a request is made to this effect by a Member State or Community institution which is a party to the proceedings or an intervener or which has submitted written observations on a reference for a preliminary ruling.[13]

It might be thought that the comparatively short terms of office, as well as the appointment procedure, would lessen the independence of the judges. This is not, however, the case. No one who has any acquaintance with the Court can doubt the complete independence of its members from any national bias. A judge does not, just because he is British, consider himself to be 'the British judge' on the Court: he is a Community judge who happens to come from Britain. There is in fact a remarkable sense of corporate identity and solidarity among the judges and advocates general and, though they may sometimes be influenced by the different traditions of their respective legal systems, no one could accuse them of taking national advantage into account; on the contrary, the Court is generally regarded as one of the most 'European-minded' institutions in the Community.

The most important protection the judges have against national pressure is the fact that there is always just one 'judgment of the court' without any separate concurring or dissenting judgments. Since, moreover, the judges swear to uphold the secrecy of their deliberations, it is never known how individual judges voted. Therefore it is impossible to accuse a judge of being insufficiently sensitive to national interests or of having 'let his government down'; no one outside the Court can ever know whether he vigorously defended the position adopted by his own country or was in the forefront of those advocating a 'Community solution'.

The background of the judges is varied: some previously held political or administrative offices; some were in private practice or were members of the national judiciary; others had academic appointments.

[11] Arts 165 EEC, 32 ECSC and 137 Euratom.
[12] Art. 95(1) of the Rules of Procedure.
[13] See Arts. 165 EEC, 32 ECSC and 137 Euratom; and Art. 95 of the Rules of Procedure. Staff cases (actions brought by officials of Community institutions against their employing institution) always go to a Chamber: Art. 95(3) of the Rules of Procedure.

Advocates General

In addition to the judges, there are also six advocates general. Although this is not required by law, the practice is for one to come from each of the four big countries and two to come from the other Member States. They have the same status as judges: the same provisions regarding appointment, qualifications, tenure and removal apply to them as to judges; they receive the same salary, and they rank equally in precedence with the judges according to seniority in office. One advocate general is appointed First Advocate General. He is elected for a one-year term in the same way as the President of a Chamber.[14] When administrative matters concerning the functioning of the Court are being discussed, the advocates general sit with the judges; but they play no part in the Court's deliberations regarding cases.

Their function has no parallel in the English legal system, though it is similar to that of a *commissaire du gouvernement* in the French *Conseil d'Etat*. In the words of the Treaty,[15] 'It shall be the duty of the Advocate-General, acting with complete impartiality and independence, to make, in open court, reasoned submissions on cases brought before the Court of Justice, in order to assist the Court . . .'. When each new case comes to the Court, it is assigned by the First Advocate General to one of the advocates general. The advocate general to whom the case is assigned, together with his legal secretary (discussed below[16]), will study the issues involved and undertake any legal research they think necessary. After the parties have concluded their submissions to the Court, the advocate general will give his opinion. This opinion is not binding on the Court, but will be considered with very great care by the judges when they make their decision. It is printed, together with the judgment, in the law reports.

Impartiality and independence are important characteristics of his office. He represents neither the Community nor any Member State: he speaks only for the public interest. He works quite separately and independently from the judges; one could say that he gives a 'second opinion' which is in fact delivered first. This opinion shows the judges what a trained legal mind, equal in quality to their own, has concluded on the matter before them. It could be regarded as a point of reference, or starting point, from which they can begin their

[14] Art. 10(1) of the Rules of Procedure.
[15] Arts 166 EEC, 32(*a*) ECSC and 138 Euratom.
[16] See pp. 54–5.

deliberations. In many cases they follow the advocate general fully; in others they deviate from his opinion either wholly or in part. But always his views will be of great value.

An advocate general's job must in many ways be more satisfying than that of a judge. A judge works as a member of a committee: any proposal he puts forward regarding a judgment must be agreed to by at least a majority of his colleagues. He cannot, therefore, put his personal stamp upon a judgment in the same way that an English judge can; and even if he succeeds in winning over his brother judges to his way of thinking on a particular issue, the result is always anonymous: no one outside the closed circle of the Court will ever know that it was his work. The advocate general, on the other hand, is on his own: his opinion is his own work (though he may receive assistance from his legal secretary) and he alone is responsible for it. He will receive praise or blame according to his deserts.

One feature of the European Court which has sometimes given rise to comment is that there is no appeal from its judgments.[17] In most cases it may be regarded as a court of first and last resort. This puts a heavy burden on the judges, a burden not made any lighter by the uneven quality of the lawyers who appear before it. The Court cannot always draw the same assistance from counsel as an English court would. In these circumstances, the role of the advocate general is especially important. His opinion could in fact be regarded as a judgment of first instance which is subject to instant and invariable appeal. It is, however, an appeal of a special nature, since the parties have no opportunity to comment on the opinion before the Court begins its deliberations.

The advocate general's opinion is usually much easier to read than the Court's judgment. The latter, being the work of a committee, is often lacking in logical rigour; its terse and formal style is unattractive – at least to those brought up in the common law tradition – while the need to achieve consensus may produce obscurities and inconsistencies. The advocate general's opinion, on the other hand, is closer in style to an English judgment, this similarity being especially marked – as one would expect – in the case of an English advocate general. In it one normally finds a discussion of the facts, reference to (and quotation from) the relevant legislative provisions, and a full consideration of previous decisions of the Court. In some cases, the advocate general will provide a short comparative survey, prepared

[17] When the Court of First Instance is established, however, the European Court will itself hear appeals from the Court of First Instance.

with the assistance of the Court 'Documentation Service', of the way the point at issue would be dealt with in the legal systems of the Member States. He will also analyse the arguments put forward by the parties and finally give his own views on the issues before the Court.

In reaching his conclusions, the advocate general is not restricted to the arguments advanced by the parties. A good example of a case in which the advocate general put forward an original solution, which had not occurred to the parties, was *Transocean Marine Paint Association* v. *Commission*.[18] This case will be considered in detail below;[19] here all that need be said of the facts is that it was an attempt to set aside a decision of the Commission which was unfavourable to the interests of the applicants. They advanced various grounds for their contention; but it was Advocate General Warner, drawing on the law of the Member States – and particularly on that of England – who proposed that it should be annulled for failure to comply with natural justice. This was accepted by the Court and the rule *audi alteram partem* was incorporated into the Community legal system as a general principle of law.

The Registrar

The Registrar of the European Court plays a more important role than his equivalent in most national systems. He is elected by the judges and advocates general by secret ballot for a term of six years and is eligible for reappointment. His functions are two-fold. The Registry is responsible for all procedural matters; documents filed with the Court are the responsibility of the Registry, which distributes them to the members of the Court and serves them on the parties. Secondly, the Registrar is in charge of the administration of the Court and is present when the Court holds an administrative meeting, though he does not have a vote. In all these activities, he is responsible to the President of the Court.

Legal Secretaries

Each judge and advocate general has one or more legal secretaries to act as his assistants. Legal secretaries usually belong to a younger generation than the judges and advocates general; they may be

---

[18] Case 17/74, [1964] ECR 1063.
[19] At pp. 147–8.

lecturers or practising lawyers and they usually spend a few years at the Court before returning to their careers in their own countries. Their main task is to carry out legal research and to assist in the preparation of opinions or other legal writing. They are chosen by the judge or advocate general for whom they work.

Specialized Services

The Court has an excellent library with materials covering the legal systems of the Member States as well as that of the Community. There is at least one lawyer from each Member State on the staff and the Research and Documentation division provides the judges and advocates general with background papers on Community law and comparative surveys of national law.

There is a Translation Directorate which translates legal documents, including the judgments of the Court and the opinions of the advocates general, into the various languages of the Court. There is also an information office and the usual personnel and financial departments.

THE COURT OF FIRST INSTANCE

Article 4, 11 and 26 of the Single European Act make provision for the establishment of a Court of First Instance attached to the European Court. It will have jurisdiction in a limited range of cases[20] and there will be an appeal on points of law to the European Court. The idea is to lessen the burden on the European Court by relieving it of less important cases, especially those involving complicated questions of fact. It is not yet decided which cases will go to the Court of First Instance, but likely candidates are staff cases, competition cases and anti-dumping cases.[21] In many respects the structure and procedure of the new court will be the same as those of the European Court.

---

[20] Actions brought by Member States or Community institutions, and preliminary references from national courts have been expressly excluded from the jurisdiction of the Court of First Instance by the Single European Act. Subject to this, its jurisdiction will be laid down by the Council decision establishing it.

[21] Certain classes of action under the ECSC Treaty may also be included. See, further, the draft decision submitted to the Council by the Court on 29 September 1987.

JURISDICTION

The European Court has no inherent jurisdiction: it has only such jurisdiction as is conferred on it by the Treaties. There are a number of specific heads of jurisdiction and a case must be brought within one of them if the Court is to hear it. The various kinds of actions will be analysed in detail in the chapters that follow; here it is enough to give an overall picture. (For a diagrammatic representation of the principal heads of jurisdiction under the EEC Treaty, see Table 5.)

There are several criteria according to which the Court's jurisdiction may be classified. The most basic distinction is between judgments and advisory opinions or rulings. The latter are very much rarer than the former, but they occur in a number of situations, for example where the Council, the Commission or a Member State requests an opinion as to whether an international agreement which the Community intends to conclude with a non-member State is compatible with the EEC Treaty. Though advisory, these opinions have legal consequences: if, in the above example, the opinion is adverse, the agreement may enter into force only if the EEC Treaty is amended to accommodate it.

As far as judgments are concerned, the most fundamental distinction is between actions begun in the European Court (direct actions) and actions begun in a national court from which a reference for a preliminary ruling is made to the European Court. This distinction is important because if an action is begun in the European Court, it will end in the European Court: the Court's judgment will constitute a final determination of the dispute between the parties and will grant any remedies that may be appropriate; it is not subject to appeal.[22]

If, on the other hand, the action is begun in a national court, it will end in a national court: the European Court's ruling will be transmitted to the national court and the latter will then decide the case. Here the European Court's ruling, though binding and not subject to appeal, is merely a determination of an abstract point of law: the European Court does not decide the case as such. The national court decides any relevant questions of fact and then applies the law – including relevant provisions of Community law as interpreted by the European Court – to the facts; it also exercises any discretion it may have as to the remedy to be given.

In spite of the limited role played by the European Court, pre-

[22] When the Court of First Instance is established, there will be an appeal (on points of law) from it to the European Court.

Table 5
The Principal Heads of Jurisdiction of the European Court under the EEC Treaty.

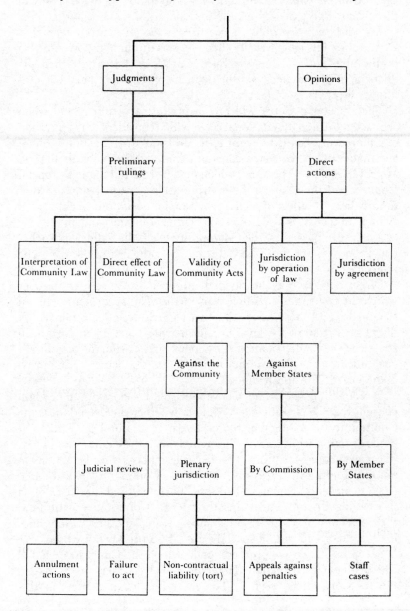

liminary rulings are of great importance because they concern the relationship between Community law and national law. It is only to the extent that it penetrates the national legal systems and confers rights and imposes obligations directly on private citizens that Community law can be really effective. It is through its power to give preliminary rulings that the European Court has established the doctrine of direct effect and the doctrine of the supremacy of Community law over national law.[23]

The European Court will give a preliminary ruling only when requested to do so by a national court which considers that a question of Community law is relevant to its decision: any court or tribunal *may* make such a request; a court or tribunal from which there is no appeal *must* do so. The issues which may be referred to the European Court are of three kinds: the interpretation of a provision of Community law, the effect of such a provision in the national legal system (which, in theory, is also a question of interpretation) and, in the case of a measure passed by the Community itself, the validity of such a provision. (Under the ECSC Treaty, only the last of these may be referred.)

Direct actions may be divided into two categories: those over which the Court has jurisdiction by virtue of an agreement between the parties and those where the Court's jurisdiction is conferred by direct operation of the law. The former are not very important in practice; the main example is actions arising out of a contract concluded by the Community which contains a clause giving jurisdiction to the European Court.

Direct actions where the Court's jurisdiction does not depend on consent may be classified according to whether the defendant is the Community or a Member State. There are a number of different kinds of action which may be brought against the Community. First, there are actions for judicial review: these may either be actions to annul a Community measure or to oblige a Community institution to pass a measure which it had previously refused to pass. Such proceedings are brought against the relevant Community institution; they may be brought by a Member State, another Community institution or – in certain special cases – by a private individual.

Secondly, there are proceedings in which the Court has what is called 'plenary jurisdiction'. Here the Court has wider powers than in the case of judicial review. The most important actions in this

[23] See Chapters 7 and 9, below.

category are actions for damages for non-contractual liability (tort), appeals against penalties imposed on private individuals for violations of Community law and actions brought by Community officials against the institution employing them.[24]

Actions for damages may be brought by either a Member State or a private individual; the applicant must prove that he has suffered loss as a result of Community action. Penalties may be imposed by the Commission where it is empowered to do so by a Community regulation. (In practice this is usually for violation of the Community competition provisions.) If the Commission imposes a penalty, the person (or firm) concerned may appeal to the European Court against both the finding that there was a violation of Community law and against the severity of the penalty. Employment disputes relating to Community staff are very numerous and take up a great deal of the Court's time, even though they are heard only by a Chamber of the Court. They are not in themselves of much interest to outsiders, though general points do arise from time to time. Many of them concern officials who object to the fact that they have been passed over for promotion or have been refused some special allowance or other benefit. Unsuccessful applicants for appointment to Community posts may also bring proceedings if they consider that the employing authority has acted improperly.

Under the EEC and Euratom Treaties, proceedings known as enforcement actions may be brought against a Member State alleged to have violated Community law. The applicant may be either the Commission or another Member State; in practice it is almost always the Commission. There is a preliminary procedure in which an opinion is given by the Commission after the Member State has explained its position: if the Member State refuses to abide by this, the Commission (or the other Member State) brings the action before the Court. (Under the ECSC Treaty, the procedure is slightly different: the Commission gives a decision instead of an opinion; this is binding and a Member State which is unwilling to comply must itself bring proceedings in the Court to have the decision set aside.)

[24] For a fuller discussion of the distinction between judicial review and plenary (unlimited) jurisdiction, see Usher, *European Court Practice*, pp. 11–12; Schermers, paragraph 567.

PROCEDURE

The procedure of the European Court is laid down partly in the Statutes of the Court (there are separate Statutes for the three Communities in the form of protocols to the ECSC, EEC and Euratom Treaties) and partly in the Rules of Procedure. The latter are drawn up by the Court itself, but have to be approved by the Council;[25] there is one set for all three Communities. They were originally modelled on those of the International Court of Justice.[26]

The two most important ways in which the procedure in the European Court differs from that in an English court are the greater importance of written documents (and the consequent down-grading of oral proceedings) and the more active role played by the Court. Both these features are generally characteristic of Continental courts.

The normal procedure in a direct action may be divided into four stages: the written proceedings, the preparatory inquiry, the oral hearing and the judgment.

The Written Proceedings

Direct actions in the European Court are begun with a document called an application, in which the applicant (plaintiff) sets out the basis of his claim. This is not served on the defendant but lodged with the Court;[27] the Registrar will serve it on the defendant, who then has one month to lodge his defence. The applicant is entitled to reply to the defence by means of a document called a reply and the defendant may answer this in a rejoinder. Then the pleadings are closed.

Admissibility

At this point the defendant may make a preliminary objection regarding admissibility. This concerns the question whether the Court is able to hear the case, in particular whether the subject-matter is within the Court's jurisdiction, whether the applicant has *locus standi*, and whether the proceedings were brought within the

---

[25] See Arts 188 EEC, 160 Euratom and 44 of the Statute of the Court (ECSC).

[26] For a consolidated version, see OJ 1982, C 39/1; there are also Supplementary Rules dealing with less important matters: see OJ 1974, L 350/29.

[27] The case officially begins at this moment and this is the cut-off date for time-limits for the commencement of proceedings. On receipt of the application, the Registrar will give the case a number, e.g. 'Case 47/77' or 'Opinion 1/75', in which the figures after the oblique stroke indicate the year when the proceedings began.

relevant time limit. A preliminary objection to admissibility is made in a separate document, to which the applicant is entitled to reply. There is a special hearing on the point and the advocate general gives an opinion. The Court will then give judgment: it may uphold the objection (in which case the action will be at an end) or dismiss it (in which case the proceedings will continue from the point where they were broken off) or the Court may decide to reserve its decision until the final judgment: in this case the main action will continue but in the end the Court may decide that it was inadmissible and reject it without going into the merits.

Preparatory Inquiry

The second stage is the preparatory inquiry. This is concerned with the determination of questions of fact. Unlike the English procedure, however, it is the Court which decides what evidence is needed. As soon as the application has been lodged, the President of the Court will assign the case to one of the Chambers and designate a judge from that Chamber as 'judge rapporteur'; the First Advocate General will then decide which advocate general will take the case. After the close of pleadings, the judge rapporteur will prepare a preliminary report dealing with the issues of fact arising in the case. The Court will then decide, at a so-called administrative meeting, what issues of fact (if any) need to be proved and what evidence is necessary for this purpose. In practice, questions of fact are not often in dispute and the Court will usually content itself with requiring the production of documents and, possibly, putting questions to the parties. Where witnesses are called, the procedure is rather different from that in an English court. The witnesses are always witnesses of the Court, not the parties. (If a party wishes a certain witness to be called, he must make a request to the Court.) A witness is summoned by an order of the Court which will indicate the facts about which he is to be examined. The witness is heard before a Chamber of the Court in the presence of the parties or their representatives; the presiding judge will examine the witness, but the parties – as well as the other judges and the advocate general – may put questions as well. The testimony is put into writing and signed by the witness after being read back to him.

English lawyers who have taken part in proceedings in the European Court are usually unimpressed with the Court's methods of taking evidence in general and examining witnesses in particular.

It is interesting to note that it was only after the United Kingdom joined the Community that counsel could put questions directly to witnesses; before that the question had to be put through the judge.

Oral Procedure

This corresponds to the 'day in court' in English procedure. However, since the evidence has already been taken at an earlier stage, it is much less important to the outcome of the case. A few days beforehand, the judge rapporteur issues his report for the hearing, which is distributed to the parties so that they can comment on it at the hearing. The report sets out the facts of the case and contains a summary of the arguments put forward by the parties.

At the hearing, counsel will address the Court and expound their contentions. After the main speeches, each side is allowed a brief reply. The judges and the advocate general may address questions to counsel. The Court then usually adjourns and the advocate general prepares his opinion; the hearing resumes at a later date for him to deliver it. The parties have no right to comment on it: the hearing is now over and the Court must consider its judgment.

Judgment

The Court always reserves judgment. The judges meet in a special deliberation room to decide on their judgment; no one other than the judges themselves may be present, not even secretaries or interpreters. The judge rapporteur has the task of preparing a draft of the judgment which is then put before the other judges; if necessary a vote is taken. The procedure is that each judge gives his opinion in turn, starting with the most junior. When a decision is finally reached, the judgment is signed by all the judges sitting and is delivered in open Court. It is also published: the operative part (formal ruling) in the Official Journal and the whole judgment, together with advocate general's opinion, in the official law reports.

Execution

In most cases the defendant is either the Community (or an institution thereof) or a Member State; in neither of these cases is it possible to obtain execution of the judgment. The judgment is binding and it is assumed that it will be obeyed. The question of execution only arises, therefore, in those rare cases where the defendant is a private individual and damages are awarded against him, or where the applicant is a private person and costs are awarded against him. In these cases the judgment creditor must go to the appropriate national court to obtain enforcement according to national procedure; enforcement is, however, automatic and the national court has no right to question the judgment.[28]

Special Procedures after Judgment

There is no appeal from judgments of the European Court; there are, however, three special procedures which, to a very limited extent, might be said to serve a similar function. These are third party proceedings, revision and interpretation. The first two allow a request to be made to the European Court to review a judgment previously given by it; under the third, the Court may be asked to clarify the meaning of its judgment.[29] Though of theoretical interest, these proceedings are rare in practice.

Third party proceedings provide a means whereby a person who was not a party to the original action may contest a judgment which is prejudicial to his rights.[30] The proceedings are begun by an application to which similar rules apply as in the case of an ordinary action and which is lodged with the Court and served by the Registrar on all the parties to the original proceedings. The third party must show that the judgment is prejudicial to his rights and give good reasons why he was unable to take part in the original action (normally this would be because it was not brought to his notice). The proceedings must be brought within two months of the publication of the judgment in the Official Journal.

When a new fact comes to light after the judgment which would have had a decisive impact on it, a party to the original proceedings may apply for revision.[31] The fact must not have been before the

[28] Arts 187 and 192 EEC, 159 and 164 Euratom, and 44 and 92 ECSC. For the procedure in the United Kingdom, see pp. 241–2, below.

[29] Clerical mistakes, errors in calculation and obvious slips in the judgment may also be corrected by the Court of its own motion or on application of a party within two weeks after the delivery of the judgment; see Art. 66 of the Rules of Procedure. A party may apply within one month for the Court to make good any omission in its judgment: Art. 67 of the Rules of Procedure.

[30] See Arts 39 EEC Statute, 36 ECSC Statute and 40 Euratom Statute; also Art. 97 of the Rules of Procedure.

[31] See Arts 41 EEC Statute, 38 ECSC Statute and 42 Euratom Statute; also Arts 93–100 of the Rules of Procedure.

Court when it gave judgment and must also have been unknown to the party making the application. The proceedings must be brought within three months of the discovery of the new fact and also within ten years of the original judgment. When an application is made, the Court first decides whether the new fact is of sufficient importance to warrant the re-opening of the case; if it decides that this is so, it will then reconsider the previous judgment in the light of the new fact. The other party is, of course, allowed to contest the application both at the stage of admissibility and when the judgment is reviewed.

An application for the interpretation of a judgment may be brought by a party to the previous case or by a Community institution even if it was not a party.[32] The request may be directed only to the actual ruling, or the reasoning on which it was based; the clarification of *obiter dicta* may not be requested.

Preliminary Rulings

The procedure is different where the European Court is asked by a national court to give a preliminary ruling. Here there are, strictly speaking, no parties; the proceedings are not regarded as contentious: the European Court views its function simply as assisting the national court. The parties to the national proceedings cannot, therefore, take the initiative: the national court sets the procedure in motion by making an order for reference and the judgment of the European Court is sent back to the national court where the case will continue on its course. The events in the European Court are only an episode in the national proceedings.

When the order for reference reaches the European Court, the Registrar will transmit copies to the parties in the national proceedings and also to the Member States, the Commission and, where a measure of the Council is in issue, to the Council. These persons and bodies may submit written observations to the Court and they may also attend the oral hearing. At the hearing, submissions are made by those attending; then the advocate general presents his opinion and judgment is given in the normal way. The parties to the national proceedings may not request revision or interpretation of the judgment; but the national court may, if it wishes, make a second reference in order to deal with a new issue or to clarify the original ruling.

[32] See Arts 40 EEC Statute, 37 ECSC Statute and 41 Euratom Statute; also Art. 102 of the Rules of Procedure.

Lawyers

The rules regarding legal representation differ according to whether the party is, on the one hand, a private person or company or, on the other hand, a Member State or Community institution.[33] In the former case, representation by a lawyer is obligatory; the only exception is that in references for preliminary rulings the national rules apply: therefore, if a party is permitted to appear in person in the court from which the reference was made, he will be allowed to do so in the European Court.

Member States and Community institutions are represented by an agent appointed for the particular case; he may be assisted by an adviser or lawyer. National governments often choose a civil servant (normally with legal qualifications) as their agent; alternatively they may brief a barrister. The Council and Commission are normally represented by a member of their legal services; sometimes outside lawyers may be briefed.

The right of a lawyer to appear before the European Court depends on national law. In direct actions, any lawyer entitled to practise before a court of any Member State may appear before the European Court; in preliminary references, anyone (even if not legally qualified) entitled to represent a party before the court or tribunal which made the reference may do so before the European Court. Agents and advisers of Member States and Community institutions may appear even if not entitled to plead in national courts.

The position regarding English lawyers is more complicated. The English texts[34] of the Statutes and Rules of Procedure use the word 'lawyer' and this is wide enough to cover both barristers and solicitors. An agreement to regulate the matter was entered into between the two professions in 1971 in anticipation of Britain's entry into the Community. Under this agreement, barristers could appear in any case, but the right of audience of solicitors was subject to restrictions. However, the Council of the Law Society rescinded the agreement on 19 June 1981 and the position now is that solicitors can probably appear in any direct action (and have done so on at least one occasion[35]); on a preliminary reference, they can appear if they have

[33] See the Statutes of the Court: Art. 17 (EEC and Euratom) and Art. 20 (ECSC); see also Arts 37, 38 and 104 of the Rules of Procedure.
[34] In other languages the provision seems more restrictive: the French text, for example, refers to 'un avocat inscrit à un barreau de l'un des États membres.'
[35] *Tither* v. *Commission*, Case 175/80, [1981] ECR 2345.

a right of audience before the court which made the reference. In practice, however, almost all English lawyers appearing before the European Court are barristers.

In direct actions the general rule is that costs are awarded to the successful party if he has asked for them. (There is an exception regarding staff cases: here the employing institution pays its own costs even if it wins.) Where costs are granted, the unsuccessful party must not only pay his own costs (e.g. lawyers' fees, travelling expenses, etc.) but also those of the successful party. In the event of a dispute, either party may apply for costs to be taxed by the Court. In preliminary rulings, on the other hand, the European Court does not award costs: they are regarded as costs in the case before the national court and any ruling made by it applies to them as well.

A person who is wholly or partly unable to meet the costs of proceedings in the European Court may apply for legal aid.[36] The application is made to the Court itself and is heard by a Chamber. Legal representation is not necessary for such an application. If legal aid is granted, the cashier of the Court pays out the sum allowed; it is, however, provided in the Rules of Procedure that the Court may order the repayment of this sum in a subsequent decision regarding costs.

Where a reference for a preliminary ruling is made from an English court, a legal aid certificate granted for the English proceedings will also cover the proceedings in the European Court.[37] Where, however, the reference is made from an English tribunal to which legal aid does not apply, for example a national insurance tribunal, the person concerned could ask the European Court to give him legal aid to cover the proceedings there.[38]

MULTILINGUALISM

One of the characteristics of the Community is that it is multilingual. Between them, the Member States have ten official languages – Danish, Dutch, English, French, German, Greek, Irish, Italian, Portuguese and Spanish. The principle of linguistic equality was not

[36] Art. 76 of the Rules of Procedure.

[37] *R.* v. *Marlborough Street Stipendiary Magistrate*, ex p. *Bouchereau* [1977] 3 All E.R. 365; see also the Legal Aid (General) Regulations 1980 (S.I. 1980 No. 1894), Reg. 52(b)(vi).

[38] Art. 104(3) of the Rules of Procedure provides that the European Court may grant legal aid on a preliminary reference in 'special circumstances'.

fully accepted in the beginning. When the ECSC Treaty was signed in 1951, Germany (and, to some extent, Italy) were in a weak political position as a consequence of the war; Britain had chosen to stand aloof from Europe. Therefore it was hardly surprising that France played the leading role and that the French language enjoyed a special position. The result was that the Treaty was drawn up in a single text in French.[39] There is no express statement that only the French text is authentic but this is generally regarded as following from the fact that it was the original.[40] Official translations were, however, made into Dutch, German and Italian and, subsequently, into the official languages of the new Member States.

The EEC and Euratom Treaties, on the other hand, are authentic in the official languages of all the Member States: they were originally drawn up in the four official languages of the original Member States and it was provided that all versions would be equally authentic.[41] When Denmark, Ireland and the United Kingdom joined the Community, it was laid down that the official translations into Danish, English and Irish would have the same status as the original versions.[42] The same steps were taken when Greece, Portugal and Spain joined the Community.[43]

All the official languages except Irish are working languages of the institutions.[44] Community legislation is published in all the working languages and it is generally accepted that all versions are equally authentic, even in the case of ECSC measures.[45] When Denmark, Ireland and the United Kingdom joined, pre-accession Community measures still in force were translated into Danish and English, and Article 155 of the Act of Accession stated that they would have the

---

[39] See Art. 100 ECSC.

[40] Thus, while Art. 160 of the Act of Accession 1972 provides for authentic versions of the EEC and Euratom Treaties in the Danish, English and Irish languages, there is no equivalent provision in the case of the ECSC Treaty: see Art. 159.

[41] See Art. 248 EEC and 225 Euratom.

[42] See Art. 160 of the Act of Accession.

[43] Art. 150 of the Act of Accession (Greece); Art. 397 of the Act of Accession (Spain and Portugal).

[44] See Arts 217 EEC and 190 Euratom, together with Regulation 1 (EEC), JO 1958, p. 385 and Regulation 1 (Euratom), JO 1958, p. 401, as amended on the accession of new Member States. As far as the ECSC is concerned, see P. Reuter, *La Communauté Européenne du Charbon et de l'Acier* (1953) at pp. 81–2, referring to an unpublished decision of the foreign ministers of the original Six, taken at a meeting in Paris on 23 and 24 July 1952, that Dutch, French, German and Italian would be the working languages.

[45] See H. Kutscher, 'Methods of Interpretation as Seen by a Judge at the Court of Justice', p. 17 (paper delivered at the Judicial and Academic Conference held at the European Court in 1976).

same authenticity as the versions in the other languages. This was also done when Greece, Portugal and Spain joined.[46]

The interpretation of multilingual texts poses particular problems. In the case of the ECSC Treaty, the French text enjoys a certain pre-eminence but this does not mean that the Court will ignore the other texts, nor that it will always give legal terms used in the Treaty the same meaning as they have in French law.[47] Normally it will look at all versions and, while giving greater weight to the French text, would be prepared to adopt an interpretation closer to one of the others if there were good reasons for doing so. Moreover, where the same term is used in the later Treaties as well, the Court will, for reasons of uniformity, try to give it the same meaning throughout. In such a situation, special weight cannot be given to the French version of the ECSC Treaty, since this would be unacceptable with regard to the other Treaties.

In the case of the other Treaties, as well as all Community legislation, each version is equally authentic. How should the Court interpret these texts? In public international law, various theories on the interpretation of multilingual treaties have been put forward. They include the following: that the least onerous version should be preferred (theory of minimum obligation); that each contracting state should be bound only by the version in its own language; and that the text in the original language should prevail.[48] Community law is not, however, a branch of international law[49] and theories which might be appropriate for the latter are not necessarily acceptable in Community law. In particular, it would be unthinkable for the obligations of Member States to vary because of differences in the texts: the unity of the Community is paramount.[50]

In practice, the European Court does not appear to have been troubled by linguistic differences in the texts. The reason is simple: even when there are no linguistic problems, the Court does not put a great deal of weight on the literal meaning of the words. Policy considerations play a particularly important role and sometimes prevail over the literal meaning even when it is clear.[51] Linguistic

---

[46] See Art. 147 of the Act of Accession (Greece) and Art. 397 of the Act of Accession (Portugal and Spain).

[47] See Dickschat, 'Problèmes d'interprétation des traités européens résultant de leur plurilinguisme' [1968] Revue Belge de Droit International 40 at 46–9.

[48] See Dickschat, op. cit., at pp. 43–4.

[49] See p. 85, below.

[50] See the quotation from *Stauder* v. *City of Ulm* given below.

[51] See pp. 77–81, below.

discrepancies are, therefore, treated in the same way as other obscurities in the text: the Court adopts the meaning which, in its view, best
accords with the purpose of the provision and the policy objectives
pursued by the Court.[52] This applies both in those cases where the
same term is used in all the versions but its meaning differs in the
various national systems and also in those cases where different terms
are used.

The chapters that follow contain many examples of the Court's
practice of choosing between the various versions on the basis of
policy objectives. Here it is sufficient to mention one: *Stauder* v. *City of
Ulm*.[53] This case, which is considered further below,[54] concerned a
Community scheme under which persons in receipt of welfare benefits could obtain butter at a reduced price on presentation of a
coupon. The scheme had been established by a Commission decision
addressed to all the Member States, and the German version stated
that the coupon had to contain the beneficiary's name; the Dutch
version was similar, but the French and Italian texts stated merely
that the coupon had to be 'individualized'.

The German authorities charged with implementing the scheme
had looked only to the German version and had issued vouchers
which had to contain the name and address of the beneficiary. The
plaintiff in the case maintained that it was a humiliation to have to
reveal his identity to the shopkeeper when he bought the butter; he
even went so far as to argue that this constituted a violation of his
human rights. He therefore brought legal proceedings in the German
courts and the case came before the European Court on a reference
for a preliminary ruling on the interpretation and validity of the
Commission decision. The Court held that it should be interpreted so
as not to require the recipient's name to be revealed. The relevant
passage of the judgment reads as follows:[55]

When a single decision is addressed to all the Member States the necessity for
uniform application and accordingly for uniform interpretation makes it impossible to consider one version of the text in isolation but requires that it be
interpreted on the basis of both the real intention of its author and the aim he
seeks to achieve, in the light in particular of the versions in all four languages.

In a case like the present one, the most liberal interpretation must prevail,

[52] See *Mij PPW Internationaal*, Case 61/72, [1973] ECR 301 (paragraph 14 of the
judgment) and *Moulijn* v. *Commission*, Case 6/74, [1974] ECR 1287 (paragraphs 10 and 11
of the judgment); see further Kutscher, op. cit., p. 20.
[53] Case 29/69, [1969] ECR 419.
[54] See p. 133.
[55] [1969] ECR at pp. 424–5 (paragraphs 3 and 4 of the judgment).

provided that it is sufficient to achieve the objectives pursued by the decision in question. It cannot, moreover, be accepted that the authors of the decision intended to impose stricter obligations in some Member States than in others.

The consequence of this judgment is that, even when a Community decision is addressed to a Member State, that State must be prepared to consider all the linguistic versions if it wants to be sure of the correct interpretation.[56]

Court Procedure

What languages may be used in Court proceedings? The question depends on what is known as the 'language of the case'.[57] Any one of the official languages of the Member States (including Irish) may be chosen, and the theory behind the rules governing the choice of language is that the Community is regarded as multilingual and consequently able to operate in any official language. Community institutions are therefore required to accommodate themselves to the needs of the other party.

In direct actions the basic rule is that the applicant has the choice of language. However, where the defendant is a Member State, or an individual or corporation having the nationality of a Member State, the language of the case is the official language of that State. (Where the Member State has more than one official language – as, for example, is the case with Belgium – the applicant may choose between them.) Except in the rare cases where a Member State brings enforcement proceedings against another Member State, the Community will always be a party to a direct action; the effect of these rules, therefore, is to benefit the other party. The Court may depart from the rules at the request of the parties; however, where the request is not made jointly by the parties, the advocate general and the other party must be heard.

In the case of a preliminary ruling, the language of the case is that of the national court or tribunal which made the reference,[58] though other Member States may submit observations in their own languages.

In general, the language of the case is used for all purposes in the proceedings, and documents in other languages must be translated

---

[56] See Kutscher, op. cit., pp. 18–19.
[57] See Art. 29 of the Rules of Procedure.
[58] Provided it is one of the official languages: it would seem that some other language – such as Welsh – would not be acceptable.

into it. Members of the Court, however, may use any official language of their choice. This applies to comments and questions during the hearing, to the judge rapporteur's report and to the advocate general's opinion. There is simultaneous translation at the oral hearing. Court publications, including law reports, are published in the working languages of the Community (i.e. in all the official languages except Irish).

It will readily be appreciated that litigants in the European Court face linguistic problems not encountered in domestic courts. The private litigant normally has the choice of language; however, a litigant who chooses, for example, Danish must be aware of the fact that most judges cannot understand this language. The precision of the pleadings may suffer on translation and at the hearing the eloquence of counsel may have little effect when it is heard through the earphones of the simultaneous translation apparatus. Clearly, a French-speaking lawyer – and to a lesser extent, an English-speaking one – will find it easier to present his case.

Drafting the Judgment

In order to maintain the secrecy of their discussions, the judges do not allow any interpreters into the deliberation room. In these circumstances multilingualism is impossible and the Court has informally adopted French as its working language.[59] This choice was made when the Court was first set up and is another example of the special position enjoyed by French in those days. Indeed the choice of French was almost inevitable in view of the fact that it was an official language of three of the six original Member States (France, Belgium and Luxembourg). Today, English is more widely spoken in the majority of Community countries, but it is unlikely, for a considerable time at least, to replace French as the working language of the Court: once made, a choice of language is hard to change, since appointments to the Court are made with this in mind.

The choice of French as the working language of the Court means that the judges speak French when they discuss their judgment. All drafting is done in French and the final version approved by the Court is in French even if this is not the language of the case. The French text of the judgment is then translated into the language of the case and this text is signed by the judges and

[59] English is sometimes used in a Chamber.

delivered in open Court. The result is that the text signed by the judges may be in a language which many of them do not understand. This throws a great deal of responsibility on those judges who are fluent in the language of the case to ensure that the translation truly reflects what was agreed on.

One drawback of the unilingual mode of operation of the Court is that it puts judges whose mother tongue is not French at a disadvantage. Most people feel less confident about giving their opinions in a group discussion if they are not fully at home in the language spoken. French-speaking judges must therefore enjoy a subtle psychological advantage over their colleagues. The use of French in the deliberation room must, moreover, work to some extent in favour of French legal thinking: it is hard to draft a judgment in French without using French legal terminology, while concepts peculiar to other systems might be ignored simply because they cannot easily be expressed in French.

Another difficulty is that, although the official version of the judgment is in the language of the case, the French language version is the one actually agreed on by the Court and therefore might be said to represent the opinion of the Court more accurately than the former. One can imagine that if there is a discussion in the deliberation room as to exactly what was decided in a previous case, it is the French text which will be examined. Consequently, a lawyer trying to convince the Court that it ought to follow its previous decision would be well advised to study the French text as well as that in his own language, even if the latter is the authentic version; where this is not the case, it is especially important not to rely exclusively on one version.

It is almost impossible for even the best translator to find a form of words with exactly the same meaning as the original; translations, therefore, can never be exact. Sometimes there is simply no equivalent word in the other language. For example, Article 40 ECSC uses the phrase '*faute de service*' in the French version; this is a French legal term which cannot be translated directly into English: the translators of the Treaty therefore had to make do with the circumlocution 'wrongful act or omission [on the part of the Community] in the performance of its functions', a phrase which entirely lacks the precise connotations of the French. (One can imagine that if the English word 'trust' were translated into French, the translators might well come up with something equivalent to 'legal relationship in which one person has a beneficial interest in property nominally owned by another', a phrase which can have little meaning for someone ignorant of English law.)

In addition to the inaccuracies which inevitably result from translation, actual mistakes sometimes occur. For example, in the English version of the judgment in *Royer*,[60] the word 'save' was omitted from the following passage: '. . . the procedure of appeal to a competent authority must precede the decision ordering expulsion [save] in cases of emergency'. This was a simple slip; a less obvious, and thus more insidious, error occurred in the *Bonsignore* case.[61] Here the phrase '*Gefährdungen der öffentlichen Ordnung*' in the authentic German version of the judgment – '*des menaces à l'ordre public*' in the French version – was mistranslated into English as 'breaches of the peace', a mistake which caused difficulties in a later case when an English court made a reference for a preliminary ruling on the same issue.[62]

THE FORM OF JUDGMENT

Judgments of the European Court consist of three main parts. The first[63] is based on the report of the judge rapporteur and contains a statement of the facts and a summary of the arguments of the parties; the second part,[64] which is usually drawn up in numbered paragraphs and set in larger print in the official version of the law reports, contains the grounds of judgment; the final part is the actual ruling.

For lawyers, the second part is the important one, since this gives the Court's reasons for its decision. After a certain amount of experimentation in the early days, the Court adopted a style based on that of the French courts. This is very formal, terse and abstract. For some time, the French version was written in the form of one long sentence, each paragraph beginning with the words '*Attendu que* . . .' ('Whereas . . .') or simply '*que*' ('that') and ending with a semicolon. These subordinate clauses would all lead up to the final ruling that, for example, the application was dismissed. This is broken up into

---

[60] Case 48/75, [1976] ECR 497, at paragraph 59 of the judgment. The authentic version of this judgment was in French.

[61] Case 67/74, [1975] ECR 297 at 307.

[62] *R.* v. *Bouchereau*, Case 30/77, [1977] ECR 1999; see *per* Advocate General Warner at p. 2024. 'Threats to public policy' would be a literal translation of the German and French texts.

[63] Headed 'Issues of Fact and Law', 'Facts' or 'Facts and Issues'. It is sometimes omitted from the European Court Reports.

[64] Headed 'Grounds of Judgment', 'Law' or 'Decision'.

separate sentences in the English version (a style now adopted in French as well) but it still reads as a series of *ex cathedra* statements, completely lacking the close reasoning of an English or American judgment.

This style was probably necessitated by the decision-making procedure adopted by the Court. For reasons discussed above,[65] the Court gives a single judgment: concurring or dissenting judgments are not permitted. However, it is the policy of the Court to involve all the judges in the drafting of the judgment in an attempt to attain the maximum consensus. Though the judge rapporteur might be expected to play a special role, the judgment is the collective work of the whole Court and it is apparently not uncommon for each sentence to be subject to lengthy discussion. Committee procedure of this kind does not lend itself to the production of a discursive judgment of the English sort.

This does not, of course, mean that a court which gives a single judgment must inevitably adopt the French style. The judgments of the Privy Council in the days before it allowed dissenting and concurring judgments are evidence of this. However, if it were desired to produce a judgment in the English style, it would be necessary to sacrifice any attempt to gain a consensus: the drafting of the judgment would have to be entrusted to a single judge – who would no doubt be the member of the court whose views most clearly represented those of the majority – and the role of the others would be limited to the suggesting of minor alterations.

Two further consequences of the attempt to attain consensus are evident in the Court's judgments. In some cases there appear to be two separate lines of reasoning, both leading to the same conclusion. Since these may be quite different, the result is disconcerting for the lawyer trying to extract the *ratio decidendi*. The reason for this appears to be that, though there was a majority in favour of the result, there were two different schools of thought as to the reasons. The inclusion of both sets of reasons appears to be an attempt to satisfy both groups.

The second expedient adopted in the case of dissension among the judges is to take the opposite course: instead of putting in something to please both groups, the Court deletes anything which might displease either. The result is that no reasons of substance are given

[65] At p. 51.

at all. Examples of both these methods of arriving at a consensus may be found below.[66]

PRECEDENT

Does the doctrine of precedent apply in the European Court? The answer is that there is no legal doctrine of *stare decisis*, but the Court does follow its previous decisions in the great majority of cases. The case law of the European Court is just as important for the development of Community law as that of English courts is for modern English law: the following chapters contain ample proof of this. The judgments of the European Court do, however, convey a misleading impression: though lawyers and the advocates general constantly cite precedents, the Court itself refers to its previous decisions only rarely. The English practice of analysing a previous case to discover its *ratio decidendi* is unknown in the judgments of the European Court. One gets the impression that the Court almost wants to play down the extent to which it follows its previous decisions: sometimes it reproduces sentences, or even whole paragraphs, from previous judgments, without quotation marks or any acknowledgment of the source. This reticence is, however, only a matter of style.

There are a number of important instances where the Court has not followed precedent. These are the result of changing circumstances or a change of opinion among the judges, possibly following criticism by the advocates general or academic writers. Where this happens, the Court does not formally overrule the earlier case or even attempt to distinguish it in the English style: it simply ignores it. Examples of cases where the Court has made a complete about-turn are given in later chapters;[67] these, however, are comparatively rare. More common are cases where the Court refines or expands doctrines previously enunciated in general terms: this, of course, is the normal way in which courts perform their task of developing the law.

The opinions of advocates general are frequently cited by lawyers (and advocates general) in cases before the Court. Do they have any weight as precedents? Obviously a great deal depends on whether the

---

[66] See *Compagnie Française* v. *Commission*, Case 64/69, [1970] ECR 221 (discussed at pp. 347–8) where two lines of reasoning were given, and *International Fruit Company* v. *Commission*, Cases 41–44/70, [1971] ECR 411 (discussed at p. 348), where virtually no reasons at all were given.

[67] See below, pp. 348–9 and 470–2.

Court itself has pronounced on the issue. The first possibility is that the Court did not consider the point in the previous case: here, in the view of two of the leading authorities on the Court, the advocate general's opinion has a value similar to that of a dictum by a single judge in the English Court of Appeal when the other judges have not commented on the matter.[68] The second possibility is that the advocate general's opinion was rejected by the Court in the previous case. Even here, it will be cited by counsel, but they will have to show that the advocate general was right and the Court wrong. In this situation, his opinion could perhaps be compared to a dissenting judgment in the Court of Appeal.[69] The third possibility is that the Court followed the advocate general: here the main value of his opinion will be to explain and clarify the judgment, something which is often necessary in view of the brevity of the Court's reasoning.

INTERPRETATION

The interpretation of the Treaties and Community legislation is one of the principal tasks of the Court. To some extent the Court's approach to this is the same as that of an English court: it looks at the words used and considers their meaning in the context of the instrument as a whole. In doing this, it tries to give the provision an interpretation which fits in with the general scheme of the instrument, though it is much more willing than an English court to depart from the literal meaning of the words to achieve this.

Beyond this, the Court makes little attempt to establish the actual subjective intention of the authors of the text. The preparatory documents (*travaux préparatoires*) for the Treaties have never been published; there are certain national materials, such as official statements by the national governments to their parliaments during ratification debates, but these are little used. As far as Community legislation is concerned, Commission proposals (including an explanatory memorandum) and the opinions of the European Parliament and the Economic and Social Committee (where these bodies have been consulted) are available, but not frequently considered by the Court. The actual discussions in the Commission and Council are secret.

[68] Brown and Jacobs, *The Court of Justice of the European Communities* (2nd ed., 1983), p. 279.
[69] Ibid.

One reason for disregarding the subjective intention of the authors of the text is that, in the case of an agreement reached after hard bargaining, there may be no common intention – only an agreement on a form of words.[70] A more important reason is that the Court prefers to interpret texts on the basis of what it thinks they should be trying to achieve; it moulds the law according to what it regards as the needs of the Community.[71] This is sometimes called the 'teleological method of interpretation', but it really goes beyond interpretation properly so-called: it is decision-making on the basis of judicial policy.

POLICY

One of the distinctive characteristics of the European Court is the extent to which its decision-making is based on policy. By policy is meant the values and attitudes of the judges – the objectives they wish to promote. The policies of the European Court are basically the following:

1. Strengthening the Community (and especially the supra-national elements in it);
2. Increasing the scope and effectiveness of Community law;
3. Enlarging the powers of Community institutions.

They may be summed up in one phrase: the promotion of European integration.

All courts are of course influenced by policy, but in the European Court policy plays a particularly important role: occasionally the Court will ignore the clear words of the Treaty in order to attain a policy objective. An example of this is *Parti Ecologiste 'Les Verts'* v. *European Parliament*,[72] which concerned a decision of the European Parliament authorizing the payment of grants from the Community budget to political parties, ostensibly to cover an information campaign to explain the work of the Parliament to the electors at the time of the 1984 elections, but in reality to contribute towards the parties' election expenses. The formula adopted for the distribution of the

[70] See the extrajudicial statement by Judge Pescatore quoted by Brown and Jacobs, p. 245.

[71] Thus Judge Kutscher (a former President of the European Court) has said extra-judicially, 'Interpretations based on the original situation would in no way be in keeping with a Community law orientated towards the future.' (H. Kutscher, op. cit., p. 22.)

[72] Case 294/83, [1987] 2 C M L R 343.

money was strongly biased in favour of those parties represented in the Parliament before the elections and discriminated against those parties seeking representation for the first time. One party in the latter category, the French Ecologists, brought proceedings in the European Court to annul the decision.

The proceedings were brought under Article 173 EEC, which provides:

The Court of Justice shall review the legality of acts of the Commission and the Council . . .

This provision is perfectly clear and does not mention acts of the Parliament; nevertheless, the Court held that acts of the Parliament are covered. It reached this conclusion in four steps. The first step was to state that the Community is based on the rule of law and acts of both the Member States and the Community institutions are subject to judicial review to ensure that they conform to the Treaty. The second step was to explain that no power had been given in the EEC Treaty to review the acts of the Parliament because, at the time when the Treaty was drawn up, the Parliament did not possess the power to pass measures which could affect the rights of third parties.[73] The third step was to point out that it subsequently obtained such powers, notably in the Budgetary Treaties and the Decision and Act on direct elections. The fourth step was to conclude that it would be contrary to the spirit and system of the Treaty if the acts of the Parliament were not now subject to review. Therefore, the Court decided, Article 173 covers acts of the Parliament.

The logic of this ruling should be fully understood: what the Court is doing is to say that the acts of the Parliament *ought* to be reviewable; therefore, they *are* reviewable. This logic, which also formed the basis of the decision in the *SPI* case (discussed below[74]), ignores the distinction between what the law ought to be and what it is, a distinction which is fundamental to the Western concept of law.

The Court's decision in the *Parti Ecologiste* case did not represent a challenge to the interests of the national governments. Where this is the case, the Court moves more carefully. A common tactic is to introduce a new doctrine gradually: in the first case that comes before it, the Court will establish the doctrine as a general principle but suggest that it is subject to various qualifications; the Court may even

---

[73] The Court pointed out that under the ECSC Treaty, where the Parliament does have such powers (see Art. 95, fourth para.), its acts are reviewable: see Art. 38.

[74] See pp. 252–3.

find some reason why it should not be applied to the particular facts of the case. The principle, however, is now established. If there are not too many protests, it will be re-affirmed in later cases; the qualifications can then be whittled away and the full extent of the doctrine revealed.

This process is well illustrated by the lines of cases concerning the treaty-making power of the Community and the doctrine of direct effect. These are both discussed below;[75] here a case will be considered which reveals in a particularly stark form the interplay between law and policy, principle and expediency: the *Second Defrenne Case*.[76] This concerned Article 119 EEC, which provides:

Each Member State shall during the first stage ensure and subsequently maintain the application of the principle that men and women should receive equal pay for equal work . . .

The first stage for bringing the Treaty into operation ended on 31 December 1961, but the Member States felt that they were not in a position to implement Article 119 by this date. They therefore held a conference which laid down a fresh time-table: the new date was 31 December 1964. This deadline was not, however, met by all the Member States and the Commission then convened various meetings and drew up a series of reports in an attempt to bring the recalcitrant governments into line. Finally the Commission announced that it would take enforcement proceedings against those Member States which had not complied by 18 July 1973, but this threat was not carried out. Then, on 10 February 1975, the Council issued a directive on equal pay which had to be implemented within one year.

In 1970, however, Gabrielle Defrenne, an air hostess who had worked for the Belgian airline, Sabena, brought proceedings against Sabena in the Belgian courts because they had paid her less than male cabin crew doing the same work. She claimed that they had no right to do this and demanded back-payment of the difference. The Belgian courts referred various questions of Community law to the European Court for a preliminary ruling; in particular, they wished to know whether Article 119 conferred rights directly on individuals, even though it had not been implemented, and, if so, from what date it did this.

These questions raised highly delicate issues. In particular, if back pay could be claimed by all women who had suffered discrimination,

---

[75] At pp. 156–62 and 188–95, respectively.
[76] *Defrenne* v. *Sabena*, Case 43/75, [1976] ECR 455.

the economic consequences would be serious: according to the United Kingdom Government, many British firms would be driven into bankruptcy if the right to equal pay were back-dated to Britain's entry into the Community.[77]

As far as the law was concerned, the principal issue was whether Article 119 was directly effective. There were quite strong reasons for believing that it was not,[78] but such a ruling would have conflicted with the Court's policy of enhancing the scope and effectiveness of Community law. On this point policy triumphed: the Court ruled that Article 119 conferred rights directly on individuals in the Member States and that the various resolutions putting off the date for implementation were of no effect. This meant that there had been a right to equal pay in the original Member States since 1 January 1962 and in the United Kingdom, Ireland and Denmark since 1 January 1973.

However, the Court felt it expedient to sweeten the pill by ruling that only those workers who had instituted legal proceedings (or made equivalent claims) before the date of the judgment could rely on the direct effect of Article 119 in order to claim back pay for periods prior to that date. Thus Miss Defrenne won her case but the Member States were shielded from an avalanche of similar claims.

This ruling neatly reconciled the Court's policy with the interests of the Member States. But it did so at the expense of legal principle: there was no possible ground in law for limiting the effect of the judgment in this way: if Article 119 was directly effective for Miss Defrenne, it must have been directly effective for all other workers; claims for back pay might be affected by national statutes of limitation, but there was no legal ground for making the date of the judgment in the *Defrenne* case decisive.[79]

---

[77] The Equal Pay Act 1970 only came into force on 29 December 1975; consequently, the Court's decision could have made employers liable for claims going back three years.

[78] See below, p. 190.

[79] The reasons given by the Court in its judgment were: first, the economic difficulties feared by the British and Irish Governments (it said that these could not affect the *future* application of the law, thereby implying that they could affect its application as regards the past); secondly, the fact that the conduct of the Member States and the views adopted by the Commission had led employers to continue their violation of the principle of equal pay; and thirdly, that the general level at which pay would have been fixed could not be known (a rather doubtful proposition). These latter arguments, however, apply just as much to workers who made claims before the *Defrenne* judgment as to those who began proceedings after it. They therefore provide no justification for the Court's ruling. It should also be pointed out that what the Court did was different from the American doctrine of prospective overruling: there an existing precedent is followed in the case at hand but notice is given that it will no longer be followed in future.

These cases are extreme examples; nevertheless they prompt the question whether it is right to allow policy to play so dominant a role. In this connection it is desirable to draw a distinction between those cases where the Court makes a choice on policy grounds between two or more legally tenable solutions and those cases where it allows policy considerations to dictate a solution that conflicts with generally accepted legal principles. The former is perfectly proper, but the latter could be criticized as going beyond the proper function of a court. It might be argued that in the case of the Community this activist approach is necessary because of the lack of a proper legislature; however, if the Community is to fulfil the expectations of its founders, it must be firmly based on the rule of law: this could be jeopardized if policy is allowed too great a role.

FURTHER READING

L. Neville Brown and Francis G. Jacobs, *The Court of Justice of the European Communities* (2nd ed., 1983).

K. P. E. Lasok, *The European Court of Justice: Practice and Procedure* (1984).

Hjalte Rasmussen, *On Law and Policy in the European Court of Justice* (1986)[80].

Schermers, Chapter 5.

John A. Usher, *European Court Practice* (1983).

H. Kutscher, 'Methods of Interpretation as Seen by a Judge of the Court of Justice' (paper presented to the Judicial and Academic Conference at the European Court in 1976).

Brown, 'The Linguistic Regime of the European Communities: Some Problems of Law and Language', (1981) 15 Valparaiso University Law Review 319.

Dickschat, 'Problèmes d'interprétation des traités européens résultant de leur plurilinguisme', [1968] Revue Belge de Droit International 40.

Slynn, 'The Court of Justice of the European Communities', (1984) 33 ICLQ 409.

Stevens, 'The Principle of Linguistic Equality in Judicial Proceedings and in the Interpretation of Plurilingual Legal Instruments:

---

[80] For a critical comment on this book, see Cappelletti, 'Is the European Court of Justice "Running Wild"?', (1987) 12 E.L. Rev. 3.

The Régime Linguistique in the Court of Justice of the European Communities', (1967) 62 Northwestern University Law Review 701.

Part II
The Community Legal System

INTRODUCTION

It is generally recognized that Community law is a separate legal system, distinct from, though closely linked to, both international law and the legal systems of the Member States. This was affirmed by the European Court in the well-known *Van Gend en Loos* case, in which it was emphasized that the Community Treaties are more than mere international agreements.[1] In addition to being treaties, they also form the constitution of the Community;[2] and the rules of law derived from them constitute the internal law of the Community.[3] In consequence of their special status, the Community Treaties will not necessarily be interpreted in the same way as ordinary treaties; nor will their effect in the Member States always be the same.[4] Another consequence is that the relations between the Member States within the Community context will not in all cases be governed by the normal rules of international law.

Though engendered by international law, Community law does not share all its characteristics; and the techniques and doctrines of Community law have more in common with branches of national law such as constitutional and administrative law than with those of international law. Community law is, however, separate from national law, even though it is applied by national courts. Thus national legislatures have no power to amend or repeal it; in the event of conflict, it will override national law; and its interpretation comes, in the last resort, within the exclusive jurisdiction of the European Court.[5]

Although it forms a coherent system, there are various purposes for

---

[1] Case 26/62, [1963] ECR 1 at 12. See also *Costa* v. *ENEL*, Case 6/64, [1964] ECR 585 at 593, where the European Court said that, unlike ordinary treaties, the EEC Treaty has created its own legal system. For a different view, see Wyatt, 'New Legal Order, or Old?', (1982) 7 E. L. Rev. 147.

[2] *Les Verts – Parti Ecologiste* v. *European Parliament*, Case 294/83, [1987] 2 CMLR 343.

[3] See *per* Advocate General Lagrange in *Fédération Charbonnière de Belgique* v. *High Authority*, Case 8/55, [1956] ECR 245 at 277.

[4] In the United Kingdom, for example, ordinary treaties are not directly applied by the courts; the Community Treaties are.

[5] According to the European Court, the Member States have limited their sovereignty, within a restricted area, in favour of the Community legal order: see the *Van Gend en Loos* case, above, note 1.

which it is necessary to make distinctions, on the basis of their origin, between different provisions of Community law. Thus proceedings for judicial review may be brought only with respect to legally binding acts of the Community institutions; in determining the validity of such acts, the Court may have regard to the relevant Treaty – EEC, ECSC, or Euratom – and 'any rule of law relating to its application'; enforcement actions may be brought against Member States for a failure to fulfil an obligation 'under' the relevant Treaty. There are also special problems as to which questions of Community law may be referred by a national court to the European Court for interpretation in a preliminary ruling; and the doctrine of direct effect depends in part on the nature of the provision in question. For all these reasons, but above all in order to delimit the extent of the system as a whole, it is necessary to analyse the sources of Community law.

In the analysis of Community law according to its sources, the most important distinction is between enacted and non-enacted law. Enacted law is law created by some authority; non-enacted law is not so created. It is, of course, true that the existence of non-enacted law is not certain unless it has been recognized by a court; and it could be argued that it, too, is created – by the courts. There are, however, important differences between judge-made law and enacted law and it is therefore reasonable to use this distinction as the basis for the classification of Community law.

Enacted Community law may be created either by a Community institution or by the Member States. The second distinction, therefore, is between acts of Community institutions (Community acts) and acts of the Member States. In this context it is important to stress that, though the most important Community institution, the Council, is composed of representatives of the Member States, its acts are Community acts, not acts of the Member States. If, on the other hand, the representatives of the Member States meet when they are *not* acting in their capacity as members of the Council, their decisions will be acts of the Member States. Such meetings may take place in the Council: the important question is not the *place* where they meet, but the *capacity* in which they meet.

Non-enacted Community law consists of the so-called 'general principles of law' – the 'common law' of the Community – which have been adopted by the European Court. They are an important source of Community law and will in all probability play an increasing role as the Community develops.

International agreements with non-member States constitute another source of Community law. They may be concluded either by the Community alone, by the Community acting jointly with the Member States or, in certain special cases, by the Member States alone. These agreements are thus either acts of the Member States or Community acts; because of their special nature, however, it is desirable to consider them separately.

It is possible, therefore, to establish the following four sources of Community law:

1. Acts of the Member States;
2. Community acts;
3. General principles of Community law;
4. International agreements with non-member States.

These will be considered in turn in the chapters in this Part of the book.

FURTHER READING

Francis G. Jacobs, *European Community Law and Public International Law – Two Different Legal Orders?* (Institut für Internationales Recht an der Universität Kiel, 1983).

Pierre Pescatore, *L'ordre juridique des Communautés européennes* (1975).

Wyatt, 'New Legal Order, or Old?', (1982) 7 E.L. Rev. 147.

Sørensen, 'Autonomous Legal Orders', (1983) 32 I C L Q 559.

3

ACTS OF THE MEMBER STATES

For purposes of discussion, acts of the Member States may be divided into three categories: the constitutive Treaties, subsidiary conventions, and acts of the representatives of the Member States.

THE CONSTITUTIVE TREATIES

The constitutive Treaties lay the foundations of the Community. They may be regarded as the constitution of the Community: they set up the various organs of the Community and grant them their powers.[1] They also contain many provisions of a non-institutional nature which would not normally be found in a constitution. These are mainly concerned with economic and social law and are evidence of the hybrid nature of the Treaties and, indeed, of the Community itself.

Which are the constitutive Treaties? They may be defined as the Treaties which created each of the three Communities – the ECSC, EEC and Euratom Treaties – together with the Treaties which amend or supplement them. The principal treaties falling within this category are as follows:[2]

1. ECSC Treaty;
2. EEC Treaty;
3. Euratom Treaty;
4. Convention on Certain Institutions Common to the European Communities;
5. Merger Treaty (Convention Establishing a Single Council and a Single Commission of the European Communities);
6. First Budgetary Treaty;

[1] Certain Council decisions are also of a constitutional nature, for example the accession decisions admitting new Member States to the ECSC or the decision providing for direct elections to the European Parliament, discussed at p. 24, above.
[2] There is no official list of these Treaties but see the European Communites Act 1972, s. 1 and Schedule 1, Part I. For the Second Budgetary Treaty, see the European Communities (Definition of Treaties) Order, 1976 (S.I. 1976 No. 217).

7. First Treaty of Accession (Denmark, Ireland and the United Kingdom);
8. Second Budgetary Treaty;
9. Second Treaty of Accession (Greece);
10. Third Treaty of Accession (Spain and Portugal);
11. Single European Act.[3]

The history and objectives of these Treaties were outlined briefly in Chapter 1; here certain legal points of a general nature will be considered.

Appended to many of the Treaties, there are certain supplementary instruments. Annexes and protocols are an integral part of the Treaty to which they relate.[4] The status of the declarations annexed to the Treaties – some of which are joint declarations on the part of all the Contracting States and some of which are unilateral declarations by one Contracting State only – is not entirely clear. Many of them were apparently intended to be only of political significance; others have an indirect legal effect. For example, certain provisions in the EEC Treaty grant rights to nationals of the Member States. The Treaty contains no definition of who is a national, and it may be assumed that the intention was that each Member State should decide who its own nationals are (subject to any relevant provisions of Community law). When the United Kingdom acceded to the Community, the Government of the United Kingdom made a Declaration regarding the definition of a United Kingdom national for Community purposes.[5] This Declaration would therefore have effect in Community law to the extent that Community law refers to national law on this matter.

The EEC and Euratom Treaties apply for an unlimited period of time; the ECSC Treaty for 50 years.[6] Each Treaty contains provisions for its amendment.[7] Under these provisions, the initiative may come from a Member State or from the Commission. In either case, a proposal for an amendment is submitted to the Council, which

[3] Decisions of the Council and agreements of the representatives of the Governments of the Member States have not been listed, even though they may amend the constitutive Treaties.

[4] See, for example, Art. 84 ECSC (which states that the Convention on the Transitional Provisions is also part of the Treaty), Art. 239 EEC and Art. 207 Euratom.

[5] This was made necessary by the complicated and confusing state of British nationality law. In 1982 it was replaced by a new Declaration, following the enactment of the British Nationality Act 1981.

[6] Arts 240 EEC, 208 Euratom, and 97 ECSC.

[7] Arts 236 EEC, 204 Euratom, and 96 ECSC.

must then decide whether to call a conference of the national governments.[8] Before deciding, the Council must consult the Parliament and – where the initiative came from a Member State – the Commission.[9] The conference is convened by the President of the Council and must act by common accord. If it decides to make amendments, these must go to the Member States for ratification in accordance with their respective constitutional requirements.

There is also a procedure laid down by Article 95 ECSC under which minor amendments to the ECSC Treaty may be made without ratification by the Member States. These amendments, which are subject to strict limitations, must first be submitted to the European Court to determine whether they comply with Article 95; then they must be approved by the European Parliament.[10] In addition, certain specific provisions in the Treaties may be amended by the Council under procedures laid down in the provisions in question.[11] In some instances, ratification by the Member States is necessary.[12]

May amendments be made only by the procedures prescribed in the Treaties, or may they also be made by means of a later treaty concluded in the normal manner? This question has evoked controversy. It has been said that there is a generally applicable rule of international law that a treaty may always be amended by a later treaty between the same parties; however, in view of the special nature of the Community Treaties, it could be argued that such a rule would not apply to them.[13] This latter opinion, which appears to be

---

[8] Under the ECSC Treaty the Council must act by a two-thirds majority; under the other Treaties an absolute majority (majority of members) is sufficient.

[9] These consultations are not required under the ECSC Treaty.

[10] The European Parliament must give its approval by a majority of three-quarters of votes cast and two-thirds of all members of Parliament. The amendment must be proposed jointly by the Commission and the Council; the latter must act by a ten-twelfths majority (following the accession of Portugal and Spain).

[11] See Arts 21 and 81 ECSC, 13, 33, 138 and 201 EEC and 76, 85, 90, 92, 108, 173, 197 and 215 Euratom.

[12] See Arts 21 ECSC, 138 and 201 EEC and 108 and 173 Euratom.

[13] See Kapteyn and VerLoren van Themaat, pp. 37–8, who point out that the Lower House of the Dutch Parliament has adopted a resolution to the effect that revision of the Treaties should take place exclusively in accordance with the amendment procedures laid down in the Treaties themselves. This was accepted by the Dutch Government. Since a subsequent treaty would have to be agreed to by each contracting party, the Dutch Government could block any attempt to amend the Treaties in this way. It is, however, pointed out by Pescatore, *L'ordre juridique des Communautés européennes* (1975), pp. 62–3, that the ECSC Treaty has, in fact, been revised on two occasions without recourse to the prescribed procedures. The first was the Treaty of 27 October 1956, which brought about certain amendments consequent on the return of the Saar to Germany, and the second was

supported by the European Court,[14] is particularly compelling if the Treaties are regarded as a constitution.[15]

A special form of amendment procedure applies when new Member States join the Community.[16] Any European state may apply for admission;[17] the application is addressed to the Council, which must act unanimously after obtaining the opinion of the Commission. In the case of the EEC, the Council must obtain the assent of the European Parliament (which acts by an absolute majority of its members) as well as consulting the Commission.[18] Under the EEC and Euratom Treaties, accession is effected by means of a treaty between the applicant state and the existing Member States; this treaty must be ratified by the Contracting States in accordance with their constitutional requirements. In the case of the ECSC, on the

the Convention on Certain Institutions Common to the European Communities, which was signed at the same time as the EEC and Euratom Treaties. The resolution of the Dutch Parliament mentioned above was in fact passed in the course of the ratification debates concerning the Treaty of 27 October 1956. The Dutch Government's undertaking did not, therefore, apply to this Treaty. It is not clear why they accepted this procedure in the case of the Convention on Common Institutions, but this Convention could perhaps be regarded as a special case, since it was closely linked with the EEC and Euratom Treaties. Pescatore takes the view that, though such a procedure is open to objections, it is nevertheless legally possible to amend the Treaties in this way, provided there is a formal agreement which is ratified by each Member State in accordance with its constitutional requirements. See also Deliege-Sequaris, 'Révision des traités européens en dehors des procédures prévues', [1980] CDE 539.

[14] *Defrenne* v. *Sabena*, Case 43/75, [1976] ECR 455 (paragraph 58 of the judgment) where the European Court said that, apart from exceptions expressly recognized in the Treaty itself, the EEC Treaty 'can only be modified by means of the amendment procedure carried out in accordance with Article 236.'

[15] This now appears to be the view of the European Court: *Les Verts – Parti Ecologiste* v. *European Parliament*, Case 294/83, [1987] 2 CMLR 343. A solution to the problem may perhaps be found if one accepts that the Community Treaties have, like a national constitution, created a new legal system: an amendment of the Treaties by other means than those prescribed in them would be invalid in terms of the Community legal system, though it might be valid in terms of international law (a separate legal system). If such an amendment nevertheless took place, and was accepted by the Community institutions, it would constitute a legal 'revolution', leading to the redefinition of the *Grundnorm* or fundamental legal principle of the system. For the application of this theory to Commonwealth constitutional law, see S. A. de Smith, 'Constitutional Lawyers in Revolutionary Situations', (1968) 7 Western Ontario Law Rev. 93.

[16] Arts 237 EEC, 205 Euratom and 98 ECSC. Although there are separate procedures under each of the three Treaties, it is doubtful whether an applicant could accede to one Treaty without also acceding to the others: see Joliet, p. 131.

[17] It is generally agreed, however, that an applicant will not be accepted as a member unless it is democratic (in the Western sense) and respects human rights: see the Declaration on Democracy issued at the meeting of the European Council in Copenhagen on 7 and 8 April 1978 (E. C. Bull. 3–1978, pp. 5–6).

[18] Art. 8 SEA.

other hand, accession is brought about by a decision of the Council (acting unanimously). The terms of accession and the consequential amendments to the original Treaties are laid down in the treaty of accession or the Council decision, as the case may be. When it joins the Community, the new Member State must also accept all existing Community law, the *acquis communautaire*.[19]

It is stated in Article 232 EEC that the provisions of the EEC Treaty will not affect either the ECSC or the Euratom Treaties. This rule is understandable in view of the fact that the scope of the former is general, while that of the latter Treaties is specific. However, though each of the Communities is autonomous, they are nevertheless interdependent: the intention was that they should form a functional unity,[20] and the Treaties are all part of the same legal system. Consequently, the European Court draws inspiration from one Treaty in interpreting another: in the absence of an indication that the authors of the Treaties intended different rules to apply in the various Communities, the Court will assume that the same rule was intended to apply in all three.[21]

SUBSIDIARY CONVENTIONS

In addition to the constitutive Treaties, there are certain other international agreements between the Member States. Where these deal with matters within the scope of the Community and were drawn up within the Community context, they may be regarded as part of Community law.

In certain cases the constitutive Treaties themselves envisage additional conventions to supplement their provisions. For example, Article 136 EEC provides that, for an initial period of five years, the details of, and procedure for, the association of the overseas countries and territories will be determined by an Implementing Convention. This Convention, which was adopted at the same time as the EEC

[19] See, for example, Arts 2–4 of the first Act of Accession, which cover acts of the Member States, Community acts and international agreements.

[20] *Campolongo* v. *High Authority*, Cases 27, 39/59, [1960] ECR 391 at 405 (see also *per* Advocate General Roemer at 417–18). See also *Luxembourg* v. *Parliament*, Case 230/81, [1983] ECR 255, where it was held that if a Community institution acts simultaneously under all three Treaties, that act may be reviewed by the Court on the basis of jurisdiction granted by any one Treaty.

[21] For examples of this, see *Meroni* v. *High Authority*, Case 9/56, [1957–58] ECR 133 at 140–1 (discussed below at pp. 113–15) and *Geitling* v. *High Authority*, Case 13/60, [1962] ECR 83 at 102.

Treaty and was annexed to it, was clearly part of Community law while it was in force.

Article 220 EEC provides that Member States 'shall, so far as is necessary, enter into negotiations with each other with a view to securing for the benefit of their nationals' various rights which are then listed. These include the recognition of companies and the recognition and enforcement of judgments. This Article has been implemented by means of conventions between the Member States which are subject to the normal national ratification processes. Two such conventions have already been signed: the Convention on Jurisdiction and the Enforcement of Judgments in Civil and Commercial Matters of 27 September 1968,[22] and the Convention on the Mutual Recognition of Companies and Legal Persons of 29 February 1968.[23] Other conventions are in preparation.

Since Article 220 imposes an obligation on Member States, and since it grants no powers to Community institutions to promulgate acts to implement it, one may reasonably conclude that the authors of the EEC Treaty intended the Member States to enter into conventions to attain its objectives. There can also be no doubt that these objectives are highly relevant to the establishment of a common market and consequently fall within the scope of the Community. For these reasons it is clear that conventions under Article 220 form part of the Community legal system.

This is confirmed by the fact that when new Member States join the EEC, they are obliged to accede to the conventions under Article 220, subject to any necessary adjustments.[24] It should also be noted that the Commission played an active role in the elaboration of the two conventions mentioned above and they were agreed to by the representatives of the Member States meeting in the Council; moreover, there are protocols to each of them granting jurisdiction to the European Court to interpret them under procedures analogous to that under Article 177 EEC.[25]

[22] OJ 1972, L 299/32. It came into force between the original six Member States on 1 February 1973. The Convention of Accession by which Denmark, Ireland and the United Kingdom became parties to it was signed on 9 October 1978 (see OJ 1978, L 304) and came into force, as far the United Kingdom was concerned, on 1 January 1987 (Civil Jurisdiction and Judgments Act 1982).

[23] Not yet in force.

[24] See, for example, Art. 3(2) of the first Act of Accession.

[25] For the protocol to the Judgments Convention, see OJ 1975, L 204/28. The protocol to the Companies Convention was also adopted on 3 June 1975 but is not yet in force. For the texts of both the protocols and an analysis of the differences between them (and a comparison with Art. 177 EEC), see Mok (1971) 8 C.M.L. Rev. 485.

However, even conventions which are not envisaged by any of the constituent Treaties may form part of the Community legal system. The most important example is the Community Patent Convention (Convention for the European Patent for the Common Market) which was signed in Luxembourg on 15 December 1975 (not yet in force).[26] The parties are the Member States and its objective is the creation of a Community patent – a single patent covering the whole of Community territory. Although express provision for such a development does not exist in the constituent Treaties, there is no doubt that the Convention is part of Community law: its subject-matter clearly falls within the scope of the EEC and, as was stated in the preamble to the Convention, its conclusion was desirable for the attainment of Community objectives; it was signed by the pleni-potentiaries of the Member States meeting in the Council; the Council itself passed a resolution urging Member States to become parties to it;[27] the Commission was closely associated with the work involved in drawing it up; and the European Court is given jurisdiction to interpret its provisions.

What would the position be if there were a conflict between a subsidiary convention and one of the constitutive Treaties? The only express provision on this question is found in the Community Patent Convention. Article 93 of this provides that no provisions of the Convention 'may be invoked against the application of any provision' of the EEC Treaty. This, however, answers the question only in the limited case of a conflict between these two instruments; in other cases the problem must be solved on the basis of general principles.

If the convention is adopted after the Treaty, it could be argued that the convention impliedly amends the Treaty and should there-fore prevail. This, however, fails to take account of the fact that both Treaty and convention are part of the Community legal system and in that system the constitutive Treaties are by their very nature of superior status: they *create* the legal system of which the conventions are a part. Moreover, the Treaties contain provisions laying down specific procedures for their amendment, procedures which were not followed when the subsidiary conventions were adopted. Whether these procedures are the only means of amending the Treaties was discussed above.[28] Whatever the answer to this question, there can be little doubt that the existence of these procedures creates a presump-

---

[26]   OJ 1976, L 17/1.
[27]   OJ 1976, L 17/43.
[28]   At pp. 90–1.

tion: if the Member States adopt subsequent agreements without going through the procedures, they may be presumed, in the absence of an express provision to the contrary, not to have intended to amend the constitutive Treaties. Consequently, one may conclude that the conventions are subordinate in status to the Treaties: in the event of conflict, a Treaty provision will prevail over a provision in a subsidiary convention.[29]

A similar argument applies where there is a conflict between a subsidiary convention and a Community act such as a regulation or directive. Community acts are adopted by the Community institutions under powers granted by the constitutive Treaties. If the subsidiary convention does not override the Treaties, it cannot affect the legislative powers conferred by them; consequently, acts adopted under those powers also cannot be affected.[30] It follows from this that, in the absence of an express provision in the convention, the Community act will prevail.

The power of Member States to conclude conventions is derived from international law and it might be thought that it would not be affected by the creation of the Communities. It has, however, been argued that Member States are precluded from entering into such conventions if the matter in question could have been dealt with by the Community itself: in other words, the existence of a Community power to regulate a given issue excludes the use of a convention.[31] When the Member States joined the Community they transferred certain powers to the Community and the European Court has held that Community power to conclude agreements with non-member States can automatically exclude national jurisdiction to do so.[32] It is probable that a similar rule applies in the case of conventions between the Member States themselves: it would be illogical if they had greater powers to enter into agreements between themselves than with third countries. Subsidiary conventions are not, however, entered into with regard to matters covered by the specific empowering provisions in the Treaties; the important question, therefore, is whether resort to conventions is precluded by the more general

[29] See Pescatore, *L'ordre juridique des Communautés européennes* (1975), pp. 143–4.

[30] See the opinion to this effect of the legal service of the Council, Document R/697/78 of 28 March 1978. It is also of interest to note that the legal service opinion states that a provision of *national* legislation enacted in implementation of a directive will also prevail over a conflicting provision in a subsidiary convention: ibid. p. 5.

[31] See Schwartz, 'Article 235 and Law-Making Powers in the European Community', (1978) 27 I C L Q 614.

[32] See pp. 158–63, below.

legislative powers contained in the Treaty, in particular Article 235. As will be seen below,[33] Article 235 is a wide provision, but it comes into play only when 'action by the Community' is necessary to attain the objectives of the Community; so, if the objective can be attained by a convention (an act of the Member States), it could be said that Community action is not necessary. An objection has been put forward to this argument that, if the authors of the Treaty had envisaged the conclusion of conventions between the Member States as an alternative to Article 235, they would have said so expressly.[34] It is true that there are a number of instances where the Treaty refers expressly to the conclusion of conventions between the Member States; but these are all cases where the Treaty lays an obligation on the Member States to attain a specific objective. Article 235, on the other hand, does not oblige the Member States to achieve any specific objective: it merely gives an additional power to attain objectives flowing from other provisions in the Treaty; consequently, there is no reason why it should make express reference to the use of conventions. In fact, one could argue that if the authors of the Treaty had intended to rule out the use of conventions they would not have referred to action *by the Community*, but merely to action. Looked at objectively, therefore, Article 235 seems to allow room for conventions; but it is far from certain that the European Court, with its policy of preferring Community action to action by the Member States, will see it this way.

ACTS OF THE REPRESENTATIVES OF THE MEMBER STATES

This is a somewhat anomalous group of acts adopted by the representatives of the Governments of the Member States, meeting in the Council. The representatives here are the delegates sent to the Council by the Member States, i.e. ministers in their respective Governments; but, since they do not act in their capacity as members of the Council when they adopt these acts, the acts are not acts of the Council but are acts of the Member States.

These acts are usually designated either 'Decision of the Representatives of the Governments of the Member States, meeting in the Council' or 'Agreement between the Representatives . . .'. They

---

[33] See pp. 104–9.
[34] Schwartz, (1978) 27 I C L Q 614 at 619–620.

are published in the Official Journal and are often signed by the President of the Council. They are an established feature of the Community – they were first used as long ago as 1954 – and they deal with a wide variety of subjects. Where they are referred to as 'agreements' they are often subject to ratification; but this is not the case where they carry the designation 'decision'. The subjects they deal with are relevant to the functioning of the Community, though they do not normally fall within any specific power to adopt a Community act.[35] The Commission often plays a part in their preparation.

What is the status of these acts? They probably all fall into one of three categories. Some of them are international agreements concluded in simplified form. In this case, they have the same status as the subsidiary conventions discussed above and, for the reasons mentioned there,[36] are part of the Community legal system.[37] Others, however, are not intended to be legally binding at all: their consequences are merely political. The well-known 'Luxembourg Accords' are probably an example. Acts falling into this category have no legal effects and are not part of any legal system, including the Community legal system. Finally, some acts of the representatives of the Member States constitute the exercise of a power conferred jointly on the Member States. For example, Article 11 of the Merger Treaty provides that members of the Commission are appointed 'by common accord of the Governments of the Member States': such appointments are made by acts of the representatives of the Member States. Acts falling into this category – though they must be adopted by unanimous agreement of all the Member States – take effect, not as international agreements, but by virtue of the Treaty provision in question. They plainly fall within the Community legal system.

---

[35] They may, however, fall within the scope of the general power contained in Art. 235 EEC; where this is so, the same objections could be raised as in the case of subsidiary conventions.

[36] However, they do not usually contain provisions giving jurisdiction to the European Court. (For exceptions to this, see Bebr, [1966] SEW at 538–9.)

[37] What was said above concerning a conflict with a Treaty provision, applies also to acts in this category.

FURTHER READING

Joliet, pp. 127–38.

Bebr, 'Acts of Representatives of the Governments of the Member States', [1966] SEW 529.

Pescatore, 'Remarques sur la nature juridique des "décisions des représentants de États Membres réunis au sein du Conseil"', ibid. p. 579.

Hauschild, 'L'importance des conventions communautaires pour la création d'un droit communautaire', [1975] RTDE 4.

Rasmussen, 'A New Generation of Community Law?', (1978) 15 C.M.L. Rev. 249.

Schwartz, 'Article 235 and Law-Making Powers in the European Community', (1978) 27 ICLQ 614.

Weiler and Modrall, 'Institutional Reform: Consensus or Majority?', (1985) 10 E.L. Rev. 316.

4

COMMUNITY ACTS

Community legislation is produced in considerable volume and can directly affect the everyday lives of ordinary citizens. This chapter is concerned with the legislative powers of the Community and the procedure to be followed.

CLASSIFICATION

Article 189 EEC lists five different kinds of act that may (if other provisions confer the power) be adopted by the Council or the Commission. These are:

1. Regulations;
2. Directives;
3. Decisions;
4. Recommendations;
5. Opinions.

Article 189 also contains a short statement of the characteristics of each kind of act. Thus a regulation is essentially legislative (normative): it lays down general rules which are binding both at the Community level and at the national level. Directives and decisions differ from regulations in that they are not binding generally: they are binding only on the person (or persons) to whom they are addressed. Directives may be addressed only to Member States but decisions may also be addressed to private citizens. According to Article 189, another characteristic of directives is that they are binding only 'as to the result to be achieved' and leave to the national authorities 'the choice of form and methods'. This suggests that directives lay down an objective and allow each national government to achieve it by the means they regard as most suitable. A decision, on the other hand, is binding in its entirety. Recommendations and opinions are not binding at all; they are not legal acts and need not be further considered.

In the Euratom Treaty, an identical classification is provided in

Article 161; but a different system is adopted in the ECSC Treaty. Article 14 ECSC lists only three kinds of act:

1. Decisions;
2. Recommendations;
3. Opinions.

The impression this gives of greater simplicity is misleading because the terminology is different: ECSC recommendations are quite different from EEC recommendations and are in fact analogous to EEC directives; the only difference is that they may be addressed to private citizens as well as Member States. Article 14 ECSC says of decisions only that they are binding in their entirety; however, the European Court has adopted a distinction, derived in part from the provisions of Article 33 ECSC, between general decisions and individual decisions: the former are equivalent to EEC regulations and the latter to EEC decisions. Like their EEC counterparts, ECSC opinions have no binding force.

These provisions give the impression of a fairly neat and tidy system in which formal designations correspond to differences in function. The differences suggest a hierarchy. Regulations (and ECSC general decisions) appear to be at the top, since they are both wide in scope, being binding on everybody, and lay down directly applicable rules. One might think that EEC decisions (and ECSC individual decisions) came next: although they bind only a limited category of persons, their obligatory quality is just as intense as that of a regulation. Directives (and ECSC recommendations), on the other hand, appear to be the weakest form: they are limited in scope and are binding only as to their objective.

Unfortunately, things are not as simple as this. The first complication is that the formal designation of an act – the label given to it by its author – is not always a reliable guide to its contents. An act may be called a regulation but bear all the characteristics of an EEC decision; or it may be called a directive but leave very little choice as to form and methods. Faced with this situation, the European Court has sometimes rejected the formal designation and looked instead at the substance of the act. If an act in the form of a regulation does not lay down general rules but is concerned with deciding a particular case, the Court may call it a 'disguised decision' and treat it for certain purposes as an EEC decision. It is not, however, clear how far the Court will go in this 'relabelling' process: so far it has done so only for the purpose of deciding questions of *locus standi* in judicial review.[1]

A second complication is that in practice the differences between the various kinds of act are not as great as might appear from the Treaty provisions. In particular, judgments of the European Court have had the effect of up-grading directives so that they are now much closer to regulations: even if they have not been implemented by the Member State to which they are addressed, they can directly confer rights on private citizens which may be invoked against public authorities.

A third complication is that the European Court has ruled that the list in Article 189 EEC is not exhaustive: it is possible to have a legally binding act which does not fall into any of the categories enumerated in the Treaty. Acts falling into this residual category are usually called, for want of a better name, acts *sui generis*. The case in which the European Court gave this ruling was the *ERTA* case,[2] which concerned the negotiations leading to the European Road Transport Agreement (ERTA) and in particular a Council 'resolution' – to use a neutral term – in which it was settled what negotiating procedure would be adopted at the conference. The Commission disagreed with the content of this 'resolution' and wished to obtain a ruling from the Court as to whether the negotiating procedure laid down in it was in accord with Community law. The only means available of bringing this issue before the Court was an action for the annulment of the 'resolution'.

One question which the Court had to decide was whether the 'resolution' could in fact form the subject of annulment proceedings.[3] If the Court had decided this in the negative, it would have been obliged to declare the proceedings inadmissible and would thus have been deprived of the opportunity to rule on the substantive issues involved, principally the capacity of the Community to conclude international agreements. The Court was, however, faced with a problem: if it decided that the 'resolution', which was not in the form of any legal act listed in Article 189 EEC, was in fact a regulation, directive or decision, it would have been obliged to annul it for lack of reasons, since there is a rule, laid down in Article 190 EEC, that

[1] See Chapter 12, below.

[2] *Commission* v. *Council*. Case 22/70, [1971] ECR 263; discussed further at pp. 158–61, below.

[3] For a general discussion of which measures are subject to annulment by the Court, see Chapter 11.

regulations, directives and decisions must state the reasons on which they are based.[4]

The Court was clearly reluctant to annul the 'resolution', since this might have meant that the negotiations for the ERTA, which had been concluded by the time the judgment was given, would have had to begin all over again. Since the Agreement had already been signed by at least some Member States, this would have been most undesirable and might have made non-member States reluctant to enter into similar negotiations in the future. In view of this, one can see the attractiveness, from a policy point of view, of declaring the 'resolution' to be a legal act *sui generis*: by holding it to be a legal act the Court was able to declare the proceedings admissible and could therefore rule on the substantive issues; and by declaring that it was *sui generis* it could hold that Article 190 did not apply to it and it need not be annulled for lack of reasons. The Court was thus able to give a judgment in which the substantive issues were decided in principle in favour of the Commission – which was all the Commission wanted – and at the same time avoid upsetting the Agreement. There were, therefore, strong policy reasons why the Court classified the 'resolution' as an act *sui generis*; had it not been for these considerations, the Court would probably have declared it to be a decision in terms of Article 189.[5]

LEGISLATIVE POWERS OF THE COMMUNITY

It is often said that the Community is based on the principle of limited powers. By this is meant that the Community institutions have no inherent powers – they possess only those powers conferred on them – and that the powers so conferred are limited in scope.[6] Proponents of this view point to the fact that most Community powers are granted by the Treaties only for the purpose of attaining clearly defined and limited objectives, such as immigration rights for migrant workers, and cannot be used for other purposes. If this were the whole story, the legislative and executive powers of the Community institutions would resemble those of Ministers in Britain.

---

[4] This rule is discussed below, pp. 119–26.

[5] This was the solution adopted in another case in which the act carried no formal designation, the *Noordwijks Cement Accoord* case, discussed below at pp. 324–6.

[6] It should be noted that Art. 189 EEC and the corresponding provisions in the other Treaties do not confer powers; they merely enumerate and define the kinds of acts which may be adopted under powers granted by other provisions.

However, there are a number of factors which call for a substantial modification of this picture. First, the empowering provisions of the Treaties are interpreted in a wide manner, in part on the basis of the theory of implied powers. This theory, which was originally developed in the constitutional and administrative law of such countries as the United States and England, and which has been recognised as a principle of international law,[7] may be expressed in both a narrow and a wide formulation. According to the narrow formulation, the existence of a given power implies also the existence of any other power which is reasonably necessary for the exercise of the former; according to the wide formulation, the existence of a given *objective* or *function* implies the existence of any power reasonably necessary to attain it.

The narrow formulation was adopted by the European Court as long ago as 1956;[8] the wide formulation was applied (with regard to the Commission) in 1987. This was in *Germany* v. *Commission*,[9] a case arising out of Article 118 EEC. Article 118 provides:

. . . the Commission shall have the task of promoting close co-operation between Member States in the social field, particularly in matters relating to . . .

This provision gives the Commission a task, but nowhere does it confer on the Commission any legislative power. The authors of the Treaty probably thought that it was not necessary. However, in 1985 the Commission, acting under Article 118, adopted a decision which obliged the Member States to consult with the Commission regarding certain matters, and to inform it of draft measures and agreements concerning the topic in question. This decision was challenged by some of the Member States, but it was upheld by the Court (except for certain provisions). The Court held that whenever a provision of the EEC Treaty confers a specific task on the Commission, that provision must also be regarded as impliedly conferring on the Commission 'the powers which are indispensable in order to carry out that task.'[10] Since the EEC Treaty confers many tasks on the

[7] See International Court of Justice Advisory Opinion on Reparation for Injuries suffered in the Service of the United Nations, [1949] ICJ 174 at 182. See further Lauwaars, pp. 94–8.
[8] *Fédération Charbonnière de Belgique* v. *High Authority*, Case 8/55, [1956] ECR 245 at 280.
[9] Cases 281, 283–5, 287/85, [1987] 1 CMLR 11.
[10] Paragraph 28 of the judgment (preliminary edition). The Court immediately went on to use the word 'necessary' instead of 'indispensable', and then applied the new doctrine in a way which suggests that it will adopt a generous view of what is 'necessary': see Hartley, 'The Commission as Legislator under the EEC Treaty', to be published in the E. L. Rev. for April 1988.

Commission, including such wide-ranging functions as that of ensuring that the provisions of the Treaty are applied,[11] this judgment is potentially very significant and could herald an era of increased Commission law-making.[12]

A second, and more severe, objection to the view that the Community is based on the principle of limited powers is that not all Treaty provisions are of the nature described above. A wider provision is contained in Article 100 EEC, which empowers the Council to issue directives 'for the approximation of such provisions laid down by law, regulation or administrative action in Member States as directly affect the establishment or functioning of the common market'.[13] Directives have been issued under this power to unify the laws of the Member States on a wide variety of subjects.

Article 100 might still be regarded as granting a specific power; but another provision clearly goes beyond this. Article 235 EEC provides:

If action by the Community should prove necessary to attain, in the course of the operation of the common market, one of the objectives of the Community and this Treaty has not provided the necessary powers, the Council shall, acting unanimously on a proposal from the Commission and after consulting the Assembly, take the appropriate measures.

Similar powers are granted by Article 95 ECSC and Article 203 Euratom. These may be regarded as an express adoption (with regard to the Council) of the wide formulation of the doctrine of implied powers; broadly speaking, it grants power to take whatever measures are necessary to attain the objectives of the Community.

In order to appreciate the precise extent of this power, the conditions prescribed for its exercise must be analysed. These may be divided into procedural and substantive requirements. The former follow the standard pattern – proposal from the Commission and consultation with the European Parliament – except that Council must be unanimous.[14]

The substantive requirements are as follows:

[11] Art. 155 EEC.
[12] The judgment only concerned the powers of the Commission; but the Council has even wider powers under Art. 235 EEC, discussed below.
[13] Under Art. 100, the Council must be unanimous, but Art. 100A, which was added by Art. 18 SEA, makes provision for qualified majority voting for the purpose of establishing the internal market, though Art. 100A(4) gives Member States a limited right to opt out.
[14] Under Art. 95(1) ECSC, the measure is adopted by the Commission but the unanimous consent of the Council must be obtained; the Consultative Committee (equivalent to the Economic and Social Committee in the EEC) is consulted, but not the Parliament.

1. The power must be used in order to attain one of the objectives of the Community;
2. Action by the Community must be necessary for this purpose;
3. The attainment of the objective must take place in the course of the operation of the common market;
4. The Treaty must not have provided the necessary powers;
5. The measure must be appropriate for the attaining of the objective.

Each of these will be considered in turn.

The objectives of the EEC are set out in Articles 2 and 3 of the Treaty; they include, in addition to more specific goals, the harmonious development of economic activities throughout the Community, a continuous and balanced expansion, an increase in stability, an accelerated raising of the standard of living and closer relations between the Member States. These objectives are broad; moreover, since Article 235 EEC does not refer expressly to Articles 2 and 3, it may be legitimate to infer additional objectives from other provisions of the Treaty.[15]

The second requirement is that action by the Community must be necessary to attain the objective. Although a determination that a Community act is necessary may seem to be a pure decision of fact, it actually involves a large measure of discretion; in the first instance at least, it will be made by the Commission and Council.

The third requirement is that the objective must be attained in the 'course of the operation of the common market'.[16] The equivalent phrases in the French and Italian texts ('dans le fonctionnement du marché commun' and 'nel funzionamento del mercato comune') mean literally 'in the functioning' of the common market. The German and Dutch texts, on the other hand, mean 'within the framework (or scope) of the common market' ('im Rahmen des Gemeinsamen Marktes' and 'in het kader van de gemeenschappelijke markt'). The latter seem slightly wider; they also make clear that the phrase cannot be given a purely temporal interpretation,[17] which might have seemed possible on the basis of the English text alone.

---

[15] Art. 95(1) ECSC contains an express reference to Arts 2, 3 and 4 ECSC, which are equivalent to Arts 2 and 3 in the EEC Treaty. This means that under the ECSC Treaty, the objectives must be drawn exclusively from these Articles.

[16] This phrase does not occur in Art. 203 Euratom.

[17] By this is meant interpreting the phrase to mean 'during the time when the common market is in operation'.

What exactly is the effect of this phrase? Article 2 EEC appears to draw a distinction between establishing the common market and 'approximating the economic policies of the Member States' (common economic policies) and it might be thought that the effect of the phrase is to limit the use of Article 235 to the former. Some writers, however, reject this view;[18] if they are correct, the phrase seems to mean no more than that the action must fall within the context of the Treaty.

The next requirement is that a specific provision of the Treaty should not have provided the necessary powers. This seems straightforward enough but in fact more problems are created by this requirement than by any other. For instance, what is the position where the Treaty expressly covers the matter in issue but grants powers which are regarded as insufficient? This question arose in *Hauptzollamt Bremerhaven* v. *Massey-Ferguson*,[19] which concerned a regulation on the valuation of goods for customs purposes. The object of this regulation, which had been enacted under Article 235, was to ensure that uniform rules were applied throughout the Community: this was clearly necessary to ensure the proper functioning of the customs union. However, Article 27 EEC is concerned with just this question, though it grants only the power to make recommendations. Since recommendations are not legally binding, it could be argued that Article 27 did not grant the necessary powers. On the other hand, it could be maintained that, since the authors of the Treaty had expressly dealt with the matter and had seen fit to give the power only to make recommendations, they must be regarded as having impliedly excluded the use of greater powers. The Advocate General, however, preferred the former argument and this was implicitly accepted by the European Court, which upheld the validity of the regulation. One can conclude, therefore, that the express grant of a power considered insufficient does not preclude resort to Article 235.

A second objection to the validity of the regulation in the *Massey-Ferguson* case was that the necessary power *was* in fact granted by certain other provisions in the Treaty, provided these were given a sufficiently broad interpretation in line with the doctrine of implied powers (narrow formulation).[20] Advocate General Trabucchi took the view, however, that the interpretation of these other powers was

[18] Marenco, 'Les conditions d'application de l'article 235 du traité CEE', [1970] RMC 147 at 150; Smit and Herzog, p. 6–289.
[19] Case 8/73, [1973] ECR 897.
[20] See *per* Advocate General Trabucchi, [1973] ECR at 913–14.

subject to doubt; therefore, even if they were sufficiently wide, recourse to Article 235 was legitimate. He expressed his opinion as follows:[21]

> Even supposing that this Regulation could have been adopted by a simpler procedure under a different rule or by implication on the basis of a number of specific rules and powers provided by the Treaty, one cannot see what damage to the public interest has been caused by the adoption of such a measure on the basis and under the procedure of Article 235. It would certainly be against the spirit of the system created by the Treaty if the Commission or the Council were to consider it necessary to act on the basis of Article 235 in a case where other provisions of the Treaty already clearly provide suitable powers of action. But we do not have to consider what legal consequences could result on such a hypothesis. In the present case, in the absence of an express and clear provision of the Treaty specifically empowering the enactment of this Regulation, one must dismiss the idea that because this provision was prudently based on the general authorizing rule of Article 235, such fact could possibly constitute an irregularity liable to render it invalid.

This was accepted by the Court; the relevant passage reads as follows:[22]

> If it is true that the proper functioning of the customs union justifies a wide interpretation of Articles 9, 27, 28, 111 and 113 of the Treaty and of the powers which these provisions confer on the institutions to allow them thoroughly to control external trade by measures taken both independently and by agreement, there is no reason why the Council could not legitimately consider that recourse to the procedure of Article 235 was justified in the interest of legal certainty. This is the more so as the Regulation in question was adopted during the transitional period.
>
> By reason of the specific requirements of Article 235 this course of action cannot be criticized since, under the circumstances, the rules of the Treaty on the forming of the Council's decisions or on the division of powers between the institutions are not to be disregarded.

Recourse to Article 235 is, however, excluded where the power to adopt the act is clearly given by another provision of the Treaty. Moreover, the second paragraph of the quotation suggests that, even in cases of doubt, it will not be permissible for the Council to use Article 235 to take over powers granted to the Commission or Parliament; nor may Article 235, with its requirement of unanimity,

---

[21] Ibid. at 914.
[22] Ibid. at 908 (paragraph 4). The phrase at the very end of this passage, 'are not to be disregarded', appears in the French text as 'ne se trouvent pas déjouées'. In the context, a better translation would have been, 'have not been prejudiced'.

be invoked where the Council could have acted under a provision requiring only a qualified majority.

This last restriction may perhaps be the explanation for the judgment in *Commission* v. *Council*,[23] a case concerning a regulation passed by the Council on the proposal of the Commission. The Commission proposal gave Article 113 EEC, which requires a qualified majority, as the legal basis of the regulation, but the Council adopted it under Article 235 because it considered that the subject-matter of the regulation was not fully covered by Article 113. The Commission brought annulment proceedings. The Court ruled that the subject-matter *was* covered by Article 113, and annulled the regulation on the ground that Article 235 cannot be used where another Treaty provision provides the necessary powers.[24] The Court expressly referred to the different voting procedures under Articles 113 and 235.

The final requisite is that the act must be appropriate. This means that it must be reasonably suitable for achieving the objective in question. It probably also means that any hardship caused must not be disproportionate to the benefits accruing from the attainment of the objective: this is in accord with the doctrine of 'proportionality', which has been adopted by the European Court as a general principle of law.[25]

It is now possible to review the effect of Article 235 as a whole. It will be seen that it confers what can only be termed a general legislative power. For this reason, the theory of limited powers does not seem to be part of Community law, except to the extent that the Community may legislate only within the general area covered by the Treaties. This consists largely of economic affairs, but social policy is also covered. It is, of course, much narrower than the area covered by federal jurisdiction in most federations – defence and foreign affairs, for example, are excluded – but it is nevertheless extensive.

This prompts the question whether there are any significant limits to the use of Article 235 within this area. One obvious limit is that measures taken under Article 235 must not go contrary to an express prohibition contained in the Treaty.

Secondly, Article 235 should not be used to adopt measures which

[23] Case 45/86, 26 March 1987 (not yet reported).
[24] An additional reason for annulment was that the regulation did not comply with Art. 190 EEC since it did not state the provision under which it was enacted: the text adopted by the Council simply referred to the EEC Treaty in general without specifying any particular Article.
[25] See below, pp. 145–7.

would constitute an amendment of the Treaty: Treaty amendments are expressly dealt with by Article 236, which, as will be remembered,[26] provides for the calling of a conference of Member States; it also lays down that any amendments must be ratified by each Member State according to its constitutional provisions. It is suggested that this procedure must be used not only where a provision of the Treaty is expressly amended, but also where the basic constitutional structure set up by the Treaty is modified.[27] These limitations are quite reasonable when one remembers that, even in a fully-fledged federation, the federal organs do not normally have power to make constitutional amendments without going through special procedures involving either a referendum or the agreement of the constituent states.

The extensive scope of Article 235 might appear of little significance in view of the rule that measures passed under it must be agreed to by all the members of the Council. This means that any Member State can veto a proposal (though an abstention will not stop the passage of the measure.)[28] However, if Article 235 did not exist, the Member States would be obliged to enter into a convention or treaty and this would be subject to ratification, which normally entails the approval of the national parliaments. The importance of Article 235, therefore, is that it allows governments to by-pass this procedure. In view of this, it is unfortunate that the European Parliament is not given a greater say when recourse is had to Article 235: instead of merely being given the right to state its opinion, it could be given the power to take the final decision jointly with the Council. A reform along these lines has already been suggested[29] but as yet there appears to be no sign of its being adopted.[30]

---

[26] See above, pp. 89–91.

[27] But see Smit and Herzog, pp. 6–291 to 6–292, where a distinction is drawn between a 'formal amendment' and measures which 'modify provisions of the Treaty by restricting or eliminating their effects'. However, the European Court's judgment in the *Massey-Ferguson* case (above) suggests that Art. 235 cannot be used to change the division of powers among the institutions of the Community.

[28] See Art. 148(3) EEC.

[29] See the Report of the Working Party examining the problem of enlargement of the powers of the European Parliament (Vedel Report), 1972, E. C. Bull., Supp. No. 4, pp. 39, 41 and 45.

[30] Art. 235 is not even included among the provisions to which the co-operation procedure applies: see Art. 6 SEA.

DELEGATION OF POWERS

So far we have been considering the powers granted to the Community institutions by the Treaties; the next question is the extent to which these powers may be delegated either to other Community institutions or to outside bodies.

From a formal point of view, a delegation takes place whenever the authority granted a power by the Treaty conveys it to some other body. This definition is not, however, wholly satisfactory, since the formal position may not always correspond with the real situation: a formal delegation may be made without any real transfer of responsibility; or, conversely, formal power may remain with the delegating authority but real power may pass out of its hands.

In order to decide whether a real delegation has taken place one must consider a number of questions. First, is the delegate granted a wide discretion or is the exercise of the power made subject to rules laid down by the delegating authority which are so restrictive that the delegate's role is merely executive? In this case the 'delegation' will be of little practical significance, since the way the power is exercised will not be affected.

Secondly, can the delegating authority exercise effective control over the delegate? This may be done in various ways. For example, it may be provided that the decision of the delegate will not come into force until it has been confirmed by the delegating authority; or the latter may be given the power to rescind it, provided it acts within a given period. This power might be exercisable by the delegating authority on its own initiative or on an appeal to it by some person or body affected by the decision. In Community law, controls of this nature are applicable when powers delegated by the Council to the Commission are exercised under the management committee procedure.[31]

Thirdly, one must consider whether the powers granted to a body are actually exercised by that body or whether the real decision is taken elsewhere. For example, the formal decision may be taken by the delegating authority and the role of the delegate may be confined to making proposals; but if the delegating authority never questions these proposals and merely rubber-stamps them, a *de facto* delegation will have taken place. Likewise, powers of control that are not in practice exercised are of little real significance.

[31] See above, pp. 12–13.

Any effective system of administrative law must take all these factors into account in deciding whether a delegation has taken place. It must also be understood that a delegation is not a question of all or nothing: it is often a matter of degree. The practical significance of the delegation will depend on the extent to which real power has been transferred.

Delegation to the Commission

Until recently, the only provisions in the Treaties expressly concerned with delegation were Articles 155 EEC and 124 Euratom. Article 155[32] reads:

In order to ensure the proper functioning and development of the common market, the Commission shall . . . exercise the powers conferred on it by the Council for the implementation of the rules laid down by the latter.

This merely requires the Commission to exercise the powers delegated to it by the Council; it contains no express authorization for such delegation. However, express authority has now been provided by Article 145 EEC as amended by Article 10 SEA, which authorizes the Council to delegate powers to the Commission to implement provisions laid down by the Council. As previously explained, such delegations are often subject to special procedures involving advisory committees; these procedures are now regulated by a frame-work decision adopted by the Council under Article 145.[33]

The validity of these procedures has been considered by the European Court in a number of cases. Though these cases were decided before the Single European Act came into force in 1987, the principles laid down in them still stand. The first was the *Köster* case,[34] which arose as follows. Acting under Article 43(2) EEC (which empowers the Council to legislate in the field of agriculture), the Council passed a regulation setting out the general principles for the organization of a common market in cereals. This regulation also made provision for the detailed rules to be laid down in measures to be adopted by the Commission under the management committee procedure.

Two objections to this were raised. First, it was pointed out that

[32] Art. 124 Euratom is virtually identical.
[33] An action by the Parliament to annul this decision was dismissed on procedural grounds: *European Parliament* v. *Council*, Case 302/87, 27 September 1988 (discussed at p. 338, below). The Court's judgment does not preclude a further challenge in other proceedings.
[34] *Einfuhr- und Vorratsstelle* v. *Köster*, Case 25/70, [1970] ECR 1161.

where measures are enacted by the Council under Article 43(2) the opinion of the European Parliament must be obtained; but when the power was delegated to the Commission, no provision for this was made. Thus the effect of the delegation was to deprive the Parliament of its right to be consulted. The Court, however, ruled that it is not necessary for all the details of regulations concerning agriculture to be enacted according to the procedure laid down in Article 43(2). It is sufficient if the general principles governing the question are set out in a measure adopted under this procedure: the details may then be laid down under a different procedure, either by the Council itself or by the Commission.

The second objection was against the management committee procedure itself. It was argued that this constituted an unwarranted restriction of the decision-making power of the Commission and jeopardized its independence. The Court, however, pointed out that the management committee could not itself take decisions; if it disapproved of a proposed measure, the only consequence was that the Commission was obliged to communicate the measure to the Council, which could then substitute its own measure for that of the Commission. The Court therefore ruled that this procedure was not contrary to the Treaty.

It will be seen from this case that the important distinction is between laying down general principles and detailed implementation; only the latter function may be delegated. However, the Court is prepared to give a wide interpretation to this concept. For example, in the *Chemiefarma* case[35], the Council adopted a regulation under Article 87 EEC which provided for fines to be levied by the Commission on firms guilty of a violation of the Community competition provisions. Article 19 of this regulation stated that firms accused of such a violation should be granted a hearing before the Commission. Article 24 delegated to the Commission the power to make detailed rules governing the procedure at such a hearing. In the case, it was objected that this entailed the power to legislate and went beyond the concept of 'implementation'. The Court held, however, that the concept of implementation includes the adoption of regulations (provisions of a legislative character). Moreover, in the *Rey Soda* case[36] the European Court said that the concept of implementation must be given a wide interpretation and that in the sphere of

---

[35] *Chemiefarma* v. *Commission*, Case 41/69, [1970] ECR 661.
[36] *Rey Soda* v. *Cassa Conguaglio Zucchero*, Case 23/75, [1975] ECR 1279.

agriculture the Council may confer on the Commission 'wide powers of discretion and action'.[37]

It is possible to conclude, therefore, that extensive discretionary powers may be delegated to the Commission, provided the empowering provision lays down the basic principles governing the matter in question. The same principle seems to apply where a Community institution delegates power to itself.[38] The significance of this is that the delegated power may be exercised by a simpler procedure than that applicable under the Treaty. For example, if the Treaty grants power to the Council to adopt regulations on a proposal from the Commission after consulting the European Parliament, the Council may – provided it lays down the general principles by means of a regulation passed under this procedure – delegate power to itself to enact implementing provisions without the involvement of the Commission or Parliament. The instrument delegating the power must, of course, be adopted under the original procedure.

Delegation to Outside Bodies

The leading case regarding delegation to bodies other than Community institutions is the *Meroni* case.[39] This concerned the scrap iron equalization fund which had been set up by the High Authority in an attempt to deal with the scrap shortage in the 1950s. The idea was to subsidize imported scrap in order to bring its price down to the level of Community scrap; the subsidies were to be paid for by a levy on all scrap users. Two bodies were set up to run the scheme, the *Office Commun des Consommateurs de Ferrailles*, which arranged the imports, and the *Caisse de Péréquation des Ferrailles Importées*, which imposed the levy and distributed the subsidies. Both bodies were incorporated as cooperatives under Belgian law.

The scheme was set up by a general decision of the High Authority which granted the two organizations their powers. There were, however, a number of ways in which the High Authority could control their activities. First, though the *Caisse* had the power to assess levy payments due from a particular firm and to issue a demand for the sum in question, it could not enforce its claims directly: if the firm failed to pay, the *Caisse* had to request the High

---

[37] See paragraphs 10 and 11 of the judgment.

[38] See the *Köster* case (above) at paragraph 6 of the judgment.

[39] *Meroni* v. *High Authority*, Case 9/56, [1958] ECR 133. The relevant part of the judgment is section III.

Authority to take a decision having executive force. Secondly, both organizations had the power to take decisions only if the members of their governing bodies were unanimous; failing this, the matter would be decided by the High Authority itself. Thirdly, all meetings of the two organizations were attended by a representative of the High Authority and he had the power to declare that any decision taken by them would be conditional on the High Authority's approval. The High Authority also had the power to call a meeting of either organization and lay proposals before it; if the proposals were not accepted within ten days, the High Authority could itself put the proposals into effect.

On paper, these powers of control appear extensive; however, according to evidence given by the High Authority in the case, they were rarely exercised. In practice the organizations had a large measure of independence.

The way the case arose was as follows. The *Caisse* had asked Meroni, an Italian steel manufacturer, to inform it of the quantity of scrap it had used, so that the *Caisse* could assess the levy payments due. Meroni failed to do this and the *Caisse* therefore told Meroni that it would make estimates of the relevant figures and assess the levy on that basis. Meroni still refused to cooperate; so the *Caisse* sent a demand for payment on the basis of the estimates. When Meroni failed to pay, the *Caisse* requested the High Authority to take a decision demanding payment. Under Article 92 ECSC this decision would be enforceable against Meroni through the Italian courts; Meroni therefore brought proceedings in the European Court to have it set aside. One of the arguments put forward was that the whole scrap equalization scheme involved an unlawful delegation of powers and was consequently invalid.

The first question the Court had to consider was whether there really had been a delegation of power to collect the levy, since the decision subject to challenge was that of the High Authority. It was, however, admitted by the High Authority that they never questioned assessments made by the *Caisse*: all they did was to rubber-stamp the *Caisse's* decision. The Court therefore held that effective decision-making power had been delegated. The next question was whether the delegation was lawful. The Court held, on three separate grounds, that it was not. First, the Court held that the High Authority had attempted to transfer wider powers than it possessed itself. By this it meant that certain obligations and restrictions which apply when the High Authority itself acts were not applicable to the *Caisse* and *Office Commun*: for example, the High Authority is obliged by the Treaty to give reasons for its decisions[40] but this obligation was not imposed on the two organizations.[41]

The second ground given by the Court was that the High Authority decision delegating powers to the two organizations did not expressly give them the power to assess the levy on the basis of an estimate of scrap used. One might have thought that this would have been covered by the doctrine of implied powers (narrow formulation),[42] but the Court ruled that a delegation of powers can never be implied. Even if the High Authority had been entitled to delegate this power, an express decision would have been necessary.

The third ground given by the Court was by far the most important: it concerned the question whether the High Authority had any power to delegate at all. The Court ruled that the High Authority possesses only very limited power to delegate to outside bodies: clearly defined executive powers may be delegated provided their exercise is subject to strict rules based on objective criteria; but discretionary powers involving extensive freedom of judgment may not be delegated. This distinction between discretionary and non-discretionary (ministerial) powers is, of course, known to English administrative law and its adoption here may be justified on the ground that the authors of the Treaties were prepared to grant extensive discretionary powers to the Commission because they had confidence in it; they might not have been prepared to see these same powers exercised by an outside body not subject to the safeguards applicable to the Commission itself.

The outcome of all this was that the High Authority decision addressed to Meroni demanding payment of the levy was quashed because it was based on a decision of the *Caisse* made under an illegal delegation of powers.[43] In view of the Court's ruling on this point, the scrap equalization scheme had to be extensively restructured.

One may conclude from this case that there is an important difference between a delegation to the Commission and a delegation to an outside body: wide discretionary powers may be delegated in the former case but not in the latter.

[40] See below, pp. 119–26.
[41] The Court also felt that decisions made by the two organizations would be immune from judicial review, but a later case established that this is not so: see *SNUPAT* v. *High Authority*, Cases 32, 33/58, [1959] ECR 127 (discussed below at pp. 136–7).
[42] See above, p. 103.
[43] The Court also gave other grounds for its decision which were not concerned with the question of delegation.

Delegation to Member States

In view of the special position of national governments in the Community structure, it is desirable to give separate treatment to the question of delegation to Member States. At the outset it is necessary to emphasize the distinction between a delegation of powers and a direction to a Member State to exercise its own powers in a particular way. The latter is very common: one form of Community act – the directive – was designed for just this purpose. Delegation of powers, on the other hand, is comparatively rare. The reason is that it is not generally necessary for powers to be transferred to Member States: they normally possess sufficient powers in their own right. If, however, Member States have given up their powers in a particular area in favour of the Community, it will be possible for powers to be transferred back to them by means of a delegation.

The leading case on the topic is *Rey Soda*.[44] This was concerned with the common organization of the market in sugar, which had been brought about by Council Regulation 1009/67. In previous cases the European Court had laid down the principle that when the market in a particular product is brought under a common organization, the Member States lose their powers to regulate it, except as regards the implementation of Community rules.[45] Under Regulation 1009/67 the Commission was given power to take measures to prevent disturbances in the market as a result of alterations in the price level. These powers were to be exercised under the management committee procedure. Acting under this provision, the Commission passed a regulation delegating to Italy the power to take measures to prevent disturbances on the Italian market as a result of the increase on 1 July 1974 of the price of sugar expressed in Italian lire. The Italian Government exercised this power by passing a decree imposing a levy on sugar stockholders. The validity of this measure was challenged in the Italian courts and the European Court had to decide on the validity of the sub-delegation to the Italian Government.

The European Court ruled that the delegation to the Commission was valid but the sub-delegation to the Italian Government was not. This ruling illustrates vividly the difference in the legal principles governing a delegation within the Community and a delegation to an outside body. The Court upheld the delegation to the Commission on

[44] *Rey Soda* v. *Cassa Conguaglio Zucchero*, Case 23/75, [1975] ECR 1279.
[45] See *per* Advocate General Mayras, ibid. at pp. 1317–8.

the ground that, since the general principles had been laid down by Council Regulation 1009/67, it was legitimate to entrust the Commission with the task of implementation, even though this involved conferring wide discretionary powers on it. But the Commission had no power to delegate these discretionary powers to the Italian Government: only strictly defined powers of execution could be sub-delegated. Thus the same principle applies in the case of a delegation to a Member State as in the case of a delegation to a body such as the *Caisse*. In the *Rey Soda* case the Court seemed to have been influenced by the fact that one effect of the sub-delegation was to remove the exercise of the power from the supervision of the management committee; but there nevertheless seems no reason to believe that the Court would apply different principles where the management committee procedure was not applicable.

Conclusions

The most important feature of the law in this area is the distinction between delegation to the Commission, which may involve wide discretionary power, and delegation to outside bodies (including Member States), which may be only of a very limited nature. Why has the European Court made this distinction? Perhaps it can be explained on the basis of the Court's underlying policy of strengthening the Community, and particularly the supranational elements in it.[46] If this is correct, one would expect the Court to be just as favourable in its attitude towards delegation to the European Parliament. So far the Court has not had occasion to rule on this.

FORM

The main requirements of form laid down by the Treaties regarding legal acts of the Council and Commission are a reference to proposals and opinions and a statement of reasons.

Proposals and Opinions

Articles 190 EEC and 162 Euratom provide (in part) as follows:

---

[46] For a general discussion of supranationalism, see above, pp. 6–7.

Regulations, directives and decisions of the Council and of the Commission . . .
shall refer to any proposals or opinions which were required to be obtained
pursuant to this Treaty.

Article 15 ECSC states:

Decisions, recommendations and opinions of the High Authority . . . shall refer
to any opinions which were required to be obtained.

These provisions are very similar. The only significant differences
are, first, that the ECSC provision applies to opinions (non-binding
acts) while the EEC provision applies only to binding acts;[47] and,
secondly, that the words 'pursuant to this Treaty' are not found in the
ECSC provision. (The omission to any reference to proposals in
Article 15 may be explained by the fact that the provision applies only
to acts of the High Authority (Commission); this, in turn, may be
explained by the fact that under the ECSC Treaty most legal acts are
adopted by the High Authority.)

Three points should be made about these provisions. The first
concerns the word 'required'. Under the EEC Treaty this is qualified
by the phrase 'pursuant to this Treaty', which suggests that requirements in measures made under the Treaty, as well as those in the
Treaty itself, are covered.[48] Delegated legislation will therefore have
to refer to proposals or opinions required by the empowering measure. Although it appears to be worded more broadly, it is doubtful
whether Article 15 ECSC is any different in this regard. Secondly, it
should be noted that the obligation in these provisions applies only to
the kinds of measures specified: legal acts *sui generis*[49] are not
covered.[50] Thirdly, it has been held by the European Court that it is
sufficient if reference is made to the fact that the opinion has been
obtained: it is not necessary to specify the contents of the opinion or to
attempt to refute any objections raised.[51]

The main cases where the obligation will apply are proposals from
the Commission and consultations with the European Parliament[52]

[47]   It must be remembered that ECSC recommendations are binding acts analogous to
EEC directives.

[48]   Lauwaars, p. 150.

[49]   Legal acts *sui generis* are discussed above at pp. 101–2.

[50]   See *Commission* v. *Council* (ERTA Case), Case 22/70, [1971] ECR 263 (paragraph 98
of the judgment). It is possible, however, that in certain cases an obligation of this kind
might apply by virtue of some other provision.

[51]   See *ISA* v. *High Authority*, Case 4/54, [1955] ECR 91 at 100. See also Lauwaars,
p. 151.

[52]   It is interesting to note that the Council has, since 1969, adopted the practice of
referring to consultations with the European Parliament even where these are *not* required:
see Parliamentary Question No. 316 of 1971, JO 1972, C 18/3 at 18/4. There is of course no
obligation to do this.

and the Economic and Social Committee. In the case of delegated legislation, reference should be made to consultations with the management committee where this procedure applies.

Reasons

By far the most important formal requirement is the obligation to give reasons. This is laid down in the same provisions. Articles 190 EEC and 162 Euratom provide:

Regulations, directives and decisions of the Council and of the Commission shall state the reasons on which they are based . . .

Article 15 ECSC provides:

Decisions, recommendations and opinions of the High Authority shall state the reasons on which they are based . . .

It is further provided by Article 5 ECSC that 'the Community shall . . . publish the reasons for its actions . . .'. This latter provision presumably applies to all organs of the Community and consequently makes up for the fact that Article 15 applies only to the High Authority.[53]

It is interesting to note that there is no *general* obligation to give reasons in the law of most Member States (e.g. England, France, Italy and Belgium) though in all these countries reasons must be given in certain cases. (In Germany and the Netherlands, on the other hand, there *is* a general obligation to give reasons for administrative acts.) The Community provision is therefore different from (some would say, in advance of) the law of many Member States. It is particularly remarkable that the requirement of reasons applies not only to administrative acts, but also to legislation (regulations). Even in Germany and the Netherlands, the requirement of reasons does not extend this far.[54]

The purpose of the requirement has been explained by the European Court in the *Brennwein* case (*Germany* v. *Commission*):[55]

In imposing upon the Commission the obligation to state reasons for its decisions, Article 190 is not taking mere formal considerations into account but seeks to give an opportunity to the parties of defending their rights, to the Court

---

[53] There are also a number of provisions applying in specific circumstances: see Arts 54(4), 66(5) and 88 ECSC and Arts 89(2), 169 and 170 EEC.

[54] See Hen, 'La motivation des actes des institutions communautaires', (1977) 13 CDE 49.

[55] Case 24/62, [1963] ECR 63 at 69.

of exercising its supervisory functions and to Member States and to all interested nationals of ascertaining the circumstances in which the Commission has applied the Treaty.

What the Court meant by this is as follows. As regards the parties, reasons will help them in two ways: if they know why the enacting authority[56] adopted the act in question, they will be able to address representations to it to persuade it to change its mind; they will also be in a better position to decide whether to bring legal proceedings to have it set aside. As regards the Court, a statement of reasons will be of assistance in deciding on the validity of the act; while third parties (including Member States) will find it useful to know the policies followed by the enacting authority so that they can appreciate the way the power is likely to be exercised in the future.

Two further purposes that will be served by the requirement of reasoning are that the European Parliament will be able to give a better-informed opinion when the draft comes before it; and the enacting institution will itself be forced to consider exactly why it is adopting the act and this might induce it to make modifications.[57]

In discussing the effect of the requirement of reasoning, two questions must be considered: the scope of the provision (to which acts does it apply?) and its content (what constitutes sufficient reasoning?). As far as the scope is concerned, the answer is given in the Treaty provisions: Article 190 EEC applies to regulations, directives and decisions of the Council and Commission,[58] while Article 15 ECSC applies to decisions, recommendations and opinions of the Commission.[59] It makes no difference whether the Council or Commission is acting under a power conferred by the Treaties or a power delegated to it by another institution.[60]

In the *ERTA* case[61] the European Court held that the requirement of reasoning did not apply to the act *sui generis* in issue there.[62]

---

[56] In *Germany* v. *Commission* the enacting authority was the Commission but the Court's statement would apply equally where it was the Council.

[57] See Lauwaars, p. 153.

[58] In the special cases covered by Arts 169 and 170 EEC, the requirement of reasoning applies also to an opinion.

[59] It must not be forgotten that Art. 5 ECSC imposes a general obligation to publish reasons on all Community institutions when they act under the ECSC Treaty.

[60] *Schwarze*, Case 16/65, [1965] ECR 877, 887.

[61] *Commission* v. *Council*, Case 22/70, [1971] ECR 263 (paragraphs 97 and 98 of the judgment).

[62] It is possible that in some cases acts *sui generis* will have to be reasoned, perhaps on the basis of a general principle of law or, in the case of the ECSC, by virtue of Article 5 ECSC. See Lauwaars, p. 152 and note 227.

However, such acts may be adopted in special circumstances only: even if the empowering provision does not specify the nature of the measure to be adopted, it is reasonable to assume that the authors of the Treaties intended that the powers conferred on the Community institutions should, in the absence of special considerations, be exercised in the form of one of the acts listed in Articles 189 EEC, 161 Euratom or 14 ECSC, as the case may be. In support of this, it should be mentioned that the act in question in the ERTA case was not adopted in terms of any provision in the Treaty: it was a resolution[63] of the Council setting out the procedure to be followed in international negotiations with non-member States. In the *ERTA* case itself the Court referred to it as 'an act of a private nature'.[64]

Finally, if the Council or Commission delegates a power which they may exercise only in the form of one of the named acts, the delegate must also exercise it in such a form or, at least, must be made subject to the same requirement of reasoning as the delegating authority. This follows from the decision in the *Meroni* case,[65] where the Court said that a Community institution cannot delegate a greater power than it possesses itself and that consequently any requirements or restrictions that apply when the delegating authority exercises the power must also be imposed on the delegate. Failure to do this renders the delegation invalid. It will be remembered that in the *Meroni* case the Court specifically mentioned the requirement of reasoning.[66]

One may conclude from the above that the requirement applies to almost all acts having legal effects. Only in exceptional cases will the Council or Commission be absolved from it.

The next question to consider is what constitutes sufficient reasons. The objectives which the requirement of reasoning is intended to serve were set out above.[67] It would seem clear, as a matter of general principle, that the test of the sufficiency of the reasons given in a particular case should be derived from these objectives: the reasons given for an act are sufficient if, but only if, they permit the attainment of these objectives.[68] To do this, they must at the very least set out the factual background which the author of the act

---

[63] The Court itself called it a 'discussion', though this term seems inappropriate in English. (The French term was *délibération*.)

[64] At paragraph 98 of the judgment.

[65] *Meroni* v. *High Authority*, Case 9/56, [1958] ECR 133. See above, pp. 113–15.

[66] See [1958] ECR at 171.

[67] Above, pp. 119–20.

[68] See Lauwaars, p. 156.

regards as relevant; they must specify the relevant legal provisions; they must state the objectives which the act is designed to attain; and they should state why, in the opinion of the enacting authority, it is desirable to attain these objectives.

An important rule laid down by the European Court is that the degree of specificity required depends on the nature of the act in question: in the case of an act of a legislative nature (regulation) it is sufficient if the reasoning is limited to broad outlines; in the case of an individual act (decision), on the other hand, more detail is required. The reason for this distinction is that a legislative act, by its very nature, is of general application. The circumstances in which it might possibly apply can never be fully known in advance; consequently, it would be impractical to expect a high degree of specificity. An individual act, however, applies only to a particular case. All the relevant facts are known and it is therefore possible to give much fuller reasons.

An indication of what is required in the case of a regulation was given by the judgment of the European Court in the *Beus* case:[69]

The extent of the requirement laid down by Article 190 of the Treaty to state the reasons on which measures are based, depends on the nature of the measure in question.

It is a question in the present case of a regulation, that is to say, a measure intended to have general application, the preamble to which may be confined to indicating the general situation which led to its adoption, on the one hand, and the general objectives which it is intended to achieve on the other.

Consequently, it is not possible to require that it should set out the various facts, which are often very numerous and complex, on the basis of which the regulation was adopted, or *a fortiori* that it should provide a more or less complete evaluation of those facts.

An example of what the Court expects in the case of a decision is provided by the *Brennwein* case (*Germany* v. *Commission*).[70] Brennwein is an alcoholic drink distilled from wine. Large quantities were produced in Germany and most of the wine was imported from outside the Community. When the common external tariff came into operation there was a substantial increase in the duty on this wine and the German Government took the view that this posed a threat to the industry. They therefore asked the Commission for a quota of 450,000 hectolitres to be imported at the old rate of duty. The

---

[69] Case 5/67, [1968] ECR 83 at 95; see also *Barge* v. *High Authority*, Case 18/62, [1963] ECR 259, 280.
[70] Case 24/62, [1963] ECR 63.

Commission took a decision granting only 100,000 hectolitres. The key passage in its reasoning was as follows:[71] 'On the basis of the existing information it has been possible to ascertain that the production of the wines in question within the Community is amply sufficient. The grant of a tariff quota of the volume requested might therefore lead to serious disturbances of the market in the products in question . . .' The Court held that this was insufficient. Instead of referring merely to 'the existing information', the Commission should have been more specific and given an indication of the evolution and size of the surpluses within the Community; secondly, it should have specified what the 'serious disturbances' were and shown why they would have resulted from the granting of the request. The decision was therefore quashed.

May the enacting authority incorporate by reference reasons given in another instrument? This happens quite often, especially in the case of agricultural measures fixing the levels of levies and refunds. These are usually changed at short notice and it is common for the measure fixing the new rate to refer back to a previous measure in which the full criteria are set out. The practice of incorporating reasons by reference has been accepted by the European Court in a number of cases.[72] In the *Schwarze* case,[73] for example, the Court upheld a Commission decision fixing the free-at-frontier price of barley, even though it contained very little reasoning, because it included a reference to a previous decision which set out the general considerations applicable to the fixing of these prices. The Court stated that less strict criteria should be applied in cases of this kind in view of the short period of time within which the Commission must act, the confidentiality of the data on which their decisions are based and the administrative difficulties which would result if detailed reasoning were required in every case.

In *Papiers Peints de Belgique* v. *Commission*,[74] on the other hand, the Commission had taken a decision imposing fines on a number of companies for breach of Article 85(1) EEC. The reasoning referred to a judgment of the European Court in a previous case. The Court held that this was insufficient: a decision under Article 85 which merely follows established policy may refer to the reasons given in a

[71] Taken from the opinion of Advocate General Roemer, at p. 72.
[72] See Lauwaars, pp. 161–2 for a summary of the cases; note that incorporation by reference was rejected in *Dalmas* v. *High Authority*, Case 1/63, [1963] ECR 303 (discussed by Lauwaars at p. 161) but accepted again in later cases.
[73] Case 16/65, [1965] ECR 877.
[74] Case 73/74, [1975] ECR 1491.

previous case, but a decision which breaks new ground – as was the case here – must be fully reasoned.

This shows that incorporation by reference is permissible only in certain cases. It is suggested that, where it is allowed, the reference should always be to a published document or, where the measure itself need not be published, to a document available to all interested parties.[75] In deciding who are to be regarded as interested parties, one should remember the Court's statement that one of the purposes of the requirement of reasoning is to enable third parties to know the policies which the Community institutions pursue and the way in which they interpret their powers.[76]

Should insufficient reasoning be excused if interested parties are subsequently informed what the enacting authority's reasons were? Against such a principle one could argue that Article 190 EEC clearly provides that measures 'shall state the reasons on which they are based': allowing incorporation by reference is stretching Article 190 to its limit; an *ex post facto* statement can in no sense be regarded as compliance. On the other hand, however, it might be said that to insist on the letter of Article 190, when the reasons are in fact known, would serve no purpose.

In the *Brennwein* case[77] the Court appeared not to regard it as sufficient that the Commission provided the relevant data in Court; however, in the *Schwarze* case[78] the Court accepted that, in certain circumstances, the requirement of reasoning will be satisfied if the parties are supplied with the information once judicial proceedings have been commenced. Although the kind of decision in issue justified a relaxation of the requirement, it is hard to accept that Article 190 has been satisfied when the party must wait not only until after the promulgation of the measure before being given the reasons, but must first commence legal proceedings. According to the Court[79], one of the purposes of the requirement of reasoning is to enable the parties to defend their rights; but they will frequently not be in a position to know whether they ought to take legal action until they have seen the reasons. Moreover, the requirement is also

[75] Lauwaars, p. 163.
[76] See above, pp. 119–20.
[77] Above.
[78] Above.
[79] See the quotation from the *Brennwein* case, set out at pp. 119–20, above.

supposed to protect third parties: they cannot be expected to commence proceedings just in order to see the reasons.[80]

A more acceptable compromise between administrative and legal requirements is to be found in *Michel* v. *European Parliament*,[81] a case concerning the rejection of an application to take part in the selection procedure for appointment to the staff of the Parliament. Here the Court annulled the decision, though the applicant had been informed of the reasons during the court proceedings. The Court stated that the reasons must in principle be given at the same time as the decision, but relaxed this requirement in view of the large number of applications (1455 out of 1740 were rejected). It held that the selection board was obliged in the letter of rejection to set out only the general criteria applied, but if the candidate asked for the particular reasons that led to his rejection, these must be supplied within the time-limit for commencing legal proceedings.

It will be evident from what has been said that the degree of detail required depends to a large extent on the circumstances of the case. Consequently, it is impossible to lay down precise rules as to what constitutes sufficient reasoning. It is, however, worth asking whether the rather ambitious objectives set out by the European Court in the *Brennwein* case are normally attained. As has been seen, the normal standards are of necessity relaxed in certain cases: in these circumstances the interests of third parties, and sometimes even of those directly involved, are liable to suffer. But are the objectives met even where these special circumstances do not exist?

The most serious problem is that the objectives set out by the Court will not be achieved unless the reasons given are the real reasons. It has, however, been said that in the everyday practice of the Commission the substantive provisions of measures are drawn up first and the reasons are added afterwards by the legal service.[82] In these circumstances there is a danger that the real reasons will not always be given: the legal service may be tempted to 'dress up' the measure by giving more acceptable reasons than those which the Commission actually had in mind. In this situation the requirement of reasons would degenerate into an empty formality.

---

[80] Other cases in which information given privately to a party has been taken into account by the Court are *Netherlands* v. *Commission*, Case 13/72, [1973] ECR 27 and *De Wendel* v. *Commission*, Case 29/67, [1968] ECR 263.

[81] Case 195/80, [1981] ECR 2861. See also *Bonu* v. *Council*, Case 89/79, [1980] ECR 553 at paragraph 6 of the judgment.

[82] Hen, 'La motivation des actes des institutions communautaires', (1977) 13 CDE 49 at 54 and 90.

One can conclude that, while the requirement of reasoning undoubtedly serves a useful purpose, the objectives set out in the *Brennwein* case are not fully attained.

PROCEDURE

The general procedure followed in the Community for the enactment of legislative measures has already been discussed.[83] It will be remembered that normally the Council adopts the measure on the proposal of the Commission after the European Parliament has been consulted. The only aspect of this that needs further consideration is the requirement of consultation. Two problems arise in connection with this: first, if the draft is amended after the consultation has taken place, must there be a further consultation on the amendment? Secondly, what is the position where the Parliament is consulted but fails to give an opinion?

The answer to the first question is that it is sufficient if all the *essential* aspects of the measure have been considered by the Parliament: an amendment of minor importance need not be sent back to the Parliament – it may even have been inspired by the Parliament's opinion – but a basic change in the content of the measure would require a fresh opinion by the Parliament.[84] One can assume that the same rule would apply where the Economic and Social Committee has to be consulted.

As far as the second question is concerned, the European Court has held that it is not enough if the Parliament is merely *asked* for its opinion: it must actually *give* its opinion.[85] Failure to fulfil this requirement will lead to the invalidity of the measure. The Court did not, however, decide what would happen if the Parliament deliberately refrained from giving an opinion in order to block the enactment of the measure. One assumes that in this case the Council could adopt the measure, provided it had exhausted all possibilities of obtaining an opinion within a reasonable time.

---

[83] At pp. 37–9, above.

[84] *Chemiefarma* v. *Commission*, Case 41/69, [1970] ECR 661 at paragraphs 68–70 of the judgment.

[85] *Roquette* v. *Council*, Case 138/79, [1980] ECR 3333; *Maizena* v. *Council*, Case 139/79, [1980] ECR 3393. See further pp. 30–2, above.

PUBLICATION AND NOTIFICATION

Under Article 191 EEC, regulations must be published in the Official Journal of the Community.[86] Directives and decisions need not be published, though in practice they often are; it is, however, provided by Article 191 that they must be notified to the persons to whom they are addressed. There are similar provisions in Article 163 Euratom. Article 15 ECSC requires decisions and recommendations which are individual in character to be notified to the person concerned; it then states that in all other cases they 'take effect by the mere fact of publication'. This may be regarded as imposing a duty to publish general decisions and recommendations in the Official Journal. One may conclude from these provisions that a general act will not take effect unless it has been published and an individual act will not be effective unless notified.[87]

Publication and notification are not, however, constitutive requirements: an act which has not been published or notified is nevertheless an act. Failure to publish or notify does not affect its existence, but only its legal consequences. This was decided by the European Court in a number of cases concerning a provision under which the High Authority was empowered to make decisions only up to a certain date. The decisions in question had been made before this date, but had been notified to the addressees only afterwards. The Court held they were valid.[88] In a similar case concerning a regulation, it was held that the validity of the measure was not affected by the fact that publication took place only after the date in question.[89]

Article 191 EEC provides that regulations will enter into force on the date specified in them or, in the absence of such a date, on the twentieth day following their publication. In practice, an earlier date is not stipulated except in cases of urgency.[90] The provision in Article 15 ECSC quoted above presumably means that, in the absence of an express provision to the contrary, a general act under the ECSC

---

[86] There is one Official Journal for all three Communities (ECSC, EEC and Euratom). It is published in each of the official languages.

[87] Since the Treaty provisions do not cover acts *sui generis*, this rule will not apply to them, unless it does so by virtue of a general principle of law.

[88] See Lauwaars, pp. 166–7 and the cases cited there.

[89] *Hauptzollamt Bielefeld* v. *König*, Case 185/73, [1974] ECR 607 (paragraphs 5–8 of the judgment). It has also been held that irregularities in the procedure for notification of a decision do not constitute a ground for its annulment: *ICI* v. *Commission*, Case 48/69, [1972] ECR 619, 652 (paragraphs 39–44 of the judgment).

[90] See Smit and Herzog, p. 5–635.

Treaty enters into force on publication. Under all three Treaties, individual acts take effect on notification.[91]

FURTHER READING

Lauwaars, Chapters II and III.

Close, 'Harmonisation of Laws: Use or Abuse of the Powers under the EEC Treaty?', (1978) 3 E.L. Rev. 461.

Lesguillons, 'L'extension des compétences de la CEE par l'article 235 du traité de Rome', [1974] Annuaire Français de Droit International 886.

Marenco, 'Les conditions d'application de l'article 235 du traité CEE', [1970] RMC 147.

Hen, 'La motivation des actes des institutions communautaires', (1977) 13 CDE 49.

Le Tallec and Ehlermann, 'La motivation des actes des Communautés européennes', [1966] RMC 179.

---

[91] It might be thought that this would mean that individual acts could never be retroactive. However, this is possible at least in those cases where the effect of the act is beneficial to the addressee: see *Rewe-Zentrale des Lebensmittel-Grosshandels*, Case 37/70, [1971] ECR 23; see also Smit and Herzog, pp. 5–644 and 5–655. This question is discussed further at pp. 139–42, below.

5

GENERAL PRINCIPLES OF LAW

In what way are 'general principles' a source of law? In answering this question, it is desirable to look for a moment at a problem of judicial psychology. In no legal system is it possible for legislation or other written sources of law to provide an answer to every question which comes before the courts. The judges are therefore obliged to create rules of law to decide the issues before them; but if their law-creating role becomes too apparent, the judges may be accused of going beyond their proper function and trespassing on the domain of the legislature. How are they to resolve this dilemma? In England the courts have traditionally resorted to the myth of the common law, the age-old tradition of customary law which, by a fiction, was regarded as being both immemorial and within the special cognizance of the judges. The European Court, on the other hand, has utilized general principles of law to cloak the nakedness of judicial law-making: the idea is that if a ruling can be shown to be derived from a principle of sufficient generality as to command common assent, a firm legal foundation for the judgment will be provided. For this reason, the European Court has developed a doctrine that rules of Community law may be derived, not only from treaties and legislation, but also from the general principles of law.

What is the origin of these general principles? They are derived from various sources, but the most important are the Community Treaties and the legal systems of the Member States. In the former case, the Court declares that a specific provision in one of the Treaties is an application of some more general principle which is not itself laid down in the Treaty. This is then applied in its own right as a general principle of law. An example of this is Article 7 EEC which prohibits all discrimination based on nationality between Community citizens as regards matters within the scope of the Treaty. This, together with other texts, has been used by the Court as the foundation for a general doctrine of equality which forbids arbitrary discrimination on any ground (discussed below).[1] Another example

---

[1] See pp. 148–50.

is Article 36 ECSC which provides that, in an appeal against a fine or penalty, the applicant may claim that the measure which he contravened is invalid. In *Meroni* v. *High Authority*[2] the applicant wished to invoke this plea in a case involving not a fine, but a levy. Article 36 could not apply but the Court held that this provision was a particular application of the general principle that all legislative measures may be challenged indirectly. This general principle was then applied to the case at hand so as to allow the applicant to challenge the measure. It will be noticed that this reasoning involves two stages: the first is inductive, in which the Court derives a general principle from specific provisions in the Treaty; the second stage is deductive – here the Court arrives at a solution to the particular issue before it by applying the general principle. It should be stressed that when the Court acts in this way the legal source of its decision is not the Treaty, but the general principle.

When the Court looks to national law for inspiration, it is not necessary that the principle should be accepted by the legal systems of all the Member States. It would be sufficient if the principle were generally accepted by the legal systems of most Member States, or if it was in conformity with a trend in the Member States so that one could say that the national legal systems were developing towards it.[3] It must again be emphasized, however, that whatever the factual origin of the principle, it is applied by the European Court as a principle of Community law, not national law.

It should also be mentioned that the Treaties themselves provide some justification for recourse to general principles as a source of law. First, there is Article 164 EEC[4] which states:

The Court of Justice shall ensure that in the interpretation and application of this Treaty the law is observed.

Since the word 'law' must here refer to something over and above the Treaty itself, it is not unreasonable to infer that this provision not only entitles, but also obliges, the Court to take general principles into account.

There is a more specific provision in Article 173 EEC. This Article

[2] Case 9/56, [1958] ECR 133. See below, pp. 397–8.
[3] See *Hoogovens* v. *High Authority*, Case 14/61, [1962] ECR 253 at 283–284, where Advocate General Lagrange said that the Court is not content to adopt the common denominator between the different systems but 'chooses from each of the Member States those solutions which, having regard to the objects of the Treaty, appear to it to be the best . . .'
[4] Arts. 31 ECSC and 136 Euratom contain similar provisions.

lays down (among other things) the grounds on which a community act may be annulled by the Court.[5] One of these grounds is 'infringement of this Treaty, or of any rule of law relating to its application'. The phrase 'any rule of law relating to its application' must again refer to something other than the Treaty itself and it has been used by the Court as the basis for the doctrine that a Community act may be quashed for infringement of a general principle of law.

The third Treaty provision is Article 215(2) EEC[6]. This is concerned with non-contractual liability (tort) and it expressly provides that the liability of the Community is based on 'the general principles common to the laws of the Member States'. This is discussed in detail in Chapter 17; all that need be said here is that, in spite of the wording of the provision, the Court is prepared to apply principles of law even if they are not found in the legal system of every Member State. In other words, it adopts the same free and independent approach to the elaboration of its case-law as in those areas where there is no express Treaty obligation to apply general principles of law. In fact, the law relating to non-contractual liability appears to be exactly the same (so far, at least) under Article 40 ECSC, which contains no reference to the general principles common to the laws of the Member States, as under Article 215(2) EEC. This illustrates the Court's willingness to apply general principles even in the absence of a specific Treaty provision.

The general principles of law are, therefore, an independent source of law and there can be little doubt that the Court would have applied them even if none of the Treaty provisions mentioned above had existed. It should not, however, be thought that the Court always makes express reference to general principles whenever it propounds new rules of law. Sometimes it simply states a rule without any express indication of its source; or it may give a justification based on policy or the general requirements of the Community legal system. However, if a formal source for such rules were required, it could always be found either on the basis of a wide interpretation of a written text or on the basis of the general principles.

What general principles has the Court so far adopted? It is impossible to enumerate them all, but some of the more important will now be discussed.[7]

---

[5] There are identical provisions in Arts 33 ECSC and 146 Euratom.
[6] There is an identical provision in Art. 188 Euratom.
[7] For a fuller discussion see Schermers, paragraphs 61–165.

FUNDAMENTAL HUMAN RIGHTS

In spite of their importance in the world today, fundamental human rights have only recently come to play a significant role in Community law. Moreover, it is probably fair to say that the conversion of the European Court to a specific doctrine of human rights has been as much a matter of expediency as conviction. The history of the matter is as follows.

One of the most strongly pursued objectives of the European Court has always been to ensure the effectiveness of Community law and this in turn has led to the doctrine of the supremacy of Community law over national law, a doctrine which the European Court has upheld with the greatest vigour. By and large, this doctrine has been accepted by the national courts; however, since the early days of the Community, German lawyers have had doubts as to whether Community law should prevail over the provisions of the German Constitution (*Grundgesetz*), especially those concerning fundamental human rights. It should be mentioned that there has been no difficulty in Germany regarding the supremacy of Community law over ordinary German law, including statutes of the Federal Parliament. However, all German laws, including federal statutes, are subordinate to the Constitution; and there is a special Federal Constitutional Court (*Bundesverfassungsgericht*) which has power to determine the constitutionality of legislation. Since their own national legislation had to comply with the principles of the Constitution, it was hardly surprising that some German lawyers took the view that Community law could not apply in Germany if it violated the fundamental human rights provisions of the *Grundgesetz*. The strong attachment of German lawyers to the concept of fundamental law, and especially fundamental human rights, is, of course, understandable in the light of recent German history.

In the 1960s, the argument that Community law should comply with the fundamental human rights provisions of the *Grundgesetz* was frequently put forward by German litigants both in German courts[8] and in the European Court. At first the European Court was unsympathetic.[9] However, it was soon apparent that the German courts found the doctrine very persuasive, and it became imperative

---

[8] For summaries of the German cases, see Brinkhorst and Schermers, *Judicial Remedies in the European Communities*, pp. 144–54 and *Supplement*, pp. 72–7.

[9] See *Stork* v. *High Authority*, Case 1/58, [1959] ECR 17 at 26; and *Geitling* v. *High Authority*, Cases 36–38, 40/59, [1960] ECR 423 at 438.

for the European Court to take action to head off a possible 'rebellion'. The solution it adopted was to proclaim a Community concept of human rights and to lay down the doctrine that the European Court would itself annul any provision of Community law contrary to human rights.

The case in which the European Court announced the new doctrine was *Stauder* v. *City of Ulm*.[10] This concerned a Community scheme to provide cheap butter for recipients of welfare benefits. The applicant received war victims welfare benefits in Germany and was therefore entitled to the cheap butter; however, he objected to the fact that he was obliged to present a coupon bearing his name and address in order to obtain the butter: he maintained that it was a humiliation to have to reveal his identity, and argued that this constituted a violation of his fundamental human rights. He therefore claimed that the Community decision in question was invalid in so far as it contained this requirement. The action was originally brought before the German courts and a reference was made to the European Court.

The European Court held that on a proper interpretation the Community measure did not require the recipient's name to appear on the coupon.[11] It then continued:[12] 'Interpreted in this way the provision at issue contains nothing capable of prejudicing the fundamental human rights enshrined in the general principles of Community law and protected by the Court.' This recognized that fundamental human rights are a general principle of Community law.

Next came the *Internationale Handelsgesellschaft* case,[13] which concerned the common agricultural policy. In order to control the market in certain agricultural products, a system had been introduced under which exports were permitted only if the exporter first obtained an export licence. When application was made for the licence, the exporter had to deposit a sum of money which would be forfeit if he failed to make the export during the period of validity of the licence. The applicants in this case, however, claimed that the whole system was invalid as being contrary to fundamental human rights. One principle invoked was that of proportionality. This is a doctrine of German constitutional law under which public auth-

---

[10] Case 29/69, [1969] ECR 419.
[11] On this aspect of the case, see above, pp. 69–70.
[12] Paragraph 7 of the judgment.
[13] Case 11/70, [1970] ECR 1125. See also *EVGF* v. *Köster*, Case 25/70, [1970] ECR 1161, at paragraph 22 of the judgment.

orities may impose on the citizen only those obligations which are necessary for attaining the public objective in question.[14] It was argued in the German *Verwaltungsgericht* (administrative court) where the proceedings commenced that the relevant Community measure was invalid for violating the German Constitution; the question of its validity was referred to the European Court.

The European Court first stated that the validity of Community measures cannot be judged according to the rules or concepts of national law: only Community criteria may be applied. Consequently, even a violation of the fundamental human rights provisions of a Member State's constitution could not impair the validity of a Community provision. Having said this, however, the Court then sweetened the pill by adding:[15]

> However, an examination should be made as to whether or not any analogous guarantee inherent in Community law has been disregarded. In fact, respect for fundamental rights forms an integral part of the general principles of law protected by the Court of Justice. The protection of such rights, whilst inspired by the constitutional traditions common to the Member States, must be ensured within the framework of the structure and objectives of the Community. It must therefore be ascertained, in the light of the doubts expressed by the Verwaltungsgericht, whether the system of deposits has infringed rights of a fundamental nature, respect for which must be ensured in the Community legal system.

The Court then examined the system in detail but concluded that no fundamental right had been violated by it.

It will be noticed that the dictum quoted above goes beyond that in the *Stauder* case in one important respect: it states that the concept of human rights applied by the Court, while deriving its validity solely from Community law, is nevertheless 'inspired' by national constitutional traditions.

A further step was taken in *Nold* v. *Commission*.[16] This case concerned a Commission decision under the ECSC Treaty which provided that coal wholesalers could not buy Ruhr coal direct from the selling agency unless they agreed to purchase a certain minimum quantity. Nold was a Ruhr wholesaler who was not in a position to meet this requirement and consequently had to deal with an intermediary. He claimed that the decision was a violation of his fundamental human rights, partly because it deprived him of a

---

[14] This doctrine has actually been adopted by the European Court as a general principle in its own right: see pp. 145–7, below.

[15] At p. 1134.

[16] Case 4/73, [1974] ECR 491.

property right and partly because it infringed his right to the free pursuit of an economic activity. He therefore brought proceedings before the European Court under Article 33 ECSC for the annulment of the decision.

The Court appeared to recognize the two rights as principles of Community law but held that they must not be regarded as absolute and unqualified: they are subject to limitations 'justified by the overall objectives pursued by the Community' and 'mere commercial interests or opportunities' are outside their scope. No infringement had therefore taken place.

In the course of its judgment the European Court made the following statement:[17]

As the Court has already stated, fundamental rights form an integral part of the general principles of law, the observance of which it ensures.

In safeguarding these rights, the Court is bound to draw inspiration from constitutional traditions common to the Member States, and it cannot therefore uphold measures which are incompatible with fundamental rights recognised and protected by the constitutions of those States.

Similarly, international Treaties for the protection of human rights on which the Member States have collaborated or of which they are signatories, can supply guidelines which should be followed within the framework of Community law.

This goes beyond the statement in the *Handelsgesellschaft* case in two respects: first, it makes clear that a Community measure in conflict with fundamental rights as expressed in the constitutions of Member States will be annulled; secondly, it reveals a new source of 'inspiration' for these rights – international treaties.

The European Court's most detailed discussion of human rights to date is to be found in *Hauer* v. *Land Rheinland-Pfalz*,[18] a case concerning a Community regulation which imposed a temporary ban on all new planting of vines. Hauer owned land in Germany which she wanted to plant as a vineyard and was prevented from doing so by the regulation. She began proceedings before the German courts and a reference was made to the European Court, which accepted as principles of Community law the right to property and the freedom to pursue a trade or profession but, after pointing out that these rights are not absolute, found that the Community measure was justified in the general interest and thus fell within an exception to the rights. The judgment is of particular interest because the European Court

[17] At p. 507.
[18] Case 44/79, [1979] ECR 3727.

not only referred to particular provisions in the constitutions of three Member States (Germany, Italy and Ireland) in order to establish that the right to property is subject to restrictions, but also analysed in some detail the relevant provisions of the European Convention on Human Rights.

This case illustrates that the Court's approach to fundamental rights is a little different from its approach to other general principles of law. The reason is that the acceptance of an express doctrine of fundamental rights was prompted by the desire to persuade the German courts to accept the supremacy of Community law even in the case of an alleged conflict with the fundamental rights provisions of the *Grundgesetz*. In view of this, national provisions are likely to be much more influential than in the case of other general principles. In fact, it is probable that the European Court would accept as a general principle of Community law a principle which is constitutionally protected in only *one* Member State. In other words, any measure which is contrary to human rights in Germany or any other Member State will be annulled by the European Court.[19] However, the European Court will never admit to applying national law as such; this is why it puts forward the notion that the Community concept of fundamental rights is merely 'inspired' by the philosophical concepts underlying the national provisions.

International treaties constitute the second source of 'inspiration' for the Community concept of fundamental human rights. If a Community measure were contrary to a human right embodied in a treaty to which a Member State was a party, the Member State might be unwilling to apply it on its territory for fear of breaching the treaty. The same considerations apply as in the case of constitutional provisions; consequently, it would probably be sufficient if a single Member State were a party to the treaty in question.

It will be remembered that in the *Nold* case the European Court spoke of treaties on which Member States have 'collaborated' or of which they are signatories. This suggests that it is not necessary for the Member State actually to be a party to the treaty: it is sufficient if it took part in the negotiations leading to its conclusion; likewise

---

[19] See *per* Advocate General Warner, *IRCA*, Case 7/76, [1976] ECR 1213 at 1237. His reasoning was as follows: Community law owes its existence to a partial transfer of sovereignty by the Member States to the Community; but since a Member State cannot be regarded as having included in that transfer the power to legislate contrary to rights protected by its constitution, it must be assumed that the Community has no power to infringe rights embodied in the constitution of *any* Member State.

signature of the treaty need not necessarily be followed by ratification. This gives the Court considerable latitude in its search for guidelines. However, if no Member State were actually a party to it, the Court would probably not feel obliged to accept every provision in the treaty.

The most important treaty in this respect is the European Convention for the Protection of Human Rights and Fundamental Freedoms. All the Member States are parties to it and there is no doubt that the rights protected by it are Community human rights. The European Court has made express reference to it on several occasions.[20] Other treaties to which it has referred are the European Social Charter of 18 November 1961 and Convention 111 of the International Labour Organization (25 June 1958).[21]

In spite of all its efforts, the European Court's attempt to head off a revolt by the German courts was not immediately successful. In the *Internationale Handelsgesellschaft* case, the German *Verwaltungsgericht* was not satisfied with the European Court's ruling and it proceeded to request a ruling from the German Constitutional Court. The Constitutional Court stated that, in the absence of a codified catalogue of human rights in Community law, it was impossible to decide whether the Community standard of human rights was adequate in terms of that laid down by the *Grundgesetz*; consequently it was not prepared to accept the European Court's ruling as conclusive. It then examined the question itself and concluded that the Community measure in question did not violate the fundamental rights provisions of the *Grundgesetz*. However, it affirmed the supremacy of the latter and alluded to the possibility that Community measures might be declared inapplicable in Germany if they violated these provisions. It was only in 1986, in the *Wünsche Handelsgesellschaft* case, that the Constitutional Court finally abandoned this position.[22]

---

[20] See, in particular, *Rutili*, Case 36/75, [1975] ECR 1219 (what restrictions may be placed on human rights); *Hauer* v. *Rheinland-Pfalz*, Case 44/79, [1979] ECR 3727 (First Protocol: right to property); *Pecastaing* v. *Belgium*, Case 98/79, [1980] ECR 691 (Art. 6: right to a fair hearing); *Valsabbia* v. *Commission*, Case 154/78, [1980] ECR 907 (First Protocol); *National Panasonic* v. *Commission*, Case 136/79, [1980] ECR 2033 (Art. 8: privacy – respect for home and correspondence); *Musique Diffusion Française* v. *Commission*, Cases 100–103/80, [1983] ECR 1825 (Art. 6: right to a fair hearing); *R.* v. *Kirk*, Case 63/83, [1984] ECR 2689 (Art. 7: non-retroactivity of penal provisions); *Johnston* v. *Chief Constable of the RUC*, Case 222/84, [1986] 3 CMLR 240 (Arts 6 and 13: right to a legal remedy).

[21] *Defrenne* v. *Sabena*, Case 149/77, [1978] ECR 1365, at paragraph 28 of the judgment.

[22] During this period the Constitutional Court never actually found any provision of Community law to be contrary to the *Grundgesetz*. For a fuller discussion of these cases, see pp. 223–5, below.

Attempts to enhance the protection of human rights have also been made by the political institutions of the Community. In 1976 the Commission submitted a report[23] to the European Parliament in which it expressed the belief that the best level of protection could be provided by the European Court through its doctrine of general principles of law, the flexibility of which would ensure that the law kept pace with changing needs. The Commission also called for a Joint Declaration by the three political institutions affirming their commitment to fundamental rights and this was made in 1977.[24]

Subsequently, however, the Commission appears to have had second thoughts and in a report published in 1979 it argued that the Community should formally adhere to the European Convention on Human Rights.[25] It also favoured a Community charter of rights (the 'codified catalogue of human rights' required by the German Constitutional Court) but recognized that this could not be achieved in the immediate future because of differences of opinion between the Member States on the definition of the social and economic rights that are most relevant to the activities of the Community. This report provoked much discussion but there does not so far seem to be any prospect of effect being given to its proposals.[26]

It is important to stress that the Community concept of human rights has so far been applied only against the Community itself. Member States are not affected by it,[27] though the same principles

[23] 'The Protection of Fundamental Rights in the European Community', E. C. Bull., Supp. 5/76.

[24] Joint Declaration by the European Parliament, the Council and the Commission, 5 April 1979, OJ 1977, C 103/1. In this they stressed the importance they attached to fundamental rights, as derived in particular from the constitutions of the Member States and the European Convention on Human Rights, and pledged to respect them in the exercise of their powers. No attempt was made to specify the rights in question. See also the Joint Declaration against Racism and Xenophobia, 11 June 1986, OJ 1986, C 158/1.

[25] 'Accession of the Communities to the European Convention on Human Rights', E. C. Bull, Supp. 2/79.

[26] On the difficulties that would arise if the Community were to adhere to the European Convention, see the House of Lords Select Committee on the European Communities, 71st Report, 'Human Rights' (HL 362, 1979/80); for a full discussion, see McBride and Brown, 'The United Kingdom, the European Community and the European Convention on Human Rights', (1981) 1 YEL 167.

[27] *Defrenne* v. *Sabena*, Case 149/77, [1978] ECR 1365; *Demirel*, Case 12/86, 30 September 1987 (not yet reported), paragraph 28 of the judgment (preliminary edition). For unsuccessful attempts to invoke the European Convention on Human Rights in the British courts on the ground that it is part of Community law, see *Allgemeine Gold und Silberscheideanstalt* v. *Commissioners of Customs and Excise* [1978] 2 CMLR 292, aff'd [1980] QB 390 (C.A.); *Surjit Kaur* v. *Lord Advocate* [1980] 3 CMLR 79 (Court of Session). See further Drzemczewski, 'The Domestic Application of the European Human Rights Convention as European Community Law', (1981) 30 ICLQ 118.

may be binding on a Member State on some other basis. The only exception is where the matter is covered by a provision of written Community law, such as a provision in one of the Treaties or in a regulation. In such a case, the provision will be interpreted in the light of the Community concept; moreover if such a provision grants rights to individuals, but these rights are subject to a proviso allowing derogations on certain grounds, any derogations thus made by the national governments should not violate the Community concept of human rights.[28] The reason is that, in derogating from the right, the Member States are acting under a power granted by the Community and are therefore subject to the same restrictions as the Community itself.

LEGAL CERTAINTY

Legal certainty – sometimes referred to as 'legal security' (*sécurité juridique*, in French) – is probably the most important general principle recognised by the European Court. It is a wide concept which cannot easily be explained in a few words, though predictability is probably the core aspect of it. The general idea of legal certainty is of course recognised by most legal systems; however, in Community law it plays a much more concrete role in the form of various sub-concepts which are regarded as applications of it. The most important of these are non-retroactivity, vested rights and legitimate expectations.

Retroactivity and Vested Rights

'Retroactivity' is a term often used by lawyers but rarely defined. On analysis it soon becomes apparent, moreover, that it is used to cover at least two distinct concepts. The first, which may be called 'true retroactivity', consists in the application of a new rule of law to an act or transaction which was completed before the rule was promulgated. The second concept, which will be referred to as 'quasi-retroactivity', occurs when a new rule of law is applied to an act or

---

[28] See *Rutili* v. *Minister of the Interior*, Case 36/75, [1975] ECR 1219 at paragraphs 31 and 32 of the judgment. This case concerned Art. 48(3) EEC which grants rights of free movement to Community workers 'subject to limitations justified on grounds of public policy, public security and public health'. See Wyatt, (1976) 1 E.L. Rev. 217 at 219–20 and (1978) 3 E.L. Rev. 483 at 486–8.

transaction in the process of completion.[29] Since the foundation of these concepts is the distinction between completed and pending transactions, it will be useful to give examples of each.

As the first example one may take a law imposing a customs duty on imported goods. Let us assume that the obligation to pay arises when the goods cross the frontier. Now, if a law is passed increasing the duty and it is provided that the new duty will apply to goods which crossed the frontier before the new law was promulgated, this will be a case of true retroactivity. Assume, however, that the new duty applies only to goods crossing the frontier after its promulgation but it applies even if the importer was legally committed to import them before the promulgation of the new law, for example by virtue of a contract. This will be a case of quasi-retroactivity.

As a second example one may take the granting of a licence by a public authority to a private citizen. If, after it has been granted, the authority withdraws it in circumstances such that the licensee is deemed never to have had a licence, one would have a case of true retroactivity. However, if it is withdrawn only for the future, but the withdrawal takes place before the expiration of its period of validity, one could say that this was a case of quasi-retroactivity.

These examples will make clear that true retroactivity can often cause severe injustice to the individual. In both the examples given, one would say that the action of the public authority was unacceptable in the absence of special circumstances. In the case of quasi-retroactivity, the injustice is much less; but nevertheless it could be quite considerable in some circumstances. The importer might have calculated his profit margins on the assumption that the rate of duty would remain constant and he might face a loss if he is obliged to absorb the new duty. Likewise, the licensee might have committed himself to a capital outlay on the assumption that the licence would remain in force for its stated period of validity. In both cases of quasi-retroactivity, however, the injustice lies not so much in the fact of retroactivity as in the fact that the legitimate expectations of the person concerned have been upset. This will occur if he had reasonable grounds for assuming that the legal position would remain unchanged and he acted to his detriment on that assumption.

The concept of vested rights is normally no more than another aspect of retroactivity. Normally, a provision which destroys vested

[29] See *per* Advocate General Roemer in *Westzucker*, Case 1/73, [1973] ECR 723 at 739. See also *Gardner & Co.* v. *Cone*, [1928] Ch. 995, *per* Maugham J. at 966. See further Letemendia, 'La rétroactivité en droit communautaire', [1977] 13 CDE 518 at 518–19.

rights will be retroactive in the strict sense: in fact, one could say that one test as to whether a law is truly retroactive is whether it affects vested rights. The problem with this formulation, however, is that it raises two very difficult questions: what constitutes a right for this purpose, and when such a right should be regarded as vested.[30]

There are two rules regarding true retroactivity: first, there is a rule of interpretation that, in the absence of a clear provision, legislation is presumed not to be retroactive;[31] secondly, there is a substantive rule that prohibits retroactivity in general, but allows exceptions where the purpose of the measure could not otherwise be achieved, provided the legitimate expectations of those concerned are respected.[32]

An example of the first rule is provided by *Société pour l'Exportation des Sucres* v. *Commission*,[33] where the Commission had passed a regulation taking away the right of exporters to obtain cancellation of their export licences. The regulation was made on 30 June 1976 and was published in an issue of the Official Journal which was dated 1 July 1976 and which should have been published on that date. However, it was delayed by a strike and appeared only on 2 July. On 1 July the applicant applied for cancellation of certain licences but this was refused on the basis of the regulation. The Court, however, interpreted the regulation as coming into force only on the date of actual publication (2 July), so that it did not apply to the applicant. This ruling was given in spite of the fact that the regulation expressly stated that it would enter into force on 1 July: the Court presumably considered that the Commission would not have included this provision if they had known that publication would be delayed; in other words, there was no intention to apply the regulation retroactively.

---

[30] For example, in *Westzucker*, Case 1/73, [1973] ECR 723, it could be argued that, when Westzucker obtained an advance fixing certificate subject to the condition that the amount of the export refund would be automatically adjusted if the intervention price changed, he obtained a vested right to an increased refund in the event of an increase in the intervention price; the better view, however, is that the right was not vested until either the intervention price was increased or until he actually exported the sugar.

[31] See *Kalsbeek* v. *Sociale Verzekeringsbank*, Case 100/63, [1964] ECR 565 at 575; *per* Advocate General Mayras in *Commission* v. *Germany*, Case 70/72, [1973] ECR 813 at 844; and *per* Advocate General Warner in *IRCA*, Case 7/76, [1976] ECR 1213 at 1237–9. This principle does not apply to procedural provisions: *Salumi*, Cases 212–17/80, [1981] ECR 2735.

[32] *Amylum* v. *Council*, Case 108/81, [1982] ECR 3107 at paragraphs 4–17 of the judgment; *Racke*, Case 98/78, [1979] ECR 69 at paragraph 20; *Rewe-Zentrale des Lebensmittel-Grosshandels*, Case 37/70, [1971] ECR 23, paragraphs 17–19. See also *per* Advocate General Roemer in *Westzucker*, Case 1/73, [1973] ECR 723 at 739; *IRCA*, Case 7/76, [1976] ECR 1213, where the Court held that true retroactivity was not involved at all, but the Advocate General considered that it was.

[33] Case 88/76, [1977] ECR 709.

Amylum v. *Council*[34] is an example of the second rule. Here, a regulation imposing a system of quotas and levies on producers of isoglucose (a kind of sugar) had been annulled in previous proceedings because the European Parliament had not been consulted. The Council then passed another regulation (after consulting the Parliament) which reimposed the system with retrospective effect. Proceedings were brought to annul the new regulation, but the Court held that the requirements for retroactivity had been met: the purpose of the regulation was to ensure that isoglucose producers were subject to the same production system as other sugar producers and this would not be the case if the regulation were not backdated; the legitimate expectations of the isoglucose producers had been respected since, in the circumstances of the case, they had good reason to expect the retrospective reimposition of the system. The regulation was therefore upheld.[35]

Legitimate Expectations

The principle of legitimate expectations is a concept derived from German law where it is known as *Vertrauensschutz*. This was originally translated into English as 'protection of legitimate confidence', a phrase which corresponds more closely to the original German and to the French *protection de la confiance légitime*. It was, however, thought that this might be misleading in English; so 'legitimate expectations' is now generally used.[36] According to this principle, Community measures must not (in the absence of an overriding matter of public interest) violate the legitimate expectations of those concerned. It is the foundation of a rule of interpretation[37] as well as a ground for annulment of a Community measure;[38] most often, however, it is used as the basis for an action for damages for non-contractual liability (tort).

What constitutes a legitimate expectation? In answering this, a

[34] Case 108/81, [1982] ECR 3107.

[35] This decision is not without disquieting implications, not least because it established the validity of a regulation which entirely nullified the effect of the Court's judgment in the earlier case.

[36] See Usher, 'The Influence of National Concepts on Decisions of the European Court', (1976) 1 E.L. Rev. 359 at 363.

[37] *Deuka* v. *EVGF*, Case 78/74, [1975] ECR 421, a case where, as in *Société pour l'Exportation des Sucres* v. *Commission* (above), the Court adopted a strained interpretation of the provision in order to protect the rights of the persons concerned without having to annul the measure.

[38] See *Töpfer* v. *Commission*, Case 112/77, [1978] ECR 1019.

number of points must be considered. First of all, an expectation is not legitimate unless it is reasonable: the question here is whether a prudent man would have had the expectation. In deciding this, one must take all the circumstances into account: for example, in the case of a measure affecting grain dealers, one must ask whether a prudent dealer of reasonable knowledge and experience would have relied on the expectation; if he would not, the expectation is not legitimate.[39]

There is also a rule that if the person concerned was not acting in the normal course of business but was trying to take advantage of a weakness in the Community system to make a speculative profit, his expectations cannot be regarded as legitimate: he should realize that the authorities will take the swiftest possible action to plug the loophole. This is well illustrated by *EVGF* v. *Mackprang*,[40] a case concerned with the intervention system for grain, under which the intervention agencies were obliged to buy grain at the intervention price. Grain could be offered to the intervention agencies in different places and there was usually no advantage to the seller in choosing one rather than another. Normally the product would be offered at the marketing centre nearest to where it was produced. However, in early 1969 there was a fall in the forward rate for the French franc in anticipation of its devaluation and it became profitable for German grain dealers to buy grain in France in order to resell it to the German intervention agency, the EVGF. This threatened to exhaust the agency's storage capacity and bring about a collapse of the intervention system in Germany. To meet this threat, the Commission adopted a decision authorizing the German Goverment to confine intervention purchases of wheat and barley to German-grown products. The decision was made on 8 May and came into force on the same day; it expressly stated that it would not apply to cereals offered to the agency before it came into force.

Mackprang was a German grain dealer who had bought wheat in France with the object of importing it into Germany and selling it to the German agency. On 8 May most of the wheat was aboard ships and barges in transit to Germany and Mackprang could not make a valid offer of this wheat because there was a rule that grain could not be validly offered while it was still in transit. When it did arrive the agency refused to buy it and Mackprang brought proceedings in the

[39] See, for example, *Union Nationale des Coopératives Agricoles de Céréales*, Cases 95–98/74, 15, 100/75, [1975] ECR 1615; *Union Malt*, Cases 44–51/77, [1978] ECR 57; and *Lührs*, Case 78/77, [1978] ECR 169.
[40] Case 2/75, [1975] ECR 607.

German courts claiming that he had had a legitimate expectation, when he bought the grain and arranged for shipment, that he would be able to sell it to the agency.

It was, however, pointed out by Advocate General Warner, when a reference to the European Court was made, that the importation of the wheat was not part of normal Community trade but was a speculative transaction of a kind which the Community provisions setting up the system had not been designed to assist. It was possible to profit from transactions of this kind only in an abnormal situation such as that resulting from the fall in the French franc. Advocate General Warner then continued:[41]

No trader who was exploiting that situation in order to make out of the system profits that the system was never designed to bestow on him could legitimately rely on the persistence of the situation. On the contrary, the only reasonable expectation that such a trader could have was that the competent authorities would act as swiftly as possible to bring the situation to an end.

This view was accepted by the Court which stated that the application of the Commission decision to cereals in transit to Germany was not an infringement of the principle of legitimate expectations but 'a justified precaution against purely speculative activities'.[42]

Where the principle of protection of legitimate expectations is used as the foundation for an action for damages, the applicant must prove not only that he had an expectation which was legitimate in the above sense, but also that he acted in reliance on it and suffered loss as the result of the Community measure. He will then be able to obtain damages under Article 215(2) EEC or the equivalent provisions in the other Treaties, unless the Community measure is justifiable by reason of an overriding matter of public interest. The leading case on this is *CNTA* v. *Commission*,[43] which is considered in detail in Chapter 17.[44]

One of the best known cases on the protection of legitimate expectations is one which at first sight appears not to involve retroactivity at all. This is *Commission* v. *Council* (first *Staff Salaries* case),[45] where the Commission brought proceedings against the Council because it felt that the latter had not given Community staff a sufficient increase in pay. Staff pay is governed by Article 65 of the

---

[41]   [1975] ECR at 623.
[42]   At paragraph 4 of the judgment.
[43]   Case 74/74, [1975] ECR 533.
[44]   See pp. 474–6, below.
[45]   Case 81/72, [1973] ECR 575.

Staff Regulations which provides for an annual review of staff salaries by the Council in the light of a report prepared by the Commission. In determining the level of pay, the Council is required to take a number of factors into account, including inflation and salary increases in the public services of the Member States. In the past, serious friction had arisen as a result of disagreement as to how these factors should be measured. Protracted negotiations then took place between the Council, the Commission and the staff associations, and a formula was eventually devised to settle the matter. This formula was embodied in a Council decision made in March 1972 and was stated to be applicable for a period of three years. When the next salary increase took place, however, the Council laid down new scales which the Commission regarded as being in breach of the formula.

The Court had to decide whether the decision containing the pay formula was legally binding on the Council. The Advocate General took the view that it was not, since a similar decision would not, in his opinion, be binding in the national legal systems. This is particularly true in England where public authorities are not generally permitted to fetter their discretionary powers by laying down in advance how they will exercise them.[46] The Court, however, decided that the decision was binding. They held that, in view of the employer-employee relationship between the Council and the staff, the latter had a reasonable expectation that the Council would abide by its undertaking regarding the formula. The new pay scales were, therefore, invalid in so far as they conflicted with it.

Finally, it should be mentioned that the European Court has stated that the principle of legal certainty imposes limits on the extent to which an individual legal act may be withdrawn. This is discussed below.[47]

PROPORTIONALITY

Proportionality is another principle derived from German law. In Germany it is called *Verhältnismässigkeit* and it is regarded as underlying certain provisions of the German constitution. Its constitutional aspect has already been mentioned in connection with fundamental human rights and it was in the *Internationale*

---

[46] For a discussion of the English law see T. C. Hartley and J. A. G. Griffith, *Government and Law*, (2nd ed.) pp. 297–300, 301–308.

[47] At pp. 439–43.

Handelsgesellschaft case (discussed above[48]) that it first made an impact on Community law, though some earlier cases could be said to have applied it in a somewhat broader sense.[49]

According to the principle of proportionality, a public authority may not impose obligations on a citizen except to the extent to which they are strictly necessary in the public interest to attain the purpose of the measure.[50] If the burdens imposed are clearly out of proportion to the object in view, the measure will be annulled.[51] This requires that there exist a reasonable relationship between the end and the means. It implies both that the means must be reasonably likely to bring about the objective, and that the detriment to those adversely affected must not be disproportionate to the benefit to the public. It is to some extent analogous to the English concept of reasonableness.

Proportionality is particularly important in the sphere of economic law, since this frequently involves imposing taxes, levies, charges or duties on businessmen in the hope of achieving economic objectives. The application of proportionality in such a situation as this is well illustrated by the *Skimmed-Milk Powder* case[52] where the Council had sought to reduce the surplus of skimmed-milk powder in the Community by forcing animal feed producers to incorporate it in their product in place of the normal protein element, soya. The drawback of this scheme was that skimmed-milk powder was approximately three times more expensive than soya. In consequence, the European Court held that the regulation embodying the scheme was invalid, partly because it was discriminatory, and partly because it offended against the principle of proportionality: the imposition of the obligation to purchase skimmed-milk powder was not necessary in order to diminish the surplus.[53]

The most striking point about the doctrine of proportionality is that it leaves a great deal to the judgment of the Court. Is the measure reasonably likely to attain its objective? Does it impose dispro-

---

[48] At pp. 123–4.

[49] See, for example, *Fédéchar* v. *High Authority*, Case 8/55, [1956] ECR 292 at 299.

[50] See *per* Advocate General Dutheillet de Lamothe in *Internationale Handelsgesellschaft*, Case 11/70, [1970] ECR 1125 at 1146.

[51] See *Balkan-Import-Export*, Case 5/73, [1973] ECR 1091 at 1112 in which the Court stated that it was not satisfied the measure in question imposed burdens which were 'manifestly out of proportion to the object in view'. See also the German decision, *Re Export of Oat Flakes*, [1969] CMLR 85 at 91.

[52] *Bela-Mühle Josef Bergman* v. *Grows-Farm*, Case 114/76, [1977] ECR 1211; see also Case 116/76 and Cases 119, 120/76, at pp. 1247 and 1269 respectively.

[53] Case 114/76 at paragraph 7 of the judgment; Case 116/76 at paragraph 24; and Cases 119, 120/76 at paragraph 7.

portionate burdens on those concerned? These are clearly questions on which opinions may frequently differ. The Court will not, of course, interfere unless there is a very clear and obvious infringement of the principle; nevertheless it is not always easy to predict when the Court will consider that that point has been reached.

THE RIGHT TO A HEARING

This principle is of interest because it was the first example of the European Court drawing on English law in the elaboration of its general principles. The case in which this occurred was *Transocean Marine Paint Association* v. *Commission*,[54] which concerned Community competition law. Article 85 EEC prohibits agreements which restrict competition but provision is made in Article 85(3) for the Commission to grant exemptions in particular cases. The agreement establishing the Transocean Marine Paint Association was *prima facie* contrary to Article 85, so an application was made to the Commission for exemption. This was initially granted, subject to conditions, for a period of ten years. When the Association applied for renewal, they were told by the Commission of certain new conditions that the Commission had in mind and were given the opportunity to make representations. They were not, however, adequately informed of one condition which was in fact imposed. For various reasons the Association objected to this condition and they brought proceedings to quash the decision granting the exemption, in so far as it imposed the condition. They put forward various grounds of invalidity but a breach of the principle of *audi alteram partem* was not one of them. It was Advocate General Warner who proposed that the case should be decided on this basis. He argued that the right to a hearing was a general principle of Community law and that it was binding on the Commission even in the absence of a specific legislative provision. He reached this conclusion after a survey of the national legal systems, in which he pointed out the important role that natural justice plays in England and was able to show that it also applies in most other Member States, though often in a less developed form.

This view was accepted by the Court which held that there is a general rule of Community law that 'a person whose interests are perceptibly affected by a decision taken by a public authority must be

---

[54] Case 17/74, [1974] ECR 1063.

given the opportunity to make his point of view known'.[55] The Court said that this rule requires that companies be clearly informed in advance of the essential features of any conditions the Commission intends to impose. Because this had not been done in the case, the condition was annulled.[56]

EQUALITY

The principle of equality finds expression in a number of provisions in the Treaties: Article 7 EEC, as has already been mentioned, prohibits discrimination on grounds of nationality; Article 40(3) EEC prohibits discrimination between producers and consumers in connection with agriculture; and Article 119 EEC provides for equal pay for equal work irrespective of sex. The European Court has, however, gone beyond these specific provisions by holding that there is a general principle of non-discrimination in Community law.[57] This does not mean that Community institutions must treat everyone alike, but that there must be no arbitrary distinctions between different groups within the Community.[58]

The *Skimmed-Milk Powder* case (discussed above[59]) was partly decided on the basis of this principle, especially as formulated in Article 40(3) EEC: the effect of making animal feed producers use skimmed-milk powder was to increase the price of animal feed and this harmed all livestock breeders; the benefits of the policy were, on the other hand, felt only by dairy farmers. Thus the policy worked in a discriminatory fashion between different categories of farmers.

[55] At paragraph 15 of the judgment. It is interesting to note that in the later case of *Mollet* v. *Commission*, Case 75/77, [1978] ECR 897, the Court spoke of a 'measure which is liable gravely to prejudice the interests of an individual' (paragraph 21), a narrower formulation than that in the *Transocean* case.

[56] For later developments, see *Oslizlok* v. *Commission*, Case 34/77, [1978] ECR 1099; *Hoffmann-La Roche* v. *Commission*, Case 85/76, [1979] ECR 461 and *Musique Diffusion Française* v. *Commission*, Cases 100–103/80, [1983] ECR 1825 (paragraphs 6–36 of the judgment); see also, Ehlermann and Oldekop, 'Due Process in Administrative Procedure' in FIDE, Reports of the 8th Congress, 1978, Vol. III, p. 11–1 at 11–3 to 11–17, and Korah, 'The Rights of the Defence in Administrative Proceedings under Community Law', [1980] CLP 73.

[57] See *Frilli* v. *Belgium*, Case 1/72, [1972] ECR 457 (paragraph 19 of the judgment) and *Sotgiu* v. *Deutsche Bundespost*, Case 152/73, [1974] ECR 153 (paragraph 11 of the judgment); see also *ECSC* v. *Ferriere Sant'Anna*, Case 168/82, [1983] ECR 1681.

[58] See *Hauts Fourneaux et Aciéries Belges* v. *High Authority*, Case 8/57, [1958] ECR 245 at 256–7; and *Union des Minotiers de la Champagne* v. *France*, Case 11/74, [1974] ECR 877 (paragraph 22 of the judgment).

[59] At p. 146.

In *Sabbatini* v. *European Parliament*,[60] the Court established sex
equality as a general principle of law. This case concerned a female
Community official who was denied a certain allowance because she
was not the 'head of the family'. The relevant provision, however,
defined this concept in such a way as to make it possible for a woman
to be regarded as head of the family only in very exceptional
circumstances, for example if her husband was incapacitated by
illness. The provision was, therefore, discriminatory and, despite the
promptings of the Advocate General, the Court held that it could not
stand.

The Court went a step further in *Airola* v. *Commission*,[61] where the
discriminatory provision was part of national law. Here, the applicant had lost her allowance because she had acquired Italian
nationality on marriage to an Italian. Under Italian Law, a foreign
woman who married an Italian man automatically acquired Italian
nationality, even if this was not her wish; but this rule did not apply to
a foreign man marrying an Italian woman. Community law had
simply given effect to Italian law for the purpose of a rule which
provided that an expatriation allowance would not be paid if the
official acquired the nationality of the country where she worked. But
the European Court ruled that Community law could not take
account of nationality acquired involuntarily under a discriminatory
provision of national law.[62]

The question of religious discrimination came before the Court in
Prais v. *Council*.[63] This concerned a woman of Jewish faith who wished
to obtain a post as a Community official. In her application she did
not mention her religion. However, when she was informed that she
would have to sit a competitive examination on a particular day, she
told the Council that the day in question was a Jewish festival and she
would be unable to attend. She asked the Council to allow her to sit
on an alternative date but this was refused on the ground that it was
essential for all candidates to sit the examination on the same date. It
was too late to change the date of the examination as the arrange-

[60] Case 20/71, [1972] ECR 345.
[61] Case 21/74, [1975] ECR 221. For a somewhat different situation, see *Van den Broeck* v.
Commission, Case 37/74, [1975] ECR 235; see also *Devred* v. *Commission*, Case 257/78,
[1979] ECR 3767.
[62] For a case involving discrimination against men, see *Razzouk and Beydoun* v. *Commission*, Cases 75, 117/82, [1984] ECR 1509 (pension rights for the husbands of deceased
Community officials).
[63] Case 130/75, [1976] ECR 1589.

ments had been completed. The examination was duly held and Mrs Prais did not attend. Another candidate was appointed.

She then brought proceedings in the European Court to annul the decision to hold the examination on a Jewish festival and to annul the result of the competition; she also asked for damages. She based her case partly on Article 27 of the Staff Regulations, which provides that officials must be selected without reference to race, creed or sex, and partly on what she claimed was a general principle of Community law prohibiting religious discrimination. The defendant accepted that freedom of religion was a general principle of Community law but maintained that its action did not constitute a violation of it.

It should be noted that the appointing authority had not been guilty of religious discrimination in the ordinary meaning of the term: there was no evidence that they knew the date in question was a Jewish festival when they originally scheduled the examination and they had certainly had no wish to create difficulties for the applicant. She, however, argued that subjective intention was not the only matter: if procedures were in fact adopted which put any candidate at a disadvantage by reason of her religion, her religious freedom had been violated.

The Court held that the appointing authority was not under an obligation to avoid holding an examination on a religious holiday if it had not been informed of the fact before the date was fixed. For this reason, Mrs Prais lost her case. However, it went on to state that, if the appointing authority is informed in advance, it should take the religious difficulties of candidates into account and endeavour to avoid holding the examination on that date. This means that, even if informed in advance, the authority is not absolutely barred from choosing such a date: but it must give reasonable weight to the desirability of not doing so and should avoid it if reasonably practicable.[64]

LEGAL PROFESSIONAL PRIVILEGE

In *AM&S* v. *Commission*[65] the European Court recognized a new general principle, that of legal professional privilege. The issue arose

[64] For a similar decision in the English Courts, see *Ostreicher* v. *Secretary of State*, [1978] 1 WLR 810; [1978] 3 All E.R. 82 (CA); see also *Ahmad* v. *ILEA*, [1977] 3 WLR 396; [1978] 1 All E.R. 574 (CA).
[65] Case 155/79, [1982] ECR 1575.

when Commission inspectors arrived one day at the offices of a British company and demanded to see their business records. This inspection was part of a general investigation into alleged anti-competitive practices in the zinc industry. It was carried out under a Community measure, Article 14 of Regulation 17, which made no mention of legal privilege. The company nevertheless refused to hand over certain documents on the ground that they were privileged. The Commission took a decision requiring the production of the documents and the company brought proceedings before the European Court to annul it.

The Court held that the confidentiality of written communications between lawyer and client, which was generally recognized in the legal systems of the Member States, would be upheld in Community law subject to two conditions: the communication must be for the purpose of the client's 'rights of defence' and the lawyer[66] must be in private practice, not an employee of the client. This latter rule has been criticized as unfair to companies employing in-house lawyers.

The procedure laid down by the European Court is as follows. If a client wishes to claim privilege, he must – without revealing the contents of the document – give the Commission sufficient information to demonstrate that the conditions have been satisfied. If the Commission does not accept this, it will take a decision requiring production of the document and, if necessary, impose a penalty for failure to comply, normally a periodic fine of a given amount for each day that the client fails to hand over the document. The client can then challenge this decision before the Court, which will decide the issue, if necessary after inspecting the document. The mere initiation of annulment proceedings will not suspend the decision but the Court may, if it thinks fit, make an interlocutory order to this effect.

In the case before the Court, the documents were legal opinions, given shortly before, and immediately after, the United Kingdom joined the Community, concerning possible conflicts with Community law – especially in the field of competition – and ways in which these could be avoided. The Court held that they were entitled to protection.

---

[66] The Court adopted the definition of 'lawyer' contained in Directive 77/249, OJ 1977, L 78/17, which covers lawyers admitted in other Member States, but not non-Community lawyers. For later developments, see Faull, (1983) 8 E.L. Rev. 411 and (1985) 10 E.L. Rev. 119.

FURTHER READING

Schermers, paragraphs 42–165.

Akehurst, 'The Application of General Principles of Law by the Court of Justice of the European Communities', [1981] BYIL 29.

Dauses, 'The Protection of Fundamental Rights in the Community Legal Order', (1985) 10 E.L. Rev. 398.

Korah, 'The Rights of the Defence in Administrative Proceedings under Community Law', [1980] CLP 73.

Lamoureux, 'The Retroactivity of Community Acts in the Case Law of the Court of Justice', (1983) 20 C.M.L. Rev. 269.

McBride and Brown, 'The United Kingdom, the European Community and the European Convention on Human Rights', (1981) 1 YEL 167.

Mendelson, 'The European Court of Justice and Human Rights', (1981) 1 YEL 126.

Weiler, 'Eurocracy and Distrust: Some Questions Concerning the Role of the European Court of Justice in the Protection of Fundamental Human Rights within the Legal Order of the European Communities', (1986) 61 Washington Law Rev. 1103.

Usher, 'The Influence of National Concepts on Decisions of the European Court', (1976) 1 E.L. Rev. 359.

6

AGREEMENTS WITH THIRD COUNTRIES

In some ways international agreements are an anomalous source of Community law. The constitutive Treaties are acts of the Member States; regulations, decisions, etc. are acts of the Community itself; general principles of law are the creation of the European Court; but international agreements have their origin outside the Community legal order and are, in part, the acts of non-member States. However, they have effects in Community law and are applied by the European Court, which has declared them to be 'an integral part of Community law'.[1] In spite of their origin, therefore, they may be regarded as a true source of Community law.

International agreements forming part of Community law may be divided into three categories. The first consists of agreements between the Community (acting alone) and one or more non-member States. This method is used where the subject-matter of the agreement falls wholly within the treaty-making competence of the Community. The second category consists of 'mixed' agreements, that is agreements between, on the one side, the Community and the Member States acting jointly and, on the other side, the non-member States. It is used when the subject-matter falls partly within the competence of the Community and partly within that of the Member States. The third category consists of agreements between the Member States (acting alone) and the non-member States. The European Court has accepted such agreements as forming part of Community law, and being binding on the Community, only in very special circumstances.

---

[1] *Haegeman* v. *Belgium*, Case 181/73, [1974] ECR 449 (paragraph 5 of the judgment).

THE TREATY-MAKING POWER OF THE EEC

Express Powers

Express treaty-making power is granted by the EEC Treaty in two cases: commercial agreements under Article 113 and association agreements under Article 238; there is also something approaching an express power in the provisions concerning co-operation with international organizations.[2] Article 228 lays down general rules regarding the procedure to be followed where the treaty-making power is exercised but does not itself confer such power.

Commercial agreements are negotiated by the Commission. Article 113(3) provides that the Commission must obtain the authorization of the Council to open negotiations; these are conducted in consultation with a special committee appointed by the Council. The Council also has the power to issue directives to the Commission. If the negotiations are successful, the agreement is concluded by the Council, acting by a qualified majority.

The power granted by Article 113 is not limited to tariff and trade agreements but covers all aspects of the Community's common commercial policy, including export aids, credit and finance, as well as the matters normally forming part of multilateral commodity agreements. It also covers development policy (aid to third world countries).[3] This power is exclusive: the Member States are precluded from entering into such agreements.

The other main area in which the Community is given express treaty-making power is association agreements. These can operate either as a preliminary to, or as a substitute for, membership of the Community. They are governed by Article 238 EEC which provides for association agreements with a non-member State, a union of States or an international organization. They are concluded by the Council, acting unanimously, after receiving the assent of the European Parliament (which acts by an absolute majority).[4]

---

[2] Arts 229–31. There is in addition a power of minor importance to enter into agreements with third countries for the recognition of travel documents issued by the Community to the members and staff of Community institutions: see Art. 7(1) of the Protocol on the Privileges and Immunities of the European Communities. (This is a protocol to the Merger Treaty: see Art. 28 of the latter.)

[3] *Commission* v. *Council*, Case 45/86, 26 March 1987 (not yet reported).

[4] *Demirel*, Case 12/86, 30 September 1987 (not yet reported), a case concerning immigration from a non-member State associated with the Community, shows that in the

The provisions on relations with international organizations (Articles 229–231) come close to granting an express treaty-making power. These require the Commission to maintain appropriate relations with international organizations in general, and the Community to establish 'all appropriate forms of co-operation' with the Council of Europe and 'close co-operation' with the OEEC (now the OECD). In the latter case, Article 231 states that the details of this will be determined 'by common accord'.

General provisions regarding the procedure to be adopted for all international agreements under the EEC Treaty are laid down by the first sub-paragraph of Article 228(1). This reads:

Where this Treaty provides for the conclusion of agreements between the Community and one or more States or an international organization, such agreements shall be negotiated by the Commission. Subject to the powers vested in the Commission in this field, such agreements shall be concluded by the Council, after consulting the Assembly where required by this Treaty.

The main importance of this is that it makes clear that all Community agreements must be negotiated by the Commission and concluded by the Council. This makes good the omission in Article 238, which fails to state expressly that the Commission negotiates association agreements.

Although the EEC Treaty gives the European Parliament a role only in the case of association agreements, it is an established practice[5] that it will be consulted in all cases.[6] The relevant committee will usually be informed by the Council when it is proposed to open negotiations and the Parliament may hold a debate on the issue. During the course of the negotiations, confidential briefings will be given to the committee by the Commission and when the negotiations are over, but before the agreement is signed, the Council will confidentially inform the committee of the substance of the proposed agreement. After the agreement has been signed, but before it is formally concluded, the Council officially informs the Parliament of its contents, though at this stage it is too late for the Parliament to influence its terms.

---

context of an association agreement the Community's treaty-making power may be wider than its internal legislative jurisdiction. In such a situation, the Community may have to rely on the Member States to pass measures to give effect to the agreement.

[5] Sometimes known as the Luns/Westerterp procedure.

[6] See Point 2.3.7 of the Solemn Declaration on European Union, signed in Stuttgart on 19 June 1983, E. C. Bull. 6–1983, p. 24 at pp. 26–27.

Implied Powers

International relations is an area which is traditionally regarded as touching the very heart of state sovereignty and it is therefore hardly surprising that the Member States have always viewed the treaty-making power of the Community with a degree of suspicion. Almost from the beginning, the Member States, and the organ which represents their collective opinion – the Council – have tried to limit the powers of the Community.

For a long time there were two rival theories regarding the Community's power to conclude treaties. On the one hand it was argued that the treaty-making power of the Community – its external competence – should reflect its internal jurisdiction. According to this doctrine of 'parallelism', as it is sometimes called, it would be illogical for the Community to have internal law-making power with regard to a certain topic and yet be unable to conclude international agreements in that field. Therefore, argued the proponents of this doctrine, the Community must be regarded as having not only those treaty-making powers expressly granted to it in the Treaty, but must in addition have such powers with regard to any topic which falls within its internal jurisdiction. This may be justified on the basis of the theory of implied powers.[7]

In the beginning, the Member States rejected this doctrine: they took the view that the EEC possesses only such external powers as are expressly granted to it by the Treaty. This standpoint may be supported by comparing the EEC Treaty with the Euratom Treaty: Article 228 EEC, the general provision covering all treaty-making by the EEC, begins with the words: 'Where *this Treaty provides* for the conclusion of agreements . . .',[8] thus suggesting that it is only in the case of an express provision that the Community may conclude international agreements. Article 101 Euratom, on the other hand, states: 'The Community may, within the limits of its powers and jurisdiction, enter into obligations by concluding agreements or contracts with a third State . . .' This implies that wherever the Community has internal competence with regard to a given question, it will also have power to enter into international agreements. The contrast between these two provisions is all the more significant in view of the fact that the two Treaties were drafted at the same time and in many instances contain identical provisions. It is hard,

---

[7] Discussed above at p. 103.
[8] Italics added.

therefore, to avoid the conclusion that the authors of the Treaties intended the EEC to have considerably more restricted treaty-making powers than Euratom.

The Member States also favoured a narrow interpretation of the provisions which expressly grant treaty-making powers. In particular, they appear to have taken the view that the provisions concerning association agreements – especially Article 238 – do not themselves confer any distinct treaty-making power: they merely regulate the way in which the power to conclude commercial agreements is exercised in a particular context.[9]

As a consequence of this, they took the position that association agreements entered into by the Community alone could deal only with tariffs and trade. Where, as was frequently the case, it was desirable to include other provisions – for example, concerning development aid – resort had to be made, in the view of the Council, to a 'mixed agreement', i.e. one concluded jointly by the Member States and the Community. Though referred to in Article 102 of the Euratom Treaty,[10] this joint procedure is not mentioned in the EEC Treaty, which appears to envisage a different solution to the problem: an amendment of the EEC Treaty so that the Community can conclude the agreement by itself. Both Article 238 and Article 228 envisage the possibility of a Treaty amendment, though neither of these provisions expressly excludes the mixed procedure.[11]

Since association agreements have almost always been more than mere commercial agreements, the mixed procedure has been frequently used, and many of the most important agreements, including the Lomé Conventions, have been concluded under it. Such agreements are first ratified by the Member States according to their respective constitutional requirements and then approved by the Council on behalf of the Community.

This difference of opinion between the Council and the Commission led to several clashes. In 1968, for example, there was a dispute as to which would conduct the negotiations for an additional protocol to the association agreement with Turkey.[12] The Commission pro-

[9] See Leopold, 'External Relations Power of EEC in Theory and in Practice', (1977) 26 ICLQ 54, 62; Costonis, 'The Treaty-Making Power of the European Economic Community', (1968) 5 C.M.L. Rev. 421, 444. There is little doubt that this view was wrong: see Costonis, op. cit., pp. 444–9.

[10] See below, pp. 170–1.

[11] The use of the mixed procedure under the EEC Treaty was, however, approved by the European Court in the *Natural Rubber Agreement* case, Opinion 1/78, [1979] ECR 2871.

[12] See Bot, 'Negotiating Community Agreements: Procedure and Practice', (1970) 7 C.M.L. Rev. 286, 296–301.

posed a compromise: it would act as spokesman for the Community with regard to those matters within the general jurisdiction of the Community and the Member State holding the presidency of the Council would speak on matters within the jurisdiction of the Member States. This was rejected by the Council which insisted that the Member State holding the presidency should speak for the Community on all matters; the Commission would be limited to explaining and supplementing the Community's position. The Commission disagreed fundamentally with this, but took no action.

A similar dispute occurred shortly afterwards regarding the Second Yaoundé Convention. Here, too, the Council was determined that the leading role in the negotiations should be played by the Member States. This issue gave rise to strong feelings and at one point the President of the Commission threatened to bring proceedings against the Council in the European Court. Eventually, however, the Commission accepted a compromise proposal, which was nevertheless regarded by most observers as a defeat for its position.[13]

These events provide the background to the first legal action between the Council and the Commission, the *ERTA* Case.[14] The history of this dispute goes back to 1962 when five of the six Member States, together with some other European countries, signed an agreement to harmonize certain social provisions relating to road transport. This agreement, normally known as the first ERTA (European Road Transport Agreement), never came into force, since it was not ratified by a sufficient number of contracting states. In 1967 negotiations started for a second ERTA and these were also conducted by the Member States. In 1969, however, the Council enacted a regulation covering much the same ground within the internal jurisdiction of the Community. The Member States were still anxious to regulate the matter on a wider basis, however, and they decided to continue the negotiations for a second ERTA.

On 20 March 1970, the Council met to discuss the matter and decided that the negotiations would be carried on by the six Member States, which would become parties to the new ERTA. It was agreed that the Member States would co-ordinate their positions and the Member State holding the presidency of the Council would act as spokesman. The Commission objected to this: they felt that they should have a role to play in view of the fact that the subject-matter of the negotiations had already been regulated internally on a Com-

---

[13] See Bot, op. cit., pp. 301–6.
[14] *Commission* v. *Council* (ERTA case), Case 22/70, [1971] ECR 263.

munity basis by the 1969 Regulation. In May 1970 they therefore brought legal action against the Council in the European Court to annul the Council resolution entrusting the conduct of the negotiations entirely to the Member States. On 1 July 1970, agreement on the new ERTA was reached and the text was declared open for signature; before the Court gave judgment, at least some of the Member States had signed it.

The jurisdictional aspects of this case have already been considered: it will be remembered that the Court eventually decided that the application was admissible since the Council resolution constituted a legal act *sui generis*.[15] As far as the substance was concerned, the main point was whether the Member States or the Community had power to enter into the agreement. This in turn depended on whether the Community has any treaty-making powers beyond those expressly granted by the EEC Treaty.

In its judgment, the Court first drew an implicit distinction between *capacity* to enter into an agreement and *authority* to do so. Capacity appears to relate to the Community's legal power to enter into an agreement; authority to the legality of its exercise of that power. For present purposes the important concept is that of authority. As regards this, the Court said that it is necessary to consider the 'whole scheme of the Treaty' as well as its substantive provisions. It then went on to say, in paragraphs 16 to 19 of its judgment:

Such authority arises not only from an express conferment by the Treaty – as is the case with Articles 113 and 114 for tariff and trade agreements and with Article 238 for association agreements – but may equally flow from other provisions of the Treaty and from measures adopted, within the framework of those provisions, by the Community institutions.

In particular, each time the Community, with a view to implementing a common policy envisaged by the Treaty, adopts provisions laying down common rules, whatever form these may take, the Member States no longer have the right, acting individually or even collectively, to undertake obligations with third countries which affect those rules.

As and when such common rules come into being, the Community alone is in a position to assume and carry out contractual obligations towards third countries affecting the whole sphere of application of the Community legal system.

With regard to the implementation of the provisions of the Treaty the system of internal Community measures may not therefore be separated from that of external relations.

---

[15] See above, pp. 101–2

This, of course, constitutes express approval of the doctrine of 'parallelism'; it is, however, expressed in a particular form: the adoption by the Community of provisions laying down common rules is the vital element bringing about a transfer of treaty-making power from the Member States to the Community. In the *ERTA* case the Court did not say that the mere *existence* of internal legislative power is sufficient: it is the *exercise* of this power which is important.[16]

Having enunciated this new principle, the Court then applied it to the facts of the case. It noted that the adoption of a common transport policy is one of the objectives laid down in Part One of the Treaty and that common rules for the attainment of this objective had been laid down in the 1969 Regulation. It followed from this that the Community obtained treaty-making power in the area covered by the Regulation when the latter came into force on 1 October 1969. This automatically entailed the loss of such power on the part of the Member States.

One might have thought that the consequence of this would have been that the Commission should have negotiated the agreement on behalf of the Community. It must not be forgotten, however, that the negotiations for the second ERTA were based on the first ERTA: the idea was merely to make such modifications as were necessary to secure its acceptance. The negotiations taken up again in 1967 were, therefore, a continuation of those which resulted in the first ERTA in 1962. Consequently, a considerable part of the negotiations had been carried out before the transfer of treaty-making power in 1969. In the circumstances, it would not have been fair to third countries if the negotiating procedure, and indeed the parties to the negotiations, had been changed at that point. In such a situation, said the Court, the Council and Commission should have agreed between themselves on appropriate methods of co-operation to ensure the most effective way of defending the Community's interests. Clearly, no such agreement was reached. The Court therefore concluded that the Council had not violated the Treaty in deciding that the negotiations would continue to be conducted by the Member States. Technically, therefore, the Commission lost the case: in reality, of course, it won a great victory.

The Court's ruling in the *ERTA* case can be fully understood only if one analyses it from a policy point of view. What the Court was

---

[16] See also paragraphs 66, 82 and, above all, 84 of the judgment. In paragraph 84 the Court expressly said that power was conferred on the Community as a result of the 1969 Regulation.

intent on doing was to enhance the Community's powers and thus reverse the trend away from Commission involvement in international negotiations. It did not, however, wish to jeopardize the agreement which had been reached on the second ERTA by ruling that it had to be renegotiated by the Commission: this would have upset the other parties and damaged the international reputation of the Community. Moreover, the Eastern Bloc was reluctant to accept the Community as a party to the agreement. The Court therefore had to find a way of upholding the Commission's contention in principle, without applying it to the facts of the case. As already mentioned, this was done by holding that a transfer of treaty-making power occurred in 1969 when the internal measure came into effect.

The same result could, however, have been achieved by ruling that the enactment of the regulation did not *confer* power on the Community but merely *deprived* the Member States of power. This could be justified by the adoption of the doctrine of parallelism in its strong form by saying that the existence of an internal power automatically implies an external power, but this power does not become exclusive until it is exercised either internally or externally. Before this, the Member States would have concurrent powers. The outcome of the *ERTA* case would have been the same, but the Commission's position in future cases would have been stronger. This was not, however, what the Court said in the *ERTA* case, though, as we shall see, it was subsequently established in later cases.

The next step came in the *North-East Atlantic Fisheries Convention* case.[17] The Convention was an international agreement entered into by seven of the nine Member States and several non-member States for the purpose of ensuring the conservation of fish stocks in the North-East Atlantic. A Fisheries Commission was set up under it and this had the power to make recommendations for conservation measures if there was a two-thirds majority in favour. These were binding on each party to the Convention unless it rejected the recommendation within a given period. Such a recommendation had been made concerning sole and plaice and this became binding under the terms of the Convention. The Netherlands, which was a party to the Convention, then enacted national measures to implement the recommendation and these included criminal provisions. The case arose when certain Dutch fishermen were prosecuted in a Dutch

[17] *Kramer*, Cases 3, 4, 6/76, [1976] ECR 1279. This case was preceded by the *Local Cost Standard* case, Opinion 1/75, [1975] ECR 1355, which did not, however, significantly develop the law on the point under consideration.

court for breach of these provisions. They argued that the Member States had no power to enter into the Convention and the Dutch legislation was therefore contrary to Community law. This raised the question whether the Convention fell within the exclusive competence of the Community.

The position regarding fisheries was that the Community had internal power but at the relevant time had not exercised that power for the purpose of conservation. However, conservation of fish in international waters is rather a special case since it is normally feasible to proceed only by way of international measures: there is no point in imposing quotas on Community fishermen if non-Community fishermen are subject to no restrictions. It is hardly surprising, therefore, that the European Court held that the Community had treaty-making power in the area. However, it went on to rule that, until the Community exercised its powers – one assumes either internally or externally – the Member States had concurrent powers. Consequently, the Dutch measure was not contrary to Community law.

In the *North-East Atlantic Fisheries Convention* case the European Court appears to have taken the position that the mere existence of internal power automatically gives rise to parallel external power; but this could be regarded as applying only in exceptional situations. In the *Inland Waterway Vessels*[18] case, however, the Court put its adoption of the new doctrine beyond doubt. After stating that the grant of internal power to attain a specific objective implies the authority to enter into international agreements where these are necessary for the attainment of that objective, it continued: 'This is particularly so in all cases in which internal power has already been used . . . it is, however, not limited to that eventuality.'[19]

The *Inland Waterway Vessels* case is interesting not only because it marks the final triumph of parallelism, but also because it throws light on two other matters. The case concerned an international agreement for the regulation of vessels on the Rhine-Moselle waterway system. The Community had internal jurisdiction in the area and could have dealt with the problem by means of a regulation. However, the Swiss were major users of the waterway and as they had to be included in the scheme, action on the international level was necessary.

[18] Opinion 1/76 *on the Laying-up Fund for Inland Waterway Vessels*, [1977] ECR 741; OJ 1977, C 107/4.
[19] Paragraphs 3 and 4 of the Court's reasoning.

The solution chosen was a mixed agreement to which the parties were the Community, Switzerland, and six of the Member States. The six contracting Member States were the three Benelux countries, Germany, France and the United Kingdom. The reason why these Member States participated in their individual capacities was that the waterways in question were already subject to two international conventions, the Mannheim Convention of 1868 and the Luxembourg Convention of 1956, and there was a potential conflict between certain provisions of the new agreement and the two earlier conventions. The six participating Member States were all parties to one or other of the earlier conventions and they undertook in the agreement to make the necessary amendments to those conventions.

On the basis of the Court's earlier decisions, one might have thought that there would have been no problem regarding the participation of the Member States. These cases hold that the implied powers of the Community are not exclusive until they have been exercised. In the *Inland Waterway Vessels* case the Court did indeed accept the participation of the Member States; however, there is a suggestion that this was only because their intervention was necessary to secure the required amendments to the earlier conventions. After referring to the necessity of amending the conventions, the Court said: 'The participation of these States in the Agreement must be considered as being solely for this purpose and not as necessary for the attainment of other features of the system.'[20] It was for this reason, said the Court, that the participation of the six Member States 'is not such as to encroach on the external power of the Community'.[21] This suggests that the Court might not have accepted the participation of the Member States if these special circumstances had not been present.

The main question in the case was something much more fundamental than either of the issues already discussed. The agreement set up an organization called the 'Laying-up Fund for Inland Waterway Vessels', which was modelled on the Community itself. According to the Statute of the Fund, it was an international public institution with legal personality. Its organs were a Supervisory Board (analogous to the Council), a Board of Management (analogous to the Commission) and a court, the Fund Tribunal. The Supervisory Board was to consist of one representative of each Member State except Ireland (which did not want to be represented)

[20] At paragraph 7.
[21] Ibid.

and one representative of Switzerland; the (non-voting) chairman was to be a representative of the Commission. Voting was normally to be by a simple majority but there was a provision that the majority had to contain the votes of at least three of the states with the greatest interest in the Fund (Belgium, Germany, France, the Netherlands and Switzerland). The Board of Management was to consist of persons appointed by the same five states together with Luxembourg; but representation was not to be equal: Germany and the Netherlands were to have four members each, Luxembourg one, and the others two each. Decisions were to be taken by a two-thirds majority.

It was provided that the Fund was to have the power, within the very narrow limits of its jurisdiction, to enact measures having direct effect in all Member States of the Community as well as in Switzerland.

The Fund Tribunal was to consist of one judge from each of the six Member States that were parties to the agreement and one from Switzerland. The intention was that the six Community judges would be appointed by the European Court from among its own members. The jurisdiction of the Tribunal was to be similar to that of the European Court and it was to have the power to give preliminary rulings on references from national courts in the Community or Switzerland.

It will be seen from this that the Fund was a supranational organization like the Community itself. Could the Community join another Community? In its opinion, the European Court held that it was possible for the Community to set up a public international institution of this kind, but it found the structure of the Fund unacceptable. In particular it considered that the Member States played too great a role – it felt that the Community institutions should have been given a greater say in the running of the Fund – and it thought that it was wrong for some Member States to be given powers which were not given to others. It also took objection to the fact that the Community judges on the Tribunal were to be appointed from among the judges of the European Court. The reason for this latter objection was that the agreement setting up the Fund was itself part of Community law and might have had to be interpreted by the European Court: if some judges of the European Court had already given a ruling on it in their capacity as members of the Fund Tribunal, they would be precluded from sitting when the issue came before the European Court. This might make it impossible for the European Court to find a quorum.

The interesting point about this opinion is that none of the points to which the European Court objected were essential characteristics of a supranational organization. It follows from this that, if the right structure were chosen, the Community might be able to become a member of such a body.[22]

Legal Proceedings

A special legal procedure is laid down by Article 228. The second subparagraph of Article 228(1) provides:

The Council, the Commission or a Member State may obtain beforehand the opinion of the Court of Justice as to whether an agreement envisaged is compatible with the provisions of this Treaty. Where the opinion of the Court of Justice is adverse, the agreement may enter into force only in accordance with Article 236.

This provision applies to all agreements to which the EEC is to be a party. In essence, it provides a power of judicial review, but this takes place before the conclusion of the agreement and is given in the form of an opinion.[23] This opinion, despite its name, has legal consequences: if it is adverse, the agreement cannot enter into force unless the EEC Treaty is amended to permit the Community to conclude the agreement.[24] Since the procedure under Article 236 for amending the Treaty is cumbersome[25] – the amendments have to be ratified by each Member State according to the requirements of its constitution – an adverse opinion will normally prevent the conclusion of the agreement. If the Court's objections are comparatively minor, however, it may be possible – if the other parties are willing – to revise the agreement in accordance with the Court's judgment.

There can be no doubt that the object of this procedure as envisaged by the authors of the Treaty was to prevent the Community from entering into agreements which are incompatible with the Treaty. The Court, however, has allowed the Commission to use it for quite a different purpose: to prevent the Member States from encroaching on the jurisdiction of the Community. The *Natural Rubber Agreement* case[26] is the best example. The International Agree-

[22] For a fuller discussion of the case, see Hartley, (1977) 2 E.L. Rev. 275.
[23] For this reason, an application under this provision will not be called, for example, 'Case 1/76', but 'Opinion 1/76'
[24] This procedure is similar to that under Art. 54 of the French Constitution.
[25] For a discussion of this procedure, see pp. 89–90, above.
[26] Opinion 1/78 of 4 October 1979, [1979] ECR 2871.

ment on Natural Rubber was a draft agreement drawn up within the framework of UNCTAD. On the Community side, the negotiations had initially been conducted jointly by the Commission and the national governments and it was intended by the latter that both the Community and the Member States should be parties. The Commission, however, felt that the matter came within the exclusive jurisdiction of the Community – it maintained that it was covered by the express treaty-making power in Article 113 – and considered that the Member States should not participate in the negotiations.

In some ways the situation was similar to that in the *ERTA* case[27] but here the Commission decided to use a different legal remedy: it brought an application under Article 228 and asked the Court for a ruling whether it would be compatible with the Treaty for the proposed agreement to be concluded in the mixed form. Since it was not disputed that the Community would be a party to the agreement, the issue before the Court was the participation of the Member States. The Member States protested at the use of the procedure for this purpose, but the Court held the application admissible, though it eventually gave a ruling which was not wholly in favour of the Commission. It held that the Member States could be parties if, but only if, it was eventually agreed that the scheme would be financed out of national funds. Until this question was decided, the Member States could continue to participate in the negotiations.

Certain features of the procedure under Article 228 are rather unusual. There is no oral hearing in the ordinary sense but the recent practice has been to hold a private hearing open only to the parties (and any Member States which are not parties). All the advocates general give opinions;[28] these are also in private and are not published. The Court then gives judgment in the normal way; this is published.

Conclusions

The authors of the EEC Treaty probably intended the EEC to have relatively limited treaty-making power (in contrast to Euratom which was intended all along to have wide powers). The Member

[27] The procedural aspects of this case were discussed above at pp. 101–2. In the *ERTA* case the Commission could not have invoked Art. 228, since that provision applies only where the Community is to be a party to the agreement.
[28] There is a mistake in the English version of Art. 108(2) of the Rules of Procedure of the European Court: 'Advocate-General' should read 'Advocates-General'.

States originally adopted a restrictive interpretation of these powers and even tried to deny the Community some of the powers which it undoubtedly possessed. In the Seventies, however, the Commission staged a counter-attack by resorting to legal action, knowing that it could count on the Court for support. The result is that the EEC now appears to possess implied powers equivalent to those expressly granted by the Euratom Treaty. The doctrine of parallelism has triumphed and the powers of the Member States have been reduced.

The series of cases by which this has been achieved is also of interest as an example of the law-making strategy of the Court. This can best be characterized as a 'step-by-step' approach: the first step, taken in the *ERTA* case, was regarded at the time as very bold – *Le Monde* published an article on 27 April 1971 asking whether the Court had exceeded its jurisdiction – but the Court nevertheless went ahead with the second step – hesitantly in the *North-East Atlantic Fisheries Convention* case and firmly in the *Inland Waterway Vessels* case: what seemed bold in 1971 had been discarded as insufficient by 1977.

Although the European Court has not so far ruled on the question,[29] there is little doubt that the doctrine of parallelism applies not only with reference to internal powers granted by the Treaty for specific objectives, but also with regard to such general powers as that contained in Article 235.[30] In fact, the Community has already concluded a number of agreements under Article 235.[31] The result is that the Community now possesses wide treaty-making powers covering virtually the whole area of the EEC Treaty.

THE TREATY-MAKING POWER OF THE ECSC

In comparison even with the rather vague provisions of the EEC Treaty, the ECSC Treaty is remarkable for its reticence on the subject of treaty-making; in fact, the Treaty proper contains nothing at all expressly authorizing the conclusion of international agree-

[29] The Court's opinion in the *Inland Waterway Vessels* case was confined to situations where the internal power is given 'for the purpose of attaining a specific object': see Opinion 1/76, [1977] ECR 741, paragraph 3 of the opinion.

[30] See the ERTA case, Case 22/70, [1971] ECR 263 at paragraph 95 of the judgment. It could even be argued that Art. 235 confers an express power: the 'appropriate measures' which the Council is empowered to take could be regarded as including international agreements.

[31] See, for example, the Convention for the Prevention of Marine Pollution from Land-Based Sources, signed in Paris on 4 June 1974, OJ 1975, L 194/6.

ments by the Community. There is no general provision along the lines of Article 228 EEC: the nearest the ECSC Treaty gets to this is Article 6(2) which states:

In international relations, the Community shall enjoy the legal capacity it requires to perform its functions and attain its objectives.

This could, of course, be interpreted as including the power to enter into international agreements – in view of its policy objectives, the European Court will probably interpret it in this way – but it gives no clue as to negotiating procedure or the method by which the agreement will be concluded. As in the EEC Treaty, there is provision (in Articles 93 and 94) for the maintenance of appropriate relations with certain international organizations; there is no mention of agreements with such organizations, but this could perhaps be implied: as early as 1953, in fact, the ECSC entered into an agreement with the International Labour Organization.[32]

More detailed provisions are to be found in the Convention on the Transitional Provisions. (This Convention, which was drawn up in pursuance of Article 85 ECSC, was intended to provide for the transition to the full operation of the common market.) Article 1(3)(*b*)(2) of this empowers the High Authority to conduct negotiations with third countries for certain purposes and similar provisions are to be found in Articles 10 and 14. However, since this Convention was intended to be merely transitional, it is hard to see how its provisions can be of relevance today. At most they could indicate that any powers implied on the basis of provisions in the Treaty itself were intended to be exercised by means of negotiations conducted by the Commission.

It is likely, however, that the European Court will apply the doctrine of parallelism to the ECSC in much the same way as in the case of the EEC; it will probably also apply the procedural provisions of the EEC Treaty to the ECSC by way of analogy. Consequently, the treaty-making power of the ECSC may well end up being much the same as that of the EEC.[33]

---

[32] JO 1953, 167.

[33] It should be mentioned that Art. 71 ECSC expressly states that the powers of Member States in matters of commercial policy will not be affected by the Treaty (save as otherwise provided therein). It might be thought that this would preserve the power of Member States to enter into commercial agreements regarding ECSC products; however, in the *Local Cost Standard* case the Court rejected the argument that Art. 71 ECSC entitled the Member States to participate in the agreement to the extent that it applied to ECSC products (see [1975] ECR at 1365). The apparent ground was that, though Art. 71 might prevent the rights of the Member States from being restricted by the ECSC Treaty, it did not prevent the EEC Treaty from imposing such restrictions.

THE TREATY-MAKING POWER OF EURATOM

The Euratom Treaty gives the Community wide treaty-making powers within the atomic energy field. This was probably necessitated by the circumstances: at the time when the Treaty was concluded, the Community countries were much less advanced in nuclear technology than the United States or Britain and the authors of the Treaty probably thought that international agreements would be required to obtain technology and materials; they may also have thought that the Community would have to enter into international agreements concerned with the security aspects of atomic energy.

The Euratom Treaty contains a special chapter on External Relations (Chapter X, Title Two). This is concerned with the treaty-making power of both the Community and the Member States; it also covers international agreements entered into by individuals or undertakings in Member States.

The treaty-making power of the Community is laid down in Article 101.[34] This gives the Community power to conclude international agreements 'within the limits of its powers and jurisdiction': in other words, the Euratom Treaty expressly applies the doctrine of parallelism. As in the case of the EEC, such agreements are negotiated by the Commission in accordance with the directives of the Council; but unlike in the case of the EEC, they are *concluded* by the Commission, though the approval of the Council must be obtained. It is, moreover, provided in the third paragraph of Article 101 that agreements may be negotiated and concluded solely by the Commission if their implementation does not require action by the Council and can be effected within the limits of the relevant budget.

The Euratom Treaty does not contain provision for a reference to the European Court to determine whether proposed Community agreements are compatible with the Treaty. It does, however, provide for an analogous procedure to test the compatibility of agreements which the *Member States* propose to conclude. This is Article 103, under which Member States are required to communicate to the Commission any agreements they propose to enter into which concern matters within the purview of the Treaty. This enables the Commission to ascertain whether the proposed agreement could impede the application of the Treaty. The Commission has one month to scrutinize the draft and make its comments known to the

---

[34] See also Arts 2(*h*), 10, 29, 46(2)(*e*) and 52. Art. 206 gives a power to conclude association agreements; it is identical in its wording to Art. 238 EEC.

Member State concerned. If the Commission raises objections, the agreement may not be concluded until the Commission's objections have been satisfied. The Member State may, however, apply to the European Court for a ruling (not an opinion, as under the EEC Treaty) as to the compatibility of the proposed agreement with the Treaty. If the Court's ruling is favourable, the Member State may go ahead with the agreement.

The procedure for an application under Article 103 Euratom is similar to that under Article 228 EEC, though there are significant differences.[35] The application may be made only by a Member State; it is served on the Commission, which may submit observations (analogous to a defence under the ordinary procedure) and these are served on the applicant. Only one advocate general is heard and, as under Article 228 EEC, the hearing takes place in private in the deliberation room. The applicant and the Commission have the right to make oral submissions.

This procedure was used for the first time in 1978 with regard to the draft Convention on the Physical Protection of Nuclear Materials, Facilities and Transports.[36] This agreement, which was drawn up under the aegis of the International Atomic Energy Agency, was to be concluded by the Member States without the participation of the Community. The object of the agreement was to ensure that nuclear materials were protected from theft and possible misuse. Many of the provisions of the agreement were clearly within the jurisdiction of the Member States – for example, those relating to criminal offences and extradition of offenders – but, in the opinion of the Commission, others impinged on areas in which the Community had direct responsibility. In particular, the Commission took the view that provisions concerning the export and import of nuclear materials could not be agreed to by the Member States acting alone. Therefore, when the text was communicated to it under Article 103 Euratom, the Commission stated in its comments that it was necessary for the Community to become a party to the agreement in addition to the Member States: such mixed agreements are expressly envisaged by Article 102 Euratom. The Belgian Government then referred the matter to the Court in order to clarify the legal position.

After a careful analysis of the terms of the draft agreement, the Court concluded that it fell partly within the jurisdiction of the Member States and partly within that of the Community. It therefore

[35] See Art. 105 of the Rules of Procedure of the Court, as amended in 1979.
[36] Ruling 1/78, [1978] ECR 2151.

ruled that the participation of the Community in the agreement was essential: the conclusion of the agreement by the Member States would be compatible with the Treaty only if the Community were also a party. The Court also stated that it would not be necessary for the other parties to the agreement to be told which parts of the agreement were within the jurisdiction of the Community and which parts within the jurisdiction of the Member States: this, they should be told, was a domestic matter for the Community.

INTERNATIONAL AGREEMENTS AND THE COMMUNITY LEGAL SYSTEM

The legal effect of international agreements with non-member States must be looked at on three levels: the international level, the Community level and the national level. The effect of an agreement on the international level depends on whether there is a binding obligation between the Community (or the Member States) on the one hand and the non-member State on the other hand. This is decided by international law. At this level, the only way in which Community law could come into play would be if international law referred a particular issue to it.

The effect of an international agreement within the Community legal system, however, is for Community law to decide. It must determine whether international agreements are a source of law within the Community legal order, and it can lay down the terms and conditions of that recognition.

The effect of an international agreement at the national level could in the same way depend on national law. However, as will be shown in Part III of this book, there is a principle of Community law (accepted – at least in great measure – by the national legal systems) that national courts must obey Community law; consequently, if Community law required the national courts to give effect to a Community treaty, they would normally comply.

The effect of a treaty obviously depends in part on its validity: a treaty can have no legal effects if it is invalid. This, however, raises two basic questions: can the European Court decide on the validity of an international agreement with a third country and, if so, what system of law will it apply?

It is suggested that, in general, the European Court would have no jurisdiction to declare invalid an international agreement with a non-member State. Unless it specifically submitted to the European Court's jurisdiction, the non-member State would not be bound by such a ruling. Consequently, all that the European Court could do would be to decide whether the agreement should be *recognized* and *applied* within the Community legal system. This could, of course, involve considering whether the agreement was valid – a question which should be decided according to international law – but no determination made by the Court would be binding on the international level.[37]

Even if the agreement is valid under international law, the European Court may refuse to apply it, either because it is not the kind of agreement which it is prepared to enforce, or because it violates a principle of Community law. It is these questions that will now be considered; in doing so, a distinction will sometimes have to be drawn between the three kinds of international agreement – those concluded by the Community, those concluded by the Member States within the general scope of the Community Treaties and those concluded jointly by the Community and the Member States (mixed agreements).

Binding the Community

Article 228(2) EEC provides that international agreements concluded by the Community are binding on the Community. This is, of course, obvious and would be the case even if it were not expressly so provided by the Treaty. The European Court has, however, gone further and laid down that international agreements entered into by the Member States can also bind the Community. The leading case on this is the third *International Fruit Company* case,[38] in which the question arose whether the Community was bound by the General Agreement on Tariffs and Trade (GATT). This is a world-wide, multilateral agreement aimed at the liberalization of international trade. It was concluded before the establishment of the Community and all the Member States are parties to it. It is concerned, as its name suggests, with tariffs and trade and thus falls within the area in

---

[37] See Pescatore, 'Les relations extérieures des Communautés européennes', (1961) (II) 103 Recueil des cours de l'Académie de Droit International de la Haye, 1 at 127–8; and *per* Advocate General Mayras in third *International Fruit Company*, Cases 21–24/72, [1972] ECR 1219 at 1234.

[38] Cases 21–4/72, [1972] ECR 1219. See also *Schlüter*, Case 9/73, [1973] ECR 1135 and *Nederlandse Spoorwegen*, Case 38/75, [1975] ECR 1439. In the latter case it was held that the Community was bound by two conventions of 15 December 1950 on customs tariffs.

which the Community has express treaty-making power. For these reasons the European Court held that the Community is bound by GATT. The key paragraph of its judgment reads as follows:[39] '. . . in so far as under the EEC Treaty the Community has assumed the powers previously exercised by Member States in the area governed by the General Agreement, the provisions of that agreement have the effect of binding the Community.' In a later case,[40] the Court said that, as regards the fulfilment of commitments under GATT, the Community has 'replaced' the Member States and it now seems generally recognized that the Community has succeeded to the rights and obligations of the Member States. The GATT is, therefore, part of Community law in the same way as treaties concluded by the Community itself.

It is not yet clear in what circumstances the Community will become bound by agreements entered into by the Member States alone but, according to Advocate General Capotorti, four conditions are necessary: first, the agreement must have been concluded prior to the EEC Treaty and all the Member States must have been parties to it when the EEC Treaty was concluded; secondly, it must have been the wish of the Member States to pledge the Community to observe the agreement, the aims of which must be shared by the Community; thirdly, action must have been taken by the Community institutions within the framework of the agreement; and fourthly, the other parties to the agreement must have recognized that powers had been transferred to the Community with regard to the subject-matter of the agreement.[41] It remains to be seen whether the Court will adopt these principles.[42]

Difficult problems can arise where the Community does not take over the rights and obligations of Member States towards third countries. Where the agreement has been concluded prior to the EEC Treaty (or, in the case of an agreement concluded by a new Member State, prior to its accession), the Community, though not bound by the agreement, is nevertheless under an obligation not to impede the fulfilment by the Member States which are parties to it of

---

[39] Paragraph 18 of the judgment.

[40] *Nederlandse Spoorwegen*, Case 38/75, [1975] ECR 1439 (paragraphs 16 and 21 of the judgment). See also *SPI*, Cases 267–9/81, [1983] ECR 801 (paragraphs 17–19 of the judgment).

[41] *Procureur Général* v. *Arbelaiz-Emazabel*, Case 181/80, [1981] ECR 2961 at 2987; see also *Attorney General* v. *Burgoa*, Case 812/79, [1980] ECR 2787 at 2815–16.

[42] If it does, the results could be strange. For example, the Community would not be bound by the European Road Transport Agreement.

their obligations under the agreement.[43] This rule, which applies even if only one Member State is a party, follows from Article 234 EEC.[44] As interpreted by the European Court,[45] this provides that the rights of the non-member States against the Member States (and the obligations of the latter towards the former) are not affected by the EEC Treaty. However, as between themselves, the rights and obligations of the Member States which are parties to the agreement are subject to the EEC Treaty.[46]

The position of the Community with regard to agreements covered by Article 234 must be distinguished from its position under agreements to which it becomes a party by succession. In the latter case the Community is bound by the agreement and is responsible to the non-member States for its fulfilment. The agreement is part of the Community legal system. In the former case, on the other hand, the Community is not bound by the agreement and is not responsible to the non-member States for its fulfilment. This is the responsibility of the Member States which are parties to it. The agreement is not part of the Community legal system, though the powers of the Community are restricted by it.[47]

The law is less clear with regard to agreements concluded subsequent to the EEC Treaty. In principle, the position should be analogous to that under Article 234, provided the subject-matter of the agreement was not, under Community law, within the exclusive competence of the Community. If the subject-matter *was* within the Community's exclusive competence at the time of the conclusion of the agreement, the European Court would probably consider that the Community's powers were not restricted by the agreement. Whether the agreement was valid at the international level would be a matter for international law.

Mixed agreements raise particular difficulties. The normal case in which a mixed agreement is concluded is where the subject-matter is regarded as falling partly within the jurisdiction of the Community and partly within that of the Member States. In such a case, is the

---

[43] *Attorney General* v. *Burgoa*, Case 812/79, [1980] ECR 2961 (paragraph 10 of the judgment).

[44] For the new Member States, see the relevant provision of the Accession Treaty, for example Art. 5 of the Act of Accession regarding the United Kingdom. For the somewhat different provisions under the Euratom Treaty, see Art. 105.

[45] *Commission* v. *Italy*, Case 10/61, [1962] ECR 1, 10.

[46] Ibid.

[47] Such an agreement would not be directly effective as a matter of Community law, though it may have direct effect under national law. It would not be covered by Art. 177 EEC.

Community bound by the whole agreement or only by the parts falling within its jurisdiction? In principle, the latter solution should be correct. If the former solution were adopted, the Community would be bound by provisions relating to an area outside its jurisdiction: this would constitute an effective modification to the Treaty and would mean that the Treaty could be amended by means of an agreement with a non-member State.[48] The latter solution, however, suffers from the disadvantage that the agreement would be split up in an awkward way: without a ruling by the Court, no one could ever be sure exactly which parts bound the Community and were therefore part of Community law.

Binding the Member States

Article 234 EEC provides that agreements concluded by the Community are binding on the Member States. Agreements concluded by the Member States which subsequently became binding on the Community would, of course, continue to bind the Member States as well. All agreements binding on the Community are consequently binding on the Member States.

Validity

When might the European Court refuse to give effect to an international agreement on the ground that it was contrary to Community law? At the present time, one cannot lay down any hard and fast rules in this regard but a few general observations may be made. In the *ERTA* case, the Court drew a distinction between the capacity of the Community to enter into international agreements and its authority to do so. If the agreement was outside the authority of the Community, its conclusion would be contrary to Community law and a ruling on this point could be obtained under Article 228 EEC. This procedure, however, can be used only before the conclusion of the agreement. If no application is made under Article 228 and the validity of the agreement arises after it is concluded, the Court would not necessarily apply the same test. In particular, it is unlikely that the agreement would be held invalid on the ground that the wrong negotiating procedure was used.

When would it be held invalid? The Court has said that the

---

[48] Pietri, 'La valeur juridique des accords liant la CEE', (1976) 12 RTDE 51 at 75. See also Ehlermann in O'Keefe and Schermers (eds), *Mixed Agreements* (1983), p. 18.

Community has capacity to enter into international agreements 'over the whole field of objectives defined in Part One of the Treaty'.[49] If the agreement was outside the capacity of the Community it would presumably be void under international law and also under Community law. Even if it came within this area, however, it is hard to see how it could be applied in the Community legal order if it directly conflicted with a provision in one of the constitutive Treaties: the powers of the Community come from the Treaties and they must be subject to the provisions of the Treaties.[50] The position would probably be the same if the international agreement was contrary to a general principle of law. If it conflicted with a Community act, on the other hand, the agreement would probably override it: in the third *International Fruit Company* case this was expressly stated by Advocate General Mayras[51] and is implicit in the judgment of the Court. One may therefore conclude – tentatively – that an international agreement entered into by the Community will be invalid if it is outside the capacity of the Community or if it conflicts with one of the constituent Treaties or (possibly) with a general principle of law.[52] It must again be stressed, however, that this relates solely to the validity of the agreement in terms of the Community legal order, not at the international level.

FURTHER READING

Jean Groux and Philippe Manin, *The European Communities in the International Order* (1985).

David O'Keefe and Henry G. Schermers (eds), *Mixed Agreements* (1983).

C. W. A. Timmermans and E. L. M. Völker, *Division of Powers between*

---

[49]   *ERTA*, Case 22/70, [1971] ECR 263 (paragraph 14 of the judgment).

[50]   See Pescatore, 'Les relations extérieures des Communautés européennes', (1961) (II) 103 Recueil des cours de l'Académie de Droit International de la Haye, 1 at 127.

[51]   [1972] ECR 1219 at 1233–4. Where a directly effective agreement conflicts with a Community act, the act will be invalid if it was subsequent to the agreement, and would probably be regarded as suspended if it was prior to it. If the agreement was not directly effective, the validity of the act might not be impaired, though it would probably have to be repealed.

[52]   As regards the ways in which such a question might come before the Court, see pp. 251–4 and 286, below. See also Pietri, 'La valeur juridique des accords liant la Communauté économique européenne', (1976) 12 RTDE 15 and 194 at 207–14.

the European Communities and their Member States in the Field of External Relations (1981).

Churchill and Foster, 'European Community Law and Prior Treaty Obligations of Member States: The Spanish Fishermen's Cases', (1987) 36 ICLQ 504.

Close, 'Self-restraint by the EEC in the Exercise of its External Powers', (1981) 1 YEL 45.

Groux, 'Le parallelisme des compétences internes et externes de la Communauté économique européenne', (1978) 14 CDE 3.

Leopold, 'External Relations Power of EEC in Theory and in Practice', (1977) 26 ICLQ 54.

Maes 'La Communauté européenne, les organisations inter-gouvernementales et les accords multilatéraux', [1977] RMC 395.

Meessen, 'The Application of Rules of Public International Law within Community Law', (1976) 13 C.M.L. Rev. 485.

Pietri, 'La valeur juridique des accords liant la Communauté économique européenne', (1976) 12 RTDE 15.

Schermers, 'Community Law and International Law', (1975) 12 C.M.L. Rev. 77.

Simmonds, 'The Evolution of the External Relations Law of the European Economic Community', (1979) 28 ICLQ 644.

House of Lords Select Committee on the European Communities, *External Competence of the European Communities* (H.L. 236, 1984/85).

Part III

Community Law and the Member States

INTRODUCTION

Part III is concerned with the relationship between Community law and national law, in particular with the application – and enforcement – of Community law in the Member States. The most important features of this relationship are the direct effectiveness of Community law in the national courts, the supremacy of Community law over national law and the procedures by which Community law can be enforced in the Member States.

At the outset it is desirable to consider whether, as a matter of general theory, it is possible to discover any principles which should govern this relationship. Does the nature of the Community as a supranational organization require any particular relationship between its law and that of the Member States? The answer to this can perhaps be obtained by considering briefly the political basis of the Community.

In contrast to past attempts, by Napoleon and Hitler for example, to unite Europe by force, the European Community is based on the consent of the Member States. Underlying this consent is the tacit assumption that all the Member States will play the game according to the same rules: national governments are prepared to accept rules of Community law which are against their interests, but benefit others, if other Member States are prepared to do the same when the balance of advantage is reversed. It follows from this that Community law must have the same meaning and effect in all Member States: it would be wrong if Community law had greater effect in one country than in another. This in turn requires that ultimate authority to decide these questions should reside in a single court whose jurisdiction extends over the whole Community. The only such court in existence is the European Court.

It also follows from these premises that Community law must override national law in the event of a conflict: if this were not so, Member States could avoid the application of Community rules disadvantageous to their interests by the simple expedient of passing conflicting legislation. Moreover, if Community law is to be directly effective – an essential characteristic of a supranational system – the

181

European Court must have the final say with regard to its validity and interpretation.

Community law would be useless if it could not be effectively enforced. This is mainly done in two ways: by private individuals in the national courts and by the Community (Commission) in the European Court. Once it is accepted that Community law is directly effective and prevails over national law, the way is open for an individual with a right under Community law – or an interest in its application – to bring proceedings in the national courts and thus make use of national legal remedies to enforce it. Alternatively, proceedings can be brought by the Commission (or another Member State) in the European Court against a Member State which fails to abide by Community law. The extent to which these procedures are effective will be considered in the following chapters.

The enforcement of Community law against private individuals raises fewer difficulties. Often this is done by a system of carrot and stick: grants or subsidies can be given to encourage activities that the Commission regards as desirable and levies imposed on those who do not conform. Import and export permits may also be withheld. In a few cases, mainly in the field of competition policy, the Commission has power to impose fines on persons who violate Community law; in other cases, Community acts require the national authorities to enact criminal measures to secure compliance with Community law.

FURTHER READING

John Usher, *European Community Law and National Law. The Irreversible Transfer?* (1981).

7

DIRECT EFFECT AND THE SUPREMACY OF COMMUNITY LAW

The purpose of this chapter is to consider the extent to which provisions of Community law must be applied by national courts – in other words, the extent to which they are part of the law of the land. Since this concerns the relationship between two legal systems, it can be looked at from two different points of view – that of Community law and that of national law. This chapter will be concerned with the position according to Community law; the national viewpoint will be discussed in the following chapter.

THE PRINCIPLE OF DIRECT EFFECT

The key concept is that of *direct effect*.[1] The European Court has, on numerous occasions, made clear what is meant by this: if a legal provision is said to be directly effective, it is meant that it grants individuals rights which must be upheld by the national courts. It should be noticed that this definition refers to *rights*, rather than to obligations, and to rights enforceable by *individuals*, rather than by public authorities. This is because the most common situation in practice is where a private citizen seeks to invoke Community law against a public authority in a Member State, usually the central government. However, a private individual may wish to invoke Community law against another private individual; and it is even possible that a national government might wish to enforce Community law against a private individual. All these questions are, of course, closely related, but the issues are not necessarily identical. In the discussion that follows the main emphasis will be put on the enforcement of Community rights by private individuals against public authorities: what is said will usually apply to the other

[1] This term, though frequently used by the European Court, is not to be found in any of the Treaties. For the term 'direct applicability', see pp. 196–7, below.

questions as well; where this is not so, separate treatment will be given to them.

As a matter of general principle, a legal provision cannot be directly effective unless two requirements are satisfied. First of all, the provision must be part of the law of the land or, to put it in a different way, it must be legally valid from the point of view of the national courts. This does not mean that it has to be part of the national legal system, in the sense that an Act of Parliament is part of the United Kingdom legal system, but merely that the national courts must recognize it as valid and binding law. The second requirement is that the terms of the provision must be appropriate to confer rights on individuals.

The meaning of these requirements may be clarified by a few examples. Assume that a revolutionary group proclaims itself the government of Britain without having effectively seized power: it may purport to make laws but, so long as the courts remain loyal to the existing government, those 'laws' will not be enforced. Likewise, if some foreign country, or an international organization, purports to legislate for Britain but their power to do so is not recognized by the British courts, their 'laws' will be of no effect, whatever their terms may be. In both cases the first requirement will not be satisfied.

An example of a situation in which the second requirement is not met is provided by section 3 of the Transport Act 1962.[2] Subsection (1) of this states: 'It shall be the duty of the Railways Board . . . to provide railway services in Great Britain . . .' and there is an analogous provision in subsection (2). But subsection (4) provides:

Subsections (1) and (2) of this section shall not be construed as imposing, either directly or indirectly, any form of duty or liability enforceable by proceedings before any court to which the Board would not otherwise be subject.

The end result is that subsections (1) and (2) are not enforceable before any British court. Other examples may be given of legal rules which, though enforceable by the appropriate public authority (for example, in England, the Crown acting through the Attorney General) may not be enforced by private individuals.

It will be apparent from these examples that the first requirement is concerned with the authorship of the provision and the form in which it was promulgated; the second relates to the contents of the measure: the former is basically a constitutional question, the latter

---

[2] See O. Hood Philips, *Constitutional and Administrative Law* (5th ed., 1973), p. 475 for further examples.

mainly a matter of interpretation – though general rules, such as those concerning *locus standi*, may also be involved.

JURISDICTION

In considering the extent to which Community law satisfies these two requirements, one must first deal with the issue of jurisdiction: which court should decide the matter – the national courts or the European Court? Although the second requirement, being a matter of interpretation, might seem to fall naturally within the jurisdiction of the European Court, the first requirement might appear to be a question for the national courts: issues of constitutional law would hardly seem appropriate for the European Court. This, however, assumes that only *national* constitutional law is in issue; once it is realized that the matter is just as much one of *Community* constitutional law, it will be apparent that the European Court's claim to jurisdiction is just as strong as that of national courts.

The issue was raised for the first time in the *Van Gend en Loos*[3] case where a private firm sought to invoke Community law against the Dutch customs authorities in proceedings in a Dutch tribunal. The tribunal made a reference to the European Court for a ruling on the question whether the provision in issue was directly effective. It was argued by the Dutch and Belgian Governments that the European Court had no jurisdiction to determine this issue as it involved questions of Dutch constitutional law. The European Court, however, rejected this argument on the ground that it was concerned only with deciding the question 'within the context of Community law' and not with determining the application of the Treaty according to the principles of Dutch national law.[4] In other words, the European Court may legitimately say that, as a matter of Community law, a given provision of Community law is directly effective. In the *Van Gend en Loos* case the European Court decided that the provision in question was directly effective, and this was accepted by the Dutch courts.

---

[3] Case 26/62, [1963] ECR 1.
[4] At pp. 10–11.

THE FIRST REQUIREMENT

Turning now from jurisdiction to substantive law, we can consider in greater detail the extent to which Community law satisfies the two requirements for direct effect. As regards the first, there can be little doubt that in principle all Community law is valid law within the Member States. However, what is far from clear is exactly on what basis this is so. There are two possible analogies on which one can draw; that of international law and that of constitutional law. The international model is the more obvious since the constituent Treaties are, after all, the creatures of international law. Here, however, one comes up against the fact that there are two distinct approaches to the application of international treaties in the national legal order: the monist and the dualist doctrines.

In simple terms, the basic thesis of the monist approach is that international law and national law are both part of one world system: they operate in different spheres but are part of the same legal structure. On this basis there is no reason why national courts should not apply international treaties, provided the appropriate constitutional procedures have been gone through to receive them into the national system. Under this doctrine the court applies the treaty as such: the national incorporation procedures – for example, assent (as distinct from enactment) by the legislature – serve merely to make it applicable in the territory concerned.

The dualist approach, on the other hand, adopts the view that international law and national law are two fundamentally different things. The view that there is one world system into which they may both be fitted is rejected. Consequently, international treaties can never be applied *as such* by the national courts. If the government concludes a treaty which requires a change in national law, the national legislature will pass legislation bringing this about. The legislation may contain provisions modelled on those of the treaty; it may even include the treaty in a schedule. But the courts will only apply those provisions as part of national law: if the version in the national legislation is different from the internationally valid version, the former will be applied (though the courts may, in cases of doubt, interpret the national implementing legislation in such a way as best to give effect to the international legal obligations created by the treaty).

It will be apparent that, while the monist view provides a possible model for the application of Community law, the dualist approach is inappropriate. In countries (such as the Netherlands) which adopt the monist doctrine, the courts may deal with Community law on the basis that it is a species of international law – albeit a rather special one – and apply rules for its recognition analogous to those applicable to ordinary international treaties. This approach is hardly suitable, however, in countries such as the United Kingdom which adopt the dualist doctrine.

The second model is that of constitutional law. This provides two possibilities: delegation of power and transfer of sovereignty. As far as the United Kingdom is concerned, the theory of delegation undoubtedly offers the easiest solution. The fact that Britain became a party to the Community Treaties could not in itself affect national law; consequently a statute, the European Communities Act, was necessary. This will be analysed in the next chapter; here it is sufficient to say that it provides that those rules of Community law which, according to Community law, are to be applied by the national courts, shall be so applied. This covers both the Treaties and Community legislation. From the standpoint of British law, the Treaties are applicable in the United Kingdom because the European Communities Act incorporated them by reference; Community legislation is applicable because the Act delegated powers to the Community to legislate for the United Kingdom.

This is not, however, the view adopted by the European Court. In the *Van Gend en Loos* case,[5] it held that the institutions of the Community are 'endowed with sovereign rights, the exercise of which affects Member States and also their citizens'.[6] It also said that Member States had 'limited their sovereign rights, albeit within limited fields' and that Community law is intended to confer rights on individuals 'which become part of their legal heritage'.[7] This is a very bold and ambitious claim but there is no doubt that it is still the view of the European Court.[8]

THE SECOND REQUIREMENT

The *Van Gend en Loos* case[9] was the first decision by the European Court on direct effect; it is also one of the most important judgments

---

[5] Case 26/62, [1963] ECR 1.
[6] At p. 12.
[7] Ibid.
[8] See also *Costa* v. *ENEL*, Case 6/64, [1964] ECR 585 at 593–4.
[9] Case 26/62, [1963] ECR 1.

ever handed down by the Court. The main issue was whether Article 12 of the EEC Treaty is directly effective. It reads:

Member States shall refrain from introducing between themselves any new customs duties on imports or exports or any charges having equivalent effect, and from increasing those which they already apply in their trade with each other.

It will be noticed that this provision is addressed to Member States: it imposes an obligation on them but does not expressly grant any corresponding right to individuals to import goods free from any duty imposed after the establishment of the EEC; nor does it state explicitly that any such duty will be invalid. For these reasons one might have thought that it would not be directly effective. The European Court, however, took the view that a provision is not prevented from being directly effective merely because it is addressed to Member States and does not expressly confer rights on private individuals.[10]

The Court instead laid down a different test:[11]

The wording of Article 12 contains a clear and unconditional prohibition which is not a positive but a negative obligation. This obligation, moreover, is not qualified by any reservation on the part of states which would make its implementation conditional upon a positive legislative measure enacted under national law. The very nature of this prohibition makes it ideally adapted to produce direct effects in the legal relationship between Member states and their subjects.

In later cases this test has been modified and refined. The suggestion that only negative obligations (prohibitions) may be directly effective has been dropped and the test may now be stated succinctly as follows:[12]

1. The provision must be clear and unambiguous;
2. It must be unconditional;
3. Its operation must not be dependent on further action being taken by Community or national authorities.

---

[10] For an affirmation of this, see *Defrenne* v. *Sabena*, Case 43/75, [1976] ECR 455 at paragraph 31 of the judgment.

[11] At p. 13.

[12] See Dashwood, 'The Principle of Direct Effect in European Community Law', (1978) 16 Journal of Common Market Studies, 229 at 231 et seq.

Clear and Unambiguous

Clarity and unambiguity are striven for by every legal draftsman; frequently, however, they are not attained. This is particularly true in the case of instruments which have to be agreed to by a number of different parties with conflicting interests, as is the case both with the constitutive Treaties and Community legislation. Like many provisions of national law, Community law is often unclear and ambiguous. This does not in itself, however, prevent its being directly effective: the European Court is there to interpret it and once this has been done the ambiguities will be resolved.

The difficulty, therefore, is not so much ambiguity, as generality and lack of precision. If the provision merely lays down a general objective or policy to be pursued, without specifying the appropriate means to attain it, it can hardly be regarded as a legal rule suitable for application by a court of law. In such cases further legislation is necessary before it can become operative.

A good example of such a provision is Article 5 EEC, which states:

Member States shall take all appropriate measures, whether general or particular, to ensure fulfilment of the obligations arising out of this Treaty or resulting from action taken by the institutions of the Community. They shall facilitate the achievement of the Community's tasks.

They shall abstain from any measure which could jeopardize the attainment of the objectives of this Treaty.

This is far too general to be directly effective by itself, though it might be suitable for application in conjunction with some other provision which spelled out more clearly what Member States were required to do, or not to do.[13]

Another example is Article 6(1) EEC, which states:

Member States shall, in close co-operation with the institutions of the Community, co-ordinate their respective economic policies to the extent necessary to attain the objectives of this Treaty.

This is clearly too vague to allow its application by national courts; in particular, no judge would wish to decide what degree of economic co-ordination is necessary to attain the objectives of the Treaty.

---

[13] However, in *Schlüter*, Case 9/73, [1973] ECR 1135 at paragraph 39 of its judgment, the European Court held that Art. 5 was not directly effective, even when combined with Art. 107. See also *Hurd* v. *Jones (Inspector of Taxes)*, Case 44/84, [1986] 2 CMLR 1 at paragraphs 47 and 48 of the judgment.

More difficult problems are raised by Article 119 EEC which requires application of the principle that 'men and women should receive equal pay for equal work'. Although it goes on to provide a definition of 'pay' and indicates what is meant by equal pay, anyone with knowledge of national legislation in this field will appreciate that the direct application of such a skeletal provision raises very substantial difficulties.

In the second *Defrenne case*[14] the European Court recognized these difficulties but it did not allow them to deflect it from its policy of maximizing the effectiveness of Community law wherever possible. The solution it adopted was to draw a distinction between 'direct and overt discrimination' on the one hand and 'indirect and disguised discrimination' on the other hand. The former, said the Court, can be identified solely by virtue of the criteria laid down in Article 119; it includes, in particular, discrimination resulting from the provisions of national legislation and collective labour agreements, as well as cases where the men and women concerned do the same work in the same establishment or service. Here the discrimination may be established by a purely legal analysis of the situation: complex judgments involving social and economic policy are unnecessary. In these cases Article 119 is directly effective. The Court admitted that there might be other cases in which the simple criteria of Article 119 would be insufficient: here further elaboration of the relevant criteria by means of Community or national measures would be necessary. One assumes that in these cases Article 119 would not be directly effective. It seems, therefore, that where the provision is only partly suitable for judicial application, it will be directly effective in part only.

The degree of precision that is necessary will of course vary according to the situation. A provision imposing obligations on private citizens – as was the case with Article 119, which, the Court ruled, applies to private employers just as much as to public ones – must of necessity attain a higher degree of precision than a measure granting rights to individuals against national authorities. In the case of criminal law, a particularly high degree of precision is essential. Thus, for example, if a Community provision required Member States to enact measures imposing criminal penalties for breach of Community law, one could hardly imagine the European Court holding that a new crime had been established by virtue of the direct

[14] Case 43/75, [1976] ECR 455. This case was discussed above at pp. 79–80.

effect of the Community provision if a Member State had failed to enact the required measures.

Unconditional

A Community provision will not be prevented from being directly effective merely because the rights it grants are dependent on some objective factor or event: once the condition is satisfied, there is no reason why the provision should not be enforced by the national courts. What is meant by the requirement of unconditionality is rather that the right must not be dependent on something within the control of some independent authority, such as a Community institution, or the Member State itself. In particular, it must not be dependent on the judgment or discretion of any such body.

An example of a situation where the judgment or discretion of a Community institution is involved is furnished by Articles 92–94 EEC. These concern state aid which distorts competition by favouring certain enterprises or products at the expense of others. This is stated by Article 92(1) to be 'incompatible with the common market' where it affects trade between Member States; certain exceptions are provided by Article 92(2) and (3). It might be thought that this was sufficiently definite to be directly effective; however, Article 93(2) makes provision for the Commission to decide whether any such aid infringes the provisions of Article 92 and to order the offending Member State to terminate it within a period of time laid down by the Commission. Moreover, Article 93(3) allows the Council to authorize any aid which might otherwise be regarded as contrary to the Treaty and, where an application is made to the Council for this purpose, any Commission proceedings under Article 93(2) must be suspended. In view of this, it is clear that Article 92(1) cannot have been intended to be directly effective: the prohibition it contains is conditional on the decisions of the Council and Commission.[15]

An extreme example of a right dependent on the discretion of a Member State would be a provision stating: 'Each Member State shall, in so far as it considers it desirable . . .' This obviously could not be directly effective: if the Member State failed to take the action in question, it could always argue that it did not consider it desirable to do so.

[15] See *Capolongo*, Case 77/72, [1973] ECR 611 at paragraphs 4–6, where the Court held that, at least as regards systems of aid in operation at the time when the Treaty went into effect, Art. 92(1) is not directly effective in the absence of a decision under Art. 93(2).

A more limited, but still significant, discretion is that which exists where Community law requires the attainment of an objective but allows the Member States to choose the means. If there are a number of quite different ways in which the objective could be attained, the discretion given to the Member States may prevent the provision from being directly effective.

An example is a Community provision[16] which requires Member States to give effect to the principle of equal treatment for men and women as regards access to employment, a provision going beyond the requirement of equal pay contained in Article 119 EEC. Among other things, this provision obliges Member States to provide a legal remedy for the victims of discrimination. In the *Von Colson* case[17] a woman who had been refused a job because of her sex argued that Community law gave her a directly effective right to demand that the court order the employer to appoint her to the post. The European Court, however, held that there were several ways in which Member States could fulfil the obligation to provide a legal remedy: for example, the victim of discrimination could be given the right to demand appointment or she could be given the right to claim damages. Any effective remedy would constitute compliance with the obligation. The discretion given to the Member States consequently prevented the obligation from being directly effective.[18]

A different kind of discretion is given in the so-called 'safeguard' clauses which occur quite frequently in different parts of the Treaty. The normal pattern is for the Treaty to grant rights, but allow the Member States to restrict these rights in special cases, it being understood that it is for the Member State concerned to decide whether the situation justifies recourse to the safeguard clause.

One example of this is Article 48(3) EEC, which grants workers the right of free movement between Member States but provides that this right is 'subject to limitations justified on grounds of public policy, public security or public health'. Since it is the national authorities who decide what the requirements of public policy are, it will be appreciated that this provision makes the right to immigrate subject to a condition dependent on the judgment of the Member State. For example, if a government decides that the activities of a

---

[16] The provision is contained in a directive, Directive 76/207, OJ 1976, L 39/40, but, as will be seen below, directives can also be directly effective where they are invoked against the state, as was the case in *Von Colson* (below).

[17] *Von Colson and Kamann* v. *Land Nordrhein-Westfalen*, Case 14/83,]1984] ECR 1891.

[18] This does not mean that other provisions in the directive are not directly effective: see the *Marshall* case, discussed below at pp. 208–11.

certain organization are against public policy, it will be entitled to invoke the proviso so as to prevent members of that organization from entering the country.

In view of this, one would have thought that the right of free movement granted by Article 48 was conditional and that, as a discretionary element is present, it could not be directly effective. In *Van Duyn* v. *Home Office*,[19] however, the European Court rejected this argument. The case concerned a Dutchwoman who wanted to enter the United Kingdom to take up a post with the Church of Scientology. Scientology might, perhaps, be described as a 'fringe religion': it is strongly supported by its adherents but disapproved of by the more established religious bodies. Some years previously the British Government had reached the conclusion that Scientology was harmful to the mental health of those involved and adopted a policy of discouraging it, though it was not made illegal. One consequence of this was that immigration permission was normally refused to known Scientologists.

When Miss Van Duyn arrived in England, she was refused permission to enter and this was justified on the basis of the public policy proviso. She then brought legal proceedings in the English courts to challenge this decision and one question which arose was whether Article 48(3) was directly effective. A reference was made to the European Court for a ruling on the issue and it was argued that the discretionary element eliminated the possibility of direct effect. The Court rejected this on the ground that the application of the proviso is 'subject to judicial control'. By this it seemed to be referring to the fact that decisions of the national authorities based on the proviso are subject to judicial review in the courts of the Member States.[20]

The difference between the situation in the *Von Colson* case and that in the *Van Duyn* case seems to be that in the former the Member States had a discretion as to how they would give effect to the right, while in the latter the right was provided by Community law and the Member States were merely given a limited power to restrict it in certain circumstances. In the former case the right was incomplete until the Member State had acted; in the latter case it was not.

---

[19] Case 41/74, [1974] ECR 1337 at paragraph 7 of the judgment.
[20] This was required by Art. 8 of Directive 64/221, OJ (Special Ed.) 1963/64, p. 117.

Not Dependent on Further Action

If the Community provision states that the rights it grants will come into effect when further action of a legislative or executive nature has been taken by the Community or the Member States, it would seem reasonable to hold that it cannot have direct effect until that action is taken. In accordance with its general policy, however, the European Court has sought to whittle this requirement down to its very minimum. It has done this by laying down a rule that if the Community provision gives a time-limit for its implementation, it can become directly effective if not implemented by the deadline.

Article 119 EEC provides an example. It states:

Each Member State shall during the first stage ensure and subsequently maintain the application of the principle that men and women should receive equal pay for equal work.

This clearly envisaged action by the Member States to bring the principle into operation, but it laid down a deadline: the end of the first stage. The Court therefore held in the second *Defrenne* case[21] that the requirement of further action did not prevent Article 119 from being directly effective thereafter.

In practice, this modification of the original rule to a large extent nullifies it, since almost all Community provisions requiring further action contain a time-limit. In such cases, the only consequence of the requirement is that direct effect is postponed until the deadline has passed.

Conclusions

The rulings of the European Court on direct effect are a good example of the Court's strategy in introducing new legal principles: in the first case in which this question arose – the *Van Gend en Loos* case – it used language which suggested that there was a fairly stringent test and that direct effect, at least in the case of Treaty provisions, was a rather rare phenomenon. Once the principle was accepted, however, the requirements were cut down: the rule regarding negative obligations was dropped and the requirements that the obligations must be unconditional and not dependent on further action were considerably qualified. The result is that direct effect may now be regarded as the norm rather than the exception.

[21] *Defrenne* v. *Sabena*, Case 43/75, [1976] ECR 455.

One can, in fact, say that the test is of an essentially practical nature: it lays down the minimum conditions for the application of almost any legal rule. In other words, the test is really one of feasibility: if the provision lends itself to judicial application it will almost certainly be declared directly effective; only where direct effect would create serious practical problems is it likely that the provision will be held not to be directly effective.[22]

The above comments concern direct effect in general. It is now desirable to change the focus of the discussion and give separate consideration to provisions derived from each of the various sources of Community law. What is said will be concerned mainly with the EEC and Euratom, but it will in most cases apply to the ECSC as well.

TREATY PROVISIONS

There is no statement in any of the Treaties as to whether Treaty provisions are directly effective.[23] It is in fact probable that the authors of the Treaties assumed that the question of direct effect would be decided by national courts according to the criteria of national law. If this is correct, the European Court's assumption of jurisdiction in this matter, as well as the liberal criteria it has adopted, constitutes a development of the very greatest importance.

REGULATIONS

Articles 189 EEC and 161 Euratom state that a regulation is 'directly applicable in all Member States'.[24] The authors of the Treaties probably intended 'directly applicable' to mean the same thing as 'directly effective'. Since there is no similar statement regarding other kinds of Community legislation, or regarding the Treaties themselves, it seems likely that they intended that regulations, and only

---

[22] See Pescatore, 'The Doctrine of "Direct Effect": An Infant Disease of Community Law', (1983) 8 E.L. Rev. 155, especially at 174–177.

[23] The existence in Arts 177 EEC and 150 Euratom of provision for a preliminary reference by a national court to the European Court for a ruling on the interpretation of Treaty provisions does not imply that such provisions may be directly effective: see below, pp. 202–3.

[24] There is no similar provision in the ECSC Treaty as regards general decisions (equivalent to EEC regulations).

regulations, would be directly effective. For reasons of policy, however, the European Court has decided that provisions in any of these instruments are capable of having direct effect. The problem then arises of reconciling this development with the wording of the Treaties, a problem which has caused much concern to legal writers[25] though not (apparently) to the Court itself. The dilemma is as follows: if one interprets 'directly applicable' to mean the same thing as 'directly effective',[26] it would seem to follow that only regulations can be directly effective. If, on the other hand, one treats the two terms as meaning something different,[27] one has to find a suitable meaning for 'directly applicable', a meaning that refers to some quality possessed by regulations but not by other instruments of Community law. This in turn has caused problems because, though such features undoubtedly exist,[28] they are neither clear-cut nor important enough to warrant a special term to describe them. In any event, it is doubtful whether the exercise is worth while, since the Court does not appear to pay much attention to the wording of the Treaties on this point and seems to use the two expressions as meaning the same thing.[29] The best solution, therefore, is to ignore the whole controversy and proceed directly to consider the features of the different instruments. This will now be done.

In view of Article 189 EEC, it might be thought that regulations are always directly effective. Very frequently this is the case – but it is not always so.[30] Take, for example, Regulation 1463/70.[31] This is

[25] For a summary of the different views, see Steiner, 'Direct Applicability in EEC Law A Chameleon Concept', (1982) 98 LQR 229.

[26] See Bebr, 'Directly Applicable Provisions of Community Law: The Development of a Community Concept', (1970) 19 ICLQ 257, *passim* and especially at pp. 266–7; and Toth, Vol. I, p. 119, note 1.

[27] This theory was first put forward by J. A. Winter in an article entitled 'Direct Applicability and Direct Effect: Two Distinct and Different Concepts in Community Law', (1972) 9 C.M.L. Rev. 425. He makes the distinction between the two terms clear at pp. 425–6 and again at pp. 435–6, though paradoxically he himself sometimes uses 'direct applicability' as if it meant 'direct effect': see, for example, pp. 427 et seq. Other authors who regard the two terms as having different meanings include Schermers, paragraphs 219 and 239; Dashwood, 'The Principle of Direct Effect in European Community Law', (1978) 16 Journal of Common Market Studies, 229 at 230; and L. J. Brinkhorst, (1971) 8 C.M.L. Rev. 380 at 390–1.

[28] See note 33, below, and the corresponding text.

[29] Pescatore, 'The Doctrine of "Direct Effect": An Infant Disease of Community Law', (1983) 8 E.L. Rev. 155, note 2.

[30] See *per* Advocate General Warner in *Galli*, Case 31/74, [1975] ECR 47 at 70 and in *Steinike und Weinlig* v. *Germany*, Case 78/76, [1977] ECR 595 at 583; and *per* Advocate General Reischl in *Ratti*, Case 148/78, [1979] ECR 1629 passim.

[31] OJ 1970 (Special Ed.) p. 482.

concerned with the introduction of recording equipment (tacho-graphs) in commercial vehicles and Article 4 states that the use of this equipment will be compulsory from a given date. Article 21(1)[32] then provides:

Member States shall, in good time and after consulting the Commission, adopt such laws, regulations or administrative provisions as may be necessary for the implementation of this Regulation.

Such measures shall cover, *inter alia*, the reorganization of, procedure for, and means of carrying out, checks on compliance and the penalties to be imposed in case of breach.

This provision clearly cannot be directly effective; in particular, it cannot be regarded as automatically creating a new criminal offence – that of driving a commercial vehicle without a tachograph. It is far too vague: it does not state exactly what will constitute the offence, who will be regarded as responsible (owner or driver), what the penalties will be or what defences will be available.

Since regulations are normally directly effective, there is usually no need for the enactment of national legislation to give effect to them. The European Court has moreover laid down a general rule that, except where they are necessary, national implementing measures are improper.[33] The reason for this is that the Court does not want the Community nature of the provision to be obscured: it must be clearly applied as a provision of Community law, not of national law. In particular the Court seems concerned about three matters. First, if the provisions of the regulation were enacted as part of a national measure, it might be thought that they took effect from the date of the national measure, rather than that of the Community measure: this could mean that the provisions would not come into force on the same date in all the Member States. Secondly, there is a danger that when the Community provisions are transformed into national law, subtle changes will be made in their content to suit national interests: in

[32] Art. 21 was renumbered Art. 23 with effect from 1 January 1978 by Art. II of Regulation 2828/77, OJ 1977, L 334/5.

[33] This rule is often justified on the ground that, under Art. 189 EEC, regulations are directly applicable. This could, therefore, indicate an appropriate meaning to give to 'directly applicable' if one wanted to distinguish it from 'directly effective', but this would then mean that not all regulations were directly applicable, which would conflict not only with Art. 189 EEC, but also with the opinion of Advocate General Warner in *R*. v. *Secretary of State for Home Affairs*, ex parte *Santillo*, Case 131/79, [1980] ECR 1585 at 1608. Moreover, the European Court has said that the fact that regulations are directly applicable does not mean that they cannot contain provisions empowering Member States to pass implementing measures: *Eridania*, Case 230/78, [1979] ECR 2749 at paragraph 34 of the judgment.

this way the uniformity of Community law would be jeopardized. Thirdly, national implementation could prejudice the European Court's jurisdiction to give a ruling on the interpretation and validity of the measure under the procedure for a preliminary reference.[34] It is true that the Court has expressly stated that its jurisdiction cannot be affected by national implementation measures;[35] nevertheless, it is conceivable that some national courts might be less ready to make a reference to the European Court if the Community provisions were incorporated in a national measure.

The doctrine that national measures are improper was first laid down in 1973 in *Commission* v. *Italy*.[36] This case concerned a Community plan to counter the chronic over-production of dairy products by the introduction of a premium for the slaughter of cows. The Italian Government had passed a decree which stated that the provisions of the relevant regulations were 'deemed to be included' in it and then proceeded to reproduce them together with certain procedural provisions of a national character.

Enforcement proceedings were taken against Italy, both because it had failed to bring the scheme into operation on time, and because certain aspects of it had not been put into effect at all. In the course of its judgment the Court made the following comments concerning the enactment of the national decree:[37]

By following this procedure, the Italian Government has brought into doubt both the legal nature of the applicable provisions and the date of their coming into force.

According to the terms of Article 189 and 191 of Treaty, Regulations are, as such, directly applicable in all Member States and come into force solely by virtue of their publication in the *Official Journal* of the Communities, as from the date specified in them, or in the absence thereof, as from the date provided in the Treaty.

Consequently, all methods of implementation are contrary to the Treaty which would have the result of creating an obstacle to the direct effect of Community Regulations and of jeopardizing their simultaneous and uniform application in the whole of the Community.

The Court went on to point out that in one respect the Italian decree had departed from the terms of Community law in that it had failed to take into account an extension of the time allowed for slaughter under

[34] See *Variola*, Case 34/73, [1973] ECR 981 at paragraph 11 of the judgment.
[35] Ibid.
[36] Case 39/72, [1973] ECR 101.
[37] Paragraph 17.

a later regulation. It then concluded:[38] 'The default of the Italian Republic has thus been established by reason not only of the delay in putting the system into effect but also of the manner of giving effect to it provided by the decree.'

The rule that national measures are improper is subject to exceptions in a number of situations. The first and most obvious exception is where the regulation itself expressly requires the Member States to take action to implement it: this was the case with Article 21 of the tachograph regulation discussed previously. Here, implementing measures are not only permitted, they are obligatory: when the United Kingdom failed to implement Article 21, it was ordered to do so by the European Court.[39]

Secondly, there may be cases in which, though the regulation does not expressly require implementation, it may impliedly permit it. This would be the case where the terms of the regulation are rather vague and provision for its detailed application is desirable. It appears that in such a case national measures will be permissible, provided they are not incompatible with the provisions of the regulation.[40]

Whether national measures are permissible in other circumstances is uncertain. One situation in which they would serve a useful function is where national provisions purport to codify the law in a particular area and thus give a complete statement of all the relevant legal rules. If a regulation impinges on that area, so that in certain cases rights may be derived from it, it might be desirable in the interests of clarity, certainty and legislative 'tidiness' for those aspects of the issue governed by the regulation to be repeated in the national provision.

A good example of this is found in the field of immigration law. In the United Kingdom, the Immigration Rules purport to give a reasonably complete statement of the immigration rights of persons who are not British citizens. Community law, of course, gives special immigration rights to Community nationals and these are embodied in the EEC Treaty and in regulations and directives. The Treaty, however, draws a distinction between employed persons (workers) and self-employed persons: the former are covered by Articles 48–51 EEC and the latter by Articles 52–58. Under Article 48(3)(*d*) the Commission is granted power to adopt a regulation to give workers

[38] Paragraph 18.
[39] *Commission* v. *United Kingdom*, Case 128/78, [1979] ECR 419.
[40] See *Bussone*, Case 31/78, [1978] ECR 2429 at paragraph 32 of the judgment.

the right to remain in the country of immigration on retirement from their job; such a regulation was passed.[41] No similar power is granted by Articles 52–58, but the Council passed a directive granting the same rights to self-employed persons.[42]

The consequence of this is that there are two Community measures, a regulation and a directive, which contain very similar provisions but cover different classes of persons. The directive obviously requires implementation and the normal way to do this in the United Kingdom would be to insert an appropriate provision in the Immigration Rules granting retired self-employed persons the right to remain in the country. But what about retired workers? If implementation of the regulation is not permitted, the end result would be rather strange: the immigration rules would expressly grant a right to self-employed persons but say nothing about workers. This could cause confusion. One possible solution would be to reproduce the terms of the Regulation in the national measures, at the same time making clear that they take effect as a regulation and not as part of the national measures.[43]

DIRECTIVES

Whatever the position may be regarding other Community measures, there is little doubt that the authors of the Treaties did not intend directives to be directly effective. This view, which was generally accepted in the early days of the EEC, follows from the concept of a directive as laid down in the EEC and Euratom Treaties: Articles 189 EEC and 161 Euratom pointedly refrain from declaring directives directly applicable. Moreover, they state that a directive is binding only 'as to the result to be achieved' but leaves 'the choice of form and methods' to the national authorities. In other words, the directive lays down an objective and leaves it to the Member States to achieve that objective according to such means as they might think fit. This clearly implies that legislative measures will be taken by the national authorities and that, though the result must be the same in all Member States, the details of the legislation

---

[41] Regulation 1251/70, OJ (Special Ed.) 1970 (II) p. 402.

[42] Directive 75/34, OJ 1975, L 14/10, passed under Art. 235 EEC.

[43] In fact the Immigration Rules grant retired workers the right to remain in the United Kingdom without making any mention of the Regulation at all: see H. C. Paper 169 of 1982/83, paragraph 147.

may vary: this is the essence of the distinction between regulations and directives. In these circumstances, one might have thought, there could be no possibility of directives having direct effect.

The First Step

The European Court, however, has decided otherwise. The first tentative step was taken in two cases decided within a couple of months of each other in 1970, *Grad*[44] and *SACE*.[45] In both these cases the role of the directive was limited to setting the date when a provision in another instrument would come into force.[46] The European Court held that this fact did not prevent the provision in the other instrument from being directly effective. It was only in a limited sense, therefore, that the directives in these cases were themselves directly effective.

The New Principle

This reasoning might have suggested that these were special cases; any such illusions were, however, dispelled when the Court decided the *Van Duyn* case in 1974.[47] The facts have already been outlined above,[48] where it was mentioned that the Court held Article 48 EEC to be directly effective. This, however, was only one issue in the case; the Court was also asked whether Article 3(1) of Directive 64/221[49] is directly effective. The purpose of this directive is to limit the discretion of Member States when they invoke the public policy proviso under Article 48 EEC, and Article 4(1) lays down that such measures must be 'based exclusively on the personal conduct of the individual concerned'. It was argued on behalf of Miss Van Duyn that this provision was directly effective and that she could therefore rely on it before the English court: she maintained that the only ground the Home Office had for refusing her admission to the United Kingdom was her membership of the Church of Scientology and she contended that this did not constitute 'personal conduct' in terms of Article 4(1).

[44] Case 9/70 [1970] ECR 825.
[45] Case 33/70, [1970] ECR 1213.
[46] In *SACE* the provision was contained in the EEC Treaty; in *Grad* it was in a decision. The ruling in the latter case that a decision can be directly effective (see pp. 211–12, below) may be thought of as foreshadowing that in the *Van Duyn* case (below).
[47] Case 41/74, [1974] ECR 1337.
[48] At p. 193.
[49] OJ 1963/64, (Special Ed.), p. 117.

This was, of course, a very different situation from that in the previous cases: here the very essence of the right was laid down in the directive. There could be no question of a 'special case': the Court was obliged to decide, as a matter of general principle, whether a directive could have direct effect. The United Kingdom Government argued that it could not, basing its argument on the provisions of Article 189 mentioned above. The European Court, however, held that directives can be directly effective.

The Court gave three arguments in support of this conclusion. The first was that it would be incompatible with the binding effect attributed to a directive in Article 189 to exclude in principle the possibility of direct effect. This argument is unsound: it is quite possible for a measure to be fully binding at the inter-state level without its being enforceable in national courts by private individuals. In such a case it could be enforced by means of an action brought in the European Court by the Commission, or by another Member State, under Articles 169–171 EEC.

The second argument was much stronger. This, however, was a policy argument, not a legal one. It was that the *effectiveness* ('*effet utile*', in French) of the measure would be greater if individuals were entitled to invoke it before the national courts. This will be considered further below.

The third argument was based on Article 177 EEC. This is the provision which governs references from national courts to the European Court. It grants the Court jurisdiction to give preliminary rulings on, among other things, the validity and interpretation of 'acts of the institutions of the Community'. The exact meaning of this phrase will be considered in Chapter 9;[50] there can, however, be no doubt that it includes decisions and directives as well as regulations. The Court argued that this implies that all such acts can be directly effective.

The Court's argument, however, assumes that a national court might require a preliminary ruling only in the case of a directly effective provision. This is not so: if a Community provision which is not directly effective is implemented by a national measure, the validity and interpretation of the latter might – under *national* law – depend on the validity and interpretation of the former. As will be shown below,[51] this is the case in the United Kingdom. Consequently, a national court might very well require a preliminary ruling

[50] See pp. 250–4, below.
[51] At pp. 240–1.

on the validity and interpretation of a Community provision which is not directly effective: the European Court has itself said that this is permissible.[52] Consequently, no inference can be drawn from the terms of Article 177.[53]

The strongest argument of a legal, or quasi-legal, nature is in fact one that was not even mentioned by the Court in the *Van Duyn* case.[54] This is an argument which may be derived from the English doctrine of Equity (and similar principles in the Civil Law). The problem in the *Van Duyn* case was that the United Kingdom Government had done nothing to implement Article 3(1) of the directive: there was no British provision stating that entry could be refused only on the basis of the personal conduct of the would-be immigrant. If this had been done, there would have been no difficulty: Miss Van Duyn could have relied on the British provision. In effect, therefore, the United Kingdom Government was seeking to deny her a right on the ground of its own failure to implement the directive. This could bring into play the principle that no one should profit from his own wrongdoing. In other words, Miss Van Duyn's rights should have been regarded as being no less than they would have been if the United Kingdom Government had fulfilled its obligation to implement the directive. This would have entailed allowing her to invoke the provisions of the directive in the English courts.

Whatever one may think about this last argument, there can be no doubt that it was on policy grounds that the Court decided to proclaim the new doctrine: the argument of *effectiveness* was what really won the day. The fact of the matter is that Member States are often very remiss in implementing directives. The Netherlands is generally regarded as one of the most conscientious of the Member States, yet a study by two Dutch authors has shown that even the Dutch have a bad record in this regard: of the 94 directives chosen for examination, almost two-thirds (60) were not implemented on time.[55] If this is the state of affairs in the Netherlands, one can expect that things will be even worse in some other countries.

---

[52] *Mazzalai*, Case 111/75, [1976] ECR 657 at 665.

[53] It is interesting to note that this argument has been abandoned in subsequent cases: see, for example, *Verbond van Nederlandse Ondernemingen*, Case 51/76, [1977] ECR 113 at paragraphs 20–4 of the judgment.

[54] It has, however, been adopted subsequently: see *Ratti*, Case 148/78, [1979] ECR 1629 at paragraph 22 of the judgment. It had previously been put forward by Advocate General Warner in *Enka*, Case 38/77, [1977] ECR 2203 at 2226.

[55] Maas and Bentvelsen, 'De tijdige uitvoering van EEG-richtlijnen in Nederland', [1978] Bestuurswetenschappen 443 at 446.

It was no doubt this problem which persuaded the Court to act. Without direct effect, a directive can be enforced only by means of an action brought in the European Court by the Commission (or by another Member State) under Articles 169–171 EEC. The difficulty is that – for reasons of manpower, if for no others – the Commission is able to handle only a small number of such cases each year: it would be quite impossible for them to bring proceedings with regard to every directive which had not been fully implemented. In some cases, moreover, pressure may be brought against the Commission to dissuade it from taking action. By declaring a directive directly effective, on the other hand, the Court can open the way for individuals to enforce it in the national courts. This has the added advantage both of shielding the Commission from political pressure and of casting on the national courts the burden of ensuring compliance.

The Importance of the Deadline

In the *Van Duyn* case the time limit for the implementation of the directive had long since passed; the significance of this date was not therefore given much emphasis. The *Ratti* case,[56] however, shows that it is in fact crucial. This concerned two directives dealing with the packaging and labelling of solvents and varnishes respectively. The first, Directive 73/173,[57] was adopted on 4 June 1973 and required Member States to implement its provisions by 8 December 1974; the second, Directive 77/728[58] was adopted on 7 November 1977 and laid down a deadline of 9 November 1979.

Mr Ratti was an Italian who ran a firm selling both solvents and varnishes in Italy. The firm decided that it would package and label its products so as to comply with the two directives, even though neither had been implemented in Italy. The matter was, however, covered by an Italian law passed in 1963 which applied to both products and was in some ways more lenient than the directives but in other ways stricter. When the firm put its products on the market, Ratti was prosecuted for failure to comply with the provisions of the Italian law. At the relevant time, the deadline for implementation of the first directive had expired but that for the second had not. Ratti

---

[56] Case 148/78, [1979] ECR 1629. For an illuminating comment, see Usher, (1979) 4 E.L. Rev. 268.
[57] OJ 1973, L 189/7.
[58] OJ 1977, L 303/23.

admitted that he had not complied with the Italian law but argued that compliance with the directives was sufficient.

The court in Milan before which the prosecution had been brought, made a reference to the European Court for a ruling on whether the directives were directly effective. The European Court held that a directive can become directly effective only when the deadline for implementation has expired; therefore, the first directive was directly effective, but the second was not. The Court held that this result was not affected by the fact that some of the varnishes had been imported from Germany, which had already implemented the second directive, and were therefore packaged and labelled in accordance with it. The result was that Community law afforded Ratti a defence to the charges relating to the solvents, but not those concerning the varnishes.

This case shows that a directive which has not been implemented cannot become directly effective before the expiry of the time limit.[59] But does this mean that it can have no effects at all before then? If the Member State purports to implement the directive before the deadline, but does so improperly, may an individual rely on the directive to correct the implementing legislation? It could be argued in support of such a contention that – though the Member State is not obliged to implement it before the expiry of the time limit – if it chooses to do so, it must comply with the terms of the directive: by purporting to implement the directive, it is voluntarily assuming the obligation at an earlier time.

Against this, however, it could be contended that, although a Member State should not be permitted to profit from its own wrongdoing, it should not, on the other hand, be prejudiced by reason of the fact that it has complied before the deadline. It remains to be seen which of these arguments gains the support of the European Court. It is, however, possible that – whatever the position may be according to Community law – the interpretation, and even the validity, of the national measure may, *as a matter of national law*, be affected by the directive. This, of course, will vary from country to country.[60]

---

[59] For the position where, after it has expired, the deadline is postponed, see *Kloppenburg*, Case 70/83, [1984] ECR 1075.

[60] In Britain a statutory instrument passed under section 2(2) of the European Communities Act might be *ultra vires* if it went beyond the obligation imposed by the directive it purported to implement. See further pp. 240–1, below.

Are Directives Now the Same as Regulations?

The granting of direct effect to directives has probably done more than any other initiative by the European Court to enhance the effectiveness of Community law. Yet there has been a price to pay: the distinction between regulations and directives has been blurred and the structure of the Treaty deformed. This, in turn, has provoked a reaction at the national level.[61] The question must therefore be asked whether any significant differences between regulations and directives still remain.

Some differences have already been mentioned. First of all, there is the date on which direct effect comes into operation: a regulation can be directly effective as soon as it comes into force, but a directive cannot be directly effective before the expiry of the time limit for implementation.

A second difference, of potentially greater significance, is that Member States are not normally either required or permitted to pass national legislation giving effect to the provisions of a regulation; in the case of a directive, on the other hand, there is the much-vaunted right to choose the 'form and methods' by which the objective of the directive will be attained.[62] There is no doubt that this applies even where the directive is directly effective; however, in such a case the discretion enjoyed by Member States could be severely restricted.

There are two reasons for this. First, the Community institutions long ago adopted the habit of enacting directives with provisions every bit as detailed and precise as those to be found in a regulation.[63] Moreover, the Court has developed a doctrine that the area of choice left to the Member States regarding the 'form and methods' of implementation depends on the objective to be achieved: in some cases, the objective will be such that this diminishes to vanishing point. For example, in *Enka* v. *Inspecteur der Invoerrechten en Accijnzen*[64] the Court stated that in the case of customs legislation absolute uniformity may be necessary. It therefore held that the relevant provision of the directive in issue had to be reproduced in exactly the same way in the implementing legislation of each Member State.[65] In

---

[61] See pp. 225–7 and 230–5, below.

[62] This is laid down in Arts 189 EEC and 161 Euratom; for the slightly different formulation applicable in the case of an ECSC recommendation, see Art. 14 ECSC.

[63] Compare, for example, Directive 75/34, OJ 1975, L 14/10, with Regulation 1251/70, OJ (Special Ed.) 1970 (II), p. 402.

[64] Case 38/77, [1977] ECR 2203 at paragraphs 11–18.

[65] For a less strict attitude, see *Commission* v. *Italy*, Case 363/85, 9 April 1987, *The Times*, 5 May 1987.

such a situation, implementation is, from the Member State's point of view, an empty exercise.[66]

It is, of course, true that there are many cases in which a real discretion will exist. It must not be forgotten, however, that some regulations have to be implemented and sometimes Member States will enjoy a significant discretion in this case as well. The tachograph regulation (discussed above[67]) is a case in point: the powers of inspection, the details of criminal procedure and the maximum penalty are all matters which, within certain limits, may be determined by the Member States.

Another possible difference which has sometimes been suggested is that, while direct effect is the normal characteristic of a regulation, it is exceptional in the case of a directive.[68] From a purely theoretical point of view this is obviously true: if the Member States carry out their obligations under Community law, there will never be occasion for a directive to have direct effect. In practice, of course, Member States do not always implement directives as they should: from the practical point of view, therefore, the important question is whether a provision is less likely to be declared directly effective simply because it is contained in a directive, rather than in a regulation.

In the *Van Duyn* case[69] the European Court said that, while regulations 'may by their very nature have direct effects', directives 'have no automatic direct effect'.[70] This suggests that such a difference does indeed exist. However, the test applied to directives is exactly the same as that adopted in the case of Treaty provisions and, though the Court gave very careful scrutiny to the provision in issue in the *Van Duyn* case, it has subsequently shown itself prepared to declare whole groups of directives directly effective *en bloc*, without even listing them individually, much less attempting to examine their provisions in order to see whether they comply with the requirements for direct effect.[71] It is, therefore, hard to discern any practical

[66] It is an exercise which must nevertheless be gone through. The Member State cannot rely on the direct effect of the directive to excuse its failure to implement it: see *Commission* v. *Belgium*, Case 102/79, [1980] ECR 1473 at paragraph 12 of the judgment.

[67] At pp. 196–7.

[68] See Brinkhorst, (1971) 8 C.M.L. Rev. 380 at 390; Dashwood, 'The Principle of Direct Effect in European Community Law', (1978) 16 Journal of Common Market Studies 229 at 241; and *per* Advocate General Reischl in *Ratti*, Case 148/78, [1979] ECR 1629 at 1650 and 1653–4.

[69] Case 41/74, [1974] ECR 1337.

[70] At paragraphs 12 and 13 of the judgment.

[71] In *Watson and Belmann*, Case 118/75, [1976] ECR 1185 the Court said that all measures adopted by the Community in application of Arts 48 to 66 of the EEC Treaty are directly effective: see the first paragraph of its formal ruling.

difference between regulations and directives on this point.

The differences discussed so far have shown themselves to be rather insubstantial; there is, however, one difference which is of great significance. This is that directives are not capable of imposing *obligations* on individuals.

Vertical and Horizontal Direct Effect

There is no doubt that both regulations and Treaty provisions are able not only to confer rights on private individuals, but also to impose obligations on them.[72] However, the European Court has held that directives can only confer rights on individuals (against the state); they cannot impose obligations on individuals (in favour of the state or other individuals). This means that directives are capable of only 'vertical' direct effect; unlike regulations and Treaty provisions, they are not capable of 'horizontal' direct effect.

The question whether it is possible for directives to have horizontal direct effect was controversial for many years. The writers were divided on the question;[73] two Advocates General came out against the possibility;[74] the Court gave hints that it shared this view;[75] finally, in *Marshall* v. *Southampton and South West Hampshire Area Health Authority (Teaching)*,[76] the Court stated explicitly that a directive 'may not of itself impose obligations on an individual' and that 'a provision of a directive may not be relied on as such against such a person.'[77] The reason given by the Court was that 'according to Article 189 of the EEC Treaty the binding nature of a directive, which constitutes the basis for the possibility of relying on the directive before a national court, exists only in relation to "each Member State to which it is addressed".'[78] In other words, a directive is not binding on

[72] As far as regulations are concerned, this follows from the terms of Arts 189 EEC and 161 Euratom, which state that regulations have general application. In the second *Defrenne* case, Case 43/75, [1976] ECR 455, the Court held that Treaty provisions can also have this effect. This has since been confirmed in numerous cases.

[73] See the list in Easson, 'Can Directives Impose Obligations on Individuals?', (1979) 4 E.L. Rev. 67 at 70, note 24.

[74] Advocate General Reischl in *Ratti*, Case 148/78, [1979] ECR 1629 at 1650; and (more clearly) Advocate General Slynn in *Becker*, Case 8/81, [1982] ECR 53 at 81.

[75] See, for example, *Becker*, *supra*, at paragraphs 17–26 of the judgment.

[76] Case 152/84, [1986] 1 CMLR 688.

[77] Paragraph 48 of the judgment. See also *Kolpinghuis Nijmegen*, Case 80/86, 8 October 1987 (not yet reported), in which the European Court held that a Member State cannot rely on the direct effect of a (non-implemented) directive in criminal proceedings against an individual; see, further, *Pretore de Salò* v. *X.*, Case 14/86, 11 June 1986 (not yet reported).

[78] Ibid.

private individuals; therefore, it cannot impose obligations on them.

This is a sound legal argument of the traditional kind. It will, however, be clear by now that the Court does not usually attach very much weight to such arguments: it is more concerned with policy. Moreover, one would have thought that the Court's policy of enhancing the effectiveness of Community law would have led it to come down in favour of horizontal direct effect. If the question had arisen for decision ten years earlier, this might well have been the result; but since then two national courts of considerable influence, the French *Conseil d'Etat* and the German *Bundesfinanzhof*, have rebelled against the whole idea that directives can have direct effect.[79] This was obviously a serious matter and, while the European Court refused to retreat from the position it had adopted, it probably considered it expedient not to press on any further. The denial of horizontal direct effect to directives can, therefore, be seen as an offer of a compromise under which the European Court will limit the direct effect of directives to vertical direct effect if national courts will accept it to that limited extent.

However this may be, there is no doubt that on purely legal grounds there are strong arguments, in addition to that put forward by the Court, against the horizontal direct effect of directives. The rationale most commonly used today to justify the direct effect of directives is that a Member State should not benefit from its own default: this cannot apply where the directive is invoked against an individual. Moreover, there is no legal requirement that directives have to be published in the Official Journal,[80] though in practice they always are.

On strictly legal grounds, however, there are strong arguments[81] against *any* direct effect being given to directives. By accepting vertical direct effect but not horizontal direct effect, the European Court has created anomalies. For example, take the case of sex discrimination in employment. There is no problem if the claim concerns equal pay: this is covered by a Treaty provision,[82] which is horizontally directly effective, so it can be invoked against a private employer. Where, on the other hand, the case concerns discrimination in some area other than pay, such as dismissals on grounds of

---

[79] For a discussion of these cases and of later developments, see below, pp. 225–7 and 230–5.

[80] Art. 191 EEC requires only that they be notified to the addressee (i.e., the Member State).

[81] See above, pp. 200–1.

[82] Art. 119 EEC.

sex, the employee must rely on a directive.[83] Since directives have only vertical direct effect, a woman employed by the state may invoke it against her employer, but a woman working for a private employer may not. Thus, for example, a nurse in an NHS hospital could rely on the directive in an English court but this would not be possible if she worked in a private hospital.[84]

A further problem concerns the exact scope of vertical direct effect. The first question is whether it matters in what capacity the state is acting. In the *Marshall* case the European Court held that it does not: it is not necessary that it should be exercising governmental powers (for example, collecting taxes); it is sufficient if it is entering into an ordinary private-law transaction, such as a contract of employment. In both cases 'it is necessary to prevent the state from taking advantage of its own failure to comply with Community law.'[85]

The second question is exactly what bodies are regarded as being part of the state. In the *Marshall* case, Advocate General Slynn said that 'state' must be taken broadly, as including all organs of the state. In matters of employment, it covers the employees of such organs and not just the central civil service.[86] The Court itself seemed to use the terms 'state' and 'public authority' interchangeably. In the *Marshall* case the claimant was an employee of an Area Health Authority, which the Court of Appeal had described as 'an emanation of the state'. It was clearly covered. The position is less certain in the case of local authorities and nationalized industries.[87] In *Marshall* the European Court said that it is for the national court to apply the principles laid down by the European Court to the circumstances of each case. This suggests that national law may have some role to play in deciding what bodies are covered. However, in view of the European Court's general policy that Community law must be applied uniformly in all Member States, it would not be surprising if

---

[83] Directive 76/207, OJ 1976, L 39/40.

[84] Cf. *Marshall, supra.*

[85] At paragraph 49 of the judgment.

[86] [1986] 1 CMLR at 701.

[87] In *Foster* v. *British Gas p.l.c.* [1987] ICR 52 an industrial tribunal held that a directive cannot be invoked against a nationalized industry (British Gas before privatization) and in *Rolls-Royce* v. *Doughty*, [1987] IRLR 447, the Employment Appeal Tribunal held that a directive could not be invoked against Rolls-Royce before privatization. However in *Rienks*, Case 5/83, [1983] ECR 4233, a case decided before *Marshall*, the European Court appeared to hold that a directive can be directly effective against the governing body of a profession in so far as the latter is 'entrusted with a public duty' (paragraph 10 of the judgment). The facts were, however, rather special: the public duty was the enrolment of a practitioner on a professional register, and the case was a criminal prosecution for illegal practice.

in later cases it were to lay down Community criteria for deciding which bodies are covered.

Even if the party against which the directive is invoked is not a public authority, and direct effect is therefore impossible, the directive may still have a decisive effect on the outcome of the case. This is because national courts are obliged, in so far as is possible, to interpret national legislation passed to implement the directive so as to give effect to it.[88] It is only where this is not possible, either because the implementing legislation is clear,[89] or because there is no implementing legislation, that the question of direct effect arises.

DECISIONS

The next question is whether an EEC or Euratom decision (or an individual decision under the ECSC) can have direct effect. It might be thought that this question was of only limited importance, since it was said previously that a decision was an executive act: the rights created by such an act would only rarely be invoked in the national courts. In fact, however, the Community institutions have not felt themselves precluded from adopting decisions of a legislative character: some of these are similar to directives and require Member States to take action in order to achieve a stated objective; others lay down general rules rather like regulations.

In view of the Court's rulings in the case of directives, it would have been surprising if it had not also declared that decisions can be directly effective. In fact this occurred first: the *Grad* case,[90] in which

---

[88] *Von Colson and Kamann* v. *Land Nordrhein-Westfalen*, Case 14/83, [1984] ECR 1891 (paragraph 26 of the judgment); see also Advocate General Slynn in *Marshall*,]1986] 1 CMLR at 698–699. Whether Community law obliges national courts to take the directive into account when interpreting other national legislation is more controversial: see Advocate General Slynn, *supra*; but see *Kolpinghuis Nijmegen*, Case 80/86, 8 October 1987 (not yet reported), where the European Court implied that it does (paragraph 12 of the judgment in the preliminary edition). In *Kolpinghuis Nijmegen* the European Court, however, said that the obligation to take the directive into account is always subject to the principles of legal certainty and non-retroactivity, principles which will be particularly important in criminal proceedings. In England, the House of Lords refused, in *Duke* v. *GEC Reliance*, [1988] 1 All E. R. 626, to 'distort the meaning' of a British statute in order to give effect to a directive which the statute was not passed to implement.

[89] See *Pickstone* v. *Freemans*, [1987] 3 WLR 811; [1987] 3 All E. R. 756; [1987] 2 CMLR 572, where the Court of Appeal held that it could not apply a directive to interpret a provision of United Kingdom legislation (because the legislation was unambiguous) but did apply it to interpret a provision of the EEC Treaty and then gave horizontal direct effect to the Treaty provision thus interpreted.

[90] Case 9/70, [1970] ECR 825.

the European Court decided that decisions can be directly effective, was decided some four years before the *Van Duyn* case.[91] The reasons given were the same.

Most of the comments made previously with regard to directives apply also to decisions. Of course a decision is different from a directive in that it can be addressed to an individual as well as a Member State. However, in view of what the Court said in the *Marshall* case (*supra*), it would seem that a decision can impose a directly effective obligation only on the addressee.[92] Where the decision is addressed to a Member State, it cannot be horizontally directly effective.[93]

GENERAL PRINCIPLES OF LAW

The general principles of Community law are not normally binding on the Member States and the question of their direct effect will arise only rarely. One special case in which they might be invoked against a Member State is where the national authorities rely on an 'escape clause', such as the public policy proviso under Article 48(3) EEC,[94] to derogate from a right granted by the Community. In such a case, the person affected might be entitled to challenge the action of the national authorities on the ground that it is contrary to a general principle of Community law.[95]

A second case in which a general principle of Community law might be invoked in a national court is where a party to proceedings claims that a Community act ought *not* to be applied on the ground that it is invalid. Here a general principle of law may furnish the ground of invalidity. In such a case, however, the national court will not decide the issue: it will refer the matter to the European Court for a ruling.[96] General principles of law will, therefore, be directly effective only in the very limited sense indicated by these two examples. They may of course affect the interpretation of some other provision which is itself directly effective, for example a provision in a regulation.

[91] See pp. 201–3, above.
[92] According to Art. 189 EEC, a decision is binding only on the person (or persons) to whom it is addressed.
[93] But see *per* Advocate General Reischl in *Unil-It*, Case 30/75, [1975] ECR 1419 at 1434.
[94] See above, pp. 192–3.
[95] See p. 139, above.
[96] See Chapter 9, especially pp. 266–7.

AGREEMENTS WITH THIRD COUNTRIES

Agreements with non-member States are obviously in a different category from the Community Treaties and Community legislation. In particular, it might be thought that international law should determine whether they were directly effective and that there would be a lack of balance and reciprocity if they were directly effective in the Community countries but not in the other countries. This argument appears originally to have had some influence,[97] but it was subsequently rejected by the European Court.[98] The position now is that international agreements with non-member States – whether they are intended to establish a special regime giving greater rights to the third country than to the Community,[99] or are reciprocal agreements of the normal type[100] – can be directly effective in the courts of the Member States of the Community, irrespective of whether they are directly effective in the non-member State. As far as one can tell, the test is the same as for the Community Treaties.[101]

The leading case is *Kupferberg*,[102] where it was argued that a German tax on wine could not apply to imports from Portugal (before Portugal joined the Community) because it conflicted with a provision in the Free Trade Agreement between the Community and Portugal. This raised the question whether the relevant provision of the Free Trade Agreement was directly effective in Germany. The European Court held that this question could not be left to the national law of each Member State because a uniform solution throughout the Community was desirable. So Community law had to

---

[97] *Bresciani*, Case 87/75, [1976] ECR 129 at 148–149 (*per* Advocate General Trabucchi) and paragraph 22 of the judgment; *Polydor*, Case 270/80, [1982] ECR 329 at 355 (per Advocate General Rozès).

[98] *Kupferberg* (discussed below); but see note 106, below.

[99] *Bresciani* (above).

[100] *Kupferberg* (discussed below).

[101] It appears to make no difference whether the agreement is concluded (on the Community side) by the Community alone, as was the case in *Kupferberg* (below), or by the Community and the Member States acting together (mixed agreement), as was the case in *Bresciani* (above), though in the latter case it could be argued that national law should determine the effect of those parts of the agreement that are outside the treaty-making competence of the Community. With regard to agreements concluded by the Member States alone which become binding on the Community by succession (such as the GATT), the European Court appears to accept the possibility of direct effect in principle, though in practice it has always ruled against it: see *International Fruit Company*, Cases 21–24/72, [1972] ECR 1219; *Schlüter*, Case 9/73, [1973] ECR 1135; *SPI*, Cases 267–9/81, [1983] ECR 801.

[102] Case 104/81, [1982] ECR 3641.

214 The Foundations of European Community Law

decide,[103] and the Court held, after examining the provision, that it was directly effective. The fact that it was probably not directly effective in Portugal was regarded as irrelevant.[104]

The result is that non-Community businessmen selling in the Community could have a more effective means of enforcing the agreement than Community businessmen exporting to the foreign country. However, the European Court has also made clear that provisions in agreements with non-member States are not to be given the same wide and policy-oriented interpretation as is given to the Community Treaties. This is so even if, as is often the case, the agreement reproduces almost exactly the wording of a provision in the EEC Treaty.[105]

The reason why the European Court has adopted this strategy appears to be as follows. When the Community enters into an agreement with a non-member State, it is under an obligation to ensure that the agreement is carried out. Frequently, however, the implementation of the agreement on the Community side will depend on the Member States. The Community could, therefore, be embarrassed in its relations with the non-member State, if the Member States failed to give effect to the agreement.

Agreements between the Community and a non-member State are, of course, binding on the Member States[106] and an action under Article 169 EEC[107] could no doubt be brought against any Member State which failed to abide by it. But this is a cumbersome remedy. By making such agreements directly effective, the European Court has established an easy means of enforcement. At the same time, by refusing to apply its normal method of interpretation to such agreements, it has ensured that non-Community countries will not be given too great an advantage.

---

[103] But the European Court said, at paragraph 17 of its judgment, that if the agreement itself provides whether or not it is to be directly effective, that will be decisive. Such provisions are not, however, normal and there was no such provision in the agreement with Portugal. In the absence of such a provision, the European Court will decide the question according to its own criteria.

[104] See paragraph 18 of the judgment.

[105] *Polydor*, Case 270/80, [1982] ECR 329; *Kupferberg* (above) at paragraphs 28–31 of the judgment. This means that the same words can mean one thing in the EEC Treaty and another in an agreement with a third country.

[106] Art. 228(2) EEC.

[107] See Chapter 10, below.

THE SUPREMACY OF COMMUNITY LAW AND THE
RESTRICTION OF NATIONAL POWERS

It is a basic rule of Community law that a directly effective provision of Community law always prevails over a provision of national law. This rule, which is not found in any of the Treaties but has been proclaimed with great emphasis by the Court, applies irrespective of the nature of the Community provision (constitutive Treaty, Community act or agreement with a non-member State) or that of the national provision (constitution, statute or subordinate legislation); it also applies irrespective of whether the Community provision came before, or after, the national provision: in all cases the national provision must give way to Community law.[108]

The second *Simmenthal* case[109] provides a good example. The facts were simple: Simmenthal imported some beef from France into Italy and was made to pay a fee for a public health inspection when the meat crossed the frontier. This was laid down by an Italian law passed in 1970; it was, however, contrary to the EEC Treaty and two Community regulations passed in 1964 and 1968 respectively. The case began in an Italian court where two points were raised by the Italian authorities: first, that the Italian law must prevail because it was passed *after* the two Community regulations; and, secondly, that even if the Italian law conflicted with Italy's treaty obligations, it had to be applied by the Italian courts until such time as it had been declared unconstitutional by the Italian Constitutional Court. This latter contention was based on a principle of Italian constitutional law according to which questions concerning the constitutionality of Italian laws had to be determined by the Constitutional Court. A reference was made to the European Court to obtain a ruling on these issues.

The European Court held that it was the duty of a national court to give full effect to the Community provisions and not to apply any conflicting provision of national legislation, even if it had been adopted subsequently. It also held that it should not wait for the national law to be set aside either by a constitutional court or by the legislature. The key passages in the judgment deserve to be quoted in full:[110]

---

[108] For a succinct survey of the relevant case law, see the opinion of Advocate General Reischl in the *Simmenthal* case, Case 106/77, [1978] ECR 629 at 651–2.

[109] Above, note 108.

[110] Paragraphs 17 and 18 of the judgment.

Furthermore, in accordance with the principle of the precedence of Community law, the relationship between provisions of the Treaty and directly applicable measures of the institutions on the one hand and the national law of the Member States on the other is such that those provisions and measures not only by their entry into force render automatically inapplicable any conflicting provision of current national law but – in so far as they are an integral part of, and take precedence in, the legal order applicable in the territory of each of the Member States – also preclude the valid adoption of new national legislative measures to the extent to which they would be incompatible with Community provisions.

Indeed any recognition that national legislative measures which encroach upon the field within which the Community exercises its legislative power or which are otherwise incompatible with the provisions of Community law had any legal effect would amount to a corresponding denial of the effectiveness of obligations undertaken unconditionally and irrevocably by Member States pursuant to the Treaty and would thus imperil the very foundations of the Community.

Three points about this should be noted: the Court's statement is limited to Treaty provisions and 'directly applicable measures of the institutions'; secondly, it does not state that conflicting national provisions are void, but merely that they are 'inapplicable'; and, thirdly, the second paragraph is concerned not only with national legislation which conflicts directly with a Community provision, but also with national laws which 'encroach upon the field within which the Community exercises its legislative power'.

As regards the first point, it is obvious that a Community provision will prevail over national legislation only if the Community provision is directly effective. The use by the Court of the term 'directly applicable' does not indicate that the principle of supremacy is limited to regulations: to the extent that they are directly effective, directives and decisions will also prevail over inconsistent national legislation. The *Ratti*[111] and *Marshall*[112] cases are both examples of the supremacy of directives over national legislation – provided the right contained in the directive is invoked against the state. It is equally clear from the cases discussed above,[113] that a directly effective provision in an international agreement will prevail over inconsistent national legislation.

The significance of the second point mentioned above is that there is, according to the European Court, a positive obligation on

---

[111] Case 148/78, [1979] ECR 1629, discussed above at pp. 204–5.

[112] Case 152/84, [1986] 1 CMLR 688, discussed above at pp. 208–11.

[113] At pp. 213–14; see, for example, *Bresciani*, Case 87/75, [1976] ECR 129.

Member States to repeal conflicting national legislation, even though it is inapplicable. This was laid down in the *French Merchant Seamen* case,[114] which concerned a French law which provided that a certain proportion of the crew on French merchant ships had to be of French nationality. This was plainly in conflict with Community law and enforcement proceedings under Article 169 EEC were brought against France. The French Government argued that the French law was not in fact applied and that, since under Community law it was inapplicable, the continued existence of the law did not constitute a violation of the Treaty. The European Court held, however, that the failure to repeal the law created 'an ambiguous state of affairs' which would make Community seamen uncertain 'as to the possibilities available to them of relying on Community law'.[115] Judgment was therefore given against France.

The discussion so far has been concerned with the situation where there is a direct conflict between Community and national law; however, the significance of the third point is that the powers of Member States can be limited even where the conflict is only indirect or potential. It has already been pointed out that in certain cases the Member States have lost the power to enter into agreements with third countries:[116] this loss of jurisdiction applies even where there is no direct conflict with Community measures. In other situations the restriction of national powers appears to be less clear-cut, though it is nevertheless real: in the field of agriculture, if the Community has introduced a common organization of the market for a given product, the Member States are precluded from adopting any measure which 'might undermine or create exceptions to it'.[117] This, too applies even in the absence of a direct conflict.

[114] *Commission* v. *France*, Case 167/73, [1974] ECR 359.

[115] See paragraph 41 of the judgment.

[116] See Chapter 6.

[117] See *Pigs Marketing Board* v. *Redmond*, Case 83/78, [1978] ECR 2347 at paragraph 56 of the judgment. For a detailed discussion of the cases in this area, see Baumann, 'Common Organizations of the Market and National Law', (1977) 14 C.M.L. Rev. 303 and Usher, 'The Effects of Common Organizations and Policies on the Powers of a Member State', (1977) 2 E.L. Rev. 428.

FURTHER READING

Schermers, paragraphs 239–263.

Bebr, 'Agreements Concluded by the Community and Their Possible Direct Effect: From International Fruit Company to Kupferberg', (1983) 20 C.M.L. Rev. 35.

Dashwood, 'The Principle of Direct Effect in European Community Law', (1978) 16 Journal of Common Market Studies 229.

Green, 'Directives, Equity and the Protection of Individual Rights', (1984) 9 E.L. Rev. 295.

Pescatore, 'The Doctrine of "Direct Effect": An Infant Disease in Community Law', (1983) 8 E.L. Rev. 155.

Steiner, 'Direct Applicability in EEC Law – A Chameleon Concept', (1982) 98 LQR 229.

Steiner, 'How to Make the Action Suit the Case: Domestic Remedies for Breach of EEC Law', (1987) 12 E.L. Rev. 102.

8

THE NATIONAL REACTION

In the previous chapter the relationship between Community law and national law was discussed from the Community side: in this chapter the same relationship will be considered from the national point of view. What was said in the previous chapter shows that Community law makes large claims: the European Court claims for itself exclusive jurisdiction to decide all questions concerning the application of Community law in the national courts and the resolution of conflicts between Community law and national law. It even claims the power to limit the scope of national law where there is no direct conflict with Community law. The principles adopted by the European Court naturally favour Community law: absolute supremacy over national law is required. And in order to achieve the greatest possible effectiveness for Community law, the European Court has been prepared to lay down rules – for example, regarding directives – which cannot have been within the contemplation of the authors of the Treaties. How have the Member States reacted to this?

THE CONSTITUTIONAL BASIS OF COMMUNITY SUPREMACY

When a country joins the Community it is obliged to reconcile its constitution with Community membership. In particular, it must make provision for the application of Community law within its territory and for the supremacy of Community law over national law. There are basically two ways in which this can be done. Those countries which follow the monist conception of international law[1] have a ready-made mechanism for the application of the Community Treaties, since they are prepared, in principle, to give direct effect to all treaties with suitable provisions. In cases of conflict with national law, monist countries will usually recognize the supremacy of treaty provisions.

[1] See pp. 186–7, above.

219

This state of affairs thus affords the possibility of accommodating Community law within the pre-existing constitutional structure of the country concerned without any constitutional amendments being necessary. Countries falling into this group include France and the Netherlands, both of which have express provision in their constitutions for the direct effect and supremacy of international treaties.[2]

The main disadvantages of this approach are, first, that it is based on the assumption that Community law is a species of international law, a view which fails to recognize its special characteristics, and, secondly, that it operates less satisfactorily in the case of Community legislation – though this can be dealt with on the basis that giving effect to a treaty necessarily entails applying measures made under the treaty.

The second possibility is for the Member State to transfer powers to the Community. This route to Community supremacy can be adopted even by countries which apply the dualist approach to international law:[3] express provision for the transfer of powers to international organizations is found in Article 24(1) of the German Constitution and Article 20 of the Danish Constitution. There is a similar provision in Article 67 of the Dutch Constitution: the Netherlands can therefore apply the Treaties on the basis of the monist theory and give effect to Community legislation under the terms of Article 67. In Italy, the constitutional position appears at first sight to be less clear-cut, but Article 11 of the Constitution, which authorizes such limitations of sovereignty as may be necessary to ensure peace and justice between nations, has been pressed into service to provide the constitutional foundation for Italian membership of the Community.[4] When Ireland joined the Community, the Constitution was specially amended to provide that nothing in it would prevent Community measures from having the force of law in Ireland.[5] Not being in a position to adopt a constitutional amendment, the United Kingdom passed a simple Act of Parliament, the European Communities Act, which made provision for the direct effect and supremacy of Community law. In neither of these two latter cases is express reference made to a transfer of powers, but something of this nature must have resulted.

---

[2]   Art. 55 of the French Constitution and Art. 66 of the Netherlands Constitution.

[3]   For the meaning of dualism, see pp. 186–7, above.

[4]   See the *Frontini* case, *Corte Constituzionale*, 27 December 1973, [1974] 2 C M L R 372, at 384–5 (paragraph 7 of the judgment).

[5]   Third Amendment to the Constitution. A further amendment was required in 1987 to enable Ireland to ratify the Single European Act.

There is, however, a certain ambiguity in some of these provisions, as a clear distinction is not always made between a mere delegation of power, which would remain subject to the ultimate control of the delegating authority, and a true transfer of sovereignty, which, though limited as regards its area of operation, would be absolute within that area. According to the European Court, only the latter fully complies with the requirements of membership.[6]

SOME SPECIAL PROBLEMS

With these general considerations in mind, we can now turn to some of the special problems of individual countries. The discussion that follows will focus on only the most important issues.

Belgium: A Triumph for Community Law

The particular interest of Belgium lies in the fact that its constitution contained no statement that international treaties have direct effect and override national law, and it was originally unclear whether it adopted the monist or dualist theory of international law. The Belgian courts therefore had to face the challenge of Community law without the support of an appropriate constitutional provision.

The test came in *Minister for Economic Affairs* v. *Fromagerie Franco-Suisse 'Le Ski'*.[7] A number of royal decrees had imposed import duties on dairy products which the respondent had been obliged to pay. However, in enforcement proceedings brought by the Commission under Article 169 EEC against Belgium and Luxembourg, the European Court had declared these duties to be contrary to the EEC Treaty.[8] They were then abolished, but the Belgian Parliament passed a statute providing that money already paid could not be recovered. The respondent objected to this and instituted legal proceedings in the Belgian courts to recover the duties it had paid. It won a judgment in its favour in the Brussels *Cour d'Appel* and the Minister appealed to the *Cour de Cassation*, the highest civil court in the country.

Two main arguments were put forward by the Minister. First, he

---

[6] See *Van Gend en Loos*, Case 26/62, [1963] ECR 1 at 12 and *Costa* v. *ENEL*, Case 6/64, [1964] ECR 585 at 593–4.

[7] *Cour de Cassation*, Belgium, 21 May 1971, [1972] CMLR 330.

[8] *Commission* v. *Luxembourg and Belgium*, Cases 90, 91/63, [1964] ECR 625.

referred to the fact that when Belgium joined the EEC, a statute was passed by the Belgian Parliament ratifying the Treaty. The effect of the Treaty in Belgium was, he argued, dependent on that statute: since the statute prohibiting recovery of the money was passed subsequent to it, the latter must prevail over the former and, therefore, over the Treaty as well: a later law always prevails over an earlier one.

The second argument put forward was that the judgment of the *Cour d'Appel* had violated a provision of the Belgian Constitution according to which only the Belgian Parliament may determine the constitutionality of a statute: the courts have no right to annul any Act of Parliament. It will be noticed that both these arguments are very pertinent to the British situation.

The *Cour de Cassation* dismissed the appeal and upheld the right of the respondent to reclaim the money. It met the first argument by declaring that when the Belgian Parliament passes a statute to ratify a treaty, that statute is merely the constitutionally prescribed method of giving assent to a treaty entered into by the Crown: the treaty does not take effect in Belgian law as part of the statute, but as a treaty. In other words, the Court declared in this case that Belgium was a monist country. Consequently, the conflict was not between two statutes, but between two instruments of a fundamentally different nature: a treaty and a statute. The Court then continued:[9]

> The rule that a statute repeals a previous statute in so far as there is a conflict between the two, does not apply in the case of a conflict between a treaty and a statute.
>
> In the event of a conflict between a norm of domestic law and a norm of international law which produces direct effects in the internal legal system, the rule established by the treaty shall prevail. The primacy of the treaty results from the very nature of international treaty law.
>
> This is *a fortiori* the case when a conflict exists, as in the present case, between a norm of internal law and a norm of Community law.
>
> The reason is that the treaties which have created Community law have instituted a new legal system in whose favour the member-States have restricted the exercise of their sovereign powers in the areas determined by those treaties.

It concluded that since the provision of Community law violated by the royal decrees, Article 12 EEC, was directly effective, it was the duty of the courts to uphold it, even when it was in conflict with a statute.

---

[9] [1972] CMLR at 373.

The second argument of the Minister was met by stating that the *Cour d'Appel* had not annulled the law prohibiting recovery but had merely declared its operation suspended to the extent of the conflict. This could be regarded as a distinction without any real difference: but once the monist position is accepted, it necessarily follows that the courts must have the power to disregard national legislation when it conflicts with a directly effective treaty provision. The truly innovative part of the judgment, therefore, was the acceptance of the monist doctrine as a part of Belgian law.

This judgment was very satisfactory from the point of view of Community law. It will not, however, be of much assistance to the British courts when they have to face a similar problem, since it is quite firmly established that the United Kingdom is a dualist country: when the British Parliament passes a statute to give effect to a treaty, the courts apply the treaty only because they are required to do so by the statute: in the United Kingdom the conflict *is* between two statutes.

Constitutional Problems in Germany and Italy

Germany and Italy, the two former Axis Powers, emerged from defeat in World War II with constitutions giving significantly more protection to fundamental human rights than those of the other Member States. This has created special problems with regard to Community law: can Community measures override national constitutional provisions and take effect in Germany and Italy even if they are contrary to fundamental human rights as understood in those countries?

In Germany, the best known case is the decision of the Constitutional Court in *Internationale Handelsgesellschaft* v. *EVGF*.[10] The background to this case was considered in Chapter 5:[11] it will be remembered that the plaintiff had asked a German administrative court to annul a decision of the EVGF based on two Community regulations; it argued that the regulations ought not to be applied in Germany as they were contrary to the fundamental human rights provisions of the German Constitution. The administrative court first made a reference to the European Court, which ruled that the validity of Community provisions should be determined according to Community law, not national constitutional law, and that the provi-

[10] *Bundesverfassungsgericht*, 29 May 1974, [1974] 2 CMLR 540.
[11] At pp. 132–4.

sions in question did not violate the Community concept of human rights.[12]

This was not, however, the end of the matter: the administrative court next made a reference to the Federal Constitutional Court (*Bundesverfassungsgericht*) for a ruling as to whether the regulations were contrary to the fundamental human rights provisions of the German Constitution. Before considering this question, the Constitutional Court had to decide whether the reference was admissible: in other words, whether Community measures are subject to the German Constitution.

The first question considered by the Constitutional Court was the relationship between German constitutional law and Community law. It took the view that Community law 'is neither a component part of the national legal system nor international law, but forms an independent system of law flowing from an autonomous legal source'[13] and concluded from this that the two legal systems were independent of each other.

The Constitutional Court next pointed out that the Community lacked a directly elected parliament[14] to which the Community organs with legislative powers were responsible on a political level and that it also lacked a 'codified catalogue of fundamental rights' comparable to that in the German Constitution. It concluded that until such time as Community protection for fundamental rights measured up to that in the German Constitution, Community measures would be subject to the fundamental rights provisions of the German Constitution.

Having thus decided the question of its own jurisdiction, the Constitutional Court next considered the substantive issue: it ruled that the Community measures in issue were not contrary to the German Constitution.

This case therefore represented a potential, rather than an actual, rebellion. In fact the Constitutional Court never found any Community measure to be contrary to the German Constitution and, after hinting at a new approach in 1979,[15] it finally ruled in 1986 that the protection of human rights in the Community had developed sufficiently to meet the requirements of the German Constitution. This

---

[12]   Case 11/70, [1970] ECR 1125.

[13]   [1974] 2 CMLR at 549 (paragraph 19 of the judgment).

[14]   At the time when the case was decided the European Parliament was not directly elected.

[15]   *Steinike & Weinlig*, 25 July 1979, [1980] 2 CMLR 531 at 537 (paragraph 12).

occurred in the *Wünsche Handelsgesellschaft* case,[16] where the Constitutional Court stated that, provided the general level of protection of human rights under Community law remained adequate by German standards, it would no longer entertain proceedings to test Community measures against the human rights provisions of the *Grundgesetz*. This particular story thus has a happy ending; in fact, citizens of the Community can be grateful to the Constitutional Court because it was its decision in the *Internationale Handelsgesellschaft* case that provided the initial impetus for the development of the Community doctrine of human rights.

Problems have also been caused by the refusal of the Federal Tax Court (*Bundesfinanzhof*) to accept the direct effect of directives. It should be explained that in Germany there are no less than five separate court systems: in addition to the ordinary courts, there are specialized courts dealing with tax, labour, social security and administrative matters. Each of these court systems is headed by a federal supreme court, the Federal Tax Court being at the top of the tax court system. Each system is independent of the others, so that the Federal Tax Court is not bound by the rulings of, for example, the Federal Administrative Court and *vice versa*. On constitutional matters, however, all courts are subject to the rulings of the Federal Constitutional Court.

The problem regarding the direct effect of directives arose when Germany was tardy in implementing a Community directive dealing with VAT. Certain provisions of this directive gave tax exemptions which were not recognised by the relevant German law. Could a taxpayer claim an exemption on the basis of the directive, even though it conflicted with German legislation?[17] In two cases, decided in 1981[18] and 1985[19] respectively, the Federal Tax Court held that this was not possible. The two cases were similar, but the second was more interesting since the judgment of the Federal Tax Court directly contradicted a ruling given by the European Court at an earlier stage of the proceedings in the case.[20] This was the *Kloppenburg* case, in

---

[16] Decision of 22 October 1986, [1987] 3 CMLR 225. The most important developments, in the eyes of the Constitutional Court, were the further elaboration by the European Court of its doctrine of fundamental rights, especially the significance now attached to the constitutions of the Member States, and the Joint Declaration of 5 April 1977 of the Parliament, the Council and the Commission.

[17] Since the defendant was the state, the issue was one of vertical direct effect only.

[18] *Bundesfinanzhof*, decision of 16 July 1981, [1982] 1 CMLR 527.

[19] *Bundesfinanzhof*, decision of 25 April 1985 (VR 123/84), *Entscheidungen des Bundesfinanzhofes* Vol. 143, p. 383 (noted by Crossland, (1986) 11 E.L. Rev. 473 at 476–479.)

[20] *Kloppenburg*, Case 70/83, [1984] ECR 1075.

which a lower tax court, the *Niedersächisches Finanzgericht*, had referred the question to the European Court and been told that the relevant provision of the directive was directly effective. The lower tax court then ruled in favour of the taxpayer. The tax authorities appealed and the Federal Tax Court reversed the lower court's judgment. Its reasoning started from the premiss that Community law could have effect in Germany only to the extent that Germany had transferred legislative powers to the Community. This transfer, permitted by Article 24(1) of the German Constitution, was limited by the terms of the EEC Treaty, which in the case of tax matters gave the Community the power to adopt only directives. According to Article 189 EEC, directives leave the Member States free to choose the form and methods of giving effect to them; so national implementing legislation is necessary for the provisions of a directive to have the force of law in the Member States. From this the Federal Tax Court concluded that directives can never have direct effect, an argument not lacking in legal logic. It supported this conclusion with references to both the *travaux préparatoires* to the EEC Treaty (in which the German Government had said that a directive cannot directly bind an individual in the absence of national legislation) and the decision of the French *Conseil d'Etat* in the *Cohn-Bendit* case (discussed below[21]). The Federal Tax Court did not allow itself to be deflected by the European Court's ruling: it said that the latter's jurisdiction under Article 177 was limited to Community law and that it did not have the power to determine which law should be applied by national courts. It also stated that the preliminary reference procedure could not be used to extend the legislative jurisdiction of the Community beyond that laid down in the Treaties.

The matter did not rest there, however, because the taxpayer, Ms Kloppenburg, then brought proceedings before the Federal Constitutional Court, which ruled that the Federal Tax Court had acted unconstitutionally: it should either have followed the ruling of the European Court or made a second reference. The third paragraph of Article 177 EEC states that a court 'against whose decisions there is no judicial remedy' is obliged to make a reference when its judgment depends on a question of Community law. The Federal Tax Court was such a court; therefore its failure to make the reference (or follow the ruling in the earlier reference) was a violation of Article 177. The reason why this violation of the EEC Treaty also constituted a

---

[21] At pp. 230–2.

violation of the German Constitution was that Article 101(1) of the latter guarantees that no one shall be deprived of his 'lawful judge'. This provision, which protects the right of the citizen to have his case heard by the lawfully constituted court having jurisdiction in the matter, was intended to prevent the establishment of special courts, which might be less impartial than the ordinary courts. The Constitutional Court had already held in the *Wünsche Handelsgesellschaft* case (*supra*) that the European Court is a 'lawful judge' in terms of Article 101(1). By deliberately refusing to make a reference to the European Court, the Federal Tax Court had deprived Ms Kloppenburg of her 'lawful judge'. Its judgment was therefore annulled.[22] Thanks to these two decisions of the Federal Constitutional Court, it now seems that the German courts have fallen into line with the rulings of the European Court.

Similar problems have arisen in Italy. In the *Frontini* case,[23] a cheese importer objected to paying a levy imposed by a Community regulation: he argued that Article 23 of the Italian Constitution, which lays down that taxes can be imposed only by, or under, a statute, precluded the application of the regulation in Italy. As the direct effect of regulations is provided for in Article 189 EEC, he claimed that the Treaty itself was incompatible with the Constitution and therefore the Italian statute providing for Italian membership of the Community was unconstitutional. A reference was made to the Italian Constitutional Court for a decision on this point.

Like the *Bundesverfassungsgericht*, the Italian Constitutional Court took the view that Community law is separate from both international law and the internal law of the Member States: it stated that Community law and national law are 'autonomous and distinct legal systems, albeit co-ordinated in accordance with the division of power laid down and guaranteed by the Treaty'. It went on to say that the provisions of the Italian Constitution apply solely to the legislative activities of the organs of the Italian State and do not apply to legislation enacted by Community institutions: these are subject to the Treaty, the constitution of the Community. Consequently the provisions of Article 23 of the Italian Constitution are inapplicable to Community measures.

The Italian Constitutional Court also considered the question of a possible conflict between Community law and fundamental human

---

[22] *Bundesverfassungsgericht*, decision of 8 April 1987 (2 BvR 687/85), [1987] Recht der Internationalen Wirtschaft 878.

[23] *Corte Constituzionale*, 27 December 1973, [1974] 2 CMLR 372.

rights. It stated – perhaps somewhat naively – that the Community's legislative power was limited to the economic field and did not apply in the civil, 'ethico-social' or political fields. Within the economic area, said the Constitutional Court, the European Court's power of judicial review under Articles 173 and 177 (1)(*b*) EEC gives ample protection to individual rights. The Constitutional Court went on to say that when the Member States, all of which adhere to the rule of law and fundamental human rights, transferred powers to the Community, they could not have intended to confer on the Community the power to enact measures violating human rights. Consequently, if ever the Treaty were interpreted in such a way as to permit the adoption of measures which violated fundamental human rights, the Constitutional Court would have to consider whether the Treaty itself was compatible with those rights: this would presumably mean that Italy's continuing membership of the Community would be called into question. However, the Italian Court stated that it would not review individual Community measures to ascertain whether they violated human rights.[24]

France: Acceptance and Rebellion

In France, statutes (*lois*) cannot be reviewed by the courts after promulgation in order to determine their constitutionality;[25] so the problems found in Germany and Italy cannot arise. Moreover, since it is provided in Article 55 of the French Constitution that international treaties have authority superior to that of any national law, one might have assumed that Community law was in a secure position in France. Unfortunately, however, this is not entirely true.

It should be explained at the outset that there are two separate court systems in France: the ordinary (judicial) courts, which deal with civil and criminal matters, and the administrative courts, which hear cases where action on the part of the administration is subject to challenge.[26] The latter may also annul legislative measures enacted

---

[24] For subsequent developments, in which the Constitutional Court further strengthened the position of Community law in Italy, see Petriccione, 'Italy: Supremacy of Community Law over National Law', (1986) 11 E.L. Rev. 320; see also Barav, 'Cour constitutionelle italienne et droit communautaire: le fantôme de Simmenthal', [1985] RTDE 313.

[25] Draft legislation may, however, be reviewed by the *Conseil Constitutionnel* before enactment to determine whether it is in accordance with the Constitution.

[26] The division of jurisdiction between the two sets of courts is actually much more complicated than this. Conflicts of jurisdiction are settled by the *Tribunal des Conflits*, which is composed of an equal number of judges from the *Cour de Cassation* and the *Conseil d'État*; the Minister of Justice, who may preside, has a casting vote.

by the executive. The highest court in the judicial order is the *Cour de Cassation*; while the *Conseil d'État* is the supreme administrative court. These two court systems have very different traditions and the most notable feature of the French reaction to Community law is the difference in attitude displayed by the judicial and administrative courts, especially by the *Cour de Cassation* and the *Conseil d'État*: while the former has sought ways of resolving the legal problems raised by French membership of the Community, the latter appears unwilling to make any compromise.

What obstacles to the application of Community law exist in France? The most important is the traditional reluctance of all French courts to question the validity of a statute and of the judicial courts to query actions of the administration, whether legislative or executive. In particular, this makes it difficult for them to refuse to apply a French law when it conflicts with Community law. A second obstacle is that Article 55 of the Constitution makes the supremacy of treaties over national legislation subject to a proviso: the treaty in question must be applied by the other party. This could make the application of Community law in France contingent on its application in other Member States.

The leading case in the *Cour de Cassation* is *Directeur Général des Douanes* v. *Société Vabre & Société Weigel*,[27] decided in 1975. The facts of the case were that Vabre had imported soluble coffee extract into France from Holland and was required to pay customs duties under a French statute passed in 1966. Since coffee extract produced in France was subject to tax at a lower rate, it claimed that it had been discriminated against contrary to Article 95 EEC. Vabre, and its agent Weigel, claimed repayment of the duties, and damages: the Paris *Cour d'Appel* upheld their claim on the ground that the EEC Treaty prevailed even over a subsequent statute;[28] a further appeal was then taken to the *Cour de Cassation*.

It was argued by the Director-General of Customs that the Paris *Cour d'Appel* had arrogated to itself the right to determine the constitutionality of a statute and this it could not do. He also pointed out that under Article 55 of the French Constitution a treaty is applicable in France only if the other country also applies it: no attempt had been made to ascertain whether the Netherlands, the country from which the coffee extract had been imported, met this condition of reciprocity. He therefore concluded that Article 55 could

---

[27] *Cour de Cassation*, 24 May 1975, [1975] 2 CMLR 336.
[28] 7 July 1973, ibid.

not be invoked to provide a basis for the application of the EEC Treaty in the case.

The *Cour de Cassation* rejected these arguments and upheld the judgment of the Paris *Cour d'Appel*. In reply to the first argument of the Director-General, the *Cour de Cassation* stated that the Community Treaties had created a separate legal order which was binding on the national courts. The second argument was rejected on the ground that Article 170 EEC grants each Member State the right to bring legal proceedings in the European Court against any other Member State which fails to apply the Treaty. Since there is thus a legal procedure to remedy any lack of reciprocity, this could not constitute a ground for not applying the Treaty.

This judgment consituted an important triumph for Community law. It should also be mentioned that the case was heard by a 'mixed chamber' of the Court, which means that the decision has especial authority in the French judicial court system.[29] Shortly afterwards, moreover, the *Cour de Cassation* held in the case of *Von Kempis* v. *Geldof*[30] that the Treaty also prevails over earlier French legislation. These rulings, therefore, firmly establish the supremacy of Community law as far as the judicial courts of France are concerned.

In the administrative courts, on the other hand, the story is rather different. Over a considerable period the *Conseil d'État* and the *tribunaux administratifs* showed themselves at best half-hearted in their loyalty towards the Community and at times downright rebellious. Then, in the *Semoules* case,[31] the *Conseil* refused to accept the supremacy of a Community regulation over a French statute passed subsequent to the regulation, a position maintained in a later case dealing with elections to the European Parliament.[32]

The *Cohn-Bendit* case[33] provides a good example of the *Conseil*

---

[29] The *Cour de Cassation* is divided into a number of chambers and cases are normally allocated to one or other of these. Specially important cases are, however, heard by a mixed chamber: this is presided over by the First President and normally includes the Presidents of several other chambers.

[30] *Cour de Cassation*, 15 December 1975, [1976] 2 CMLR 152.

[31] *Conseil d'État*, 1 March 1968, [1970] CMLR 395. In this case the Conseil appeared to accept the view of the *Commissaire du Gouvernement* (analogous to an advocate general in the European Court) that French courts cannot refuse to apply a statute because it conflicts with a treaty. For a fuller discussion of the attitude of the French administrative courts towards Community law at this time, see Weiss, 'Self-Executing Treaties and Directly Applicable EEC Law in French Courts', 1979/1 LIEI 51 at 69–71 and 73–4.

[32] *Conseil d'État*, 22 October 1979, [1980] AJDA 39, a case concerning a conflict between the EEC Treaty and a subsequent French statute. (The position would probably be different in the case of an *earlier* statute.)

[33] *Conseil d'État*, 22 December 1978, Dalloz, 1979, p. 155.

d'État's attitude towards Community law. Daniel Cohn-Bendit, sometimes referred to in the press as 'Danny the Red', was a German citizen, born and permanently resident in France. He was a student of sociology at Paris-Nanterre University and became one of the leaders of the student revolt of May 1968. On 24 May 1968, the French Minister of the Interior (equivalent to the Home Secretary) issued a deportation order against him on the ground that his presence in France was contrary to the public good (*ordre public*). He therefore had to leave. Some years later, in 1975, Cohn-Bendit wanted to return to France in order to take up an offer of employment which had been made to him. He requested the Minister to rescind the deportation order but this was refused, without any proper reason being given, by a decision of 2 February 1976.

Cohn-Bendit challenged this refusal in proceedings brought before the Paris *Tribunal Administratif*: he argued that the Minister's refusal was contrary to Article 48 EEC and infringed, in particular, Article 6 of Directive 64/221.[34] Article 48 gives Community citizens a right to enter another Community country in order to take employment but makes this right subject to limitations 'justified on grounds of public policy, public security or public health'. Directive 64/221, however, gives Community citizens various rights when the public policy proviso is invoked; one of these, laid down in Article 6, states that the immigrant must be given the reasons for the decision, unless this would be contrary to the interests of state security. The *Tribunal Administratif* made a reference to the European Court for the interpretation of these provisions and stayed the proceedings until an answer was received.

By making this order, the *Tribunal Administratif* implicitly recognized that the Directive could be invoked by Cohn-Bendit. The Minister refused to accept this and appealed to the *Conseil d'État* against the order of reference. Shortly before judgment was given, however, the Minister revoked the deportation order. One might have thought that this is would have been the end of the matter, but the *Conseil d'État* went ahead and delivered a very surprising judgment: it allowed the appeal on the ground that, under the EEC Treaty, directives cannot be invoked by individuals in the national courts in order to challenge an individual administrative decision; Cohn-Bendit could not, therefore, invoke Directive 64/221 before the court. The interpretation of the Directive was consequently irrelevant to the proceedings.

---

[34] OJ (English Edition) 1963/64, p. 117.

It is, of course, true that there are good reasons for thinking that the authors of the Treaty did not intend directives to have direct effect: in this respect, there is a great deal to be said in favour of the *Conseil d'État's* interpretation of the Treaty. However, the doctrine of the direct effect of directives had been firmly established by the date of the *Cohn-Bendit* judgment[35] and the *Conseil* was perfectly well aware of it. This judgment was a clear and deliberate act of defiance: by rejecting the authority of the European Court – even where it could be said to have gone beyond the Treaty – the *Conseil d'État* struck a blow at the foundations of the Community.

The result of the *Cohn-Bendit* case is that the direct effect of directives is not recognized by the administrative courts in France.[36] This means that an individual administrative act (a decision by an administrative authority dealing with a particular case) cannot be challenged on the ground that it is contrary to a directive. The *Conseil d'État* has, however, held that legislation adopted by the French Executive (but not statutes passed by the French Legislature) will be annulled if it conflicts with the result to be achieved under a directive. This follows from the *Conseil d'État's* interpretation of Article 189 EEC. It considers that a directive cannot be directly effective since it cannot confer rights directly on individuals; but since it is binding on the Member States as to the result to be achieved, it can constitute the foundation for an action to annul a decree or other administrative measure of a legislative nature.[37] Thus in one case a ministerial order permitting the hunting of turtle doves was annulled because it conflicted with the objective of a directive on the protection of birds.[38]

The contrast in attitudes between the *Conseil d'État* and the *Cour de*

---

[35] It had also been clearly laid down that Directive 64/221 was directly effective: see, for example, *Van Duyn* v. *Home Office*, Case 41/74, [1974] ECR 1337; *Bonsignore*, Case 67/74, [1975] ECR 297; *Rutili*, Case 36/75, [1975] ECR 1219; *Royer*, Case 48/75, [1976] ECR 497; and *Watson and Belmann*, Case 118/75, [1976] ECR 1185.

[36] See also *Tribunal Administratif*, Paris, 2 December 1980, Dr Fisc. 1981, No. 2384; *Conseil d'État*, 28 November 1980, Dr Fisc. 1980, No. 21 comm. 1121; *Conseil d'État*, 25 February 1981, [1981] Recueil Dalloz Sirey (Informations Rapides) 331; *Conseil d'État*, 13 December 1985, [1985] Recueil des Décisions du Conseil d'État 515. The judicial courts, on the other hand, seem to be prepared to accept the direct effect of directives: see *Grunert*, Case 88/79, [1980] ECR 1827, a reference from the *Tribunal de Grande Instance*, Strasbourg.

[37] Such actions must be brought within a short time-limit (usually two months) by a person with the requisite interest. In addition, it seems that a directive may be used as the basis for an indirect challenge (*exception d'illégalité*) to such a measure.

[38] *Conseil d'État*, 7 December 1984, [1985] RTDE 187. The proceedings were brought by various conservationist groups, including an organization for the protection of birds. See also *Conseil d'État*, 28 September 1984, [1984] RTDE 759; *Conseil d'État*, 6 March 1987, *Fédération Française des Sociétés de Protection de la Nature* (not yet reported).

Cassation is most strikingly reflected in a group of cases concerning monetary compensatory amounts ('m.c.a.'s'). The details of the cases were complicated but the essential facts were simple. In the circumstances of the cases, m.c.a.'s took the form of levies payable on exports of agricultural products. They were imposed by Community regulations but were collected by the national governments. In France, m.c.a.'s on exports to other Community countries were payable to the French Customs, while m.c.a.'s on exports to non-member States were collected by a French governmental agency called ONIC. This difference had one important consequence: disputes regarding the amount payable fell within the jurisdiction of the administrative courts when ONIC was involved but, by virtue of a special provision of French law, came within the jurisdiction of the judicial courts when the Customs were the collecting agency. In the end, this difference turned out to be crucial.

The first group of cases concerned three exporters, Roquette, Maïseries de Beauce and Providence Agricole. Roquette had exported within the Community and had been obliged to pay m.c.a.'s to the French Customs. It then brought proceedings before a judicial court, the *Tribunal d'Instance* of Lille, to recover the payments, claiming that the relevant regulations were invalid. The other two exporters had similar claims against ONIC and they sued in the administrative courts (in Orléans and Châlons-sur-Marne, respectively). All three courts made preliminary references to the European Court asking for a ruling on the validity of the regulations in question. The European Court gave similar judgments in all three cases: it held that the regulations were invalid, but went on to declare that this would not enable the charging of m.c.a.'s to be challenged with regard to the period prior to the date of the judgment.[39] This meant that money already paid could not be recovered.

This judgment was controversial because, though Article 177 EEC gives the European Court the power to declare a Community act invalid, there is no express power to rule on the consequences of such invalidity or to declare a regulation invalid for the future but valid for the past. Article 174, second paragraph, does give such a power, but it applies only to annulment actions under Article 173. The European Court, however, said that Article 174, second paragraph, applies 'by analogy' to rulings under Article 177.

[39] *Roquette* v. *French Customs*, Case 145/79, [1980] ECR 2917; *Maïseries de Beauce* v. *ONIC*, Case 109/79, [1980] ECR 2883; *Providence Agricole* v. *ONIC*, Case 4/79, [1980] ECR 2823.

When the proceedings recommenced in France the result was the same in each case: the three courts each ruled that the jurisdiction of the European Court was limited to answering the questions asked by the French courts. They had asked whether the regulations were invalid; they had not asked what the consequences of invalidity were. In answering a question which had not been asked, the European Court had gone beyond its jurisdiction and its ruling on this point was not binding on the French courts. They each ruled that the m.c.a.'s had to be repaid.[40]

These judgments went on appeal. In the case of Roquette, the appeal went first to the *Cour d'Appel* of Douai (which upheld the lower court's judgment)[41] and then to the *Cour de Cassation*. In the other two cases the appeal went to the *Conseil d'État*.

The *Conseil d'État* upheld the judgments of the lower courts.[42] It said that the European Court's ruling on the consequences of invalidity, being outside the scope of the questions asked, was not binding on the French court. The *Cour de Cassation*, on the other hand, reached the opposite conclusion. It said that the European Court's ruling on the consequences of invalidity should have been followed.[43]

These cases had an interesting sequel. Another French exporter, which (before the European Court's judgments in the earlier cases) had paid m.c.a.'s to both ONIC and the French Customs, decided to bring proceedings to recover them. It sued ONIC in the Paris *Tribunal Administratif* and the Customs in the Paris *Tribunal d'Instance*. The latter made a reference to the European Court asking expressly whether the invalidity of the regulations entitled the exporter to claim a refund. The European Court gave the same answer as in the previous cases but this time there could be no objection that it had gone beyond the questions asked.[44] The *Tribunal d'Instance* therefore

---

[40] *Tribunal d'Instance*, Lille, 15 July 1981, [1982] Recueil Dalloz Sirey (Jurisprudence) 9 (*Roquette*); *Tribunal Administratif*, Orléans, 23 February 1982, [1982] Recueil des Décisions du Conseil d'État 471 (*Maïseries de Beauce*). The judgment of the *Tribunal Administratif*, Châlons-sur-Marne, has not been reported, but was the same as that of the *Tribunal Administratif*, Orléans.

[41] *Cour d'Appel*, Douai, 19 January 1983, [1983] Gazette du Palais 292.

[42] *Conseil d'État*, 26 July 1985, [1985] Recueil des Décisions du Conseil d'État 233; [1985] AJDA 615; [1986] RTDE 158 (*Maïseries de Beauce*); *Conseil d'État*, 13 November 1985 (*Providence Agricole*) (not reported).

[43] *Cour de Cassation*, 10 December 1986, [1986] RTDE 195.

[44] *Société des Produits de Maïs* v. *French Customs*, Case 112/83, [1985] ECR 719.

ruled that the exporter was not entitled to a refund.[45]

The *Tribunal Administratif*, on the other hand, made no reference to the European Court. It held that ONIC was obliged to repay the money.[46] This judgment went on appeal to the *Conseil d'État*, where it was argued that the European Court's ruling on the reference from the Paris *Tribunal d'Instance*, as well as similar rulings on references from courts in other Member States, should be followed. The *Conseil d'Etat* rejected this with the curt statement that the European Court's rulings, having been made in the course of proceedings in other courts between different parties, were not binding on the Paris *Tribunal Administratif*. The appeal was dismissed.[47]

Even if one accepts the view that the earlier judgments of the European Court were not binding, it could still be argued that the *Conseil d'État* should itself have referred the question to the European Court: under Article 177 EEC a court from which there is no appeal is obliged to refer any question on the interpretation of the EEC Treaty or on the validity or interpretation of a Community act. It is possible that the *Conseil d'État* considers that Article 177 does not cover a question concerning the consequences of the invalidity of a Community act. Opinions may differ as to whether a power to rule on the validity of an act includes the power to rule on the consequences of its invalidity; but since this involves the interpretation of Article 177, and therefore raises a question on the interpretation of the EEC Treaty, it is itself covered by Article 177. The *Conseil d'État* should, if it had entertained doubts on the matter, have made a preliminary reference to the European Court asking whether the obligation under Article 177 to refer questions on the validity of Community acts includes an obligation to refer a question on the consequences of the invalidity of such an act.[48] The *Conseil d'État's* failure to do this is indicative of its determination to prevent the European Court from using its power to interpret the Treaty as a means of extending its jurisdiction.

[45] *Tribunal d'Instance*, First Arrondissement, Paris, 11 July 1986 (not reported). The *Tribunal d'Instance*, which was differently constituted when it gave this judgment from the way it had been when it made the reference, was nevertheless unable to resist criticizing the European Court's ruling for lack of legal logic and almost seemed to regret that the European Court had been asked the questions on the consequences of the invalidity of the regulations.

[46] *Tribunal Administratif*, Paris, 17 May 1983 (not reported).

[47] *Conseil d'État*, 13 June 1986, [1986] RTDE 533.

[48] The *Conseil d'État* would probably justify its attitude on the basis of the *acte clair* doctrine (as to which, see pp. 270–2, below) but it is doubtful whether this doctrine can legitimately be applied in such a case.

COMMUNITY LAW IN THE UNITED KINGDOM

The United Kingdom was faced with three problems of a constitutional nature when it joined the Community in 1973; two of these were of comparatively minor singificance but the third was, in theory at least, almost insuperable. The first is that the United Kingdom has a largely unwritten constitution; consequently, provision for membership could not be made by means of a constitutional amendment (as was done in the Republic of Ireland). Secondly, the attitude of the United Kingdom towards international law is strictly dualist: there is no general rule of law allowing treaties to take effect in the internal legal system. These problems could be, and were, overcome by means of a special Act of Parliament; what could not be overcome in this way was the principle of Sovereignty of Parliament, the fundamental doctrine of the British Constitution.

The European Communities Act

The European Communities Act 1972 was passed by Parliament to make provision for Britain's membership of the Community. An Act of Parliament was necessary for a number of purposes, but above all to make Community law applicable in the national legal system: without the European Communities Act, the Community Treaties and Community legislation – though binding on the United Kingdom at the international level – would have been of no effect internally. This was made clear by Lord Denning MR in the following *dictum* from *McWhirter* v. *Attorney-General*,[49] a case decided before the Act had been passed: 'Even though the Treaty of Rome has been signed, it has no effect, so far as these Courts are concerned, until it is made an Act of Parliament. Once it is implemented by an Act of Parliament, these Courts must go by the Act of Parliament.'

This shows that the doctrine adopted by the Belgian *Cour de Cassation* in the *Fromagerie 'Le Ski'* case[50] does not apply in the United Kingdom: the European Communities Act is not merely the means by which Parliament gave assent to the Treaties (something which is not strictly necessary in British constitutional law),[51] it also provides

[49] [1972] CMLR 882 at 886.
[50] See pp. 221–3, above.
[51] It is, however, normal practice (and possibly a constitutional convention) for treaties requiring ratification by the Crown to be laid before Parliament 21 days before they are ratified (the 'Ponsonby Rule'): see (1924) 171 H.C. Debates, cols 2001–2004.

the legal foundation for the direct effect of Community law in the United Kingdom. Because of this, the provisions of the Act are of special importance.

The Community Treaties

Section 1(2) of the Act defines what is meant by the 'Community Treaties' (usually referred to in the Act as 'the Treaties'). In this definition, a distinction is drawn between, on the one hand, the accession and pre-accession treaties and, on the other hand, the post-accession treaties. The accession treaties are the Treaty of Accession, by which the United Kingdom acceded to the EEC and Euratom, and the Decision of Accession, by which the United Kingdom acceded to the ECSC. These were both agreed to on 22 January 1972; this is the vital date for distinguishing pre-accession from post-accession treaties: treaties concluded before this date are 'pre-accession' and those concluded after it are 'post-accession'.

The full list is as follows:

1. The six pre-accession constitutive Treaties (listed by name);[52]
2. Any treaty entered into by any of the Communities before 22 January 1972 (with or without any of the Member States);[53]
3. Any treaty entered into by the Member States (with or without any other country) before 22 January 1972 as a treaty ancillary to any of the above;[54]
4. The Treaty of Accession;
5. The Decision of Accession (ECSC);
6. The Treaty and Decision relating to the accession of Greece (added by an amendment under the European Communities (Greek Accession) Act 1979);
7. The Decision of the Council of 7 May 1985 on the Communities' system of own resources (added by an amendment under the European Communities (Finance) Act 1985);
8. The undertaking by the Representatives of the Governments of the Member States meeting within the Council on 23 and 24 April 1985 to make payments to finance the Communities' budget for 1985 (added by an amendment under the European Communities (Finance) Act 1985);

[52] See Schedule 1, Part I, items 1–6. They are set out at p. 88, above.
[53] Ibid. item 7.
[54] Ibid.

9. The Treaty and Decision relating to the accession of Spain and Portugal (added by an amendment under the European Communities (Spanish and Portuguese Accession) Act 1985);
10. The Single European Act 1986 (Title II and certain other provisions only) (added by an amendment under the European Communities (Amendment) Act 1986);
11. Any Treaty entered into by any of the Communities after 22 January 1972 (with or without any of the Member States);
12. Any treaty entered into by the United Kingdom after 22 January 1972 as a treaty ancillary to any other Community treaty.

Most of these items are self-explanatory, but some require a brief explanation.

It will be noticed that No. 2 is the pre-accession counterpart of No. 11: these concern international agreements with third countries concluded by the ECSC, EEC or Euratom. The Member States may, or may not, be joint parties with the Community: in other words, the so-called 'mixed agreements' are included. No. 3 is similar to No. 12: these refer to agreements concluded by the Member States which are ancillary to the other Community treaties and would include decisions of the representatives of the governments of the Member States, subsidiary conventions and amendments to the constitutive Treaties.

It is provided by section 1(3) that an Order in Council may declare a treaty to be a 'Community Treaty', and such a declaration is conclusive. An Order in Council is not, however, necessary: an agreement which falls within the definition of a 'Community Treaty' will be so regarded, even without a declaration. There is, however, one exception: a post-accession treaty *entered into by the United Kingdom* (other than a pre-accession treaty to which the United Kingdom accedes on terms settled on or before 22 January 1972)[55] will not be regarded as a 'Community Treaty' unless it is so specified in an Order in Council of which a draft has been approved by resolution of each House of Parliament.[56]

---

[55] See Art. 3(1) of the Act of Accession: agreements falling within Art. 3(2) would not come within this exception as the terms had to be agreed to at a later date. Thus the United Kingdom's accession to the Convention on Jurisdiction and the Enforcement of Judgments in Civil and Commercial Matters required a Convention of Accession, signed in 1978, which amended the original Convention: see OJ 1978, L 304.

[56] For an (unsuccessful) attempt by a private citizen to prevent an agreement between the Member States from being so specified, see *R* v. *HM Treasury*, ex parte *Smedley* [1985] QB 657 (CA).

This provision gives Parliament control over three classes of agreement:[57] first, it covers agreements concluded by the Member States between themselves – new constitutive Treaties (including treaties amending or supplementing existing constitutive Treaties), subsidiary conventions and acts of the representatives of the Governments of the Member States meeting in the Council (in so far as these constitute international agreements); secondly, it applies to so-called 'mixed agreements' (agreements between, on the one side, the Community and the Member States and, on the other side, third countries); and thirdly, it could apply to agreements between the Member States and third countries which are binding on the Community and consequently part of Community law (assuming this is possible). In all these cases, parliamentary approval will normally be required in the other Member States as well.

Direct Effect

Section 2(1) of the Act makes provision for the direct effect of Community law in the United Kingdom. It reads as follows:

All such rights, powers, liabilities, obligations and restrictions from time to time created or arising by or under the Treaties, and all such remedies and procedures from time to time provided for by or under the Treaties, as in accordance with the Treaties are without further enactment to be given legal effect or used in the United Kingdom shall be recognised and available in law, and be enforced, allowed and followed accordingly; and the expression 'enforceable Community right' and similar expressions shall be read as referring to one to which this subsection applies.

Three comments may be made about this: first, it provides for the direct effect of both the Community Treaties (as previously defined) and Community legislation ('rights . . . created or arising . . . *under*[58] the Treaties'); secondly, it includes future Community law ('from time to time created'); and thirdly, it makes clear that Community law determines whether a particular provision is directly effective ('as *in accordance with the Treaties*[59] are without further enactment to be given legal effect').

[57] In one special case, Parliament must give its approval by statute: under s. 6(1) of the European Assembly Elections Act 1978, it is stated that no treaty providing for any increase in the powers of the European Parliament may be ratified by the United Kingdom unless it has been approved by Act of Parliament. For an example of such approval, see the European Communities (Amendment) Act 1986, s. 3(4), which concerned the increases in the powers of the European Parliament contained in the Single European Act.

[58] Italics added.

[59] Italics added.

In view of the wide definition given to 'Community Treaties', section 2(1) covers all forms of written Community law. The only provisions of Community law which might not be covered are the general principles of law; but these only rarely apply in the national courts and could probably be brought within the terms of section 2(1) on the ground that they are impliedly based on the Treaties and therefore arise 'under' the Treaties.[60]

Implementation

Section 2(2) makes provision for the implementation of Community law by means of subordinate legislation. This may be done either by Order in Council or by regulation made by a Minister or department designated for this purpose by Order in Council.[61] In both cases the measure must be in the form of a statutory instrument[62] and must be approved by Parliament.[63]

This power may be used for the following purposes:

1. Implementing any Community obligation of the United Kingdom;
2. Enabling any such obligation to be implemented;
3. Enabling any rights enjoyed, or to be enjoyed, by the United Kingdom under, or by virtue of, the Treaties to be exercised;
4. Dealing with matters arising out of, or related to, any such obligation or rights or the coming into force, or the operation from time to time, of the above.

'Community obligation' means an obligation 'created or arising by or under the Treaties'.[64] It follows from this that the power is dependent on the existence of a right or obligation under the Community Treaties (as previously defined) or under Community legislation[65] and can be used only for purposes subordinate to such right or obligation. Consequently, if the British Government uses this power to implement a Community provision but misconstrues that

---

[60] See Chapter 5.

[61] See the European Communities (Designation) Order 1973, S I 1973, No. 1889.

[62] Schedule 2, paragraph 2(1) and s. 1(1) of the Statutory Instruments Act 1946.

[63] If the instrument has not been approved in draft by each House of Parliament, it will be subject to annulment by negative resolution of either House: European Communities Act, Schedule 2, Paragraph 2(2).

[64] Schedule 1, Pt. II.

[65] A right or obligation under Community legislation would constitute a right or obligation arising 'under' the Treaties.

provision so that the implementing measure goes substantially beyond the provision, the implementing measure may be ruled *ultra vires* by the British courts. Where the Community provision turns out to be invalid, there will of course be no Community obligation to implement; therefore, the implementing measure will be even more clearly invalid. It follows from this that, in order to determine the validity of the implementing measure under British law, the British court may have to make a reference to the European Court under Article 177 EEC in order to obtain a ruling on the interpretation or validity of the Community provision. This will be the case even where the Community provision is not directly effective.

It is provided by section 2(4) of the Act that implementing measures made under section 2(2) may include 'any such provision (of any such extent) as might be made by Act of Parliament'.[66] There are, however, four things which are expressly prohibited. These are specified in Schedule 2, paragraph 1, which provides that the power may not be used:

(a) to impose or increase taxation;
(b) to enact retroactive legislation;
(c) to sub-delegate legislative power (except to make rules of procedure for any court or tribunal);
(d) to create any new criminal offence punishable with imprisonment for more than two years or punishable on summary conviction with imprisonment for more than three months or with a fine of more than £400 (if not calculated on a daily basis) or with a fine of more than £5 per day.

If it is necessary to do any of these things to implement Community law, an Act of Parliament will have to be passed.

Enforcement of Judgments

The European Communities (Enforcement of Community Judgments) Order 1972,[67] which was made under section 2(4) of the Act, makes provision for the enforcement in the United Kingdom of

---

[66] It is not entirely clear what the purpose of this provision is, but it is possible that it was intended to exclude the common law presumptions applicable to delegated legislation (other than those given statutory force in Schedule 2, paragraph 1.) For a general discussion of these presumptions, see T. C. Hartley and J. A. G. Griffith, *Government and Law* (2nd ed., 1981), pp. 360–362); but see Lawrence Collins, *European Community Law in the United Kingdom* (3rd ed.), pp. 85–87, where a different view is put forward. It would seem also that implementing measures under section 2(2) may repeal an Act of Parliament passed prior to the European Communities Act.

[67] S I 1972, No. 1590.

judgments of the European Court and of decisions of the Council or Commission imposing fines or penalties. The judgment or decision must be registered by the High Court (after the Secretary of State has appended an enforcement order) and is then enforced in the same way as an ordinary High Court judgment.

Supremacy of Community Law[68]

Section 2(4) of the European Communities Act also provides that 'any enactment passed or to be passed, other than one contained in this Part of this Act, shall be construed and have effect subject to the foregoing provisions of this section . . .'. Now, the foregoing provisions of section 2 include section 2(1), which states that directly effective Community law must be recognized and enforced in the United Kingdom; consequently, it seems that Parliament intended that all Acts of Parliament, both past and future, should be subordinated to Community law. This view is strengthened by section 3(1), which states that any question as to the 'effect' of any of the Treaties or of Community legislation must be decided 'in accordance with the principles of any relevant decision of the European Court'. One such principle is, of course, that of the supremacy of Community law.

There is no doubt that these provisions are effective as regards United Kingdom legislation passed prior to the European Communities Act: Parliament can obviously state that all previous legislation is subject to the provisions of a new statute. The same applies to delegated legislation made under a statute passed prior to the European Communities Act, even if the delegated legislation itself was adopted after the European Communities Act: the force and effect of delegated legislation can never be greater than that of the empowering statute itself.

The real problem concerns statutes passed after the European Communities Act. It is true that, under section 2(4), these are also subject to Community law; however, the principle of Sovereignty of Parliament intrudes at this point and limits the effectiveness of this provision. The doctrine of the Sovereignty of Parliament is the fundamental principle of the British Constitution: it states that there are no legal limits to the legislative power of Parliament, except that Parliament cannot limit its own powers for the future. It follows from this that section 2(4) must be ineffective if it was intended to deprive

---

[68] For a more detailed discussion of this topic, see the article by Clarke and Sufrin listed below under 'Further Reading'.

Parliament of the power to pass legislation which would override Community law: Parliament is constitutionally unable to deprive itself of this power.

Does this mean that post-accession Acts of Parliament must prevail over Community law? If this were so, it would be a very serious matter: it would mean that the United Kingdom would be constitutionally unable to accept the obligations of Community membership. Fortunately, this is not the case. Section 2(4) lays down a rule of interpretation – and in view of the United Kingdom's membership of the Community, it is a very strong rule – that Parliament is to be presumed not to intend any future statute to override Community law. Therefore, Community law will always prevail unless Parliament clearly and expressly states in a future Act that it is to override Community law. This, of course, would constitute a repudiation of the Treaty and would lay the United Kingdom open to proceedings in the European Court for violation of a Treaty obligation. Responsibility would then rest with Parliament, not with the courts. The position was clearly expressed by Lord Denning MR in *Macarthys Ltd* v. *Smith*.[69] where he said:

If the time should come when Parliament deliberately passes an Act with the intention of repudiating the Treaty or any provision in it or intentionally of acting inconsistently with it and says so in express terms then I should have thought that it would be the duty of our courts to follow the statute of our Parliament. I do not however envisage any such situation ... Unless there is such an intentional and express repudiation of the Treaty, it is our duty to give priority to the Treaty.[70]

From the point of view of Community law, this may not be as satisfactory a situation as that prevailing in some of the other Member States, but in practice priority will be given to Community law: in view of the high degree of party discipline in the House of Commons, it is unlikely that Parliament would repudiate the

[69] [1979] 3 All E.R. 325 at 329. See also *per* Lawton LJ at p. 334. In subsequent proceedings in the same case, Lord Denning made the point even more forcefully: see [1981] 1 All E.R. 111 at 120. For an earlier statement by Lord Denning, see *Shields* v. *E. Coomes (Holdings) Ltd*, [1979] 1 All E.R. 456, 461–462; [1978] 1 WLR 1408, 1414 (CA).

[70] In *Garland* v. *British Rail Engineering Ltd*, [1983] 2 AC 751; [1982] 2 All E.R. 402; [1982] 2 WLR 918, the House of Lords expressly refrained from considering the correctness of this approach. It was sufficient for the purposes of that case to affirm that post-accession statutes should, if reasonably capable of bearing such a meaning, be construed so as to be consistent with Community law. See also *National Smokeless Fuels Ltd* v. *IRC*, [1986] 3 CMLR 227; but see *Duke* v. *GEC Reliance*, [1988] 1 All E.R. 626 (HL).

Treaties unless the Government itself had decided on such a course of action.

FURTHER READING

Ganshof van der Meersch, 'Community Law and the Belgian Constitution' in St John Bates *et al.* (eds), *In Memoriam J.D.B. Mitchell* (1983), p. 74.

Koopmans, 'Receptivity and its Limits: The Dutch Case', *ibid*, p. 91.

Buffet-Tchakaloff, La France devant la Cour de Justice des Communautés Européennes (1985).

Clarke and Sufrin, 'Constitutional Conundrums: The Impact of the United Kingdom's Membership of the Communities on Constitutional Theory' in Furmston *et al.* (eds), *The Effect on English Domestic Law of Membership of the European Communities and of Ratification of the European Convention on Human Rights* (1983), p. 32.

Schermers, paragraphs 224–38.

Simon, 'L'effet dans le temps des arrêts préjudiciels de la CEE: enjeu ou prétexte d'une nouvelle guerre des juges?' In *Liber Amicorum P. Pescatore* (1987)

Boulouis, 'L'applicabilité directe des directives. A propos d'un arrêt Cohn-Bendit du Conseil d'Etat', [1979] RMC 104.

Constantinesco, Soler-Couteaux and Simon, 'Chronique de jurisprudence administrative française intéréssant le droit communautaire', to be published in [1988] RTDE.

La Pergola and Del Duca, 'Community Law and the Italian Constitution', (1985) 79 American Journal of International Law 598.

Maresceau, 'The Effect of Community Agreements in the UK under the European Communities Act 1972', (1979) 28 ICLQ 241.

Mitchell, Kuipers and Gall, 'Constitutional Aspects of the Treaty and Legislation relating to British Membership', (1972) 9 C.M.L. Rev. 134.

Petriccione, 'Italy: Supremacy of Community Law over National Law', (1986) 11 E.L. Rev. 320.

Simon and Dowrick, 'Effect of EEC Directives in France: The Views of the Conseil d'État', (1979) 95 LQR 376.

Trindade, 'Parliamentary Sovereignty and the Primacy of Community Law', (1972) 35 MLR 375.

Wade, 'Sovereignty and the European Communities', (1972) 88 LQR 1.

Weiss, 'Self-Executing Treaties and Directly Applicable EEC Law in French Courts', 1979/1 LIEI 51.

9

PRELIMINARY REFERENCES

It has already been explained why a supranational political entity such as the Community cannot function effectively unless there is a single court with power to decide all questions of Community law.[1] This means that the European Court must have jurisdiction to decide such questions when they arise in national court proceedings. How is this to be done? The authors of the Treaties shrank from allowing an appeal from the national courts to the European Court and settled instead for a half-way house: a preliminary reference.

There are two major differences between an appeal and a reference. First, in the case of an appeal the initiative lies with the parties: the party who is dissatisfied with the court's judgment decides whether to appeal and then takes the necessary procedural steps. The court *a quo* normally has no further say in the matter and cannot prevent the appeal from being lodged.[2] Secondly, the appeal court decides *the case*, even though the appeal may be on limited grounds only, and it has the power to set aside the decision of the court *a quo*; normally it can then substitute its own decision for that of the lower court.[3] These features are not found in the procedure for a preliminary reference: the court *a quo* decides whether the reference should be made and only specific issues are referred to the European Court. Once it has decided these, the European Court remits the case to the national court for a final decision.

This procedure puts the European Court in a weaker position than the supreme court in a federation. It suggests that the national courts are not subordinate to the European Court, but co-equal: the relationship is not one of hierarchy, but of co-operation. This com-

---

[1] See pp. 181–2, above.

[2] In some cases, however, the parties may appeal only with the leave of the court *a quo* or the appeal court: this is the position in the case of appeals from the English Court of Appeal to the House of Lords.

[3] In some Continental countries, for example France, the position is different in the case of an appeal in cassation: if the Court of Cassation allows the appeal, it quashes the lower court's judgment and then sends the case to another *Cour d'Appel* – not the one from which the appeal came – for a new decision.

promise solution is typical of the Community and illustrates its hybrid character.

The relevant provisions are Articles 177 EEC, 150 Euratom and 41 ECSC. The first two are in virtually identical terms, but the ECSC provision is very much more restricted. Article 177 EEC reads[4]

> The Court of Justice shall have jurisdiction to give preliminary rulings concerning:
>
> (*a*) the interpretation of this Treaty;
> (*b*) the validity and interpretation of acts of the institutions of the Community;
> (*c*) the interpretation of the statutes of bodies established by an act of the Council, where those statutes so provide.
>
> Where such a question is raised before any court or tribunal of a Member State, that court or tribunal may, if it considers that a decision on the question is necessary to enable it to give judgment, request the Court of Justice to give a ruling thereon.
>
> Where any such question is raised in a case pending before a court or tribunal of a Member State, against whose decisions there is no judicial remedy under national law, that court or tribunal shall bring the matter before the Court of Justice.

It will be seen from this that, under the EEC and Euratom Treaties, questions both of interpretation and validity may be referred to the European Court: references for interpretation may be made with regard to both the Treaty and Community acts, but references for a ruling on validity may be made only in the case of the latter. Since the Treaties are, in a sense, the constitution of the Community, it is understandable that their validity cannot be challenged in terms of the Community legal order.

One of the most important issues that may be referred to the European Court is not, however, expressly mentioned in Article 177: this is the *effect* of a Community provision. In theory, the direct effect of Community provisions, as well as the supremacy of Community law over national law, are regarded by the European Court as being aspects of interpretation (though in reality they go a long way beyond what is normally regarded as interpretation). The result is that three issues may be referred for a ruling – interpretation, effect and validity – though the latter applies only in certain cases. Questions of fact and of national law may not be referred, nor may the European Court rule

---

[4] The only way in which Art. 150 Euratom differs from this is that in paragrah 1(*c*) the words 'save where those statutes provide otherwise' replace 'where those statutes so provide'.

on the *application* of the law to the particular case – though the exact borderline between interpretation and application is at the best of times uncertain.

Article 41 ECSC is short: it states simply that the European Court has 'sole jurisdiction to give preliminary rulings on the validity of acts of the High Authority and of the Council where such validity is in issue in proceedings brought before a national court or tribunal'. Validity is therefore the only issue that may be referred: there is no way in which a national court can obtain a ruling on the interpretation or effect of ECSC law.[5]

WHICH PROVISIONS MAY BE REFERRED?

Articles 177 EEC and 150 Euratom cover three kinds of provision: (a) the Treaty; (b) acts of Community institutions; and (c) statutes of bodies established by an act of the Council. The first two items will be discussed below, but a word should be said here about the third. What is meant by this? In Community law the word 'statute' normally refers to the instrument governing the working of some body or institution: the statute of the European Court, for example, provides for the appointment of judges, the composition of the court and certain procedural matters; the statute of the European Investment Bank provides for the setting-up of the Bank, the powers of the Board of Governors and various other matters. If, therefore, the word 'statute' in paragraph 1(c) of Articles 177 EEC and 150 Euratom refers to the instrument setting up the body, it will by definition be an act of the Council.

The significance of this is that acts of the Council are already covered by paragraph 1(b). Therefore, the effect of paragraph 1(c) is not to add to the jurisdiction of the European Court, but to restrict it: all that paragraph 1(c) does is to limit the scope of paragraph 1(b). First of all, under Article 177(1)(c) a preliminary ruling may be given regarding a statute *only if that statute so provides*, while under Article 177(1)(b) acts of the Council may in all cases be referred; therefore, Article 177(1)(c) prevents a reference regarding a statute which does not so provide. (Under Article 150(1)(c) Euratom the position is slightly different: a preliminary ruling may be made *except where the statute provides otherwise*; consequently, its effect is that a prohibition in

[5] For the position under the EEC and Euratom Treaties, see pp. 266–7, below.

such a statute would deprive the European Court of jurisdiction, even though a similar prohibition in any other act of the Council would be ineffective.) The second consequence of paragraph 1(*c*) is that it prevents the Court from ruling on the *validity* of such a statute: under paragraph 1(*b*) the validity of a Community act may normally be decided on a preliminary reference, but this is not possible where the act constitutes the statute of a body.

In practice, the important provisions of the first paragraph of Articles 177 EEC and 150 Euratom are sub-paragraphs (*a*) and (*b*). The effect of these can best be considered by looking in turn at each of the sources of Community law.

Treaties

The words 'this Treaty' in Article 177(1)(*a*) EEC cover the EEC Treaty and all Treaties amending or supplementing it.[6] The Euratom Treaty, and all Treaties amending or supplementing it, are covered by Article 150(1)(*a*) Euratom. The ECSC Treaty, however, may not be referred, as it contains no equivalent provision. The result is that provisions in any of the constitutive Treaties dealing with the EEC and Euratom may be referred, but not those dealing with the ECSC.

Subsidiary Conventions

In some cases – for example, the Convention on Jurisdiction and the Enforcement of Judgments in Civil and Commercial Matters – these subsidiary conventions are envisaged by the EEC Treaty. Nevertheless, they cannot be regarded as forming part of it; therefore, they are not covered by the words 'this Treaty' in Article 177(1)(*a*).[7] However, some conventions, including the Judgments Convention, themselves make provision for preliminary references to the European Court.[8]

[6] With regard to the instruments by which new Member States accede to the Community, see, for example, Art. 1(3) of the Treaty of Accession 1972, which brings that Treaty and the Act of Accession annexed to it within the scope of Art. 177 EEC.
[7] See *Hurd* v. *Jones (Inspector of Taxes)*, Case 44/84, [1986] 2 CMLR 1, in which the European Court held that the agreements between the Member States setting up European Schools in various Community countries were not covered by Art. 177.
[8] See pp. 92–3, above.

Acts of the Representatives of the Member States

By definition, these are not acts of a Community institution and are therefore excluded from paragraph 1(*b*); nor are they part of the EEC or Euratom Treaties. Consequently, they fall outside Articles 177 EEC and 150 Euratom and cannot be referred to the European Court. This is not very serious, however, because national courts would not normally have occasion to consider them.

Community Acts

These are covered by Articles 177(1)(*b*) EEC, 150(1)(*b*) Euratom and 41 ECSC[9]. In the case of EEC and Euratom measures, the reference may be on either interpretation or validity; but ECSC acts may be referred only as regards validity. Article 41 ECSC applies only to acts of the Commission or Council; but the other two Treaties refer simply to acts of 'the institutions of the Community'. In practice, most Community acts are adopted by either the Commission or the Council but there is no doubt that acts of the European Parliament, and even of the Court itself, are also covered.[10]

It should be noted that all the provisions mentioned above refer simply to 'acts': it is not necessary that the act be directly effective. As was explained above,[11] a national court might have good reason for referring an act that was not directly effective for a ruling on its validity or interpretation.[12] It follows from this that all binding acts are covered, including acts *sui generis*.[13] May non-binding acts, such as EEC recommendations or opinions, be referred? Since they are generally regarded as 'acts',[14] they should in theory be included: in some cases a national court might consider that the interpretation of

---

[9] But Art. 177 does not cover international agreements concluded by national organizations to give effect to a directive: *Demouche*, Case 152/83, 6 October 1987 (not yet reported), a case concerning an agreement between national motor insurance bureaux on the 'green card' system.

[10] See, further, Schermers, paragraph 742.

[11] At pp. 240–1.

[12] In *Haaga*, Case 32/74, [1974] ECR 1201, a German court asked for a reference on a directive, which was not directly effective, in order to elucidate the meaning of a national implementing measure; the European Court had no hesitation in giving the ruling. See also *Mazzalai*, Case 111/75, [1976] ECR 657 at 665.

[13] It was held in the *ERTA* case (*Commission* v. *Council*, Case 22/70, [1971] ECR 263) that in act *sui generis* is an 'act' for the purpose of Art. 173 EEC (see pp. 101–2, above); consequently, it must also be an 'act' for the purpose of Art. 177.

[14] This follows by implication from Arts 173 EEC and 146 Euratom, which speak of 'acts . . . other than recommendations or opinions'.

a national measure depends on that of a non-binding Community act.[15]

General Principles of Law

These cannot form the subject matter of a reference as they are neither part of the Treaties nor Community acts. As far as national courts are concerned, however, general principles of law are not normally applicable in the abstract, but only in conjunction with a provision of written Community law. If a suitable Treaty provision or Community act provides a peg on which to hang the general principle, the latter could be interpreted in the course of a reference regarding the former.

Agreements with Non-Member States

Since these are clearly not part of the EEC or Euratom Treaties, they will be covered only if they are regarded as acts of Community institutions. As has already been explained, agreements between the Community and non-member States are normally concluded by the Council:[16] in the *Haegeman* case[17] the European Court seized on this as a ground for regarding such agreements as Community acts. The Court therefore ruled that the Association Agreement between the Community and Greece was covered by Article 177(1)(*b*).

Is this view justified? First, it should be pointed out that there is a distinction between an international agreement and a national measure passed by one of the contracting parties to conclude or ratify the agreement: the latter is simply the constitutionally required method of giving assent to the agreement. In the *Haegeman* case the Court mentioned that the Association Agreement had been concluded by means of a Council decision. However, it was not the Council decision that the Court interpreted, but the Agreement itself. The two should not be confused.

It should also be noted that the party to the agreement on the Community side is the Community itself – the EEC, Euratom or ECSC, as the case may be – not the Council. Such agreements, therefore, do not constitute acts of an *institution* of the Community, as

---

[15] See Schermers, paragraphs 302 and 740.
[16] See pp. 154–5, above. Under Art. 101(3) Euratom, agreements may in certain cases be concluded by the Commission.
[17] Case 181/73, [1974] ECR 449.

required by Article 177(1)(*b*): they are acts of the Community. Even if one takes the view that one cannot distinguish the Community from its institutions, moreover, it is still doubtful whether agreements are covered by Article 177(1)(*b*): this provision was surely intended to apply to unilateral acts, not bilateral acts such as international agreements.[18]

Whatever view one takes of the *Haegeman* case, there can be no doubt that its reasoning can apply only if the Community formally becomes a party to the agreement by means of an act of one of its institutions. This would seem to exclude the possibility that the European Court could take jurisdiction under Article 177 to interpret an international agreement such as the General Agreement on Tariffs and Trade, to which the Community has not formally adhered, even though the European Court has held that the Community has become bound by the GATT because it succeeded to the rights and obligations under it of the Member States.[19] Yet the European Court, in one of the most blatantly policy-based judgments it has ever given, has ruled that the GATT *is* covered by Article 177.

This occurred in the *SPI* case,[20] where the Italian *Corte Suprema di Cassazione* expressly asked the European Court whether the GATT fell within the scope of Article 177.[21] The European Court's answer was not based on the wording of Article 177, which it did not even quote, but on pure policy.[22] It started with the proposition that the GATT, like all agreements binding on the Community, should receive a uniform interpretation throughout the Community: any

[18] This is the view of Advocate General Trabucchi who said in *Bresciani*, Case 87/75, [1976] ECR 129 at 147 that a convention is of necessity a bilateral or multilateral legal instrument and, as such, 'does not lend itself to identification with the acts of the Community executive, which are inherently unilateral'. Advocate General Trabucchi concluded that the *Haegeman* judgment therefore means that, in Community law, international agreements are not binding on private individuals as such, but only by virtue of an act of a Community institution (i.e., the decision or regulation formally concluding the agreement). It appears from this that the Advocate General regards the Community as adopting an essentially dualist approach to international law. This seems to be the only way in which the European Court's judgment in *Haegeman* can be justified; but the view that the Community adopts a dualist approach to international law does not seem consistent with the general tenor of the Court's judgments, especially its decision in the *SPI* case (below), nor does it seem to be borne out by the wording of the decisions or regulations themselves.

[19] See pp. 172–3, above.

[20] Cases 267–269/81, [1983] ECR 801. See also *Singer and Geigy*, Cases 290, 291/81, [1983] ECR 847.

[21] This was in a reference under Art. 177. Since it involved the interpretation of the EEC Treaty, this question was of course covered by Art. 177.

[22] The relevant passages are contained in paragraphs 14–19 of the judgment.

divergence in its application in the different Member States would compromise the unity of the Community's common commercial policy and create distortions in trade within the Community. The Court then characterised its jurisdiction under Article 177 on a functional basis: it referred to it as 'the jurisdiction conferred upon the Court in order to ensure the uniform interpretation of Community law.'[23] It was then able to conclude that Article 177 must cover the GATT.[24]

The Court's rhetoric in this case was beguiling, but it should not be allowed to obscure the nature of the Court's reasoning. The Court was saying, quite simply, that because it would be desirable for the GATT to be covered by Article 177, therefore it *is* covered. This is the reasoning of politics, not law.[25]

It should be noted that the Court stated in the *Haegeman* case that it had jurisdiction to interpret the agreement *within the framework of Community law*;[26] it also said that the agreement constituted an act of a Community institution *in so far as it concerned the Community*.[27] These phrases make it clear that the Court was interpreting the agreement only in so far as it applied as part of Community law and was not claiming that its interpretation was binding on the other party to the agreement. This is clearly right: if the other contracting state felt that the European Court had misinterpreted the agreement and that as a result it was not being properly applied on the Community side, it would be entitled to complain that the Community was failing in its obligations under the Treaty and, if this produced no results, to resort to the remedies available under international law.

It should also be noted that if, as the Court stated, an international agreement between the Community and a non-member State is an act of a Community institution in terms of Article 177(1)(*b*), it follows that the European Court must have jurisdiction to rule on its validity as well as on its interpretation. It would hardly be appropriate, however, to apply the same criteria as in the case of a unilateral Community act (namely, the grounds laid down in Article 173 EEC) and one would expect the European Court to exercise this jurisdic-

---

[23] Paragraph 15.
[24] The Court stated that this was the case only from 1 July 1968, the date on which the Common Customs Tariff came into force in the Community. (It was on this date that, according to the Court, the Community took the place of the Member States with regard to the GATT.) Prior to this date, only the national courts could interpret the GATT.
[25] For a discussion of the Court's use of policy arguments, see pp. 77–81, above.
[26] Paragraph 6 of the judgment.
[27] Paragraph 4 of the judgment.

tion with caution. The Court's ruling would, of course, apply only within the Community legal order: it would not be binding on the other party to the agreement.

The Association Agreement with Greece, which featured in the *Haegeman* case, was concluded jointly by the Community and the Member States on the one side and by Greece on the other. This was because it was considered to fall partly within the treaty-making jurisdiction of the Community and partly within that of the Member States. It is strange that the Court did not seem to think that this affected its jurisdiction to interpret the agreement. The clause of the agreement in issue in *Haegeman* was plainly within the jurisdiction of the Community, but if it had been within that of the Member States, would the Court still have been entitled to interpret it?[28]

WHICH COURTS ARE COVERED?

Article 177 EEC draws a distinction between courts which *may* make a reference and those which *must* do so: the former are covered by the second paragraph and the latter by the third. Under Article 41 ECSC, on the other hand, the position is rather different. It seems clear that any 'national court or tribunal' *may* request a ruling on a question of validity; however, since the European Court has exclusive jurisdiction to decide such questions, it would appear that national courts and tribunals are *obliged* to request a ruling whenever a determination of such a question is necessary for proceedings before the national court. It seems, therefore, that under the ECSC Treaty the power to refer and the obligation to refer are co-terminous: what is said below on the power to refer under the EEC Treaty will, therefore, apply under the ECSC Treaty to both the power and the obligation to refer.

Power to Refer

Article 177(2) EEC states that 'any court or tribunal of a Member State' may request a ruling. This, therefore, lays down two require-

---

[28] See *Demirel*, Case 12/86, 30 September 1987 (not yet reported), where this question was raised by the British and German Governments, but not decided.

ments: the body making the request must be a court or tribunal and it must be 'of a Member State'.[29]

What are the essential characteristics of a court or tribunal? It is generally recognized that this is a question which must be decided by Community law: it is not decisive whether the body is recognized as a court under national law.[30] It does not matter what the body is called: according to the European Court, the important question is whether it performs judicial functions.[31] The concept of a 'judicial function' is notoriously difficult to pin down[32] but one would normally regard a body as being judicial if it had power to give binding determinations of the legal rights and obligations of individuals. One would often expect to find a dispute between two parties (*lis inter partes*) and a procedure under which the determination was made on the basis of evidence and legal argument. One cannot, however, regard these characteristics too rigidly. Although courts are normally concerned with declaring the rights of parties, they do have discretionary powers and to that extent exercise functions which might not be regarded as strictly judicial. Moreover, courts also hear non-contentious proceedings and do not always operate under normal adversary procedure: the European Court has, in fact, held that a reference can be made in *ex parte* and interlocutory proceedings.[33] On the other hand, one would not usually regard a body as judicial if its functions were purely advisory, investigatory or conciliatory, nor if they were legislative or executive. In addition to these requirements,

[29] The view has been put forward that a body may be entitled to make a reference even if it is not covered by Art. 177(2). The argument is that Art. 177(2) is not an exhaustive statement of the power to refer: Art. 177(1) should, according to this view, be regarded as independently conferring a power to make a reference: see Mok, 'Should the "First Paragraph" of Art. 177 of the EEC Treaty by Read as a Separate Clause?', (1967–68) 5 C.M.L. Rev. 458, where this theory is considered but ultimately rejected. There seems little doubt in fact that the drafters of the Treaty intended that the second and third paragraphs should define the scope of the general principle laid down in the first: a body that is not a court or tribunal would not, therefore, be covered by Art. 177.

[30] *Per* Advocate General Gand in *Vaassen*, Case 61/65, [1966] ECR 261 at 281. It follows from this that the question whether a particular body is a court or tribunal for the purposes of Art. 177 may itself be referred to the European Court, either by the body in question or by another body, for example a court hearing an appeal against the first body's decision to refer or not to refer.

[31] *Politi* v. *Italy*, Case 43/71, [1971] ECR 1039 at paragraph 5; *Simmenthal*, Case 70/77, [1978] ECR 1453 at paragraph 9.

[32] See S. A. de Smith, *Judicial Review of Administrative Action*, (4th ed., 1980, by J. M. Evans), pp. 80–7.

[33] See *Politi* v. *Italy*, Case 43/71, [1971] ECR 1039; *Birra Dreher* v. *Italian Finance Administration*, Case 162/73, [1974] ECR 201; and *Hoffman-La Roche* v. *Centrafarm*, Case 107/76, [1977] ECR 957 at paragraph 4 of the judgment.

the body should enjoy some measure of official recognition; it should in some sense be part of the state machinery.

There are a number of cases in which the European Court has considered these questions. In the first, it had to decide whether a body whose decisions were in theory only advisory came within the terms of Article 177(2). This was the Dutch *Raad van State* (Council of State) which is in effect the supreme administrative court in the Netherlands. In strict law, however, the application for review is made to the Crown, which is advised by the *Raad van State*. Like the Privy Council, the *Raad van State* has a judicial committee which functions as a court and operates according to normal judicial procedure. The European Court had no difficulty in accepting the *Raad van State* as a court for the purpose of Article 177, thus showing that the reality of the matter is more important than the theory.[34] This does not, however, mean that a body whose decisions were in fact, as well as in theory, only advisory could make references to the European Court.

The requirement of official authority has been considered by the European Court in several cases. The first is *Vaassen*,[35] which concerned a reference from a body in the Netherlands, officially described as an 'arbitration tribunal' (*scheidsgerecht*), which settled disputes regarding the pension fund for the mining industry. Although the pension scheme was set up privately by organizations representing employers and workers in the industry, it was approved both by the minister responsible for mining and the minister responsible for social security, the latter's approval being necessary for the purpose of obtaining exemption from the national social insurance scheme. This meant that any subsequent changes in the rules of the scheme also required ministerial approval. The members of the arbitration tribunal were appointed by the minister and it operated according to adversary procedure of the normal judicial type. By virtue of a regulation of the Council of the Mining Industry – a public body – all eligible persons were obliged to be members of the scheme and any disputes concerning rights under the scheme had to be taken to the arbitration tribunal for decision. These features indicate that the *scheidsgerecht* was not really an arbitral body: as was pointed out by

[34] *Nederlandse Spoorwegen*, Case 36/73, [1973] ECR 1299. The jurisdictional problem was discussed by Advocate General Mayras at pp. 1317–20. An interesting possibility raised by this case is whether the Parliamentary Commissioner for Administration in Britain could make a reference.

[35] Case 61/65, [1966] ECR 261.

Advocate General Gand, it was 'a judicial body duly representing the power of the state, and settling as a matter of law disputes concerning the application of the insurance scheme . . .'[36]. In these circumstances, it is hardly surprising that the European Court held that it was a court or tribunal within the meaning of Article 177.

The *Broekmeulen* case[37] involved similar issues. It concerned a body in the Netherlands called the Appeals Committee for General Medicine. This body heard appeals from the General Practitioners Registration Committee, which registered G Ps wishing to practise in the Netherlands. Both bodies were set up by the Royal Netherlands Society for the Promotion of Medicine. Though a private association of doctors, the Society had a large degree of control over the practice of medicine in the Netherlands and G Ps were not recognized for the purposes of Dutch social security legislation unless they were registered with the Society; so, from a practical point of view, it was impossible to practise without registration.

The Appeals Committee was constituted as follows: one third of its members were appointed by the medical faculties of the Dutch universities, one third by the Society and one third by the Dutch Government. It followed adversary procedure and legal representation was allowed.[38] It was not, however, a court or tribunal under Netherlands law; nevertheless the European Court held that it could make a reference under Article 177.

Both these cases concerned bodies which enjoyed a significant degree of official recognition and to some extent carried out a public function. Where this is not the case, the situation will be different. Thus, the European Court has held that a private arbitrator, deriving his powers from an arbitration clause in a contract freely entered into by private parties, cannot make a reference under Article 177, even though he is obliged to decide the case according to the law and his awards are enforceable through the judicial system.[39] It is also doubtful whether a purely domestic tribunal, operating under the rules of a private association, could make a reference unless some measure of official recognition was accorded to it.

---

[36] At p. 282.

[37] Case 246/80, [1981] ECR 2311.

[38] In some circumstances there may have been a right of appeal to the courts from its decisions, but no such appeal had ever been made.

[39] *Nordsee* v. *Reederei Mond*, Case 102/81, [1982] ECR 1095. The result of this ruling is that the only way in which a point of Community law raised in an arbitration can be referred to the European Court is through an appeal to a court, which can then make the reference. For a case in which this occurred, see *Bulk Oil* v. *Sun International* [1984] 1 W L R 147 (C A).

The *Borker*[40] case concerned a slightly different issue, which related more to the nature of the proceedings than to that of the body making the reference. Borker, a member of the Paris Bar, had been refused permission by a German court to appear before it. He considered that this was contrary to Community law and complained to the Paris Bar Council, which made a reference to the European Court. Since the Paris Bar Council has no jurisdiction to decide who can appear before a German court, the proceedings before it could not lead to a 'decision of a judicial nature'. The European Court therefore ruled that it could not accept the reference.

The question of the nature of the proceedings sometimes also involves that of the appropriate point at which to make the reference, since the nature of the proceedings may undergo a change at a certain point – for example, from investigatory (administrative) to judicial. This can happen in criminal proceedings, where one might regard the judicial phase as commencing when a suspect is arrested, or perhaps when he is charged.

These issues arose in an Italian case known, revealingly, as *Criminal Proceedings against a Person or Persons Unknown.*[41] The proceedings began when Italian anglers, concerned at the high level of pollution in a river, complained to the local *Pretore*, who instituted criminal proceedings under Italian anti-pollution legislation against a person or persons unknown. (According to the European Court, a *Pretore* is a judge who combines the duties of public prosecutor and investigating judge.) The *Pretore* made a reference to the European court on the interpretation of a directive that was relevant to the case.

Since no one had so far been charged, it could have been (and was) argued that the reference was premature: the proceedings had not yet assumed a judicial character. The European Court, however, accepted the reference, saying that it is for the national court to decide when the reference should be made.[42]

The most controversial case on this issue is *Foglia* v. *Novello.*[43] This was a reference by an Italian court in an action between two Italians

---

[40] Case 138/80, [1980] ECR 1975.

[41] Case 14/86, judgment of 11 June 1987, The Times, 20 June 1987 (also cited as *Pretore di Salò* v. *X*). See also *Pretore of Cento* v. *A Person or Persons Unknown*, Case 110/76, [1977] ECR 851.

[42] This was in spite of the fact that, as the European Court recognised, some of the *Pretore's* duties were not of a strictly judicial nature.

[43] Case 104/79, [1980] ECR 745. See also the earlier case of *Mattheus* v. *Doego*, Case 93/78, [1978] ECR 2203, where the parties to a private contract tried to make the European Court give a ruling on the admission of Spain and Portugal to the Community.

who had entered into a contract of sale requiring delivery of the goods in France. The contract provided that the buyer would not be responsible for the payment of any taxes imposed in contravention of Community law. The goods were duly delivered. The seller was required to pay a consumption tax in France and claimed reimbursement from the buyer. The latter refused on the ground that the tax was contrary to Community law. Thus the Italian courts were required to decide whether the French tax was in accordance with Community law.

There were in fact grounds for believing that the whole transaction was contrived in order to raise a test case. For this reason, the European Court refused to accept the reference, stating that there was no genuine dispute between the parties. The Italian court, which had to give judgment in the case, was unwilling to accept this and made a second reference; but the European Court remained adamant.[44]

This ruling could be criticized because, whatever the motives of the parties, the Italian court was faced with what, on the surface at least, was a genuine dispute. Moreover, the bringing of a test case is a recognized device for obtaining a ruling on a disputed question of law.

In between the two rulings in *Foglia* v. *Novello*, two other references were made to the European Court by courts in Italy. In both these cases, *Chemial* v. *DAF*[45] and *Vinal* v. *Orbat*,[46] the facts were similar to those in *Foglia* v. *Novello*, except that the disputed tax was Italian, not French. In the first case, the Advocate General (Mr Mayras) regarded the case as covered by the decision in *Foglia* v. *Novello* (No. 1), and urged the Court to refuse to give a ruling. In *Vinal* v. *Orbat*, however, a different Advocate General (Mr Reischl) said that the Court should accept the reference, first, because the action was not *manifestly* bogus and, secondly, because it was an *Italian* tax that was in issue. In both the cases, the Court accepted the reference, thus suggesting that it agreed with Advocate General Reischl's opinion. In fact it seems likely that the real reason for its decision in *Foglia* v. *Novello* was one of policy: it did not wish to offend France by allowing the lawfulness of its taxes to be challenged by such round-about means, rather than by the more normal route of an enforcement

---

[44] Case 244/80, [1981] ECR 3045.
[45] Case 140/79, [1981] ECR 1.
[46] Case 46/80, [1981] ECR 77.

action under Article 169 EEC.[47] This view is supported by the fact that in *Foglia* v. *Novello* (No. 2) the Court said that special vigilance was required where the legislation of one Member State is subject to challenge in the courts of another Member State.[48]

The second requirement of Article 177(2) is that the court or tribunal must be 'of a Member State'. Besides suggesting that the body should have some official standing, this also means that it must be *in* a Member State.[49] Foreign (non-Community) courts are clearly excluded; it is also doubtful whether international courts come within the terms of the provision, though some authors consider that they should be allowed to make references.[50]

Where a body has the right to make a reference under Community law, it cannot be deprived of that right by national law. This is illustrated by the *Rheinmühlen* cases,[51] which concerned an attempt by a German cereal exporter to obtain an export rebate under Community law. The *Hessisches Finanzgericht* (Hessian Tax Court) ruled against Rheinmühlen, which then appealed to the highest German court in these matters, the *Bundesfinanzhof* (Federal Tax Court). The *Bundesfinanzhof* quashed the judgment and held that Rheinmühlen was entitled at least to a rebate at a lesser rate. The case was then sent back to the *Hessisches Finanzgericht* for a decision on certain questions of fact.

Under German law, the Hessian court was bound by rulings of the Federal court on points of law. The *Hessisches Finanzgericht* was not, however, prepared to accept the ruling in this case, as questions of Community law were involved. It therefore made a reference to the European Court for an interpretation of the relevant provision; it also asked the European Court for a ruling on the question whether it is permissible for a lower court to make a reference when the case has been sent back to it by a higher court after an earlier judgment has been set aside.

---

[47] Or by means of a reference by a *French* court.

[48] Paragraph 30 of the judgment in Case 244/80. *Foglia* v. *Novello* has given rise to a considerable literature. For some of the articles, see 'Further Reading' at the end of this chapter.

[49] Courts in dependencies of a Member State which are within the territorial scope of the Treaty as laid down in Art. 227 EEC should, however, be allowed to make references. Thus the courts of Gibraltar, for example, should be entitled to request preliminary rulings with regard to those Community provisions which apply to Gibraltar.

[50] See Schermers, paragraph 701. It is hard to accept Professor Schermers' view that the European Court of Human Rights can be seen as part of the judiciary of the Member States.

[51] Cases 166/73, [1974] ECR 33 and 146/73, [1974] ECR 139.

Rheinmühlen then appealed to the *Bundesfinanzhof* against the Hessian court's order referring the case to the European Court and the *Bundesfinanzhof* itself made a reference to the European Court: it asked whether Article 177 gives lower courts an unfettered right to refer, or whether it is subject to national provisions under which lower courts are bound by the judgments of superior courts. This was of course substantially the same as the second question referred by the Hessian court.

The European Court held that the power of a lower court to make a reference cannot be abrogated by a provision of national law: it stated that the lower court must be free to make a reference if it considers that the superior court's ruling could lead it to give judgment contrary to Community law. This means that national rules of *res judicata* do not apply to Community law. On all questions of Community law, including the question of supremacy, the European Court must be the final authority.

It is interesting to note that the Advocate General, Mr Warner, went even further: he suggested that there ought not even to be a right of appeal against an order for reference. In his view, such a right of appeal itself fettered the power of the lower court to make a reference. On this point, however, the European Court did not follow him. The position is, therefore, that national law cannot take away the right given in Article 177(2), but this does not prevent the lower court's order for reference from being quashed on appeal. The consequences of this are considered below.[52]

Obligation to Refer

Article 177(3) EEC lays down an obligation to refer with regard to a court or tribunal of a Member State 'against whose decisions there is no judicial remedy under national law'. Which courts are covered by this? Two points of view exist as to the meaning of the phrase: according to the 'abstract theory', the only courts within the scope of the provision are those whose decisions are *never* subject to appeal; according to the 'concrete theory', on the other hand, the important question is whether the court's decision *in the case in question* is subject to appeal. This distinction can be very important where, for example, there is a right of appeal only if the sum of money in issue is more than a certain amount.

[52] See pp. 275–7.

The wording of Article 177(3) itself favours the abstract theory: if the authors of the Treaty had intended the decisive point to be whether there was a right of appeal in the particular case in question, they would not have put the word 'decisions' into the plural. The use of the plural suggests that the general position regarding appeals is the criterion. Another argument may be derived from considerations of national legal policy: the reason why rights of appeal are limited in certain cases is to prevent proceedings from becoming too drawn-out and to keep costs within reasonable bounds. These objectives might be jeopardized if national courts were obliged to make a reference to Luxembourg even where the sum in issue was small or the case was generally of limited importance.

The policy of Community law, on the other hand, places paramount importance on maintaining uniformity of interpretation of Community provisions: this could be undermined if it were possible for a case involving Community law to run its course without a reference being made. Some of the most important judgments of the European Court have in fact been handed down in cases involving very small sums of money.[53] There is, moreover, an *obiter dictum* of the European Court supporting the concrete theory: this was in *Costa* v. *ENEL*,[54] a reference from a *giudice conciliatore* (magistrate) in Italy. Although the decisions of a *giudice conciliatore* are appealable in some cases, there was no right of appeal against the decision in the proceedings in question because the sum of money involved was so small. In the course of its judgment, the European Court said, with reference to Article 177:[55] 'By the terms of this Article, however, national courts against whose decisions, *as in the present case*, there is no judicial remedy, must refer the matter to the Court of Justice . . .' This suggests that the European Court considers that Article 177(3) refers to the highest court in the case, rather than the highest court in the country. This view seems preferable, though the matter cannot be regarded as settled.[56]

Special difficulties arise with regard to the English Court of Appeal. Decisions of the Court of Appeal may be taken on appeal to the House of Lords only if the leave of either the Court of Appeal or the House of Lords is obtained. Clearly, if the Court of Appeal is prepared to grant leave to appeal in a particular case, it would not be

---

[53] In *Costa* v. *ENEL* (below), for example, the sum in dispute was less than £2.
[54] Case 6/64, [1964] ECR 585.
[55] At p. 592 (italics added).
[56] See *per* Advocate General Capotorti in *Hoffman-La Roche* v. *Centrafarm*, Case 107/76, [1977] ECR 957 at 979–80.

under an obligation to make a reference to the European Court: it would, on any theory, be outside Article 177(3). But what if it refuses leave to appeal?

Assuming that the concrete theory is correct, there are two possible solutions: on the one hand, it could be argued that, if a reference is appropriate, the Court of Appeal is obliged *either* to make the reference *or* to grant leave to appeal to the House of Lords.[57] If it does neither, it would be in breach of Article 177(3). On the other hand, the position could be saved if the House of Lords itself granted leave. In other words, if the Court of Appeal both refuses to make a reference and refuses leave, the House of Lords would be obliged – if the concrete theory is correct – to grant leave to appeal.[58]

In *Bulmer* v. *Bollinger*[59] there is a *dictum* by Lord Denning M R that the Court of Appeal is *never* obliged to make a reference; this point was, however, expressly left open by the other two judges.[60] In the later case of *R.* v. *Henn and Darby*,[61] however, the point actually arose. The accused were convicted by the court of first instance and appealed on the ground that Community law provided a defence to the charge. They asked the Court of Appeal (Criminal Division) to refer the relevant provisions of the Treaty to the European Court for interpretation. The Court of Appeal refused to do so; it dismissed the appeal and refused leave to appeal to the House of Lords. The judgment contains no discussion of the question whether the Court of Appeal was obliged to refer the matter to Luxembourg.[62] The accused then petitioned the House of Lords for leave to appeal: this was granted and a reference was made to the European Court.

An interesting question prompted by this case is whether the appellants in a situation of this kind could ask the House of Lords,

[57] See Jacobs and Durand, *References to the European Court* (1975), p. 163; and Jacobs, 'Which Courts and Tribunals are Bound to Refer to the European Court?', (1977) 2 E.L. Rev. 119 at 121.
[58] See Jacobs, (1977) 2 E.L. Rev. 119 at 121.
[59] [1974] 2 All E.R. 1226 at 1233.
[60] See *per* Stephenson LJ at p. 1241. Stamp LJ agreed with the judgment of Stephenson LJ. Moreover, in the subsequent case of *Hagen* v. *Moretti*, [1980] 3 C M L R 253 at 255, there is an express statement by Buckley LJ that the Court of Appeal is obliged to refer, if leave to appeal is unobtainable. On the other hand, in *Pickstone* v. *Freemans*, [1987] 3 W L R 811; [1987] 3 All E. R. 756; [1987] 2 C M L R 572 (C.A.), Purchas LJ said (at pp. 591, 599) that the Court of Appeal is not obliged to refer; however, leave to appeal to the House of Lords was granted.
[61] [1978] 3 All E.R. 1190 (C A); [1980] 2 All E.R. 166 (E C J and H L).
[62] It was suggested by the House of Lords that the Court of Appeal considered the point too clear to warrant a reference: see [1980] 2 All E.R. at 196–7, *per* Lord Diplock. This appears to be a reference to the *acte clair* doctrine, discussed below at pp. 270–2.

when petitioning for leave to appeal, to refer to the European Court the question whether a court in the position of the House of Lords is obliged to grant leave to appeal in cases where a point of Community law is in issue and the court *a quo* has refused to make a reference. It could be argued that, since the House of Lords is – on any theory – covered by Article 177(3), it would be obliged to refer *that question* to the European Court. If the European Court ruled in favour of the appellants, the House of Lords would have to grant leave to appeal and refer the substantive question.

This argument is attractive, but it could founder on the word 'pending' in Article 177(3). The obligation to refer arises only if the case is 'pending' before a court against whose decisions there is no judicial remedy. Can a case be said to be 'pending' before the House of Lords when leave to appeal has not yet been granted? One could, perhaps, answer this by contending that in the situation under consideration the 'case' is not the appeal itself but the application for leave to appeal: this certainly would be pending before the House of Lords. Interestingly enough, under Article 177(2) it is sufficient if a question of Community law is 'raised' before a court and the court considers that a decision on it is necessary to enable it to give judgment. It seems, therefore, that the House of Lords would at least have the *power* to make a reference before granting leave, even if it is not obliged to do so. If it would otherwise be inclined to refuse leave to appeal, it would be desirable for it to make a reference.[63]

Up to now it has been assumed that the question is simply one of appeal; but it will be remembered that the phrase in the Treaty is 'judicial remedy'. This clearly does not cover a non-judicial remedy, such as the prerogative of mercy, but would it cover judicial review? Decisions of a National Insurance Commissioner, though not subject to appeal, may be quashed in proceedings for judicial review for error of law. Does this constitute a 'judicial remedy'?[64] According to a decision by a National Insurance Commissioner, it does,[65] but the point has never been considered by the European Court. Since the

---

[63] Different issues arise with regard to a Divisional Court in criminal cases, since there is no appeal from its judgment if it refuses to certify a point of law for consideration by the House of Lords. For a case in which it was argued that the third paragraph of Art. 177 applied to it, but which was decided on the basis of the *acte clair* doctrine (discussed below at pp. 270–2), see *S A Magnavision N F* v. *General Optical Council (No. 2)*, [1987] 3 C M L R 262 (DC).

[64] For a detailed discussion of this question, see Jacobs, 'Which Courts and Tribunals Are Bound to Refer to the European Court?', (1977) 2 E.L. Rev. 119.

[65] *Re a Holiday in Italy*, [1975] 1 C M L R 184.

High Court can make a reference on an application for judicial review,[66] there would seem to be no reason why the Commissioner should be obliged to refer. However, an application for judicial review can be made only with leave of the High Court; so the same problems as with the Court of Appeal arise again.

What is the position where the judgment may be reconsidered in other proceedings? This occurs if an interim order is given in interlocutory proceedings: the order may not be appealable in the interlocutory proceedings, but is subject to review in the main action.

The point arose in *Hoffman-La Roche* v. *Centrafarm*,[67] in which the plaintiff had applied to the German courts for an interim order to prohibit the defendant from marketing pharmaceutical products with a particular trademark. Centrafarm maintained that it had a right under Community law to market the products, but the court of first instance granted the order. On appeal, Centrafarm asked the *Oberlandesgericht Karlsruhe* to refer the relevant provisions of Community law to the European Court. The *Oberlandesgericht* was apparently unwilling to make the reference unless it was obliged to do so; it therefore referred three questions to the European Court: the first concerned the interpretation of Article 177(3) itself and was aimed at discovering whether it applied in interlocutory proceedings; the other two related to the substantive issues in the case, but the *Oberlandesgericht* stated that these were to be answered only if the ruling on the first question meant that a reference was obligatory. This rather unusual procedure could have caused the European Court some embarrassment; however, it dealt with the matter by confining the proceedings in the first instance to the question relating to Article 177, the other two questions being left over for later consideration.

The judgment of the *Oberlandesgericht* was not appealable within the context of the interlocutory proceedings, but was subject to review in the main proceedings. In other words, any ruling on a point of Community law made by the *Oberlandesgericht* could be challenged subsequently in the main proceedings. Under German law, the defendant could, moreover, compel the plaintiff to institute the main action. In view of this, it was fair to say that the judgment of the *Oberlandesgericht* was not final, except in a temporary sense.

The European Court began its judgment by expressly affirming

[66] It has in fact done so: see *R.* v. *National Insurance Commissioner,* ex parte *Warry*, Case 41/77, [1977] ECR 2085.

[67] Case 107/76, [1977] ECR 957. For an enlightening comment, see Jacobs, (1977) 2 E.L. Rev. 354.

that interlocutory proceedings are covered by Article 177(2): the summary and urgent character of these proceedings does not deprive the court of the *power* to make a reference. This is clear enough (though it had been doubted by the German court); but what about Article 177(3): does the possibility of review in the main action constitute a 'judicial remedy'?

In deciding this question, the Court started from the premiss that the function of Article 177(3) 'is to prevent a body of national case law not in accord with the rules of Community law from coming into existence in any Member State'. This suggests that the important thing is that, *at some stage in the course of the national proceedings*, there should be an obligation to refer. In accordance with this, the Court therefore held that there is no obligation to make a reference in interlocutory proceedings for an interim order, even if there is no appeal against that decision in the context of those proceedings, provided the decision is subject to review in subsequent proceedings which may be instituted by, or at the request of, either party.

This last point is, of course, crucial: if the ruling cannot be reconsidered in the main proceedings, or if each party is not given the right to insist that those proceedings take place, the judgment in the interlocutory proceedings will not be subject to a 'judicial remedy'. It is of course true that in practice interlocutory orders are often allowed to stand. But this is because the losing party does not consider it worth while to contest the order further. The same thing happens in ordinary proceedings: a court gives a judgment which is subject to appeal, but the unsuccessful party decides not to appeal. In both cases, however, the party against whom judgment is given has the *right* to take the matter further.

Preliminary Rulings on Validity

It has already been pointed out that under Article 41 ECSC the European Court has exclusive jurisdiction to rule on the validity of an act of the Commission or Council. This means that no national court may declare an ECSC act invalid: *any* national court before which the issue is raised must refer it to the European Court.

There is no equivalent provision under the EEC or Euratom Treaties, but the European Court has achieved the same result by judicial decision. This was in the *Foto-Frost*[68] case, where it said that,

---

[68] Case 314/85, 22 October 1987 (not yet reported).

while national courts may declare a Community act valid, they have no power to declare it invalid.[69] The decision was justified on the basis of policy considerations, the desirability of safeguarding the uniform application of Community law being the most important.[70]

WHEN SHOULD A REFERENCE BE MADE?

Two separate, but related, questions must now be considered. First of all, in what circumstances does the power, or obligation, to refer come into existence? Secondly, where the court has the power to refer, but is not obliged to do so, how should it exercise its discretion? The first question concerns the law; the second relates to judicial policy.[71]

The Law

Article 177(1) states which questions may be referred to the European Court; this has already been discussed. Article 177(2) then provides that where 'such a question' is raised, the court may make a reference 'if it considers that a decision on the question is necessary to enable it to give judgment'. Here the phrase 'such a question' refers back to Article 177(1) and means those questions of Community law covered by that provision. Consequently, there are two requisites which must be fulfilled before Article 177(2) comes into operation: an appropriate question of Community law must be *raised* before the court; and a decision on that question must be *necessary* to enable it to give judgment.

At first sight it appears that, under Article 177(3), only the first requisite need be met: Article 177(3) states merely that where 'any such question is raised', the court must refer the matter to the European Court. Here the phrase 'any such question' could be read as meaning the same thing as 'such a question' in Article 177(2) and therefore referring back to Article 177(1). However, it would be

---

[69] The case was decided under Art. 177 EEC, but the ruling would also apply to the Euratom Treaty. The position is therefore the same under all three Treaties.

[70] It is interesting to note that some years ago the European Court proposed that the Treaties should be amended to incorporate such a rule: see *Suggestions of the Court of Justice on European Union*, E. C. Bull., Supp. 9/75, p. 17 at p. 21. This proposal was not put into effect, and the Court apparently decided to take the necessary action itself.

[71] On both these questions, see Jacobs, 'When to Refer to the European Court', (1974) 90 LQR 486.

absurd if a court were obliged to refer a question which was quite
irrelevant to the proceedings; therefore, 'any such question' must
refer back to the second paragraph of Article 177 and mean any
question which falls within that provision, i.e. a question of Community law on which a decision is necessary to enable the court to
give judgment.[72] It follows from this that the same two requisites
apply under Article 177(3).

What is the meaning of these two requisites? The first could
suggest that a reference cannot be made unless one or other of the
parties has raised a point of Community law: the phrase 'raised *before*
any court' could be read as precluding the court itself from raising the
point of its own motion. This, however, seems an unduly restrictive
interpretation and has been rejected by the European Court, which
has ruled that a reference may be made by the national court of its
own motion.[73]

The second requisite is that the national court must consider that a
decision on the question is necessary to enable it to give judgment.
Two points should be noted at the outset: it is not a *reference* to the
European Court which must be necessary, but a *decision* on the
question; secondly, the Treaty makes clear that this is a question for
the national court to decide and, unless Community law is clearly
inapplicable to the case,[74] the European Court will not question
whether the reference is necessary.[75]

When is a decision necessary in order to give judgment? Clearly,
the outcome of the case must be dependent on the decision: as Lord
Denning has said,[76] if the Community point is decided in one way,
judgment for one party must result; if it is decided in another way,
judgment must be given for the other party. This does not, however,
mean that everything must hinge on the Community point: it would
be sufficient if the final judgment were in any way different, even if it
were a question only of the measure of damages or terms of the order.

[72] See *Bulmer* v. *Bollinger*, [1974] 2 All E.R. 1226 at 1234, *per* Lord Denning M R, and the
decision of the Dutch *Hoge Raad* (the highest civil court in the Netherlands) in the *Reinvoorde*
case, 7 April 1970, [1973] C M L R 175 (paragraph 20); see also Schermers, paragraph 726.
[73] *Salonia*, Case 126/80, [1981] E C R 1563 (paragraph 7 of the judgment); see also R S C
Ord. 114, r. 2(1); The Criminal Appeal (References to the European Court) Rules 1972, S I
1972, No. 1786, r. 3(1); Crown Court Rules 1982, SI 1982 No. 1109, r. 29(2); County Court
Rules 1981, Ord. 19, r. 11 (2).
[74] See *Rijksdienst voor Werknemerspensioenen* v. *Vlaeminck*, Case 132/81, [1982] E C R 2953.
[75] See Jacobs and Durand, op. cit., p. 159 and cases cited in notes (q) to (t). See also
Pierik, Case 117/77, [1978] E C R 825.
[76] In *Bulmer* v. *Bollinger*, [1974] 2 All E.R. 1226 at 1234; but see *Foglia* v. *Novello*,
discussed at pp. 258–60, above.

If, on the other hand, the judgment would be exactly the same however the Community point was decided, a decision on it would not be necessary for the judgment.

What if the Community point would be conclusive only in certain circumstances? Two examples may be given of such a situation. Assume that one party bases his case exclusively on a provision of Community law, but that provision would be applicable only if certain contested facts are established. Before those facts have been established, the court cannot be certain whether a decision on the Community point is necessary or not: if the facts cannot be established, the outcome of the case would be the same irrespective of how the Community point was decided. Until evidence has been heard, therefore, the Community point is only potentially decisive.

The second example is a case where one party puts forward two quite separate grounds each of which, if established, would make good his claim. If one ground is based on Community law and one on national law, the court cannot tell whether the Community point is decisive until it has decided the other point: if the party can win on that, it would not matter which way the Community point was decided; only if the national point goes against him, would the Community point become decisive.

The problem in both these situations is that, until the other matters have been decided, the Community point would dispose of the case only if it was decided in one particular way. In the first example, it would dispose of the case if it were decided against the person relying on Community law: in such a case, he would lose even if he succeeded in establishing his contentions of fact. In the second example, on the other hand, the Community point would dispose of the case only if it were decided in favour of the person relying on it: he would then win even if the other point went against him.

What should a court do in such a situation? It could be argued that the court cannot make a reference until the other matters have been decided: unless it does this, it cannot be certain that a decision on the Community point is really necessary.[77] This, however, is too restrictive an interpretation.[78] From a practical point of view, it might be

[77] *Per* Lord Denning M R in *Bulmer* v. *Bollinger* [1974] 2 All E.R. 1226 at 1235 (letters d and e). In Lord Denning's view, the court should decide the facts before making the reference.

[78] Lord Denning's view to the contrary (above) has been subject to widespread criticism and was not accepted in *R.* v. *Plymouth Justices,* ex p. *Rogers,* [1982] 3 W L R 1; [1982] 2 All E.R. 175; [1982] 3 C M L R 221 (D C); see also *Polydor* v. *Harlequin Record Shops,* [1980] 2 C M L R 413 (C A); see further Schermers, paragraphs 722–724 and the authors cited there in note 120.

much better in some cases to decide the Community point first. If it is fairly simple, but the other matters are complex, it could be less expensive and more expeditious to make an immediate reference to the European Court. It is suggested, therefore, that 'necessary' should be interpreted to mean that the point *could* be decisive. In other words, it should be sufficient if a decision on the point is potentially decisive: it should not have to be proved that it would be decisive in all possible eventualities. If this interpretation is accepted, the national court would then be able to decide for itself when to make the reference.[79]

What is the position where the point has already been decided by the European Court in a previous case? The European Court has ruled that in such a case the national court is not obliged to make a reference even if it is a court against whose decisions there is no judicial remedy under national law.[80] In such a situation the point can be regarded as settled and the case would be exempted from Article 177(3): according to the European Court, the authority of the previous ruling would deprive the obligation under Article 177(3) of its purpose 'and thus empty it of its substance'.[81] However, the European Court is not bound by its own previous decisions and if the national court thought that the previous judgment was wrong and wanted the European Court to reconsider the matter, it would be entitled to make the reference.[82] The existence of a previous ruling, therefore, removes the obligation to refer, but does not affect the power to refer.

Some lawyers push this argument further and apply the same rule where the Community provision is regarded as clear, even if the European Court has not ruled on it. This is the so-called '*acte clair*' doctrine, according to which a clear provision (*acte clair*) does not require 'interpretation' and therefore falls entirely outside the scope of Article 177 as a whole. If there is no doubt as to the meaning of the provision, it is argued, there can be no 'question' on which a decision is necessary: all the court has to do is to apply the provision.

This doctrine has something to recommend it from a common-sense point of view and has attracted the support of some eminent

[79] As far as the English High Court is concerned, it is expressly stated in RSC Ord. 114, r. 2(1) that the order may be made at any stage in the proceedings.
[80] *Da Costa*, Cases 28–30/62, [1963] ECR 31 at 38; *CILFIT*, Case 283/81, [1982] ECR 3415 (paragraphs 13–15).
[81] *Da Costa* (supra).
[82] Ibid.

jurists.[83] However, it is a well-known fact that what is clear to one set of lawyers can be extremely doubtful to another set of lawyers. This is especially true where the two groups belong to different legal traditions or look at the law from different points of view. In the case of Community law in particular, the policy-oriented approach of the European Court can produce very different results from the more traditional methods of an English judge.

This controversy is important only with regard to Article 177(3): since a lower court is not in any case obliged to make a reference, it would be entitled to refrain from doing so on the ground that the provision is sufficiently clear. In the case of a court against whose decisions there is no judicial remedy, however, the question is crucial: is such a court exempted from the obligation to refer if it considers that the provision does not require interpretation?

In spite of its dangers, the *acte clair* doctrine has been fairly widely accepted by national courts in the Community[84] and in 1982 it gained the approval of the European Court, though this approval was subject to so many conditions that one might think the Court was really trying to kill the idea.[85] The case in question was *CILFIT*[86], where the European Court said that even a court covered by Article 177(3) is not obliged to make a reference where the answer is 'so obvious as to leave no scope for any reasonable doubt'.[87] It qualified this, however, by saying that the national court must be convinced that the answer would be equally obvious to a court in another Member State and to the European Court. In deciding whether the answer is obvious, the national court must compare the different versions of the text in the various Community languages. It must also bear in mind that legal concepts and terminology do not necessarily

[83] See, for example, Lagrange, 'The Theory of the Acte Clair: A Bone of Contention or a Source of Unity?', (1971) 8 C.M.L. Rev. 313.

[84] Schermers, paragraph 729 and the references he gives in note 129. The Commission has also expressed its acceptance of the doctrine: see European Parliament, Question 608/78, 31 January 1979, O J 1979, C 28/9. Lord Denning gave the doctrine his approval in *Bulmer* v. *Bollinger*, [1974] 2 All E.R. 1226 at 1235, and it was applied in *SA Magnavision N V* v. *General Optical Council* (*No. 1*), [1987] 1 C M L R 887 and (*No. 2*), [1987] 2 C M L R 262 (both Div. Ct); see also *R* v. *Secretary of State for Social Services*, ex p. *Bomore Medical Supplies* [1986] 1 C M L R 228 (CA). However, in *R.* v. *Henn*, [1980] 2 All E.R. 166 at 196–7, the House of Lords went no further than to say that a reference need not be made where the point is covered by an 'established body of case law' of the European Court. It also stressed the pitfalls of applying English canons of statutory interpretation to Community law.

[85] See Rasmussen, 'The European Court's *Acte Clair* Strategy in *CILFIT*', (1984) 9 E.L. Rev. 242.

[86] Case 283/81, [1982] ECR 3415.

[87] At paragraph 16 of the judgment.

have the same meaning in Community law as in national law. The European Court concluded by saying that 'every provision of Community law must be placed in its context and interpreted in the light of the provisions of Community law as a whole, regard being had to the objectives thereof and to its state of evolution at the date on which the provision in question is to be applied'.[88] Put more simply, the national court must remember the European Court's habit of giving great weight to policy.[89]

It is not hard to see that full compliance with these requirements is virtually impossible. In particular, the obligation to compare the text in its different linguistic versions could cause great difficulties. In the absence of expert evidence, an English court could not compare, for example, the Greek and Danish texts. The importance of this is, however, beyond doubt since it can often happen that a text which appears straightforward in one language may be ambiguous (or mean something different) in another. An example in point is *Koschniske*,[90] in which a Dutch social security tribunal had to interpret a Community regulation which contained, in the Dutch text, the word '*echtgenote*'. The English version of the regulation uses the word 'spouse' and all the other texts use a word which can apply to both a husband or a wife; the Dutch word, however, can apply only to a woman: it means 'wife'. (The masculine form is '*echtgenoot*'.) The question before the Dutch tribunal was whether the term could cover a husband. On the basis of the Dutch text alone, it might have seemed clear that it could not. Fortunately, the tribunal made a reference to the European Court which ruled, after considering all the versions of the provision, that it covered both a husband and a wife. If the tribunal had interpreted the provision for itself without considering the other versions of the text, it would have made a serious mistake.

Discretion

A court has a discretion only if its decisions are subject to an appeal or other judicial remedy. Assuming this to be the case, how should the

---

[88] Paragraph 20 of the judgment.
[89] In some cases the European Court will even give an 'interpretation' that is clearly at variance with an unambiguous text. For examples, see *Parti Ecologiste 'Les Verts'* v. *European Parliament* (discussed at pp. 77–8, above) and the *SPI* case (discussed at pp. 252–3, above).
[90] Case 9/79, [1979] ECR 2717. See further, pp. 68–70, above.

discretion be exercised?[91] This is, of course, a question for the national courts themselves, but among the factors which they may wish to take into consideration are the following. Should the facts be decided first? In many cases this will be desirable,[92] but in some it may be better to obtain a ruling from the European Court right at the outset: until that has been obtained, it might not be clear what facts *are* relevant.

Referring a case to Luxembourg will involve a delay in the proceedings. In some cases a lower court might feel that the time factor is so important that it would be justified in deciding the point itself. However, if the case is taken on appeal, a reference may well be made in the end and the result might be that a final judgment takes even longer to obtain. In some interlocutory cases, for example an application for an injunction pending trial, the best course might be for the court to grant the order and at the same time make the reference. This will protect the plaintiff's position while the Luxembourg proceedings are taking place.

The difficulty and importance of the point, as well as the expense of a reference in comparison to the amount at stake, will also be considered, though there have been cases where points of great public importance have been decided in actions involving only very small sums of money.[93] Finally, the wishes of the parties will not be ignored, but it must be remembered that the decision to refer is that of the court, not the parties.

---

[91] For a general discussion, see *Bulmer* v. *Bollinger*, [1974] 2 All E.R. 1226 at 1235–1236; *Church of Scientology of California* v. *Customs and Excise Commissioners*, [1981] 1 All E.R. 1035 (C A); *R.* v. *Plymouth Justices*, ex p. *Rogers*, [1982] 3 W L R 1; [1982] 2 All E.R. 175; [1982] 3 C M L R 221 (D C); *Customs and Excise Commissioners* v. *Samex*, [1983] 1 All E.R. 1042; [1983] 3 C M L R 194; see also Jacobs, 'When to Refer to the European Court', (1974) 90 L Q R 486. In *R.* v. *Henn*, [1980] 2 All E.R. 166 at 196, the House of Lords said that in a criminal trial on indictment it will rarely be proper for the trial court to make a reference.

[92] See *Irish Creamery Milk Suppliers Association* v. *Ireland*, Cases 36, 71/80, [1981] E C R 735, where, however, the European Court stressed that it was for the national court to decide when to make the reference. See also the English cases cited in the previous note.

[93] See note 53, above.

PROCEDURE

English Courts

In England provision for preliminary references has been made in the rules of procedure of the most important courts.[94] However, even where this is not the case, any court or tribunal covered by Article 177 may make a reference: its power to do so derives from the Treaty and section 2(1) of the European Communities Act; the procedural details may be fixed by the court itself under its inherent power to regulate such matters.[95] The discussion which follows is based on RSC Ord. 114, which applies to the High Court and the Court of Appeal; similar provisions are applicable in the other courts for which special provision has been made and the Rules of the Supreme Court would no doubt furnish a model for those courts and tribunals for which no special provision has been made.

It is expressly provided that an order for reference may be made by the court on application by either party, or of the court's own motion. It is also expressly stated that it may be made at any stage of the proceedings:[96] thus there is no requirement in the Rules that the evidence must he heard before a reference may be made.[97] An application by a party for an order may be made either before, or at, the hearing; in the former case it is made by motion.[98]

If the court decides to make the reference, the order will contain a schedule in which the request for a ruling and the questions asked will be set out. The proceedings will then be stayed (unless the court orders otherwise) until the European Court has given its ruling.[99] The Senior Master of the Supreme Court (Queen's Bench Division) will transmit the order to the European Court.[100]

[94] For the High Court and Court of Appeal, RSC Ord. 114; for the Court of Appeal, Criminal Division, The Criminal Appeal (References to the European Court) Rules 1972 (SI 1972 No. 1786); for the county court, the County Court Rules 1981, Ord. 19, r. 11; and for the Crown Court, The Crown Court Rules 1982, SI 1982 No. 1009, r. 29.

[95] Jacobs and Durand, *References to the European Court* (1975), pp. 164 and 167.

[96] A reference cannot, however, be made after delivery of judgment, even if the order of the court has not yet been drawn up: *SA Magnavision NV* v. *General Optical Council (No. 2)*, [1987] 2 CMLR 262 (Div. Ct.).

[97] RSC Ord. 114, r. 2(1).

[98] RSC Ord. 114, r. 2(2).

[99] RSC Ord. 114, r. 4.

[100] RSC Ord. 114, r. 5. The rule that the order for reference is transmitted by the Senior Master of the Supreme Court applies not only to the High Court and Court of Appeal, but also to the other courts for which express provision for preliminary references has been made: see SI 1972 No. 1786, r. 4; Crown Court Rules 1982, r. 29(4); County Court Rules 1981, Ord. 19, r. 11 (5).

The Reference

The form and content of the reference are not covered by the rules of procedure of either the English courts or the European Court. However, certain general practices have grown up. Normally the order for reference will contain a brief summary of the facts of the case (in so far as these have already been established), an account of the procedure followed prior to the reference, the order sought by the plaintiff, the matters raised in defence, the main arguments of the parties on the Community point and the reasons of the court for making the reference.[101] Sometimes the national court will indicate its own interpretation of the provision in question. Where national law is relevant, the national court should give a clear statement of the provisions in question: the European Court has no power to rule on national law, but a knowledge of the relevant national provisions may be useful in order to define the exact issues at stake.

The European Court has no jurisdiction, in proceedings for a preliminary reference, to rule on the *application* of Community law to the facts of the case: all it can do is to interpret Community law and, in the case of Community acts, rule on their validity. For this reason the questions put to the European Court should be phrased in an abstract way: the Court should, for example, be asked whether a particular provision of Community law is to be interpreted as having a particular meaning, rather than asked whether it provides a defence to the charge in the case. The European Court, however, adopts a very flexible approach and will not refuse to give a ruling on the ground that questions are improperly phrased: it will simply decide what questions should have been asked and then proceed on the basis that those are the questions referred. In this way it can get to the substance of the matter with the minimum of formality and delay.

Appeals against an Order for Reference

Is it legitimate for national law to provide for a right of appeal against an order for reference? It has already been mentioned that in the *Rheinmühlen* case[102] Advocate General Warner suggested that the

---

[101] Jacobs and Durand, op. cit., 169; see also Collins, *European Community Law in the United Kingdom* (3rd ed.) pp. 155–163. These matters will be covered in greater detail in the file of the case, which is also sent to the European Court: Jacobs and Durand, op. cit., p. 176.

[102] Cases 146, 166/73, [1974] ECR 33 at 43–7.

existence of a right of appeal constituted an improper fetter on the power of a national court to make a reference. This was rejected by the European Court, which ruled that the order for reference remains 'subject to the remedies normally available under national law'.[103] The mere fact that an appeal has been lodged will not, however, deter the European Court from going ahead with the reference: only if the order for reference is withdrawn by the court which made it, or is set aside by a higher court, will the European Court decline to give a ruling.[104]

As was pointed out by Advocate General Warner in the *Rhein-mühlen* case, this rule could mean that the European Court would give unnecessary rulings: if the appeal is allowed after the ruling has been made, the ruling will not be applied by the national court. This is not, however, likely to occur very often, as the time needed for a ruling by the European Court will normally be greater than that for an appeal against the order for reference; moreover, the most likely reason for the appeal to be allowed is that the appellate court might think that the Community point is not relevant to the proceedings: if this is the case, the European Court's ruling will not be applied anyway. Normally, the appeal will be decided before the case is heard by the European Court and the existence of a right of appeal is therefore more likely to prevent the European Court from giving unnecessary judgments.

---

[103] [1974] ECR at 147, paragraph 3. The words 'normally available' could suggest that it is improper to make special provision for an appeal against an order for reference (as is done, for example, under RSC Ord. 114, r. 6): see Jacobs and Durand, op. cit., p. 171; for the view that the special features of the appeal procedure laid down by RSC Ord. 114 do not prevent the right of appeal from being regarded as a normal remedy, see Collins, op. cit., p. 152. It is interesting to note that Advocate General Warner's view seems to have found favour in Ireland, where the Irish Supreme Court held in *Campus Oil* v. *Minister for Industry and Energy* [1984] 1 CMLR 479, that Art. 177 is part of domestic Irish law and *under Irish law* precludes any appeal against an order for reference. Irish law made no express provision for an appeal and the Supreme Court said that the Irish Parliament lacks the power to make such provision. The Supreme Court was aware of the *Rheinmühlen* case but considered it irrelevant since it was deciding the matter under Irish law. See, further, O'Keefe, 'Appeals against an Order to Refer under Art. 177 of the EEC Treaty', (1984) 9 E.L. Rev. 87.

[104] [1974] ECR at 147, paragraph 3. See also *BRT* v. *SABAM*, Case 127/73, [1974] ECR 51 at paragraph 9 of the judgment and *Simmenthal*, Case 106/77, [1978] ECR 629 at paragraph 10 of the judgment. See also *De Geus* v. *Bosch*, Case 13/61, [1962] ECR 45, where the Court held that the mere fact that one of the parties had appealed against the order for reference did not preclude it from hearing the case. In *Chanel* v. *Cepeha*, Case 31/68, [1970] ECR 403, however, the court which made the reference informed the European Court that an appeal had been lodged and stated that the effect of this under national law was to suspend the order for reference. The European Court thereupon stayed the proceedings. Subsequently, the parties agreed to a settlement and the appeal was allowed; the European Court then removed the case from the register.

In England, special provision is made for appeal against an order for reference made by the High Court. RSC Ord. 114, r. 6 states that an order for reference is deemed to be a final decision, so that an appeal lies to the Court of Appeal without leave; notice of appeal must, however, be served within 14 days. Under RSC Ord. 114, r. 5, the order will not be transmitted to the European Court until this time limit has expired and, if an appeal is lodged, until after it has been disposed of; consequently, most of the questions discussed in the previous paragraphs are unlikely to arise in the case of references from English courts.[105] It is also possible to appeal against a *refusal* to make an order for reference but, as this would be an interlocutory appeal and no special provision is made for it in the Rules of Court, leave would have to be obtained from either the High Court or the Court of Appeal.[106] It seems rather strange that special provision is made for appeal against an order to refer, but not against a refusal to make such an order;[107] however, it will always be possible to renew the request for a reference if the case itself is taken on appeal.

The European Court

The procedure in the European Court was discussed in Chapter 2. The parties – together with the Member States, the Commission and, where one of its acts forms the subject matter of the proceedings, the Council – have the right to submit written observations and make oral submissions. However, the issues before the Court are determined by the order for reference and the role of the parties in this regard is limited to making suggestions to the Court as to how the reference should be interpreted. As was mentioned previously, the Court does not pay excessive regard to the exact wording of the questions submitted by the national court but tries rather to get to the heart of the matter. If the case can be disposed of without answering all the questions posed by the national court, the European Court will do this: for example, if the European Court is asked questions concerning the validity and interpretation of a Community measure,

---

[105] A similar provision applies to the county court: see CCR 1981, Ord. 19, r. 11 (5). For a suggestion that these provisions are incompatible with Community law, see Jacobs and Durand, op. cit., pp. 171–172 and Usher, *European Court Practice*, pp. 163–164; *contra* Collins, op. cit., p. 152.

[106] *Bulmer* v. *Bollinger* [1974] 2 All E.R. 1226 at 1233 (*per* Lord Denning MR) and at 1241 (*per* Stephenson J).

[107] It was suggested by Stephenson J in *Bulmer* v. *Bollinger* [1974] 2 All E.R. 1226 at 1241 that the failure of RSC Ord. 114, r. 6 to deal with this was an oversight.

it will not concern itself with the interpretation if it holds the measure invalid.

The European Court has no jurisdiction to give rulings which bind the national court on questions of fact. It often cannot decide the relevant points of law without some basis of fact, but it normally relies on the national court to supply this. For these reasons, the European Court is not normally required to make findings of fact in preliminary references. There are, however, exceptions: for example, if the validity of a Community act is in issue, the Court may have to decide a question of fact in order to determine whether the Community act is valid. In this situation the Court will decide the question of fact according to its normal procedure, if necessary hearing witnesses, and then rule on the validity of the measure.[108] The national court is bound by the ruling on the point of validity, though not (presumably) on the findings of fact on which it was based.

In its judgment, the European Court will, after setting out the facts and background to the case, discuss the questions posed and give the reasons for its rulings on the various issues. At the end of its judgment, it will give formal rulings on the questions asked, or state that certain questions do not require an answer.[109] As was mentioned above, if the questions are put in an improper form, the Court will answer them as if they had been properly put. Sometimes two or more questions will be answered together. Occasionally the Court will answer more than was asked.[110]

INTERPRETATION AND APPLICATION

It has already been pointed out that the European Court has power to interpret Community law but not to apply it to the facts of the case. The precise distinction between interpretation and application is, however, very elastic and the European Court appears to make use of this elasticity for its own purposes. Thus, if it is asked to interpret a Community provision, it may satisfy itself with a general indication of the provision's meaning and then state that it is a question of fact, to be decided by the national court, whether a particular case comes

[108] See *per* Advocate General Warner in *EMI*, Case 51/75, [1976] ECR 811 at 854. A case in which such questions of fact had to be decided was *Milac*, Case 131/77, [1978] ECR 1041.

[109] The formal rulings must be interpreted in the light of the reasons: *Bosch*, Case 135/77, [1978] ECR 855 (paragraph 4).

[110] For the problems caused by this in France, see pp. 233–5, above.

within its scope: in such a situation, the effective determination of the case rests with the national court. On the other hand, however, it might give such a precise and specific interpretation that the national court is left with nothing more to do, other than to give a formal judgment. Its choice between these two approaches seems to depend on policy (though one might surmise that the Court would incline towards the first alternative if its members were unable to agree among themselves on the precise interpretation of the provision).

The distinction between these approaches may be made clear by two examples. The first is *Walrave and Koch* v. *Union Cycliste Internationale*,[111] which concerned motor-paced cycle racing. In this sport, one person rides ahead on a motorcycle and is followed by another on a racing bicycle, the former being called the 'pacer' and the latter, the 'stayer'. The idea is that the pacer creates a slip-stream and if the stayer remains within it, he can achieve considerable speeds. The case arose because the body controlling the sport made a rule that pacer and stayer had to be of the same nationality. The two plaintiffs, who were both professional pacers, felt that the rule would make it difficult for them to obtain work. They therefore brought proceedings in a national court for a declaration that the rule was contrary to Community law. The EEC Treaty prohibits discrimination against workers, self-employed persons and providers of services, and the European Court, to which a reference was made under Article 177 EEC, had no difficulty in finding that professional sportsmen were covered by the relevant provisions. However, they took the view that, notwithstanding the prohibition against discrimination, national teams could be selected on the basis of nationality. The question, therefore, was whether pacer and stayer constituted a team or whether the stayer was the only competitor and the pacer a mere auxiliary, like a trainer or coach. Instead of giving a clear answer, however, the European Court merely stated:[112] '. . . it is for the national court . . . to decide in particular whether in the sport in question the pacemaker and stayer do or do not constitute a team.' This left everything to the national court.

This may be contrasted with another case also concerning the rights of Community immigrants, *Cristini* v. *SNCF*.[113] Under Article 7(2) of Regulation 1612/68 it is provided that a Community national working in another Member State is entitled to the same 'social

---

[111] Case 36/74, [1974] ECR 1405.
[112] At paragraph 10 of the judgment.
[113] Case 32/75, [1975] ECR 1085.

advantages' as national workers in the country of immigration. A French court asked the European Court whether a French provision entitling large families[114] to a special card giving them the right to reduced fares on the French railways was a 'social advantage' within the meaning of the Regulation.

The European Court might have given some vague definition of a 'social advantage' and left it to the French court to decide whether this covered the French provision. Instead it went right to the point. After first disclaiming any power to 'apply the Community rule to a specific case', it stated:[115] '. . . Article 7(2) of Regulation (EEC) No. 1612/68 of the Council must be interpreted as meaning that the social advantages referred to by that provision include fares reduction cards issued by a national railway authority to large families . . .' This clearly left nothing more to be decided by the national court.

EFFECTS OF PRELIMINARY RULINGS

After the European Court has given judgment, the case is sent back to the national court which made the reference. The proceedings will then continue in the national court from the point at which they were suspended. The national court is not obliged to apply Community law – it may eventually decide the case on other grounds – but if it does apply it, it is bound by the European Court's ruling.[116]

What is the effect of the ruling in *subsequent* cases? As was mentioned above,[117] if the same issue arises again in a later case in the courts of the Member State from which the reference was made, or in the courts of another Member State, the ruling may be applied again without it being necessary to make a new reference. This is so even if the court concerned is one from which there is no appeal. On the other hand, the court is not *precluded* from making a reference if it wishes. It might do this if it considers the previous ruling mistaken and would like the European Court to reconsider the matter. As no strict doctrine of precedent operates in Community law, the European Court could in theory overrule its previous decision; in practice, however, it would be very unlikely to do so, since individuals and courts in the Member States might have relied on it.

---

[114] Families with three or more children under the age of 18.
[115] At paragraph 19 of the judgment; see also the formal ruling.
[116] *Milch-, Fett- und Eierkontor*, Case 29/68, [1969] ECR 165 (paragraph 3 of the judgment).
[117] See p. 270.

Are all courts and tribunals in Member States *bound* by the ruling unless and until it is overruled in a later judgment? It is suggested that this is the case: even if the court in question is not covered by Article 177(3), it should be obliged either to follow the ruling or to make a new reference.[118] It would be improper for it simply to depart from the ruling because it thought that it was wrong. This is certainly the position in the United Kingdom, where it is provided by section 3(1) of the European Communities Act that any question as to the meaning or effect of any of the Treaties, or as to the validity, meaning or effect of any Community instrument, must, if not referred to the European Court for a ruling, be decided in accordance with the principles laid down by any relevant decision of the European Court.[119]

FURTHER READING

Collins, *European Community Law in the United Kingdom* (3rd ed., 1980), Chapter 3.

Jacobs and Durand, *References to the European Court* (1975).

Schermers, Chapter 4.

Schermers *et al.* (eds), *Article 177 EEC: Experiences and Problems* (1987).

Alexander and Grabandt, 'National Courts Entitled to Ask Preliminary Rulings under Article 177 of the EEC Treaty: The Case Law of the Court of Justice', (1982) 19 C.M.L. Rev. 413.

Barav, 'Some Aspects of the Preliminary Rulings Procedure in EEC Law', (1977) 2 E.L. Rev. 3.

Barav, 'Preliminary Censorship? The Judgment of the European Court in Foglia v. Novello', (1980) 5 E.L. Rev. 443.

Barav, 'Imbroglio préjudiciel', [1982] RTDE 431.

Bebr, 'Article 177 of the EEC Treaty in the Practice of National Courts', (1977) 26 ICLQ 241.

Bebr, 'The Possible Implications of *Foglia* v. *Novello* II', (1982) 9 C.M.L. Rev. 421.

---

[118] This point has not been considered by the European Court; for references to academic writings and national court judgments (both *pro* and *contra*), see Schermers, paragraphs 759–761. See, in particular, Trabucchi, 'L'effet "erga omnes" des décisions préjudicielles rendues par la Cour de justice des Communautés européennes', [1974] RTDE 56.

[119] The position regarding preliminary rulings on the validity of a Community act is discussed further in Chapter 14.

Bebr, 'Arbitration Tribunals and Article 177 of the EEC Treaty', (1985) 22 C.M.L. Rev. 489.

Dashwood and Arnull, 'English Courts and Article 177 of the EEC Treaty', (1984) 4 YEL 255.

Gray, 'Advisory Opinions and the European Court of Justice,' (1983) 8 E.L. Rev. 24.

Jacobs, 'When to Refer to the European Court', (1974) 90 LQR 486.

Lagrange, 'The Theory of the Acte Clair: A Bone of Contention or a Source of Unity?', (1971) 8 C.M.L. Rev. 313.

O'Keefe, 'Appeals against an Order to Refer under Article 177 of the EEC Treaty', (1984) 9 E.L. Rev. 87.

Rasmussen, 'The European Court's *Acte Clair* Strategy in *CILFIT*', (1984) 9 E.L. Rev. 242.

10

ENFORCEMENT ACTIONS

There are two ways in which Community law can be enforced against national governments. The first is through action taken by private individuals in the national courts. This is possible only through the application of the doctrine of direct effect; but as long as that doctrine is accepted by the national courts, it provides a very effective means of enforcing Community law: its particular advantages are that it puts no strain on Community manpower, and national governments are not likely to disobey the rulings of their own courts. Its main limitations are that it applies only with regard to directly effective provisions – though the European Court is now prepared to hold most provisions directly effective – and then only if an individual or company whose interests are affected is prepared to take legal action. So far the Commission has not itself brought proceedings in national courts in order to secure compliance with Community law, nor does it appear to be prepared to give financial assistance to would-be litigants for this purpose.

One situation in which national proceedings are appropriate is where a national government purports to restrict the freedom of action of its citizens in a way which is contrary to Community law. It may do this by making it a criminal offence to do something which is covered by a Community right: in such a case the accused can plead Community law as a defence and a preliminary reference will normally be made to the European Court to determine whether the provision should be interpreted in the way suggested by the accused; if the European Court decides that it should, he will be acquitted. Thus, for example, when the Irish Government imposed restrictions on fishing in Irish waters which were contrary to Community law, a Dutch fisherman was able to invoke Community law as a defence to a charge of illegal fishing.[1]

Another possibility is that the national government will take administrative action contrary to some provision of Community law.

[1] *Minister for Fisheries* v. *Schoenenberg*, Case 88/77, [1978] ECR 473. Parallel proceedings under Art. 169 EEC were also brought: see *Commission* v. *Ireland*, Case 61/77, [1978] ECR 417.

For example, in 1977 the Ministry of Agriculture in Britain imposed a ban on the importation of main-crop potatoes. A Dutch potato exporter challenged this by applying for a declaration in the High Court that the ban was contrary to Community law. A reference was made to the European Court, which held that this was indeed the case.[2] The ban was then lifted.

A third possibility is that the national authorities will refuse to grant an individual a benefit to which he is entitled under Community law. The *Cristini* case, discussed in the previous chapter,[3] provides an example of the way in which national proceedings and a reference under Article 177 EEC can be used by the person concerned to vindicate his rights.

This way of proceeding is of great importance and will be very valuable to the individual concerned; it is not, however, sufficient in itself to ensure the effectiveness of Community law in all cases. The second way in which Community law can be enforced against national governments is by direct proceedings against the Member State concerned. Special provision is made for this in the Treaties and it was originally thought by many to be the only way in which Community law could be enforced.[4]

The relevant provisions are Articles 88 ECSC, 169–171 EEC and 141–143 Euratom. As is often the case, the EEC and Euratom provisions are identical, but there are important differences under the ECSC. Under all three Treaties, however, the procedure can be divided into two distinct stages: the administrative stage, in which the Commission plays the main part, and the judicial stage, in which the European Court gives a ruling.

The most important difference between the ECSC Treaty and the later Treaties is that under the former the administrative stage is concluded by a Commission decision recording the Member State's violation; this decision is binding and if the Member State wishes to contest it, it must bring proceedings before the European Court.

Under the EEC and Euratom Treaties, on the other hand, the Commission merely delivers an opinion: this is not binding and if the

---

[2] *Meijer* v. *Department of Trade*, Case 118/78, [1979] ECR 1387. A parallel action under Art. 169 was brought in this case as well: *Commission* v. *United Kingdom*, Case 231/78, [1979] ECR 1447. In both this and the Irish fisheries case the proceedings under Art. 169 were, as things turned out, unnecessary.

[3] At p. 279.

[4] See, for example, the arguments advanced by the Dutch and Belgian Governments in *Van Gend en Loos*, Case 26/62, [1963] ECR 1.

Member State fails to abide by it, the Commission must bring the matter before the Court.

A second difference is that under the ECSC Treaty the procedure may be set in motion only by the Commission, while under the EEC and Euratom Treaties another Member State may also initiate it. This is, however, rare in practice: it is thought that a direct clash between two Member States could create bad feeling and, as the Commission is normally quite happy to take action, Member States are usually prepared to leave it to the Commission.

It should also be mentioned that, besides the general enforcement procedures laid down by the Treaty provisions referred to above, there are certain special procedures which apply only in the case of violations of particular rules of Community law. The main examples are found in Articles 93,[5] 100A(4), 180 and 225 EEC and Articles 38 and 82 Euratom. These provisions lay down variants of the normal procedure which replace the latter in the circumstances indicated.

The bulk of this chapter will be taken up with a discussion of the normal enforcement procedure against Member States – that is to say, the procedure initiated by the Commission under the general enforcement provisions mentioned previously: the rights of Member States, and of private individuals, to take action will be dealt with separately; the special enforcement procedures will be considered only incidentally.

WHAT CONSTITUTES A VIOLATION?

Provisions Covered

What constitutes a violation of Community law for the purpose of an enforcement action? What provisions of Community law may be enforced by means of this procedure? Under all three Treaties the proceedings may be brought only if a Member State has failed 'to fulfil an obligation under this Treaty': only a violation of such an obligation will, therefore, provide the foundation for an enforcement action.[6]

[5] For a discussion of this procedure, see Dashwood, 'Control of State Aids in the EEC: Prevention and Cure under Art. 93', (1975) 12 C.M.L. Rev. 43 at 53–7.
[6] It should be noted that the French version of the Treaty seems wider than the English. It reads: 'Si la Commission estime qu'un État membre a manqué à une des obligations qui lui incombent en vertu du présent Traité . . .' It could be argued that 'obligations arising by virtue of the Treaty' covers all the obligations resulting from Community membership.

What is covered by this? Clearly, a violation of a provision in one of the constitutive Treaties (the ECSC, EEC and Euratom Treaties, together with any amending and supplementing Treaties) would be included. A violation of an obligation contained in Community legislation enacted under the Treaties would likewise be covered: violation of the legislation would constitute a violation of the Treaty provision empowering its enactment. Moreover, a violation of a provision in an agreement between the Community and a non-member State could reasonably be regarded as a violation of the constitutive Treaty under which the Community was empowered (expressly or impliedly) to conclude the agreement. This is particularly clear in the case of the EEC in view of Article 228(2), which states that international agreements concluded under the procedure laid down in Article 228(1) are binding on the Member States.[7] It is hard to see how international agreements between the Member States and third countries could be covered, even if, as in the case of the GATT, they are binding on the Community.[8] Article 228 EEC would not apply in such a case as it covers only 'agreements between the Community and one or more States'. However, in view of the blatant disregard for the words of the Treaty displayed by the European Court in the *SPI*[9] case, one cannot rule out the possibility that it would hold these agreements to be covered by Article 169.

What is the position with regard to an agreement concluded jointly by the Community and the Member States on the one side and one or more non-member States on the other side? It will be remembered that these 'mixed agreements' are normally entered into where the matters dealt with are thought to fall partly within the jurisdiction of the Community and partly within that of the Member States.[10] If this is so, a breach by a Member State of an obligation under a mixed agreement could form the subject-matter of an enforcement action if the obligation fell within the jurisdiction of the Community, but should not do so otherwise.

Agreements between the Member States themselves (other than the constitutive Treaties) pose similar problems. A decision of the representatives of the Governments of the Member States meeting in

[7] It is true that Art. 228(1) commences with the words 'Where this Treaty provides for the conclusion of agreements between the Community and one or more states . . .' but this could be regarded as including implied provision for the conclusion of an international agreement; there is little doubt that the European Court would take this view.

[8] See pp. 172–3, above.

[9] Cases 267–9/81, [1983] ECR 801: see pp. 252–4, above.

[10] See pp. 153 and 174–5, above.

the Council cannot constitute an obligation under the ECSC, EEC or Euratom Treaties if, on its true construction, it is no more than an international agreement in simplified form.[11] The same is true of subsidiary conventions, except perhaps in the case of conventions entered into under Article 220 EEC. This requires Member States to 'enter into negotiations with each other with a view to securing for the benefit of their nationals' certain advantages, such as the simplification of formalities regarding the enforcement of judgments given in other Community countries.[12] The Convention on Jurisdiction and the Enforcement of Judgments in Civil and Commercial Matters[13] was concluded in consequence of this provision. It could be argued that a breach of the Judgments Convention (or any other convention concluded to give effect to Article 220) would constitute a violation of Article 220 itself. If this is correct, an enforcement action under Article 169 could then be brought.

Is this argument justified? Its main weakness is that an international convention derives its validity directly from international law and is an independent source of obligations: it would be artificial to regard obligations under a convention concluded to give effect to Article 220 as deriving from Article 220. On the other hand, it could be maintained that these conventions are part of the Community legal system and the unity and coherence of that system would be compromised if they could not be enforced in the same way as other provisions of Community law. In view of its policy objectives, one might expect the European Court to find this latter argument more attractive.

Whatever the answer to this problem may be, there can be little doubt that subsidiary conventions not envisaged by Article 220 cannot be enforced under Article 169. In view of this, it is hardly surprising that the Community Patent Convention provides for its own enforcement procedure. This differs from that under Article 169 EEC in that the Commission has no role to play: Article 101 of the Community Patent Convention provides that any dispute between Contracting States concerning the interpretation or application of the convention which has not been settled by negotiation must first be submitted to a body set up under the convention, the Select Commit-

[11] See pp. 96–7, above.
[12] Under Art. 3(2) of the Act of Accession, the United Kingdom undertook to accede to the conventions provided for in Art. 220 EEC which had already been signed by the original Member States.
[13] For both the original, and the amended, text, see OJ 1978, L 304.

tee of the Administrative Council; if the Select Committee is unable to bring about agreement between the States concerned within six months, any one of them may submit the dispute to the European Court for a ruling.[14]

Difficulties also arise with regard to obligations derived from general principles of law: unless they can be regarded as in some way inherent in the constitutive Treaties, they would not fall within the scope of an enforcement action.[15] Though binding on the Community, these principles are not normally applicable to Member States; consequently this problem is not likely to arise very often. What could easily happen, however, is that a Member State might be bound by an express provision of Community law and the European Court might have recourse to a general principle of law in order to interpret the provision: in this situation the general principle would be indirectly applicable to the Member State and a breach of it would also constitute a violation of the express provision. In such a case, of course, no difficulties would arise.

Violations by the Legislature or Judiciary of a Member State

What is the position where the violation of Community law is the result of action (or failure to act) on the part of the national legislature or courts? For example, the national parliament may fail to pass legislation introduced by the government to give effect to a Community obligation, or it may insist on enacting legislation contrary to Community law. A violation by the courts could take a number of forms: they could refuse to give direct effect to a provision of Community law; they could refuse to make a reference to the European Court even where bound to do so under Article 177(3); or they could refuse to accept that Community law overrides national law in the event of a conflict. Is the national government responsible for these violations?

---

[14]   For the text of the Convention (which is not yet in force), see OJ 1976, L 17.

[15]   It should, however be noted that both Mertens de Wilmars and Verougstraete, 'Proceedings against Member States for Failure to Fulfil their Obligations', (1970) 7 C.M.L. Rev. 385 at 388 (paragraph 5) and Barav, 'Failure of Member States to Fulfil their Obligations under Community Law', (1975) 12 C.M.L. Rev. 369 at 377 consider that general principles of law are covered by Art. 169, though neither gives any satisfactory reasons to support this opinion. Professor Schermers takes the view (paragraph 514) that a breach of a general principle will be covered only if the Member State was acting in the performance of Community functions: in this situation the general principle could normally be regarded as implicitly contained in the written provision under which the Member State was acting.

The short answer to this question is that, although the national government appears before the Court in enforcement actions, the actual defendant is the state, not the government.[16] Since the legislature and judiciary are organs of the state just as much as the government is, there is no reason in principle why a violation of Community law by the legislature or courts should not engage the responsibility of the state in the same way as a violation by the executive. There have, in fact, been cases in which national legislation was required in order to comply with Community law and the national government introduced a bill and did all in its power to secure its enactment, but the national legislature failed to pass it: in these cases the national government argued before the European Court that it was absolved from responsibility for the violation of Community law as it had done everything it could to get the measure approved. The Court, however, rejected these arguments on the ground given above.[17]

Similar arguments can be used in the case of the judiciary, but so far no enforcement action has been brought for a violation of Community law by the national courts, though – as was shown in Chapter 8 – there have been several occasions on which such violations occurred.[18] In practice, the Commission has shown itself loath to institute proceedings in such cases.[19] It seems that this is partly

---

[16] See *per* Advocate General Warner in *Cremonini*, Case 815/79, [1980] ECR 3583 at 3621–3622, and in *R. v. Bouchereau*, Case 30/77, [1977] ECR 1999 at 2020. There appears to be one exception to this, *Commission* v. *Government of the Italian Republic*, Case 16/69, [1969] ECR 377, but this is thought to be a mistake: see Schermers, paragraph 539. The Court itself gave judgment against the 'Italian Republic', not the Italian Government.

[17] See *Commission* v. *Belgium*, Case 77/69, [1970] ECR 237 and *Commission* v. *Italy*, Case 8/70, [1970] ECR 961. In the former case the Court said that a Member State is responsible even for the actions of 'a constitutionally independent institution' (paragraph 15 of the judgment): this phrase could cover the courts as well as the legislature.

[18] Notably by the French *Conseil d'État*: see pp. 230–5, above.

[19] Proceedings against Germany were apparently commenced after the decision of the *Bundesverfassungsgericht* in the *Internationale Handelsgesellschaft* case but they were not pursued: see Schermers, paragraph 541, note 630, citing *Europe*, 27 December 1974, No. 1657, p. 9. When the French *Conseil d'État* refused to make a reference to the European Court in the *Semoules* case (1 March 1968, [1970] CMLR 395), the Commission evidently considered whether action under Art. 169 should be taken against France: see the Commission's replies to Parliamentary Questions 28/68 (OJ 1968, C71/1) and 349/69 (OJ 1970, C20/4). In *Meyer-Burckhardt* v. *Commission*, Case 9/75, [1975] ECR 1171, 1187, Advocate General Warner said that proceedings can be brought under Art. 169 where a national court covered by Art. 177(3) fails to make a preliminary reference when required to do so by that provision; but he made clear that the Commission has a discretion whether or not to initiate the procedure and said that proceedings should 'not lightly be undertaken'. For references to the views of writers on this question, see Barav, 'Failure of Member States to Fulfil their Obligations under Community Law', (1975) 12 C.M.L. Rev. 369 at 379–80.

because the independence of the judiciary might appear to be undermined by such proceedings and partly because the effective application of Community law depends to a great extent on the co-operation of the national courts. This is normally given, but if relations between the European Court and the national courts were soured by proceedings in which the former appeared to sit in judgment over the latter, the national judges might change their attitude. This would have very serious consequences.

The European Court has also ruled that constitutional difficulties are no excuse for a failure to fulfil an obligation under the Treaty.[20] If the defendant Member State is a federation, it will not constitute a defence to show that the violation was due to the action of a constituent state, such as a German *Land*.[21] The same rule would apply with regard to a violation by the legislature, executive or judiciary of a dependency of a Member State, provided it was covered by the Treaty. Thus the United Kingdom would be liable for a violation by Gibraltar, the Channel Islands or the Isle of Man.

THE ADMINISTRATIVE STAGE

The administrative stage of the proceedings is covered by the first paragraph of Articles 169 EEC, 141 Euratom and 88 ECSC. The EEC and Euratom provisions state:

If the Commission considers that a Member State has failed to fulfil an obligation under this Treaty, it shall deliver a reasoned opinion on the matter after giving the State concerned the opportunity to submit its observations.

Article 88 ECSC is similar except that it requires the Commission to record the Member State's failure in a reasoned decision.

The use of the word 'shall' in these provisions suggests that the Commission is under an obligation to deliver the opinion or take the decision. (This contrasts with the second paragraph of the EEC and Euratom provisions, where it is stated that if the Member State does not comply with the opinion, the Commission 'may' bring the matter before the European Court.) However, this obligation can arise only

---

[20] See *Commission* v. *Italy*, Case 100/77, [1978] ECR 879 (paragraph 21 of the judgment).

[21] See *Casagrande* v. *Munich*, Case 9/74, [1974] ECR 773: this was a reference under Art. 177, but the European Court made clear that Community law is binding at all levels in a Member State. The position would be the same in the case of a violation by a local authority.

if two conditions are fulfilled: the Commission must consider that a breach has taken place and the Member State must have been given an opportunity to submit its observations.

The structure of the Treaty provision suggests that the normal order of events will be: first, the Commission concludes that a violation has taken place; then it allows observations to be submitted; and finally it delivers the opinion. However, no reasonable administrative authority would reach a definite conclusion on a matter as important as this until *after* it had considered the Member State's observations: it is an essential part of the *audi alteram partem* doctrine that the hearing must precede the decision. Therefore, the correct order of events should be: first the observations; then the conclusion that there has been a violation; and finally the delivery of the opinion. However, the Commission would not ask the Member State for its observations unless it had reason to believe that a breach might have taken place. Therefore, the formal request for observations must itself be preceded by a preliminary determination that a violation appears to have occurred.

In fact, the whole administrative stage can be subdivided into two distinct phases: the informal phase and the formal phase. In the informal phase the Commission investigates a possible breach and considers whether there is sufficient evidence to justify the commencement of formal proceedings. This informal investigation will be conducted with discretion: the Commission will try to avoid press publicity and the embarrassment that might result for the defendant Member State. Informal discussions with the Member State will be held in an attempt to ascertain the facts and to reach a settlement. Only when the Commission feels that the factual and legal issues have been fully investigated will it consider whether to move on to the formal phase. It will then decide either that further proceedings are not warranted, in which case the matter will be at an end, or it will decide that sufficient evidence of a violation exists to justify the commencement of the formal phase.

The formal phase will begin with a formal request to the Member State to submit its observations. This formal communication specifies what the Member State is alleged to have done wrong and which rule of Community law has been infringed;[22] it will also lay

---

[22] The Member State must be told in clear terms, either in the formal communication or at an earlier stage, exactly what the allegations against it are; otherwise the whole proceedings could be nullified: see *Commission* v. *Denmark*, Case 211/81, [1982] ECR 4547 (paragraphs 5–12 of the judgment); see also *Commission* v. *Italy*, Case 309/84, [1987] 2 CMLR 675.

down a time limit for the submission of observations. Further discussions may take place after the Member State's observations have been received: the Commission is always anxious to reach an amicable settlement, if this is possible. Only when it becomes clear that the Member State is not prepared voluntarily to accept the Commission position, will the Commission issue the reasoned opinion (or decision) formally recording the violation.

Commission Discretion

Must the Commission issue a formal opinion or decision to record every failure to observe the Treaty that comes to its notice? Or does it have a discretion as to which cases it will pursue? As was shown above, the Treaty suggests that the Commission has no discretion once it has concluded that a violation has taken place. However, it was also shown that the Commission will normally reach such a conclusion only after a fairly complex procedure of investigation and consultation has taken place. Before this has happened, the Commission will not be in a position to reach a definite conclusion; and before such a conclusion is reached, the obligation to deliver the opinion or take the decision will not arise.

The important question, therefore, is whether there is any obligation on the Commission to set the investigatory procedure in motion whenever it appears, either on the basis of information arising in the course of the Commission's normal operations or as a result of representations made by some outside person or body, that there are reasonable grounds for believing that a violation might have occurred. Articles 169 EEC, 141 Euratom and 88 ECSC contain no direct statement that such an obligation exists. It would not, however, be unreasonable to take the view that an implied obligation exists to consider with an open mind whether investigations should begin. This view is supported by Articles 155 EEC and 124 Euratom, which provide that the Commission 'shall ensure that the provisions of this Treaty and the measures taken by the institutions pursuant thereto are applied'. (The equivalent provision under the ECSC Treaty, Article 8, is weaker: it states merely that the Commission has the duty of ensuring that the objectives set out in the Treaty are attained.)

Before considering the existence and limits of any obligation that may exist regarding the setting in motion of the enforcement procedure, however, it would be desirable to turn for a moment from legal principle to practicalities. First, it should be noted that a large number of contraventions of Community law takes place. There is evidence to suggest that many directives are implemented by the Member States only after the time limit has expired.[23] When implementation does take place, it is not always wholly satisfactory.[24] The scope for enforcement actions is therefore very large: since the Commission has only limited staff available, it is not possible for it to investigate every suspected violation.

Secondly, there is a tendency for national governments to resent the initiation of enforcement proceedings against them. As was once said by Advocate General Roemer,[25] this procedure puts the Member State's prestige in issue: no one likes to be accused of having broken the law. Since the Community mechanism functions only if there is mutual trust and good will between the Member States and Community institutions, excessive resort to enforcement actions might do more harm than good. It must not be forgotten, moreover, that under the EEC and Euratom Treaties there is no provision for sanctions: there is always a danger, therefore, that a Member State will simply ignore any ruling given against it.

In view of these considerations, it would be unreasonable to hold that there is an absolute obligation on the Commission to commence enforcement proceedings in every case where a violation may have occurred. On the other hand, however, it would be wrong to assume that there is no obligation at all. The true position seems to be that the Commission has a discretion but is also subject to a duty. The duty is to take the most appropriate action to ensure that Community law is obeyed; the discretion concerns the determination of what is most appropriate in the circumstances.[26] This discretion must, however, be exercised according to the correct criteria.

In *Commission* v. *France*[27] (Euratom case) Advocate General Roemer indicated some of the situations in which the Commission might be justified in not initiating the enforcement procedure: where there is a possibility that an amicable settlement may be achieved if formal proceedings are delayed; where the effects of the violation are

---

[23] As regards the Netherlands, see Maas and Bentvelsen, 'De tijdige uitvoering van EEG-richtlijnen in Nederland', [1978] Bestuurswetenschappen 443.

[24] For a survey of the implementation in the United Kingdom and the Netherlands of Community obligations in the field of immigration, see T. C. Hartley, *EEC Immigration Law* (1978), Chapters 6 and 7.

[25] *Commission* v. *France*, Case 7/71, [1971] ECR 1003 at 1026.

[26] *Commission* v. *France* (above) at paragraph 5 of the judgment.

[27] [1971] ECR at 1025.

only minor; where there is a major political crisis which could be aggravated if proceedings are commenced with regard to matters of secondary importance; and where there is a possibility that the Community provision in issue might be altered in the near future. These are only examples: the basic principle is that the Commission must balance the harm caused by non-compliance with the law against the embarrassment and inconvenience that could result from bringing proceedings.

One study suggests that the circumstances in which the Commission refrains from action can be grouped into three categories.[28] The first concerns isolated acts by national officials which are of only limited importance: here the Commission will not normally take action if there is no evidence of a general administrative practice and if redress can be obtained through the national courts (though the availability of such a remedy does not, in law, preclude resort to an enforcement action[29]). Secondly, the Commission has not so far brought proceedings regarding violations of Community law by national courts. This was discussed above.[30] Finally, action will not be taken where this would inflame a politically sensitive situation.

A decision not to press on with action in these circumstances would not normally be unreasonable. However, one cannot help feeling that there are also other situations in which the Commission fails to initiate proceedings: for example, the Commission's failure to secure implementation of Article 119 EEC, as revealed in the second *Defrenne* case,[31] cannot easily be fitted into any of the categories listed above – unless one regards the principle of equal pay for men and women as politically too hot to handle.

Recording the Violation

After it has considered any observations submitted by the Member State within the time-limit laid down in the request, the Commission must finally decide whether a violation has occurred. If it considers that it has, it will record this infringement in a reasoned opinion or decision. The main function of this is to specify exactly what the Member State has done wrong. If the matter subsequently goes to the

---

[28] Evans, 'The Enforcement Procedure of Art. 169 EEC: Commission Discretion', (1979) 4 E.L. Rev. 442 at 449–55.
[29] *Commission* v. *Italy*, Case 31/69, [1970] ECR 25 (at paragraph 9 of the judgment).
[30] At pp. 289–90.
[31] See pp. 79–80 and 190, above.

European Court, the opinion or decision serves as a definition of the issues before the Court: the Commission cannot raise any violations which are not set out in it.

The Commission is also obliged to give its reasons for concluding that the Member State has infringed the Treaty. As was explained in Chapter 4,[32] there is a general obligation for all EEC and Euratom regulations, decisions and directives and for all ECSC decisions, recommendations and opinions to contain reasons. Therefore, it was not strictly necessary for Article 88 ECSC to lay down that the decision must be reasoned; in the case of the EEC and Euratom Treaties, on the other hand, there is no general requirement that opinions must contain reasons: the provision to this effect in Articles 169 EEC and 141 Euratom shows that an opinion recording a Treaty violation is a very special kind of opinion.

What was said in Chapter 4 concerning the general requirement to give reasons applies here as well, though the main function served by the requirement in enforcement proceedings will be to help the defendant Member State decide whether it would be worth while contesting the matter before the Court. The statement of reasons should therefore contain sufficient detail to enable it to do this. Moreover, as the opinion or decision is of a quasi-judicial nature, one would expect a fuller statement than in the case of a legislative or administrative act.[33]

The Commission is also obliged to set a time-limit within which the Member State must end the violation. The significance of this is slightly different under the ECSC Treaty compared with the two later Treaties. Under Article 88 ECSC, sanctions may be imposed if the Member State has not ended its infringement within the period set by the Commission.[34] Under the EEC and Euratom Treaties, on the other hand, there is no provision for sanctions: the opinion is not binding and if the Member State fails to comply, the Commission must bring the matter before the Court; it may only do this, however, after the expiry of the time-limit.[35] The time-limit therefore gives the

[32] See pp. 119–26.
[33] The European Court has said that the extent of the obligation to give reasons depends on the nature of the act: it is more extensive in the case of an individual act than a legislative act: see pp. 122–5, above. In the case of a judicial act, it should be more extensive still.
[34] If the Member State takes legal proceedings, however, sanctions cannot be imposed until the Court has given judgment. In practice, the Member State always does take legal proceedings.
[35] Arts 169(2) EEC and 141(2) Euratom.

Member State a period of grace within which it is protected from the threat of sanctions or legal proceedings.[36]

The reasoned opinion or decision also specifies what action may be taken by the Member State to end its infringement. However, as the opinion or decision is merely declaratory – it simply records a violation – the Commission cannot impose any new obligation on the Member State:[37] the Member State can therefore choose what measures it takes, so long as the infringement is in fact terminated.

Time-Limit for Commission Action

There is no time-limit for the initiation of proceedings or for the delivery of the reasoned opinion or decision: it falls within the Commission's discretion to decide when to act. This is illustrated by a case under Article 141 Euratom, *Commission* v. *France*.[38] The case concerned Title II, Chapter VI of the Euratom Treaty, which contains various provisions designed to ensure that all users of nuclear fuels in the Community can obtain reasonable supplies. A special Supply Agency was set up to control the supply of nuclear materials. The French Government, however, took the view that these provisions lapsed after seven years, as they had not been confirmed by the Council under Article 76(2) Euratom. In 1965 it therefore informed French undertakings that the provisions of Chapter VI were no longer applicable: the French Government itself ceased to comply with them. In particular, it did not inform the Supply Agency of contracts it had concluded for the procurement and supply of nuclear materials. The Commission considered, however, that Chapter VI was still in force and in 1970 it commenced proceedings under Article 141: France was invited to submit observations; a reasoned opinion was given declaring France guilty of a violation of the Treaty; and, after France had failed to comply with it within the period laid down, an action was instituted before the European Court.

[36] The reasoned opinion cannot, however, affect the rights of third parties. A finding that no violation occurred does not preclude proceedings in the national courts by private individuals, nor does it prevent the European Court from ruling against the Member State in a reference from a national court under Art. 177 EEC: see *Essevi*, Cases 142–143/80, [1981] ECR 1413, at paragraphs 13–18 of the judgment.

[37] See *Netherlands* v. *High Authority*, Case 25/59, [1960] ECR 355 at 373–5. This case concerned the ECSC Treaty; the position is even clearer under the EEC and Euratom Treaties, since the reasoned opinion is not legally binding.

[38] Case 7/71, [1971] ECR 1003.

One argument put forward by the French Government was that the proceedings had been started too late. It maintained that it had made its views known in 1965 and that it was not open to the Commission to wait so long before bringing the action. The Court rejected this contention. It held:[39]

The action for a declaration that a State has failed to fulfil an obligation provided for by Article 141 of the Treaty, does not have to be brought within a predetermined period, since, by reason of its nature and purpose, this procedure involves a power on the part of the Commission to consider the most appropriate means and time-limits for the purposes of putting an end to any contraventions of the Treaty.

The action was therefore declared admissible; the Court went on to hold that Chapter VI had not lapsed: it gave judgment against France.

Consequences of Procedural Defects

It will be seen from what has been said that there are a number of procedural requirements which must be complied with by the Commission: the Member State must be given a fair opportunity to submit its observations (this involves both giving it sufficient information regarding the case it must meet and allowing a reasonable time for the observations to be communicated); the opinion or decision must be properly reasoned; and the Member State must be given a reasonable period to end its violation. What happens if the Commission violates one of these requirements?

The consequences of a procedural defect vary according to the Treaty involved. Article 33 ECSC provides that a Commission decision may be annulled by the Court for infringement of an essential procedural requirement.[40] The reasoned decision could therefore be attacked on purely procedural grounds, irrespective of the rights and wrongs of the substantive issue. If it were annulled, the Commission would have to start the procedure all over again. The only proviso is that the defect must be sufficiently serious. Failure to give sufficient reasons or an infringement of the *audi alteram partem* principle would justify annulment: the Court has already held that both these requirements are 'essential'.[41]

[39] Paragraph 5 of the judgment.
[40] This is discussed in detail at pp. 411–13, below.
[41] See p. 413, below.

The position is somewhat different in the case of the EEC and Euratom Treaties. Here the Commission delivers an opinion instead of a decision. An opinion is not subject to annulment proceedings;[42] so it cannot be challenged for infringement of a procedural requirement. However, if the Commission brings the matter before the Court, the Member State may raise the procedural infringement. If this is sufficiently serious, it should constitute a bar to the action: it would be reasonable to regard the procedural requirements laid down in Articles 169 EEC and 141 Euratom as essential preconditions for the admissibility of an enforcement action.[43]

THE JUDICIAL STAGE

The delivery of the reasoned opinion or decision marks the end of the administrative stage. Next comes the judicial stage: here the matter is put before the European Court for a final ruling. Under the EEC and Euratom Treaties the legal proceedings are brought by the Commission. There is no deadline for the commencement of the action but the Commission must wait until after the expiry of the time-limit given in the reasoned opinion.[44] Under the ECSC Treaty, on the other hand, the action is brought by the Member State: the time-limit for this is two months from the date on which the reasoned decision was notified to it. It is not clear why a time-limit is laid down in the one case but not in the other.

Under all three Treaties the Court has full jurisdiction to consider all the issues. The proceedings are not a review of the opinion or decision: the Court considers *de novo* whether the violation has occurred. As will be seen in Chapter 15, the powers of the Court in review proceedings are restricted: it may annul the measure in question on limited grounds only; its power to review the Commis-

---

[42] *Lütticke* v. *Commission*, Case 48/65, [1966] ECR 19; see also *Commission* v. *France*, Cases 6, 11/69, [1969] ECR 523 (paragraphs 35–7 of the judgment). For a suggestion that there may be exceptions to this rule, see Schermers, paragraph 522.

[43] In *Commission* v. *Italy*, Case 7/61, [1961] ECR 317, the Court appeared to consider an allegation that the opinion did not contain sufficient reasons as going to the admissibility of the enforcement action; and in *Commission* v. *Italy*, Case 31/69, [1970] ECR 25, the Court said that the opportunity to submit observations was 'an essential procedural requirement' (paragraph 13 of the judgment); see also *Commission* v. *Germany*, Case 325/82, [1984] ECR 777 (paragraph 8 of the judgment).

[44] The European Court cannot extend or reduce the time limit set by the Commission: *Commission* v. *Italy*, Case 28/81, [1981] ECR 2577.

sion's evaluation of a situation is restricted; and the only remedy it can grant is a declaration of invalidity: it cannot substitute its decision for that of the Commission. These restrictions do not apply when the Court exercises plenary jurisdiction. However, the scope of the proceedings is limited to the infringements specified in the reasoned opinion or decision: the Commission cannot raise new allegations before the Court.[45]

The time factor can be important. Proceedings cannot be brought under the EEC and Euratom Treaties if the breach is terminated before the deadline laid down in the reasoned opinion: but what happens if it is terminated after the deadline but before judgment is given? This occurred in *Commission* v. *Italy*[46] (*Pork Imports* case) where the Court ruled that it did not constitute a bar to the action.[47] Proceedings cannot, on the other hand, be brought regarding a violation which had not yet occurred when the Commission invited the Member State to submit its observations, even though the Commission may have had reason to believe that it was contemplated.[48]

Member States often put forward ingenious defences to excuse their failure to abide by Community law.[49] Normally these get short shrift from the Court. It is no defence to argue that the Commission or Council is also in breach of the Treaty with regard to the same subject matter, or that the act complained of was in retaliation for a comparable violation by another Member State:[50] '*tu quoque*' is no defence in Community law. Nor may a Member State complain that

---

[45] See, for example, *Commission* v. *Italy*, Case 166/82, [1984] ECR 459 (paragraph 16 of the judgment).

[46] Case 7/61, [1961] ECR 317 at 326.

[47] There are various reasons why the Commission might wish to continue with the action: for example, it might want to obtain a ruling to clarify the matter in case the violation is repeated at a later stage. In practice, however, it will usually drop the proceedings once the breach is remedied.

[48] See *Commission* v. *Italy*, Case 31/69, [1970] ECR 25 (paragraphs 11–14 of the judgment); see also *Commission* v. *Italy*, Case 309/84, [1987] 2 CMLR 657.

[49] For a fuller discussion, see Schermers, paragraphs 523–38a.

[50] See *Commission* v. *Luxembourg and Belgium*, Cases 90, 91/63, [1964] ECR 625 at 631, where it was held that failure by the Community to carry out its obligations does not justify the Member States' taking the law into their own hands, and *Steinike und Weinlig*, Case 78/76, [1977] ECR 595, where the Court held that a breach by a Member State of an obligation under the Treaty cannot be justified by the fact that other Member States have also failed to fulfil the obligation in question (paragraph 24 of the judgment). *Commission* v. *France*, Case 26/69, [1970] ECR 565, suggests, however, that a Member State might be excused if it was not engaged in an act of retaliation but, through no fault of its own, was forced into violating the Treaty by a wrongful act on the part of the Community.

other Member States were doing exactly the same thing and no proceedings were brought against them.[51] In general, the Court, though willing to consider policy issues, is not impressed by technical, legalistic defences.

If the Court finds the allegations proved, it will give judgment against the Member State. Under the EEC and Euratom Treaties, this takes the form of a declaration that the Member State has failed to fulfil an obligation under the Treaty. The Court will, of course, specify what act or omission is the source of the violation. The Court has no power specifically to order the Member State to do, or not to do, something;[52] nor, if the violation takes the form of national legislation contrary to Community law, can it declare the legislation invalid.[53] This does not, however, mean that the Member State is not obliged to comply with the judgment. Articles 171 EEC and 143 Euratom state:

If the Court of Justice finds that a Member State has failed to fulfil an obligation under this Treaty, the State shall be required to take the necessary measures to comply with the judgment of the Court of Justice.

This makes clear that the judgment, though declaratory in nature, is binding: the Member State is obliged to terminate the violation found by the Court, though it can choose the way in which this will be done.

Under the ECSC Treaty the position is slightly different: the Court will simply reject the Member State's action. This has the effect of affirming the Commission's reasoned decision, which is of course binding. The way will then be open for the imposition of sanctions.

REMEDIES WHERE THE COMMISSION FAILS TO ACT

It was said previously that the Commission has a discretion whether to set the enforcement procedure in motion, but there is a duty to exercise that discretion properly. What remedies exist if the Com-

[51] See *Germany* v. *Commission*, Cases 52, 55/65, [1966] ECR 159 at 170–2.
[52] This does not apply in the case of interim orders (discussed below). The Court might, of course, try to help the Member State by suggesting ways in which it could bring the violation to an end.
[53] In *Commission* v. *Italy* (second *Art Treasures* case), Case 48/71, [1972] ECR 527 (paragraphs 7–9 of the judgment) the Court emphasised that national authorities should not apply national legislation that is incompatible with Community law: this, of course, is a simple re-iteration of the doctrines of direct effect and the supremacy of Community law discussed in Chapter 7.

mission fails in that duty? This question must be considered separately with regard to the different Treaties.

Under the ECSC Treaty a simple remedy exists: an action can be brought under Article 35 to obtain a ruling by the Court that the Commission has failed to fulfil an obligation under the Treaty by not taking a decision under Article 88 recording the Member State's violation. This action may be brought by another Member State or by a private individual or firm with appropriate standing. The details of actions under Article 35 ECSC are considered in Chapter 13; it is sufficient here to say that any producer of coal or steel who is affected by the violation would have *locus standi* to bring proceedings.

The most likely reason why the Commission would have declined to act would be that it did not consider that the Member State had committed a breach of the Treaty: if the applicant can show that this conclusion was based on an error of fact or law, the Court will give judgment against the Commission. Likewise, if the Commission decided that proceedings were not opportune, and this conclusion was reached on the basis of improper considerations or was otherwise a misuse of the Commission's powers, the Court will grant a remedy. Under Article 35 ECSC, the remedy consists of the annulment of the implied decision refusing the applicant's request for action: the Court cannot directly order the Commission to take a decision under Article 88, but Article 34 ECSC requires the Commission to 'take the necessary steps to comply with the judgment'.

An example of this procedure is furnished by *De Gezamenlijke Steenkolenmijnen in Limburg* v. *High Authority*.[54] Here an organization of Dutch coal mining enterprises brought proceedings against the Commission because the latter had failed to take a decision under Article 88 declaring that Germany had violated the Treaty by using public funds to finance a bonus for German miners. The Dutch mining undertakings considered that this gave the German mines an unfair competitive advantage over the Dutch mines and was contrary to Article 4(*c*) ECSC, which prohibits state aids or subsidies. The European Court held that the applicant had sufficient interest in the matter to be entitled to bring the proceedings. The Commission had decided not to act because it considered that the German measures were not contrary to the Treaty; the Court, however, held that this was wrong and gave judgment for the applicant.

This procedure can be used not only against the government of

---

[54] Case 17/57, [1959] ECR 1.

another Member State, but also against one's own government. This happened in *Groupement des Industries Sidérurgiques Luxembourgeoises* v. *High Authority*,[55] where a group of Luxembourg steel producers complained that the High Authority had failed to take action against the Luxembourg Government when the latter had enacted measures requiring all industrial users of coal to pay a levy, which was then used to subsidize sales to domestic users. The applicant in this case was held to have sufficient interest to bring the proceedings, though it lost on the merits.

Under the EEC and Euratom Treaties, this remedy is not available. This is because the reasoned opinion, unlike the reasoned decision under the ECSC Treaty, is not legally binding and hence not a reviewable act.[56] If an opinion is given, it cannot be challenged under Article 173 EEC or 146 Euratom;[57] nor can a failure to give an opinion be attacked under Article 175 EEC or 148 Euratom.[58] This is not important as far as Member States are concerned since Articles 170 EEC and 142 Euratom give Member States the right to bring proceedings themselves. Private individuals, on the other hand, are clearly in a much less advantageous position under the EEC and Euratom Treaties than under the ECSC Treaty.

Are any other remedies available? In *Vloeberghs* v. *High Authority*[59] a Belgian coal dealer suffered loss because the French Government refused to allow the entry into France of a consignment of coal which Vloeberghs had imported into Belgium from outside the Community. He maintained that the French had violated the Treaty and asked the Commission to take action under Article 88. They refused. Vloeberghs was unable to use the procedure under Article 35 because, as a coal dealer and not a coal producer, he lacked *locus standi* under Articles 33 and 35 ECSC. He therefore brought an action for damages against the Commission and claimed compensation for the loss he had suffered through not being able to export the coal to France. He lost the action in the end, but there was no suggestion in the case that such actions are not available in principle. If this is so,

---

[55] Cases 7, 9/54, [1954–56] ECR 175.

[56] This concept is discussed in Chapter 11.

[57] See note 42, above.

[58] It is assumed that a reviewable omission under Arts 175 EEC and 148 Euratom is an omission to adopt a reviewable act: see pp. 375–8, below. There can be no doubt that a private individual cannot challenge a failure to give an opinion: under Arts 175 EEC and 148 Euratom, a non-privileged applicant can bring proceedings only if the defendant institution has failed to address to him an 'act other than a recommendation or an opinion'.

[59] Cases 9, 12/60, [1960] ECR 197.

this means of redress could prove valuable to private individuals, especially those who lack standing to bring proceedings under Article 33 or 35.[60]

Can actions in tort (or 'non-contractual liability', as it is called in Community terminology) be brought under the EEC and Euratom Treaties? In principle, there seems to be no reason why the position should be any different from that under the ECSC Treaty: the distinction between an opinion and a decision is not relevant in actions for damages. In *Denkavit* v. *Commission*,[61] a private firm sued the Commission for damages for loss caused by the fact that deliveries of feeding-stuffs had been stopped at the Italian frontier. The Italian authorities had done this on the ground that the potassium nitrate content of the feeding-stuffs was higher than that permitted under an 'urgent note' which had been issued by the Italian Minister of Health a year previously. Denkavit claimed that the 'urgent note' violated the Treaty and that the Commission was partly to blame for the situation, as it had acted too slowly in taking measures to require Italy to revoke the note.

The Advocate General, Mr Mayras, was unsympathetic to this claim.[62] The Court, however, did not dismiss it out of hand but considered it on its merits: it eventually concluded that the Commission's tardiness – it did eventually take action – was excused by the legal uncertainties and scientific doubts which existed at the time. The Court said, however, that the 'urgent note' constituted an obstacle to trade between Member States and that it was 'necessary to consider whether the Commission, by conduct for which there was no justification, did not improperly contribute to the maintenance of that obstacle and thereby incur liability'.[63] This suggests that in principle such an action can be brought.

It is interesting to note that in an earlier case, *Meyer-Burckhardt* v. *Commission*,[64] Advocate General Warner came down against such a possibility. He maintained that it would be wrong for the Court to decide whether the Member State had infringed the Treaty if that State was not a party to the proceedings and did not enjoy the

---

[60] For a fuller discussion of the case, see pp. 469 and 480–1, below.

[61] Case 14/78, [1978] ECR 2497.

[62] See [1978] ECR at pp. 2515–16.

[63] Paragraph 8 of the judgment. See also *Lütticke* v. *Commission*, Case 4/69 [1971] ECR 325, which concerned the special procedure under Art. 97(2) EEC. This case is discussed at pp. 471–2, below. See further *Société d'Initiatives et de Coopération Agricoles* v. *Commission*, Case 114/83, [1984] ECR 2589; *GAARM* v. *Commission*, Case 289/83, [1984] ECR 4295.

[64] Case 1/75, [1975] ECR 1171.

safeguards provided for in Article 169.[65] This is a serious objection; nevertheless it must be pointed out that it applies equally in proceedings under the ECSC Treaty, both in the case of an action for damages and an action for a remedy for failure to act under Articles 33 and 35.[66]

ACTIONS BY MEMBER STATES

Under the EEC and Euratom Treaties – but not under the ECSC Treaty – an enforcement action may be brought by a Member State. The procedure is laid down in Articles 170 EEC and 142 Euratom. These provisions, which are identical, read as follows:

A Member State which considers that another Member State has failed to fulfil an obligation under this Treaty may bring the matter before the Court of Justice.

Before a Member State brings an action against another Member State for an alleged infringement of an obligation under this Treaty, it shall bring the matter before the Commission.

The Commission shall deliver a reasoned opinion after each of the States concerned has been given the opportunity to submit its own case and its observations on the other party's case both orally and in writing.

If the Commission has not delivered an opinion within three months of the date on which the matter was brought before it, the absence of such opinion shall not prevent the matter from being brought before the Court of Justice.

The first steps under this procedure are clear enough. The applicant requests the Commission to deliver a reasoned opinion on the alleged infringement. The Commission must comply with this request within three months; otherwise the applicant may commence proceedings before the Court without waiting for the opinion. The procedure before the Commission is similar to that under Article 169 EEC but the rights of the Member States are more extensive: each party is entitled both to present its own case and to comment on that of the other party; moreover these proceedings are both written and oral.[67]

---

[65] [1975] ECR at p. 1190.

[66] It should also be said that the question at issue would not be whether the Member State had in fact violated the Treaty, but whether there were sufficient grounds to justify the commencement of proceedings.

[67] The English text is ambiguous as to whether the words 'both orally and in writing' in the third paragraph of Art. 170 EEC apply only to the observations on the other party's case or also to the submission of the Member State's own case. The French text, however, makes clear that it applies to both. It reads: 'La Commission émet un avis motivé après que les États intéressés aient été mis en mesure de présenter contradictoirement leurs observations écrites et orales.'

It is less clear exactly what happens after the opinion has been given – assuming that it is duly given within the three month period. There are several possibilities. Assume, first, that the opinion is to the effect that there has been no infringement: is this the end of the matter or may the applicant persist in its claim and bring the case before the Court? It would seem that it can:[68] the first paragraph of Article 170 EEC gives Member States a general right to bring proceedings. This is qualified by the second paragraph, which lays down a procedural condition, but this condition is satisfied once the matter has been 'brought before the Commission' and the latter has been given an opportunity (three months) to deliver its opinion: there is no requirement that the opinion must be favourable to the applicant's case. Once the opinion has been given, the procedural conditions are satisfied and the general right in the first paragraph then has full application.[69]

What happens if the opinion is that the defendant has committed a breach? There is no statement in the Treaties that the opinion must set a time-limit within which the defendant must cease the violation. Could this be implied by analogy with Articles 169 EEC and 141 Euratom? Some writers consider this to be so,[70] but it is hard to see what function such a time-limit would serve, since the applicant would not be obliged to wait for the expiration of the period before going to the Court.

Further difficulties could arise if the Commission upholds the applicant's claim only in part. Say the applicant alleges that the defendant has broken the Treaty in three ways but the Commission rejects two of these complaints and upholds only the third: if the defendant then complies with the opinion, can the applicant nevertheless go to the Court with regard to the first two complaints? If the applicant can go to the Court when the opinion is wholly against him – as was suggested above – it would be strange if he could not do the same when the opinion is partly in his favour and partly against him. It seems, therefore, that the defendant cannot necessarily obtain immunity from legal action by complying with the opinion, as he can under Article 169. This means that the opinion has little significance under Article 170, except as an indication to the Court of how the Commission views the matter.[71]

---

[68] Mertens de Wilmars and Verougstraete, op. cit., (1970) 7 C.M.L. Rev. 385 at p. 393.
[69] There is no time-limit for bringing the action.
[70] Mertens de Wilmars and Verougstraete, op. cit., at p. 393.
[71] It is possible, however, that the Commission might feel obliged to intervene in the Court proceedings in support of its opinion, as it did in *France* v. *United Kingdom* (below).

As was mentioned previously, the procedure under Article 170 is very little used. The first case under it to go to judgment was an action brought by France against the United Kingdom in which it was claimed that certain fish conservation measures adopted by Britain were contrary to the Treaty. The Commission was asked by France to give an opinion and, after the parties had put forward their views in writing, it held a hearing at which the parties could present their cases orally. It then gave an opinion which stated that the United Kingdom had infringed the Treaty. (No time-limit was set for ending the infringement nor were any suggestions made as to what action would be sufficient to bring this about.) France then took the matter before the Court and the Commission applied for leave to intervene in support of France.[72] This was granted. The hearing then proceeded in the normal way; judgment was given against the United Kingdom.[73]

INTERIM MEASURES

When Member States break the Treaty – as they sometimes do quite consciously – they usually intend their action to be only temporary: they know they will have to come into line eventually but try to put it off as long as possible. Delaying tactics are consequently the order of the day: if an illegal subsidy or import ban can be kept in force long enough, it may have served its purpose. Member States therefore play for time in their negotiations with the Commission and the Commission tries to hurry the procedure along. In this situation the ability to apply for an interim order from the Court would be a very useful weapon for the Commission. Is this possible?

Articles 186 EEC and 158 Euratom state simply:[74]

The Court of Justice may in any cases before it prescribe any necessary interim measures.

This rather uninformative provision gives no indication of what kinds of interim measures may be prescribed but it has come to be accepted

---

[72] See the Statute of the Court, Arts 37 (EEC) and 38 (Euratom).

[73] *France* v. *United Kingdom*, Case 141/78, [1979] ECR 2923.

[74] There is a similar provision in Art. 39 ECSC (last paragraph). However, as the reasoned decision under Art. 88 ECSC is binding, the Member State is obliged to obey it while proceedings are pending, unless the Court, acting under a power also provided in Art. 39 ECSC, suspends its application. An interim order could perhaps be obtained if the Member State failed to abide by it.

in cases involving private persons and Community institutions that something in the nature of an English interlocutory injunction can be granted, though such applications do not often succeed.[75] Is a similar remedy available against a Member State?

In *Commission* v. *United Kingdom* (*Pig Producers* case)[76] the issue was put to the test. The British Government had instituted a subsidy scheme for United Kingdom pig producers to help them compete against imports subsidized by the Community. The British Government informed the Commission of its intention to grant the subsidy but, contrary to Article 93(3) EEC, it put the scheme into operation without waiting for the Commission to decide whether the scheme was compatible with the common market in terms of Articles 92 and 93. On 17 February 1977 the Commission adopted a decision under Article 93 requiring Britain to terminate the subsidy scheme forthwith. Britain did not comply and the Commission then brought an enforcement action under Article 93(2).

The enforcement action was commenced on 11 March 1977; on 12 May the Commission asked the Court to make an interim order requiring Britain to stop paying the subsidy until judgment in the main action had been given. On 21 May the Advocate General gave his opinion: he put forward three reasons why the order should not be granted. First, he considered that the comparatively long delay before the Commission made its request suggested that the matter was not sufficiently urgent to justify an interim order; secondly, he was afraid that irreparable damage might be suffered by British pig producers if the subsidy was ended prematurely; and thirdly, he doubted whether the Court had jurisdiction to make an interim order against a Member State. In enforcement actions the judgment takes the form of a declaration that the Member State has failed to fulfil an obligation under the Treaty; the Court does not expressly order the Member State to do anything, though Article 171 EEC requires the Member State to take the 'necessary measures' to comply with the judgment: if the final judgment is only declaratory, can the Court grant an interim order specifically requiring the Member State to do something?

The Advocate General's hesitations were not shared by the Court:

---

[75] See Gray, 'Interim Measures of Protection in the European Court', (1979) 4 E.L. Rev. 80 at 96–8, where it is pointed out that, at the time of writing, only 16 out of 54 applications had been successful. In competition cases, however, the chances of success are greater than in other proceedings involving private parties.

[76] Cases 31, 53/77R, [1977] ECR 921.

on the same day that he had given his opinion, the Court gave its decision: it ordered the United Kingdom to end the subsidy forthwith.[77] Few reasons were given: the Court hinted that the Commission might have had good cause for not applying immediately for an interim order (it was presumably trying to settle the matter by negotiation) and it suggested that an order would not necessarily have irreversible consequences for British producers (Britain could re-instate the scheme retroactively if it won the action). No consideration was given to the Advocate General's doubts as to whether the Court had power to make the order: the Court simply assumed that it did.

This judgment broke new ground: the Court now exercises wider powers in interim proceedings than it possesses when it gives a final judgment.[78] However, the wording of Article 186 provides some justification for the Court's position: it refers to 'any' cases before the Court and empowers it to prescribe 'any necessary interim measures'.

The day after the decision in the *Pig Producers* case, the Court gave judgment on another application for an interim order against a Member State. Ireland had introduced fisheries conservation measures which the Commission regarded as being contrary to the Treaty. Proceedings under Article 169 EEC were brought and at the same time an application was lodged for an interim order requiring Ireland to suspend the operation of the measures, which prohibited fishing by boats above a given size. Nine days later, the Court gave judgment: it held that there was serious doubt as to whether the Irish measures were compatible with Community law (mainly because they operated in a discriminatory fashion) and decided that suspension of the measures appeared justified in principle; however, it considered that their abolition could have harmful effects on conservation unless they were replaced by other measures and it therefore deferred a decision for a month in order to give the parties an opportunity to reach agreement on alternative measures.[79]

Reconsideration of the matter was postponed several times at the joint request of the parties until the Commission reported that the

---

[77] The British Government in fact ceased making payments towards the end of June: see Wainwright, (1977) 2 E.L. Rev. 349 at 350.

[78] It might be thought that the fact that the proceedings were brought under Art. 93 EEC made them a special case; but the Court's judgments in *Commission* v. *Ireland* (below) suggest that the position is exactly the same in an enforcement action brought purely under Art. 169.

[79] *Commission* v. *Ireland*, Case 61/77R, [1977] ECR 937.

negotiations had broken down. At this time a new government had just taken office in Ireland and it asked for a further adjournment in order to familiarize itself with the case. The Court was not, however, prepared to grant this and it ordered Ireland to suspend the measures within five days (this extra time was granted to allow it to adopt alternative measures; these had to be approved by the Commission).[80]

The use of interim measures against Member States seems now to be established. The procedure is basically the same as that applicable when such measures are requested against a private party or Community institution.[81] Two points should, however, be noted: although the application for interim relief may be made at the same time as the application commencing proceedings in the main action, it may not be made before this;[82] secondly, in both the cases discussed above, the application was heard by the full Court – not by the President alone, as is normally the case – and an opinion was given by the Advocate General.[83] In later cases, however, the normal procedure was used.[84]

There are three main considerations which the Court will take into account when deciding whether to grant an application for interim relief.[85] First, it will consider the likelihood of the proceedings being successful: no order will be made if the claim in the main action is manifestly unfounded. Secondly, it must be shown that the need for the order is urgent.[86] Thirdly, the Commission will normally be required to demonstrate that irreparable damage to the Community interest will occur if the order is not given, but the defendant may attempt to show that irreparable damage to its interests will ensue if the order *is* granted.

---

[80] *Commission* v. *Ireland*, Case 61/77R, [1977] ECR 1411.

[81] See John A. Usher, *European Court Practice* (1983), Chap. 10.

[82] See the Rules of Procedure of the European Court, Art. 83(1), which states that the application is admissible only if it is made 'by a party to a case before the Court and relates to that case'.

[83] Rules of Procedure, Art. 85 (third paragraph). Where the application is heard by the President, the Advocate General does not give an opinion.

[84] See *Commission* v. *Italy*, 154/85R, [1986] 2 CMLR 159 and *Commission* v. *Belgium*, Case 293/85R, [1986] 1 CMLR 594.

[85] See *per* Advocate General Mayras in *Commission* v. *United Kingdom*, Cases 31, 53/77R, [1977] 921 at 931–5 and *per* Advocate General Reischl in *Commission* v. *Ireland*, Case 61/77R, [1977] ECR 937 at 953–4.

[86] In *Commission* v. *Ireland*, however, Advocate General Reischl took the view that the mere fact that the Irish measures were actually being applied was sufficient to establish the requisite degree of urgency (at p. 954).

RESTITUTION AND DAMAGES

If the Member State could be forced to undo its action, delaying tactics would serve no purpose. In some situations this might be impossible, but if the violation consisted of an illegal subsidy or an unlawful tax, restitution might be feasible. This could occur under national law simply as a result of the Court's judgment in the enforcement action: for example, the European Court's decision in *Commission* v. *Luxembourg and Belgium*[87] that import duties imposed by the Belgian Government on dairy products were in violation of Community law was followed by a successful action by importers to reclaim money already paid.[88] (Such actions are, of course, based on the doctrine of direct effect and could succeed even without enforcement proceedings having been brought; where this is the position, a reference will normally be made to the European Court under Article 177.)

In some cases, however, national law will make no provision for restitution. Where this is so, can the Member State be forced to repay, or reclaim, the money? The difficulty here is that a judgment under Article 169 EEC does no more than declare that the defendant Member State has failed to fulfil an obligation under the Treaty: as was mentioned previously, it does not (except in the case of interim measures) order the Member State to take any specific action. Article 171 EEC requires the Member State to take 'the necessary measures to comply with the judgment of the Court of Justice' but it is generally assumed that it is for the Member State itself to decide what these are. Although it must end its infringement, it is not clear to what extent Article 171 obliges the Member State to attempt to undo its past misconduct.

One possibility would be for the Commission to request the Member State to ensure that restitution takes place. If it refuses, new enforcement proceedings could be commenced for a breach of Article 171: in this way, the Court could be asked to rule on the matter. So far, the Commission does not appear to have resorted to this procedure.

In *Commission* v. *Germany*[89] (*Kohlegesetz* case) the Commission tried a different tactic. The German Government had made provision for

---

[87] Cases 90, 91/63, [1964] ECR 625.
[88] *Minister for Economic Affairs* v. *Fromagerie Franco-Suisse 'Le Ski'*, *Cour de Cassation*, Belgium, 21 May 1971, [1972] CMLR 330 (discussed above at pp. 221–3).
[89] Case 70/72, [1973] ECR 813.

certain investment grants which the Commission regarded as contrary to Article 92 EEC. On 17 Febraury 1971 the Commission adopted a decision requiring Germany to cease paying the grants: the German Government complied, but only after a certain period of time. The Commission regarded this delay as unacceptable and brought proceedings under Article 93: it asked the Court not only for a declaration that Germany had failed to comply with the decision of 17 February 1971, but also for a ruling that it was obliged to obtain repayment of grants made after the promulgation of the decision.

The German Government objected to the admissibility of this second claim but the Court overruled the objection. The Court pointed out that the Commission has the power, when it rules that an aid is contrary to the Treaty, to require the Member State to abolish or alter it: this is specifically stated by Article 93(2). It then said: 'To be of practical effect, this abolition or modification may include an obligation to require repayment of aid granted in breach of the Treaty, so that in the absence of measures for recovery, the Commission may bring the matter before the Court.'[90]

It might be thought that this applied only under the special procedure laid down by Article 93 EEC, but the Court went out of its way to dispel any such idea: it expressly said that in an action under Articles 169–171, the Commission can apply for a declaration that 'in omitting to take specific measures' the Member State has failed to fulfil an obligation under the Treaty. It then continued:[91]

Since the aim of the Treaty is to achieve the practical elimination of infringements and the consequences thereof, past and future, it is a matter for the Community authorities whose task it is to ensure that the requirements of the Treaty are observed to determine the extent to which the obligation of the Member State concerned may be specified in the reasoned opinions or decisions delivered under Articles 169 and 93(2) respectively and in applications addressed to the Court.

This suggests that in its decision (under Article 93) or reasoned opinion (under Article 169) the Commission may specify what remedial measures are required: failure to carry these out would itself be a breach of the Treaty. For example, the Commission could say in its reasoned opinion that the Member State had violated the Treaty (i) by applying an illegal tax and (ii) by not repaying money already collected. If the Member State refused to comply, the Court could grant a declaration in similar terms.

[90] At paragraph 13 of the judgment.
[91] Ibid.

In *Commission* v. *Germany* the Court decided in the end that the Commission had failed to establish its case, so the order sought by the Commission was not granted. For many years thereafter, the Commission made no further attempts to obtain restitution. The reasons for this are not clear but there can be no doubt that restitution would give rise to serious problems if the recipients did not know that the grants were contrary to Community law. It was perhaps for this reason that in *Commission* v. *Germany* the Commission requested repayment only of those grants made after the decision of 17 February.

In 1980, however, the Commission announced a change of policy regarding state aid to industry: it said that in future it would require repayment of aid granted without first informing it, as required by Article 93(3) EEC.[92] The Commission also announced that in cases where this occurred it would publish a notice in the Official Journal warning the recipients of the risks involved.

The first time this new policy was put to the test, however, something rather strange occurred. A Commission decision was adopted requiring Belgium to reclaim illegal aid granted to a factory making wall coverings.[93] Some months later, however, a 'corrigendum' was published deleting the provisions requiring repayment.[94] So Belgium did not have to reclaim the aid.

In 1983 the Commission tried again. The case also concerned Belgium; this time it was aid to a manufacturer of ceramic sanitary ware. The Commission decision required Belgium to reclaim the aid. Belgium did not comply and the Commission brought legal proceedings. The Court upheld the Commission decision.[95] It remains to be seen, however, whether restitution will be ordered in proceedings under Articles 169–170.

Where the Treaty violation consists of, say, an import ban, there can be no question of restitution. Could the Member State be required to pay damages in such a case? In the course of the dispute over the French Government's refusal to obey the Court's judgment in the '*Sheepmeat*' case (discussed below), the British Government spoke of the possibility of obtaining damages. It could perhaps be argued that failure to compensate British exporters was itself a

---

[92] See OJ 1983, C 318/3.
[93] Decision 82/312, OJ 1982, L 138/18.
[94] OJ 1982, L 289/35.
[95] *Commission* v. *Belgium*, Case 52/84, [1987] 1 CMLR 710. For further discussion, see Flynn, (1983) 8 E.L. Rev. 297 at 308–310 and (1984) 9 E.L. Rev. 365.

violation of the Treaty, either because there is an independent obligation to compensate the victims of illegal acts, or because of Article 171. When the dispute was settled, however, the claim for damages was dropped.[96]

EFFECTIVENESS[97]

It is not easy to give a complete assessment of the effectiveness of the enforcement procedure because one cannot know how often the Commission never even commences formal proceedings. Statistics are, however, available for cases in which formal proceedings are begun and there are a number of interesting facts which emerge. First, there has been a great increase in the number of proceedings commenced. Up until the late Sixties, the number of cases in which formal proceedings were begun was less than 30 each year. This increased gradually in the following decade. Then in the late Seventies there was a dramatic increase when the figure climbed to over 200 per year. This increase was due both to a larger number of Treaty violations and to a tougher policy on the part of the Commission. Whereas previously proceedings were brought only as a last resort, from 1977 onwards the policy was to commence proceedings much more as a matter of course whenever there were grounds for suspecting that an infringement had taken place.[98]

A second interesting fact is that only a small proportion of cases (less than 10 per cent) continue to the point where judgment is given: the great majority are settled. A third interesting fact is that, if the case does go as far as judgment, the procedure usually takes several years from the date when the Member State is asked to give its comments. There are several cases in which it has dragged on for more than five years.[99]

If judgment is given against the Member State, it may be some time – occasionally as long as several years – before the defendant

---

[96] The request for damages was made to the Commission. The idea was that the Commission would ask the Court to make a declaration that France's failure to pay compensation was a violation of the Treaty. The sum claimed was approximately £20 million: see *The Times*, 11 January 1980.

[97] The factual information on which the following paragraphs are based is to be found in Audretsch, *Supervision in European Community Law* (2nd ed., 1986), especially at pp. 350–400.

[98] Ibid. pp. 279–289.

[99] Ibid. pp. 367–375. The average seems to be 2–3 years.

314 The Foundations of European Community Law

complies with the judgment.[100] Where compliance is unduly delayed the Commission may bring a second action, claiming that the failure to obey the first judgment is itself a violation of the Treaty.[101]

This tactic was used against France in the notorious '*Sheepmeat*' case, which began when France (with some justification on legal and social grounds) refused to admit imports of lamb and mutton from other Member States, principally Britain. The Commission brought proceedings and in due course the Court gave judgment against France.[102] The French Government, however, made clear that they would not comply with the judgment until the Council agreed to a Community support system which would protect French farmers, a measure blocked by Britain.

The Commission then brought new proceedings and applied for an interim order requiring France to admit British lamb without restrictions. Surprisingly, this was refused by the Court on the ground that it would substantially duplicate the previous judgment and would not, therefore, be 'necessary', as required by Article 186 EEC.[103] In fact, one suspects that the Court, knowing that any order it gave would be ignored, decided that it would be better to save what was left of its tattered authority by refusing the order. In the end the case never went to a final judgment: Britain agreed to a Community regime for lamb and mutton in exchange for concessions on its budgetary claims; France then lifted the ban on imports.

What can be done if a Member State defies the Court? Under Article 88 ECSC provision is made for the imposition of sanctions: money payable to the delinquent Member State may be withheld or other Member States may be authorized to take action 'to correct the effects of the infringement'. These sanctions are authorized by the Commission but the assent of the Council (acting by a two-thirds majority) must be obtained. In fact, no sanctions have ever been imposed. Under the EEC and Euratom Treaties there is no provision for sanctions.

In conclusion, one can say that the enforcement procedure is

---

[100] In at least half the cases it appears that the defendant fails to comply within a year of the judgment. In one case, *Commission* v. *Italy*, Case 79/72, [1973] ECR 667, the judgment had still not been obeyed after ten years: Audretsch, pp. 395–396.

[101] Art. 171 EEC requires a Member State to comply with a judgment under Arts 169 and 170. Failure to comply is, therefore, a violation of Art. 171. For a list of cases in which a second judgment has been obtained, see Audretsch, p. 688. Several years normally elapse between the two judgments.

[102] *Commission* v. *France*, Case 232/78, [1979] ECR 2729.

[103] Cases 24, 97/80R, [1980] ECR 1319.

effective in the great majority of cases. In a small number of cases, Member States see fit to break the rules and even to defy the Court. When this occurs, the matter passes outside the realm of the law and becomes political. In such a situation, coercion of the Member State by the Community is hardly practical; this is inevitable in view of the basic political nature of the Community. Only concerted action by the other Member States – or a compromise solution – will bring the violation to an end.

FURTHER READING

H. A. H. Audretsch, *Supervision in European Community Law* (2nd ed., 1986).

Schermers, paragraphs 491–554.

Barav, 'Failure of Member States to Fulfil their Obligations under Community Law', (1975) 12 C.M.L. Rev. 369.

Ebke, 'Enforcement Techniques within the European Communities', (1985) 50 Journal of Air Law and Commerce 685.

Evans, 'The Enforcement Procedure of Article 169 EEC: Commission Discretion', (1979) 4 E.L. Rev. 442.

Gray, 'Interim Measures of Protection in the European Court', (1979) 4 E.L. Rev. 80.

Mertens de Wilmars and Verougstraete, 'Proceedings against Member States for Failure to Fulfil their Obligations', (1970) 7 C.M.L. Rev. 385.

Oliver, 'Enforcing Community Rights in the English Courts', [1987] 50 MLR 881.

Steiner, 'How to Make the Action Suit the Case: Domestic Remedies for Breach of EEC Law', (1987) 12 E.L. Rev. 102.

Part IV
Administrative Law

INTRODUCTION

The Rule of Law is fundamental to all systems of constitutional law. It is so fundamental, in fact, that if it does not exist in at least its most basic form – that governmental authorities not only enforce the law but are also bound by it themselves – there can be no constitutional law. Constitutional law is, after all, the system of legal rules regulating governmental authority and the relations between citizens and the state.

The Rule of Law in this basic sense is, of course, a principle of the Community. However, if the concept is to attain its full realization, more is required than this. In addition, the legality of governmental action should be subject to determination by an independent, impartial adjudicatory body – in short, by a court. In the Community, the appropriate body is the European Court. How far may the Court pass judgment on the actions of the Community authorities? This raises the question whether the Community possesses a system of administrative law to provide the citizen with a remedy in the event of a legal dispute with the Community. This involves three main issues: whether the European Court may review (and, if necessary, quash) Community measures, whether it may require the Community to act where its failure to act is a violation of the law and, finally, whether it is possible to enforce obligations in contract, quasi-contract and tort against the Community.

With regard to the first issue, a distinction must be made between a direct challenge and an indirect challenge to a Community act. The object in the former is to obtain a declaration of invalidity. The object of the latter, on the other hand, is something quite different, and the validity of the act arises for decision only because the main question before the court depends on it: the challenge to the act is merely a preliminary step in a procedure leading to a decision on a different issue.

This distinction is important as regards the way the proceedings are instituted. As might be expected, a declaration of invalidity can be obtained only in proceedings specially instituted for this purpose under the relevant provision in the Treaty. In the case of an indirect challenge, on the other hand, the direct object of the proceedings is, and must be, something other than the determination of the validity of the act. In other words, an indirect challenge is made when the act in question is applicable to, or otherwise relevant in, proceedings concerned with something else and it is argued that the act should not be applied on the ground that it is invalid. The Court will then consider its validity. If it finds it invalid it will refuse to apply it. The purpose of making an indirect challenge, then, is to induce the Court not to apply the act to the proceedings.

An important point to note is that, while a direct challenge can be made only before the European Court, an indirect challenge may be made both before a national court and before the European Court. If it is made before a national court the question of the validity of the act will be referred to the European Court for a preliminary ruling.

It will be seen from this that there are three procedural mechanisms or 'avenues of review' by which the question of validity can be brought before a court: a direct challenge before the European Court; an indirect challenge before the European Court; and an indirect challenge before a national court. However, an essential principle is that, whatever avenue of review is used, the *substantive* question before the court is always the same: the validity of the act.

If proceedings are brought to quash a Community act (direct challenge) the first question that must be considered is jurisdiction. Closely related to this is the concept of *locus standi* (standing). Jurisdiction is concerned with the power of the Court to hear the case. Looked at from the point of view of the applicant, *locus standi* relates to his right to bring the proceedings, his right to appear before the Court and put his case to it. In other words, if there is an admittedly unlawful act, the question still arises who has the right to ask the Court to quash it.

However, if one looks at it from the point of view of the Court it appears as an aspect of jurisdiction: does the Court have the power to hear proceedings brought by *this* applicant? Thus, from the Court's point of view one can distinguish two kinds of jurisdiction. The first is concerned with the Court's power to hear a case concerning a particular subject-matter. This is jurisdiction *ratione materiae* (regarding the subject-matter). The second, otherwise known as *locus standi*, is jurisdiction *ratione personae* (regarding the person who is bringing the proceedings). There is also a third kind of jurisdiction: jurisdiction *ratione temporis* (regarding the time of the proceedings). This is concerned with the question: can the Court hear proceedings brought *at this time?* The importance of this is that there are strict time-limits for bringing proceedings: if the application is too late, the Court will not be able to hear it. The time limit in annulment actions is one month under Article 33 ECSC and two months under Article 173 EEC.

The second issue mentioned above concerns an unlawful failure to act. In one sense a remedy for failure to act is simply the obverse of an annulment action. In fact, however, the matter is more complicated. If an annulment action is successful, the Court will declare the act void; but if proceedings for failure to adopt an act are successful, the Court merely declares that the defendant's failure is contrary to the Treaty: it cannot itself adopt the act. For this reason an indirect challenge is not possible in the case of inaction: in collateral proceedings the Court cannot be asked to decide the case on the basis that the act in question has been adopted. This means that the remedies open to the individual are more restricted in the case of a failure to act.

The third issue concerns the enforcement of Community obligations, in particular the right to obtain damages from the Community.

These are the matters that will be considered in this final part of the book.

11

REVIEWABLE ACTS

The first question concerns jurisdiction *ratione materiae*: over what matters does the Court have jurisdiction? Review proceedings are brought for a particular purpose: to have the Court *declare void an act of the Council or Commission*. This is laid down in Articles 173 and 174 EEC.[1] The former provides:

> The Court of Justice shall review the legality of acts of the Council and the Commission other than recommendations or opinions. . . .

And Article 174 states:

> If the action is well founded, the Court of Justice shall declare the act concerned to be void. . . .

It should be noted that in Community law there is no procedure equivalent to the English action for a declaration (or injunction). The Court cannot consider the legal position of the applicant in the abstract. If the action is brought under Article 173 the applicant must find some 'act' of the Commission or Council to be the subject-matter of the proceedings: he can then ask the Court to declare it void. Without this, the Court lacks jurisdiction *ratione materiae*. The first question therefore is concerned with the concept of an 'act'.

Article 173 EEC refers to 'acts . . . other than recommendations or opinions'. It will be remembered that Article 189 EEC[2] lists five kinds of act which the Council and Commission and empowered to pass. These are:

1. regulations,
2. directives,
3. decisions,
4. recommendations,
5. opinions.

The European Court has, however, held that this list is not exhaustive. There is also an innominate class of acts *sui generis*. These acts,

---

[1] Identical provisions are contained in Arts 146 and 147 Euratom.
[2] Identical provisions are contained in Art. 161 Euratom.

since they are 'acts other than recommendations or opinions', are subject to review under Article 173 EEC.[3]

What are the essential characteristics of reviewable acts under Article 173? These can be discovered by looking at the two classes of acts that are excluded: recommendations and opinions. It is stated in Article 189 EEC that these 'shall have no binding force'. Regulations, directives and decisions, on the other hand, are all stated to have binding force. It is a reasonable inference, therefore, from the provisions of the Treaty – and this has, in fact, been confirmed by the European Court on numerous occasions – that the essential characteristic of a reviewable act under the EEC Treaty is that it must have binding force or, to put it another way, it must have *legal effects*.

It is interesting to contrast the ECSC Treaty. Article 33 ECSC states:

The Court shall have jurisdiction . . . to have decisions or recommendations of the High Authority declared void. . . .

In other words it gives a positive, rather than a negative, definition of a reviewable act. It will be remembered[4] that, under Article 14 ECSC, decisions under the ECSC are equivalent to either regulations or decisions of the EEC while recommendations under the ECSC are broadly equivalent to EEC directives. They are legally binding and are not the same thing as EEC recommendations. It will thus be seen that, by referring to decisions and recommendations, Article 33 ECSC is referring to the ECSC equivalents of EEC regulations, directives and decisions. The only difference, therefore, is that acts *sui generis* are reviewable under the EEC Treaty but not under the ECSC Treaty.

It is interesting to speculate why the authors of the EEC Treaty defined reviewable acts by means of a negative definition. Did they consider that the list in Article 189 EEC was not exhaustive? This is unlikely since, until the decision of the European Court in the ERTA case, it was generally believed that the list *was* exhaustive.[5] Perhaps it was merely thought to be a more elegant style of drafting and the authors of the Treaty did not intend to widen the scope of the Court's jurisdiction. If this is so, the decision of the European Court in

---

[3] See pp. 101–2, above.
[4] See above, p. 100.
[5] See the opinion of Advocate General Roemer in the *Noordwijks Cement Accoord* case, Cases 8–11/66, [1967] ECR 75 and 95, followed by Advocate General Dutheillet de Lamothe in *ERTA*, Case 22/70, [1971] ECR 263 at 287.

the ERTA case brought about an effective modification of the Treaty.

It was stated above that under the EEC Treaty the European Court has jurisdiction to review any act that has legal effects. Under the ECSC Treaty reviewable acts must also have this quality (Article 14 ECSC says that both decisions and recommendations are legally binding) though they must in addition be classifiable as decisions or recommendations. Under both Treaties, therefore, the characteristic of having legal effect is basic to the concept of a reviewable act.

What does 'having legal effect' mean? One might say that an act has legal effect if it alters the legal position of some person. A person's legal position is the sum total of his legal rights and obligations (in a broad sense). In other words, to have legal effect, an act must produce a change in somebody's rights and obligations.

THE *NOORDWIJKS CEMENT ACCOORD* CASE

One of the best illustrations of the way this principle applies in practice is the *Noordwijks Cement Accoord* case.[6] In order to grasp the issues in this case it is necessary to have some understanding of the Community law relating to competition. The relevant provision in the EEC Treaty is Article 85. Paragraph 1 of this prohibits agreements between undertakings which restrict competition in the common market. In order to put teeth into this, the Council (acting under a power granted by Article 87 EEC) made Regulation 17, which imposes fines on undertakings guilty of violating Article 85(1). It was, however, realized by the authors of the Treaty that not all restrictive agreements were bad; so provision was made in Article 85(3) for exemptions to be granted to agreements that are economically beneficial. Such exemptions are granted by the Commission after an examination of the agreement in question.

The procedure established by Regulation 17 is that all restrictive agreements must be notified to the Commission, which then has the task of deciding whether they violate the provisions of Article 85(1). If they do not, there is of course no problem: the agreement is quite valid. If it does come within the prohibition in Article 85(1), the Commission must then decide whether an exemption under Article

---

[6] Cases 8–11/66, [1967] ECR 75.

85(3) should be granted. It is only if the Commission refuses to grant such an exemption that the firms concerned are liable to be fined.

The problem with this procedure is that it may take a considerable time for the Commission to reach a decision on these two points. What are the firms to do in the meantime? If they decide not to operate the agreement, which may eventually be held lawful, they will suffer commercially. But if they carry out the agreement and it is finally held unlawful, they might be subject to heavy fines. This difficulty was understood by the authors of Regulation 17 and it is therefore provided in Article 15(5) of the Regulation that undertakings will enjoy an immunity from fines from the time when the agreement is notified until the Commission reaches its decision. This, of course, gives the firms full protection; but it appears to have been thought too favourable to them. So it was provided in Article 15(6) of the Regulation that the immunity will cease to apply once the Commission has informed the firms, *after a preliminary examination*, that the agreement appears to violate Article 85(1) and that there appear to be no grounds to justify an exemption under Article 85(3). Once the firms receive this communication, they continue to operate the agreement at their own risk: if eventually it is held to be lawful, well and good; otherwise they will be subject to fines.

In the *Nordwijks Cement Accoord* case the companies concerned had notified their agreement to the Commission. In due course they received a letter under Article 15(6) of Regulation 17. It stated:

The Commission subjected the agreement in question to a provisional examination. It reached the conclusion that the conditions for the application of Article 85(1) of the Treaty were met and that application of Article 85(3) to the said agreement, in the form in which it was notified, was not justified.

The letter then went on to inform the companies that the immunity from fines would cease as from the receipt of the letter. The companies concerned brought proceedings under Article 173 EEC to quash the decision contained in the letter.

It was argued by the Commission that the proceedings were inadmissible because the Court had no jurisdiction *ratione materiae*: no 'act' was in existence which could be quashed. The letter, they said, contained a mere *opinion* by the Commission, which would be subject to reconsideration and which was not legally binding. It was not, therefore, a reviewable act.

The Court rejected this contention. After pointing out that the effect of the decision was to remove the immunity provided by Article 15(5), they stated:[7]

This measure deprived them of the advantages of a legal situation which Article 15(5) attached to the notification of the agreement, and exposed them to a grave financial risk. Thus the said measure affected the interests of the undertakings by bringing about a distinct change in their legal position. It is unequivocally a measure which produces legal effects touching the interests of the undertakings concerned and which is binding on them. It thus constitutes not a mere opinion but a decision.

The proceedings were therefore held to be admissible.

This judgment shows that it is sufficient if the act has only a contingent effect on the legal position of those concerned.[8] The immunity taken away by the decision was in the nature of an insurance policy: if in the end the agreement was held not to infringe Article 85, the immunity would – with hindsight – turn out to have been unnecessary. Only if this was not the case would the applicant's legal rights have been affected by the decision.

LEGAL EFFECT

In most cases it will be fairly obvious whether or not an act of a Community institution has legal effects. Some examples have already been given. However, there are a number of difficult cases that have been brought to light in judgments of the European Court. This section is devoted to a discussion of them.

First, a fairly obvious case: if a legal act merely confirms a previous act, it does not change anyone's legal position. It has no legal effect.[9] This does not apply, however, if after the adoption of the first act there has been a fundamental change in the circumstances such that the legal effect of the first act is modified.[10] In particular, this will be the case where the judgment of a court obliges the authority to reconsider the first act.[11]

More difficult problems arise where an authority adopts an act which binds the authority as to how it will act in the future. Since this may deprive it of a power – the power to act differently – it can affect

---

[7]   Ibid. at p. 91.
[8]   See also *Deshormes* v. *Commission*, Case 17/78, [1979] ECR 189 (at paragraphs 8–17 of the judgment).
[9]   See *SNUPAT* v. *High Authority*, Cases 42, 49/59, [1961] ECR 53 at 75–6.
[10]   See *ERTA*, Case 22/70, [1971] ECR 263 at paragraph 66 of the judgment and *per* Advocate General de Lamothe at p. 286.
[11]   *SNUPAT* v. *High Authority*, loc. cit., note 9, above.

the legal position of those who would benefit from the exercise of the power. The matter is difficult, however, because the authority may be able to revoke the act. Nevertheless, if the authority is bound by the act until it is revoked, it is probably accurate to regard it as a reviewable act.

An example of this is the case of *Lassalle* v. *European Parliament*.[12] In this case a Community official on the staff of the European Parliament brought proceedings[13] to annul a Notice of Vacancy for the post of Head of Division in the division in which he worked. The Notice specified that one of the qualifications for the post was a 'perfect knowledge of Italian'. There was no actual reason why the holder of the post had to have a perfect knowledge of Italian and this was, in fact, a disguised way of saying the job was reserved for an Italian national. This requirement would have precluded Lassalle from being a candidate and he therefore wished to have the Notice quashed. The admissibility of the application was not in fact contested by the defendant and was not therefore discussed in detail by the Court. However, the Advocate General stated:[14]

. . . the notice of vacancy in this instance contains various conditions which limit the choice which the administration will have eventually to make. In short, it is limiting its choice in advance and, in so doing, is taking a decision which, when published, has an immediate adverse effect on servants who, like the applicant, do not fulfil one or other of the required conditions . . .

The Notice was, therefore, a reviewable act.

Another difficult problem arises where the procedure laid down for taking a decision involves a number of steps, each step being itself a sort of preliminary decision. It might, for example, be required that, before the final decision is taken, the opinion of certain bodies should be obtained. The question is whether each of these preliminary decisions should be regarded as a reviewable act or whether they should be regarded as being subsumed in the final decision. From an analytical point of view, the correct answer to this question might depend on the exact requirements of the law. If it is provided merely that the opinion of a certain body must be *taken into account* by the

---

[12] Case 15/63, [1964] ECR 31. See also *Küster* v. *European Parliament*, Case 79/74, [1975] ECR 725 (at paragraphs 4–8 of the judgment) and *De Roubaix* v. *Commission*, Case 25/77, [1978] ECR 1081 (at paragraphs 6–9 of the judgment).

[13] The proceedings were brought under Art. 91 of the Staff Regulations (Regulation 31/1962, JO 1962, 1385): see Art. 179 EEC. The issue, however, was the same as under Art. 173 EEC or 33 ECSC.

[14] At p. 41.

authority making the final decision, it might seem that the preliminary decision does not affect anyone's legal position and is not,
therefore, a reviewable act. If, on the other hand, the law states that
the authority making the final decision cannot decide in a certain way
unless a *favourable opinion* is given by some other body, the preliminary
decision will restrict the power of the body giving the final decision.
In such a case the preliminary decision should be regarded as a
reviewable act.

This, however, is not the view which has been taken by the Court.
In the case of *Huber* v. *Commission*[15] the Court had to consider a
problem concerned with the establishment of a Community official.
Under the Staff Regulations the opinion of the Establishment Board
had first to be obtained. It was moreover provided that the decision-
making authority, the Committee of Chairmen, could not establish
an official unless the report of the Establishment Board was favourable. In *Huber* v. *Commission* the report was unfavourable and the
Advocate General stated that, since the appointing authority was
legally precluded from establishing an official if the report of the
Establishment Board was unfavourable, this report was a reviewable
act.[16] It took away the power to establish from the Committee of
Chairmen and thus put an end to the official's chances of establishment. The Court, however, rejected this opinion and held that the
report was not a reviewable act, on the ground that it was not
separable from the final decision.[17]

This ruling is questionable from the legal point of view but it
probably did little harm on the facts of the case since the Court made
clear that the report could be challenged in the course of proceedings
to annul the final decision. Moreover, the applicant would benefit in
one respect, since the time limit for bringing the proceedings would
begin only on the date of the final decision. The result of this and
subsequent cases is that preliminary decisions of this kind are not
reviewable in their own right.[18] To come within this rule, the
preliminary decision must not affect the applicant's rights independently of the final decision. Its only legal consequences must be its
effects on the final decision.[19]

[15] Case 78/63, [1964] ECR 367. This was also a case under the Staff Regulations: see note 13 above.
[16] Ibid. at p. 383.
[17] At pp. 375–6.
[18] See also *Weighardt* v. *Euratom Commission*, Case 11/64, [1965] ECR 285 at 298.
[19] In the *Noordwijks Cement Accoord* case (above) the Commission argued that the decision in its letter was a mere preliminary decision, but the Court rejected this because the decision had immediate legal consequences which were independent of the final decision.

The leading case is now *IBM* v. *Commission*,[20] another decision under EEC competition law. The Commission decided to open proceedings against IBM for abuse of a dominant position and they wrote IBM a letter informing it of this and inviting it to put its case. A statement of objections, specifying what IBM was alleged to have done, was enclosed. This communication was a necessary preliminary to any decision against a defendant in such proceedings. IBM, however, objected to the proceedings on a number of grounds extrinsic to the substance of the case. In particular, it alleged that the statement of objections lacked clarity (it said that it had no clear idea what it was alleged to have done), that the decision to bring proceedings had not been taken by the Commissioners themselves but by an official and that the proceedings were contrary to international law because the Commission was attempting to apply Community law extraterritorially. There were obviously great advantages in obtaining a decision on these points before the substance of the action was dealt with; so IBM brought an annulment action against the decision to commence proceedings and against the statement of objections.

The Court, however, held that these were not reviewable acts: they were mere preliminary decisions which could be challenged only in the course of a review of the final decision. The Court justified this on the ground that the consequences of the decision to bring proceedings were either wholly favourable to IBM (for example, it precluded proceedings by the national authorities) or merely paved the way for later steps in the procedure.

This judgment may have been correct in terms of the previous case law of the Court but it had unfortunate consequences for IBM because it meant that IBM had to incur the great expense of fighting the case on the merits before it could raise its preliminary objections.

Another case in which the Commission raised the 'preliminary decision' argument was *AKZO* v. *Commission*.[21] This was also a competition case, in which the Commission decided to show certain documents to the complainant in the case. The company against which the proceedings had been brought, AKZO, claimed that the documents contained confidential information which it did not want business rivals to see; it therefore brought an annulment action against the Commission's decision to show the documents to the complainant. This time the Court held the proceedings admissible: the decision directly affected AKZO's right to confidentiality, inde-

---

[20] Case 60/81, [1981] ECR 2639.
[21] Case 53/85, [1987] 1 CMLR 231.

pendently of the final decision. Moreover, a right to challenge the decision on the documents in the course of a review of the final decision would not constitute an adequate remedy because by then the damage would already have been done.

It was pointed out earlier that one of the defects of Community law is that it has no equivalent to the English action for a declaration. The European Court has, however, tried to alleviate this by ruling that a statement of future intention by the Commission or Council is a reviewable act. In strict logic this would be the case only if the authority was bound by its statement; however, this could have undesirable consequences as the persons concerned could be deprived of a remedy. A few examples will make this clear. In the case of *Fédération Charbonnière de Belgique* v. *High Authority*,[22] the High Authority wrote to the Belgian Government and told them that continued grants of equalization aid for the Belgian coalfields would be conditional on the Belgian Government's taking certain steps. This obviously meant that the subsidies would be withdrawn if the steps were not taken. Strictly speaking, nobody's legal rights were affected because the High Authority was not (presumably) bound by its statement. Yet it was obviously desirable that the mining companies should be allowed to obtain a ruling on the validity of the High Authority's decision as soon as it was made, rather than making them wait to see what action the High Authority took if the Belgian Government refused to comply. A declaration would have been the appropriate remedy. In the absence of such a remedy the Court had to characterize the High Authority's letter as a reviewable act. This is what it did. It justified its ruling as follows:[23]

In its letter of 28 May 1955 the High Authority accepted that equalization aid must be accompanied by a series of measures to be adopted by the Belgian Government. Furthermore, it considers that the Belgian Government ought to apply four measures, indicated at points (a), (b), (c) and (d). The action referred to under (d) is, therefore, one of the series of measures which the Belgian Government would be obliged to take if the circumstances so required. The High Authority has thus unequivocally determined the attitude which it had decided to take henceforth should the circumstances mentioned under point 2(d) of the letter arise. In other words, it has laid down a rule to be applied if necessary. It must therefore be seen as a decision within the meaning of Article 14 of the Treaty.

[22] Case 8/55, [1956] ECR 245.
[23] [1956] ECR at 257.

Another example is the case of *Algera* v. *Common Assembly*.[24] The plaintiffs were all officials of the Common Assembly of the ECSC who had been appointed on fixed-term contracts. When the Staff Regulations for Community employees were adopted, the plaintiffs were offered permanent appointments under them. They were, however, unwilling to accept the gradings they were offered. A letter was written to them on behalf of the Assembly noting their rejection of their gradings and stating that if they continued in this attitude they would be regarded as only temporary employees and would lose various benefits. The Court held that this letter constituted a reviewable act because it specified with all necessary precision what action the Common Assembly intended to take if the plaintiffs continued to refuse the grading offered.[25]

The European Court has in fact adopted a general doctrine that any statement by a Community institution as to the action it intends to take in given circumstances is a reviewable act provided it is definite and unequivocal. The fact that the institution is not legally bound by such a statement appears to be immaterial. It is obviously desirable that the persons affected should be able to test the legality of the action proposed and they are entitled to assume that the authority means what it says. Thus, though strictly speaking, such a statement of intention may not be a legal act, it is desirable on policy grounds that it should be treated as such in the absence of provision for an action to obtain a declaration.

VOID AND VOIDABLE ACTS

Up to now nothing has been said about the validity of acts. This is obviously important because it might be thought that an invalid act could have no legal effect. However, in Community law the general rule is that invalid acts are voidable, not void. In other words, they have legal effects unless and until they are set aside by the European Court. Since the question of jurisdiction is decided at the beginning of the hearing, it is clearly proper, in the case of a voidable act, to assume its validity for the purpose of deciding whether it has legal effects.

The rule that invalid acts are normally voidable and not void is important for another reason as well. It will be remembered that

---

[24] Cases 7/56, 3–7/57, [1957] ECR 39.
[25] [1957] ECR at 54.

there is a very short time period for bringing proceedings to quash an act. Once this has gone by, the act can no longer be annulled. An invalid act which is immune from review for this reason is not, however, the same as a valid act, since it may be subject to indirect challenge.[26] However, this right is limited; so for some purposes a voidable act which has not been annulled within the time-limit has the same effect as a valid one.

The reason for the rule that invalid acts are merely voidable, and also for the very short period within which a challenge may be brought, is said to be a desire to protect legal certainty. If an act of a public authority has the appearance of being valid, it is desirable that it should be treated as such unless and until it is annulled; and the period of uncertainty is restricted as much as possible by having a short time-limit. However, if the act is quite patently and obviously invalid – for example, if it is made by an authority which could not possibly have the power to make it – legal certainty is no longer in issue. In such a case the act may be regarded as being void, 'non-existent' in Community terminology.

This has two important consequences. First, paradoxical as it may seem, the European Court will have no jurisdiction to quash it. Since it is non-existent, it can have no legal effects; therefore it is not a reviewable act. If proceedings are brought to annul such an 'act', the Court will declare them inadmissible: it will lack jurisdiction *ratione materiae*. This is quite logical, though it may seem strange to the Anglo-Saxon mind that an act which is vitiated by a significant but not obvious fault may, being merely voidable, be quashed by the Court; but that an 'act' which is patently invalid, being absolutely void, cannot be annulled. In practice, however, this is not as serious a draw-back as it might appear since, if the Court gives a judgment stating that the case is inadmissible because the 'act' is non-existent, the practical effect will be the same as a declaration of invalidity. (And costs may even be granted to the applicant – who is technically the losing party – if he can show that the defendant was at fault in leading him to believe that the 'act' was in fact legally effective.)[27]

The second consequence of the 'act' being non-existent is that the expiry of the time-limit cannot give it even the shadow of validity. It is always open to indirect challenge since, once it is shown to be

---

[26] See Chapter 14.

[27] See *Lemmerz-Werke* v. *High Authority*, Cases 53, 54/63, [1963] E.C.R 239 at 249. In this case the applicant had to pay a quarter of the costs and the defendant, three-quarters. In the *Tubes de la Sarre* case (below), on the other hand, the applicant had to pay all the costs.

non-existent, no court is entitled to take cognizance of it. The passage of time can never confer validity on it.[28]

It is not easy to say precisely in what circumstances an act will be non-existent but the European Court has said that the defects of the act must be particularly serious and obvious.[29] Normally, the invalidity of the act must be apparent on its face. In *Société des Usines à Tubes de la Sarre* v. *High Authority*[30] the European Court held that the absence of reasons renders an act non-existent. However, this has not been followed in later cases[31] and cannot now be regarded as good law. The two cases in which an act probably would be non-existent are where it is clearly and obviously *ultra vires*, for example if it deals with a subject matter completely outside the scope of the Treaties,[32] or if there are such major procedural defects in its enactment that it could not be said to have been adopted by the authority.

The latter situation was considered by the European Court in *Lemmerz-Werke* v. *High Authority*[33] in which the Court had to decide whether certain letters constituted reviewable acts under Article 33 ECSC. The High Authority had previously issued a general decision (Decision 22/60) prescribing the form that decisions had to take.[34] One of these requirements was that the decision had to be signed by a member of the High Authority on its behalf. The letters, which were signed merely by an official of the High Authority, did not comply with these requirements and the Court held that they did not constitute decisions and were not, therefore, reviewable. It gave its reasons as follows:[35]

According to Article 14, decisions shall be taken by the High Authority, that is to say by its members sitting as a body. As such decisions are 'binding in their entirety' however, they must show that they are intended to have legal effects upon those to whom they are addressed.

[28] See further, Chapter 14, below.

[29] *Consorzio Cooperative d'Abruzzo* v. *Commission*, Case 15/85, 26 February 1987 (not yet reported) (paragraph 10 of the judgment). See further *Algera* v. *Common Assembly*, Cases 7/56, 3–7/57, [1957] ECR 39 at 60–1.

[30] Cases 1, 14/57, [1957] ECR 105.

[31] See, for example, *Nold* v. *High Authority*, Case 18/57, [1957] ECR 121, and the *Noordwijks Cement Accoord* case, Cases 8–11/66, [1967] ECR 75. The *Tubes de la Sarre* case might still stand in the special case of a reasoned opinion (equivalent to a decision) under Art. 54(4) ECSC.

[32] *Commission* v. *France (Rediscount Rate case)*, Cases 6, 11/69, [1969] ECR 523.

[33] Cases 53, 54/63, [1963] ECR 239.

[34] On this see *Krupp* v. *Commission*, Cases 275/80, 24/81, [1981] ECR 2489; see also *National Carbonising* v. *Commission*, Cases 109, 114/75, [1977] ECR 381 at 388 *per* Advocate General Mayras.

[35] Ibid., p. 248.

It follows from the natural meaning of the word that a decision marks the culmination of procedure within the High Authority, and is thus the definitive expression of its intentions.

Finally, it is necessary for the legal protection of all those affected that they should be able to identify by its very form a decision which involves such serious legal consequences, in particular a compulsory time-limit for exercising the right of instituting proceedings against it. In particular, for a measure to amount to a decision, those to whom it is addressed must be enabled clearly to recognize that they are dealing with such a measure.

It follows therefore from all these considerations that a decision must appear as a measure taken by the High Authority, acting as a body, intended to produce legal effects and constituting the culmination of procedure within the High Authority, whereby the High Authority gives its final ruling in a form from which its nature can be identified.

Any measure, therefore, which in particular, does not appear to have been debated and adopted by the High Authority and authenticated by the signature of one of its members, cannot be regarded as a decision.

It is not easy to know to what extent the principles laid down in this passage are based on Decision 22/60 as distinct from the Treaty itself. The judgment was not expressly based on Decision 22/60, and the Court was careful to point out that the absence of an inessential requirement of form will not prove fatal as long as the 'fundamental conditions underlying the concept of a decision within the meaning of the Treaty' are satisfied. This suggests that the judgment was, at least in part, independent of Decision 22/60. If this is so, it must now be regarded as of doubtful authority in so far as it requires the signature of a member of the Commission: it would be unreasonable if the Commission could not delegate decision-making powers to its staff, and there have been a number of cases in which the Court has recognized that letters signed by Commission officials can constitute reviewable acts.[36] Nevertheless, the general idea expressed in the quotation is still valid, especially the principle that the nature of the act must be apparent on its face; it must also be clear that it has been adopted according to appropriate procedures.

[36] For instance, in the *Noordwijks Cement Accoord* case (above, note 5); see further Usher, (1984) 9 E.L. Rev. 261 at 262. It is interesting to note that in *Kohler* v. *Court of Auditors*, Cases 316/82, 40/83, [1984] E C R 641, a case under the Staff Regulations, the European Court held that an oral decision can be a reviewable act: see Usher, loc. cit.

ACTS OF THE COUNCIL AND OF THE COMMISSION

Article 173 EEC makes provision for the review of acts only of the Council and Commission.[37] The European Court, however, has decided to read this provision as if it also covered acts of the European Parliament.[38] The circumstances in which this occurred were explained in Chapter 2.[39] It is impossible to predict whether the European Court will extend Article 173 still further, but for the moment one must say that acts only of the Council, Commission and Parliament are reviewable under the EEC Treaty.

Under the ECSC Treaty, Article 33 covers the acts of the Commission (High Authority) only. Article 38 ECSC provides for the review (on limited grounds) of acts of the Council and Parliament, but only if the applicant is a Member State or the Commission.[40]

The existence of different provisions in the different Treaties could cause difficulties. There is, of course, no problem if the measure is passed under one Treaty only. But what if a single measure is passed simultaneously under all three Treaties? This happened in *Luxembourg* v. *European Parliament*,[41] where the European Parliament passed a resolution that it would hold its future sessions in Strasbourg. It has previously held some of its sessions in Luxembourg, and the Luxembourg Government wished to challenge the resolution. The case arose before the European Court had 'rewritten' Article 173 EEC so as to cover the Parliament; so the apparent position was that acts of the European Parliament could be reviewed only under the ECSC Treaty.

There is only one Parliament for all three Communities and the future sessions would concern all three. Could the resolution be reviewed on the basis of one Treaty only? The Parliament maintained that it could not. It argued that in passing the resolution it had made a single and indivisible use of its powers under all three Treaties. The Court, however, held that the resolution could be annulled on the basis of Article 38 ECSC alone. It therefore appears that where an institution's activities are not confined to one Treaty alone, the remedies given by any relevant Treaty can be used to challenge the

[37] Art. 146 Euratom is the same.
[38] *Parti Ecologiste 'Les Verts'* v. *European Parliament*, Case 294/83, [1987] 2 CMLR 343.
[39] See pp. 77–8.
[40] Art. 38 ECSC could not be applied in *Parti Ecologiste 'Les Verts'* v. *European Parliament* because there the applicant was a political party.
[41] Case 230/81, [1983] ECR 255.

measure.[42] It seems also that if an act is annulled under Article 38 ECSC, it is annulled for all three Communities: it cannot be regarded as annulled for the ECSC but still operative for the other Communities.[43]

What happens if a Community institution, the acts of which are reviewable, delegates power to some other body? Will the acts of this other body be reviewable? There will, of course, be no problem if the power is delegated to another Community institution whose acts are also reviewable. For example, if the Council delegates power to the Commission (as is envisaged by Article 145 EEC), the European Court will have jurisdiction to review any act adopted under the delegated power.

A more difficult problem arises where power is delegated to a body specially set up by a Community institution. An example of this occurred under the ECSC Treaty where the High Authority set up two subordinate bodies, the *Office commun des consommateurs de ferrailles* (OCCF) and the *Caisse de péréquation de ferrailles importés* (CPFI). The function of these organisations, which were both established as co-operatives under Belgian law, was to administer the subsidy system for steel scrap.[44] This was financed by a levy[45] on all steel-making enterprises and it was the job of the *Caisse* to determine how much each enterprise had to pay.

In the case of *SNUPAT* v. *High Authority*,[46] a steel-making firm, SNUPAT, was in dispute with the *Caisse* as to the amount it owed under the levy. On 12 May 1958 the *Caisse* wrote to SNUPAT rejecting its contentions and stating that it owed a certain sum. The *Caisse* was empowered to do this under the High Authority's Decision 2/57, Article 12(2), which authorized it to collect payments under the levy. In the event of an enterprise failing to pay, the *Caisse* would ask the High Authority to take a decision which would be enforceable against the enterprise by virtue of Article 92 ECSC.

One of the issues in the case was whether the *Caisse's* letter was a reviewable act in view of the fact that it originated, not from the High

[42] See also *Municipality of Differdange* v. *Commission*, Case 222/83, [1984] ECR 2889 (paragraph 6 of the judgment).

[43] In the case being discussed, the resolution was not annulled, but in a similar case decided the following year, *Luxembourg* v. *European Parliament*, Case 108/83, [1984] ECR 1945, a later resolution of the Parliament was annulled. On the background to these cases, see pp. 27–8, above.

[44] This scheme is discussed further at pp. 113–15, above.

[45] The authority to impose levies was granted by Art. 49 ECSC. See also Art. 50(2) ECSC.

[46] Cases 32, 33/58, [1959] ECR 127.

Authority, but from the *Caisse* (which the Court referred to as the CPFI). After deciding that a notification of this kind created an obligation on the enterprise (and thus had legal effects) the Court said:[47]

> Article 33 of the ECSC Treaty only provides for actions against decisions of the High Authority. It is therefore necessary to examine whether decisions adopted by the CPFI are equivalent to decisions of the High Authority.
>
> In this regard there must be taken into consideration the fact that the CPFI was an organ of a financial arrangement set up by the High Authority and that it held its powers from the latter.
>
> Moreover, as has been found above, notifications from the CPFI in fact constituted the final administrative decision, which the High Authority could have avoided if it had made provision for administrative appeals against the deliberations of the Brussels agencies under clearly defined conditions.
>
> Therefore, it must be accepted – and to do otherwise would be to deprive the undertakings of the protection afforded them by Article 33 of the ECSC Treaty – that the decisions adopted by the CPFI under Article 12(2) of Decision No 2/57 rank as decisions of the High Authority and, as such, are open to applications for annulment under the conditions laid down in Article 33.
>
> The contested decision is individual in character and concerns the applicant.
>
> Therefore the application against the letter of 12 May 1958 is admissible.

One can perhaps generalize from this judgment by saying that if a Community institution which has the power to take reviewable decisions delegates that power to another body, the Court will not be precluded from reviewing the acts adopted under the power merely because they are in the name of the other body. The only exception to this is that if the delegation of powers is patently illegal, the Court may hold the act of the subordinate body to be non-existent.

FURTHER READING

Lauwaars, pp. 256–61.
Schermers, paragraphs 287–324.
Waelbroeck, 'La notion d'acte susceptible de recours dans la jurisprudence de la Cour de Justice des Communautés européennes', [1965] CDE 225.

---

[47] [1959] ECR at 137–8.

12

LOCUS STANDI

PRIVILEGED APPLICANTS

The first paragraph of Article 173 EEC[1] states that the European
Court has jurisdiction in actions for judicial review brought by a
Member State, the Council or the Commission. It appears to be
implicit in this paragraph that no question of *locus standi* can arise: the
'privileged' applicants covered by it always have *locus standi*, even to
challenge a decision addressed to someone else.

Article 173 provides for the review of acts only of the Council and
Commission. It will be remembered, however, that in *Parti Ecologiste
'Les Verts'* v. *European Parliament*[2] the European Court decided that
Article 173 should be regarded as covering the acts of the European
Parliament as well.[3] In view of this, it was argued by the Parliament
that it should also benefit from the unlimited standing conferred on
privileged applicants by the first paragraph of Article 173, but this
was rejected by the Court in a decision which must be regarded as
a major set-back for the Parliament.[3a] The Court also said that the
Parliament is not a 'legal person' within the meaning of the second
paragraph of Article 173; consequently, the Parliament cannot bring
proceedings under either paragraph.

Under the first paragraph of Article 33 ECSC, only acts of the
High Authority may be challenged; and in such proceedings the
Member States and the Council always have *locus standi*. Article 38
ECSC allows proceedings to be brought against an act of the
Assembly (Parliament) or Council. These may be brought only by a
Member State or the High Authority and only on limited grounds.

The justification for giving privileged applicants unlimited *locus
standi* is that *every* Community act concerns them. In this respect a
parallel may be drawn with the Crown (represented by the Attorney-

---

[1] Art. 146 Euratom is identical to Art. 173 EEC: everything in the text regarding the
EEC applies equally to Euratom.
[2] Case 294/83, [1987] 2 CMLR 343.
[3] See above, pp. 77–8.
[3a] *European Parliament* v. *Council*, Case 302/87, 27 September 1988 (not yet reported).

General) in English administrative law. This idea of universal interest is justified in the case of Community institutions; in the case of the Member States it can be explained only on the basis of the hybrid nature of the Community, half-way between an inter-governmental organisation and a federation.

NON-PRIVILEGED APPLICANTS: BASIC REQUIREMENTS UNDER THE EEC TREATY

Applicants who do not fall into the 'privileged' category are dealt with in the second paragraph of Article 173 EEC. This reads:

Any natural or legal person may . . . institute proceedings against a decision addressed to that person or against a decision which, although in the form of a regulation or a decision addressed to another person, is of direct and individual concern to the former.

It will be immediately apparent from this that the rights of ordinary persons to bring proceedings are restricted. The first point to note is that they may bring proceedings against only one kind of legal act: a decision. This is clearly stated in the provision.

It is obvious that this provision – especially the phrase, 'a decision . . . in the form of a regulation' – would not make sense unless it was understood that there is a distinction between the form of an act and its essential nature. This is in fact the case, as has been stressed many times by the European Court: neither the form in which an act is adopted nor the designation which it gives itself is conclusive as to its essential nature.[4]

This distinction between form and substance can give rise to ambiguity. When the Treaty uses the word 'decision', one might not be sure whether it means 'an act in the form of a decision' (a decision in the formal sense) or 'an act which is in substance a decision' (a decision in the material sense). One assumes, of course, that in normal circumstances these two will be the same thing: normally the author of the act will adopt it in its correct form and give it its correct designation. Nevertheless, there can be exceptional cases in which this is not so.

It is stated in Article 173(2) that there are three situations – and, since the Court regards this provision as exhaustive, only three – in

---

[4] See, for example, *Confédération Nationale des Producteurs de Fruits et Légumes* v. *Council*, Cases 16, 17/62 [1962] ECR 471 at 478–9.

which non-privileged applicants may bring review proceedings. These are where the challenged act is:

1. a decision addressed to the applicant;
2. a decision in the form of a regulation;
3. a decision addressed to another person.

It is clear that in the second case the word 'decision' means an act which is in substance a decision. What about cases 1 and 3? The decision in the *Noordwijks Cement Accoord* case[5] shows that case 1 is also concerned with a decision in the material sense. In this case, it will be remembered, the challenged act was a letter addressed to the applicants which withdrew the immunity from fines which they had hitherto enjoyed. The letter was not a decision in the formal sense and the Commission argued that it was not a reviewable act at all. The Court, however, found that it was a decision in the material sense and ruled that the proceedings were therefore admissible.

There is no reason to doubt that case 3 also refers to a decision in the material sense. In other words, any act, irrespective of its form, that is addressed to either the applicant or any other person (including, it has been held,[6] a Member State) may be the subject of proceedings brought by a private person, provided it is in substance a decision.[7] If this is correct, it would mean that an act in the form of a directive could be open to challenge by a non-privileged applicant. What is the position where the act, being a decision in the material, but not the formal, sense, is not addressed to anyone? If it is in the form of a regulation, there is, of course, no problem. It comes under case 2. If this is not the case – for example, if the act is not in any recognized legal form – it would seem at first sight that it could not be challenged by a private person. One hopes, however, that the Court would not adopt such an excessively literal interpretation of the text and would hold the application admissible, provided the other requirements of Article 173(2) were met. This would be clearly in accord with the spirit of the text.

What are these other requirements? In the case of a decision addressed to the applicant there are none. In all other cases, however, it must in addition be shown that the decision is of direct and

---

[5] Cases 8–11/66, [1967] ECR 75; discussed at pp. 324–6, above.

[6] *Plaumann* v. *Commission*, Case 25/62, [1963] ECR 95.

[7] However, though the Court has been prepared to hold that an act which is not in the form of a decision is in substance a decision, it has not so far applied the process in reverse and ruled that an act in the form of a decision is in substance some other kind of act: see pp. 351–3, below.

individual concern to the applicant, in which case he might be regarded as a sort of *de facto* addressee.[8] One can, therefore, summarize the position by saying that a private person may challenge an act that is in essence a decision, provided it is either addressed to him or is of direct and individual concern to him.

It has just been said that a person directly and individually concerned by an act may be regarded as a *de facto* addressee. If the act is in fact addressed to another person (case 3), must the applicant prove that the other person is an addressee in form only and not an addressee in substance at all? The wording of paragraph 2 of Article 173 might suggest this: '. . . a decision which, although in the form of a regulation or a decision addressed to another person . . .' In spite of this, however, the European Court has never required an applicant under case 3 to show that the actual addressee is not genuinely affected by the act.[9] It is, of course, quite possible that two people might be directly and individually concerned by an act, possibly in different ways, and if this is the case there is no reason why both should not have *locus standi* to challenge it: it should not be necessary for the applicant to prove an *exclusive* interest.

In any proceedings brought by an ordinary litigant, it is an essential requirement that the challenged act be shown to be a decision in the material sense. How is this to be done? What *is* the essential nature of a decision? These are not easy questions to answer, but one can start off by pointing out that a decision is a reviewable act. It can, therefore, be distinguished from opinions and other non-reviewable acts by the test of legal effect (discussed in the last chapter.) This is what occurred in the *Noordwijks Cement Accoord* case[10] where the Commission argued that the act in question was an opinion. Once this possibility was ruled out on the ground that it had legal effects, the Court assumed that it was a decision.

The problem can, therefore, be reduced to one of distinguishing a decision from the other kinds of reviewable act: a regulation, directive or act *sui generis*. In fact the European Court has never had to consider the possibility that the act in question might be a directive or act *sui generis*. The normal sort of case is one in which the alternative classification is a regulation and for this reason the tests formulated

---

[8] See *Municipality of Differdange* v. *Commission*, Case 222/83, [1984] ECR 2889 (paragraph 9 of the judgment).

[9] *Plaumann* v. *Commission*, Case 25/62, [1963] ECR 95 at 113, *per* Advocate General Roemer; *Eridania* v. *Commission*, Cases 10, 18/68, [1969] ECR 459 at 490, *per* Advocate General Roemer.

[10] See note 5, above.

by the Court have all been adopted with this purpose in mind.

The European Court has held that the word 'decision' in Article 173 has the same meaning as in Article 189 EEC.[11] No doubt the same applies to the word 'regulation'. It is useful, therefore, to compare the two provisions in Article 189.[12] The provision concerning decisions states:

A decision shall be binding in its entirety upon those to whom it is addressed.

It should be noted that the phrase 'those to whom it is addressed' in this provision must include what were previously termed '*de facto* addressees' as well as actual ones; otherwise it would be impossible to have a decision in the form of a regulation.

Article 189 also provides:

A regulation shall have general application. It shall be binding in its entirety and directly applicable in all Member States.

These two statements, which are not very satisfactory as definitions, nevertheless suggest a distinction: a decision is binding only on its addressee (actual or *de facto*); a regulation is binding generally.

The European Court has used this distinction as the foundation for its pronouncements on the subject. Thus, in *Confédération Nationale des Producteurs de Fruits et Légumes* v. *Commission*,[13] the first major case on this question, the Court expressed itself as follows:[14]

Under the terms of Article 189 of the EEC Treaty, a regulation shall have general application and shall be directly applicable in all Member States, whereas a decision shall be binding only upon those to whom it is addressed. The criterion for the distinction must be sought in the general 'application' or otherwise of the measure in question.

The essential characteristics of a decision arise from the limitation of the persons to whom it is addressed, whereas a regulation, being essentially of a legislative nature, is applicable not to a limited number of persons, defined or identifiable, but to categories of persons viewed abstractly and in their entirety. Consequently, in order to determine in doubtful cases whether one is concerned with a decision or a regulation, it is necessary to ascertain whether the measure in question is of individual concern to specific individuals.

In these circumstances, if a measure entitled by its author a regulation contains provisions which are capable of being not only of direct but also of individual concern to certain natural or legal persons, it must be admitted, without prejudice to the question whether that measure considered in its entirety

---

[11] *Confédération Nationale* case, note 4 above.
[12] Art. 161 Euratom contains identical provisions.
[13] Cases 16, 17/62, [1962] ECR 471.
[14] At pp. 478–9.

can be correctly called a regulation, that in any case those provisions do not have the character of a regulation and may therefore be impugned by those persons under the terms of the second paragraph of Article 173.

Putting the matter in very crude and general terms, one might say that a regulation lays down general rules; a decision is concerned with individual cases. This basic distinction is well known to administrative lawyers and acts falling into the former category are variously known as 'legislative', 'normative', or 'general' acts; those in the latter category are usually called 'individual', 'executive' or 'administrative' acts.[15] A regulation, therefore, is a normative act; a decision is an individual one.

The next requirement is that of individual concern. Article 173 states that, if the applicant is not the addressee of the decision, the proceedings will be inadmissible unless he is *individually concerned* by it. The meaning of this was explained by the Court in *Plaumann* v. *Commission* as follows:[16]

Persons other than those to whom a decision is addressed may only claim to be individually concerned if that decision affects them by reason of certain attributes which are peculiar to them or by reason of circumstances in which they are differentiated from all other persons and by virtue of these factors distinguishes them individually just as in the case of the person addressed. In the present case the applicant is affected by the disputed decision as an importer of clementines, that is to say, by reason of a commercial activity which may at any time be practised by any person and is not therefore such as to distinguish the applicant in relation to the contested decision as in the case of the addressee.

In this case, the act in question was a decision of the Commission addressed to the German Government refusing permission to lower the duty on imported clementines. The applicant was an importer of clementines. He was affected by the decision, but only as a member of a general class: any other importer of clementines would be affected in the same way. He was, therefore, not individually concerned and consequently lacked *locus standi* to bring the proceedings.

Direct concern relates to causation: there must be a direct link of cause and effect between the act and its impact on the applicant. If the applicant is not affected, or if the effect is more directly caused by

---

[15] See, for example, S. A. de Smith, *Judicial Review of Administrative Action* (4th ed. by J. M. Evans, 1980), pp. 71–6; J. A. G. Griffith and H. Street, *Principles of Administrative Law* (5th ed., 1973), pp. 14, 62–6. Some of these terms are, unfortunately, ambiguous. For example, an 'administrative act' can mean either an act of an administrative nature (as in the text) or an act (of whatever nature) adopted by an administrative authority.

[16] Case 25/62, [1963] E C R 95 at 107.

344 The Foundations of European Community Law

the act of some other authority, such as a Member State, he will not
be directly concerned by the Community act.

Having examined the requirements for *locus standi* under Article
173, second paragraph, in a fairly theoretical way, we must next look
at the relationship between these requirements; then we shall be able
to see how they apply in practice.

THE RELATIONSHIP BETWEEN THE REQUIREMENTS

The structure of Article 173, second paragraph, indicates that, except
in the case of a decision addressed to the applicant, there are three
separate requirements for *locus standi*: first, the act must be a decision
in the material sense; secondly, the applicant must be individually
concerned by it; and thirdly, he must be directly concerned by it.
There is no doubt that the third requirement raises quite separate
issues, but it will be apparent from what has been said that the test for
deciding whether an act is a decision, and the test for establishing
individual concern, are very similar.[17] Thus in the passage from the
Confédération Nationale case quoted above,[18] the Court said that the
criterion for determining whether a measure is a decision or a
regulation is whether or not it is of individual concern to specific
individuals. In later cases, however, a difference has emerged between the two tests, though the tests themselves have not been
applied consistently. The test for deciding whether an act is a
regulation or decision is based on the terms in which it is expressed. If
it applies to abstractly defined categories of persons, it is a true
regulation; if, however, it applies only to named, or individually
identified, individuals, it is a decision.

The test for individual concern, on the other hand, focuses on the
persons whose legal rights are affected by the measure. The question
to consider is whether they are affected as members of an open or a
closed category. An open category is one the membership of which is
not fixed and determined when the measure comes into force; a closed
category is one the membership of which *is* fixed and determined.

---

[17] In *Greek Canners* v. *Commission*, Case 250/81, [1982] ECR 3535 at 3544–3545,
Advocate General Sir Gordon Slynn said that the two tests were 'analogous'. On the other
hand, Advocate General Warner had said earlier, in the *Japanese Ball-Bearing* cases, Cases
113/77, etc., [1979] ECR 1185 at 1243, that the tests were separate and independent, a
view repeated in *Calpak* v. *Commission*, Cases 789, 790/79, [1980] ECR 1949 at 1970–1971;
see, further, Usher, (1984) 9 E.L. Rev. 263 at 264.

[18] See pp. 342–3.

The *Plaumann* case[19] (discussed above)[20] provides an example. Plaumann was affected by the measure in his capacity as a fruit importer. Since anyone can import fruit, and the measure would have applied to any new importer who commenced operations after it came into effect, the category was an open one; therefore, Plaumann was not individually concerned by it. If, on the other hand, the act had applied only to persons who had imported a given quantity of fruit during a stipulated period prior to the enactment of the measure, the category would have been closed. If Plaumann had been such a person, he would have been individually concerned.

It is easy to see that the test for distinguishing between a regulation and a decision is stricter than that for individual concern. If the applicant is named or otherwise individually identified in the measure, so that the first test is satisfied, it must necessarily follow that he will be individually concerned as well. On the other hand, it is quite possible for the second test to be satisfied, even if the first is not. This will occur when the measure, though framed in general terms, applies only to a closed category of persons. An example of this is a measure which applies only to persons who imported fruit during a certain period in the past.

The way in which the Court uses these tests is very interesting. Where the act is in the form of a regulation, the Court may decide to deal first with the question whether the act is a true regulation. If it does this, it almost always applies the first test, and almost invariably finds that the measure is in substance a regulation. The application is then declared inadmissible on *locus standi* grounds and there is no need to consider individual concern.[21]

However, in other cases the Court skips over the question whether the measure is a true regulation, and proceeds directly to the question of individual concern. It then applies the second test and quite often finds it satisfied. When this occurs, it does not consider whether the act is really a decision. It simply declares the application admissible (provided direct concern is also established).[22] In view of this, it is hard to avoid feeling that the Court decides first whether it wants the

[19] Case 25/62, [1963] ECR 95.

[20] See p. 343.

[21] See *Compagnie Française Commerciale et Financière* v. *Commission*, Case 64/69, [1970] ECR 221, and the cases mentioned below at pp. 347–9.

[22] See *CAM* v. *Council and Commission*, Case 100/74, [1975] ECR 1393; *Roquette* v. *Council*, Case 138/79, [1980] ECR 3333; *Agricola Commerciale Olio* v. *Commission*, Case 232/81, [1984] ECR 3881.

application to be admissible and then applies whichever test will produce the desired result.

INDIVIDUAL CONCERN AND THE NATURE OF A DECISION

In the pages that follow an attempt will be made to analyse the decisions of the European Court. Since the reasons given by the Court are often scanty and sometimes conflicting, a distinction will be introduced which does not appear to have been adopted by the Court itself. This is between proceedings to annul acts of a quasi-judicial nature and proceedings to annul acts based purely on policy and discretion. Cases falling into the former category are those in which the Community institution adopting the act is bound by clear rules, and the final determination depends largely on questions of fact. A semi-judicial procedure is followed. The main cases falling into this category concern competition, dumping and state aids; they will be given separate treatment in the section entitled 'Quasi-judicial Determinations'. The preceding subsections will be concerned only with acts based on policy and discretion; most of these concern agriculture.

Small Groups

The first situation to consider is where the measure is drafted in general terms but the persons affected, though members of a theoretically open category, in fact consist of a small and easily identifiable group. This situation arises quite frequently and the Court almost always denies *locus standi*. *KSH* v. *Council and Commission*[23] is an example. This concerned an act in the form of a regulation which applied to isoglucose, a form of sugar made from starch. The persons concerned were the producers of isoglucose. They were in theory a general class but in fact there were only very few of them. Their number was unlikely to increase, since heavy capital investment was necessary and some of the technology involved was protected by patents. It was probable that the relevant Community officials were aware of their identity. Nevertheless, the Court ruled that the measures were true regulations; so the producers had no *locus standi*.

---

[23] Case 101/76, [1977] ECR 797. See also *Zuckerfabrik Watenstedt* v. *Council*, Case 6/68, [1968] ECR 409.

Spijker v. *Commission*[24] shows that the Court adopts the same approach where the act is in the form of a decision (addressed to someone other than the applicant). The case arose when the Commission adopted a decision addressed to the three Benelux countries, banning imports into those countries of brushes manufactured in China. The persons concerned – brush importers in the Benelux countries – were an open category, but the applicant was in fact the only person in the three countries who imported Chinese brushes. Moreover, there was evidence indicating that the decision was passed expressly to deal with him (he was suspected by the Netherlands Government of having previously committed a major fraud by making a false declaration regarding the origin of the product). For these reasons, Advocate General Rozès considered that the applicant had *locus standi*; but the Court applied the standard theory and held that he was not individually concerned.

Binderer v. *Commission*[25] also appears rather unfair. Binderer, a firm of wine merchants, had asked the Commission whether Community law prohibited the use of certain German words to describe wines grown in Hungary and Yugoslavia. The Commission replied that it did not. Binderer then took steps to import the wines but the Commission subsequently passed a regulation prohibiting the use of the terms in question. Binderer brought proceedings to annul the regulation but the Court held that it lacked *locus standi*. It is true that Binderer was affected by the regulation only as a member of an open category – wine importers – but in view of the fact that Binderer had previously consulted the Commission and apparently relied on their reply, the Court might have found that it had been sufficiently singled out to be given *locus standi*.

Open and Closed Categories: Regulations

There have been a number of cases in which a measure, though framed in abstract terms, has applied (in whole or in part) to a closed category of persons. We will first consider the cases where the measure was in the form of a regulation. The earliest such case was *Compagnie Française Commerciale et Financière* v. *Commission*,[26] which was decided in 1970. Most of the provisions of the regulation in issue

---

[24] Case 231/82, [1983] ECR 2559. But for a more liberal decision, see *Control Data Belgium* v. *Commission*, Case 294/81, [1983] ECR 911.
[25] Case 147/83, [1985] ECR 257.
[26] Case 64/69, [1970] ECR 221.

applied to open categories of persons, but one provision, which was of
a transitional nature, only affected French exporters who had entered
into contracts before 11 August 1969, had registered them with the
French authorities by 18 August, but had not carried them out when
the regulation was made on 22 August. Such persons were a closed
category and their identity could have been ascertained by the
Commission when it adopted the regulation. For this reason, Advocate General Roemer considered that the exporters had *locus standi* to
challenge the provision in question, but the Court held that the
measure, including the provision subject to challenge, was a true
regulation, which could not be challenged by a private applicant.

The next case, *International Fruit Company* v. *Commission*,[27] concerned the procedure for importing apples from non-member States.
Under this, importers had to apply in advance to the national
authorities for an import licence. Each week the national authorities
would collate the applications made during the previous week and
pass the details to the Commission. The Commission would then
enact a measure in the form of a regulation, laying down rules for
deciding the applications in question. These measures concerned
only a closed category of persons: those who had made applications
during the preceding week. One such applicant brought annulment
proceedings and the Court held that the relevant provision was in
reality a bundle of decisions. The application was held admissible. In
this case the measure as a whole concerned a closed category, unlike
in the previous case. It is also worth noting that once the Court had
decided that the measure was really a decision, it affirmed individual
concern without further discussion.

Four years later, in 1975, the Court decided *CAM* v. *Commission*,[28]
in which the facts were almost indistinguishable from those in the
Compagnie Française case. Advocate General Warner considered that
the Court should follow its earlier ruling and therefore concluded that
the application was inadmissible. The Court, however, decided
to consider first the question of individual concern. It applied the
closed category test and, on finding this satisfied, held the application
admissible. There was no express finding that the measure was a
decision; the Court must have assumed that this followed from its
finding on individual concern.

The same approach was adopted in *Exportation des Sucres* v.

[27] Cases 41–44/70, [1971] ECR 411.
[28] Case 100/74, [1975] ECR 1393.

Commission,[29] decided in 1977, and in *UNICME* v. *Council,*[30] decided in 1978. (In the latter case the regulation applied to an open category, and the application was consequently inadmissible, but the Court made clear that the vital question was individual concern under the closed category test: it said that if direct and individual concern can be established, it is unnecessary to consider whether the measure is in substance a decision or a regulation.[31])

At this point it might have been thought that the law was settled: the *Compagnie Française* case could have been dismissed as an early aberration and one could have concluded that the closed category test had triumphed. In succeeding cases, however, the Court swung back to the approach in the *Compagnie Française* case. The first such case was *Beauport* v. *Council and Commission,*[32] decided in 1979. Here, the entire regulation applied to a closed category, sugar refineries which had previously been allocated a sugar quota. Advocate General Warner considered that the measure was a disguised decision, but the Court ruled that it was a true regulation. Later cases decided along the same lines include *Wagner* v. *Commission,*[33] *Calpak* v. *Commission,*[34] *Moksel* v. *Commission*[35] and *Deutz und Geldermann* v. *Council.*[36] The position now seems to be that where the measure is in the form of a regulation and does not fall into the quasi-judicial category discussed below, the Court will normally apply the abstract terminology test and not concern itself with whether a closed category is involved. As might be expected, there are few cases in which this test can be satisfied.

The only cases since the beginning of 1980 (other than those in the quasi-judicial category) in which the Court has allowed a private applicant to challenge an act in the form of a regulation appear to be *Roquette* v. *Council,*[37] *Agricola Commerciale Olio* v. *Commission*[38] and

---

[29] Case 88/76, [1977] ECR 709.

[30] Case 123/77, [1978] ECR 845.

[31] See paragraph 7 of the judgment.

[32] Cases 103–109/78, [1979] ECR 17.

[33] Case 162/78, [1979] ECR 3467. On this and the following cases, see the helpful article by Rosa Greaves, 'Locus Standi under Art. 173 EEC when Seeking Annulment of a Regulation', (1986) 11 E.L. Rev. 119.

[34] Cases 789, 790/79, [1980] ECR 1949.

[35] Case 45/81, [1982] ECR 1129.

[36] Case 26/86, 24 February 1987 (not yet reported).

[37] Case 138/79, [1980] ECR 3333. Other aspects of this case are discussed at pp. 31–2, above.

[38] Case 233/81, [1984] ECR 3881.

Salerno v. *Commission and Council*.[39] The last of these was a staff case concerning the re-employment of officials of an organization which was about to be dissolved. This may explain why the Court held the application admissible. The other two cases both involved rather special circumstances. The facts in *Roquette* were similar to those in *Beauport* in that the measure concerned a closed category of persons, isoglucose producers who had previously been awarded a quota. On the basis of the more recent cases, this would not in itself have been enough to ensure *locus standi*. However, there was an annex, which was an integral part of the regulation, which listed the producers by name and stated exactly what their quotas would be under the new rules laid down by the regulation. The Court therefore concluded that the producers were directly and individually concerned by the regulation; the application was consequently admissible. (It is interesting to note that *Roquette* challenged the regulation only in so far as it fixed its quota, but the Court went on to annul the whole regulation, on the ground that the Parliament had not been consulted.)

It could be argued that in *Roquette* the measure was in substance a decision even under the abstract terminology test, though the Court did not expressly decide it on that ground. In *Olio*, however, it is hard to see how the test could have been satisfied. The case concerned the procedure for disposing of surplus stocks of olive oil held by the intervention authorities. A Commission regulation was passed providing for the sale of the oil by tender. This duly took place and, as the sale was greatly oversubscribed, lots were drawn. Then the Commission realized that, due to a change in market conditions, the successful tenderers stood to make large profits. So two further regulations were passed cancelling the sale. These were challenged before the Court by the successful tenderers. The Court declared that, though the letters of allocation (which declared the successful tenderers owners of the oil) had not yet been sent, there was nothing further to negotiate and both sides were committed to going through with the transaction: 'the situation between the parties to the sale was determined'.[40] For these reasons, said the Court, the measures were of direct and individual concern to the applicants. The applications were ruled admissible without any express finding that the measures were really decisions.

---

[39]   Cases 87, 130/77, 22/83, 9, 10/84, [1985] E C R 2523. The point referred to in the text arose in Case 22/83.

[40]   Paragraph 11 of the judgment.

This judgment shows that, even in cases outside the quasi-judicial category, the Court can still adopt a liberal attitude. It should, however, be emphasized that the only persons concerned by any part of the measures were members of a closed category (successful tenderers) and, though title had not yet passed, the successful tenderers could be regarded to some extent as having had vested rights; moreover, it is unlikely that they could have obtained a remedy by any other means.

Open and Closed Categories: Decisions

Where the act is in the form of a decision, a different picture emerges. In this situation the Court has never considered whether the act might be a disguised regulation: it has always taken for granted that it is correctly designated, and examined only whether the applicant is directly and individually concerned. The closed category test is applied to decide the latter question.

The first case to consider is *Toepfer* v. *Commission*,[41] decided in 1965. The applicants in this case were a group of German grain dealers who, on 1 October 1963, applied to the relevant German authority for import licences. There was a variable levy on imports and the applicable rate (in the circumstances of the case) was that prevailing when the application was made. On 1 October 1963 the rate was zero. The German authority realized, however, that because of a change in market conditions, the importers were liable to make large profits; so they decided to reject all applications until the levy rate had been increased. They therefore told the importers that their applications would be refused and they asked the Commission to confirm this decision. On the same day, the Commission raised the levy rate as from 2 October. On 3 October the Commission took a decision, addressed to Germany, confirming the ban with regard to applications made on 1–4 October, inclusive. The dealers brought proceedings to annul this decision.

The position here was that the category of persons affected by the decision was partly closed (those who had already applied) and partly open (those who would apply during the remainder of the period covered by the ban). The Court held that the dealers who had applied on 1 October were affected differently from the others because, if they resubmitted their applications when the ban expired,

---

[41] Cases 106–107/63, [1965] ECR 405.

they would have to pay an increased levy. From this the Court concluded that the 1 October applicants were individually concerned. This case is interesting because it shows that if a measure in the form of a decision affects an open category of persons, but contained within that open category there is a closed category the members of which are affected in a significantly different way, the latter will be individually concerned.

A similar result was reached in *Bock* v. *Commission*.[42] Bock applied to the relevant German authority for a permit to import Chinese mushrooms. The German authority told him that this would be refused as soon as authorization had been obtained from the Commission. The Commission then took a decision authorizing the refusal of import permits, including those for which applications had already been made. Bock asked the Court to annul only the provision applying the decision to such applications. Since the persons affected by this provision were a closed category, the Court held that Bock was individually concerned, though it was less clear than in the previous case that such persons were affected differently from later applicants.

The situation was similar in *Piraiki-Patraiki* v. *Commission*,[43] decided in 1985. This concerned a Commission decision (based on Article 130 of the Greek Act of Accession) permitting France to impose restrictions on imports of cotton yarn from Greece. The decision was challenged by a number of Greek manufacturers, some of whom had entered into contracts to export cotton to France which had not been carried out when the decision was taken. The Court held that these exporters were individually concerned. It said that Article 130 imposed an obligation on the Commission to take the interests of such exporters into account and, since the Commission had not done so, it annulled the decision to the extent to which it applied to them.

In theory, the form in which an act is adopted should make no difference to *locus standi*. Enough has been said, however, to show that it *can* make a difference: this may be illustrated by comparing the three cases just discussed with some of those considered under the previous heading.[44] If the abstract terminology test were applied, the decisions in issue in *Toepfer*, *Bock* and *Piraiki-Patraiki* might well be

---

[42] Case 62/70, [1971] ECR 897.
[43] Case 11/82, [1985] ECR 207.
[44] At pp. 347–9. See, for example, *Moksel* v. *Commission*, Case 45/81, [1982] ECR 1129.

regarded as disguised regulations. The Court's unwillingness to reclassify such acts is, therefore, of considerable significance.[45]

Special Considerations

In addition to the matters already discussed, there are a number of special considerations that appear to influence the European Court, though the Court itself may not always acknowledge them. The first, which has been alluded to in some judgments,[46] is whether there is any alternative remedy open to the applicant. (Such a remedy would normally be in the national courts, which could refer the matter to the European Court under Article 177 EEC.) The second consideration, which is more speculative and does not appear to have been mentioned by the Court, is whether there is any alternative applicant who would have an interest in challenging the measure. The third, which is also speculative, is whether the applicant has a strong case on the merits and, in particular, whether the case raises issues of general importance.[47]

Each of these factors is of only limited weight by itself, but if they are all found together, they could well tip the balance. Thus if a plainly illegal act were challenged by an applicant who had no alternative means of bringing the matter before the Court, and if the only persons with *locus standi* would have no interest in bringing proceedings, the Court might well feel obliged to stretch a point in order to declare the application admissible.

This is perhaps the explanation for *Parti Ecologiste 'Les Verts'* v. *European Parliament*.[48] The facts of this case were outlined above,[49] where it was explained that the European Parliament had adopted a

[45] In *Piraiki-Patraiki* the Court expressly said that it was not necessary to go into the legal nature of the decision (paragraph 5 of the judgment). In *Plaumann*, Case 25/62, [1963] ECR 95, the Commission argued that its decision was in substance a normative act but the Court held that it was an individual act. The nearest the Court seems to have come to reclassifying a decision was in *Spijker* v. *Commission*, Case 231/82, [1983] ECR 2559, where it said, in paragraph 9 of its judgment, that, with regard to importers, the decision was a 'measure of general application'.

[46] See *Alusuisse* v. *Council and Commission*, Case 307/81, [1982] ECR 3463 (paragraph 13 of the judgment); *Spijker* v. *Commission*, Case 231/82, [1983] ECR 2559 (paragraph 11 of the judgment); *Allied Corporation* v. *Commission*, Cases 239, 275/82, [1984] ECR 1005 (paragraph 15 of the judgment); *Union Deutsche Lebensmittelwerke* v. *Commission*, Case 97/85, 21 May 1987 (not yet reported) (paragraph 12 of the judgment).

[47] It is noticeable that when the Court makes a particularly liberal ruling on the question of admissibility, it frequently goes on to annul the measure.

[48] Case 294/83, [1987] 2 CMLR 343.

[49] See pp. 77–8.

decision to use public money to subsidize the election expenses of the parties fighting the forthcoming elections. The decision, however, discriminated against parties which were not already represented in the Parliament. In other words, the parties already in the Parliament awarded the bulk of the money to themselves. Clearly they would have no interest in challenging the decision. On the other hand, parties not already represented were affected by the decision only as members of an open category. According to the normal rules, such parties would not be individually concerned. However, since there was no adequate alternative remedy, the Court granted standing to one such party, the Parti Ecologiste. It pointed out that if standing were restricted to parties already represented (a closed category), the result would be unequal protection for parties competing in the same election. After surmounting other obstacles, the Court held the application admissible, and went on to annul the decision.[50]

QUASI-JUDICIAL DETERMINATIONS

The concept of a quasi-judicial determination is not one recognized by the European Court, but it has become increasingly clear that it is not possible to make sense of the cases unless one adopts some such notion. An attempt was made earlier to explain what was meant by it.[51] The core idea of the concept is that the determination is to a large extent made on the basis of objective considerations and is the culmination of a procedure which has judicial features. Such determinations are predominantly decisions of fact and law, rather than discretionary decisions. There are, moreover, persons who could be regarded as being, in some sense, parties to the proceedings. Once one acknowledges that someone is a 'party' to the proceedings which resulted in the determination, it is easy to conclude that he should have *locus standi* to challenge it.

Competition Proceedings

The first example is a decision whether a firm has violated Community competition law. Articles 85 and 86 EEC prohibit certain activities and the Commission has the task of ensuring compliance.

---

[50] On other aspects of the case, see pp. 77–8 and 338, above.
[51] See p. 346.

The essence of the procedure is that the Commission first conducts an investigation and then holds a hearing at which the firm whose conduct is under consideration is invited to appear and present its case. Such a firm could therefore be regarded as the defendant. The determination takes the form of a decision addressed to the defendant. It may exonerate the defendant or find that it has violated the law. In the latter case a fine may be imposed. Since the decision is addressed to the defendant, it can clearly challenge it before the Court under Article 173.

What about the victim of the alleged malpractice? Community law allows anyone with a 'legitimate interest' to lodge a complaint with the Commission. Such a complainant is granted various procedural rights and may be entitled to participate in the hearing.[52] Can a complainant bring proceedings under Article 173 to challenge the final determination, especially if it exonerates the defendant?

This question came before the Court in 1977 in *Metro* v. *Commission*.[53] Metro was a self-service wholesaler dealing in electronic goods, which complained that another firm, SABA, was acting in violation of Article 85 because its conditions of sale, which applied to all its dealers, had the effect of precluding self-service wholesalers from distributing its products. The Commission investigated this complaint and took a decision exonerating SABA.

Metro wished to have this decision annulled. Since it was not the addressee of the decision (though it had been informed of it), it had to show that it was directly and individually concerned. One might have thought that it was not individually concerned because the persons affected by the decision were an open category – all self-service wholesalers in electronic goods wishing to handle SABA's products. The Court, however, held the proceedings admissible. It pointed out that the decision had been adopted as a result of Metro's complaint and said that it was in the interests of a 'satisfactory administration of justice' that anyone entitled to make a complaint should be allowed to institute proceedings against a decision dismissing the complaint. This case therefore establishes that in competition proceedings a complainant is regarded as individually

---

[52] See Regulation 17, OJ (Special Edition) 1959–62, p. 87, Art. 3(2)(b) and Art. 19(2); see also Regulation 99/63, OJ (Special Edition) 1963/64, p. 47, Art. 5 and Art. 7.

[53] Case 26/76, [1977] ECR 1875. See also *Demo-Studio Schmidt* v. *Commission*, Case 210/81, [1983] ECR 3045 and the second Metro case, *Metro* v. *Commission*, Case 75/84, [1987] 1 CMLR 118.

concerned by the final decision even if it is affected by it in the same way as other members of an open category.[54]

Anti-Dumping Proceedings

The second example concerns measures adopted in the course of anti-dumping proceedings. (Dumping is a form of unfair competition in international trade, usually involving selling in different markets at different prices, particularly exporting at a lower price than that applicable on the home market.) A special difficulty arises here because the normal remedy for dumping is an anti-dumping duty, which under Community law has to be imposed by regulation. The problem is that if the Court were to hold that such a measure was a true regulation, any application by an individual to annul it would be inadmissible on *locus standi* grounds; but if the Court were to hold that the measure was really a decision, it could be argued that it should be annulled for having been adopted in the wrong form.[55] This dilemma may explain the differing views expressed by the Court: in *Alusuisse* v. *Commission*[56] it implied that a measure can be simultaneously both a regulation and a decision (even though a previous case had expressly said that this is impossible[57]), while in *Allied Corporation* v. *Commission*[58] it described the anti-dumping regulation in issue as having a 'legislative character',[59] but nevertheless allowed a private applicant to challenge it. Clearly the Court has been searching for a formula which will enable it to find a satisfactory solution to the *locus standi* question, without at the same time obliging it to annul the measure. This is probably impossible, if the requirements of Article 173 are respected. In any event, the Court appears tacitly to have abandoned the rule that a private applicant cannot challenge a true regulation: in anti-dumping cases direct and individual concern are now the only criteria for *locus standi*.

The procedure in anti-dumping cases is analogous to that in

---

[54] However, if the Commission closes the investigation without taking a formal decision, the complainant has no remedy: *GEMA* v. *Commission*, Case 125/78, [1979] ECR 3173.

[55] See Usher, (1984) 9 E.L. Rev. 263 at 264.

[56] Case 307/81, [1982] ECR 3463 (paragraph 9 of the judgment).

[57] *Moksel* v. *Commission*, Case 45/81, [1982] ECR 1129 (paragraph 18 of the judgment). This discrepancy is all the more surprising in view of the fact that both these cases were decided by the Third Chamber, with the same judges sitting on each occasion.

[58] Cases 239, 273/82, [1984] ECR 1005 (paragraph 11 of the judgment). This was a judgment of the Full Court.

[59] Paragraph 11 of the judgment.

competition cases.[60] The status of complainant is fully recognized and proceedings are not normally initiated without a complaint. The role of defendant is more ambiguous because anti-dumping duties are usually imposed on all goods of the relevant kind from the country in question. This means that all exporters of such goods in the foreign country, as well as importers in the Community, could be regarded as having an interest in the proceedings. Public notice is given of the initiation of proceedings and all exporters and importers known to be concerned are informed individually by the Commission. They have the right to make representations in writing and are normally entitled to make oral representations as well. The Commission usually invites them to give evidence and Commission inspectors may visit their plants. Firms that participate in the procedure in this way could be regarded as parties.

The first judgment to consider is that in the *Japanese Ball-Bearing* cases.[61] This concerned a challenge to a Council regulation imposing an anti-dumping duty on all ball-bearings manufactured in Japan. The duty was, however, suspended for so long as the four major producers (who were named in the regulation) carried out an undertaking to raise their prices. Did the four producers have *locus standi* to challenge the regulation? According to the normal principle, they were not individually concerned because they were affected by the regulation only as members of an open category – exporters of Japanese ball-bearings. The Court nevertheless held that they had *locus standi* since they were named in the regulation, the purpose of which was to ensure that they carried out their undertakings.

The *Japanese Ball-Bearing* cases were concerned with a rather unusual situation, but *Allied Corporation* v. *Commission*[62] has now clarified and broadened the law. It establishes that exporters may challenge a regulation laying down an anti-dumping duty either if they were identified in the measure *or* if they were 'concerned by the preliminary investigations',[63] i.e. took part in the Commission investigation.[64]

[60] For a full description of the procedure, see J. F. Beseler and A. N. Williams, *Anti-Dumping and Anti-Subsidy Law* (1986), Chapter 8.

[61] *NTN* v. *Council*, Case 113/77, [1979] ECR 1185; *ISO* v. *Council*, Case 118/77, [1979] ECR 1277; *Nippon Seiko* v. *Council and Commission*, Case 119/77, [1979] ECR 1303; *Koyo Seiko* v. *Council and Commission*, Case 120/77, [1979] ECR 1337; and *Nachi Fujikoshi* v. *Council*, Case 121/77, [1979] ECR 1363.

[62] Cases 239, 275/82, [1984] ECR 1005.

[63] Paragraph 12 of the judgment.

[64] It is interesting that in the *Allied Corporation* case the Commission informed the Court that it was in favour of the exporters' actions being held admissible because otherwise Community exporters to the United States might not be allowed to challenge anti-dumping measures against their goods: see paragraph 9 of the judgment.

Importers, on the other hand, are in a different position: they are normally the persons obliged to pay the import duty, so they (unlike exporters) will have a remedy in the national courts. This is probably the reason why they are not accorded *locus standi* under Article 173 unless they are named in the regulation or special circumstances apply.[65] It seems that, in their case, participation in the investigation is not sufficient.[66]

Complainants are treated more generously.[67] (Like exporters, they have no alternative remedies.) *Timex* v. *Council and Commission*[68] concerned a regulation imposing an anti-dumping duty on mechanical watches from the Soviet Union. The proceedings had been initiated after a complaint by a British trade association on behalf of Timex, the only British manufacturer. Timex participated in the investigation and the duty was fixed in the light of the effect of the dumping on Timex, which was named in the preamble to the regulation. Timex, however, thought that the duty was too low and brought proceedings to annul the regulation. It was argued by the defendants that Timex was not individually concerned because it was affected only as a member of an open category – manufacturers of mechanical watches in the Community. However, the Court held that Timex had *locus standi*: the regulation was 'a decision which is of direct and individual concern to Timex'.[69] In view of this it seems likely that complainants will be given the same rights as exporters.

State Aid

State aid which distorts competition is (generally speaking) contrary to Community law and Article 93 EEC lays down a procedure for determining when a violation has occurred. This involves an investigation by the Commission, followed by a decision addressed to the Member State alleged to have granted the aid. That Member State

[65] See paragraph 15 of the judgment in the *Allied Corporation* case; see also *Sermes* v. *Commission*, Case 279/86, Order of 8 July 1987 (not yet reported).

[66] See *Alusuisse* v. *Council and Commission*, Case 307/81, [1982] ECR 3463, paragraphs 12 and 13 of the judgment. In *Allied Corporation* the importer (Demufert) was not named in the regulation, though it may have been involved in the investigation.

[67] *FEDIOL* v. *Commission*, Case 191/82, [1983] ECR 2913, establishes that a complainant has a remedy where the Commission fails to initiate proceedings, something not available to the complainant in competition cases: see note 54, above.

[68] Case 264/82, [1985] ECR 849.

[69] Paragraph 16 of the judgment. In paragraph 12, however, the Court said that anti-dumping regulations are 'legislative in nature and scope, inasmuch as they apply to traders in general'.

can clearly challenge the decision under Article 173,[70] but can a complainant do so? The status of complainant is not given formal recognition in the same way as in the case of competition and anti-dumping proceedings, but in practice competitors of the firms receiving the aid are allowed to participate in the investigations.

In *COFAZ* v. *Commission*,[71] COFAZ and three other French fertilizer producers complained through their trade association to the Commission that their Dutch competitors were receiving aid from the Dutch Government. The Commission investigated the matter and the French firms played some part in the proceedings. Eventually the Commission concluded that no aid was involved and it took a decision, addressed to the Dutch Government, terminating the proceedings. COFAZ challenged this decision but the Commission argued that it was not individually concerned because it was affected only in its capacity as a fertilizer producer, an open category. The Court, however, held the application admissible. It said that firms playing a part in the procedure comparable to that of a complainant should have *locus standi*, provided their position in the market was significantly affected by the aid.

Conclusions

The cases discussed show that where a quasi-judicial determination is challenged, the Court adopts a much more liberal attitude than it does where the proceedings concern a discretionary act. Not only is the closed category test often ignored but, in the case of anti-dumping regulations, the Court does not even concern itself with the nature of the act. All this is in stark contrast to the position where discretionary acts are involved, especially if they are in the form of a regulation.

DIRECT CONCERN

As explained above, direct concern raises issues of cause and effect. The main situation in which it is important is where the effect of the decision on the applicant depends on the discretion of another

---

[70] But see *Comité de Développement et de Promotion du Textile et de l'Habillement* v. *Commission*, Case 282/85, 10 July 1986 (not yet reported) where the statutory body administering the aid was held not to have *locus standi*.
[71] Case 169/84, [1986] 3 CMLR 385.

person.[72] Thus if a Community institution grants a discretionary
power to another authority (e.g. a Member State), the mere fact that
the power would, if exercised, affect the applicant does not mean that
he has *locus standi* to challenge the decision granting it: the inter-
position of an autonomous will between the decision and its effect on
the applicant means that he is not *directly* concerned. Moreover, since
a negative act is treated in the same way as a positive act for the
purpose of jurisidiction, a decision by a Community institution
refusing to grant a discretionary power cannot be challenged by those
who would have been affected by its exercise, had it been granted.

The best case to illustrate these principles is *Alcan* v. *Commission*.[73]
The facts in the *Alcan* case were that, under the relevant provisions,
Member States could apply to the Commission for a quota of
unwrought aluminium imports at a reduced rate of duty. In October
1968 the Belgian Government made a request for such a quota for the
year 1968 and a request for an increased quota was made in December 1968. In May 1969 the Commission took a decision addressed to
the Belgian Government rejecting the request. The question was
whether the applicants, Alcan and two other aluminium-refining
companies in Belgium, could challenge this decision.

Two points about the situation should be noted: first, that if the
quota had been granted, the Belgian Government would not have
been obliged to allow the quantity of unwrought aluminium in
question to be imported at the reduced rate. In other words, the
Commission would merely have given an authorization: the Belgian
Government would have had a discretion whether or not to make use
of it. Secondly, since the Commission's decision was not made until
May 1969, and the quota was for the year 1968, the effect of the
authorization (if it had been given by the Commission and put into
effect by the Belgian Government) would merely have been that
companies which had imported aluminium in 1968 would have been
able to claim a refund on duty paid by them. In view of this latter fact,
Advocate General Gand considered that the applicants were individually concerned; but both he and the Court took the view that they
were not directly concerned because, even if the authorization had

---

[72] Problems can also arise where the contested act is one giving aid to a competitor
(*Eridania* v. *Commission*, Cases 10, 18/68, [1969] ECR 459) or refusing to prevent a
Member State from doing so (*COFAZ* v. *Commission*, Case 169/84, [1986] 3 CMLR 385).
This in turn raises the question whether there must be an effect on the applicant's *rights*, or
whether an effect on his *interests* is sufficient. Community law has not yet come to terms with
this problem.

[73] Case 69/69, [1970] ECR 385. See also *Mannesmannröhren-Werke* v. *Council*, Case
333/85, 17 March 1987 (not yet reported).

been granted, the Belgian Government might have decided not to use it. It was probably unlikely, in the circumstances, that this would have happened – why would the Belgian Government have made the request if they had not intended making use of it? – but the theoretical possibility was enough to eliminate *locus standi*.

If, however, the power is not discretionary, or if it is exercised first and confirmed afterwards, those affected by its exercise will be directly concerned by the act conferring or confirming it. An example of the first situation is the *International Fruit Company* case (discussed above[74]). It will be remembered that, under the provisions then in force, persons wishing to import table apples were required to obtain an import permit from the national authorities. Each week the national authorities would inform the Commission of the number of applications for permits made to them during the preceding week. The Commission would then adopt an act (which the Court held to be a bundle of decisions, though it was in the form of a regulation) which laid down a formula for deciding how the applications should be dealt with. The national authorities then granted import permits on the basis of the formula. The Court held that, since the formula left no discretion to the national authorities, an applicant for a permit was directly concerned by the Commission's decision.

An example of the second situation is the *Toepfer* case,[75] which also concerned import permits but the system in operation was different. Normally all applications had to be granted by the national authorities; but on this occasion the national authorities had decided to apply 'safeguard measures' and this entitled them to refuse applications, provided that their decision to apply the 'safeguard measures' was confirmed by the Commission. The applicant applied for a permit; the German authorities declared that safeguard measures were to be applied; the Commission confirmed this; and the applicant was then informed that his application was rejected. Since the Commission's decision confirming the measures was taken after the German authorities' decision to apply them, the applicant was, the Court held, directly concerned by the Commission's decision: at the time when it was taken, an independent will no longer stood between the decision and its effect on the applicant.[76]

---

[74] See above, p. 348.

[75] See above, pp. 351–2.

[76] The position might be different in the case of someone who applied for a permit *after* the Commission's decision was taken. Even if the Commission authorised the continuance of the 'safeguard measures' for a certain period of time subsequent to its decision, the national authorities would, presumably, retain the discretion to revoke them sooner.

A more difficult case relating to this problem is *Bock* v. *Commission*,[77] which concerned import permits for mushrooms. At the time in question, the German Government had a policy of excluding imports of mushrooms that originated in the People's Republic of China. It was not, however, easy to give effect to this policy when the mushrooms were already in free circulation in another Member State. For, although such imports could not be made without an import permit, the German authorities were obliged to grant such a permit within a reasonable time (normally four days) after the application, unless they first obtained authorization from the Commission to suspend the issue of permits.

In the case, Bock lodged his application for a permit on 4 September 1970. On 11 September the German authorities told the Commission that they had received an application for an import permit for Chinese mushrooms and they requested authorization to exclude imports of such mushrooms 'including the import envisaged by the import application in question'. On the same day the German authorities informed Bock that his application would be rejected as soon as the Commission had given its authorization. On 15 September the Commission made a decision addressed to the German Government authorizing the excluding of Chinese mushrooms, including those for which applications for import permits were pending.[78] Bock's application was then formally rejected. He brought proceedings to quash the decision in so far as it applied to applications already pending.

The Commission objected to the admissibility of the case on the ground that Bock was neither individually nor directly concerned. The Court, however, held the application was admissible. It considered Bock individually concerned because his application was lodged before the decision was made. In so far as the decision applied to such applications (and it was challenged only to the extent that it did) the persons affected were ascertainable when the decision was made. The Court also considered that Bock was directly concerned: the German authorities had already informed him that his application would be rejected as soon as authorization had been obtained and the authorization had been requested for precisely this purpose.

One might criticise this decision on the ground that the German authorities were, nevertheless, still legally entitled not to make use of

[77] Case 62/70, [1971] ECR 897.
[78] There was some dispute as to the correct interpretation of this part of the decision but the Court held that this is what it meant.

the authorization. They had been given a discretionary power. It is true that they would not have asked for the pcwer if they had not intended using it and they clearly did intend using it with regard to Bock's application. But they could have changed their minds. After all, in the *Alcan* case one could have argued that the Belgian Government would not have asked for the authorization unless they had intended using it. Yet the Court held, in that case, that the applicant was not directly concerned.

These two cases are obviously very similar. However, there are two important differences between them. The first was that the German authorities had expressly told Bock that, if they obtained the authorization, it would be used to reject his application. There was no evidence that this was so in the *Alcan* case. The second difference was that in the *Alcan* case the Belgian Government had been acting in the interests of Alcan and the other importers in making the application. One might almost say that it had been acting on their behalf. Since the importers and the Member State were 'on the same side', so to speak, it would not have been unreasonable to regard the interests of the importers as sufficiently protected by the right of the Belgian Government to bring proceedings to set aside the decision. As it was a privileged applicant, there could have been no objections to the Belgian Government's *locus standi*. The fact that the Belgian Government did not bring an application suggests either that it did not consider it would meet with success or that it had changed its mind about the desirability of making use of the authorization. In the *Bock* case, on the other hand, the German Government was obviously acting against the interests of the importer. Bock could not look to his Government to bring an application to quash the decision. So if he had been refused *locus standi* there would have been no possibility that the legality of the decision would have been challenged (except in the somewhat unlikely circumstance of an application by another Member State, perhaps Holland, the country from which the import was to have been made).

The first distinguishing fact was recognized by the Court itself and is obviously relevant. The second was not alluded to by the Court, but it may have been influenced by it. It is obviously a factor of great practical importance, though it is hardly something that could have been expressly stated by the Court.

A later case, which is similar to *Bock* but probably goes further, is *Piraiki-Patraiki* v. *Commission*.[79] The facts of this case were outlined

---

[79] Case 11/82, [1985] ECR 207.

earlier:[80] it will be remembered that the Commission took a decision authorizing France to exclude Greek cotton yarn. Since France was not legally obliged to exercise the power, it could be argued that the Greek exporters who challenged the decision were not directly concerned by it. However, France was already exercising a very restrictive system of licences for such imports and the Court said that the possibility that France might decide not to make use of the authorization was 'entirely theoretical';[81] so the applicants were held to be directly concerned.

NON-PRIVILEGED APPLICANTS: THE ECSC TREATY

Paragraph 2 of Article 33 of the ECSC Treaty differs in important respects from paragraph 2 of Article 173 EEC. It provides:

> Undertakings or the associations referred to in Article 48 may ... institute proceedings against decisions or recommendations concerning them which are individual in character or against general decisions or recommendations which they consider to involve a misuse of powers affecting them.

In some respects this is narrower than Article 173(2) EEC; but in other, more important, respects it is wider.

The first way in which it is narrower is as regards the persons who may institute proceedings. Article 173(2) gives this right to 'any natural or legal person' – i.e. anyone – but Article 33(2) restricts it to two classes of person: undertakings and associations. There is a definition of 'undertakings' in Article 80 ECSC. This states:

> For the purposes of this Treaty, 'undertakings' means any undertaking engaged in production in the coal or the steel industry within the territories referred to in the first paragraph of Article 79 ...

Article 48 makes clear that the 'associations' referred to are associations of 'undertakings' as defined by Article 80.[82] In other words, the only applicants (other than those in the privileged category) who are permitted to bring proceedings under Article 33 are firms engaged in production in the coal and steel industries together with their trade associations.

The second way in which the ECSC Treaty is narrower is that

---

[80] See p. 352.
[81] Paragraph 9 of the judgment
[82] See *Groupement des Industries Sidérurgiques Luxembourgeoises* v. *High Authority*, Cases 7, 9/54, [1956] ECR 175 at 190–192.

under Article 33 only the acts of the Commission may be challenged; Article 173, on the other hand, applies to the acts of both the Commission and the Council. Article 38 ECSC provides for review of acts of the Council and of the Parliament, but it grants *locus standi* only to the Member States and the Commission. So non-privileged applicants do not have the right to challenge Council acts under the ECSC.[83] However, the legislative and executive powers of the Community are, under the ECSC Treaty, granted almost exclusively to the Commission, in the sense that the author of most ECSC acts is the Commission (though the Council often has a power of veto). Consequently, this limitation is more apparent than real.

The ECSC Treaty is, on the other hand, more liberal with regard to the kinds of act that may be challenged. Article 33 allows non-privileged applicants to bring proceedings to quash two categories of acts: 'decisions and recommendations . . . which are individual in character' and 'general decisions and recommendations'. Individual decisions under the ECSC are equivalent to EEC decisions. Recommendations under the ECSC are, of course, different from EEC recommendations: they are legally binding and are analogous to EEC directives.[84] Their inclusion is not, however, a very significant extension: ECSC recommendations can, unlike EEC directives, be addressed to private firms as well as to Member states; it would, therefore, have been strange if they had not been included.

A more important difference between the two provisions is with regard to the second category. General decisions are normative acts, equivalent to EEC regulations.[85] These general acts may be challenged by non-privileged applicants under the ECSC Treaty, but only on one ground: they must involve a misuse of powers affecting the applicant. Misuse of powers is the most difficult of the four grounds to establish; nevertheless, the fact that non-privileged applicants may proceed at all against normative acts is in striking contrast to the EEC Treaty.

Another way in which Article 33(2) is wider in scope is with regard to *locus standi*. In the case of individual acts, all that Article 33(2) requires is that the challenged act should concern the applicant; that concern need not be individual or direct. This is an important difference. Where the challenged act is general, it must be shown that

[83] On the interplay between the EEC and ECSC Treaties, where the one allows a challenge and the other does not, see pp. 335–6, above.
[84] See above, p. 100.
[85] Ibid.

the misuse of powers 'affects' the applicant. Again, it need not affect him individually or directly.

It is interesting to look at some of the most important decisions on these points to see how the Court has interpreted this text. This will throw valuable light on the EEC Treaty because the authors of Article 173 had these decisions in mind when they drafted the latter Article.

The first case to consider is *Groupement des Industries Sidérurgiques Luxembourgeoises* v. *High Authority*.[86] This case, which was decided in 1956, concerned a decree enacted by the Luxembourg Government establishing two official bodies called the *Office Commercial* and the *Caisse*. The decree provided that the former would have the sole right of importing coal into Luxembourg and that a levy on all sales of coal to industrial enterprises in Luxembourg had to be paid to the latter. The plaintiffs in the case were a group of Luxembourg steel producers. They wrote to the High Authority requesting it to adopt a decision declaring that the *Office's* monopoly of coal imports and the levy were both illegal. No action was taken by the High Authority during the two months following receipt of this request; consequently, under the provisions of Article 35 ECSC, they were deemed to have passed a decision refusing to comply with it.[87] The plaintiffs, therefore, brought proceedings in the Court to have this implied decision set aside.

Since the plaintiffs did not allege a misuse of power, they had to prove, in order to establish the admissibility of the proceedings, that the decision was individual and that it concerned them.

In order to discover whether these conditions were met, it is necessary to see what the decision would have been if it had been express. It would have stated that the monopoly enjoyed by the *Office Commercial* and the levy payable to the *Caisse* were not contrary to Community law. Such a decision would obviously have affected the legal position of these two bodies by confirming their powers. From their point of view it would have been an individual act. But the decision would also have affected the legal position of coal importers and coal users: it would have confirmed that they were not legally entitled to import coal and that they were obliged to pay the levy. Since they would have been affected as members of an open category, the decision would, from their point of view, have been normative (general).

---

[86] Cases 7, 9/54, [1956] ECR 175.
[87] See Chapter 13.

The Advocate General (Mr Roemer) stated that, in his opinion, the implied decision was individual but that, in so far as it concerned the legality of the *Office Commercial's* import monopoly, the applicants lacked *locus standi* because their interest in the matter was not peculiar to them: it was shared with all other users of coal and coal dealers. What the Advocate General was saying – if one might use the terminology of the EEC Treaty – was that the applicants were not individually concerned.[88]

The Advocate General's opinion, which seems hard to sustain on the basis of the English text of Article 33, was probably inspired by the German text. There is, unfortunately, a discrepancy between the French, Italian and, subsequently, the English texts, on the one hand, and the German and Dutch, on the other. The former all speak of individual decisions or recommendations concerning the applicant; the latter, however, refer to decisions or recommendations concerning the applicant individually – a more restrictive formulation.[89] This divergence would be troublesome were it not for the fact that under the ECSC Treaty the French text alone is authentic.

The Court rejected the Advocate General's opinion. They held that the applicants had *locus standi*. It is sufficient, they said, if the decision possesses the characteristics of an individual decision and it is 'not necessary for the decision to manifest this character in relation to the applicant'.[90] In other words, the Court confirmed that individual concern is not necessary under the ECSC Treaty.

The other case is *Fédération Charbonnière de Belgique* v. *High Authority*[91] (discussed in the previous chapter).[92] One of the issues in this case was the right of a non-privileged applicant to challenge a general decision (normative act). It was argued by the defendant that this could not be done unless the decision was general in form only, i.e., if it was an individual decision disguised as a general decision. This contention was rejected by the Court. It said: 'A disguised individual decision remains an individual decision, since its nature

---

[88] See [1956] ECR 175 at 215.

[89] The texts are: French: '. . . contre les décisions et recommandations individuelles les concernant . . .'; Italian: '. . . contro le decisioni e le raccomandazioni singole che le concernono . . .'; German: '. . . gegen die sie individuell betreffend Entscheidungen und Empfehlungen . . .'; Dutch: 'tegen de hen individueel betreffende beschikkingen en aanbevelingen . . .'.

[90] [1956] ECR at 192.

[91] Case 8/55, [1956] ECR 245.

[92] See p. 330, above.

depends on its scope rather than on its form. . . . The Court considers that Article 33 clearly states that associations and undertakings may contest not only individual decisions but also general decisions in the true sense of the term.'[93]

The interesting point about these two cases is that when the authors of the EEC Treaty drafted Article 173, they incorporated into the text of that Article precisely those ideas which had been rejected by the Court in its interpretation of the ECSC Treaty. It is not enough, under the EEC Treaty, that the act is individual, it must also be of individual concern to the applicant. (It might be mentioned that the idea of direct concern was also mooted by Advocate General Roemer in the *Groupement des Industries Sidérurgiques Luxembourgeoises* case, though he considered that this requirement was met on the facts of the case.[94]) Moreover, under Article 173 EEC only an act *in the form of* a regulation may be challenged by a non-privileged applicant: the unsuccessful contention of the High Authority in the *Fédération Charbonnière* case was adopted in the text of the EEC Treaty.

It is clear, therefore, that the authors of the EEC Treaty made a deliberate choice in favour of a more restrictive system. They apparently thought that Article 33 ECSC, as interpreted by the Court, was too liberal. The reasons for this are not altogether clear but they are probably related to the general weakening of the supranational elements in the EEC as compared with the ECSC. It is possible, moreover, that the authors of the EEC Treaty (representatives of the national governments) thought it unnecessary to provide for such extensive judicial control of the Commission (since its powers were less) and undesirable to have too much judicial control of the Council (since this represented the Member States). It is also possible that the Court interpreted the ECSC Treaty more liberally than had been intended by its authors, though this is doubtful.

FURTHER READING

G. Bebr, *Development of Judicial Control of the European Communities* (1981).

P. van Dijk, *Judicial Review of Governmental Action and the Requirement of an Interest to Sue* (1980), Chapter 7.

[93] [1956] ECR at 257–8.
[94] [1956] ECR at 214–15.

Schermers, paragraphs 264–286 and 388–423.

Dinnage, 'Locus Standi and Article 173 EEC', (1979) 4 E.L. Rev. 15.

Fromont, 'L'influence du droit français et du droit allemand sur les conditions de recevabilité du recours en annulation devant la Cour de Justice des Communautés européennes', (1966) 2 RTDE 47.

Greaves, 'Locus Standi under Article 173 EEC when Seeking Annulment of a Regulation'', (1986) 11 E.L. Rev. 119.

Harding, 'Decisions Addressed to Member States and Article 173 of the Treaty of Rome', (1976) 25 ICLQ 15.

Harding, 'The Private Interest in Challenging Community Action', (1980) 5 E.L. Rev. 354.

Kovar and Barav, 'Le recours individuel en annulation', (1976) 12 CDE 68.

Rasmussen, 'Why is Article 173 Interpreted against Private Plaintiffs?', (1980) 5 E.L. Rev. 112.

Stein and Vining, 'Citizen Access to Judicial Review of Administrative Action in a Transnational and Federal Context', (1976) 70 Americal Journal of International Law 219.

13

FAILURE TO ACT

A remedy for a wrongful failure to act is provided by Articles 175 EEC[1] and 35 ECSC. Article 175 EEC reads as follows:

> Should the Council or the Commission, in infringement of this Treaty, fail to act, the Member States and the other institutions of the Community may bring an action before the Court of Justice to have the infringement established.
>
> The action shall be admissible only if the institution concerned has first been called upon to act. If, within two months of being so called upon, the institution concerned has not defined its position the action may be brought within a further period of two months.
>
> Any natural or legal person may, under the conditions laid down in the preceding paragraphs, complain to the Court of Justice that an institution of the Community has failed to address to that person any act other than a recommendation or an opinion.

It will be noticed that this provision bears a fairly strong resemblance to Article 173 EEC. The first paragraph in both Articles is concerned with the rights of so-called 'privileged applicants'. The second paragraph of Article 175, which deals with procedure and time-limits, corresponds to the third paragraph of Article 173; the third paragraph of Article 175 deals with the rights of non-privileged applicants and this parallels the second paragraph of Article 173.

The most obvious difference between the two Articles is that proceedings cannot be brought under Article 175 unless the applicant has first addressed a request for action to the defendant. The defendant must be given two months to comply and the action may then be brought within the following two months. Another difference is that only one ground of review is laid down by Article 175, while under Article 173 there are four. (The grounds of review under both Articles are discussed in Chapter 15).

Article 35 ECSC reads as follows:

> Wherever the High Authority is required by this Treaty, or by rules laid down for the implementation thereof, to take a decision or make a recommendation and fails to fulfil this obligation, it shall be for States, the Council, undertakings

---

[1] Art. 148 Euratom is identical to Art. 175 EEC and everything in the text regarding the latter applies also to the former.

or associations, as the case may be, to raise the matter with the High Authority.

The same shall apply if the High Authority, where empowered by this Treaty, or by rules laid down for the implementation thereof, to take a decision or make a recommendation, abstains from doing so and such abstention constitutes a misuse of powers.

If at the end of two months the High Authority has not taken any decision or made any recommendation, proceedings may be instituted before the Court within one month against the implied decision of refusal which is to be inferred from the silence of the High Authority on the matter.

Although the arrangement of the paragraphs is somewhat different, this provision has very close links with Article 33 ECSC. In fact, Article 33 provides the basis for actions under Article 35: according to Article 35(3), the Commission is deemed to have passed an 'implied decision of refusal' if it has not taken action within one month of the request. The proceedings before the Court then take the form of an action to annul this implied decision and are, of course, governed by Article 33. This fiction of an implied decision is the most important difference between the ECSC and EEC provisions.

From a theoretical viewpoint, it is quite clear that proceedings to quash a legal act, and proceedings to require a public authority to take action, are two aspects of the same legal remedy. The similarities between the two sets of provisions in each of the Treaties indicate that the authors of the Treaties were well aware of this. It is no surprise, therefore, that the European Court has adopted this doctrine as a general principle. Thus in *Chevalley* v. *Commission*[2] it was not clear whether the application should have been under Article 175 or under Article 173. The action had originally been brought under Article 175 but, in the course of the hearing, the applicant had requested the Court to consider it as an application under either Article 175 or Article 173, depending on which the Court considered appropriate. In its judgment, however, the Court did not regard it as necessary to characterize the proceedings as being under either one or the other, since the two Articles 'merely prescribe one and the same method of recourse'.[3] Under the ECSC Treaty, of course, this identity is inherent in the very nature of Article 35.

[2] Case 15/70, [1970] ECR 975.
[3] Paragraph 6 of the judgment. For similar statements by the Advocates General, see: *Mackprang* v. *Commission*, Case 15/71, [1971] ECR 797 at 802 (*per* Advocate General Dutheillet de Lamothe); *Nordgetreide* v. *Commission*, Case 42/71, [1972] ECR 105 at 116 (*per* Advocate General Roemer); *Compagnie d'Approvisionnement* v. *Commission*, Cases 9, 11/71, [1972] ECR 391 at 414 (*per* Advocate General Dutheillet de Lamothe); and *Holtz & Willemsen* v. *Council*, Case 134/73, [1974] ECR 1 at 14 (*per* Advocate General Reischl).

The principle that the two Articles are concerned with essentially the same remedy, which for the sake of brevity will henceforth be referred to as the 'unity principle', is not of merely theoretical interest but has a very important practical consequence. It implies that the conditions and limitations applicable to the remedy should be the same under the two procedures, except to the extent that different rules are a necessary consequence of the inherent differences between an act and a failure to act, between commission and omission. Subject to this exception, one would expect the applicant to have the same rights in Article 175 proceedings as he has in Article 173 proceedings: any restriction or limitation which is not justifiable on this basis must, therefore, be regarded as a shortcoming in the legal system of the Community.

Before analysing the detailed rules to see whether any such shortcomings exist, it is, however, necessary to consider one further general matter: the concept of a 'negative decision'.

NEGATIVE DECISIONS

A 'negative decision' is a decision of a public authority in which it decides not to act in a particular way. A rejection of a request is the most common example. From a strictly theoretical viewpoint, a negative decision would be a reviewable act – an act having legal effects – only if it was binding on the authority, in the sense that it precluded the authority, at least for a period, from changing its mind and taking the action in question. In such a situation the authority will have lost the power to take the action in question. Where this is not the case, however, the decision will have no legal effects: in law the legal position of the authority and of the person making the request will be the same as before. Normally, of course, a negative decision is not binding on the authority making it.

It will, however, be remembered that the European Court has departed from strict theory by ruling that a statement by a Community institution as to how it intends to act in the future, even if it is not legally binding on the institution, is to be regarded as a reviewable act if it is definite and unequivocal.[4] As was explained above, this was necessitated by the absence in Community law of anything corresponding to the English action for a declaration. Were it not for

---

[4] See pp. 330–1, above.

Failure to Act 373

this doctrine, it would be impossible for the legality of a proposed course of action to be challenged until it was actually carried out.

Since a negative act is no more than a (negative) statement of future intention, it is not surprising that the European Court has adopted a general doctrine that a negative act which is sufficiently clear and precise constitutes a reviewable act, provided the act which the Community institution has refused to adopt would itself have been reviewable.[5] If, for example, the Commission informs a citizen that it will not address a decision (in the technical sense) to him, the citizen would be able to challenge the refusal in annulment proceedings, since the decision, if it had been taken, would have been reviewable.

A negative act is, moreover, classified for the purpose of *locus standi* in the same way as the positive act. Thus if a private individual requests the Commission to pass a regulation and the Commission refuses, the negative decision containing the refusal is regarded for review purposes as a general (normative) act, even though the refusal is addressed solely to the person concerned. He cannot, therefore, challenge it in review proceedings, since, as was pointed out in Chapter 12, non-privileged applicants have no *locus standi* under the EEC Treaty to challenge a general act.[6]

This attitude makes sense if one realizes that a challenge to a negative act is in reality an application for a remedy for a failure to act; consequently, it is really directed at the respondent's failure to adopt the requested act and it is therefore right that questions of *locus standi*, as well as questions of reviewability, should be determined with reference to that act. This may be clearly demonstrated by considering the effect of a judgment in favour of the applicant. A declaration by the Court that a negative act is invalid would be meaningless, were it not for the fact that the respondent must then adopt the act which it had previously refused to adopt. This follows from Article 176(1) EEC which states:

The institution whose act has been declared void or whose failure to act has been declared contrary to this Treaty shall be required to take the necessary measures to comply with the judgment of the Court of Justice.

[5] *De Gezamenlijke Steenkolenmijnen in Limburg* v. *High Authority*, Case 30/59, [1961] ECR 1 at 15; and *Lütticke* v. *Commission*, Case 48/65, [1966] ECR 19 at 31, *per* Advocate General Gand.

[6] *Nordgetreide* v. *Commission*, Case 42/71, [1972] ECR 105.

If the negative act has been quashed because the respondent had no right to refuse to take the action required, the 'necessary measures' would clearly be the adoption of the act in question.

An action to annul a negative decision is, therefore, a remedy for failure to act; nevertheless in form it is still an action to annul and it is governed by Article 173 EEC and not by Article 175. The latter Article comes into play only when the respondent omits even to give a definite refusal. To an English lawyer, it might seem strange that a remedy under Article 175 is barred by an outright refusal: in proceedings under English law for *mandamus* such a refusal would, if anything, strengthen the plaintiff's case. However, the approach adopted by Community law will have no serious consequences as long as the rights of the applicant are the same in either case. This is another reason why the principle of unity should be upheld.

In practice it may sometimes be uncertain whether a refusal is sufficiently clear and definite to constitute a reviewable act. This was the difficulty in the *Chevalley* case (mentioned above) and it was for this reason that the applicant brought his action in the alternative under either Article 175 or Article 173. There appears to be no objection to this, provided the applicant follows the preliminary procedure required by Article 175 (the request for action) and he complies with the time-limit applicable under each Article.

This problem cannot arise under the ECSC Treaty, since actions under Article 35 ECSC proceed on the basis of an implied decision of refusal. In other words *all* remedies under the ECSC Treaty for failure to act take the form of an annulment action directed against a negative decision: if that decision is express the proceedings will be brought under Article 33 alone; if it is implied, they will be brought under Article 33 in conjunction with Article 35. The only difficulty which may face the applicant is to decide which decision should form the object of his action in those cases where he has been given a reply but he is doubtful whether it is sufficiently clear and definite to constitute an express refusal. In this case, proceedings could be brought in the alternative against either the reply or the implied decision of refusal.

PARTIES TO THE PROCEEDINGS

Article 175 EEC makes provision for proceedings to be brought only against the Council and the Commission, but it is likely that the

European Court will 'extend' Article 175 to cover proceedings against the Parliament, as it has done in the case of Article 173.[7] The first paragraph of Article 175, which concerns privileged applicants, provides that the Member States and 'the other institutions of the Community' may bring proceedings. This latter phrase covers the Council, the Commission and the Parliament.[8] The Court is probably also covered, though it is not likely to commence proceedings.

The third paragraph of Article 175 grants a limited right of action to non-privileged applicants. 'Any natural or legal person' may bring proceedings on this basis, subject to the rules concerning *locus standi*, which will be discussed below.

Under the ECSC Treaty, the only party against which an action under Article 35 may be brought is the Commission. This, of course, is in line with annulment actions under Article 33. Article 38, however, grants a limited right to bring annulment actions against the Council and the Parliament; but there is no provision allowing proceedings for failure to act against these institutions.

Article 35(1) ECSC states that the Member States, the Council, undertakings or associations,[9] 'as the case may be', have the right to initiate the preliminary proceedings (request for action). Since Article 35 ECSC is based on the fiction of an implied decision, the proceedings before the Court will be governed by the same rules of *locus standi* as actions under Article 33 ECSC. Therefore, the Member States and the Council will have the status of privileged applicants; and undertakings and associations will have the status of non-privileged applicants.

REVIEWABLE OMISSIONS

What kinds of act may the Commission or Council be required to perform by means of proceedings under Article 175? In other words, what kind of omission is reviewable? This question is, of course, the negative equivalent of the question discussed in Chapter 11: what acts are reviewable? From the point of view of theory (unity principle) one would expect the answer to be that only an omission to

---

[7] See pp. 77–8, above.

[8] *European Parliament* v. *Council*, Case 13/83, [1985] ECR 1513.

[9] Art. 80 ECSC states that 'undertaking' means an undertaking engaged in production in the coal or steel industry; Art. 48 makes clear that an 'association' is an association of 'undertakings' as so defined.

adopt a reviewable act – an act having legal effects – would be reviewable under Article 175. In order to facilitate discussion, this view will henceforth be referred to as the 'narrow interpretation' while the view that other kinds of omissions are also reviewable will be called the 'wide interpretation'.

The narrow interpretation is clearly correct under the ECSC Treaty: Article 35 expressly refers to a failure to 'take a decision or make a recommendation' and decisions and recommendations are the only reviewable acts under Article 33. (It will be remembered that an ECSC decision is the equivalent of either a decision or regulation under the EEC Treaty and an ECSC recommendation is analogous to an EEC directive: it is legally binding and is quite different from an EEC recommendation.) The EEC Treaty, however, is less clear.

Article 175 EEC refers in its first paragraph simply to a failure 'to act'. This contrasts with Article 173(1) which applies only to 'acts . . . other than recommendations or opinions'. Does the fact that non-binding acts (recommendations and opinions) are not expressly excluded in Article 175(1) mean that a failure to adopt such an act may be challenged by proceedings under Article 175? It could, of course, be argued that 'act' in Article 175(1) is impliedly limited to a reviewable act; but this could be countered by reference to Article 175(3). This provision, which is concerned with proceedings by non-privileged applicants, refers to 'any act other than a recommendation or an opinion': if the word 'act' in Article 175(1) is impliedly limited to a reviewable act, it would be unnecessary expressly to exclude a recommendation or an opinion in Article 175(3). It seems, therefore, that an analysis of the text lends support to the wide interpretation and this is the view of many writers.[10]

The objection to such a conclusion is that it conflicts with the unity principle: if the action to annul and the action for a remedy for failure to act are, as the European Court has confirmed, merely different aspects of the same remedy, how can the subject-matter of the second be so much wider than that of the first? Such a result would completely negate the unity principle.

In an attempt to meet this objection, Professor H. G. Schermers has put forward an ingenious argument.[11] He accepts that legal remedies should be based on 'positive rules of law' and states that this

---

[10] Schermers, paragraphs 328 and 483; Toth, 1975/2 L I E I at p. 80. Further citations are given in Barav, op. cit., p. 59, note 1; Barav himself, however, rejects this view.

[11] Schermers, paragraph 328.

requirement is met in the case of an action to annul by the rule that the challenged act must be legally binding. In the case of an omission, however, he states that the requirement is satisfied if the *provision which requires the act to be taken* is legally binding. This, however, treats as equivalent two quite different things: the act or omission which is the subject-matter of the proceedings and the rule of law which has allegedly been violated by the defendant in adopting, or failing to adopt, the act in question. It is quite true that an action for failure to act will be unsuccessful unless the omission constituted a violation of Community law: the defendant cannot be required to act unless there is an obligation to act. Likewise, in an action for annulment, the act adopted by the defendant must be illegal: the defendant must have violated a binding rule of Community law if the Court is to annul it. But this is quite a different matter from the nature of the act or omission itself. A non-binding act will not be reviewable under Article 173 just because it violates a binding provision of Community law; likewise, a failure to adopt a non-binding act cannot, without violating the unity principle, be the subject-matter of an action under Article 175: if the same principles are to apply to proceedings under the two Articles, only an omission to adopt an act with legal effects can constitute a reviewable omission.

In addition to the argument based on principle, there is a powerful practical argument to support the narrow interpretation. Assume that failure to give an opinion, or to adopt some other non-reviewable act, could constitute the basis of proceedings under Article 175. Before the matter can be brought before the European Court, the defendant must be called upon to act. When this occurs, all the defendant has to do is to inform the applicant in clear and unequivocal terms that it will not comply with his request. This refusal would bar the action under Article 175 since the defendant would thereby have 'defined its position'. It would not, on the other hand, constitute a reviewable act in itself, since a negative act – a refusal – is reviewable only if the act which the defendant refuses to adopt would itself be reviewable.[12] Consequently, an express refusal would always constitute a bar to proceedings for a remedy for failure to adopt a non-reviewable act.

There is, moreover, reason to believe that the European Court itself supports the narrow interpretation. In the *Chevalley* case,[13] it said: 'The concept of a measure capable of giving rise to an action is

---

[12] *Lütticke* v. *Commission*, Case 48/65, [1966] ECR 19.
[13] Case 15/70, [1970] ECR 975 at 979.

378 The Foundations of European Community Law

identical in Articles 173 and 175, as both provisions merely prescribe one and the same method of recourse.' The statement that the concept of a reviewable act[14] is identical in the two provisions must, of course, be taken to mean that the one is the negative of the other, i.e., that a reviewable omission under Article 175 is the failure to adopt an act reviewable under Article 173. It has been objected, however, that as the *Chevalley* case concerned an action brought by a non-privileged applicant, the statement should be regarded as applicable only to such proceedings.[15] However, the statement was derived by the Court from the principle that Articles 173 and 175 both give expression to the same legal remedy – the unity principle – and it ought therefore to be equally applicable to all actions under Article 175.

Preliminary Acts

If the narrow interpretation is correct, a problem could arise with regard to what is sometimes called a 'preliminary act', in other words an act which is the first step in the adoption of some other act. This concept was discussed in Chapter 11 where it was suggested that the reviewability of such a preliminary act should depend on whether or not it has legal effects.[16] For example, if the law provides that the final act cannot be adopted until some other body has been consulted, it would be wrong to regard the opinion of this other body as a reviewable act, since it is not binding on the authority empowered to adopt the final act. If, on the other hand, the final act can be adopted only if the other body gives its consent, then the 'opinion' of that other body would have legal effects and ought to be regarded as reviewable. However, as was pointed out in Chapter 11,[17] the European Court has taken the view that, even in this case, such a preliminary act will not necessarily be a reviewable act. This does not normally have serious consequences, however, because the preliminary act may be reviewed in the context of proceedings to annul the final act.

Unfortunately, this will not always be possible in the case of a failure to act. If the preliminary act and the final act are both adopted by the same body, there will be no problem: the action for a remedy

[14] A 'measure capable of giving rise to an action', in the original French text 'acte pouvant donner lieu à recours', means a reviewable act.
[15] Toth, 1975/2 LIEI at pp. 79–80.
[16] Above, pp. 326–31.
[17] Ibid.

for failure to act can be brought against the body in question and, though the complaint will be that the defendant failed to adopt the final act, its failure to adopt the preliminary act can be considered as an incidental issue. Where, however, the preliminary act is the responsibility of a different body, proceedings cannot be brought against the body responsible for the final act, since it can raise the defence that it is not empowered to adopt the act in question until the preliminary act has been performed; since the latter is not its responsibility, it could not be held to blame for the failure to act.

This is more than a theoretical problem. Most of the legal acts which the Council is empowered to adopt may be enacted only on the basis of a proposal from the Commission. A Commission proposal for a regulation, decision or directive to be adopted by the Council is a preliminary act of the kind under consideration. If the Commission fails to make such a proposal, the Council is powerless to act. There ought, therefore, to be a remedy if the Commission, in violation of the Treaty, fails to make a proposal. If the wide interpretation is accepted, there will be no difficulty; but if the narrow interpretation is correct, it becomes necessary to consider whether such a proposal constitutes a reviewable act.

As was pointed out above, there are strong theoretical grounds for regarding a Commission proposal as a reviewable act: by making the proposal, the Commission confers a power on the Council to adopt the act in question. The cases in which the Court has held preliminary acts not to be reviewable all concerned acts of some internal body within a Community institution. It is suggested that where the preliminary act and the final act are adopted by different Community institutions, the Court should adopt the theoretically sounder view and rule that such preliminary acts are reviewable.[18] This would enable the Court to grant a remedy where the Commission wrongfully fails to make a proposal.

Failure to Repeal an Act

Assume that a Community institution adopts a legal act and, after the time-limit for challenging it in annulment proceedings has passed, the applicant requests the institution to repeal it on the ground that it violates Community law. If the Community institution does not comply with this request, may the applicant bring proceed-

[18] See Barav, op. cit., pp. 60–1.

ings for a remedy for failure to act? In support of such an application it could be argued that, since all Community institutions are obliged to respect the law, there is a legal obligation to repeal any act which is inconsistent with Community law, even if the time-limit for an annulment action has expired. Moreover, since the repealing act would clearly have legal effects, the controversy over the wide and the narrow interpretations would not affect the matter.

The European Court has, however, ruled that this cannot be done. The leading case under the EEC Treaty is *Eridania* v. *Commission*,[19] in which an Italian sugar-refining concern brought proceedings to challenge three Commission decisions granting aid to its competitors. The applicant claimed that these decisions were illegal and requested the Commission to revoke them. When this request was not met, it brought two actions: first, proceedings under Article 173 to annul the decisions (Case 10/68); secondly, proceedings under Article 175 for a remedy for the Commission's failure to revoke the decisions (Case 18/68). These two actions were joined and the Court decided them both in a single judgment. Case 10/68 was declared inadmissible because the applicant lacked *locus standi*: the decisions were not addressed to the applicant and the applicant was not, in the opinion of the Court, directly and individually concerned by them. Case 18/68 was also declared inadmissible. The reasoning of the Court was as follows:

This application concerns the annulment of the implied decision of rejection resulting from the silence maintained by the Commission in respect of the request addressed to it by the applicants seeking the annulment or revocation of the three disputed decisions for illegality or otherwise because they are inappropriate.

The action provided for in Article 175 is intended to establish an illegal omission as appears from that article, which refers to a failure to act 'in infringement of this Treaty' and from Article 176 which refers to a failure to act declared to be 'contrary to this Treaty'.

Without stating under which provision of Community law the Commission was required to annul or to revoke the said decisions, the applicants have confined themselves to alleging that those decisions were adopted in infringement of the Treaty and that this fact alone would thus suffice to make the Commission's failure to act subject to the provisions of Article 175.

The Treaty provides, however, particularly in Article 173, other methods of recourse by which an allegedly illegal Community measure may be disputed and if necessary annulled on the application of a duly qualified party.

To admit, as the applicants wish to do, that the parties concerned could ask

---

[19] Cases 10, 18/68, [1969] ECR 459 at 482–3.

the institution from which the measure came to revoke it and, in the event of the Commission's failing to act, refer such failure to the Court as an illegal omission to deal with the matter would amount to providing them with a method of recourse parallel to that of Article 173, which would not be subject to the conditions laid down by the Treaty.

This application does not therefore satisfy the requirements of Article 175 of the Treaty and must thus be held to be inadmissible.

Some authors[20] have suggested that this judgment lays down that there is no obligation on Community organs to repeal an invalid act. This, however, is not justified: all the Court decided was that it had no jurisdiction to consider the question in proceedings brought under Article 175. The ruling was procedural, not substantive. This is also clear from the ruling in an earlier case under the ECSC Treaty, *Meroni* v. *High Authority*[21] (fifth *Meroni* case), in which the Court stated that 'an applicant cannot be permitted, by using the procedural artifice of an action for failure to act, to ask for the annulment of decisions which might have been declared void if proceedings had been instituted within the time-limit laid down in the third paragraph of Article 33'.

The Court's objection to the use, for this purpose, of proceedings for a remedy for failure to act is that it would allow a decision to be challenged after the expiry of the time-limit for annulment actions. This is what the Court meant in the *Eridania* case when it said that, if this procedure were allowed, applicants would be provided with a method of recourse 'which would not be subject to the conditions laid down by the Treaty'. This cannot refer to the *locus standi* provisions, since these are the same in actions for a remedy for failure to act as in annulment actions (see below).

It is interesting to note in this connection that the *Eridania* case (Case 18/68) could in fact have been decided on the ground of *locus standi*. This was the ground on which the annulment action (Case 10/68) was decided; but the same reasoning could have been applied to the action for a remedy for failure to act. The third paragraph of Article 175 EEC allows a non-privileged applicant to bring proceedings only where the respondent has failed to address an act *to him*. The applicant's request in the *Eridania* case was for the revocation of the three decisions and this could have been done only by passing three further decisions revoking the earlier ones. These latter decisions would have been addressed to the same persons as the earlier ones,

---

[20] See Schermers, paragraph 457.
[21] 21–26/61, [1962] ECR 73 at 78.

382 The Foundations of European Community Law

namely the recipients of the aid (the rival firms) and the Italian Government. Eridania was not, therefore, asking the Commission to address an act to it; moreover, since the original decisions were not – in the Court's view – of direct and individual concern to Eridania, the repealing decisions would also not have been of direct and individual concern to it. Consequently, it had no greater *locus standi* in the Article 175 proceedings than it had in the Article 173 proceedings.

It should also be pointed out that the rationale given by the Court is not entirely sound. The purpose of the short time-limit in annul-ment actions is the protection of persons who have relied on the act in question – the principle of legal certainty – and it is to uphold this principle that the Court does not allow acts to be challenged by means of proceedings for a remedy for failure to act. However, where the act is repealed, the interests of these persons could, in some cases at least, be protected by means of transitional provisions in the repealing measure. Moreover, it should be remembered that the repeal of an act need not be retroactive, while the annulment of an act normally has the effect of rendering it void *ab initio*. Consequently, repeal does not pose the same threat to legal certainty as annulment.

Whatever view one takes of this, there is one special case in which it is possible that the Court *will* allow the action. This is where the act in question is originally quite valid, but subsequently becomes incom-patible with Community law as a result of a later development. If this development takes place more than two months after the publication, or notification, of the act, it will not be possible to bring proceedings under Article 173. In such a case an action under Article 175 will be the only possibility and it would be a particularly appropriate remedy since an act which was validly passed, but which sub-sequently became illegal, ought more properly to be repealed than annulled. A *dictum* by Advocate General Roemer in the *Eridania* case suggests that an exception might exist in such a case.[22]

THE REQUEST FOR ACTION

The most important procedural difference between actions for a remedy for failure to act and annulment actions is that in the former case there is a special preliminary procedure which must be gone through before the application may be made to the European Court.

[22] [1969] ECR at 494.

This procedure, which applies under the ECSC Treaty as well as under the EEC Treaty, consists of a formal request to the defendant to take action. The request must state clearly what action is required.[23] This is important since, when the case goes before the Court, the applicant can complain only that the defendant failed to take the action previously requested.

It must also be made clear that the request is being made in terms of Article 175 EEC, or Article 35 ECSC, and that the applicant considers the defendant legally obliged to take the action required.[24] For this reason, 'request' is probably too mild a term to use: 'demand' might be more appropriate. It would be desirable, therefore, for the applicant to refer expressly to the Treaty or to state that legal proceedings will be taken if the required action is not forthcoming.

After the request for action has been made, the defendant institution has a period of two months to comply. Only if this period expires without action by the defendant may the application be made to the Court. There is, however, a time-limit for this application: under Article 175 EEC it must be brought within two months; under Article 35 ECSC the period is only one month. These time-limits (which run from the end of the initial two-month period) are very short and the action will be declared inadmissible if it is brought either too early or too late. This could cause difficulties for the applicant if he is uncertain whether a particular communication constitutes a formal request for action or not: if he goes to Court and it transpires that it does not, his application will be declared inadmissible and he will have to pay costs; but if he fails to institute proceedings within the time limit and it is subsequently established that the communication did constitute a request for action, he will have lost the right to bring proceedings. (It is not clear whether he could start the procedure all over again with a new request for exactly the same action; the Court might hold his right of action had been time-barred.)

What is the purpose of this special procedure? In answering this question it must be remembered that an important difference between an act and an omission is that while one can say exactly what the contents of an act are and when it came into existence, this is not always so easy in the case of an omission. The function of the special procedure is to make good this deficiency: the omission is deemed to have taken place at the end of the first two-month period and its

---

[23] *Nuovo Campsider* v. *Commission*, Case 25/85, 6 May 1986 (not yet reported).
[24] Ibid.

contents are defined by the terms of the request. The purpose of the
procedure is, therefore, formally to put the respondent in default.[25] It
is interesting to note that there is a similar preliminary procedure
where the Commission brings proceedings against a Member State
for a failure to comply with an obligation under Community law: see
Chapter 10, above.

Time-Limit for Making Request

It will be noticed that the Treaties lay down no time-limit within
which the request for action must be made. This is quite logical if one
accepts that the failure to act is established only when the preliminary procedure has been completed. In spite of this, however, the
European Court has stated, in *Netherlands* v. *Commission*,[26] that the
preliminary procedure must be initiated within a 'reasonable time'.
The case arose in the following circumstances. The French Government had drawn up a plan for restructuring the iron and steel
industry, which entailed low-interest Government loans to iron and
steel producers. The French Government informed the Commission
of this in September 1966 and the Commission had to consider
whether the plan contravened the ECSC Treaty, especially Article
4(c), which prohibits state subsidies and aids. The Commission
reached a provisional conclusion that the plan was not contrary to the
Treaty and informed the other Member States of this in June 1967.
The Netherlands Government immediately expressed its reservations and in April 1968 it requested the Commission to define its
position further. After further consideration, the Commission
reached a final conclusion that the plan did not violate Community
law and it informed the Netherlands Government of this on 9
December 1968. A year and a half later, on 24 June 1970, the
Netherlands Government made a formal request in terms of Article
35 ECSC that the Commission take a decision under Article 88
ECSC to the effect that the French plan involved violations of
Community law; the Commission did not comply and the Netherlands then brought the action.[27]

[25] There are, of course, some cases in which this is not necessary, for example where the
law lays down both the content of the action and the date by which it must be performed. In
these cases the only function of the procedure will be to give the respondent the opportunity
to comply with the request before legal proceedings are brought.

[26] Case 59/70, [1971] ECR 639.

[27] It might be thought that the Commission decision that the plan did not contravene
Community law (communicated to the Dutch Government on 9 December 1968) consti-

The Court, however, held that the application was inadmissible because the period of 18 months between the communication of 9 December 1968 and the request for action of 24 June 1970 was too great.[28] The Court began its reasoning by mentioning that Article 35 ECSC lays down no time limit for bringing the request for action. It then continued:[29]

It follows, however, from the common purpose of Articles 33 and 35 that the requirements of legal certainty and of the continuity of Community action underlying the time-limits laid down for bringing proceedings under Article 33 must also be taken into account – having regard to the special difficulties which the silence of the competent authorities may involve for the interested parties – in the exercise of the rights conferred by Article 35.

These requirements may not lead to such contradictory consequences as the duty to act within a short period in the first case and the absence of any limitation in time in the second.

This view finds support in the system of time-limits in Article 35, which allows the Commission two months in which to define its position, and the interested party one month in which to institute proceedings before the Court.

Thus it is implicit in the system of Articles 33 and 35 that the exercise of the right to raise the matter with the Commission may not be delayed indefinitely.

If the interested parties are thus bound to observe a reasonable time-limit where the Commission remains silent, this is so *a fortiori* once it is clear that the Commission has decided to take no action.

It will be noticed that the Court purports to base its argument on the unity principle: if there is a time-limit under Article 33, there should also be such a limit under Article 35. However, there *is* a time-limit under Article 35: this is the period of one month within which the action must be brought. This runs, of course, from the end of the two month period, that is from the date on which the defendant is

tuted a reviewable act since it was a refusal to take a decision under Art. 88. However, in an earlier case, *De Gezamenlijke Steenkolenmijnen in Limburg* v. *High Authority*, Case 17/57, [1959] ECR 1, the European Court had ruled that a determination of this kind does not constitute a reviewable act because Art. 88 gives the power only to take a decision that a violation *has* occurred: there is no power to take a decision that a Member State has *not* violated the Treaty. This judgment, which is hardly in conformity with the general doctrine of the Court on negative acts, seems to have established a special rule that a decision by the Commission not to act under Art. 88 cannot be challenged in annulment proceedings. Consequently, the communication of 9 December 1968 could not impair the right of the Dutch Government to bring the proceedings for failure to act.

[28] It is interesting to compare this with the decision in *Commission* v. *France* (Euratom), Case 7/71, [1971] ECR 1003, decided a few months later, in which the Court refused to lay down a time limit where a *Member State* fails to comply with the Treaty: see paragraph 5 of the judgment and *per* Advocate General Roemer at p. 1026.

[29] [1971] ECR at 653.

formally deemed to be in default. The proposition that there must be a time-limit for making the *request* can be deduced from the unity principle only if one accepts that the cause of action arises at some earlier date; but this cuts away the justification for the preliminary procedure.

The proposition accepted by the Court was considered by Advocate General Roemer. He rejected it on the ground that the adoption of a period of limitation of no specific length – that the request must be made within a *reasonable* time – was contrary to the principle of legal certainty.[30] How can the parties know where they stand if they cannot be sure how long the period of limitation is?

The principle of legal certainty was, of course, one of the principles invoked by the Court in support of its ruling. This was because the justification usually given for the short time-limit under Article 33 is that, by annulling an apparently valid legal act, the Court could upset the legitimate expectations of persons who relied on it; therefore, in order to limit as much as possible the uncertainty caused by annulment actions, the period within which they may be brought should be as short as possible. However, as was pointed out above, the analogy between Articles 33 and 35 does not hold good at this point, since proceedings under Article 35 do not result in any *retrospective* change in the legal rights of the persons concerned: the annulment of a legal act invalidates it from the moment when it was adopted; but an order under Article 35 merely requires the respondent to adopt an act in the future. Such an act need not be retrospective.

It is true that in the special case of a decision under Article 88 ECSC legal expectations could be upset if the Commission is required to take action. Such a decision could oblige a Member State to modify or abandon a scheme which might have been in operation for some time. There is no time-limit within which the Commission must commence proceedings under Article 88; but if the Commission has informed the Member State that it considers its action to involve no violation of Community law, it would not be unreasonable for the persons concerned to believe that the matter has finally been settled.[31] However, even if the imposition of a time-limit for an action

---

[30] Ibid. at p. 658.

[31] In *Netherlands* v. *Commission* this point was considered by Advocate General Roemer but rejected on the ground that the French Government had put their plan into operation before the Commission decision had been made. It could not, therefore, be said that they had relied on the decision: see ibid. at pp. 658–9.

for a remedy for failure to act is justified in the case of proceedings under Article 88, there is no reason why it should apply to all proceedings under Article 35 ECSC or Article 175 EEC. Yet the extract from the judgment quoted above clearly shows that it was the Court's intention to lay down a general rule.

A final difficulty raised by the judgment, in so far as it applies outside the context of Article 88, concerns the moment when the 'reasonable period' begins to run. In *Netherlands* v. *Commission* it began when the Dutch Government was informed that the Commission had reached a final decision not to take action. Paragraph 19 of the judgment (quoted above) makes clear, however, that the time-limit can apply even where no such decision is taken. But the Court gave no indication when it would begin to run in such a case. Uncertainty on this point, coupled with uncertainty as to the length of the 'reasonable period', could create intolerable difficulties for an applicant. It could, moreover, have the undesirable consequence that applicants would feel obliged to commence the procedure at the earliest possible moment, thus forcing the defendant institution to take a decision before they were ready to do so. For these reasons, it is unfortunate that the Court did not restrict its ruling to cases involving Article 88 ECSC.[32]

DEFINITION OF POSITION

According to Article 175 EEC, the action for a remedy for failure to act is admissible only if the defendant institution has not 'defined its position' within the two months following the request for action. By this is meant a clear and definite statement by the defendant either accepting or rejecting the request (or accepting it in part or to a limited extent.)[33] Some writers[34] see in this provision a danger that, by means of a carefully worded reply, the defendant could block a right of action that would have existed if the defendant had merely remained silent.

If this were true it would be a most serious matter. But is it true? It will be remembered that under the doctrine of the negative act

[32] The problem cannot arise in the case of Art. 169 EEC because proceedings under Art. 175 cannot be used with regard to Art. 169: see p. 302, above.

[33] See *European Parliament* v. *Council*, Case 13/83, [1985] ECR 1513 (paragraph 25 of the judgment).

[34] Toth, 1975/2 LIEI at pp. 82–3; see also Barav, op. cit., p. 61, note 5. For a view close to that adopted in the text, see Schermers, paragraph 456.

(discussed above) a refusal of a request is a reviewable act provided the act which the defendant was asked to adopt would itself have been reviewable. The only proviso is that the statement of refusal must be clear and definite; but there is no reason to doubt that a statement which is not sufficiently clear and definite to constitute a negative act would not constitute a definition of position either. It was suggested above that proceedings under Article 175 can be brought only with regard to a failure to adopt a reviewable act: this is the only kind of omission that is reviewable. If this is correct it means that, even if the defendant remains silent, the application will be admissible only if the action requested is the adoption of a reviewable act and the applicant has the appropriate *locus standi* (*locus standi* is discussed below). If there is an express refusal, the refusal will be a reviewable act under Article 173, provided these self-same conditions are met. It follows, therefore, that there should be no gap: if the omission is reviewable under Article 175, the definition of position will be reviewable under Article 173.

There are two decisions of the European Court which are said to contradict this. The first, *Lütticke* v. *Commission*,[35] concerned an attempt by a private firm to induce the Commission to take proceedings against Germany under Article 169 EEC for an alleged violation of the Treaty. As was seen in Chapter 10, these proceedings begin with a preliminary procedure analogous to the request for action under Article 175: the Commission delivers a reasoned opinion, after first giving the Member State the opportunity to submit its observations; if the Member State fails to accept the opinion, the Commission may bring an action before the Court. This procedure is very different from that under Article 88 ECSC: there, the Commission takes a *decision*, instead of giving an opinion, and this decision is binding on the Member State unless it is set aside by the Court in proceedings brought by the Member State. Under the EEC Treaty, the opinion is not binding: it is merely a prelude to proceedings by the Commission.

In the *Lütticke* case the applicant requested the Commission to commence the procedure under Article 169; but the Commission took the view that Germany had not infringed the Treaty and therefore refused to take action. The applicant then brought proceedings before the Court under Article 173 to quash the negative decision of refusal; alternatively it asked for a remedy under Article 175.

The Court held the application inadmissible. In so far as it was

[35] Case 48/65, [1966] ECR 19.

based on Article 173, it was inadmissible because the refusal to act was not a reviewable act. The reason for this was that no measure taken by the Commission during the preliminary procedure under Article 169 – neither the request to the Member State to submit its observations, nor the reasoned opinion – has any binding force. In other words, the acts which the applicant requested the Commission to perform were not reviewable acts; therefore, the Commission's refusal to perform them could not be a reviewable act. The application was also inadmissible in so far as it was based on Article 175, because the refusal constituted a definition of position.

The important point to note about this case is that the result would have been exactly the same if the Commission had remained silent instead of giving an express refusal. The basic reason why the application was inadmissible was that there was no reviewable omission. The argument put forward above – that only the failure to adopt a legal act constitutes a reviewable omission – is not accepted by some writers; but there can be no dispute that it is correct in at least the case of an application by a non-privileged applicant. Under Article 175(3), a private applicant, as was *Lütticke*, may bring proceedings only if 'an institution of the Community has failed to address to that person any act other than a recommendation or an opinion'. Since *Lütticke* had not asked the Commission to address such an act to him, his application would have been inadmissible irrespective of whether the Commission had defined its position or not. This case does not, therefore, reveal any gap in the Treaty or in the legal protection available to individuals.

The other case is *Nordgetreide* v. *Commission*.[36] Here the applicant had requested the Commission to amend a regulation dealing with monetary compensatory amounts. The Commission refused to make the amendment and the applicant brought proceedings under Article 173 to quash the refusal; alternatively, he asked for a remedy under Article 175. The Court stated that, since the measure to be amended was a regulation, the amending measure would also be a normative act. It will be remembered from the discussion of *locus standi* in Chapter 12 that private persons, such as *Nordgetreide*, have no capacity to challenge a normative act; moreover, as the Court pointed out, the amending measure would not have affected the applicant directly and individually. Since he would have had no *locus standi* to challenge the act requested, he likewise had no *locus standi* to challenge the

---

[36] Case 42/71, [1972] ECR 105.

negative decision refusing to adopt it. The application was, therefore, declared inadmissible in so far as it was based on Article 173; in so far as it was based on Article 175, it was inadmissible because the Commission's refusal constituted a definition of position.

Here too, however, the position would have been exactly the same if the Commission had remained silent. *Nordgetreide* would still have lacked *locus standi* since he had not asked the Commission to address an act *to him*: the amendment to the regulation would not have been such an act. This case, too, reveals no gap in the law.[37]

It should be mentioned that the position is even clearer under Article 35 ECSC. There it is laid down that the only reviewable omission is a failure to adopt a decision or recommendation (equivalent to a directive under the EEC Treaty). Article 35(3) does not use the phrase 'defined its position' but says instead that proceedings may be brought if the Commission has not taken any decision or made any recommendation within the two month period. It follows that only if it constitutes a decision or recommendation will an express refusal block an action for a remedy for failure to act.

LOCUS STANDI

It will be remembered from Chapter 12 that, in proceedings under Article 173 EEC, privileged applicants always have *locus standi*; non-privileged applicants, on the other hand, may challenge only a decision addressed to them or a decision (which may be in the form of a regulation) which is of direct and individual concern to them. The position under Article 175 EEC is similar: privileged applicants always have *locus standi*; but a non-privileged applicant has *locus standi* only where the defendant institution has 'failed to address' to him 'any act other than a recommendation or an opinion'.

In interpreting this provision, the first point to note is that the word 'act' can mean only a reviewable act: this follows from the decision in the *Chevalley* case.[38] Secondly, it might be thought that a non-privileged applicant could challenge a regulation or directive as well as a decision; but, since a regulation or directive could never be

---

[37] A case which does cause concern is *GEMA* v. *Commission*, Case 125/78, [1979] ECR 3173. The reasons in this case are unsatisfactory but the result could be justified on the ground that the Commission was not under an obligation to take the decision requested by the applicant.

[38] See above, p. 371.

addressed to him – a regulation is not addressed to anyone, since it has general application, and a directive is addressed only to a Member State – it follows that he can never have *locus standi* to challenge an omission to adopt such acts.[39]

Under Article 173, however, what is important is not the *form* of the act, but its *essential nature*. Therefore, it should not matter that the act is in the form of a regulation, provided that in substance it is an individual act (decision). One can conclude, therefore, that a private person has *locus standi* to challenge such an act, so long as it is 'addressed' to him.

What is meant by 'addressed'? Must the act be formally addressed to him or is it sufficient if he is directly and individually concerned by it? It will be remembered from the discussion in Chapter 12 that this is sufficient under Article 173, and it was said that in such a case the person concerned was a '*de facto*' addressee. If one accepts the unity principle, the same rule should apply under Article 175 and this would seem to follow from the *Chevalley* case.[40] Moreover, although the Danish, French, Irish and German texts of Article 175 are the same as the English, the Dutch and Italian texts suggest that this wider interpretation is legitimate: these texts state that a non-privileged applicant may bring proceedings where the defendant institution has failed to adopt an act other than a recommendation or opinion 'with respect to him'.[41]

This wider view has been strongly supported by Advocate General Dutheillet de Lamothe in *Mackprang* v. *Commission*.[42] In that case the Commission had argued in favour of the narrow interpretation, i.e. that the act requested must be one which would be *formally addressed* to the applicant. Advocate General de Lamothe replied to this contention as follows:

The Commission's argument on this point comes up against a very strong objection. If the concept of a measure against which individuals could bring proceedings were different in scope with regard to the application of Article 173 from that with regard to the application of Article 175 the result would be that, in certain cases, the existence or absence of a judicial remedy would depend on the actions of the Community authorities to which the request was submitted.

[39] As regards regulations, see *per* Advocate General Roemer in *Nordgetreide* v. *Commission*, Case 42/71, [1972] ECR 105 at 116.
[40] See above, pp. 371–2.
[41] Schermers, paragraph 446.
[42] Case 15/71, [1971] ECR 797 at 807–8. But see *per* Advocate General Slynn in *Lord Bethell* v. *Commission*, Case 246/81, [1982] ECR 2277 at 2295–2296 (and the statements by other advocates general there cited).

If those authorities replied to the request either by accepting it or by rejecting it, the author of the request would be entitled to proceed under Article 173, even if he is not the addressee of the measure adopted or requested, provided that this measure is of direct and individual concern to him.

On the other hand, if the Community authorities did not reply to the person concerned he would, according to the Commission's argument, be deprived of any method of recourse if he is not the addressee of the measure requested, *even if the latter is of direct and individual concern to him.*

It is obviously difficult to justify making the existence or absence of a judicial remedy depend on the action or inaction of the administrative body to which a request is submitted.

In view of these arguments, it is suggested that the applicant should be regarded as the addressee either if the act would have been formally addressed to him or if he would have been the '*de facto*' addressee, i.e. if it would have concerned him directly and individually.[43] The position would then be the same as under Article 173.

There can be no doubt that this is the position under Article 35 ECSC, since this Article is based on the concept of an implied negative decision. In theory, all proceedings under Article 35 are actions to quash a decision of refusal; consequently the *locus standi* provisions of Article 33 are always applicable.

FORM OF JUDGMENT

Under Article 173 the consequence of a successful action is that the provision in question is declared void by the Court. In proceedings under Article 175, however, the Court has no power itself to promulgate the act which the defendant wrongfully failed to pass: all it can do is to declare that the failure to act was contrary to the Treaty. However, Article 176 EEC provides that the defendant institution 'shall be required to take the necessary measures to comply with the judgment of the Court of Justice'. This obliges the defendant to take action; but it still retains such measure of discretion as to the form and content of the act as is granted to it under the provision requiring the act to be performed. The position is the same under Article 34 ECSC.

---

[43] It is significant that in *Lord Bethell* v. *Commission*, Case 246/81, [1982] ECR 2277, the Court four times used phraseology suggesting acceptance of this wider view: it referred to the adoption of an act 'in relation to' the applicant (paragraph 13 of the judgment), 'in respect of' him (paragraphs 15 and 16) and 'with regard to' him (paragraph 16).

FURTHER READING

Schermers, paragraphs 431–58.
Barav, 'Considérations sur la spécificité du recours en carence en droit communautaire', [1975] RTDE 53.
Toth, 'The Law as it Stands on the Appeal for Failure to Act', 1975/2 LIEI 65.

14

INDIRECT CHALLENGE

An indirect challenge to the validity of an act is a challenge made in the course of proceedings not instituted for that purpose. The object of the proceedings must, therefore, be something other than the annulment of the act and the court must have jurisdiction on some ground independent of the indirect challenge. The purpose of an indirect challenge is to require the court to decide the case on the basis that the act in question is invalid; consequently the challenge may be made only if the act is *relevant* to the proceedings.[1] It follows as a matter of theory, therefore, that an act is susceptible to indirect challenge whenever it is relevant to the proceedings, but is not itself the subject-matter of the proceedings.

Another name for an indirect challenge, often used by writers on Community law, is 'plea of illegality'. This indicates that a party to proceedings has contended that an act is illegal and therefore invalid.[2] It is a translation of the French term, *exception d'illégalité* (sometimes mistranslated as 'exception of illegality'). It does not, however, convey the idea quite so well as 'indirect challenge', which expresses both the fact that the validity of the act is under attack and that the challenge is incidental to the primary object of the proceedings.

Since Community law is applied at the national level as well as at the Community level, an indirect challenge to a Community act may be brought in a national court as well as in the European Court. When this occurs, the question of the validity of the act is referred to the European Court under Article 177(1)(*b*) EEC, Article 150(1)(*b*) Euratom or Article 41 ECSC. Once the European Court has made a ruling, the case goes back to the national court, which will give judgment on the basis of the decision of the European Court.

Some writers take the view that the issues involved where the European Court makes a decision under this procedure are fundamentally different from those where the indirect challenge is made

---

[1] See *Italy* v. *Commission*, Case 32/65, [1966] ECR 389.

[2] Most writers, however, use this term only where the challenge is made in proceedings brought in the European Court and not where it is made in a national court.

in proceedings brought initially in the European Court.[3] This view derives some justification from the fact that different Treaty provisions are applicable and also from the fact that the relationship between Community law and national law is involved. However, at a more fundamental level the issues are identical, since the legal nature of an indirect challenge is the same irrespective of the court in which it is brought. For this reason, the general principles of indirect challenge will be discussed in this chapter in the context of both kinds of procedure.

The theoretical possibility of an indirect challenge (which may, of course, be brought by either applicant or defendant) could arise in almost any proceedings in the European Court. Thus, in an annulment action under Article 173 EEC, the validity of the act subject to direct challenge could depend on the validity of another act and an indirect challenge could be made against this. For example, the former act might have been adopted on the basis of powers delegated by the latter. Other questions which could in theory depend on the validity of an act which is not itself the subject-matter of the proceedings are: in an action under Article 175 EEC for a remedy for failure to act, the obligation to act; in actions arising out of a contract (Article 181 EEC), the validity of the contract; in actions in tort (Articles 178 and 215(2) EEC), the lawfulness of the allegedly wrongful act; in enforcement actions against a Member State under Article 169 EEC, the existence of the obligation which the Member State is alleged not to have fulfilled; and in appeals against penalties under Article 172 EEC, the validity of the measure that the appellant is alleged to have violated. In a national court the question could arise whenever Community law was relevant to the proceedings, for example when a party claims a right based on a directly effective Community measure or when a national measure is enacted in implementation of a Community measure.

Theoretically, the potential scope for indirect challenge is wide. The question to be considered in this chapter is whether it may be invoked whenever appropriate, or whether there are restrictions on its use. In particular, there is the question whether it should be regarded as available in all cases where it is not excluded by express

---

[3] See Bebr, 'Examen en validité au titre de l'article 177 du traité CEE et cohésion juridique de la Communauté', [1975] CDE 379 at 417–20. Many writers, however, accept the basic identity between the two cases: see Arendt, 'La procédure selon l'article 177 du traité instituant la Communauté Economique Européenne', (1965) 13 SEW 383 at 409; Mertens de Wilmars, 'La procédure suivant l'article 177 CEE', (1965) 13 SEW 437 at 444; for further references, see Bebr, op. cit., p. 417, note 110.

enactment (as is the case in English law) or whether it may be invoked only where there is express authorization in the Treaties.

TREATY PROVISIONS

EEC

The EEC Treaty contains two provisions dealing with indirect challenge.[4] The first is Article 184, which reads:

Notwithstanding the expiry of the period laid down in the third paragraph of Article 173, any party may, in proceedings in which a regulation of the Council or of the Commission is in issue, plead the grounds specified in the first paragraph of Article 173, in order to invoke before the Court of Justice the inapplicability of that regulation.

This is a classic description of an indirect challenge. The grounds of invalidity are, as in English law, exactly the same as in the case of a direct challenge. If successful, the effect of the challenge is that the act is not applied in the case in question.

Although Article 184 is expressed in general terms, it nevertheless contains two limitations: first – and most important – it applies only to regulations; secondly, it applies only where the challenge is made in the course of proceedings in the European Court (this is not clear from the wording of Article 184 but was laid down by the European Court in *Wöhrmann* v. *Commission*[5]). The first of these restrictions raises fundamental issues which will be discussed below; the second, however, is easily explained by virtue of Article 177.

Article 177(1)(*b*) EEC is the second Treaty provision dealing with indirect challenge. It makes provision for national courts to refer to the European Court questions concerning 'the validity . . . of acts of the institutions of the Community'. Since the national courts have no power to hear a direct challenge to the validity of Community acts, this must refer to an indirect challenge; it therefore implicitly accepts that an indirect challenge may be made before a national court. It should be noted that this provision does not lay down any limitations as to the kind of act that may be challenged, provided it is a Community act.[6]

---

[4] Arts 156 and 150 Euratom are identical to Arts 184 and 177 EEC; everything said in the text with regard to the EEC applies equally to Euratom.

[5] Cases 31, 33/62, [1962] ECR 501.

[6] See pp. 250–1, above.

ECSC

In the ECSC Treaty the question of an indirect challenge in the national courts is dealt with in Article 41. This reads:

The Court shall have sole jurisdiction to give preliminary rulings on the validity of acts of the High Authority and of the Council where such validity is in issue in proceedings brought before a national court or tribunal.

This is the equivalent of Article 177(1) (*b*) EEC.

There is no exact equivalent in the ECSC Treaty of Article 184 EEC. The only other provision in the ECSC Treaty is Article 36(3), which has a very limited scope. Article 36 ECSC is concerned with the imposition of penalties by the Commission on firms or individuals for breach of Community law, and Article 36(2) grants a right of appeal from such a penalty to the European Court. Article 36(3) then states:

In support of its appeal, a party may, under the same conditions as in the first paragraph of Article 33 of this Treaty, contest the legality of the decision or recommendation which that party is alleged not to have observed.

Thus if a party is fined for breach of Community law, he may attack the decision by alleging that the provision against which he offended is invalid. This is, of course, an indirect challenge.

Article 36(3) deals with an indirect challenge only in one kind of proceeding: an appeal against a penalty. However, in the case of *Meroni* v. *High Authority*[7] the European Court held that such a challenge can be made in other proceedings as well. Meroni was a steel-producing enterprise which was a user of scrap iron. On 24 October 1956 the High Authority (Commission) took a decision requiring Meroni to pay a sum of money by way of a levy. Meroni brought proceedings under Article 33 ECSC to quash this decision on the ground that the whole levy scheme, set up by a general decision (equivalent to an EEC regulation) adopted on 26 March 1955, was illegal. This plea involved an indirect challenge to the general decision in the course of an annulment action against an individual decision. Since the levy was in no sense a penalty, but was a form of tax, there could be no question of applying Article 36(3). The European Court held, however, that there was a general principle of Community law allowing an indirect challenge: Article 36

---

[7] Case 9/56, [1958] ECR 133 (discussed further at pp. 113–15, above); see also Case 10/56, [1958] ECR 157; and *Compagnie des Hauts Fourneaux de Chasse* v. *High Authority*, Case 15/57, [1958] ECR 211.

was merely an application of this principle to one particular case. It rejected the argument that the express recognition of the principle in that one case impliedly excluded its application in other cases. In reaching this conclusion, the Court drew support from the fact that general recognition had been given to the principle in Article 184 of the EEC Treaty.

While the decision in the *Meroni* case seems to extend the scope of Article 36(3) to proceedings other than appeals against penalties, the decision in a later case, *Dalmas* v. *High Authority*,[8] limits the kind of act against which the challenge may be made. Unlike the *Meroni* case, this *was* an appeal against a penalty and Article 36 was, therefore, directly relevant. In the course of the appeal against the decision imposing the penalty, Dalmas wished to make an indirect challenge to an *individual* decision addressed to it some time previously. The Court held, however, that a party cannot make an indirect challenge to an individual decision addressed to him, once the time-limit for a direct challenge (under Article 33 ECSC) has passed.

These cases establish that, as in English law, the right to make an indirect challenge is not dependent on an express Treaty provision: it is a general principle of law. However, unlike in English law, this general principle does not apply in all cases. The next question to consider is the scope of the principle and the restrictions to which it is subject.

WHAT ACTS MAY BE CHALLENGED?

Here the crucial distinction is between normative (general) acts and individual acts. This distinction was discussed in Chapter 12:[9] regulations under the EEC Treaty and general decisions under the ECSC Treaty are normative acts; EEC decisions and ECSC individual decisions are individual acts. However, it is not the form of the act which is decisive but its substance; therefore an act in the form of a regulation may turn out to be, in substance, a decision (individual act) and *vice versa*. This same distinction applies with regard to indirect challenge: in *Simmenthal* v. *Commission*[10] the European Court held that an act which was not in the form of a regulation, but was

---

[8] Case 21/64, [1965] ECR 175.
[9] See pp. 341–3, above.
[10] Case 92/78, [1979] ECR 777 (paragraphs 39–41 of the judgment).

normative in substance, should be treated as a regulation for the purpose of an indirect challenge under Article 184 EEC.

There are no problems as far as normative acts are concerned. The right to make an indirect challenge to a normative act in proceedings before the European Court is laid down by Article 184 as regards the EEC Treaty and, as far as the ECSC Treaty is concerned, has been established by the cases mentioned above. There has never been any doubt that a normative act is subject to indirect challenge in the national courts. This means that normative acts are open to indirect challenge in all courts.

In the case of individual acts, on the other hand, the position is complex. It is settled that the addressee of an individual act may not challenge it indirectly in the European Court. It is also clear that a person who is *not* the addressee of an individual act may challenge it indirectly in a national court: thus, for example, if the Commission addresses a decision to a Member State empowering it to take certain action, and the Member State takes that action, a person affected by it may make an indirect challenge to the Commission decision in the course of proceedings brought in the national courts to challenge the validity of the action of the Member State.[11]

It is not, however, settled whether a person other than the addressee of an individual act may challenge it in the European Court or whether a person who *is* the addressee may challenge it in the national courts. It is, of course, true that Article 184 EEC refers only to regulations, thus suggesting that decisions may never be challenged indirectly in the European Court, and that Article 177(1)(*b*) EEC refers simply to 'acts of the institutions of the Community', thus implying that decisions may in all cases be challenged indirectly in the national courts. However, what was said above regarding the ECSC Treaty shows that the exact words of the Treaty provision are far from decisive, especially where – as here – general principles of law are concerned. It is therefore necessary to consider these two questions from a wider perspective.

European Court: Individual Acts Addressed to Another Person

Can a non-privileged applicant (private citizen) make an indirect challenge in the European Court to an individual act addressed to

---

[11] See, for example, *Gesellschaft für Getreidehandel* v. *EVGF*, Case 55/72, [1973] ECR 15. See also *Handelsvereniging Rotterdam*, Cases 73, 74/63, [1964] ECR 1, especially *per* Advocate General Roemer at pp. 20–2.

400 The Foundations of European Community Law

another person? In order to answer this question it is desirable to consider the rationale for the rule that the addressee of an individual act may not challenge it indirectly in the European Court.

In the *Dalmas* case, where this rule was first laid down, the ground given was that, if the rule did not exist, the time-limit on annulment actions under Article 33 ECSC (direct challenge) would be of no effect: the addressee would be able to postpone challenging the decision until it was enforced against him, even if this were after the one month time-limit. But why is it necessary to have a time-limit?

In answering this question, one should first point out that there is no inherent reason, applicable in all cases, why there should be a short time-limit. In England, as a matter of general principle, an indirect challenge may be brought, even against an individual act addressed to the person concerned, without regard to any particular time-limit.[12] In practice, however, the right to challenge the acts of a public authority is often taken away by an 'ouster clause'. This is a provision in a statute that any decision taken under the statute may not be called into question in any court. This precludes any challenge, either direct or indirect. Sometimes, on the other hand, the ouster clause permits a challenge to a named court or tribunal within a limited period of time, and then precludes all further challenges.

The reason why such clauses are enacted in England, and why the very short time-limit is imposed under Articles 33 ECSC and 173 EEC, is that reliance may have been placed on the validity of the act by someone other than the person seeking to challenge it, and the reasonable expectations of this person might be upset if the act is subsequently held to be invalid. The usual example given is a compulsory purchase order under which land is acquired by a public authority for building, say, a hospital. If the owner of the land could wait until the hospital had been built before challenging the validity of the order, the results would obviously be very unfortunate. In such cases, therefore, it is usual to allow him a short time to make the challenge and to preclude any challenge thereafter.

This example shows that, in some cases at least, it is desirable to have a strict time-limit for challenging a legal act, and this rationale – which is an aspect of the principle of legal security – is applicable to an indirect challenge as well as to a direct challenge. However, it applies just as much to normative acts as to individual acts and, if it were the only relevant principle, it would preclude all indirect

---

[12] See for example *Cooper* v. *Wandsworth Board of Works* (1863) 14 C B (N.S.) 180 and *R.* v. *Fulham Rent Tribunal* [1951] 2 K B 1, *per* Devlin J at p. 10.

challenge once the time-limit had expired. There is, however, another relevant principle – the principle of legality – which requires that no effect should be given to invalid acts. If this principle were fully applied, indirect challenge would be allowed in all cases.

Since these two principles conflict, a compromise must be found; and the form this compromise takes, in Community law, is to allow an indirect challenge in the case of a normative act but not in the case of an individual act addressed to the person making the challenge. There are two reasons why it is more serious to deny the right to make an indirect challenge in the former case than in the latter. First, as was seen in Chapter 12, non-privileged applicants have no right to make a direct challenge to a normative act; therefore, if they were denied the right to make an indirect challenge to such an act, they would have no right to challenge it at all.

Secondly, if an act is addressed to a person and he is informed of it – under Article 191 EEC a decision must be notified to the addressee and takes effect only on notification – it is reasonable to assume that he is aware of its import; consequently, he may reasonably be required to make his challenge within a given time-limit. If, on the other hand, no such notification takes place – normative acts merely have to be published in the Official Journal – it is quite possible that he will be unaware of its existence or, even if he knows that it has been adopted, may not appreciate its full import. Consequently, he might fail to challenge it within the stipulated time-limit.

Now, it will be noticed that the scope of the second of these two policy arguments is wider than that of the first. If one accepted only the first argument – that is, if one took the view that a litigant should be permitted to make an indirect challenge only against an act which he could not have challenged directly even if he had taken proceedings within the time-limit – one would conclude, first, that a privileged applicant could never make an indirect challenge under any circumstances and, secondly, that a non-privileged applicant could make an indirect challenge only to a normative act or an individual act which is not addressed to him and which does not concern him directly and individually. The reason for excluding a privileged applicant (Community institution or Member State) is that it has *locus standi* to make a direct challenge to *any* act; the reason a non-privileged applicant should be allowed to challenge indirectly only the acts mentioned above is that he has *locus standi* to make a direct challenge to an individual act which either is addressed to him or which concerns him both directly and individually.

If, on the other hand, one also accepted the second policy argument, one would allow an indirect challenge against any normative act, irrespective of whether or not the applicant was a privileged applicant; and in addition one would allow it against an individual act which was not addressed to the person wishing to make the indirect challenge. In this case, direct and individual concern would be irrelevant.

Although the question under discussion has not yet been directly considered by the European Court, its judgment in *Simmenthal* v. *Commission*[13] indicates that it accepts the first of these two policy arguments. In that case the Court said:[14]

... Article 184 of the EEC Treaty gives expression to a general principle conferring upon any party to proceedings the right to challenge, for the purpose of obtaining the annulment of a decision of direct and individual concern to that party, the validity of previous acts of the institutions which form the legal basis of the decision which is being attacked, if that party was not entitled under Article 173 of the Treaty to bring a direct action challenging those acts by which it was thus affected without having been in a position to ask that they be declared void.

The Court then went on to apply this principle to the case of an act which, though not in the form of a regulation, was normative in substance and was therefore not open to direct challenge by non-privileged applicants. However, there is no reason to doubt that the Court would also apply it to the case of an individual act which was not addressed to the party in question and which could not have been challenged by him under Article 173 because it was not of direct and individual concern to him.

The acceptance of this argument by the Court is to be welcomed. Moreover, in the *Universität Hamburg* case[15] (discussed below),[16] the Court also accepted the second policy argument. This case was admittedly concerned with an indirect challenge in the national courts, but the policy argument applies equally in both cases. In view of the uncertainty still surrounding the rules for *locus standi* under Article 173 EEC, it would be unfair if a person who had thought that he was not entitled to make a direct challenge to an act were told by the Court after the expiry of the time-limit that no indirect challenge was possible because he could, after all, have challenged it under Article 173.

[13] Case 92/78, [1979] ECR 777.
[14] At paragraph 39 of the judgment.
[15] Case 216/82, [1983] ECR 2771.
[16] See pp. 403–5.

National Courts: Challenge by the Addressee

May the addressee of an individual act challenge it in the national courts? The policy arguments discussed above suggest fairly clearly that he should not be permitted to do so. It is by no means certain, however, that this is so. In *De Bloos* v. *Bouyer*[17] the question was discussed by both the Commission (in the course of its observations) and by the Advocate General, but neither was able to come to any very definite conclusions; the Court itself did not consider the point.

In the later case of *Commission* v. *Belgium*,[18] however, the Court gave a hint of how it views the matter. This was an enforcement action brought under the special procedure relating to state aids laid down in Article 93(2) EEC. The Commission had taken a decision addressed to Belgium and, when this was not complied with, it brought the matter before the Court. The Belgian Government tried to make an indirect challenge to the decision but, since the decision was an individual act addressed to Belgium, the Court had no difficulty in deciding that it could not do this. At the end of the judgment the Court considered one of the arguments put forward by the Belgian Government. This was that as the decision could be challenged in the national courts and a reference made to the European Court under Article 177(1)(*b*), it ought also to be open to challenge in proceedings brought directly in the European Court. The answer given by the European Court was as follows:[19]

Although it is true that the validity of a Community measure may be called in question by means of the procedure for obtaining a preliminary ruling referred to in Article 177 of the Treaty, in spite of the expiry of the period laid down in the third paragraph of Article 173, such a procedure, which is laid down in respect of all measures adopted by the institutions and corresponds solely to the requirements of the national courts, is nevertheless subject to objectives and rules different from those which govern the applications referred to in Article 173 of the Treaty, and cannot justify a derogation from the principle of the time-barring of applications as a result of the expiry of the periods within which proceedings must be brought, without thereby depriving Article 173 of its legal significance.

Although this stops short of saying directly that the Belgian Government could itself have challenged the decision in the national courts, it could be regarded as suggesting that this might be so.

The *Universität Hamburg*[20] case, on the other hand, could be re-

[17] Case 59/77, [1977] ECR 2359.
[18] Case 156/77, [1978] ECR 1881.
[19] At paragraph 25 of the judgment.
[20] Case 216/82, [1983] ECR 2771.

garded as implying that the addressee of a decision cannot challenge it indirectly in the national courts. In this case, the Court allowed the University of Hamburg to make an indirect challenge in the German courts against a decision which (though addressed to the German Government) concerned it directly and individually and which could, therefore, have been challenged directly by the University under Article 173 EEC.[21] The reasons the Court gave for this ruling are instructive. It said that the University might not have been aware of the decision before the expiry of the time-limit under Article 173 because the Commission was not obliged to inform the University or even to publish the decision; consequently the University might not have been able to exercise its right to challenge the decision directly. The same reasoning would apply in most cases where the decision was not addressed to the person concerned, but it would not apply where he was the addressee. This suggests, therefore, that the addressee of a decision cannot challenge it individually in the national courts.

WHO MAY MAKE THE CHALLENGE?

Are privileged applicants (Community institutions and Member States) ever entitled to make an indirect challenge, or are they precluded from doing so by virtue of their status, irrespective of the nature of the act involved? It was mentioned above that the first of the two policy arguments would preclude privileged applicants from ever making an indirect challenge but the second would permit them to do so unless the act in question were addressed to them.

The only case so far in which this question has arisen was *Italy* v. *Commission.*[22] Here Italy brought proceedings under Article 173 to quash a Council regulation, and also made an indirect challenge against two other regulations. The question was raised by the Commission whether a Member State is entitled to make an indirect challenge but the Advocate General, Mr Roemer, stated that a Member State should have the same rights as other applicants. He based his opinion on two arguments: first, Article 184 is expressed in general terms and provides that 'any' party may make the challenge; and secondly, he said that the Member State might not have exer-

---

[21] This was established in *Control Data Belgium* v. *Commission*, Case 294/81, [1983] ECR 911.
[22] Case 32/65, [1966] ECR 389.

cised its right to make a direct challenge because the defects of the regulation might not have been fully apparent until it was applied in a particular case.[23] The European Court did not deal with the point; it rejected the challenge on the ground that the regulations in question were not relevant to the issue before the Court.[24]

IN WHAT PROCEEDINGS MAY THE CHALLENGE BE MADE?

It was shown above[25] that the theoretical conditions for an indirect challenge could occur in almost any kind of proceedings. Are there in fact any limitations on the proceedings in which the challenge may be made? So far, the European Court has allowed the challenge to be made in annulment actions, actions under Article 35 ECSC for a remedy for failure to act,[26] staff actions under Article 179 EEC[27] and proceedings in a national court. There is no doubt that it may also be made in an appeal against a penalty: under the ECSC Treaty this is expressly covered by Article 36(3).

It has, on the other hand, been suggested that an indirect challenge cannot be made in enforcement proceedings.[28] This is by no means certain. There have been several cases, of which *Belgium* v. *Commission* is one, in which it was held that in enforcement actions a Member State cannot make an indirect challenge to an individual act addressed to it,[29] but this is equally true in all proceedings. It is possible that the European Court may eventually decide that a Member State, as a privileged applicant, is precluded from making an indirect challenge in any proceedings; apart from this, however, there is no

[23] [1966] ECR at 414.

[24] The Court did, however, repeat the words of Art. 184 EEC ('any party may . . .') and some writers have taken this as an indication that the Court accepted the Advocate General's opinion: see Schermers, paragraph 467 and Barav. 'The Exception of Illegality in Community Law: A Critical Analysis', (1974) 11 C.M.L. Rev. 366 at 372. This view, however, may involve reading too much into the judgment.

[25] At pp. 395–6.

[26] *SNUPAT* v. *High Authority*, Cases 32, 33/58, [1959] ECR 127 at 139.

[27] *Sabbatini* v. *European Parliament*, Case 20/71, [1972] ECR 345.

[28] See Schermers, paragraph 462.

[29] The case most often cited as authority for the supposed rule is *Germany* v. *High Authority (Railway Tariffs* case), Case 3/59, [1960] ECR 53. However, the measures against which the German Government wished to make the indirect challenge – the decisions of 12 February 1958 – were individual acts addressed to Germany. It was for this reason that the Court held that no indirect challenge could be made: see p. 61 of the judgment where the Court refers to Case 9/56 (this was the *Meroni* case discussed in the text at p. 397, above). See also *per* Advocate General Roemer at p. 67 where the same point is made even more clearly.

reason why enforcement actions should be any different from other proceedings.

ON WHAT GROUNDS MAY THE CHALLENGE BE MADE?

Article 184 EEC makes clear that where the challenge is made in the European Court the grounds of review are exactly the same as in the case of a direct challenge under Article 173. At one time there was some doubt whether this was also true in the case of a challenge in the national courts in view of the fact that Article 177(1)(*b*) EEC and Article 41 ECSC speak of the 'validity' of an act, while Articles 173 EEC and 33 ECSC use the word 'legality'. Is there any difference between validity and legality? In the *Handelsvereniging Rotterdam* case[30] it was suggested by the German Government in its observations that 'validity' had a much more restricted meaning than 'legality' and that in proceedings under Article 177(1)(*b*) the Court could consider only whether or not the act was non-existent (void) and not whether it might be merely voidable. (It will be remembered from the discussion in Chapter 11 that invalid Community acts are normally voidable and not void: the latter is the case only in very special circumstances where the act lacks any semblance of validity.[31])

This argument was rejected by Advocate General Roemer who took the view that the same grounds of review apply as in the case of a direct challenge.[32] The Court did not specifically consider the problem but it has never given any indication that narrower grounds should be applied under Article 177, and in the third *International Fruit Company* case[33] it expressly stated that the grounds of review under Article 177 cannot be restricted. One can conclude, therefore, that the grounds of review are identical in all cases.[34]

[30] Cases 73, 74/63, [1964] ECR 1.
[31] See pp. 331–4, above.
[32] [1964] ECR at 19–20.
[33] Cases 21–24/72, [1972] ECR 1219 (paragraph 5 of the judgment).
[34] It is argued by Professor Schermers (paragraph 478) that there is an exception where the Community act is contrary to an international agreement which is not directly effective. In the third *International Fruit Company* case (above) the European Court held that this could not be a ground of review under Art. 177(1)(*b*) (see also *Schlüter*, Case 9/73, [1973] ECR 1135 (paragraphs 24–31 of the judgment) and *Bresciani*, Case 87/75, [1976] ECR 129 (paragraphs 15–26 of the judgment).) Professor Schermers considers that it would be a ground of review under Art. 173. However, this is doubtful since it would go against the logic of the judgment in *International Fruit*. The reason why the European Court ruled that the GATT was inapplicable in national courts was that it considered that the Contracting States had not intended to confer legal rights on individuals; the fact that its

THE EFFECT OF A SUCCESSFUL CHALLENGE

Since the purpose of an indirect challenge is to persuade the court to decide the case before it on the basis that the act subject to the indirect challenge is invalid, it might be thought that a successful challenge could have no consequences beyond the case in question: unlike a ruling in an annulment action, it would have no *erga omnes* effect. In practice, however, it appears to have much the same effect, since the European Court has held that when an act has been declared invalid on a reference from a national court, though that ruling is binding only on the court which made the reference, 'it is sufficient reason for any other national court to regard that act as void',[35] (though such court may, if it wishes, refer the matter to the European Court again[36]). The strong implication of this judgment is that a ruling of invalidity is binding on other national courts, unless the European Court rescinds it on a subsequent reference – an unlikely occurrence. Moreover the European Court has also ruled, on a reference from a national court, that an act may be invalid for the future but valid for the past.[37] Such a ruling would be pointless if it was not applicable in later cases.

FURTHER READING

Schermers, paragraphs 459–482.
Barav, 'The Exception of Illegality in Community Law: A Critical Analysis', (1974) 11 C.M.L. Rev. 366.
Bebr, 'Judicial Remedy of Private Parties against Normative Acts

---

provisions were, if not subject to further negotiation, at least sufficiently flexible to allow for their adaptation to special circumstances was an indication of this. But if the GATT was intended only to create rights and obligations between the Contracting States, there is no reason why it should be effective at the Community level any more than at the national level: the international level is the only plane on which it could apply. This seems to have been the view of the Advocate General: see [1972] ECR 1239–40.

[35] *International Chemical Corporation*, Case 66/80, [1981] ECR 1191 (first paragraph of the ruling).

[36] This could be to ask the European Court to reconsider its previous ruling; a more likely reason would be to request clarification on the temporal effect of the ruling (whether it applies only to the future or also to the past).

[37] *Providence Agricole de la Champagne*, Case 4/79, [1980] ECR 2823; *Maïseries de Beauce*, Case 109/79, [1980] ECR 2883; *Roquette*, Case 145/79, [1980] ECR 2917. See pp. 233–4, above.

of the European Communities: The Role of the Exception of Illegality', (1966) 4 C.M.L. Rev. 7.

Bebr, 'Examen en validité au titre de l'article 177 du traité CEE et cohésion juridique de la Communauté', [1975] CDE 379.

Bebr, 'Preliminary Rulings of the Court of Justice: Their Authority and Temporal Effect', (1981) 18 C.M.L. Rev. 475 (especially pp. 475–483).

Harding, 'The Impact of Article 177 of the EEC Treaty on the Review of Community Action', (1981) 1 YEL 93.

Trabucchi, 'L'effet "erga omnes" des décisions préjudicielles rendues par la Cour de justice des Communautés européennes', [1974] RTDE 56.

15

GROUNDS OF REVIEW

When the applicant has finally overcome all jurisdictional hurdles and problems of admissibility, he must then convince the Court that the measure ought to be annulled. To do this, he must establish one or other of the grounds of review set out, in identical terms, in Articles 173 EEC, 33 ECSC and 146 Euratom. These grounds apply not only in direct actions for annulment, but also in the case of an indirect challenge.[1] The grounds of review are four in number:

1. lack of competence;
2. infringement of an essential procedural requirement;
3. infringement of the Treaty or any rule of law relating to its application;
4. misuse of powers.

These grounds are derived from French administrative law; this does not, however, mean that they will necessarily be applied in the same way in Community law as in French law: the legal traditions of all the Member States, as well as the special circumstances of the Community, will be taken into account by the European Court.

It will be noticed that these grounds are broad and general; they also overlap to a considerable extent. In fact, if the third ground were given a sufficiently extensive interpretation, it could cover all the other three. For this reason, the European Court does not always pay very much attention to determining which ground is involved and, even when the measure is annulled, it is not always expressly stated which of the four formal grounds provided the basis.[2] There is nothing improper in this so long as it is clear that the case comes within at least one of them.

---

[1] See p. 406, above.
[2] There are some exceptional cases where it does matter which ground is applied. The most important is when a non-privileged applicant challenges a general measure under Art. 33 ECSC; here only misuse of powers may be invoked.

THE FORMAL GROUNDS

Lack of Competence

Here 'competence' means legal power to adopt an act. The principle of the Treaties is that institutions have no power to adopt an act unless they are authorized to do so by a Treaty provision: the Community has no inherent legislative or executive power. For every act, therefore, it must be possible to point to a Treaty provision (or to another legal act in turn based on a Treaty provision) which provides its legal foundation. If there is no such foundation, the act will be annulled for lack of competence. The equivalent concept in English law is *ultra vires*.

Although this ground of review raises fundamental issues, it is not very often invoked. This is largely because it is not very easy – except, perhaps, in cases of delegation – to establish that the enacting authority lacked competence. It will be remembered from the discussion in Chapter 4 that the European Court gives a wide interpretation to empowering provisions in the Treaties; the theory of implied powers also extends the competence of the Council and Commission.[3] On top of this, Article 235 EEC (and its equivalents) are of such wide scope that, except in the case of matters wholly outside the ambit of the Treaty, it is almost always possible to find a legal foundation for a Council act.[4]

When the Council and Commission adopt legal acts they state, in the preamble to the act, the provision which constitutes its legal foundation. This should make it easy to discover whether the act is within the competence of the enacting authority. However, there is a catch. This statement is usually in the form: 'Having regard to the Treaty establishing the European Economic Community and in particular Article . . . thereof.' In other words, the legal foundation specified is not merely the Article expressly referred to but also any other Article in the Treaty.[5] It might seem to follow that, if the act is challenged on the ground that the Article expressly referred to does not in fact authorize it, the enacting institution could put forward another Treaty provision as an alternative foundation (provided any

---

[3] See pp. 103–4, above.

[4] Art. 235 EEC is discussed in Chapter 4, pp. 103–4.

[5] However, if the preamble merely refers to the EEC Treaty without specifying any particular Article, the measure will be annulled for violation of an essential procedural requirement: *Commission* v. *Council*, Case 45/86, 26 March 1987 (not yet reported), discussed above at p. 108.

special procedural requirements of the latter have been complied with). Whether this is correct, however, remains to be seen.

It is interesting in this connection to note that in one instance the Council changed the stated legal foundation *ex post facto* by means of a later measure. The original measure was Regulation 947/71[6] which stated in its preamble that it was enacted on the basis of the EEC Treaty 'and in particular Article 103 thereof'. Subsequently, this Regulation was amended by Regulation 2746/72.[7] This latter Regulation was itself enacted on the basis of the EEC Treaty 'and in particular Articles 28, 43, 103 and 235 thereof'. Besides amending the substantive provisions of Regulation 974/71, it also provided that the part of its preamble setting out its legal foundation should be replaced with the following: 'Having regard to the Treaty establishing the European Economic Community and in particular Articles 28, 43 and 235 thereof.'

The strange point about this is that Article 103, which was the sole expressly stated ground of Regulation 974/71 in its original form, was not even mentioned in the new version of the preamble, even though the amending Regulation was itself stated to be based on it (together with other provisions). This suggests that the Council had doubts as to whether Regulation 974/71 could, even in its original form, be founded on the basis of Article 103. It is also interesting to note that the Council included Article 235 among the list of provisions expressly mentioned. Presumably the idea was that if the other Articles provided a sound foundation, the Regulation would be valid on that basis; if not, then Article 235 could be legitimately invoked since it could be said that the Treaty had 'not provided the necessary powers'.[8]

Infringement of an Essential Procedural Requirement

This ground of invalidity includes requirements which may be regarded as procedural in the strict sense, such as a requirement to consult another authority, and also requirements concerning the form of the measure – for example, the requirement to give reasons.

The requirement may be laid down either in the Treaty or in secondary legislation (for example, in the case of delegation, a requirement to consult); it may also be prescribed by a general

---

[6] JO 1971, L 106/1.
[7] JO 1972, L 291/148.
[8] See pp. 104–9, above.

principle of law. An example of the latter is the principle of *audi alteram partem*, which was held in the *Transocean Marine Paint* case[9] to be binding on the Commission even in the absence of an express legislative provision.[10]

It will be noticed that only an 'essential' procedural requirement is a ground of annulment. The distinction between essential and non-essential requirements, which was adopted from French administrative law,[11] is similar to the English distinction between procedural provisions that are mandatory and those that are merely directory. The philosophy behind this distinction is the same in all three systems: to invalidate an act for an insignificant procedural defect would unduly hamper administrative activity and would encourage excessive formalism and 'red tape', which in turn would stifle initiative and slow down the administrative process; on the other hand, not to annul for any formal defect at all would be detrimental to good administration and would prejudice the rights of individuals. The law therefore tries to achieve a compromise by restricting the sanction of invalidity to those cases where an important provision has been violated.

This compromise has many advantages; but it has the disadvantage of uncertainty: how does one tell whether a requirement is to be regarded as essential or not? Community provisions laying down procedural requirements do not normally state whether their infringement will lead to invalidity. Therefore, one must look to the function of the provision and to the likely consequences if it is not observed. Thus, if failure to observe it could affect the final content of the act, one would be justified in concluding that it was an essential requirement. For example, a requirement to consult another body, or to grant the person concerned a hearing, is classifiable as essential on the basis of this test: the facts and arguments that would be brought to the notice of the enacting authority through this procedure could induce it to alter the content of the measure.

It would be a mistake, however, to conclude that this is the sole test: procedural requirements which have no possible effects on the content of the act can also be classified as essential. For example, the most important objectives of the requirement to give reasons are, according to the European Court, to help the persons concerned

[9] Case 17/74, [1974] ECR 1063.
[10] See pp. 147–8, above.
[11] The term used in French law for an essential procedural requirement is *'une forme substantielle'*; this is also the term used in the French version of the Treaties.

defend their rights, to help the Court exercise its supervisory functions and to enable third parties to appreciate the way in which the enacting authorities use their powers.[12] None of these considerations relates to the content of the measure:[13] yet nothing could be more firmly established than that the requirement to give reasons is an essential procedural requirement.

The most important requirements so far held to be essential are the requirement to give reasons, the requirement to state the provision under which the measure is adopted,[14] the requirement to grant a hearing (*audi alteram partem*),[15] the requirement to attain assent,[16] and the requirement to consult.[17] The requirement that a Council measure be based on the proposal of the Commission would obviously also be essential. It seems fairly clear that the requirement laid down in Article 190 EEC (and equivalent provisions in the other Treaties) that measures must refer to any proposals or opinions obtained pursuant to the Treaty[18] would also be held to be essential: this is contained in the same Treaty Articles as the requirement to give reasons and would probably be classified in the same way. The position is less certain concerning the requirements of publication and notification.[19] There can be no doubt that failure to publish or notify will prevent the measure from coming into force but it is not clear whether it would justify annulment.[20]

---

[12] See pp. 119–20, above.

[13] It is, of course, true that another function of the requirement to give reasons is to clarify the enacting authority's objectives in adopting the measure; thus the discipline of formulating the reasons could induce it to reconsider the content of the measure. To this extent, the classification of this requirement as essential could be justified on the basis of the first test. This function has not, however, been mentioned by the European Court and it must be regarded as secondary.

[14] *Commission* v. *Council*, Case 45/86, 26 March 1987 (not yet reported).

[15] *Transocean Marine Paint* v. *Commission*, Case 17/74, [1974] ECR 1063.

[16] *Klöckner-Werke* v. *Commission*, Case 119/81, [1982] ECR 2627 (paragraph 6 of the judgment). This case concerned the duty to attain the assent of the Council under Art. 58(1) ECSC.

[17] *Italy* v. *High Authority*, Case 2/54, [1954] ECR 37 at 51–2 (duty under Art. 60(1) ECSC to consult the Consultative Committee); *Netherlands* v. *High Authority*, Case 6/54, [1955] ECR 103 at 112; *Roquette* v. *Council*, Case 138/79 [1980] ECR 3333 and *Maizena* v. *Council*, Case 139/79, [1980] ECR 3393 (duty to consult the European Parliament).

[18] See pp. 117–19, above.

[19] Discussed above, pp. 127–8.

[20] See Vandersanden and Barav, p. 211.

Infringement of the Treaty or of any Rule of Law Relating to its Application

If narrowly interpreted, this ground applies only to those cases where the act subject to challenge violates an express prohibition – in contrast to lack of competence, which applies in the absence of any relevant provision – but if given a wide interpretation it overlaps with virtually every other ground of annulment, since each could be said to involve an infringement of some rule of Community law. For this reason, it is almost always pleaded by litigants in addition to any other ground they might think appropriate.

What does it cover? First, it covers all provisions in the relevant Treaty – EEC, ECSC or Euratom – and all other Treaties amending or supplementing it; consequently it covers all the constitutive Treaties.[21] Secondly, it covers 'any rule of law' relating to the application of any of those Treaties. At first sight, the meaning of this phrase may give rise to doubt. The Dutch version of the Treaty uses the phrase, *enige uitvoeringsregeling daarvan*, which means 'any rule executing it'.[22] This suggests that the phrase applies only to implementing provisions, but this is too narrow an interpretation: the European Court has made clear that it applies to all rules of Community law other than those found in the constituent Treaties.

Each of the following is a possible source of rules of law relating to the application of the Treaty:[23]

1. Community acts (including acts *sui generis*);
2. Subsidiary conventions (provided they are part of the Community legal system);
3. Acts of the representatives of the Member States (in so far as they are legally binding);
4. Treaties with third countries binding on the Community (whether entered into by the Community or by the Member States);
5. The general principles of Community law.

Each of these will be considered in turn.

Violation of another Community act will be a ground of annulment if that other act was binding on the author of the act subject to challenge. This will occur where the latter is delegated legislation and also in those cases where the principle of legal certainty (protection of

---

[21] See Chapter 3, pp. 88–9, above.
[22] Schermers, paragraph 378.
[23] See Vandersanden and Barav, pp. 188–201.

legitimate expectations) requires that the author of the act subject to challenge abide by some previous act adopted by it. The *Staff Salaries* case[24] (discussed above)[25] furnishes an example of this: the Court there annulled a measure of the Council providing salary increases for Community staff because it violated a previous Council decision laying down the formula on the basis of which future salary increases were to be calculated. The Court held that the principle of legitimate expectations required the Council to adhere to its previous decision.

The question whether a subsidiary convention prevails over a Community act has already been discussed; the matter is not free from doubt but it was suggested that it probably does not.[26] If this is correct, violation of such a convention will not be a ground of annulment; but if the European Court takes the opposite view, there is no doubt that it would annul the act in question for violation of a rule of law relating to the application of the Treaty. It will also be remembered that acts of the representatives of the Member States are in some cases a species of international agreement between the Member States.[27] In such cases they will be of a similar status to the subsidiary conventions.

International agreements with non-member States concluded by the Community, or otherwise binding on it, are also covered; so any Community act contrary to such an agreement would be annulled by the Court, provided that the agreement was directly effective.[28]

The general principles of Community law play an important part in annulment actions.[29] An infringement of such a principle is a ground of invalidity except in those cases where the principle is merely interpretive or intended only to fill gaps in Community legislation.

Misuse of Powers

Though of great theoretical interest, this ground is only very rarely established in practice. It is derived from French administrative law

---

[24] *Commission* v. *Council*, Case 81/72, [1973] ECR 575.

[25] At pp. 144–5.

[26] See pp. 94–5, above.

[27] See pp. 96–7, above.

[28] *International Fruit Company*, Cases 21–24/72, [1972] ECR 1219 (paragraph 5 of the judgment); *Schlüter*, Case 9/73, [1973] ECR 1135 (paragraphs 24–31 of the judgment); *Bresciani*, Case 87/75, [1976] ECR 129 (paragraphs 15–26 of the judgment). It has been suggested that in the case of a direct challenge, the agreement need not be directly effective, but this is doubtful; see p. 406, note 34, above.

[29] See Chapter 5, above.

– where it is known as *détournement de pouvoir* – but is also found, in one form or another, in the legal systems of most Western countries. A misuse of powers is the exercise of a power for a purpose other than that for which it was granted.[30] It is a well established ground of invalidity in English administrative law, where it is usually referred to, more informatively, as 'improper purpose'.

Unlike the other grounds of invalidity, which are objective in character, misuse of powers is subjective: in order to establish it, one has to discover what the subjective purpose – the motive or intention – was of the authority exercising the power.[31] For this reason, misuse of powers is more difficult to prove than other grounds: in the absence of a document emanating from the authority which indicates its purpose in adopting the measure, the applicant may have to rely on inference from the content of the measure and the general circumstances prevailing when it was enacted.[32] It is not, however, necessary to prove bad faith: an authority may quite innocently misuse its powers if it fails to appreciate the purpose for which they were given.

Under the ECSC Treaty, misuse of powers plays a special role which in some ways puts it above the other grounds of invalidity. First, it will be remembered that where a non-privileged applicant challenges a general decision or recommendation (normative act), he may do so only on one ground: misuse of powers affecting him;[33] secondly, where the Commission is obliged to evaluate the economic situation in order to decide how to exercise its powers, the Court may

---

[30] See *Netherlands* v. *High Authority*, Case 6/54, [1955] ECR 103 at 116; *Compagnie des Hauts Fourneaux de Chasse* v. *High Authority*, Case 15/57, [1958] ECR 211 at 230.

[31] In some of its earlier judgments, however, the European Court seems to have veered away from the pure doctrine of misuse of powers and allowed an objective element to enter its reasoning. Thus in *Hauts Fourneaux et Aciéries Belges* v. *High Authority*, Case 8/57, [1958] ECR 245 at 256, the Court said that violation of the principle of equality could constitute misuse of power; while in other cases there is a suggestion that lack of foresight could lead to misuse of power: see *Fédéchar* v. *High Authority*, Case 8/55, [1956] ECR 292 at 303, and *Chambre Syndicale de la Sidérurgie Française* v. *High Authority*, Cases 3, 4/64, [1965] ECR 441 at 454–5; see further, Vandersanden and Barav at pp. 207–8. This extended concept of misuse of powers (which appears to have been derived from German law: see Dickschat, 'Problèmes d'interprétation des traités européens résultant de leur plurilinguisme', [1968] Revue Belge de Droit International 40 at 47,) was probably adopted by the Court because of the special role played by misuse of powers in the ECSC Treaty, particularly with regard to the right of non-privileged applicants to challenge normative measures. By applying the wider concept, the Court could extend the right of non-privileged applicants to obtain judicial review under Art. 33 ECSC.

[32] The Court has said that the misuse of powers must be established 'on the basis of objective, relevant and consistent facts': see *Gutmann* v. *Commission*, Cases 18, 35/65, [1966] ECR 103 at 117 and *Lux* v. *Court of Auditors*, Case 69/83, [1984] ECR 2447 (paragraph 30 of the judgment).

[33] See p. 365, above.

not review the Commission's assessment except where it is alleged that the Commission has misused its powers or has manifestly failed to observe the provisions of the Treaty or any rule of law relating to its application. This latter provision is discussed below.[34]

It will be apparent that misuse of powers is closely related to the doctrine of proportionality. This is one of the general principles of Community law (discussed above in Chapter 5);[35] it requires that burdens imposed on the citizen be proportionate to the objective pursued: the means chosen must be reasonably likely to attain the objective and the detriment inflicted on those concerned must not be disproportionate to the general benefit. The difference between proportionality and misuse of powers is that proportionality is purely objective: the terms of the measure are balanced against the objective of the provision under which it was adopted; in the case of misuse of powers, on the other hand, the subjective intention of the author of the act is the relevant factor. If the authority is genuinely pursuing the proper objective, but uses inappropriate means, the measure will be annulled for lack of proportionality; if the objective is improper, misuse of powers will be the correct ground of review. However, though the two doctrines are quite distinct in theory, they can easily merge in practice, since the fact that the measure is inappropriate for the attainment of its ostensible objective will suggest that this was not the objective which its author was trying to attain.

In what circumstances will misuse of powers apply? French writers sometimes divide it into two categories, primary *détournement de pouvoir* and secondary *détournement de pouvoir*. The former comprises those cases where the power is not used in the public interest at all, but is used for some private objective of its author, perhaps to advance his own interests or to spite someone he dislikes. For example, if an official were refused a particular post because the decision-maker wished to appoint his girl-friend, one would have a case of primary misuse of powers.[36]

Secondary misuse of powers occurs where the objective pursued is in the public interest but it is not one which the author of the act is entitled to pursue. The case of *Gutmann* v. *Commission*[37] furnishes a good example of this. The applicant in this case was a Euratom

---

[34] At pp. 425–7.

[35] At pp. 145–7.

[36] Cf. *Mirossevich* v. *High Authority*, Case 10/55, [1956] ECR 333. Here similar allegations were made but were not proved.

[37] Cases 18, 35/65, [1966] ECR 103.

official who was transferred from the Research Centre at Ispra to Brussels on the basis of a provision authorizing the transfer of an official 'in the interests of the service'. The Court held, however, that this was not the real reason for the decision to transfer him: it was actually taken for disciplinary purposes. The decision was, therefore, annulled for misuse of powers.

Another case in which the plea was successfully invoked was *Giuffrida* v. *Council*.[38] This concerned an official called Signor Martino, who held an appointment at a particular grade, even though for many years he had performed duties appropriate to an official of a higher grade. In an attempt to remedy this anomalous situation, the Council organized a competition for a post at the higher grade. The sole object of this was, by the Council's own admission, to allow Signor Martino to be appointed to a post corresponding to his duties. Two officials applied, Signor Martino and the applicant in the case, Signor Giuffrida; Signor Martino was appointed and Signor Giuffrida brought proceedings to annul the appointment. The Court held that the objective of any recruitment procedure, including an internal competition, should be to appoint the best man for the job; by deciding in advance whom they would appoint, the Council was guilty of a misuse of powers. The appointment was therefore quashed.

A misuse of powers may also occur if an authority, for an improper reason, adopts a measure under one provision, when another provision would have been more appropriate. This was recognized by the Court in *Compagnie des Hauts Fourneaux de Chasse* v. *High Authority*, where it said:[39] 'In this connexion it must be recognized that there might have been a misuse of powers if the High Authority had been faced with a situation covered by the procedure in Article 59 and, in order to evade the safeguards provided for in Article 59, had nevertheless deliberately decided to make use of Article 53(b) and of the financial arrangements provided for therein.' This rule would not, of course, apply if both provisions were appropriate and the authority's choice was not made on improper grounds.

It is important to note that a measure will not be annulled for misuse of powers if the improper purpose had no effect on its

[38] Case 105/75, [1976] ECR 1395. See also *Fabrique de Fer de Charleroi* v. *Commission*, Cases 351, 360/85, 29 September 1987 (not yet reported), a case involving steel quotas in which the Commission adopted criteria designed to help a particular Member State rather than to spread the burden fairly among all steel enterprises.

[39] Case 15/57, [1958] ECR 211 at 231. The Court actually found that misuse of powers had not been proved.

substance. After all, why should a measure be quashed if it would have been enacted in exactly the same terms even if its author had not been pursuing an illegitimate objective? Consequently, it will be valid if pursuit of the proper purpose would inevitably have led to the same result.[40]

It follows from the above rule that if the authority has two objectives, one proper and one improper, the measure will not be annulled if the proper objective was the decisive one. In such a case, the improper objective will have no influence on the outcome. In *Fédéchar* v. *High Authority*[41] the Court said:

Even if one unjustified reason were included among those which justify the action of the High Authority, the decision would not for that reason involve a misuse of powers, in so far as it does not adversely affect the basic aim of [the provision under which it was taken].

This statement suggests that so long as the legitimate aim is attained, the presence of an improper purpose will be of no consequence. It seems to extend the rule slightly, since the improper purpose may have had some effect on the terms of the measure, even if it did not prevent the fulfilment of the legitimate objective. In other cases, there are suggestions that, where several motives are present, the applicant must prove that the improper motive was the sole, or at least the dominant, one.[42]

THE TIME FACTOR

In all annulment actions, the validity of the act must be determined on the basis of the situation existing at the time when it was adopted. A measure cannot, therefore, be annulled because of a subsequent event. This is logical in view of the fact that annulment is normally retroactive: the Court declares the act to have been invalid *ab initio*.[43] It follows from this that an act cannot be annulled on the ground that it is in conflict with a superior rule of law contained in a measure enacted at a subsequent date. The superior measure will, of course,

---

[40] *Fédéchar* v. *High Authority*, Case 8/55, [1956] ECR 292 at 300–1.

[41] Case 8/55, [1956] ECR 245 at 301. See also *France* v. *High Authority*, Case 1/54, [1954] ECR 1 at 16.

[42] See the *Fédéchar* case, Case 8/55, [1956] ECR 292 at 303; and *Hauts Fourneaux de Chasse* v. *High Authority*, Case 2/57, [1958] ECR 199 at 232. Compare the English decision of *R.* v. *Brixton Prison Governor, ex parte Soblen* [1963] 2 QB 243 (Lord Denning's judgment).

[43] See pp. 434–5, below.

prevail and the first act will be inapplicable to the extent of the conflict; but the Court will not annul it.

These principles can be illustrated from the case law of the European Court. *Schroeder* v. *Germany*,[44] for example, concerned a Community measure passed in order to limit imports of tomato concentrate from Greece. It was argued that the measure was not appropriate to achieve its objective – it was enacted under a power to pass 'appropriate' measures – because it could easily be circumvented. In dealing with this point, the Court said that the matter had to be approached on the basis of what was known when the measure was introduced: 'retrospective considerations of its efficacy' could not be taken into account.[45]

In the *Compagnie d'Approvisionnement* case,[46] the measure in issue was intended to counteract the effects of the devaluation of the French franc and it did this, in part, by granting subsidies to French exporters of agricultural produce. The applicant, which was a French exporter, maintained, however, that the subsidies were not high enough. One of its objections to the measure was that it infringed the principle of equality, since it was less generous than another regulation passed at a later date granting subsidies to German and Dutch importers consequent on a revaluation of the German and Dutch currencies. It alleged that this constituted discrimination against French exporters. The Court, however, ruled that the validity of the first regulation could not be called into question on the basis of subsequent events; consequently a comparison with the later measure could not be used to establish discrimination.[47]

This latter case raises some interesting issues: if two measures are passed dealing with situations which are sufficiently similar to bring the principle of equality into play, the possibilities of annulment might depend on which is passed first. If the less favourable measure is passed after the more favourable, it could be annulled for violation of the principle of equality. If, on the other hand, the less favourable measure is passed first, it is doubtful whether either could be annulled on this ground: the less favourable measure could not be annulled because of the time factor; the more favourable would not be quashed because the persons benefiting from it would not wish to

---

[44] Case 40/72, [1973] ECR 125.
[45] At paragraph 14 of the judgment.
[46] Cases 9, 11/71, [1972] ECR 391.
[47] At paragraph 39 of the judgment.

challenge it and those covered by the less favourable measure would normally lack *locus standi*.

Is there no remedy in the latter case? One possibility is that those covered by the less favourable measure might request the enacting institution to amend it to bring it into line with the other measure; if this request were not met, proceedings could be brought for a remedy for failure to act. It will be remembered that in *Eridania* v. *Commission*[48] the Court ruled that an action for failure to act cannot be used for the purpose of obliging a Community institution to repeal an invalid act. It was, however, suggested above[49] that there should be an exception to this rule where the act was initially valid but subsequently became incompatible with Community law as a result of a later development. If such an exception exists, the case where the less favourable measure is passed first would be precisely the situation in which it should be applied.

INTEREST

The (rather strict) rules of *locus standi* applicable in Community law were discussed in Chapter 12: is it sufficient if these are satisfied and it is thus established that the applicant has a legally-recognized interest in the annulment of the act; or must he also prove an interest in each ground of annulment pleaded? In the national systems of the Community countries there is a sharp divergence on this point:[50] in French, Belgian and Italian law the view is taken that it is enough that the applicant has an interest in the annulment of the measure itself. If this is the case, he is entitled to put forward any ground recognized by law. In England, Scotland, Denmark, the Netherlands and Germany, on the other hand, the applicant must, in at least some cases, show that he has an interest in the ground pleaded. This latter view has prevailed in Community law, at least with regard to staff cases.

In *Marcato* v. *Commission*[51] a Commission official, who had been unsuccessful in his application for a more senior post, brought proceedings to annul the competition for the appointment. One of his

[48] Cases 10, 18/68, [1969] ECR 459.
[49] See pp. 379–82.
[50] See the opinion of Advocate General Warner in *Deboeck* v. *Commission*, Case 90/74, [1975] ECR 1123 at 1140–1.
[51] Case 37/72, [1973] ECR 361.

objections was that the notice of competition did not lay down an age limit for candidates, as was required by the Staff Regulations. The applicant was, in fact, the second oldest of the candidates and, as the Commission pointed out, an age limit of 50 or 60 would not have eliminated any of the candidates, while a limit of 40 would have eliminated the applicant himself. The Commission therefore argued that he could not object to the absence of an age limit, since his interests were not affected. This argument was fiercely rejected by Advocate General Mayras (a Frenchman) on the basis of the standard French doctrine. The Court, however, accepted it. The relevant passage of the judgment reads:[52] 'The setting of an age limit could only have resulted either in eliminating the applicant himself from the competition, which would have been directly contrary to his interest, or else in eliminating other, possibly qualified, candidates, which in the circumstances cannot be regarded as a legitimate interest of his.' The interesting point to note is that it is not enough for the applicant to have an actual interest in the ground pleaded; his interest must also be regarded as *legitimate*. Presumably the Court considered that the rule regarding age limits had been enacted solely in the interests of the service and not in order to benefit rival candidates.[53]

Two other examples may be briefly mentioned.[54] In *De Dapper* v. *Parliament*[55] another unsuccessful candidate complained that the persons who were appointed to the post had remained in the same grade: the Court held that only *they* could complain about this. In *Deboeck* v. *Commission*[56] an unsuccessful candidate objected to the fact that the notice of competition had not been preceded by a notice of vacancy. The function of a notice of vacancy is to allow the appointing authority to consider whether the post might not be filled by transfer or promotion instead of by competition. The applicant, however, was not eligible for transfer or promotion to the post: her

---

[52] Paragraph 6 of the judgment.

[53] A similar argument has been adopted in a number of English decisions: see, for example, *R.* v. *Commissioners of Customs and Excise*, ex parte *Cooke and Stevenson* [1970] 1 All E.R. 1068.

[54] See also *Alfieri* v. *Parliament*, Case 35/64, [1965] ECR 261 at 267; *Serio* v. *Commission*, Case 115/73, [1974] ECR 341 at 349 and *De Vleeschauwer* v. *Commission*, Case 144/73, [1974] ECR 957 at 986.

[55] Case 29/74, [1975] ECR 35 at 40.

[56] Case 90/74, [1975] ECR 1123.

only chance of appointment lay in a competition; therefore, she was not entitled to object.[57]

It is not entirely clear exactly when an applicant will be regarded as not having an interest in a particular ground but it is probably legitimate to formulate the rule as follows: where the complaint is that the author of the act failed to do something, the applicant will not be entitled to object if he would have been no better off if the omission had not occurred; where, on the other hand, something was done which ought not to have been done, the applicant will be able to rely on the irregularity only if his interests were prejudiced. An applicant will not, moreover, be regarded as affected unless he has a *legitimate* interest: an interest would probably be regarded as legitimate only if it was one which the rule of law violated might reasonably be supposed to have been intended to protect.

The cases do not indicate the scope of the rule. It will apply most often to procedural irregularities, but it appears also applicable to defects of substance: the allegations in *Marcato*, and even more so in *De Dapper*, go beyond what could be regarded as procedure. However, there must be some cases in which it would not apply. Where a serious illegality is alleged, the Court will normally investigate it of its own motion; consequently it will be irrelevant whether or not the applicant has an interest. The rule can therefore apply only to less serious irregularities; in such cases its application is entirely justifiable.

MISTAKE OF FACT

A decision of fact is a determination whether or not a particular state of fact exists. It is quite different from a decision to act, though the two kinds of decision are frequently linked: the power to adopt a measure may be dependent on the prior existence of a situation of fact. The enacting authority must then determine the question of fact before it can exercise the discretionary power. If, however, it makes a wrong decision of fact it may enact a measure when it has no power to do so: such a measure will be invalid and will be quashed by the European Court if appropriate proceedings are brought. The formal

---

[57] Another possible objection to the omission was that it might have meant that certain potential candidates would not have known of the competition; but this did not affect the applicant: she *did* know of it.

ground of annulment will usually be infringement of the Treaty or of a rule of law relating to its application.

A good example is provided by *Barge v. High Authority*.[58] This was another of the many cases under the ECSC Treaty concerning the scrap iron equalization scheme. It will be remembered that under this scheme imported scrap was subsidized and the subsidy paid for by a levy on all users of scrap, both imported and home-produced.[59] Since the levy was based on the quantity of scrap used, the High Authority had to determine this before it could decide how much was owed by any given firm. Where the firm failed to provide the relevant figures, the High Authority was obliged to make an estimate of scrap used. This was what occurred in the *Barge* case, where the estimate was based on the amount of electricity used by the steel foundry in question. The High Authority then passed two decisions; one set out the estimated quantities of scrap used and the other fixed the amount due by way of the levy. These decisions were challenged by Barge who succeeded in proving that the assessment of scrap consumed was inaccurate. The Court thereupon quashed both decisions.

Where a Community institution makes a mistake concerning a purely factual question of this kind, the Court will always quash the measure if its validity is dependent on the decision of fact. However, in many cases the relevant question is not one of 'pure' fact, but is rather an evaluation or judgment based on facts. For example, there are a number of provisions giving the Commission power to adopt measures if a given situation has produced 'economic difficulties' in a particular Member State or if there is a threat of 'serious disturbances' to the market in a given product. Clearly, a determination by the Commission that economic difficulties exist or that serious disturbances are threatened is a decision of a somewhat different nature from a determination that a particular firm has consumed X tons of ferrous scrap.

A decision of this kind is a complex determination containing, first, a number of purely factual decisions – for example, on the level of imports, exports, prices, profits, etc. – and, secondly, an evaluation of the situation thus revealed in which it is decided that these 'primary' facts either establish, or do not establish, the existence of economic.

[58] Case 18/62, [1963] ECR 259. See also *Milac*, Case 131/77, [1978] ECR 1041 (where the question of fact on which the validity of the measure depended was whether the price of one product was dependent on that of another) and *per* Advocate General Mayras in *Westzucker*, Case 57/72, [1973] ECR 321 at 351.

[59] See pp. 113–14, above.

difficulties or a threat of serious disturbances, as the case may be. Though factual in one sense, this evaluation depends on the Commission's judgment, exercised on the basis of its experience. Though it does not, strictly speaking, involve a discretion,[60] it does contain a subjective element. Since the European Court lacks the political and economic expertise of the Commission and Council, it would be inappropriate if it were too ready to review it.

The ECSC Treaty

In view of these considerations, it is not surprising to find that the ECSC Treaty contains a provision imposing restraint on the Court. This is contained in Article 33 and reads as follows:

The Court may not, however, examine the evaluation of the situation, resulting from economic facts or circumstances, in the light of which the High Authority took its decisions or made its recommendations, save where the High Authority is alleged to have misused its powers or to have manifestly failed to observe the provisions of this Treaty or any rule of law relating to its application.

A number of comments may be made on this provision. First, it applies only to the Commission's *evaluation* of the situation, not to its findings of primary fact. If these are wrong – for example, if the Commission uses inaccurate statistics – the Court will be entitled to quash the measure.

Secondly, the provision refers only to the evaluation of *economic* facts; however, the Court has adopted a similar attitude of restraint with regard to evaluations of other kinds where the Community institution, either because of greater expertise or special knowledge of the situation, is in a better position to make a judgment. Thus, the Court will be slow to review a decision of a Community institution on the professional competence of an official of that institution.[61] This may be illustrated by *Leroy* v. *High Authority*,[62] an action brought by a

[60] See *per* Advocate General Gand in *Germany* v. *Commission*, Case 50/69R, [1969] ECR 449 at 458.
[61] See *Kergall* v. *Common Assembly*, Case 1/55, [1955] ECR 151 at 157 (the assessment of professional competence is normally a matter for the administration); *Mirossevich* v. *High Authority*, Case 10/55, [1956] ECR 333 at 342 (it is within the discretion of the competent authority to assess the aptitude of candidates for their duties but the Court may review the methods by which such assessment is made); and *Bourgaux* v. *Common Assembly*, Case 1/56, [1956] ECR 361 at 368 (the question as to which of five officials whose posts had been abolished were to be given three new posts was within the discretion of the Assembly, but it could be challenged on the ground of misuse of powers).
[62] Cases 35/62, 16/63, [1963] ECR 197.

temporary official of the High Authority who had been refused permanent status. The refusal of the Establishment Board to recommend that he be given a permanent appointment was made on the basis of a report on Leroy drawn up by his superior. In the course of the proceedings, Leroy sought to attack the assessment of his professional competence contained in the report. On this point, the Court ruled as follows:[63]

It must be stressed that the applicant's criticisms are not directed against the material accuracy of findings of fact which are capable of objective verification, nor against assessments which may be objectively reviewed, but against complex value-judgments the merits of which, by their very nature and subject, cannot be reviewed by the Court. For this reason this complaint must be rejected without any examination of the accuracy of the criticisms contained in the establishment report.

It will be noticed that Article 33 does not impose an outright ban on the Court's reviewing the determination; it merely gives the Commission a certain margin of error: a clear mistake can still result in annulment. Thus if the Commission makes its determination with the wrong objectives in mind, or takes into account irrelevant considerations, or fails to take into account relevant considerations, it will be guilty of a misuse of powers. The Court may review the determination to see whether this is established. Likewise, if the determination is clearly unwarranted on the basis of the primary facts, it would be quashed on the ground that the Commission had 'manifestly failed to observe' Community law.

When the Commission takes a decision of this kind it will be obliged to set out the findings of primary fact on which its evaluation is based. If it fails to do this, the measure will be quashed for lack of reasons. It will always be open to the parties to challenge these primary findings of fact: if it is shown that they are incorrect, the measure will be quashed, unless some alternative basis for it can be established. Secondly, if the Commission has misinterpreted a relevant legal concept – for example, 'economic difficulties' or 'serious disturbances' – the measure will also be annulled (unless, again, the error is immaterial). It is, of course, the Court which decides on the correct interpretation of these concepts; moreover, it also decides on the extent to which they should be legally defined. For example, the Court could say that the meaning of 'economic difficulties' is purely a matter of judgment; or it could lay down precise rules for determining

[63] Ibid. at 207.

whether or not such difficulties exist. The more the Court lays down such rules, the less margin of appreciation it leaves the Commission.

The EEC Treaty

The EEC Treaty contains no equivalent to the provision in Article 33 ECSC quoted above and at first the Court was prepared to consider the relevant economic data in some detail. One case in which this occurred was *Italy* v. *Commission*,[64] which concerned the problems caused by the increasing numbers of Italian refrigerators imported into France after 1961. The French invoked Article 226 EEC and asked the Commission for permission to take protective measures. The Commission then took a decision allowing France to impose a special duty on Italian imports. Under Article 226, the Commission was entitled to authorize protective measures only where 'difficulties arise which are serious and liable to persist in any sector of the economy'. The Italian Government brought proceedings for the annulment of the Commission's decision and in the course of these proceedings challenged the Commission's finding that this requirement had been satisfied. In dealing with this question, the Court gave quite detailed consideration to the relevant economic factors; however, it did so only in order to discover whether the Commission had misinterpreted the concept of serious difficulties.

In *Toepfer* v. *Commission*[65] the Court appeared to go further. The facts of this case have already been discussed;[66] here it will be sufficient to recall that the Commission had been slow to increase the levy on maize imports into Germany when the new French harvest came on to the market. Certain German grain importers were quick to take advantage of this and put in applications for import permits for fairly large quantities of maize (in all, approximately 125,000 metric tons, about 8–10 per cent of annual imports). The German intervention agency tried to block this by immediately asking the Commission for authorization to suspend all maize imports. This was granted.

Toepfer was one of the German importers who challenged the Commission decision granting the authorization. Under the relevant provision, the Commission could give authorization only if the imports in question threatened to cause 'serious disturbances' to the

[64] Case 13/63, [1963] ECR 165.
[65] Cases 106, 107/63, [1965] ECR 405.
[66] See pp. 351–2, above.

market. Toepfer claimed that this was not the case and that the decision was consequently invalid for an infringement of the Treaty or a rule of law relating to its application. In ruling on this, the Court analysed the economic data and concluded that the quantity of maize in question was not sufficient to cause serious disturbances even if it were sold at low prices. The decision was therefore annulled.

In this case the Court seems to have gone close to reviewing the Commission's evaluation of the situation, though it could be argued that the evidence showed that the Commission had misconceived the idea of 'serious disturbances'. In fact, though the Court did not decide the case on this basis, it could be maintained that there had really been a misuse of powers by the Commission: it had not actually been concerned with preventing a collapse of the market but rather with depriving the importers of the financial 'killing' they had expected. However, the evidence was probably insufficient to establish this.

The first express reference in an EEC case to the doctrine of restraint is probably a statement by Advocate General Dutheillet de Lamothe in 1971 in *Rewe-Zentrale*.[67] This case was concerned with Article 226 EEC and it is desirable to say a little more about this provision in order to appreciate the remarks of the Advocate General. Article 226 was applicable only during the transitional period before the common market was fully established and was intended as a safeguard provision to deal with emergencies. Where it was established to the satisfaction of the Commission that such a situation had arisen, it was for the Commission to decide what measures were necessary. In deciding this, the Commission was obliged by Article 226(3) to give priority to 'such measures as will least disturb the functioning of the common market'. Advocate General de Lamothe began his discussion by commenting that, though Article 226 does not confer a discretion on the Commission, it grants it a wide power of appraisal, which is, however, subject to review by the Court.[68] He then continued:[69]

I consider that it follows from this that, apart from a major infringement of a procedural requirement or a misuse of powers, decisions taken by the Commission in implementation of Article 226 are unlawful only in the following cases: first, where the Commission's appraisal is based on substantially incorrect facts.

[67] Case 37/70, [1971] ECR 23.
[68] See also *per* Advocate General Gand in *Germany* v. *Commission*, Case 50/69R, [1969] ECR 449 at 458.
[69] [1971] ECR at 42.

The illegality is thus established. Secondly: where, although the Commission's appraisal is based on substantially correct facts, it is nevertheless *clearly* wrong. Thirdly: where a measure derogating less substantially from the rules of the common market would *clearly* have sufficed to remedy the situation which called for the employment of Article 226.

The Court itself made no direct reference to the doctrine in *Rewe-Zentrale*. Two years later, however, such a reference was made in *Westzucker*.[70] This case concerned a Commission decision suspending payment of a grant. In reviewing the validity of this decision, the Court said that the Commission enjoyed a 'significant freedom of evaluation' in fixing the level of the grant. It then continued:[71] 'When examining the lawfulness of the exercise of such freedom, the courts cannot substitute their own evaluation of the matter for that of the competent authority but must restrict themselves to examining whether the evaluation of the competent authority contains a patent error or constitutes a misuse of power.' This formula has been repeated in later cases.[72] In *Racke*,[73] however, the Court expanded on it by adding to the two grounds of review already established – patent error and misuse of power – a third ground: that the competent authority had clearly exceeded the limits of its power of evaluation.[74] One can conclude from this that the position under the EEC Treaty is now the same as that under the ECSC Treaty: the absence of an express provision in Article 173 is irrelevant.

FAILURE TO ACT

Special considerations apply where the action is for a remedy for failure to act. First, it is necessary to draw a distinction between a negative decision (a decision refusing to act) and failure even to reply to a request for action. Since the former is technically an act, and the proceedings technically an action for annulment, the grounds of review will in theory be those set out in Articles 173 EEC, 33 ECSC and 146 Euratom. However, since the proceedings are in reality designed to require the defendant to act, certain grounds will be

[70] Case 57/72, [1973] ECR 321.
[71] Paragraph 14 of the judgment.
[72] See *Deuka*, Case 78/74, [1975] ECR 421 at paragraph 9 of the judgment.
[73] Case 136/77, [1978] ECR 1245 at paragraph 4 of its judgment.
[74] The English text of the judgment mistranslates the French word *appréciation* as 'discretion'; it should, of course, be 'evaluation': compare the French and English texts of Art. 33 ECSC.

inappropriate. For example, an applicant would hardly plead lack of competence: if the defendant has no competence in the matter, it would not be able to perform the act in question even if it wanted to; so any proceedings would be in vain. A negative decision may, on the other hand, be attacked on procedural grounds (including natural justice) or for defects of form (including lack of reasoning); however, if it is annulled on one of these grounds the applicant might find that he has won a hollow victory: the defendant may simply take the same decision over again after complying with the relevant requirements.

Where the defendant fails even to reply to the request for action, there can obviously be no question of pleading lack of form or failure to comply with the appropriate procedure: non-action, by its very nature, has no form, and no procedure applies to it. As in the case of a negative act, lack of competence is also inappropriate. This leaves only two possible grounds: infringement of the Treaty or any rule of law relating to its application and misuse of powers.

When will these grounds apply? Articles 175 EEC and 148 Euratom state, in identical terms:

Should the Council or the Commission, in infringement of this Treaty, fail to act, the Member States and the other institutions of the Community may bring an action before the Court of Justice to have the infringement established.

This suggests that infringement of the Treaty is the only ground that may be pleaded.

Article 35 ECSC, on the other hand, appears more extensive. It provides:

Whenever the High Authority is required by this Treaty, or by rules laid down for the implementation thereof, to take a decision or make a recommendation and fails to fulfil this obligation, it shall be for the States, the Council, undertakings or associations, as the case may be, to raise the matter with the High Authority.

The same shall apply if the High Authority, where empowered by this Treaty, or by rules laid down for the implementation thereof, to take a decision or make a recommendation, abstains from doing so and such abstention constitutes a misuse of powers.

This provision makes a clear distinction between two cases: a requirement to act and a power to act. Since this distinction is, in fact, basic to the whole question of a wrongful omission, these two situations will be discussed separately.

Requirement to Act

Here there must be an obligation on the defendant to adopt a legal act. The main problem concerns the source of the obligation. Obviously an obligation contained in one of the constitutive Treaties will be sufficient: the phrase 'this Treaty' in Articles 175 EEC, 35 ECSC and 148 Euratom covers each of those Treaties together with any amending or supplementing Treaties. Obligations contained in secondary legislation (Community acts) are expressly covered in the ECSC Treaty; there can be little doubt, however, that the phrase 'in infringement of this Treaty' in the other Treaties covers them as well, since an infringement of a measure passed under a Treaty is also an infringement of the Treaty itself: if a Treaty empowers a Community institution to enact legislation, it impliedly provides that it must be obeyed by other institutions – the essence of legislation is, after all, that it is legally binding. The lack of an express reference to subordinate legislation in the EEC and Euratom Treaties is, therefore, of no significance. The same is probably true of an international agreement binding on the Community.

Will an obligation derived from a general principle of law be sufficient? In so far as the ECSC is concerned, it could be argued that general principles of law are covered by the concept of rules laid down for the implementation of the Treaty: there is no doubt that they are covered by the equivalent phrase in Article 33 ECSC. Under the other Treaties the position is more doubtful; it is, however, possible that the European Court might hold that the obligation to respect the general principles of law is inherent in all the Treaties. Articles 164 EEC and 136 Euratom could perhaps be invoked for this purpose.

Power to Act

It might be thought that no remedy for failure to act could be obtained where there is merely a discretionary power to act. For various reasons, however, this is not the case. First of all, a power is almost always coupled with a duty, even if this duty is no more than to consider, with an open mind, whether the power should be exercised. Public authorities are not given powers to be exercised according to whim: a public authority must exercise its powers for the public good; and it must ascertain the public good according to the criteria laid down by law. Consequently, whenever granted a power, it must be willing to consider – in appropriate cases – whether to exercise it or not. This obligation applies to Community institutions as much as to any other public authorities. Therefore, if the power is granted by the Treaty or a provision of Community legislation, the institution will be guilty of an infringement of the Treaty if it fails to give the matter proper consideration.

Secondly, if the authority does apply its mind to the matter, but decides not to act, it will violate the law if it reaches its decision improperly. If it acts for the wrong motive, or takes improper considerations into account, or fails to take proper considerations into account, it will be guilty of a misuse of powers. Such misuse of powers will normally be the consequence of a mistake of law or of fact.

This situation is expressly covered in the second paragraph of Article 35 ECSC (quoted above). There is no equivalent provision in the other Treaties; but here, too, it is legitimate to consider the matter impliedly covered by the phrase 'infringement of this Treaty'. If the Treaty (or Community legislation passed under the Treaty) gives a discretionary power, there is an implied obligation to exercise that power according to the proper criteria. A misuse of that power is therefore an infringement of the empowering provision in the same way that a failure to consider whether it should be exercised is an infringement of it.[75]

CONCLUSIONS

It will be apparent from what has been said that the grounds of review are sufficiently flexible in Community law to give the European Court a wide measure of discretion. The way it exercises that discretion will depend to a large degree on judicial policy. For this reason, a purely legal analysis will not necessarily enable one to predict the outcome of a case.

FURTHER READING

Schermers, paragraphs 310–15 and 331–84.
Auby, 'The Abuse of Power in French Administrative Law', (1970) 18 Am. Jo. Comp. L. 549.
K. P. E. Lasok, 'Judicial Review of Issues of Fact in Competition Cases', [1983] European Competition Law Review 85.

[75] See Vandersanden and Barav, pp. 242–3.

Rigaux, 'Pouvoir d'appréciation de la Cour de Justice des Communautés Européennes à l'égard des faits', in *Miscellanea Ganshof van der Meersch* (1972), Vol. II, p. 365.

Waelbroeck, 'Examen de Jurisprudence 1955 à 1971', [1971] Revue Critique de Jurisprudence Belge 513 at 540–6.

16

ANNULMENT AND REVOCATION

ANNULMENT

Retroactivity

The basic principle of Community law is that invalid acts are voidable, but annulment is retroactive. This means, first, that invalid acts which are not annulled are valid to the extent that they cannot be challenged indirectly; and, secondly, that if they *are* annulled, they are deemed never to have existed. Moreover, since an annulment operates *erga omnes*, its effects apply equally to persons who were not parties to the annulment proceedings.[1] These principles are, however, subject to exceptions. The first is that in certain rare cases an act will be absolutely void – in Community terminology, 'non-existent' – in which case annulment is neither necessary nor, indeed, possible, since the act is treated for all purposes as if it had never been adopted.[2]

Secondly, the principle that annulments are retroactive does not apply in certain cases. This is because retroactivity could have unfortunate consequences, especially in the case of a normative measure (regulation), since persons might have relied on it in good faith; moreover, other measures may have been taken under it and, if the validity of these other measures depends on that of the annulled measure, they will be invalid too.

Since this could conflict with the principle of legal certainty, one aspect of which is non-retroactivity, there is a provision in the EEC

---

[1] It follows logically from these principles that once an act has been annulled, a subsequent action to annul it, even if brought by another party, should be declared inadmissible for lack of jurisdiction *ratione materiae*: there is no longer anything left to annul. However, the Court has not been consistent on this point: compare *Italy* v. *High Authority*, Case 2/54, [1954] ECR 37; *Assider* v. *High Authority*, Case 3/54, [1955] ECR 63; *ISA* v. *High Authority*, Case 4/54, [1955] ECR 91; *Italy* v. *High Authority*, Case 20/59, [1960] ECR 325 and *Netherlands* v. *High Authority*, Case 25/59, [1960] ECR 355. See, further, Liliane Plouvier, *Les Décisions de la Cour de Jusice des Communautés Européennes et leurs Effets Juridiques* (1975), pp. 96–100.

[2] See pp. 331–3, above.

Treaty[3] which enables the Court to avoid such a consequence in the case of a regulation. This is Article 174(2) EEC which, after providing that an act against which a successful challenge has been made will be declared void, states:

In the case of a regulation, however, the Court of Justice shall, if it considers this necessary, state which of the effects of the regulation which it has declared void shall be considered as definitive.

This rather obscure provision allows the Court to limit the retroactive effect of the annulment in appropriate cases.[4] It could apply where the Commission acted under the regulation, for example by conferring benefits on particular individuals: the Court could then declare that benefits already conferred would not be affected by the annulment of the regulation.

In the *Staff Salaries* case[5] the Court made a much more striking use of Article 174(2). This was a case brought by the Commission against the Council to establish whether the annual salary increase granted to Community officials was large enough. The case was discussed above,[6] and it will be remembered that the Council had decided, after discussions with the Commission and the Staff Associations, that future salary increases would be based on an agreed formula. However, when the next increase was made, it was – in the opinion of the Commission – below the minimum permissible under the formula. Now, the only way in which the Commission could bring the issue before the Court was to institute an action for the annulment of the Council regulation setting out the new salary scales. The action was successful: the Court ruled that the formula was binding on the Council and the new scales were indeed too low. However, the Court was then faced with a problem: if it annulled the regulation, the staff would not be entitled to *any* increases until such time as a new regulation was adopted. To avoid this, the Court resorted to Article 174(2) EEC and ruled that the annulment would be projected into the future so that the regulation would continue in force until such time as a new measure was promulgated; only then would it take effect.

---

[3] There is an identical provision in the Euratom Treaty (Art. 147(2)) but no equivalent in the ECSC. It is probable, however, that the Court will hold that it has a similar power under the general principles of law.

[4] See *per* Advocate General Dutheillet de Lamothe in *Compagnie d'Approvisionnement* v. *Commission* Cases 9, 11/71, [1972] ECR 391 at 411.

[5] *Commission* v. *Council*, Case 81/72, [1973] ECR 575.

[6] At pp. 144–5 and 415.

Compliance with the Judgment

Another provision of importance is Article 176 EEC. This states:[7]

The institution whose act has been declared void . . . shall be required to take the necessary steps to comply with the judgment of the Court of Justice.

There is a similar provision in Article 34 ECSC:

If the Court declares a decision or recommendation void, it shall refer the matter back to the High Authority. The High Authority shall take the necessary steps to comply with the judgment . . .

What are these steps likely to be? Besides the obvious fact that the Commission or Council will no longer operate or enforce the annulled act, positive action may have to be taken to undo the effects of past enforcement. In addition to the payment of damages (discussed below in Chapter 17) it may be necessary to withdraw subordinate acts adopted on the basis of the annulled measure. This is discussed further below.[8]

It should be noted that if the act was annulled on merely *formal* grounds – for example, for lack of natural justice or failure to give reasons – the enacting authority will not normally be precluded from re-enacting it according to the correct procedure. Subject to the principle of legal certainty, it could even be retroactive.[9] If, on the other hand, the measure was annulled for some reason of substance, such as lack of competence, infringement of the Treaty or misuse of powers, re-enactment will not normally be permissible. It may, however, be necessary to replace it with a new measure containing different provisions.

Partial Annulment

The Court is not bound always to annul the whole measure: where the invalidity affects only certain provisions, and these provisions are severable from the rest of the instrument, it may annul them only. A provision will not be severable if the rest of the instrument will not make sense without it; nor will it be severable if the purpose of the instrument will be prejudiced to such an extent that the enacting institution would probably not have adopted it at all if it had known that the provision in question was illegal.

---

[7] Art. 149 Euratom contains an identical provision.
[8] See pp. 439–43.
[9] *Amylum* v. *Council*, Case 108/81, [1982] ECR 3107; *Roquette* v. *Council*, Case 110/81, [1982] ECR 3159; *Tunnel Refineries* v. *Council*, Case 114/81, [1982] ECR 3189.

Transocean Marine Paint Association v. *Commission*[10] is a good example of the problems which can arise where the application is for the annulment of only part of a decision. The applicants in this case had applied to the Commission for exemption from the provisions of Article 85 EEC and had been granted it subject to certain conditions, one of which was that the Commission had to be informed of any financial links between the members of the association and other firms. The association maintained that this condition was unjustifiable and brought proceedings to have it annulled. The Court decided that it should be annulled because the Commission had not given the association advance warning that they had the condition in mind. The association were thus precluded from putting their case to the Commission before the decision was made. The Court held that this infringed the rules of natural justice.

The difficulty then confronting the Court was that if they merely annulled the condition, the association might be in too favourable a position: even they were prepared to concede that the Commission were entitled to be given *some* information. The solution put forward by Advocate General Warner was to interpret Article 176 EEC along the same lines as Article 34 ECSC. It will be remembered that the latter provision expressly allows the Court to refer the matter back to the enacting authority. He therefore proposed that the condition should be annulled and referred back to the Commission, which could then reconsider the matter and possibly replace it with a less onerous requirement. This suggestion was followed by the Court.

Rejection of Application

Finally, it should be mentioned that the *rejection* of an application to annul does not definitively establish the validity of the measure; in particular, it does not preclude a new application by another party based on different grounds of invalidity.[11]

[10] Case 17/74, [1974] ECR 1063; discussed at pp. 147–8, above.

[11] In *Assider* v. *High Authority*, Case 3/54, [1955] ECR 63 the application was directed against various measures, all of which had been the subject of a previous application in which some had been annulled and others not. The position regarding the measures already annulled was considered above. As regards the others, the Court merely referred to the previous judgment and stated that, as no new grounds of invalidity had been put forward, the application would be dismissed. It is not entirely clear whether the previous judgment operated as *res judicata*, in the sense that it precluded a reconsideration of the arguments previously advanced, or whether it would be open to the applicant in the new proceedings to attempt to make the Court change its mind, perhaps by bringing new evidence. The fact that the application was held *admissible*, suggests that the latter alternative may be correct. There is, however, no doubt that a fresh application may be made on *different* grounds.

INDIRECT CHALLENGE

In theory, a declaration of invalidity resulting from an indirect challenge is applicable only to the case in question; in practice, however, its effects are much wider than this.[12] To this extent, it has been assimilated to an annulment. In addition, the Court has applied Articles 174 and 176 by analogy to declarations of invalidity under Article 177, thus narrowing the differences between the two remedies even more.

In the *Quellmehl and Gritz* cases,[13] the Council had given a subsidy both to starch producers and to the producers of two competing products, quellmehl and gritz. It subsequently passed a regulation withdrawing the subsidy from quellmehl and gritz, but not from starch. The quellmehl and gritz producers brought proceedings in the national courts and a reference was made to the European Court, which held that it was contrary to the principle of equality to subsidize the one and not the other. It did not, however, hold the regulation invalid (which would have allowed the quellmehl and gritz producers to succeed in their claim for payment of the subsidies). Instead, the Court ruled that the Council had to pass a new regulation either restoring the subsidy to the quellmehl and gritz producers or withdrawing it from the starch producers. It subsequently justified this ruling on the basis of Article 176.[14]

In the *Maize* cases,[15] the Commission had passed a regulation applying a system for calculating monetary compensatory amounts for maize products. In proceedings resulting from a reference under Article 177 EEC, the European Court held the regulation invalid. However, it applied the second paragraph of Article 174 by analogy to enable it to hold that its ruling would not affect the payment of m.c.a.'s on transactions prior to its judgment. In effect, this meant that the regulation was annulled prospectively but not retrospectively.[16]

---

[12] See p. 407, above.

[13] *Ruckdeschel,* Cases 117/76, 16/77, [1977] ECR 1753; *Moulins de Pont-à-Mousson,* Cases 124/76, 20/77, [1977] ECR 1795.

[14] See the *Maize* cases, note 15, below.

[15] *Providence Agricole* v. *ONIC,* Case 4/79, [1980] ECR 2823 (paragraphs 42–46 of the judgment); *Maïseries de Beauce* v. *ONIC,* Case 109/79, [1980] ECR 2883 (paragraphs 42–46 of the judgment); *Roquette* v. *French Customs,* Case 145/79, [1980] ECR 2917 (paragraphs 50–55 of the judgment).

[16] For the reaction to this in the French courts, see pp. 233–5, above.

REVOCATION

The power of a Community institution to revoke or withdraw an act adopted by it is subject to limitations resulting from the principle of legal certainty.[17] The operation of this principle appears to depend on whether the act is individual (a decision) or general (a regulation). Since all the Court's judgments have been concerned with the former, the discussion that follows will be limited to these.

Lawful Acts

In considering the limitations required by the principle of legal certainty, it is necessary to distinguish between lawful (valid) acts and unlawful ones. A lawful individual act conferring rights on private persons cannot be revoked retroactively. Whether it can be revoked prospectively depends on its terms: if it purports to give a right for a fixed period of time – for example, an appointment to a post until retirement, or a licence for a stated period – it cannot, if valid, be revoked at all.[18] If, on the other hand, it was never intended to be irrevocable – for example, a temporary appointment – it may be revoked according to its terms (complying with any applicable period of notice).

Algera v. *Common Assembly*[19] provides an example of this principle: Miss Algera had been a temporary official with the Common Assembly (European Parliament). Then the Assembly addressed a decision to her admitting her to the benefits of the statute of service – which meant that she was given a permanent appointment. Later the Assembly purported to revoke this decision; but the Court held that it had no power to do this: the decision was an individual one conferring a right; since it was valid, it could not be revoked without the beneficiary's consent.

Unlawful Acts

The question of revocation cannot arise if the act has been annulled, or if it falls within the rare class of non-existent (absolutely void) acts.[20] If neither of these is the case, and if the time-limit for an

[17] See pp. 139–45, above.
[18] See *per* Advocate General Lagrange in the *Hoogovens* case (below) [1962] ECR at 282.
[19] Cases 7/56, 3–7/57, [1957] ECR 39.
[20] See pp. 331–3, below.

annulment action has expired, the act will produce the same affects as a valid act (except to the extent that it can be challenged indirectly). It then becomes important to know whether it may be withdrawn.

An unlawful individual act may always be revoked prospectively, even if it purported to be irrevocable for a given period. In the *Algera* case, for example, the Assembly's decision also conferred a certain grade on Miss Algera. This provision of the decision was, however, unlawful and the Court held that it could be effectively revoked.[21]

The circumstances in which an unlawful individual act may be revoked retrospectively are complex. The leading cases are *SNUPAT* v. *High Authority*[22] and *Hoogovens* v. *High Authority*.[23] Both these cases concerned the ECSC scrap iron equalization scheme, which was the subject of several cases already discussed.[24] It will be remembered that the idea was to keep down the price of ferrous scrap by means of a subsidy on imported scrap, this subsidy to be paid for by a levy on all users of ferrous scrap, both imported and non-imported. The levy, however, only applied to scrap *bought* by a firm, not to scrap arising from its own resources. This distinction was the subject of much dispute, especially as regards the situation where the scrap came from another firm closely linked to the user.

SNUPAT was a steel producer which had close links with the Renault car firm and it used a great deal of scrap provided by the latter. It maintained that it should be exempt from the levy on this, but the High Authority ruled that this scrap could not be regarded as arising from its own resources. This ruling was confirmed by the Court.[25] Having failed in this move, SNUPAT then raised objections to the fact that an exemption had been given to two other steel producers – the Dutch firm, Hoogovens, and the Italian firm, Breda Siderurgica: it argued that its own contributions were that much greater by reason of the exemptions granted to these other firms.

The exemptions given to these two firms had been granted by individual decisions taken by the High Authority and addressed to the firms in question. SNUPAT therefore requested the High Authority to revoke them with retroactive effect. The High Authority did not reply to this request; and SNUPAT then brought proceed-

[21] See also *Simon* v. *Court of Justice*, Case 15/60, [1961] ECR 115; *Elz* v. *Commission*, Case 56/75, [1976] ECR 1097; and *Herpels* v. *Commission*, Case 54/77, [1978] ECR 585 (at paragraph 38 of the judgment).
[22] Cases 42, 49/59, [1961] ECR 53.
[23] Case 14/61, [1962] ECR 253.
[24] See above, pp. 113–15.
[25] *SNUPAT* v. *High Authority*, Cases 32, 33/58, [1959] ECR 127.

ings under Article 35 ECSC for the annulment of the implied decision of the High Authority rejecting this request.

The Court ruled that the exemptions were indeed unlawful. The next question was whether they should be revoked retrospectively: there was little point in revoking them prospectively since the whole equalization scheme had by then been wound up. The two firms argued that retroactive revocation would conflict with the principle of legal certainty; but the Court held that this principle does not have absolute validity where the measure in question is invalid: it must be balanced against the principle of legality.

The Court stated that retroactive revocation will be proper where the original decision was taken on the basis of incorrect or incomplete information supplied by the person concerned or where the public interest in legality otherwise outweighs the private interest in legal certainty. Applied to the facts of the case, the latter test involved balancing the interests of the two firms, which had relied in good faith on the validity of the exemptions in the conduct of their business, against the Community interest in the proper functioning of the equalization scheme, which would have been prejudiced if some scrap users had been able to avoid paying their proper contributions. The Court held that the weighing-up of these considerations, as well as the determination of the relevant questions of fact, lay in the first instance within the jurisdiction of the High Authority. It therefore annulled the implied decision refusing to revoke the decisions and remitted the matter to the High Authority for it to decide whether the revocation should be retroactive.

After investigating the facts and giving careful consideration to the conflicting policy issues, the High Authority decided on retroactive revocation of the decisions.[26] It did this by means of decisions addressed to the firms concerned. Hoogovens objected and brought proceedings to annul the decision addressed to it.

The first point made by Hoogovens was that the High Authority had not found that any misleading or incomplete information had been supplied by Hoogovens and it could not, therefore, be regarded as responsible for the situation. This, however, merely removed one possible ground on which it could have been decided to make the revocation retroactive: it did not rule it out altogether.

A more substantial point concerned the time factor. The decision granting the exemption had been taken on 18 December 1957; the

---

[26] The firms concerned were given the right to put their views to the High Authority before it reached its decision.

decision revoking it was made on 14 June 1961: Hoogovens argued that this gap of three and a half years was unreasonably long. In the course of his opinion, Advocate General Lagrange considered the significance of the time factor in national law. He pointed out that French law draws a distinction between decisions which create legal rights – for example, an appointment to a post in the public service – and decisions which merely *declare* the rights which the person already had. Constitutive decisions, even if unlawful, can be annulled only during the period within which an annulment action can be brought; the only exception is where the decision was the result of fraud on the part of the addressee. Invalid declaratory decisions, on the other hand, may be revoked at any time, though in some cases the person concerned may be entitled to sue the administration for damages if it was guilty of maladministration. The Advocate General proposed that the French rule should be adopted in the case of constitutive decisions but in the case of declaratory decisions the Court should apply the principle of weighing up the conflicting interests.

The Court followed this in part only. It held that delay is never an absolute bar to retroactivity but is only one factor to be taken into consideration. In the case of a constitutive decision, considerable weight will be attached to it; where the decision is merely declaratory it will be of less significance. In the case at hand, the Court found that the decision was merely declaratory: the High Authority had no power to give special privileges to any firm; it had to apply the law as it was.[27] Consequently, the delay did not prevent retroactive revocation, especially as Hoogovens must have known for a long time that the exemptions were disputed. The High Authority could not, moreover, be blamed for having originally thought that Hoogovens was entitled to an exemption, since the correct interpretation of the relevant provision 'proved to be very debatable'. The Court therefore upheld the High Authority's decision that the revocation should be retrospective.

[27] Though it purports merely to state the existing situation, it should not be thought that a declaratory decision cannot affect the legal position of those concerned: if it is wrong it will (unintentionally) grant rights to those concerned; if this were not the case it would be unnecessary to revoke it. This is because an invalid legal act, unless it is non-existent, is effective until annulled or revoked (except in so far as it may be challenged indirectly). This point is further illustrated by the fact that in the earlier case of *SNUPAT* v. *High Authority*, Cases 32, 33/58, above, where the Court rejected SNUPAT's claim to an exemption, it held that a decision regarding the levy is a reviewable act. It will be remembered from Chapter 11 that a measure cannot constitute a reviewable act unless it affects the legal position of those concerned.

These principles were developed further in *Lemmerz-Werke* v. *High Authority*.[28] In this case the Court indicated that an important question to ask in weighing up the conflicting interests is whether it was justifiable for the person concerned to think that the decision was final and definitive. In answering this question, two considerations should be borne in mind: did the person concerned have reason to suspect that the decision might be invalid; and had an unreasonably long period of time elapsed between the original decision and the revocation? The Court also stated that, even if the person concerned was not justified in thinking that the decision had finally settled the matter, the enacting authority might still be precluded from revoking it retroactively if they had been guilty of 'a breach of their duty to act with care and accuracy' – in other words, maladministration.[29]

In *Consorzio Cooperative d'Abruzzo* v. *Commission*,[30] unreasonable delay *was* held to bar revocation. This concerned a Commission decision giving a grant to an organization in Italy. In the original draft of the decision, the amount of the grant was approximately four billion lire. Then the Commission decided to reduce it to approximately three billion, and it informed the recipient. Owing to unexplained circumstances, however, the first draft was enacted by mistake. Some two and a half years later, the Commission withdrew the decision and replaced it with another giving the lesser sum. The recipient brought proceedings to annul the latter decision. The Court held that an unlawful decision may be revoked only if the revocation occurs within a reasonable time and the author of the decision has sufficient regard to how far the addressee may have been led to rely on the lawfulness of the measure.[31] On the facts of the case, the recipient of the grant might reasonably have relied on the validity of the decision since it had no way of knowing what had happened: it probably thought that the Commission had decided, after all, to give it the larger sum. Moreover, the delay in withdrawing it was excessive, since the Commission could have discovered its mistake within a few days. The second decision was therefore annulled.

[28] Case 111/63, [1965] ECR 677.
[29] At p. 692.
[30] Case 15/85, 26 February 1987, *The Times*, March 23, 1987.
[31] This statement of the law was first put forward in *Alpha Steel* v. *Commission*, Case 14/81, [1982] ECR 749 (paragraph 10 of the judgment). In this case, the Commission addressed a decision to the applicant, imposing certain restrictions on it. The applicant brought proceedings to annul the decision. While these were pending, the Commission withdrew the decision and replaced it with one which was even more restrictive. The Court held that the first decision could be revoked: since the applicant had challenged it, the applicant could not argue that it had been led to rely on the lawfulness of the decision.

FURTHER READING

Schermers, paragraphs 316–18.

Toth, II, pp. 92–6.

Bebr, 'Preliminary Rulings of the Court of Justice: Their Authority and Temporal Effect', (1981) 18 C.M.L. Rev. 475.

Brown, 'Agrimonetary Byzantinism and Prospective Overruling', (1981) 18 C.M.L. Rev. 509.

Harding, 'The Impact of Article 177 of the EEC Treaty on the Review of Community Action,' (1981) 1 YEL 93.

Toth, 'The Authority of Judgments of the European Court of Justice: Binding Force and Legal Effects', (1984) 4 YEL 1.

Waelbroeck, 'May the Court Limit the Retrospective Operation of its Judgments?', (1981) 1 YEL 115.

17

COMMUNITY OBLIGATIONS

This chapter is concerned with the liability of the Community in contract, quasi-contract (restitution) and tort.

CONTRACT

The two main questions regarding contracts entered into by the Community are the jurisdiction of the European Court and the law to be applied.

Jurisdiction of the European Court

The jurisdiction of the European Court with regard to Community contracts is laid down by Article 181 EEC:[1]

The Court of Justice shall have jurisdiction to give judgment pursuant to any arbitration clause contained in a contract concluded by or on behalf of the Community, whether that contract be governed by public or private law.

It will be seen that this provision uses the phrase 'arbitration clause', thus suggesting that the European Court has jurisdiction only as an arbitrator. The significance of this is that in many countries the activities of arbitrators are subject to the supervision of the courts. There cannot, of course, be any question of this with regard to the European Court; so it would have been better if the Treaty had not used the terminology of arbitration. A preferable phrase would have been 'jurisdiction clause', which is used in private international law to describe a provision in a contract conferring jurisdiction on the courts of a particular country.

It should also be noted that the provision does not state that the 'arbitration clause' must refer only to disputes arising out of the contract in which it is contained. A common clause would be of this type (for example, 'all disputes arising out of this contract shall be

---

[1] Art. 153 Euratom contains an identical provision; everything in the text regarding the EEC applies equally to Euratom. Art. 42 ECSC is almost identical.

445

heard by the Court of Justice of the European Communities') but it may also be possible for the parties to enter into a contract conferring jurisdiction on the European Court to hear disputes arising out of *another* contract.

If the European Court does not have jurisdiction by virtue of such a clause, the national courts will be entitled to hear the case. This follows from Articles 183 EEC, 155 Euratom and 40(3) ECSC[2]

If a case was brought before the European Court and it was asserted by the applicant that the Court had jurisdiction on the basis of an 'arbitration clause', it might be necessary for the Court to consider whether the clause in question was valid. There is no indication in the Treaty as to the form which the clause should take, though the requirement in Article 38(6) of the Rules of Procedure that a copy of the clause must be submitted with the application implies that it should be in writing. It is suggested that the best solution would be for the Court to apply the rules laid down in Article 17(1) of the Convention on Jurisdiction and the Enforcement of Judgments in Civil and Commercial Matters,[3] which was concluded by the Member States pursuant to Article 220 EEC.[4] This provides that an agreement conferring jurisdiction must be 'either in writing or evidenced in writing or, in international trade or commerce, in a form which accords with practices in that trade or commerce of which the parties are or ought to have been aware'. These rules are binding only on national courts but there is no reason why the European Court should not apply them by analogy. This is especially appropriate since the European Court has jurisdiction to interpret the Convention on a reference from a national court for a preliminary ruling.

Choice of Law

What law will be applied to a Community contract? Article 215(1) EEC and Article 188(1) Euratom purport to deal with this problem but do so in an unsatisfactory way. They read:

The contractual liability of the Community shall be governed by the law applicable to the contract in question.

---

[2] These provisions state that national courts are entitled to hear actions against the Community except where the European Court has jurisdiction.

[3] For both the original and amended texts, see OJ 1978, L 304.

[4] It is one of the subsidiary conventions: see pp. 92–3, above.

In so far as it is more than a mere tautology, this means only that the liability of the Community is governed by the same law as governs the contract as a whole. This is, of course, what one would have assumed to be the case anyway. The provision does, however, have some value – though of a purely negative kind – in that it makes clear that the Community claims no special privileges or immunities.[5] There is no equivalent provision in the ECSC Treaty but there is no reason to doubt that the position is the same under it.

An inference may, perhaps, be drawn from what Article 215(1) does *not* say: it does not expressly empower the European Court to build up a Community law of contract. This omission is noteworthy in that the second paragraph of Article 215, which deals with non-contractual liability, envisages the creation of a Community law of tort. It states that the non-contractual liability of the Community is to be governed by 'the general principles common to the laws of the Member States'. The contrast between these two paragraphs of Article 215 might, therefore, suggest that contractual liability is not governed by Community law.

If the applicable law is national law, the choice of the appropriate system must be determined by the rules of private international law. If a national court has jurisdiction it will apply the same rules as in an ordinary case. But what should the European Court do? There are no Community rules of conflict of laws; so the European Court will have to create such a system by synthesizing the national systems. This can best be done by applying the rules in the Convention on the Law Applicable to Contractual Obligations (1980), even though, at the time of writing, it is not in force.[6]

In practice the Commission always insists on the insertion of a choice-of-law clause in its contracts. The validity and effect of such a clause has been disputed in only one case – on the ground that the contract was more closely connected with the law of another country and contained express references to the law of that country – but the Court upheld it, saying that an express choice of law prevails over all other considerations.[7]

When the European Court applies the law of a Member State, it

[5] See P. J. Verdam, 'De privaatrechtelijke contractuele aansprakelijkheid der EEG', in *Volkenrechtelijke opstellen aan Prof Dr Gesina H. J. van der Molen* (International Law Essays in Honour of Gesina H. J. van der Molen) p. 169 at 174–5.

[6] OJ 1980, C 266.

[7] *Commission* v. *CO.DE.MI*, Case 318/81, [1985] ÉCR 3693 (see paragraph 21 of the judgment). This is in accordance with the Contractual Obligations Convention, though the Court made no reference to the Convention.

decides questions of law on the basis of its own knowledge, after hearing argument, even if no judge from the country in question is sitting on the case.[8] It does not require expert evidence, as would an English court if it had to apply foreign law.[9]

Different principles apply in the case of contracts of employment of Community officials.[10] In two early cases the European Court classified these as public law contracts. In the first of these cases, *Kergall* v. *Common Assembly*,[11] the applicant was a senior administrative official working for the Common Assembly (European Parliament). The Court held that his contract of employment was a public law contract since he was required to perform 'public law functions' and his contract referred to the internal regulations of the Common Assembly. In *Von Lachmüller* v. *Commission*[12] the applicants worked in the translation service of the Commission. After the Court had established that the Commission was a public authority (public law corporation), it continued:[13]

Moreover, those contracts were concluded to enable the Language Service of the Commission to function properly. The work of that service, which is responsible for ensuring that the contents of the acts of the Commission shall be identical in the four official languages of the Community, constitutes an important element in the procedure which has as its purpose the formulation in each language of those acts; thus that service is of the same public nature as the Commission itself.

Therefore the contracts at issue come under public law and are subject to the general rules of administrative law.

It appears from these extracts that it does not necessarily follow that all contracts of employment with Community institutions will automatically be classified as public law contracts. In both these judgments the Court went to some pains to establish that the work performed by the applicants was of a governmental nature. It might be legitimate to conclude that where this is not the case the contract will be governed by private law.[14]

The consequence in these cases of the Court's characterization of

---

[8] See, for example, *Commission* v. *CO.DE.MI* (above) and *Pellegrini* v. *Commission*, Case 23/76, [1976] ECR 1807 (decided under Art. 188(1) Euratom.)

[9] On possible limits to the application of national law, see *Commission* v. *Tordeur*, Case 232/84, [1985] ECR 3223.

[10] Such cases are rare because Community officials do not normally hold office on a contractual basis.

[11] Case 1/55, [1955] ECR 151.

[12] Cases 43, 45, 48/59, [1960] ECR 463.

[13] At p. 473.

[14] Cf. *Porta* v. *Commission*, Case 109/81, [1982] ECR 2469.

the contract as public was that it was governed by administrative law. There was no suggestion in either case that national administrative law was to be applied; so one must conclude that where public law is applicable, it will be *Community* public law. This was not expressly stated but, since the Court decided the cases on the basis of legal rules that were not stated to be those of any national system, one can reach no other conclusion. If this is correct, it means that the classification of a contract as public not only affects the kind of law applicable (public rather than private) but also the legal system – Community, rather than national, law.

QUASI-CONTRACT

Most Western legal systems recognize a form of liability based on the principle of unjust enrichment. According to this principle, if the plaintiff can show that the defendant was unjustly enriched at his expense, the defendant is liable to make restitution to the extent that he has been enriched. This principle of liability is distinct from both contract and tort. Some English authorities have stated that its basis is a fictitious promise to make restitution (hence the term 'quasi-contract'); but since the promise *is* fictitious, it cannot realistically be regarded as a form of contractual liability. It differs from tortious liability in two respects. First of all, the basis of a tort is usually thought to be a wrongful act – though liability without fault might seem an exception to this – and the liability to make restitution is independent of any wrongful act. Secondly, in tort the measure of liability is, as a basic rule, the extent of the loss suffered by the plaintiff; in unjust enrichment it is the extent to which the defendant was enriched.

Does this form of liability apply to the Community? This is obviously a matter of some practical importance, since a common situation in which liability might arise is where money is paid on the mistaken assumption that it is owed. It could easily happen that a person might pay a sum of money to a Community institution; thinking that he was legally obliged to pay it, and it might turn out later that there was no such obligation. Is the Community obliged to return it?

Substantive Law

There is no provision in the Treaties expressly dealing with quasi-contract, but since this species of liability is generally recognized in the law of the Member States it would be reasonable to expect that it would be accepted as one of the general principles of law applied by the European Court. This is, in fact, the case and there have been a number of decisions in which the European Court has given effect to the doctrine. Most of these are staff cases and a typical example is *Wollast* v. *EEC*,[15] in which a Community employee was illegally dismissed from her job. The Court annulled her dismissal with the result that she was entitled to receive pay for the period since the dismissal. She had not, however, done any work during this period and she had thus been able to avoid certain expenses that she would otherwise have incurred; for example, she had not had to employ domestic help for her three young children. The Court held that she had been unjustifiably enriched at the expense of the Community and ordered that a deduction of 15 per cent. be made from her salary for the period in question.

A different situation arose in *Mannesmann* v. *High Authority*,[16] where a scrap-iron subsidy had been wrongly paid and the High Authority tried to recover it by taking a decision requiring Mannesmann, the user of the scrap, to refund it. Mannesmann brought proceedings under Article 33 ECSC to quash the decision. The European Court accepted that the High Authority had the power to recover the money on the basis of quasi-contract; nevertheless, it quashed the decision because the subsidy had been paid not to Mannesmann, but to his supplier.

Jurisdiction

The next problem to consider is that of jurisdiction. The cases in which the doctrine has been applied so far have all been ones in which the Court has had jurisdiction on some ground not specifically related to quasi-contract: in the staff cases it was Article 179 EEC which gives the Court jurisdiction in any dispute between the

[15] Case 18/63, [1964] ECR 85. See also *Degreef* v. *Commission*, Case 80/63, [1964] ECR 391 and *Willame* v. *Commission*, Case 110/63, [1965] ECR 649. In *Danvin* v. *Commission*, Case 26/67, [1968] ECR 315, a Community servant claimed that the Community had been unjustly enriched at his expense but was unable to establish that he had suffered any loss.
[16] Cases 4–13/59, [1960] ECR 113.

Community and its servants (within the limits and under the conditions laid down in the Staff Regulations and the Conditions of Employment); in *Mannesmann* the issue arose incidentally in the course of review proceedings. The case where a private citizen has a claim against the Community in quasi-contract is not covered by either of these provisions and the question arises whether there is any general ground of jurisdiction applicable to actions in quasi-contract against the Community.

The only possibility under the EEC Treaty is Article 178. This gives jurisdiction in disputes relating to 'compensation for damage' under Article 215(2). The latter provision talks of non-contractual liability, rather than tortious liability, and might therefore be thought to cover quasi-contract as well as tort. However, Article 178 itself is concerned only with compensation for damage and Article 215(2) requires the Community to 'make good any damage caused' by its institutions. This suggests that the basis of the liability covered by these provisions is the loss suffered by the plaintiff, rather than the enrichment of the defendant. The equivalent provision under the ECSC Treaty is Article 40. This provides even less scope for quasi-contract. Not only does it talk about 'pecuniary reparation . . . to make good any injury' caused by the Community, but it also makes liability dependent on a wrongful act or omission.

There is one possible way round these difficulties. One could argue as follows: it is true that the duty to make restitution is not based on fault and that the measure of liability is not the extent of the plaintiff's loss but the extent of the defendant's enrichment; but the failure of the defendant to make voluntary restitution once the true situation becomes known could be regarded as a fault and the loss suffered by the plaintiff as a result would be the amount which the defendant should have paid, i.e. the amount by which he was enriched.

It must be admitted that this argument is a strained one and it seems probable that the authors of the Treaty did not have quasi-contract in mind when they drafted these provisions.[17] It is nevertheless possible that the European Court may decide, for policy reasons, that it would be desirable for it to have jurisdiction to hear actions in quasi-contract against the Community and if this were so they might consider that a wide interpretation of these provisions was the best way of achieving this.

[17] It is interesting to note that it was stated by counsel for the Commission in argument in *Roquette* v. *Commission*, Case 26/74, [1976] ECR 677 at 681, that quasi-contract was 'foreign to the action for compensation for damage under Art. 215 of the EEC Treaty'.

If the non-contractual liability provisions are eventually held not to cover quasi-contractual obligations, there is another way in which an applicant might be able to bring his case before the European Court. This is by means of an indirect route: he would make a request to the Community institution in question to repay the money, and if it refused he would bring proceedings under Article 173 EEC or Article 33 ECSC to ask the Court to quash the decision rejecting his request. The ground of invalidity put forward would be the infringement of a rule of law relating to the application of the Treaty, which covers the infringement of general principles of law,[18] including the principle of unjust enrichment. If the Community institution failed to make a decision in response to the request for a refund, proceedings for a remedy for failure to act could be brought. Either way the applicant could require the Court to consider whether his claim was well-founded.[19] If he succeeded, the defendant institution would be 'required to take the necessary measures to comply with the judgment'.[20] This would include the payment of the sum.

The only objection that could be raised against this procedure is that a decision by a Community institution granting, or refusing to grant, repayment of a sum of money by which the Community was unjustly enriched might not be regarded as a reviewable act. The concept of a reviewable act was considered above,[21] and it will be remembered that the basic rule is that an act is not reviewable unless it has legal effects; in other words, it must cause some change in the legal rights and duties (using these terms in a wide sense) of the applicant. It could be argued that, in the situation under consideration, a decision by the Community institution would not have legal effects since, if the applicant's claim were justified, he would be legally entitled to be paid anyway: a negative decision could not take away his right and a positive decision could not give him a greater right.

It is doubtful whether this argument is justified. From a practical point of view a decision in the applicant's favour would be of the greatest value to him; even from a theoretical viewpoint it is not certain that his legal position would be unaltered, since a positive decision could be regarded as creating a new legal right and this

[18] See pp. 414–15, above.
[19] This procedure was used by the applicant in *Haegeman* v. *Commission*, Case 96/71, [1972] ECR 1005, but the claim was held inadmissible on other grounds. For a discussion of the case, see pp. 486–7, below.
[20] Art. 176 EEC; see also Art. 34 ECSC.
[21] See Chapter 11.

could have consequences as regards the remedies open to him, including the time-limit for bringing proceedings. Moreover, the European Court has shown itself willing in the past to give more weight to practical considerations than theory in deciding what constitutes a reviewable act.

In conclusion, it should be mentioned that if it finally turns out that the European Court has no jurisdiction to hear quasi-contractual claims, the way would then be open for proceedings against the Community in the national courts.[22]

TORT

Community tort liability is dealt with in Articles 178 and 215(2) EEC and Article 40(1) and (2) ECSC.[23] Article 178 EEC merely provides that the European Court will have jurisdiction to decide disputes relating to compensation for damage as provided for in Article 215(2). The latter provides as follows:

> In the case of non-contractual liability, the Community shall, in accordance with the general principles common to the laws of the Member States, make good any damage caused by its institutions or by its servants in the performance of their duties.

The provisions of Article 40(1) and (2) ECSC are slightly different:[24]

> Without prejudice to the first paragraph of Article 34, the Court shall have jurisdiction to order pecuniary reparation from the Community, on application by the injured party, to make good any injury caused in carrying out this Treaty by a wrongful act or omission on the part of the Community in the performance of its functions.
>
> The Court shall also have jurisdiction to order the Community to make good any injury caused by a personal wrong by a servant of the Community in the performance of his duties. The personal liability of its servants towards the Community shall be governed by the provisions laid down in their Staff Regulations or the Conditions of Employment applicable to them.

The differences between the EEC and ECSC Treaties are set out in the Table below. This shows that certain phrases are found in one and not in the other and also that there are differences between

---

[22] See Arts 183 EEC, 155 Euratom and 40(3) ECSC.

[23] Arts 151 and 188(2) Euratom are identical to Arts 178 and 215(2) EEC: everything in the text regarding the EEC applies equally to Euratom.

[24] Art. 40(2) is as substituted by the Merger Treaty, Art. 26. The reference, in Art. 40(1), to Art. 34 is discussed at pp. 468–9, below.

equivalent phrases. Most of these differences are without significance; the one exception concerns the question of fault.

Comparison of EEC and ECSC Treaties

	EEC	ECSC
1.	compensation for damage (Article 178)	pecuniary reparation from the Community (Article 40(1))
2.	in accordance with the general principles common to the laws of the Member States (Article 215(2))	
3.		on application by the injured party (Article 40(1))
4.	the Community . . . shall make good any damage (Article 215(2))	make good any injury (Article 40(1))
5.	caused by its institutions (Article 215(2))	caused in carrying out this Treaty by *a wrongful act or omission* on the part of the Community *in the performance of its functions* (Article 40(1)) *Note: the words italicized are the translation of the French phrase, 'une faute de service'.*
6.	or [caused] by its servants in the performance of their duties (Article 215(2))	caused by a personal wrong by a servant of the Community in the performance of his duties (Article 40(2))

Apart from this, both provisions contain the same elements. First, there must be an act or omission on the part of the Community; secondly, the applicant must have suffered damage; and thirdly, the damage must have been caused by the act or omission. The ECSC Treaty includes a fourth element: fault. Thus, in the case of an act by the Community, it must be established that the Community was guilty of a *faute de service* (translated as 'a wrongful act or omission . . . in the performance of its functions'). In the case of an act by a Community servant, it must be shown that he had committed a *faute personnelle* ('personal wrong'). The EEC Treaty, on the other hand, makes no mention of fault. It does, however, provide that Community liability will arise in accordance with the general principles common to the laws of the Member States. These principles do, of course, depend to a large extent on fault; but liability without fault is not unknown.

Before discussing these elements in detail, it is worth considering some preliminary matters. First of all, it should be noted that there is no limitation on the persons who may sue. The restrictive provisions of judicial review are absent here. This applies under the ECSC Treaty just as much as under the EEC Treaty. It will be remembered that under Article 33 ECSC, together with Articles 48 and 80, the only private applicants permitted to bring applications for review are producers of coal and steel and their associations; this restriction does not, however, apply in the case of tort actions.[25] Thus, a *distributor* of coal or steel, while unable to bring review actions under Article 33 ECSC, can sue under Article 40 ECSC. Nor does the short time-limit within which review proceedings must be brought apply here. The period of limitation in tort actions is five years.[26]

The second question concerns the person against whom the action should be brought. Article 215(2) EEC says that 'the Community' must make good the damage and Article 40 ECSC also states that liability rests on the Community. However, the Community can act

---

[25] *Vloeberghs* v. *High Authority*, Cases 9, 12/60, [1961] ECR 197 at 214. For a discussion of other aspects of this case, see p. 469, below.

[26] Art. 43 of the Statute of the Court of Justice of the EEC, Art. 40 of the Statute of the ECSC, and Art. 44 of the Statute of Euratom. The last sentence of these provisions suggests that the period may be reduced if an application is made to the relevant institution of the Community, but this is not the case: the European Court held in *Kampffmeyer* v. *Commission*, Cases 5, 7, 13–24/66, [1967] ECR 245 at 259–60, that the period can never be less than five years. But an application to the institution can interrupt the running of time provided it is followed by the bringing of proceedings under Art. 173; the period is also interrupted by the institution of proceedings before the Court. See further *Giordano* v. *Commission*, Case 11/72, [1973] ECR 417. The expiry of the limitation period is not a bar to proceedings where the applicant only belatedly became aware of the event giving rise to the damage he suffered and did not have a reasonable time to commence proceedings before the limitation period expired: *Adams* v. *Commission*, Case 145/83, [1985] ECR 3539 (paragraphs 48–51 of the judgment). See also *Birra Wührer* v. *Council and Commission*, Cases 256, 257, 265, 267/80, 5/81, [1982] ECR 85, which held that time cannot start to run before the damage has occurred, even if the defendant's act took place some time previously.

only through its institutions. Which institution should represent the Community before the Court? In the case of *Werhahn* v. *Council and Commission*[27] it was argued (by the Commission) that the Commission should always fulfil this role. This contention was based on Article 211 EEC which provides that, in legal proceedings *in national courts*, the Community will be represented by the Commission. The Commission argued that this provision should be applied by analogy to proceedings in the European Court; but this was rejected by the Court which held:[28] '. . . it is in the interests of a good administration of justice that where Community liability is involved by reason of the act of one of its institutions, it should be represented before the Court by the institution or institutions against which the matter giving rise to liability is alleged.' The case itself concerned a regulation enacted by the Council on the proposal of the Commission. Since both these institutions were responsible for the regulation which was the alleged wrongful act, the applicant had brought the action against both of them. The Court held that this was quite correct.

One can conclude from this that the action must be brought against the Community as represented by the institution which is responsible for the act or omission which forms the basis of the proceedings. Where there is joint responsibility, both institutions concerned must be named as defendants. If, therefore, the Council can adopt a legal act only on the proposal of the Commission (which is the normal situation), both are responsible.

In proceedings under Article 215(2), the Court must give judgment in accordance with the 'general principles common to the laws of the Member States'. Since the Community is a public authority, it is to the law of *public* tort liability in the Member States that we must look.[29] In most Member States (including Britain) the liability of public authorities in tort is governed, in principle, by the same law as that of private individuals. But there are always a number of special rules which apply to public authorities so that even in these countries there are significant differences between the law applied in the public and the private spheres. In France, on the other hand, there is a completely separate system of public (administrative) tort law.

It is important to note that the Treaty refers to 'general principles',

---

[27] Cases 63–9/72, [1973] ECR 1229.

[28] At paragraph 7 of the judgment.

[29] See *per* Advocate General Roemer in *Plaumann* v. *Commission*, Case 25/62, [1963] ECR 95 at 116–17 and *per* Advocate General Gand in *Kampffmeyer* v. *Commission*, Cases 5, 7, 13–24/66, [1967] ECR 245 at 352.

not 'rules', of law. It is, in fact, widely recognized that the Court is not obliged to look for the lowest common denominator and find the Community liable only where liability would exist under the legal system of each of the Member States.[30] Such a solution would stunt the growth of Community law. What is required is that the Court should look to the very general principles which apply in all the Member States – such as causation, damage, fault and risk – and build up from these principles a system of law suited to the needs of the Community. The particular rules applied at the Community level need not necessarily be found in a majority of national systems and, where the special character of the Community so requires, it may even be permissible to apply rules not found in any national system. This means that the national systems are no more than a starting point for the judges in the European Court. They must, of course, respect the general legal tradition common to the Member States but they are not bound to adopt specific solutions. This gives the Court considerable scope for a creative approach.

In the ECSC Treaty there is no reference to the law of the Member States. Article 40 has, however, adopted two concepts of French law which play a leading role in the French system of administrative liability, *faute de service* and *faute personnelle*. The fact that these concepts are drawn from French law does not mean that they are to be applied in Community law in exactly the same way as in French law.[31] In interpreting them, French law obviously has a special role to play since they originated in that system; but once they became part of Community law the umbilical cord was cut and they became independent of any national system. The result is that in interpreting Article 40 ECSC the European Court will look to the national law of the Member States to exactly the same extent as in the case of Article 215(2) EEC; the absence of a specific provision to this effect will not inhibit a law-finding procedure that the European Court applies in all branches of the law.[32]

---

[30] See *per* Advocate General Roemer in *Zuckerfabrik Schöppenstedt* v. *Council*, Case 5/71, [1971] ECR 975 at 989 and *per* Advocate General Gand in *Sayag* v. *Leduc*, Case 9/69, [1969] ECR 329 at 340.

[31] See *per* Advocate General Roemer in *Plaumann* v. *Commission*, Case 25/62, [1963] ECR 95 at 117.

[32] For a general discussion, see Usher, 'The Influence of National Concepts on Decisions of the European Court', (1976) 1 E.L. Rev. 359.

Acts Imputable to the Community

The first basic requisite of Community liability in tort is that there should be an act imputable to the Community. The concept of an act in this context is very wide. It includes a physical act (e.g. driving a motor car), an act intended to have legal effects (e.g. a regulation), a verbal statement,[33] and anything else that is capable of causing harm to others. It also includes a failure to act (omission) provided there was a duty to act. The special problems which arise in connection with acts intended to have legal effects are considered below.[34]

Under Article 215(2) EEC, an act is imputable to the Community either if it is an act of an institution of the Community ('. . . damage caused by its institutions') or if it is an act of a servant of the Community and is performed in the course of his duties ('. . . damage caused . . . by its servants in the performance of their duties'.) Article 40(1) ECSC refers to an 'act . . . on the part of the Community' and Article 40(2) ECSC to an injury caused 'by a servant of the Community in the performance of his duties'. The differences between the provisions of the two Treaties are no more than verbal.

The Treaties therefore recognise two categories of act for which the Community is responsible: acts performed by the Community itself (through its institutions) and acts performed by Community servants. Since Community institutions act through their servants (officials) it will be seen that there is a considerable overlap between these two categories. To an English lawyer, indeed, it might seem that the first category is entirely covered by the second and is therefore otiose. This is not entirely true, however, since there are certain acts which are more properly described as acts of the institution itself rather than of its officials. The best example consists of formal (official) acts, i.e., those performed by the official organ of the institution, such as decisions of the Commission or Council, or resolutions of the Parliament. The category would also include acts performed jointly by a number of officials over a period of time, for example monitoring of market conditions or supervision of subordinate authorities. The importance of the recognition by the Treaties of acts of the institutions themselves as a separate category is that an applicant in an action for damages does not have to name the official responsible; nor does it matter if no official was responsible. This is particularly important in the case of a failure to act: it is enough to

[33] See p. 467, below.
[34] See pp. 468–83.

show that there was a duty on the institution to act; it need not be shown that any individual official was responsible.

In order to prove that an act of an official is imputable to the Community, it must be shown that the act was performed in the course of his duties. This concept will be familiar enough to English lawyers. It is interesting to note, however, that in its original form, Article 40(2) ECSC contained a more restrictive provision. This provided for an action *against the official* in the European Court in those cases where he had caused damage by a personal wrong in the performance of his duties. Community liability existed only where the injured person was unable to obtain redress from the servant. Article 40(2) ECSC was changed to its present form by Article 26 of the Merger Treaty. This brought it into line with the EEC Treaty.

The only case in which the European Court has had to consider what is meant by an act performed in the course of an official's duties was *Sayag* v. *Leduc*.[35] Mr Sayag was an engineer employed by Euratom who was instructed to take Mr Leduc and another person, who were both representatives of private undertakings, on a visit to the installations at Mol in Belgium. He decided to drive them there in his private car and was given a travel order for this purpose. (The significance of the travel order was that it meant that his expenses would be paid by the Community.) While he was driving them, he was involved in a traffic accident in which he and his passengers were injured. The passengers brought an action for damages in the Belgian courts against Sayag, but it was argued that he was acting in the performance of his duties when driving the car and that this meant that the action should have been brought against the Community instead.[36] The Belgian *Cour de Cassation* ordered that a preliminary reference be made to the European Court to determine what is meant by the phrase 'in the performance of their duties' in Article 188(2) of the Euratom Treaty (equivalent to Article 215(2) EEC).

The Court, following Advocate General Gand, gave a restrictive interpretation to the phrase. It ruled:[37]

By referring at one and the same time to damage caused by the institutions and to that caused by the servants of the Community, Article 188 indicates that the Community is only liable for those acts of its servants which, by virtue of an

---

[35] Case 9/69, [1969] ECR 329.
[36] This argument assumes that Community liability excludes individual liability, though this is by no means entirely certain: see note 40, below.
[37] [1969] ECR at 335–6.

internal and direct relationship, are the necessary extension of the tasks entrusted to the institutions.

In the light of the special nature of this legal system, it would not therefore be lawful to extend it to categories of acts other than those referred to above.

A servant's use of his private car for transport during the performance of his duties does not satisfy the conditions set out above.

A reference to a servant's private car in a travel order does not bring the driving of such car within the performance of his duties, but is basically intended to enable any necessary reimbursement of the travel expenses involved in the use of this means of transport to be made in accordance with the standards laid down for this purpose.

Only in the case of *force majeure* or in exceptional circumstances of such overriding importance that without the servant's using private means of transport the Community would have been unable to carry out the tasks entrusted to it, could such use be considered to form part of the servant's performance of his duties, within the meaning of the second paragraph of Article 188 of the Treaty.

It follows from the above that the driving of a private car by a servant cannot in principle constitute the performance of his duties within the meaning of the second paragraph of Article 188 of the EAEC Treaty.

It follows from this that the liability of the Community for the acts of its servants is narrower than that of most Member States (except Germany) for the acts of their servants.[38] It is hard to see any justification for this.

Where the Community is not liable it is, of course, possible to sue the servant in his personal capacity. Such proceedings must be brought in the national courts and are governed by national law. Community officials enjoy immunity from suit in national courts in respect of 'acts performed in their official capacity',[39] but it is hard to see how this can apply where the Community is not itself liable.[40]

[38] See the comparative survey made by Advocate General Gand, ibid. at pp. 340–1, where it is shown that in most of the original six Member States liability for the acts of public servants is wide. The only exception is Germany. In France there is authority relevant to the actual point at issue: it has been held that the state can be liable as a result of an accident caused by an official driving his private car on official business: *Bourrée*, C E, 26 July 1944, Rec. Lebon, p. 217.

[39] Protocol on the Privileges and Immunities of the European Communities (a protocol to the Merger Treaty), Art. 12(a). It is provided in Art. 18 that the immunity must be waived by the Community whenever such waiver is not contrary to the interests of the Community.

[40] See *per* Advocate General Gand in an earlier case between the same parties, *Sayag* v. *Leduc*, Case 5/68, [1968] E C R 395 at 408. In this case the Court held that Sayag was not entitled to immunity, but it made clear (in the last paragraph of its judgment) that the immunity of the servant and the liability of the Community are separate questions. It is therefore possible, though unlikely, that in some cases they may both be liable. This would be the case only if it is possible for a Community official to be acting in the performance of his duties (the test for Community liability) without at the same time acting in his official capacity (the test for immunity).

Another problem concerns the extent to which the Community will be liable for the torts of other authorities which act on its behalf or to which it delegates powers. The Treaties say nothing regarding the liability of the Community for the acts of its agents and it is uncertain – especially in view of the restrictive attitude taken towards liability for the acts of servants – how far the Court will impute to the Community the acts of an agent. It will be remembered, however, that in the field of judicial review the Court held, in *SNUPAT* v. *High Authority*,[41] that, where the Community set up a subordinate body and delegated powers to it, the acts of that body could be regarded as acts of the delegating institution for the purpose of review. Might not a similar rule apply in the case of tort liability?

In *SNUPAT* v. *High Authority*, the High Authority had set up two subordinate bodies, the *Office commun des consommateurs de ferrailles* (OCCF) and the *Caisse de péréquation de ferrailles importés* (CPFI), which were both incorporated under Belgian law, to administer an equalization scheme for ferrous scrap. Under this scheme, imported scrap was subsidized and the cost was met by a levy on all scrap users. The CPFI had demanded that SNUPAT pay a certain sum of money under the levy and SNUPAT brought an action in the European Court under Article 33 ECSC to annul the demand. The Court ruled that decisions of the CPFI should be imputed to the High Authority for the purpose of the admissibility of the action.

A later case, *Worms* v. *High Authority*,[42] raised the question of liability in tort. Mr Worms was a Dutch scrap dealer who claimed that he had suffered damage because the OCCF had refused to do business with him. He sued the High Authority under Article 40 ECSC and the Court had to decide whether the Community could be liable for the acts of the OCCF. In its judgment the Court pointed out that the CPFI and the OCCF had different functions: the former had executive functions concerning the equalization scheme while the latter's functions were normally of a commercial nature and were concerned with the purchase of scrap on the open market. The Court then stated:[43]

When carrying on its strictly commercial activities, the OCCF, a Belgian company under private law, is governed by national law. It is only in cases where the OCCF's acts concern the functioning of the equalization scheme, and on

---

[41] Cases 32, 33/58, [1959] ECR 127. See pp. 336–7, above.
[42] Case 18/60, [1962] ECR 195.
[43] Ibid, at p. 204.

that account have the character of a public duty, that they can be considered as directly giving rise to the liability of the High Authority.

The Court went on to hold that the buying of scrap was an activity of a purely commercial nature and any damage caused by the OCCF's refusal to do business with a particular dealer was not the responsibility of the High Authority. Worms would have to sue the OCCF directly in the national courts.

From this it may be concluded that where a Community institution delegates governmental powers to some other body, the acts of that body in the exercise of those powers may be imputed to the Community; but where such a body carries out functions which are not of a governmental nature, its acts will not be imputable to the Community. This distinction between governmental and non-governmental functions appears to be akin to that between public law and private law activities. Buying goods in the open market is a commercial (private law) activity; but collecting levies is a public law function and acts performed in this field would be imputable to the Community.

Worms v. *High Authority* appears to establish, therefore, that there are in fact *three* categories of acts which may be imputed to the Community: acts of Community institutions; acts of Community servants in the performance of their duties; and acts of other bodies performed in carrying out governmental (public) functions delegated to them by a Community institution.[44]

Damage and Causation

Once the existence of an act (or omission) imputable to the Community has been established, the next requisite is that it should have caused damage to the applicant. The European Court has never laid down any general principles as to the kinds of loss for which compensation may be claimed or the way in which damages will be calculated. Instead it has proceeded on an *ad hoc* basis and tried to reach a result that was just in the circumstances. For this reason, and because there have, in fact, been very few actual awards of damages, it is impossible to do more than make a few brief comments.

The Court has shown itself willing to award compensation to firms for financial losses. In *Kampffmeyer* v. *Commission*,[45] for example, it was

[44] As to whether the Community could be liable for acts of Member States, see Schermers, 'The Law as it Stands on the Appeal for Damages', 1975/1 LIEI 113 at 133-4.
[45] Cases 5, 7, 13-24/66, [1967] ECR 245. This decision is discussed further at pp. 463-4, 481-2, and 484-6, below.

held that where, as a result of unlawful Community action, a firm was forced to break a contract, the cancellation fees incurred might be recovered from the Community; and in *CNTA* v. *Commission*[46] it was held that a firm was entitled to compensation for losses caused by currency fluctuations where the Community was responsible for its having been exposed to this risk. It also seems probable, though it has not been finally decided, that compensation may be obtained for losses resulting from unlawful assistance given by Community institutions to competitors.[47]

In the *Kampffmeyer* case (above) the question also arose whether an applicant could claim for loss of profit. A number of German grain dealers had applied for permits to import maize from France into Germany at a time when, because of the zero rate of levy, it was possible to make substantial profits. The German authorities wrongfully refused to grant the permits and the Commission upheld this action. The Court ruled that the Community was liable in principle to compensate the dealers for their losses. The dealers who claimed for loss of profit fell into two categories: some had concluded contracts to buy grain in France and had cancelled them when import permits were refused; others had not concluded contracts before applying for permits. As regards the first category, the Court was prepared to award damages for loss of profit but it stated that, in view of the speculative nature of the transactions, it would award them only a sum equal to ten per cent of what they would have had to pay by way of the levy if they had imported the maize after the levy rate had been raised to a normal level. Since their profits would probably have been at least equal to the normal levy rate, they were being awarded, in effect, only ten per cent of the profits they could have made. Though it was reasonable to take into account the element of risk involved in transactions of this nature, this seems an excessively large reduction. The second category of applicants fared even worse: they were awarded no damages at all. The reason given by the Court was that their transactions lacked 'any substantial character'; but this does not seem entirely justifiable since they had taken a concrete step by applying for an import permit. Their decision not to conclude

---

[46] Case 74/74, decision of 14 May 1975, [1975] ECR 533; decision of 15 June 1976, [1976] ECR 797.

[47] There have been several cases in which damages have been claimed on this basis but they have all been dismissed on other grounds. See, for example, *Bertrand* v. *Commission*, Case 40/75, [1976] ECR 1; and *Roquette* v. *Commission*, Case 26/74, [1976] ECR 677. These cases show that proof of causation in this situation will be difficult.

contracts until the permits had been obtained might be viewed as nothing more than normal business prudence.

In staff cases the Court has been prepared to award damages for anxiety and hurt feelings in the case of Community employees who have been wrongfully dismissed or otherwise unfairly treated.[48] The sums granted under this head have usually been small.

It is now settled that it is possible to bring proceedings before the damage has actually occurred: in such a case the applicant can obtain a declaration that he is entitled in principle to compensation.[49] This is possible, however, only if the damage is imminent and there is a high degree of certainty that it will take place. This would normally mean that the cause of the damage (the Community action) must already have occurred even if its consequences have not yet been fully realized.[50] The importance of this ruling is that it enables persons affected by Community measures to challenge them as soon as they have taken place and thus obtain a ruling as to their legality. In other words, an action for a declaration under Article 215(2) EEC could be used as a substitute for a review action under Article 173 EEC; this could be valuable in view of the limitations placed on the right of private individuals to bring review proceedings.[51]

Where damages are calculated in one currency (for example, the European currency unit) and awarded in another (for example, the national currency of the applicant) the appropriate date for conversion is that of the judgment.[52] If, as is often the case, the Court first gives an interlocutory judgment on the question of liability and, if the parties are unable to reach agreement, fixes the amount of damages in a later judgment, the relevant date is that of the interlocutory judgment.[53] Interest is usually awarded from the date of the interlocutory judgment.[54]

The European Court has had little to say about the problem of causation. One situation which raises the question of remoteness is where a Member State acts in violation of the Treaty and thereby causes loss to the applicant. If the Commission was aware of the facts

---

[48] See, for example, *Algera* v. *Assembly*, Cases 7/56, 3–7/57, [1957] ECR 39 and *Willame* v. *Commission*, Case 110/63, [1965] ECR 649. However, time begins to run for limitation purposes only when the damage actually occurs: *Birra Wührer* v. *Council and Commission*, Cases 256, 257, 265, 267/80, 5/81, [1982] ECR 85.

[49] *Kampffmeyer* v. *Council and Commission*, Cases 56–60/74, [1976] ECR 711.

[50] See *per* Advocate General Reischl, ibid. at p. 753.

[51] See Chapter 12.

[52] *Dumortier* v. *Council*, Cases 64, 113/76, 167, 239/78, 27, 28, 45/79, [1982] ECR 1733.

[53] Ibid.

[54] Ibid.

but failed to take enforcement proceedings against the Member State, can the applicant bring an action in tort against the Commission on the ground that its failure to act was the cause of its loss? There have been several cases in which such proceedings have been brought, but they have all been dismissed on other grounds.[55] In some of them, however, the European Court appeared to accept that liability can arise in this way.[56]

Fault

Under the ECSC Treaty fault is an essential element of liability. There is no such requirement under the EEC Treaty, but up to now the European Court has always required the proof of fault in actions under Article 215(2). It considered the possibility of non-fault liability in *Compagnie d'Approvisionnement* v. *Commission*,[57] which concerned the measures taken after the devaluation of the French franc in 1969. In order to minimize disruption to the Common Agricultural Policy, the Council decided (among other things) that the French Government would grant subsidies on imports of cereal products. The amount of the subsidies was to be fixed by the Commission and this was done by two Commission regulations. The applicants were cereal dealers who claimed to have suffered loss because the subsidies were fixed at too low a level to compensate for the devaluation of the franc. They put forward various arguments in order to establish the liability of the Community, including an argument based on the French doctrine of equal apportionment of public burdens (*l'égale répartition des charges publiques*) under which the state may be liable in certain circumstances in the absence of fault. To establish liability under this head in French law it is necessary to show that measures taken by the state have placed an abnormal and unjustifiably severe burden on certain individuals who have thus been required to make a disproportionate sacrifice in the general interest.

[55] See *Vloeberghs* v. *High Authority*, Cases 9, 12/60, [1961] ECR 197 (discussed below at p. 469); *Lütticke* v. *Commission*, Case 4/69, [1971] ECR 325; *Bertrand* v. *Commission*, Case 40/75, [1976] ECR 1; *Denkavit* v. *Commission*, Case 14/78, [1978] ECR 2497; *Société d'Initiatives et de Coopération Agricoles* v. *Commission*, Case 114/83, [1984] ECR 2589, and *GAARM* v. *Commission*, Case 289/83, [1984] ECR 4295.

[56] See the *Vloeberghs* case, [1961] ECR at 216 (also *per* Advocate General Roemer at p. 240) and the *Denkavit* case, [1978] ECR 2497 at paragraph 8 of the judgment. See further at pp. 302–4, above.

[57] Cases 9, 11/71, [1972] ECR 391; see also *Biovilac* v. *EEC*, Case 59/83, [1984] ECR 4057 (paragraphs 27–30 of the judgment), where reference was also made to the German concept of '*Sonderopfer*'.

Advocate General Mayras considered this argument but decided that the applicants had not met the conditions imposed by French law.[58] The Court also rejected it without ruling on whether or not non-fault liability is part of Community law:[59] 'Any liability for a valid legislative measure is inconceivable in a situation like that in the present case since the measures adopted by the Commission were only intended to alleviate, in the general economic interest, the consequences which resulted in particular for all French importers from the national decision to devalue the franc.' In other words, the disputed measures did not impose a burden on the applicants; they gave them a benefit. Therefore no question of liability under this head could arise.

Non-fault liability continues to be a possibility under the EEC Treaty but the general tenor of the Court's judgments in cases under Article 215(2) makes clear that it will apply only in special circumstances: the normal rule is that fault must be established. What is meant by fault? In broad terms it means that the act or omission which forms the basis of the action must be wrongful. In the case of an omission this means that there must have been a duty (as distinct from a mere power) to act; in the case of a positive act it means either that the action was wrongful in itself or that it was carried out in a wrongful way.

In general, any malfunctioning of the administrative system can constitute a *faute de service*. One could perhaps say that there is a legal duty on Community institutions (and on other institutions to which Community functions are delegated and for whose acts the Community is responsible) to carry out their functions in a sensible and efficient manner – in other words, a duty of a good administration. Consequently, any breach of this duty could be a *faute de service*, for example: failure to adopt procedures necessary for the efficient functioning of the service, failure to supervise subordinate officials or outside bodies to whom functions have been delegated, failure to obtain all the facts before making a decision, taking a decision on the basis of erroneous or irrelevant facts, giving misleading information to the public, failure to give necessary information to the public, delay or lack of foresight – in short, everything which English lawyers sum up under the heading of 'maladministration'. In addition, of course, a violation of any written or unwritten rule of law may also

---

[58] At pp. 422–3.
[59] Paragraph 46 of the judgment.

constitute a *faute de service*, provided the rule in question is intended for the protection of individuals.[60]

It should not, however, be thought that *any* deviation from the standard of an ideal service constitutes a *faute de service*. The concept, after all, carries a connotation of blameworthiness and it is therefore necessary to consider whether the short-coming in question is excusable. For example, in the case of a decision of fact (i.e., a judgment whether a certain state of facts exists) the institution concerned may be excused if it makes a mistake, provided it adopted the correct procedures and reached the conclusion which seemed indicated in the light of the information to hand.[61] A good example is to be found in the case of *Richez-Parise* v. *Commission*.[62] The applicants in this case were a number of officials of the EEC who had been given incorrect information concerning their pensions and had thereafter resigned from the service and taken certain decisions regarding their financial rights. The information in question was based on an interpretation of the relevant legal provisions and at the time at which it was given the Commission had no reason to believe that it was wrong. Subsequently the Commission discovered that their interpretation was of doubtful validity but they took no immediate steps to inform the applicants of this. It was only some time later, after the applicants had committed themselves as regards the form in which they would take their accrued pension entitlements, that the position was rectified. The European Court held that the initial interpretation was not itself a wrongful act since the mistake was excusable, but the failure to correct it as soon as the Commission became aware of the true position was a *faute de service*.

While a *faute de service* occurs where the administrative organ is itself defective, a *faute personnelle* applies where the individual officer acts wrongfully: where he fails to carry out instructions or acts negligently or illegally or in bad-faith – in other words, where the short-coming is one of the individual rather than of the service.

The best known case in which Community liability has been established, and one of the few cases in which substantial damages have been awarded, is *Adams* v. *Commission*.[63] While employed by a Swiss pharmaceutical company (Hoffman-La Roche), Adams had,

[60] See pp. 480–2, below.

[61] See *per* Advocate General Gand in *Kampffmeyer* v. *Commission*, Cases 5, 7, 13–24/66, [1967] ECR 245 at 275–7.

[62] Cases 19, 20, 25, 30/69, [1970] ECR 325. For another case on misleading information, see *Compagnie Continentale France* v. *Council*, Case 169/73, [1975] ECR 117.

[63] Case 145/83, [1985] ECR 3539.

after requesting confidentiality, given the Commission documents which showed that the company was violating Community competition law. The Commission then brought proceedings against the company and as a result it was fined. Subsequently the company discovered, partly as a result of documents supplied by the Commission, that Adams was the informant.

Under Swiss law Adams had committed a criminal offence by revealing the company's secrets to the Commission. By this time Adams had ceased to work for Hoffman-La Roche and gone to live in Italy. However, he came to Switzerland on a visit and the company had him arrested. The Swiss police kept him in solitary confinement and did not allow him to communicate with his family. As a result, his wife, who had also been interrogated, committed suicide. After his release (he was convicted but given a suspended sentence) he sued the Commission for damages.

The Court held that the Commission was bound by a duty of confidentiality and that it had violated this, in particular by not warning Adams when it discovered that Hoffman-La Roche was planning to have him prosecuted. However, they held that Adams was partly to blame for his own misfortune (for example, by returning to Switzerland) and they decided that liability should be apportioned equally between him and the Commission. The Commission was, therefore, ordered to compensate him to the extent of one half of the damage suffered.[64]

LIABILITY FOR ACTS INTENDED TO HAVE LEGAL EFFECTS

Special considerations apply where the alleged wrongful act on the part of the Community is an act intended to have legal effects, i.e. a reviewable act as defined in Chapter 11. Under the ECSC Treaty there is a provision directly covering this situation, Article 34 ECSC. This provides that where a decision (equivalent to an EEC regulation or decision) or recommendation (analogous to a directive under the EEC Treaty) is annulled, the Commission (High Authority) must, if the decision or recommendation involves fault of such a nature as to render the Community liable, pay damages to any

---

[64] The amount of damages was settled in negotiations between the parties. According to *The Times* of 18 October 1986, Adams eventually accepted £200,000 (£100,000 for mental anguish and £100,000 for economic loss) plus £176,000 for costs.

undertaking or group of undertakings which has suffered direct and special harm. The term 'undertaking' is defined in Article 80 ECSC as a producer of coal or steel in the Community. This means that only a restricted group of applicants can resort to Article 34; moreover, they cannot do so unless the decision or recommendation has first been annulled.

Article 34 probably applies where there has been a failure to act, since under Article 35 ECSC an unlawful failure to take a decision or make a recommendation gives rise – provided the required procedure is followed – to an implied decision refusing to act, which may itself be annulled under Article 33 ECSC. Article 34 could then be invoked.

In view of the limited scope of Article 34, the question arises whether it is possible to bring an ordinary tort action under Article 40. This would provide a remedy in cases where the applicant is unable to bring an annulment action because he has no *locus standi*.

The question came before the Court in *Vloeberghs* v. *High Authority*,[65] where a coal distributor brought an action for damages against the Commission on the basis of Article 40 ECSC, because the Commission had failed to take a decision requiring the French Government to allow his coal to enter France. The Commission claimed that the action was inadmissible, arguing that Article 34 provides the sole means of obtaining damages for loss caused by an act intended to have legal effects. It urged the Court not to allow Article 40 ECSC to be used as a means of circumventing the restrictions on judicial review imposed by Articles 33 and 35. As a coal distributor (not a producer), Vloeberghs was of course precluded from bringing action under Article 35.

The Court, however, rejected the Commission's argument. It pointed out that review actions and tort actions are quite separate remedies and that there is no reason why the restrictive conditions of the former should apply to the latter. The Court stated that it was not necessary for the applicant first to bring proceedings under Article 35. It expressly left open the question whether the same would apply where the basis of the action was a positive act rather than an omission, but it is hard to see how a different solution could be justified since the reasoning adopted by the Court would be equally applicable.

In the EEC Treaty the nearest equivalent to Article 34 ECSC is Article 176. This reads:

---

[65] Cases 9, 12/60, [1961] ECR 197. For further discussion of this case, see pp. 302–3 above.

The institution whose act has been declared void or whose failure to act has been declared contrary to this Treaty shall be required to take the necessary measures to comply with the judgment of the Court of Justice.

This obligation shall not affect any obligation which may result from the application of the second paragraph of Article 215.

This gives no right to damages – unless the payment of damages were regarded as a 'necessary measure'[66] – but in view of its second paragraph it cannot hinder an action in tort.

The 'Plaumann Doctrine'

The first case concerned with liability for a reviewable act under the EEC Treaty was *Plaumann* v. *Commission*.[67] This case was discussed in Chapter 12.[68] It will be remembered that the German Government had applied to the Commission for permission to lower the duty on clementines from 13 per cent to 10 per cent. The Commission took a decision addressed to Germany refusing this request. Plaumann was a German importer of clementines who claimed that the Commission's refusal was illegal. He brought proceedings under Article 173 EEC for the annulment of the decision and also under Article 215(2) EEC for damages. The amount claimed in damages was a sum equal to the additional duty he had had to pay.

It will be remembered from the discussion in Chapter 12 that the review proceedings were declared inadmissible on the ground that Plaumann lacked *locus standi*. The Court declared the tort action admissible but dismissed it on the merits. It gave its reasons as follows:[69]

The conclusions of the applicant ask for payment of compensation equivalent to the customs duties and turnover tax which the applicant had to pay in consequence of the Decision against which it has at the same time instituted proceedings for annulment. In these circumstances it must be declared that the damage allegedly suffered by the applicant issues from this Decision and that the action for compensation in fact seeks to set aside the legal effects on the applicant of the contested Decision.

In the present case the contested Decision has not been annulled. An administrative measure which has not been annulled cannot of itself constitute a

---

[66] According to Advocate General Roemer in *Nordgetreide* v. *Commission*, Case 42/71, [1972] ECR 105 at 115 the Court does not have the power to specify what measures must be taken to comply with its judgments.
[67] Case 25/62, [1963] ECR 95.
[68] See pp. 343–5, above.
[69] [1963] ECR at 108.

wrongful act on the part of the administration inflicting damage upon those whom it affects. The latter cannot therefore claim damages by reason of that measure. The Court cannot by way of an action for compensation take steps which would nullify the legal effects of a decision which, as stated, has not been annulled.

The action brought by the applicant must therefore be dismissed as unfounded.

This reasoning will be familiar: exactly the same argument was put forward by the Commission in *Vloeberghs* v. *High Authority*. The argument rejected by the Court in that case was accepted in *Plaumann*. It is unclear why the Court changed its ground within so short a time (two years). What should, however, be emphasized is that this restrictive approach was in no way required by the Treaty: there is nothing in the EEC Treaty suggesting that a reviewable act which has not been quashed cannot form the basis of an action in tort; nor is this principle derived from the legal systems of the Member States.[70] As the Court said in the *Vloeberghs* case, actions for damages and applications for review are quite separate proceedings with different objectives.

This decision was subject to heavy criticism[71] but it was almost eight years before the Court had an opportunity to reconsider it. This first occurred in *Lütticke* v. *Commission*,[72] in which a German company sued the Commission for damages because it had failed to address a directive or decision to Germany requiring it to modify certain taxes which the company had been obliged to pay. The Commission contended that the action was inadmissible because it was intended to establish a failure to act on its part and its effect would be to circumvent the limitations imposed by Article 175 EEC on the application for a remedy for failure to act. This, of course, was precisely the argument unsuccessfully put forward in *Vloeberghs* and adopted by the Court in *Plaumann*. This time the Court rejected it. Its words were:[73]

The action for damages provided for by Article 178 and the second paragraph of Article 215 was established by the Treaty as an independent form of action with a particular purpose to fulfil within the system of actions and subject to conditions for its use, conceived with a view to its specific purpose. It would be contrary to the independent nature of this action as well as to the efficacy of the general

[70] See *per* Advocate General Roemer in *Zuckerfabrik Schöppenstedt* v. *Council*, Case 5/71, [1971] ECR 975 at 990 and the authors there cited.

[71] Ibid. at p. 991.

[72] Case 4/69,]1971] ECR 325.

[73] Paragraph 6 of the judgment.

system of forms of action created by the Treaty to regard as a ground of inadmissibility the fact that, in certain circumstances, an action for damages might lead to a result similar to that of an action for failure to act under Article 175.

So the action was declared admissible (though it was dismissed on the merits on the ground that the Commission's failure to act was not wrongful).

The position was confirmed in *Zuckerfabrik Schöppenstedt* v. *Council*,[74] where the act in question was a Council regulation which provided for compensation for stock-holders of sugar who had suffered loss as a result of the price changes that came about when a Community régime for sugar was introduced. The terms of this regulation did not, however, entitle the applicant, a German company, to any compensation. It claimed that this was wrong and sued the Council for damages. The Council contested the admissibility of the action on the ground that, in practical terms, its result would be the nullification of the legal effects of the regulation. This, it argued, would undermine the system of judicial review set up by Article 173 EEC under which private persons are not entitled to challenge the validity of regulations. The Court rejected this argument on the basis of the same reasoning as in the *Lütticke* case. It seems, therefore, that the point is now settled.[75]

The significance of this should be emphasized. The rule in *Plaumann* was more than a procedural one. It has already been shown that the rules of admissibility for applications to annul and applications for a remedy for failure to act are extremely strict: the narrow concept of *locus standi* and the short time-limit impose stringent limitations on the right to bring these proceedings.[76] Therefore, if it had been accepted that such proceedings were a necessary precondition for an action for damages, the latter action would have been likewise restricted and Community liability would have been severely limited.

[74] Case 5/71, [1971] ECR 975.
[75] The argument was put again in a few subsequent cases but was always rejected by the Court. See, for example, *Compagnie d'Approvisionnement* v. *Commission*, Cases 9, 11/71, [1972] ECR 391 (paragraphs 3–7 of the judgment) and *Merkur* v. *Commission*, Case 43/72, [1973] ECR 1055 (paragraphs 3 and 4 of the judgment). It appears, however, that the *Plaumann* doctrine still applies where the applicant claims not compensation for loss actually suffered, but the sum that would have been payable if the measure had not been adopted: see *Krohn* v. *Commission*, Case 175/84, [1987] 1 CMLR 745 (paragraphs 30–34 of the judgment); *Birke* v. *Commission and Council*, Case 543/79, [1981] ECR 2669 (paragraphs 23–28 of the judgment); *Bruckner* v. *Commission and Council*, Case 799/79, [1981] ECR 2697 (paragraphs 14–20). In such a case, however, the action would not really be in tort.
[76] See Chapter 12, above.

The 'Schöppenstedt Formula'

The *Schöppenstedt* case is important not only because it marked the final removal of the shackles imposed by *Plaumann*; it was also the first case in which the European Court made a general statement of the principles governing Community liability for a normative act. This statement, which will be referred to henceforth as the '*Schöppenstedt* formula', has been repeated, with small verbal differences, in most subsequent cases.[77] In a later version it reads as follows:[78] 'The Court of Justice has consistently stated that the Community does not incur liability on account of a legislative measure which involves choices of economic policy unless a sufficiently serious breach of a superior rule of law for the protection of the individual has occurred.'

According to its terms, the formula applies where the source of liability is a legislative measure involving choices of economic policy. The concept of a 'legislative act' (also called a 'normative' or 'general' act) has already been discussed in the context of judicial review.[79] It will be remembered that such an act is to be distinguished, not on the basis of its form, but on the basis of its substance. It is an act which lays down general rules which apply to an indefinite category of persons. It will normally take the form of a regulation. Acts of an individual nature (decisions), on the other hand, are not covered by the formula: nevertheless it is doubtful whether the position is so very different where the action is based on such an act.

For the formula to apply, the act must also involve 'choices of economic policy'. This means two things: the act must be a discretionary one and it must be concerned with economic matters. As regards the first characteristics, it is hard to imagine a legislative act that is not discretionary. As regards the second, most Community legislation concerns economic matters since the Community is an economic one. It is true that some measures are less directly economic than others – a regulation prohibiting discrimination against foreign workers is less obviously economic than one imposing a levy on imported products – but it is unlikely that the former kind will give rise to actions for damages.

Where it applies, the formula lays down three requisites for liability:

[77] For a full discussion of the formula, see W. van Gerven, 'De niet-contractuele aansprakelijkheid van de Gemeenschap wegens normatieve handelingen', [1976] SEW 2.

[78] *HNL* v. *Council and Commission*, Cases 83, 94/76, 4, 15, 40/77, [1978] ECR 1209 at paragraph 4 of the judgment.

[79] See pp. 342–3, above.

1. There must be a breach of a superior rule of law;
2. The breach must be sufficiently serious;
3. The superior rule of law must be one for the protection of the individual.

It should be noted that these are necessary conditions for liability; they are not sufficient conditions: the general rules concerning damage and causation must also be satisfied. All the formula does is to spell out the circumstances in which an act of the kind under consideration will be regarded as wrongful for the purpose of founding an action in tort. It does not concern itself with the other elements of tortious liability.

First Requisite

The first requisite is that there must be a breach of a superior rule of law. Any rule of Community law should constitute a 'superior rule of law' for this purpose, provided it is binding on the author of the allegedly tortious act: in other words, if it would constitute a ground of annulment under Article 713 EEC (or the equivalent provisions in the other Treaties) it should constitute a superior rule of law for the purpose of tort liability.

An example of a case in which the Court held that a general principle of law was sufficient for this purpose is *CNTA* v. *Commission*.[80] This case arose out of the system of monetary compensatory amounts (m.c.a.'s), which were intended to compensate for fluctuations in exchange rates. These payments had originally been granted on exports of colza seed from France but on 26 January 1972 the Commission passed a regulation which abolished the system as from 1 February. The applicant was a French firm which had entered into a number of export contracts before the regulation was passed and these were to be performed after the ending of the scheme. It claimed that it had entered into the contracts on the assumption that m.c.a.'s would be payable and had calculated its price on that basis. It argued that it had suffered loss by reason of the sudden ending of the scheme without warning and without any provision being made for transactions which were in the process of completion when it came into force. It therefore sued the Commission for damages.

[80] Case 74/74, [1975] ECR 533.

In order to establish liability it had to prove that the Commission had been guilty of a wrongful act. It claimed that the regulation was such an act because it infringed the principle of legal certainty and in particular the principle of the protection of legitimate expectations (*Vertrauensschutz*).

The Court stated that, though the system of m.c.a.'s could not be regarded as furnishing a guarantee to exporters that they would not suffer loss as a result of fluctuations in the exchange rate, it nevertheless had the effect in practice of shielding them from such a risk. Consequently, even a prudent exporter might decide not to cover himself against it. The Court then continued:[81]

> In these circumstances, a trader may legitimately expect that for transactions irrevocably undertaken by him because he has obtained, subject to a deposit, export licences fixing the amount of the refund in advance, no unforeseeable alteration will occur which could have the effect of causing him inevitable loss, by re-exposing him to the exchange risk.
>
> The Community is therefore liable if, in the absence of an overriding matter of public interest, the Commission abolished with immediate effect and without warning the application of compensatory amounts in a specific sector without adopting transitional measures which would at least permit traders either to avoid the loss which would have been suffered in the performance of export contracts, the existence and irrevocability of which are established by the advance fixing of the refunds, or to be compensated for such loss.
>
> In the absence of an overriding matter of public interest, the Commission has violated a superior rule of law, thus rendering the Community liable, by failing to include in Regulation No 189/72 transitional measures for the protection of the confidence which a trader might legitimately have had in the Community rules.

The Court went on to hold, however, that the Community was not liable to pay the full amount of the m.c.a.'s applicable to the transactions in question. The Community's obligation was solely to ensure that the exporter did not make an actual loss on the transaction as a result of a change in the exchange rate. In later proceedings[82] it was established that payment for the shipments had been made in French francs. Therefore CNTA had suffered no loss and it consequently obtained no damages.

It is important to note that the Court did not hold the regulation invalid. If it had done so, CNTA would have been entitled to the m.c.a.'s at the normal rate. The wrongful act was not the passing of the regulation but the failure either to give reasonable notice to interested parties that the system would soon be ended or, alterna-

[81] Paragraphs 42–4 of the judgment.
[82] [1976] ECR 797.

tively, to include transitional provisions to protect exporters who had already committed themselves. It was this omission which violated the principle of the protection of legitimate expectations which, according to the Court, was a superior rule of law in the terms of the *Schöppenstedt* formula.

Second Requisite

The second requisite is that the breach must be sufficiently serious. Later cases have shown that this is the most important aspect of the *Schöppenstedt* formula and it constitutes the most difficult hurdle for the applicant to surmount. The first decision to consider is *HNL* v. *Council and Commission*,[83] more commonly known as the second *Skimmed-Milk Powder* case. This arose out of the over-production of milk in the Community and the creation of a skimmed-milk powder 'mountain'. In an attempt to get rid of this, the Council passed a regulation obliging animal feed producers to purchase skimmed-milk powder from the intervention agencies. The idea was that skimmed-milk powder would replace soya as a source of protein in the animal feed. The drawback of this, however, was that skimmed-milk powder was much more expensive than soya and the consequence of the scheme was that farmers had to pay more for their animal feed.

The farmers objected and various actions were brought to contest the legality of the regulation. Some were brought in the national courts and referred to the European Court under Article 177; others were actions for damages brought in the European Court. Judgment was given first in the cases under Article 177: the Court ruled that the regulation was invalid because it obliged the producers to purchase skimmed-milk powder 'at such a disproportionate price that it was equivalent to a discriminatory distribution of the burden of costs between the various agricultural sectors' without being justifiable for the purpose of disposing of the stocks of skimmed-milk powder.[84] In other words, the regulation offended against the principles of non-discrimination and proportionality.[85]

The following year the Court gave judgment in the tort actions. Since the regulation had already been ruled invalid, there could be no dispute regarding the first requirement of the *Schöppenstedt* formula;

---

[83] Cases 83, 94/76, 4, 15, 40/77, [1978] ECR 1209.
[84] See paragraph 3 of the judgment. See further *Bela-Mühle*, Case 114/76; *Granaria*, Case 116/76; and *Ölmühle Hamburg*, Case 119, 120/76, [1977] ECR 1211 et seq.
[85] See pp. 148–50 and 145–7, above.

nor did the Court have any difficulty in holding that the third requirement was satisfied. The difficulties centred around the second requirement: was the violation sufficiently serious?

It might have been thought that if the violation were serious enough to result in a ruling that the regulation was invalid, it would be serious enough to justify the award of damages; but the Court held that this was not the case. A ruling of invalidity merely satisfies the first requirement in the *Schöppenstedt* formula; it does not necessarily satisfy the second. The Court tried to justify this strict approach by pointing out that in national law it is only in exceptional cases that public authorities incur liability for legislative measures. It may be doubted, however, whether analogies with national law are very apposite in this regard, since the democratic element is largely absent in the Community legislative process.

The Court then stated that in a legislative field involving wide discretion, the Community will not be liable unless the institution concerned has 'manifestly and gravely disregarded the limits on the exercise of its powers'. The requirement of a serious violation has thus been enlarged: applicants must now establish a *manifest* and *grave* violation. The Court held that these requirements were not satisfied in the case. It gave four reasons: first, the regulation affected a wide category of persons, namely all buyers of protein animal feed; secondly, the price increase had only a limited effect on production costs; thirdly, the increase was slight in comparison with increases caused by fluctuations in world prices; and lastly, the effect of the regulation on profits did not exceed the normal level of risk inherent in activities in the agricultural sectors concerned.

One can conclude from this that liability will not result from measures of this kind unless the violation of the law has a serious impact on the interests of the applicants. The last three factors mentioned are all concerned with the degree of harm suffered by the victims. The first factor indicates that liability will be less likely to result where the loss is spread over a wide class of persons than where it is concentrated on a small number of victims.

The *HNL* case was followed a year later by a group of cases concerning two rather unusual products, quellmehl and gritz.[86] The former is made from maize or wheat and is used in bread production

---

[86] *Dumortier* v. *Council*, Cases 64, 113/76, 167, 239/78, 27, 28, 45/79, [1979] ECR 3091; *Ireks-Arkady* v. *Council and Commission*, Case 238/78, [1979] ECR 2955; *DGV* v. *Council and Commission*, Cases 241, 242, 245–250/78, [1979] ECR 3017; *Interquell* v. *Council and Commission*, Cases 261, 262/78, [1979] ECR 3045.

to keep the dough damp; the latter is also derived from maize and is
used in brewing. The history of these cases started some years ago
when the Community decided to subsidize starch in order to enable it
to compete with synthetic products. Starch is, however, to some
extent interchangeable with quellmehl and gritz and the subsidy
enabled it to undercut quellmehl in baking and gritz in brewing. To
prevent this, the subsidies were granted to the latter products as well.

The trouble started when the Council passed a regulation withdrawing the subsidies for quellmehl and gritz but not for starch. The
quellmehl and gritz producers objected and brought actions in the
national courts. In references under Article 177 EEC the European
Court ruled that the Council had been guilty of discrimination in
treating quellmehl and gritz differently from starch.[87] The Council
then restored the subsidies, but only from the date of the Court's
judgment. The quellmehl and gritz producers claimed that they
should have been back-dated to when they were originally withdrawn and brought proceedings under Article 215(2) for compensation for the loss they had suffered during the period when they were
without subsidies.

There was again no difficulty in proving that the regulations which
withdrew the subsidies violated a superior rule of law for the protection of the individual. Was the violation manifest and grave? The
Court held that it was. Its reasons were not very clear but it
emphasized that the quellmehl and gritz producers were a small,
clearly-defined group and stated that the loss they had suffered went
beyond the risks normally inherent in their business. The Court
therefore ruled that they were entitled to damages based on the
amount of the subsidy they would have received if they had been
treated on the same basis as the starch producers. However, this was
to be reduced to the extent to which they had been able to pass on any
part of the loss to their customers.[88]

This decision may be contrasted with the judgment given by the
Court only two months later in the *Isoglucose* cases.[89] Isoglucose is a
recently-developed product which has already featured in several
cases. It is a sweetener which competes with sugar in a certain sector

[87] *Ruckdeschel*, Cases 117/76, 16/77, [1977] ECR 1753 and *Moulins de Pont-à-Mousson*, Cases 124/76, 20/77, [1977] ECR 1795.
[88] The Court did not actually fix the amount of damages: this was left over for determination in later proceedings. See, further, [1982] ECR 3271 and 3293.
[89] *Amylum and Tunnel Refineries* v. *Council and Commission*, Cases 116, 124/77, [1979] ECR 3497; *KSH* v. *Council and Commission*, Case 143/77, [1979] ECR 3583 (second *Isoglucose* cases).

of the market (soft drinks, jams and similar products). It was first put on the market in 1976 and the Community authorities immediately took steps to meet the threat it posed to sugar, a product which was in surplus and building up a 'mountain'. The result was a regulation imposing on isoglucose a levy of such large proportions that, according to the producers, it would have made all production uneconomical. Two of the main factories were in England and proceedings were brought in the English courts to challenge the validity of the regulation. The European Court held, on a reference under Article 177, that the regulation infringed the principle of equality because it discriminated against isoglucose in comparison with sugar.[90] The levy was then withdrawn with retroactive effect.

This did not, however, end the troubles of the isoglucose manufacturers. They had been obliged to suspend production while the levy dispute was pending: if the levy had been upheld, their plants would have had to switch to other products or close entirely. They had therefore incurred heavy expenses from lost production and financial overheads. Hardest hit was the Dutch firm Koninklijke Scholten-Honig (KSH) which had been forced into liquidation. It had constructed a large plant at Tilbury which had been sold at a loss. It claimed that its total loss resulting from the imposition of the levy was over 147 million guilders (over £30 million). The other two producers, Amylum and Tunnel Refineries, had suffered less but their losses were still quite considerable: Amylum claimed over 100 million Belgian francs and Tunnel Refineries over £1 million. No one could contend that these losses were within the normal risk of manufacturing even a new product.

The producers therefore brought actions for damages. There was again no problem with the first and third requisites under the *Schöppenstedt* formula, but was the violation manifest and grave? On the basis of the tests in the previous cases, one would have thought that it was. Isoglucose manufacturers were an even more restricted group than quellmehl and gritz producers: their numbers were limited by the heavy investment required and the fact that some of the technology involved was still under patent. Moreover, the impact of the regulation on their business was little short of catastrophic.

In spite of this, the Court held that they were entitled to no compensation. Its reasoning was sparse – suggesting that the judges were divided among themselves – and no consideration was given to

---

[90] *Royal Scholten-Honig*, Cases 103, 145/77, [1978] ECR 2037 (first *Isoglucose* cases).

the degree of harm suffered; instead the Court concentrated on the extent to which the law had been violated. One would have thought that this was at least as great as in the previous case – the Court itself said that the charges borne by the isoglucose manufacturers were 'manifestly unequal' as compared to those imposed on sugar producers – but the Court ruled that the defendants' errors were not of such gravity that their conduct could be regarded as 'verging on the arbitrary' (a point on which opinions might differ).

It now appears that the requirement that the violation be manifest and grave has two aspects to it: one is the degree of harm suffered and the extent to which it is concentrated on a small group of victims; the other is the extent to which the law has been violated. Only if the defendant's conduct verges on the arbitrary will the Community be liable. This represents a more stringent criterion than was applied in the earlier cases: no mention of arbitrariness was made in the *Quellmehl and Gritz* cases; nor could it be contended that the degree of discrimination in those cases was greater than in the *Isoglucose* cases. It seems likely, therefore, that it will be even more difficult to obtain damages in the future.

Third Requisite

The third requisite is that the rule of law infringed must be one for the protection of the individual. None of the recent cases sheds much light on this, except that the principles of proportionality, legitimate expectations and non-discrimination are all regarded as being for the protection of the individual. What the requirement appears to mean is that the purpose of the violated rule must be to benefit individuals of the category to which the applicant belongs. If this is correct, the requirement is no more than a restatement of a principle which has already been applied in cases decided before *Schöppenstedt*.

The principle was first laid down in *Vloeberghs* v. *High Authority*.[91] This case was discussed above and it will be remembered that it concerned a legal act of a non-normative kind, namely a failure to take a decision under Article 88 ECSC. Vloeberghs was a Belgian coal dealer which had a number of customers in France to whom it wanted to sell coal which it had imported from America and which was in stock in Belgium. The French authorities refused to allow the coal to enter France. Vloeberghs regarded this as a violation of the

---

[91] Cases 9, 12/60, [1961] ECR 197.

Community Obligations 481

Community principle of free circulation of goods which, it claimed, applied to coal originating outside the Community provided that it had been lawfully imported into a Member State. It therefore asked the High Authority to institute enforcement proceedings against France under Article 88 ECSC. When the High Authority failed to do so, Vloeberghs brought proceedings against it for damages on the ground that the High Authority's failure to act was a violation of the Treaty, especially Article 8 ECSC which imposed a duty on the High Authority to ensure that the objectives of the Treaty were attained.

The Court accepted that the principle of free circulation of goods applied to coal originating outside the Community provided it had been lawfully imported into a Member State. However, it stated that this principle had been established in the interests of Community production and, though it had been extended to coal produced outside the Community, it was not intended to benefit it and those dealing in it: the purpose of extending the principle to imported coal was merely to ensure that measures taken to restrict the movement of imported coal did not indirectly impede the circulation of Community coal. Consequently, though the High Authority owed a duty to Community producers to enforce the principle of free circulation, it owed no such duty to dealers in non-Community coal. The action was therefore dismissed.

Another case in which this question arose was *Kampffmeyer* v. *Commission*.[92] This case is discussed in detail elsewhere[93] and it is sufficient to say here that the applicants were German grain importers who had applied to the relevant German authority for licences to import maize from France. Under Article 22 of Regulation 19, the German authority could refuse such applications only if a serious disturbance of the market was threatened. Any such decision had to be confirmed by the Commission which was under an obligation not to confirm it unless it considered that this condition was fulfilled. In the case, the German authority suspended imports and this decision was confirmed by the Commission. The applicants then sued the Community for damages.

The Court held that the condition laid down in Article 22 of Regulation 19 had not, in fact, been fulfilled and that the Commission decision confirming the German measures was consequently invalid. Was the rule of law violated (Article 22 of Regulation 19) intended to

[92] Cases 5, 7, 13–24/66, [1967] ECR 245.
[93] See pp. 463–4, above and pp. 484–6, below.

benefit the applicants? The Court held that it was. Its reasoning was as follows:[94]

> With regard to the argument that the rule of law which is infringed is not intended to protect the interests of the applicants, the said Article 22, together with the other provisions of Regulation No 19, is directed, according to the wording of the fourth recital in the preamble to the regulation, to ensuring appropriate support for agricultural markets during the transitional period on the one hand, and to allowing the progressive establishment of a single market by making possible the development of the free movement of goods on the other. Furthermore, the interests of the producers in the Member States and of free trade between these States are expressly mentioned in the preamble to the said regulation. It appears in particular from Article 18 that the exercise of freedom of trade between States is subject only to the general requirements laid down by its own provisions and those of subsequent regulations. Article 22 constitutes an exception to these general rules and consequently an infringement of that article must be regarded as an infringement of those rules and of the interests which they are intended to protect. The fact that these interests are of a general nature does not prevent their including the interests of individual undertakings such as the applicants which as cereal importers are parties engaged in intra-Community trade. Although the application of the rules of law in question is not in general capable of being of direct and individual concern to the said undertakings, that does not prevent the possibility that the protection of their interests may be – as in the present case it is in fact – intended by those rules of law. The defendant's argument that the rule of law contained in Article 22 of Regulation No 19 is not directed towards the protection of the interests of the applicants cannot therefore be accepted.

The task of determining the purpose of a legal rule often involves more than pure legal analysis and for this reason it is impossible to lay down general rules. It is, however, interesting that the Court in the above passage expressly rejected two arguments. First, the fact that a provision has been enacted in the general interest does not mean that it cannot *also* have been intended to protect the interests of particular individuals. It is sufficient, therefore, if it is intended *in part* to protect their interests. Secondly, the fact that an individual would not have *locus standi* to challenge it in review proceedings, because it is not of direct and individual concern to him,[95] does not necessarily mean that the provision is not intended to protect his interests.

---

[94] [1967] ECR at pp. 262–3.
[95] See Chapter 12, above.

Conclusions

It was said earlier that the advantage of a tort action is that it is not subject to the restrictive conditions applicable to actions for judicial review, especially the short time-limits and the strict rules for *locus standi*. It will be apparent from what has been said, however, that tort actions based on reviewable acts are hardly ever successful, at least to the extent of leading to an award of damages. Nevertheless, an applicant may regard the action as worthwhile if he obtains no more than a statement by the Court that the Community measure is illegal: this will normally have the same practical effect as a successful annulment action.

CONCURRENT LIABILITY: THE COMMUNITY AND THE MEMBER STATES

The question to be considered here concerns the extent to which the liability of the Community is affected by the fact that there is concurrent liability on the part of a national authority. This problem arises very frequently, since it is normal practice for Community policies to be carried out by national authorities. Policy decisions are taken by Community institutions and the requisite legal acts are adopted; but the implementation of these policies is usually entrusted to agencies of the national governments acting on behalf of the Community. The citizen usually deals with the latter and if he suffers damage it is usually through the instrumentality of these authorities. If, therefore, he is forced to pay a sum of money that is not due, or refused a grant to which he is entitled, it is the national authority which acts or fails to act. The root cause of the trouble may be some act or failure to act on the part of the Community but, since the matter is implemented by the national authority, the possibility arises of a right of action against the national authority as well as against the Community. The action against the national authority may be in tort, quasi-contract (restitution) or on the basis of a statutory obligation, and will have to be brought in the national courts, as there is no provision for a private person to sue a national government in the European Court.[96]

---

[96] Actions against a Member State in the European Court may be brought only by the Commission or another Member State: Arts 169 and 170 EEC and 141 and 142 Euratom. Such actions may not be brought at all under the ECSC Treaty.

Will the existence of such a remedy affect any right of action the applicant may have against the Community in the European Court? Obviously he cannot be allowed to obtain compensation twice over. So any compensation already obtained in the national courts will have to be deducted from what he is awarded in the European Court. But what will happen if no compensation at the national level has yet been obtained either because no proceedings have been instituted or because they are still pending?

The first occasion on which the Court had to consider this problem was in *Kampffmeyer* v. *Commission*.[97] This case, which has already been discussed,[98] concerned German grain dealers who had been refused permits to import maize from France into Germany. By the time the ban was lifted, the import levy had been increased; so those dealers who went through with their transactions were forced to pay a sum which would not otherwise have been payable. The decision to ban imports was taken by the German Government but it was approved, as required under Community law, by the Commission. In earlier proceedings[99] the Court annulled the Commission decision; now the importers brought proceedings against the Commission for damages. The Court held that by approving the German measures in circumstances in which they were not justified the Commission had committed a wrongful act which could result in liability. The Court was prepared to consider compensation only for those importers who had concluded contracts to buy maize in France before the applications for import permits had been refused. The loss suffered fell into two categories: in some cases the grain bought had subsequently been imported and the levy paid; in others the contracts had been cancelled. In the former cases the loss suffered was equal to the levy paid; in the latter it was equal to the payments involved in cancellation plus loss of profit.[100]

As far as concurrent liability was concerned, there were two possible grounds on which a claim could be made against the German authorities. One was quasi-contract (restitution). This applied only where the maize had been imported into Germany and the levy paid. The Court pointed out that the levy was paid into the German treasury and that it might be possible to recover it through

---

[97] Cases 5, 7, 13–24/66, [1967] ECR 245. See also *Becher* v. *Commission*, Case 30/66, [1967] ECR 285.

[98] See pp. 463–4 and 481–2, above.

[99] *Toepfer* v. *Commission*, Cases 106, 107/63, [1965] ECR 405; discussed at pp. 351–2, above.

[100] The question of damages is discussed further at pp. 463–4, above.

proceedings in the German courts. It therefore ruled that this possibility must first be exhausted before it would consider awarding damages under this head against the Community.

The second possible cause of action against the German authority was in tort. The German decision to ban imports was illegal and the German authority was consequently just as much at fault as the Commission: the Germans had imposed the ban; the Commission had confirmed it. Proceedings against the German Government had, in fact, already been instituted but the German court had stayed them to await the outcome of the Community proceedings. The European Court held that before it could decide the extent of the Community's liability, the German courts should be given the opportunity to decide whether the German authority was liable. It therefore stayed the proceedings.

Was this decision justifiable? It seems clear that the basic premise of the judgment was that primary liability rested on the German authority and that Community liability was only subsidiary.[101] There was considerable justification for this view as regards the levy since, under the provisions applicable at that time, such levies were not handed over to the Community. If there was a right under German law to recover the levy, it was not unreasonable to regard this aspect of the claim as one where Community liability was subsidiary.

The ruling on the tort issue, however, is hard to justify. This was a case of joint liability and there was no obvious reason why the liability of the Community should be subsidiary to that of the German authorities. The German proceedings had already been stayed to await the outcome of the Community action; now the European Court was staying the Community action to wait for the German court to give judgment. What if neither was prepared to act first? The European Court was sacrificing the interests of the applicants, who should have been permitted to sue whichever joint tortfeasor they chose, in order to shift the liability onto the German authority. The Court's justification for this was that it was necessary in order to 'avoid the applicants' being insufficiently or excessively compensated for the same damage by the different assessment of two different courts applying different rules of law'.[102] The

---

[101] See *per* Advocate General Gand in *Becher* v. *Commission*, Case 30/66, [1967] ECR 285 at 305.

[102] [1967] ECR at 266.

German court could, of course, have given exactly the same reason for its ruling.

It is hard to know why the Court adopted this approach.[103] Perhaps it thought that if it were more liberal it would be swamped by actions for damages; perhaps it was afraid that the Commission would be outmanoeuvred by the German authorities and the Community would end up having to meet the whole of the claim itself. Whatever the reasons, the decision produced totally unsatisfactory results for the applicants, who struggled for years to obtain a remedy.[104]

It was not until five years later that the problem again came before the European Court. This was in *Haegeman* v. *Commission*,[105] decided in 1972. Haegeman was a Belgian firm which imported wine from Greece. A countervailing duty had been imposed on these imports by a Community regulation and Haegeman claimed that this was illegal as it was contrary to the association agreement between the Community and Greece. It therefore wrote to the Commission and requested the return of the money it had paid. When this was refused it brought proceedings under Article 173 EEC to quash the decision refusing to refund the money.

It should be noted that the countervailing duty, though imposed by Community regulations, was collected by the Belgian authorities. In this respect it was similar to the levy in *Kampffmeyer*. There had, however, been an important development since that decision. The Council Decision of 21 April 1970 on the Replacement of Financial Contributions from Member States by the Communities' Own Resources[106] provided that as from 1 January 1971 the revenue from certain levies and duties would go to the Community. According to the Court, the countervailing duty in question came within the scope of this provision. In other words, while in *Kampffmeyer* the levies were paid into national funds, in *Haegeman* the money went into the Community treasury.[107]

---

[103] It should be noted that the solution adopted by the Court had been rejected by Advocate General Gand: see [1967] ECR at 278–9.

[104] See Schermers, 'The Law as it Stands on the Appeal for Damages', 1975/1 LIEI 113 at 135 and Boulouis and Chevallier, *Grands arrêts de la cour de justice des communautés européennes*, Tome 1, p. 417, note A1 (1974). After 9 years the majority of the applicants did, in fact, obtain compensation in the German courts; but some had still not exhausted the remedies under national law: see Durand, 'Restitution or Damages: National or European Court?', (1975–6) 1 E.L. Rev. 431 at 433.

[105] Case 96/71, [1972] ECR 1005.

[106] Decision 70/243, JO 1970, L94.

[107] It is not clear from the case whether all the payments were made after 1 January 1971 but the Court assumed in its judgment that all the payments went into Community funds.

One would have thought that this new factor would have greatly strengthened the case for holding that the Community was under an obligation to refund the money. The Court, however, ruled that because the collection of these funds was a matter for the national authorities, claims for refunds had to be made to them. Any ensuing litigation would then be brought in the national courts. The Commission was, therefore, not obliged to consider Haegeman's application and the annulment action was inadmissible.

This reasoning is hard to accept. The fact that the mechanics of collection are a matter for national provisions and the collection is carried out by national officials does not affect the question of who is liable to make repayment. The duties were imposed by Community provisions and collected on behalf of the Community. The national authorities were agents of the Community and the money was handed over to the Community. If the duties were illegal, it was the Community, not the national authorities, which was unjustly enriched. It was, therefore, unjustified to hold that the national authorities alone were liable to make restitution.[108]

Haegeman also claimed damages in tort for various losses he had suffered as a result of the imposition of the duty, but the Court held that, as the question of Community liability depended on the legality of the duty, this claim would be dismissed 'at the present stage'. It is not entirely clear what was meant by this but it seems that the Court intended that Haegeman should first establish the illegality of the levy through proceedings in the Belgian courts with a reference to the European Court under Article 177 EEC. Then, if it were successful in this, it could return to the European Court with its tort action.

It is interesting that in a case decided only a few months before, *Compagnie d'Approvisionnement* v. *Commission (No. 2)*,[109] Advocate General Dutheillet de Lamothe had given careful consideration to just this possibility. In this case the applicants, who were French dealers in cereals, complained that a subsidy, granted under a Council regulation, had been fixed by the Commission at too low a level. They therefore brought proceedings against the Commission under Article 215(2). One argument put forward by the Commission was that the action was inadmissible because the applicants should first have brought proceedings in the French courts to establish that the Commission regulation fixing the level of the subsidy was illegal. This would have been referred under Article 177 EEC to the

---

[108] But see Joliet, *Le contentieux*, p. 228.
[109] Cases 9, 11/71 [1972] ECR 391.

European Court and a ruling on the point would have been made.
Only if this were successful, argued the Commission, could the
applicants bring their action against the Community.

Advocate General Dutheillet de Lamothe rejected this argument.
First, he pointed out that in view of the various levels of the national
court system through which the case would have to pass, it might well
be over five years before the matter was finally concluded. By this
time the period of limitation for the action against the Community
would have expired. (In his view there was no ground on which the
running of time could be interrupted in these circumstances.) He also
pointed out the extreme difficulties which similar doctrines had
caused in France and other countries and suggested that the end
result could be a denial of justice. Finally he stated that there was
nothing in the Treaty to justify such a procedure.

The Court declared the action admissible. Thus, though it did not
explicitly deal with this particular point, it implicitly rejected the
Commission's argument. One wonders why, so soon afterwards, it
should have required Haegeman to make what Advocate General
Dutheillet de Lamothe had referred to as the 'long march' through
the national courts.

However, in a similar case decided a year after *Haegeman*, *Merkur* v.
Commission,[110] the European Court held that the action was admissible. It said that as it already had the case before it, it 'would not be in
keeping with the proper administration of justice and the requirements of procedural efficiency to compel the applicant to have
recourse to national remedies and thus to wait for a considerable
length of time before a final decision on his claim is made.'[111] It is
hard to regard this ruling as anything other than a rejection of the
decision in *Haegeman*.[112]

For the next few years little was heard of the *Haegeman* ruling and
one might possibly have thought that it had been quietly forgotten. In
one case, *Holtz and Willemsen* v. *Council and Commission*,[113] it was
argued by the Commission that the applicant's claim (for a subsidy)
should have been brought in the national courts. This was rejected by
Advocate General Reischl[114] and the Court, though it did not deal

[110] Cases 43/72, [1973] ECR 1055.
[111] Ibid., at paragraph 6 of the judgment.
[112] See Van Gerven, 'De niet-contractuele aansprakelijkheid van de Gemeenschap
wegens normatieve handelingen', [1976] SEW 2 at 7–8.
[113] Case 153/73 [1974] ECR 675.
[114] [1974] ECR at 700–1.

with the point, found the proceedings admissible. In *CNTA* v. *Commission*[115] the point was not even really argued.

In 1975, however, the Court again changed tack[116] and since then there have been many cases in which the applicant has been sent to the national courts. The case law now seems to have stabilized itself sufficiently for it to be possible to give a statement of the legal position. To do this it is necessary to distinguish between three separate situations: first where the applicant's loss lies in the fact that he was unlawfully obliged to pay a sum of money to the national authority; secondly, where his loss lies in the fact that the national authorities unlawfully refused to make a payment to him; thirdly, where his loss is of some other kind. In the first situation his right of action against the national authority will be in quasi-contract (restitution); in the second it will be on the basis of a statutory obligation; in the third it will be in tort. Each situation will be considered separately.

Restitution

Where the applicant's loss consists in the fact that he was unlawfully obliged to make a payment to the national authority, he will normally have a remedy in quasi-contract against the national authority. In such a situation, he will not be entitled to bring proceedings against the Community even if the national authority acted as agent for the Community and handed the money over to it. In *Kampffmeyer*[117] the proceedings in the European Court were held admissible and the Community was held liable in principle; in the later cases the proceedings were held inadmissible. The latter is the rule today.

Statutory Obligation

The second situation is where the national authority has wrongfully refused to make a payment to the applicant. In spite of the earlier cases discussed above,[118] the general rule now is that such an action

---

[115] Case 74/74, [1975] ECR 533 (discussed at pp. 474–6, above).
[116] The doctrine was resurrected (somewhat ambiguously) in *Grands Moulins des Antilles* v. *Commission*, Case 99/74, [1975] ECR 1531 and (more emphatically) in *IBC* v. *Commission*, Case 46/75, [1976] ECR 65. For a discussion of these, and later, cases, see Hartley, 'Concurrent Liability in EEC Law: A Critical Review of the Cases', (1977) 2 E.L. Rev. 249.
[117] See pp. 484–6, above.
[118] See pp. 487–9.

will be inadmissible, even if the basis of the obligation was a Community measure, and the national authority obtained its funds from the Community.

No National Remedy

In both the situations discussed so far, the position is different where no procedure exists for the applicant to obtain a remedy in the national courts. The most important case in which this will occur is where the sole cause of the problem is the failure of the Commission or Council to adopt a legal act. In such a case, the applicant cannot bring proceedings in the national court and ask it to decide the case on the basis that the measure has been enacted. Not even the European Court can do this: in actions for a remedy for a failure to act, all it can do is to declare that the defendant's failure to act is contrary to the Treaty.[119] In these circumstances there is, therefore, no procedure under which the applicant can bring his complaint before the national courts. Since the alternative would be a denial of justice, the European Court has, after some hesitation,[120] held that proceedings can be brought directly before it against the appropriate Community institution. Thus if, for example, Community law imposes a duty on the Commission to pass a regulation granting an export subsidy whenever the currency of a Member State is devalued, and the Commission fails to pass the regulation, an exporter who would have been entitled to benefit from the subsidy may sue the Commission before the European Court.[121]

This situation must be contrasted with another situation, superficially similar but in fact very different, in which the right to receive

[119] See p. 392, above.

[120] See *Roquette* v. *Commission*, Case 26/74, [1976] ECR 677. This case concerned an exporter who had been obliged to pay a levy under a provision of Community law. The levy was collected by the national authority and handed over to the Commission. The exporter considered that he had not been liable to make the payment and brought proceedings for its recovery, with interest, in both the national courts (against the national authority) and the European Court (against the Commission). The national court made a reference under Art. 177 EEC and the European Court gave a ruling in favour of the exporter (see *Roquette* v. *France*, Case 34/74, [1974] ECR 1217). The national court then ordered the repayment of the sum in question but refused to award interest, partly on the ground that the Community had had the use of the money during the period in question. The exporter then continued his action against the Commission in the European Court in order to obtain the interest. The European Court, however, held this claim inadmissible on the ground that it was ancillary to the claim for the repayment of the levy, a claim which was within the exclusive jurisdiction of the national courts.

[121] See *Unifrex* v. *Commission and Council*, Case 281/82, [1984] ECR 1969.

the subsidy already exists by virtue of a previous regulation, but the right is wrongfully withdrawn by a later regulation. Here a remedy would normally exist in the national courts since the exporter could sue the national authority responsible for payment of the subsidy and argue that the later regulation is invalid and of no effect. A reference could be made to the European Court and, if it upheld this contention, the earlier regulation would still be in force and would entitle the exporter to receive the subsidy.[122]

Tort

In an action in tort the applicant is claiming not a specific sum of money, but compensation for loss suffered. It now appears to be settled that if this is the true nature of his claim, he can proceed directly against the Community in the European Court.

This is shown by *Dietz* v. *Commission*.[123] Dietz was a German firm which entered into a contract to export sugar to Italy. After the contract was made but before it was performed, a levy was introduced on imports into Italy. The result was that Dietz made a loss on the transaction, and it brought an action against the Community in the European Court on the ground that the sudden imposition of the charge was a violation of the principle of the protection of legitimate expectations.

It will be remembered that in the *CNTA* case, which had been decided a couple of years previously, the Court had ruled that a claim of this nature is possible.[124] As that case made clear, however, an applicant in Dietz's position cannot claim a full refund of the levy; all it can claim is the amount of any actual loss – not loss of profit – that it suffered. For this reason Dietz's claim was not for a fixed sum but was a true tort action; consequently it was admissible.

The *Quellmehl and Gritz* cases establish this even more firmly. It will be remembered[125] that the essence of the claim was that subsidies had been withdrawn from quellmehl and gritz but not from starch. Since starch was in competition with quellmehl and gritz, this constituted discrimination. The Court, however, held that the quellmehl and gritz producers did not have a claim to the subsidy as such; all they were entitled to was compensation for the loss they had

---

[122] See *IBC* v. *Commission*, Case 46/75, [1976] ECR 65.
[123] Case 126/76, [1977] ECR 2431.
[124] See pp. 474–6, above.
[125] See pp. 477–8, above.

suffered (though on the facts of the case it came to the same thing). This, too, was a true tort action and was therefore admissible.[126]

It should, however, be noted that in both these cases the role of the national authorities was limited to carrying out the Community measure according to its terms and it is by no means certain, especially in view of the judgment in the third *Skimmed-Milk Powder* case,[127] that they would have been jointly liable with the Community. It follows that the position might be different where they clearly were joint tortfeasors, as in *Kampffmeyer* v. *Commission*.[128]

FURTHER READING

Joliet (*Le contentieux*), pp. 243–271.

Schermers, paragraphs 569–636.

Barav, 'La répétition de l'indu', [1981] CDE 507.

Bridge, 'Procedural Aspects of the Enforcement of European Community Law through the Legal Systems of the Member States', (1984) 9 E.L. Rev. 28.

Durand, 'Restitution or Damages: National Court or European Court?', (1975–6) 1 E.L. Rev. 431.

Harding, 'The Choice of Court Problem in Cases of Non-Contractual Liability under EEC Law', (1979) 16 C.M.L. Rev. 389.

Lewis, 'Joint and Several Liability of the European Communities and National Authorities', [1980]. Current Legal Problems 99.

Oliver, 'Enforcing Community Rights in the English Courts', (1987) 50 MLR 881.

---

[126] See also, *Zuckerfabrik Bedburg* v. *EEC*, Case 281/84, 14 January 1987 (not yet reported) (paragraphs 10–12 of the judgment).

[127] *Granaria*, Case 101/78, [1979] ECR 623.

[128] See pp. 484–6, above.

INDEX